D0987540

A DICTIONARY OF
LITURGY & WORSHIP

A
DICTIONARY
OF
LITURGY &
WORSHIP

EDITED BY
J G DAVIES

SCM PRESS LTD

334 00313 X

First published 1972
by SCM Press Ltd
26–30 Tottenham Road London N1 4BZ
Seventh impression 1984

Typeset by Filmtype Services Limited, Scarborough
and printed in Great Britain by
Richard Clay (The Chaucer Press) Ltd,
Bungay, Suffolk

PREFACE

Ritual would appear to be natural to man. When even birds and animals engage in it, as for example in sex play, it is not surprising to discover that human beings practise it almost universally. This formalization of natural actions lies at the basis of worship, which is the expression in corporate gatherings of adoration, praise and thanksgiving to God in response to his activity in the world. This response precedes doctrinal formulation, so that one may say that worship is primary and theology secondary. In Christian terms, this means that the early church worshipped Christ long before it had reached an intellectual understanding of his person and work. It is this sequence that explains the Latin tag *lex orandi, lex credendi,* i.e. what is to be believed is derived from the practice of worship. Consequently, worship has always been regarded as the living heart of any religion. Because of this centrality, a knowledge of worship is essential for a sympathetic appreciation of all religious movements.

Worship can be either 'free' or formal. In the latter case it is offered according to fixed rites and it is customary to use the term 'liturgy' in reference to these. Liturgy also bears a narrower sense in that it can refer in particular to the eucharist as the church's corporate and official act of worship. Because of this distinction, it has seemed appropriate to use both worship and liturgy in the title of this *Dictionary.*

As a reference book, this present volume is intended to provide background knowledge about worship for those who are regularly involved in it or would learn something about it. It seeks to concentrate upon the information that Christians today need in order to participate with understanding in the worship of the traditions to which they belong. At the same time, it aims to assist them to appreciate traditions and contemporary practices other than their own, familiarity with which is required to further the cause of ecumenical cooperation.

The separate articles are not confined to simple definitions, but give the historical background to the subject treated and seek to relate this to the contemporary scene. However, while a reliable factual content is essential, emphasis is laid upon its interpretation, with particular reference to the principles upon which the practice, object, etc. is founded or used. In this way the reader will be enabled to understand not only what has been or is done but why it has been or is done. Hence, the *Dictionary* is concerned not only with the structures but also with the rationale of worship, the tracing of patterns and influences, and the underlying basis.

The entries relate not only to the historic Christian churches, such as the Anglican, the Lutheran, the Presbyterian and the Roman Catholic, but also to those bodies which have intimate links with the biblical and Christian inheritance, such as the

Pentecostals and the Unitarians. In addition, accounts are given of the worship of other major world religions, e.g. Judaism and Islam.

In order to ensure representative accounts, the contributors to the *Dictionary* have been chosen from recognized liturgical experts within the different churches, so that, for example, Eastern Orthodox scholars have written on subjects pertaining to their own church, similarly Old Catholics, etc. The result of this is that some of the major articles are composite. The accounts of baptism, matrimony, liturgies, etc., are divided into sections, each one detailing the practice of a major denomination. The opening three sections of each composite article are in historical sequence, so that the first is devoted to the patristic period, the second to Eastern Orthodoxy, and the third to Roman Catholicism, medieval and modern; the remainder follow in alphabetical order, beginning with Anglicanism.

One consequence of this composite authorship is that different viewpoints are expressed, so that, e.g. in the entry on 'Ordination', varied and sometimes conflicting understandings of the subject are to be found. This lack of uniformity is inevitable if the positions of the several Christian churches are to be presented faithfully. Not only has each contributor been left free to give his own denominational interpretation, but no attempt has been made to achieve a consensus on matters of minor importance; e.g. the date of the *Apostolic Tradition* of Hippolytus is variously given, according to the predilection of the individual writers, as $c.215$, $c.217$ or even $c.222$.

While the majority of entries are devoted to the principal aspects of liturgy and worship, others treat of its ancillaries, e.g. its architectural setting, vestments, etc.

Worship today is, of course, not simply a matter of history. The Liturgical Movement, to which a major article is devoted, and the many revisions that are currently being produced witness to a desire to formulate patterns of worship relevant to contemporary man. But to say this is to recognize that worship is undergoing a crisis. To some it has lost its meaning. Hence the need, which is emphasized in several entries, for experimental forms, for attention to the problems of indigenization, to secularization, to the relation of liturgy and culture and liturgy and mission.

It is hoped that the *Dictionary* will be found useful by several types of reader. It is intended to appeal to church leaders, clergy and ministers, to laity and to students who wish to increase their understanding of the history and contemporary practice of worship and liturgy.

The selection of topics is always a difficult task. What one would include, another would omit. The existence of companion volumes, such as the *Theological Word Book of the Bible* (1950) and *A Dictionary of Christian Theology* (1969), has enabled the editor to have a greater latitude than would otherwise have been the case, for it has seemed unnecessary to repeat what is to be found in these works of reference. While he must bear the responsibility for the final choice, he is grateful to those who have given their advice and to all the contributors, without whose ready cooperation this project could not have been completed.

J. G. DAVIES

CONTRIBUTORS

The Rev. Dr Henry Ashworth, OSB
Books, Liturgical 3. Medieval and Roman Catholic

The Rev. Dr Frank Baker
Love Feast

The Rev. Dr John M. Barkley
Baptism; Burial 12. Reformed; Ordination 13. Reformed

Dr B. B. Beach
Baptism 15. Seventh-day Adventist; Books, Liturgical 15. Seventh-day Adventist;
Burial 13. Seventh-day Adventist; Liturgies 15. Seventh-day Adventist (Communion
Service); Matrimony 13. Seventh-day Adventist; Ordination 14. Seventh-day
Adventist; Seventh-day Adventist Worship

The Rev. Dr Eugene Brand
Liturgies 9. Lutheran; Lutheran Worship

Dr F. F. Bruce
Baptism 13. Plymouth Brethren; Burial 11. Plymouth Brethren; Liturgies 13.
Plymouth Brethren; Matrimony 11. Plymouth Brethren; Plymouth Brethren

The Rev. C. O. Buchanan
Burial 4. Anglican; Liturgies 4. Anglican

Dr H. Ellsworth Chandlee
Baptism 4. Anglican; Liturgical Movement, The

The Rev. Joseph Connelly
All Saints; All Souls; Ember Days; Fast Days; Ferial; Mariological Feasts; Rogation
Days; Saints' Days

The Rev. Dr Gilbert Cope
Colours, Liturgical; Gestures; Postures; Vestments

General Frederick Coutts
Salvation Army

Dr Maurice A. Creasey
Quaker Worship

The Rev. J. D. Crichton
Altar, Stripping of; Altar, Washing of; Ashes; Asperges; Baptism 3. Medieval and
Roman Catholic; Bible Services; Books, Liturgical 2. Roman Catholic; Liturgies 3.
Medieval and Roman Catholic; Mass, High; Mass, Low; Matrimony 3. Medieval
and Roman Catholic; New Fire; Ordination 3. Medieval and Roman Catholic;
Paschal Vigil; Roman Catholic Worship; Tenebrae; Unction

The Rev. Canon G. J. Cuming
Books, Liturgical 4. Anglican; Churching of Women; Commination; Matrimony 4. Anglican; Sick, Visitation of the

The Rev. Dr Horton Davies
Baptism 7. Congregational; Books, Liturgical 7. Congregationalist; Burial 6. Congregationalist; Congregationalist Worship; Liturgies 7. Congregationalist; Matrimony 6. Congregationalist; Ordination 7. Congregationalist

The Rev. Professor J. G. Davies (Editor)
Ablutions; Absolution; Aisle; Alms; Amen; Apse; Architectural Setting; Atrium; Baptistery; Basilica; Bible, Use of in Worship; Blessing; Books, Liturgical 1. The Early Church; Books, Liturgical 9. Lutheran (2) United States; Burial 1. The Early Church; Calendar; Canticles; Cathedral; Centralized Building; Ceremonial; Chancel; Chapel; Choir (Architectural); Commixture; Communion; Consecration of Churches; Crucifix; Dedication; Dismissal; Disposal of Eucharistic Remains; Easter Garden or Sepulchre; Eucharist; Font; Fraction; Gallery; Invocation; Lavabo; Lord's Supper; Martyrium; Matrimony 1. The Early Church; Mission and Worship; Mixed Chalice; Narthex; Nave; Office Hymn; Ordination 1. The Early Church; Orientation; Rite; Ritual; Rubrics; Sacristy; Sanctuary; Secularization and Worship; Sentences; Tract; Transept; Vestry; Words of Administration

The Rev. F. Debuyst
Architectural Setting (Modern)

Peter Dickinson
Music, Modern; Organ

The Rev. Dr C. W. Dugmore
Canonical Hours

The Rev. Canon J. D. C. Fisher
Baptism 1. Patristic; Catechumen, Catechumenate; Insufflation

The Rev. P. V. Fisher
Culture and Worship

The Rt. Rev. J. H. Foy
Moravian Worship

The Rev. Dr R. H. Fuller
Lectionary; Sermon

The Rt. Rev. T. S. Garrett
Church of South India Worship

The Rev. A. Raymond George
Anniversary; Baptism 10. Methodist; Books, Liturgical 10. Methodist; Burial 9. Methodist; Extempore Prayer; Methodist Worship; Ordination 10. Methodist; Prayer Meeting

W. Jardine Grisbooke
Agnus Dei; Anaphora; Antidoron; Baptism 2. Orthodox; Books, Liturgical 2. Orthodox; Cathedral Office; Collect; Consecration Prayer; Diptychs; Doxology;

Enarxis; Entrance, Great; Entrance, Little; Incense; Intercession; Kyrie; Litany; Liturgies 2. Orthodox; Lord's Prayer; Oblation; Ordinary; Orthodox Worship; Presanctified Mass; Proper; Prothesis; Sanctus; Shinto Worship; Silent Prayer; Suffrages; Super Oblata; Synaxis; Trisagion

The Rev. Dr E. R. Hardy
Coptic Worship

Andrew Heley
Baptism 8. Jehovah's Witnesses; Books, Liturgical 8. Jehovah's Witnesses; Burial 7. Jehovah's Witnesses; Jehovah's Witnesses' Worship; Liturgies 8. Jehovah's Witnesses; Matrimony 7. Jehovah's Witnesses; Ordination 8. Jehovah's Witnesses

The Rev. Dr Peter Hinchcliff
Acolyte; Bishop; Cantor; Celebrant; Chairman of District; Crucifer; Deacon; Deaconness; Elder; Lay Preacher; Lector; Local Preacher; Presbyter; Reader; Server; Superintendent; Thurifer

Dr W. J. Hollenweger
Camp Meeting; Experimental Forms of Worship; Liturgies 12. Pentecostal; Open-Air Meeting; Ordination 12. Pentecostal; Pentecostal Worship; Spirituals

The Rev. Clifford Howell, SJ
Vernacular

The Rev. Dr E. Bolaji Idowu
Indigenization

The Rev. R. C. D. Jasper
Anglican Worship; Canon; Ordination 4. Anglican; Procession

The Rev. Dr F. Kalb
Books, Liturgical 9. Lutheran

Archdale A. King
Benediction; Concelebration; Exposition; Forty Hours Devotion; Reservation; Rosary; Sacred Heart; Stations of the Cross; Veneration of the Cross

The Rev. Dr J. A. Lamb
Books, Liturgical 14. Reformed; Liturgies 14. Reformed; Matrimony 12. Reformed

The Rev. Paul Lazor
Burial 2. Orthodox; Matrimony 2. The Orthodox Church; Ordination 2. Orthodox

The Rev. Dr Allan A. McArthur
Advent; Ascension Day; Ash Wednesday; Christmas; Corpus Christi; Easter; Epiphany; Good Friday; Holy Saturday; Holy Week; Lent; Low Sunday; Octave; Palm Sunday; Pentecost; Quinquagesima; Sunday; Transfiguration; Trinity Sunday

The Rev. Dr Kilian McDonnell
Baptism 12. Pentecostal; Books, Liturgical 12. Pentecostal

The Rev. Dr W. D. Maxwell
Reformed Worship

The Rev. Brian A. Newns
Burial 3. Medieval and Roman Catholic; Epistle; Exorcism; Gospel; Last Gospel; Lesson

Dr Alfred Niebergall
Burial 8. Lutheran; Matrimony 8. Lutheran

The Rev. Dr Geoffrey Parrinder
Buddhist Worship; Hindu Worship

The Rev. A. E. Peaston
Unitarian Worship

The Rev. Thomas Phelan
Offertory

The Rev. Canon Ronald Pilkington
Papal Rites

The Rev. Dr C. E. Pocknee
Alms-Dish; Altar; Altar Hangings; Altar Rails; Ambo; Aumbry; Baldachin; Bells; Candles, Lamps and Lights; Cathedra; Chalice and Paten; Chrismatory; Ciborium; Corporal; Cross; Cruet; Fan; Frontal; Iconostasis; Lectern; Monstrance; Pall; Paschal Candle; Pew; Piscina; Pulpit; Purificator; Pyx; Reredos; Rostrum; Screen; Stoup; Tabernacle; Thurible; Tower; Veil

Dr Jacob Posen
Jewish Worship

The Rev. Kurt Pursch
Baptism 11. Old Catholic; Books, Liturgical 11. Old Catholic; Burial 10. Old Catholic; Liturgies 11. Old Catholic; Matrimony 10. Old Catholic; Old Catholic Worship; Ordination 11. Old Catholic

Bernarr Rainbow
Carol; Chants; Choir (Musical); Hymns 2. Vernacular

The Very Rev. Dr Alan Richardson
Creed, Creeds

The Rev. Alec Robertson
Antiphon; The Chants of the Proper of the Mass; Church Modes; The Divine Office: Gregorian Chant; Hymns 1. Latin; Motet; Music in the Mass of the Roman Rite; Notation and Rhythm; Polyphony; Psalmody; Psalm Tones; Responsorial Psalmody and Responsories

Dr Albert E. Rüthy
Baptism 11. Old Catholic; Books, Liturgical 11. Old Catholic; Burial 10. Old Catholic; Liturgies 11. Old Catholic; Matrimony 10. Old Catholic; Old Catholic Worship; Ordination 11. Old Catholic

The Rev. Peter Selby
Prayer

Dr E. J. R. H. S. von Sicard
Baptism 9. Lutheran; Ordination 9. Lutheran

The Rev. Dr John E. Skoglund
Baptist Worship; Burial 5. Baptist; Liturgies 5. Baptist; Ordination 5. Baptist

John B. Taylor
Islamic Worship

The Rev. C. Tol
Baptism 11. Old Catholic; Books, Liturgical 11. Old Catholic; Burial 10. Old Catholic; Liturgies 11. Old Catholic; Matrimony 10. Old Catholic; Old Catholic Worship; Ordination 11. Old Catholic

The Rev. David Tripp
Covenant Service; Watch Night

The Rev. Paul Verghese
East Syrian Worship; Ethiopian Worship; Mar Thoma Church Worship; West Syrian Worship

Dr Keith Watkins
Baptism 6. Christian Church (Disciples of Christ); Books, Liturgical 6. Christian Church (Disciples of Christ); Christian Church (Disciples of Christ) Worship; Liturgies 6. Christian Church (Disciples of Christ); Ordination 6. Christian Church (Disciples of Christ)

The Rev. Canon E. C. Whitaker
Ante-Communion; Bidding Prayer; Confirmation; Harvest Thanksgiving; Three-hours Service

Dr James F. White
Baptism 10. Methodist; Liturgies 10. Methodist; Matrimony 9. Methodist; Methodist Worship 2. USA

The Rev. Stephen Winward
Baptism 5. Baptist; Books, Liturgical 5. Baptist; Matrimony 5. Baptist

Dr Thomas F. Zimmerman
Assemblies of God Churches' Worship

ACKNOWLEDGMENTS

We are grateful to the following for permission to reproduce copyright illustrations: A.C.L., Brussels, *Plate 35; L'Art Sacré*, Paris, *Fig. 10;* James Austin, *Plate 5;* Bernsen's International Press Service Ltd., *Plate 41;* D. X. Botte, *Plate 15;* James Brooks, *Plate 10;* Courtauld Institute of Art, *Plates 7 & 8;* Graphion, London, *Plate 31;* Louis Grossé Ltd. *Fig. 25;* C. V. Hancock, *Plates 6 & 27;* The Mansell Collection, *Plates 1 & 3;* Fritz Metzger, Zürich, *Plate 13;* National Gallery, London, *Plate 39;* Pax House, Ipswich, Suffolk, *Plate 22;* Otto Pfeifer, Lucerne, *Plates 14, 42 & 43;* Poppe, Bad Kissingen, *Plate 11;* Rheinisches Bildarchiv, *Plate 12;* Victoria & Albert Museum, Crown Copyright, *Plates 34 & 40;* Colin Westwood, *Plate 23;* C. D. & A. Willmott, *Plate 2.*

ABBREVIATIONS

AV   Authorized Version (King James Version) of the Bible
BCP   *Book of Common Prayer*
DCT   *Dictionary of Christian Theology*, ed. Alan Richardson, 1969
DTC   *Dictionnaire de Théologie Catholique*, ed. A. Vacant, E. Mangenot and
           E. Amann, 1903-50
ET   English translation
IKZ   *Internationale Kirchliche Zeitschrift*
NEB   New English Bible
NT   New Testament
OT   Old Testament
RV   Revised Version of the Bible
TDNT *Theological Dictionary of the New Testament*, ET of *TWNT*, trans. and
           ed. Geoffrey W. Bromiley, 1964 ff.
TWNT *Theologisches Wörterbuch zum Neuen Testament*, ed Gerhard Kittel,
           1933 ff.
WCC   World Council of Churches

Ablutions

The ceremonial cleansing of the eucharistic vessels and of the minister's fingers after communion. In the patristic period this took place in the sacristy (q.v.) when the service was ended (*see* **Disposal of Eucharistic Remains**). But in the tenth and eleventh centuries it became customary to do this immediately after the act of communion itself, i.e. before the end of the service proper. This transference of the ablutions to a position within the mass was realized in two stages. The first stage comprised the washing of the priest's hands, the water being poured down the piscina (q.v.). The second stage involved the cleaning of the chalice with the consumption of the liquid used. The ablutions as finally evolved were the product of the fusion of these two, and so the Roman practice, regulated by the missal of Pope Pius V, requires the cleansing of the chalice with wine and then of the fingers and chalice with wine and water.

W. Lockton, *The Treatment of the Remains at the Eucharist after Holy Communion and the Time of the Ablutions*, 1920.

EDITOR

Absolution

A formal act of pronouncing the forgiveness of sins. In the early church this was a public event, in the sense that sinners were reconciled in the presence of the congregation, after they had previously made private confession; the church leaders were thus acting upon the commission of Christ to 'bind' and 'loose' (Matt. 16.19; 18.18). By the side of this public system of discipline, there was also the practice of confessing one's sins privately to a spiritual director without absolution. In the Celtic monasteries of the sixth century these two systems were amalgamated, the absolution, in front of the congregation, being transferred to private confession. The confession (q.v.) of sin entered the liturgy soon after the year 1000 and the accompanying absolution was either declaratory or precatory, i.e. God's forgiveness was either declared or prayed for. In the thirteenth century the indicative form was adopted, i.e. 'I absolve you'.

Absolution continues to be given privately, e.g. in the Anglican, Lutheran, Orthodox and Roman Churches. Liturgically it is included in most services, such as the daily offices (q.v.) or in the eucharist.

EDITOR

Acolyte

Strictly one of the minor orders of the ministry, the office existed in the church in Rome by the middle of the third century. It was subsequently introduced into the other parts of Western Christendom and is still one of the stages through which aspirants to the priesthood in the Roman Catholic Church pass. In this sense it is part of the ordained ministry. The acolyte's functions were originally similar to those of the modern server (q.v.) and included the carrying of ceremonial lights. The term is commonly used by Anglicans to denote anyone who carries a torch or candle in liturgical processions.

P. HINCHLIFF

Adoration *see* Prayer (1)

Advent

The word 'Advent' is derived from a Latin root which means 'coming' or 'arrival', and the season was developed in the Western Church as a preparation for the festival of the Nativity. Councils held in Gaul in the sixth century refer to a penitential period of six weeks before Christmas. There was fasting on Mondays, Wednesdays and Fridays. But the season was already known to Gregory of Tours in the latter part of the preceding century. It may be affirmed that fifth-century Gaul was the place of origin of the fully-organized period of six Sundays, and that the structure of Advent, with regard to its length, was modelled on Lent. Various lectionaries dating from the seventh and eighth centuries, or representing the use of that time, show the six-Sunday pattern in Gaul and north-west Italy. At a greater distance from Gaul, that is, in Spain, north-east Italy and south Italy, we find five Sundays, clearly representing a modification of the original structure. One of the lectionaries noted above is derived from *Reginensis 9*, a seventh-century manuscript, containing a complete table of lessons from the Pauline epistles, an early witness to the Ambrosian liturgy of Milan. The table begins with the Christmas vigil and lists the lessons of a six-Sunday Advent at the end of the lectionary. Similarly, with reference to a lectionary not taken into account above, it is evident that also at Rome liturgical conservatism ensured that the inclusion of Advent, a practice introduced from elsewhere, did not at that stage succeed in disturbing the pattern of a lectionary which traditionally began with Christmas. For the Würzburg manuscript, *Mp. th. fol. 62*, containing in a table of epistles the oldest Roman lectionary and the usage of the early seventh century, commences with Christmas and places a five-Sunday Advent at the end. The logic of the invention of Advent had not been completely accepted. Eventually at Rome Advent was reduced from five to four Sundays. As the Roman rite gradually triumphed over the native uses of the West the four-Sunday Advent became the norm, and the original structure of six Sundays was almost completely obscured.

A. A. McArthur, *The Evolution of the Christian Year*, 1953; A. A. McArthur, *The Christian Year and Lectionary Reform*, 1958.

A. A. MCARTHUR

Adventist Worship
see Seventh-day Adventist Worship

Agape *see* Love Feast

Agnus Dei

The anthem *Agnus Dei*, for many centuries sung between the fraction (q.v.) and communion in the Roman mass, has recently been restored to its original purpose as a *confractorium*, i.e. anthem to be sung during the fraction. It appears to have been introduced into the Roman rite in the seventh century, perhaps during the pontificate of Sergius I (687-701), for it is clearly of Eastern origin – the word 'lamb' is commonly used in the Eastern liturgies to designate both Christ and the consecrated bread of the eucharist, and the West Syrian liturgy contains *confractoria* which speak of 'the Lamb of God who takes away the sins of the world' – and this was a period of considerable Eastern, and especially Syrian, influence at Rome: Syria had recently been overrun by the Moslems, and many Syrian clergy found their way to Rome, among them Pope Theodore I (642-9), while Sergius I was a Syrian by descent.

A prayer addressed specifically to Christ present in the eucharist as a sacrificial offering, the anthem originally comprised simply as many repetitions as necessary of the single sentence 'O Lamb of God, that takest away the sins of the world, have mercy upon us'. When the fraction was shortened through the introduction of unleavened bread, the number of repetitions was fixed at three, probably about the middle of the ninth century, and during the tenth and eleventh centuries, when the fraction had all but disappeared, and the anthem in practice therefore accompanied the kiss of peace (q.v.) immediately following, the third clause was given the appropriately variant ending it has had ever since – '. . . of the world, grant us peace'. As early as the eleventh century, too, a further variant appears, which has also persisted: at requiem masses, the first and second petitions end '. . . grant them rest', and the third 'grant them rest everlasting'.

J. A. Jungmann, *The Mass of the Roman Rite*, II, 1955, pp. 332-40.

W. JARDINE GRISBROOKE

Aisle

The lateral division of a church, being the part on either side of the nave (q.v.). In the patristic period in certain areas it was customary to assign the south aisle to the men and the north to the women. The application of this word to the gangways up the centre of a nave or elsewhere is of course incorrect, and the expression 'centre aisle' is a contradiction in terms.

EDITOR

Alb *see* Vestments (1*a*)

All Saints

Many martyrs and non-martyrs were unrecorded and therefore unhonoured on earth. On the other hand, places like Antioch and Rome had more known martyrs than there were days of the year. So a common feast for all martyrs was instituted, and this is the origin of the later All Saints feast. A feast of All Martyrs was observed on Easter Friday in Syria at the beginning of the fifth century, and the octave day of Pentecost was the day for a similar feast in the Byzantine liturgy. In Rome, Boniface IV had the relics of many martyrs moved from the catacombs to the Pantheon, and on 13 May 610, he consecrated the building as *St Maria ad Martyres*. This became known as the feast of All Martyrs and All Saints and of Our Lady. These three feasts, especially the Syrian one, were closely connected with the Easter season and therefore with Christ's victory. This paschal connection was broken and eventually rather lost sight of after the Roman feast of 13 May was transferred in 835 to 1 November, with the title of All Saints.

J. CONNELLY

All Souls

Most Christians who were remembered each year were neither martyrs nor confessors – people not distinguished by their death or by their way of life. At such anniversaries the eucharist was offered, not in thanksgiving as for the martyrs, but in petition to God and in the hope that God would give the departed to share in the victory of the risen Christ. The funeral service is a glowing testimony to Christian hope in a 'blessed resurrection' and to Christian love for departed relatives and friends.

Besides the funeral or anniversary rites, a general commemoration or *memento* of the dead is found in the eucharistic prayer of liturgies. There has also been for centuries a day set apart for the general commemoration of the dead. Easter Saturday was designated in the Syrian rite as a 'memorial day of all priests and monks and of all the faithful departed'. This shows the connection between Easter and the liturgy of the dead, and between All Saints and All Souls.

There is evidence of many local 'memorial days' in the West in earlier centuries, but All Souls, as now observed, is due to Odilo of Cluny. This solemn 'memorial day', first kept in Cluniac houses (from about 1000), eventually became an official part of the Roman rite.

During the 1914-18 war Benedict XV allowed priests to celebrate the eucharist three times on All Souls' Day (2 November). This permission was given partly because of the 'useless slaughter' of the war and also because the confiscation of church property at, and since, the Reformation had made it impossible to carry out the obligations for anniversary masses which had been the conditions of so many gifts and legacies.

J. CONNELLY

Alleluia *see* Chants of the Proper of the Mass

Alms

Ultimately derived from the Greek word *eleemosune* meaning 'mercy', the term alms refers to charitable gifts. The necessity for generous giving was recognized by the first Christians as the right response to Christ's own self-giving (II Cor. 8.9). The presentation of these gifts early became an integral part of worship, especially at the eucharist associated with the offertory (q.v.), and they were a portion of the offerings made either in kind or in money.

At the present day the tendency is to speak of the 'collection' and the word 'alms' has a certain archaic character. In liturgical usage, however, the correct phrase would be 'the collection of alms'.

EDITOR

Alms-dish

The duty of sharing material things with those less fortunately placed occupies a prominent place in the teaching of the OT and NT (Matt. 6.3-4; Acts 11.27-30), and the subject is often mentioned by early Christian writers, such as Justin Martyr and Cyprian. In earlier times the method was sometimes to collect alms (q.v.) for the poor outside the church; in many English medieval churches there was an alms-chest with a slot in the lid, as at Heckfield, Yorkshire. Pope Innocent III ordered such chests to be placed in English churches in the time of King John for collections for the Crusades. In the time of King Edward VI many of the alms-chests disappeared, but there remained the poor men's box.

Some commentators have wrongly concluded that the alms-dish or basin was entirely an innovation of the post-Reformation rites introduced in the English prayer book; but this is incorrect, as there are fifteenth-century examples still extant, and there are references to such dishes in the fourteenth century (*Test. Ebor.* i. 114, Surtees Soc.).

It is, however, interesting to notice the changes that have taken place in the method of collecting alms in the various editions of the English prayer book: That of 1549 says, 'While the clerks do sing the Offertory, so many as are disposed shall offer to the poor men's box, everyone according to his ability.' But in the 1552 book the rubric was altered thus, 'Then shall the Churchwardens or some other by them appointed gather the devotion of the people, and put the same into the poor men's box.' It was not until 1662 that the present custom appeared, following the Scottish Liturgy of 1637, 'The deacon or (if no such be present) one of the churchwardens shall receive the devotions of the people there present, in a bason provided for that purpose. And when all have offered, he shall reverently bring the said bason, with the oblations therein, and deliver it to the presbyter, who shall humbly present it before the Lord, and set it upon the Holy Table.'

This was a return in principle to the custom of earlier centuries when the elements of bread and wine as well as other offerings in kind were brought up by the people and received on tray-shaped patens (*see* **Chalice and Paten**).

C. E. POCKNEE

Almuce *see* Vestments (2e)

Altar

Derived from the Latin *altare*, the word means a place or structure where sacrifice is offered. In Christian worship it is associated with the chief act of Christian worship, the Lord's Supper, the eucharist, the holy communion or the mass.

There can be little doubt that at the institution of the sacrament of the Lord's body and blood in the Upper Room Jesus presided at a wooden table; and that structures of this kind were used in the house-churches when the eucharist was celebrated on the first day of the week during the first three centuries of the Christian era. References to the eucharist in the NT are not frequent since it was the normal function of the Christian assembly on Sundays.

It has been mistakenly supposed that the term 'altar' can only be applied to a structure of stone rather than wood. Paul, referring to the disorders at Corinth in connection with the eucharist, speaks of 'the Lord's table' (I Cor. 10.21); but this is an oblique reference to the sacrament itself rather than to the structure of the table. The writer of the Epistle to the Hebrews says, 'We have an altar from which those who serve the tent have no right to eat' (Heb. 13.10). There can be little doubt that the writer is referring to the eucharist in distinction from the sacrifices of the old covenant. It is important to take note that he refers not simply to an altar in the new dispensation but to a place where eating takes place, a sacrificial act. In the Greek text of this passage the term for altar is the normal term used to describe both Jewish and pagan altars of sacrifice in the Septuagint, e.g. Lev. 6.9 and Judg. 6.25. The fact that this term is applied to the eucharist is of considerable significance. The reference to the eucharist as 'a pure sacrifice' by the writer of the *Didache*, ch. 14, about AD 100, also underlines this fact. Ignatius of Antioch in his epistles, written about 107, also makes numerous references to the altar (the same term) and the eucharist, thus 'Be careful to use one eucharist, for there is one flesh of our Lord Jesus Christ, and one cup for union with his blood, one altar, as there is one bishop' (*Ep. Phil.* 4.1). The Greek fathers during the first four centuries sometimes use the term 'table' and sometimes 'altar' for the structure upon which the eucharist is celebrated. The Latin fathers, such as Tertullian and Cyprian in the third century, also use the terms *mensa* and *altare* for the eucharistic table. Augustine of Hippo (d. 430) uses the term *altare* in connection with a wooden table (*Ep.* 185), thus disproving the idea that a distinction was drawn between a communion table of wood and a sacrificial altar of stone. Wooden altars seem to have been of various shapes, square, round and semi-circular.

There can be little doubt that the custom of having stone altars is directly connected with the celebration of the eucharist at or near the tomb of a saint in the catacombs, thus linking altar with tomb. With the building of permanent churches in the fourth century at Rome, Jerusalem and elsewhere, the idea was carried a step further and the altar was built over the martyr's or confessor's tomb or shrine. Hence the words *martyrium* (q.v.) or *confessio*. In the more important churches the body of a celebrated saint was buried under the altar, but in the smaller churches which were used simply as a place of assembly for public worship it became the custom to require that some kind of relic associated with a saint should be buried in a cavity in the top of the altar. In some instances a consecrated host was used instead. Thus eventually it became the more usual custom to require that no altar was used without such relics.

While in the first three centuries the mere fact of celebrating the eucharist on an altar-table was considered to be sufficient to hallow it, it gradually came to be the custom that no altar should be used without its formal consecration by a bishop. This consisted in the placing of relics in the altar, to which we

Plate 1
Altar with ciborium
c. 1000, Castel S. Elia,
Italy

have alluded; in addition, the altar-top had five crosses engraved on it and these were anointed with chrism by the bishop (*see* **Consecration of Churches**). Nevertheless, it is possible to produce evidence for the use of altars which had received no such consecration. Also, we know that wooden altars were in use in England until quite late in the Middle Ages.

In the earlier centuries the altar was of equal dimensions, i.e. it was cube-shaped. Prominence was given to this type of altar by surmounting it with a canopy mounted directly on four columns, and known as a ciborium (*see* Plate 1). This kind of canopy and its columns were made of wood, stone, or precious metal. In the West, as the centuries went on, the altar tended to be lengthened,

until in the late Middle Ages we find very long altars such as that at Tewkesbury Abbey (13 ft) and that of the Lady Chapel at Ely (over 16 ft). The result was that the ciborium resting on its four columns became dismembered; the posts or columns remained round the ends of the lengthened altar, while the canopy became suspended as a separate tester hanging from the roof. Sometimes the posts were surmounted by carved angels holding candles. This type of altar was more prevalent in northern Europe, and it has been mistakenly termed an 'English altar', as though it was something peculiar to the Church of England.

Another development in Western Christendom in the Middle Ages was the multiplication of altars in churches associated with guilds and fraternities, in contrast to the primitive era when there was only one altar and one celebration of the eucharist in any one church on any one day. In this respect the Eastern Orthodox Church, with its one altar and one eucharist on any one day, has remained closer to the primitive church.

For many centuries, too, except possibly in churches of the East Syrian rite, the altar was normally free-standing and accessible on all sides. In the West, however, the altar came to be placed against a wall or screen. In the greater churches such as abbeys and cathedrals, this screen often separated the altar from the reliquary containing the body of the patron saint, as we can still see at Westminster Abbey and St Albans Cathedral. The separation of the altar from the saint's reliquary in the later Middle Ages was to permit the crowds to pray at the shrine of the saint without interrupting the service in progress at the high altar.

The placing of candlesticks (see **Candles, Lamps and Lights**) and a cross (q.v.) on the altar was also a very late innovation in the West, the candlesticks and cross originally being used in processions and placed on the pavement around the altar. Only at the end of the Middle Ages did these ornaments sometimes come to be set upon the altar. The idea that all altars must have a cross standing on them is an error of the nineteenth-century ecclesiologists. Also, the custom of having precisely six candlesticks on the altar was a development that arose from the Counter-Reformation movement in the Roman Church in the sixteenth century. Nor did flower vases find a place on the holy table in olden times, but flowers were thrown on the pavement before the altar and not crammed into vases to decline in a state of putrefaction.

At the Reformation many stone altars were destroyed and replaced by wooden tables because stone altars had become associated with a particular view of the eucharistic sacrifice. Through a revived biblical theology and the wider study of comparative religion we realize that both medievalists and Reformers were too limited in their conception of sacrifice which they associated exclusively with death or immolation. Today we should prefer to say that the sacrifice of Christ recalled in the eucharist is the whole of his atoning work culminating in the cross, resurrection and ascension.

J. Braun, *Der Christliche Altar*, 2 vols, 1924; D. R. Dendy, *The Use of Lights in Christian Worship*, 1959; C. E. Pocknee, *The Christian Altar*, 1963.

C. E. POCKNEE

Altar Hangings

In the first two centuries of the Christian era it is unlikely that the table at which the eucharist was celebrated was regarded as a permanent feature and ornament. But in the third century, rooms came to be adapted permanently in the larger houses as the eucharistic room, and the altar-table was looked upon as the focal point of Christian worship (see **Architectural Setting**). Over the table was thrown a cloth of silk, damask or brocade which enveloped it on all sides, the altar (q.v.) being cube-shaped in structure at that time. As time went on, this cloth was decorated with emblems in embroidery and with jewels; John Chrysostom in the fourth century had to give a warning that too much attention should not be paid to this kind of thing. We can see, in a sixth-century mosaic in the church of San Vitale, Ravenna, a depiction of an altar arrayed in this kind of altar-cloth or pall.

Over the decorated cloth there was spread at the time of the offertory (q.v.) the fair linen cloth upon which the eucharist was celebrated. The altar arrayed in this vesture was regarded as the symbol of Christ in the midst of his church.

This type of throw-over altar cloth was revived in the Church of England in the seventeenth century and has somewhat misleadingly come to be termed a 'Jacobean' altar frontal; but it is, as we have stated, a revival of the vesture of the early Christian centuries.

In the second part of the Middle Ages in the West, when altars came to be placed close to screens and walls, the throwover cloth was abandoned for a frontal (q.v.), a flat silk cloth which was suspended on the side of the altar visible to the congregation.

In the earlier centuries there were also silk or damask curtains suspended on rods between the columns or posts that supported the ciborium (see **Baldachin**). These curtains were also embroidered and decorated with jewels in the larger and more affluent churches. In the later Middle Ages, when the altar came to be lengthened, these curtains were hung between the riddel-posts that enclosed the ends of the altar, while at the back of the altar, if there was not a reredos (q.v.) of wood or stone, a cloth with embroidered figures and emblems was hung. This back-cloth is properly termed a *dorsal* or *super-frontal*.

A fair linen cloth is spread on the top of the altar at the time of the celebration of the eucharist. As the shape of the altar has changed over the course of the centuries, this cloth has had to be adapted in form to meet such changes. (*See* Plate 2.)

P. Dearmer, *The Linen Ornaments of the Church,* [2]1950; C. E. Pocknee, *The Christian Altar*, 1963; The Warham Guild, *The Warham Guild Handbook*, rev. ed., 1963.

C. E. POCKNEE

Altar Rails

Altar rails were unknown in England before the Reformation and they began to come into use in the last part of the reign of Queen Elizabeth I. But a considerable impetus was given to their use by William Laud who, first as Dean of Gloucester in 1616, and later as Bishop of Bath and Wells and then Bishop of London, and finally as Archbishop of Canterbury in 1634, insisted that the altar should be placed in the traditional position in the sanctuary (q.v.) and fenced off with rails to protect it from irreverence. The purpose of these rails was to protect the altar from profanity. They were provided with a gate in the middle and the closeness of the balusters to one another was to prevent dogs from getting into the sanctuary. To quote the words of Bishop Wren of Norwich, 'the Rayle be made before the Communion Table reaching crosse from the north wall to the south wall, neere one yarde in height, so

Plate 2   Altar with carved reredos and riddel posts, vested with frontal and frontlet, Tring, England

thick with pillars that doggs may not gett in'. The purpose of these rails, therefore, was not to provide a support for the communicants to lean against when they received holy communion. Indeed, the height of these seventeenth century rails makes them inconvenient for the kneeling communicant.

During the Commonwealth period some of these rails were destroyed and had to be replaced at the Restoration of 1660. Many of the rails erected in the nineteenth century are of poor design. In the present century some of these have been replaced by kneeling benches for the communicants. But liturgical reforms now taking place seem to indicate that both rails and benches alike may become obsolete with the increasing custom of standing to receive holy communion. It should be realized that for over a thousand years throughout Christendom the normal posture for receiving holy communion was that of standing; only in the thirteenth century did the custom of kneeling come into fashion in connection with the introduction of the ceremony of the elevation of the host. Standing at the holy communion has never been abandoned in the Eastern Orthodox rite.

C. E. POCKNEE

Altar, Stripping of

A rite that took place at the end of the liturgy on Maundy Thursday. The altar cloth(s) and frontal were removed during the recitation of Ps. 21 (22).

From a very early time altars which were simple and unpretentious structures were covered with a single cloth, for such was the custom of the Roman empire at the time. Of this we have probably the first witness in the Gnostic *Acts of Thomas* (5th act, ch. 49), and by the fourth century Optatus of Milevis certainly refers to the linen cloth. This was removed without ceremony at the end of the eucharist and the altar stood bare throughout the week. This remained the custom for centuries, although by the sixth century, at least in some places (e.g. Ravenna), the altar was richly clothed. This practice, together with the later allegorizing tendencies, led to a symbolic interpretation of the rite.

There were two factors that led to the development of the rite summarily described above. (1) The altar itself came to signify Christ's body and the cloth(s) and frontal or pallium the members of Christ's body, namely Christians. (2) The place in the

Passion according to St John (which was and is still sung on Good Friday) where Ps. 21 (22) is quoted (John 19. 23, 24) led to a *dramatization* of the rite. By the second half of the eighth century (*Ordo Romanus* XXVII), two deacons standing at either end of the altar took away the cloth 'in the manner of thieves', furtively. Later still (*Ordo Romanus* XXXI – *c*. 850-900), the cloth was taken from the altar at the words 'They divided my vesture among them'. In the tenth century the rite was associated with the rending of the veil in the Temple, and two cloths were prepared which at the appropriate moment were parted and taken away.

The rite then signified the stripping of Christ before his crucifixion and the separation of Christ from his members, the church. All this was summed up in the (allegorical) commentaries of Beleth (d. 1165) and Durandus of Mende (d. 1296), with sundry additions. For the former, the rite signified the kenosis of Christ who in the passion was stripped of his glory, his stripping by the soldiers before crucifixion and the abandonment of him by the apostles. The rite reminds Durandus of Isa. 53 and of the rending of the Temple veil. The ancient action, then, of removing the cloth from the altar after every eucharist and then on Maundy Thursday without ceremony was now transferred to that day with the significance that it symbolized the stripping of Christ before his crucifixion. Combined with the washing of the altar (q.v.), it ultimately signified the church's mourning for its dead Lord.

In the revision of the Holy Week liturgy of 1970, there has been a return to the earliest tradition. Both on Maundy Thursday and Good Friday the cloth is removed without ceremony.

J. D. CRICHTON

Altar, Washing of

A rite now observed only at St Peter's, Rome, on Maundy Thursday, it was, in the Middle Ages, practised very generally (e.g. Spain, France, England) at least in cathedrals and larger churches on the same day.

Originally it was a utilitarian rite whose purpose was to clean the whole church in preparation for the celebration of the Easter festival. Thus Isidore of Seville (*De Ecclesiasticis Officiis*, I, 29) speaks of the altars, walls, floors and vessels being washed on Maundy Thursday. This statement is juxtaposed to one referring to the Lord's washing of his disciples' feet, thus discreetly suggesting a symbolism: the church in the person of the disciples is washed, cleansed from sin.

A Gallic writer, St Eloy or Eligius of Noyon (588-659), repeats this statement, which would seem to indicate that the custom was common at this time to Spain and Gaul. It does not appear in the Roman books until the tenth-century *Romano-Germanic Pontifical* (ed. C. Vogel, 1963, vol. II, p. 57) where Isidore's words are reproduced almost *verbatim*. It would seem to be a clear inference that the custom came from Spain through France to Rome under German influence. Thence it spread throughout Europe. It is found in J. Beleth (d. 1165) and in Durandus of Mende (d. 1296), the Sarum books and in the English writer John Myrc (fl. 1400), who provides a commentary on the Sarum use.

Symbolism. As can be seen from the origin of the observance (*see above*), its meaning is partly suggested by its place in the Holy Week liturgy. It was associated with the commemoration of the Last Supper and of the Passion. But during all the Middle Ages the altar acquired an ever richer symbolism and became more and more the focus of attention. It became the principal symbol of Christ. At its consecration, five crosses were carved in the table (*mensa*) to represent the five wounds of Christ, and the cloths and covering (frontal or *antependium*) were regarded as the members of Christ's (mystical) body. The stripping of the altar (q.v.) was a sign of death and, as the present rite (*see below*) indicates, the washing with wine and water signifies the mourning over the dead Christ. In other words, it is a funeral rite.

But the medieval writers, after their fashion, allegorized the rite. Thus for Beleth, the washing with wine and water signifies the blood of redemption and the water, the water of regeneration. There is naturally a reference to the water and blood that flowed from Christ's side, and there is the comment that the church washes the altar because his body was sprinkled with blood and water on the cross. The branches or sprigs with which the wine and water were spread over the altar suggest the crown of thorns, and therefore the branches must have rough leaves. But he also refers to the cleaning of the floor with similar branches, and this symbolizes our being cleansed from vice. Durandus repeats much of this, sometimes using the very words

of Beleth, and offering very little of his own. In the Sarum use we note that it was the five crosses themselves that were washed, thus emphasizing that it was a funeral rite. John Myrc repeats Beleth and Durandus.

The twigs or branches were scattered upon the altar after the washing, and even in recent times, the palms from the previous Palm Sunday were put on the (now unwashed) altars (*see* Herbert Thurston, *Lent and Holy Week*, 1904, pp. 302f.).

The present rite. It is performed by seven canons of St Peter's after the last office of Maundy Thursday. With the other clergy of the basilica, they go in procession to the Altar of the Confession, Ps. 21 (22) is intoned and the canons then pour wine mixed with water on the altar. The cardinal archpriest approaches and with a branch of yew spreads it over the altar and the canons do likewise. Afterwards, they dry the altar with sponges and towels. All now retire from the altar and kneel while the responsory *Christus factus est* (Phil. 2.8) is sung. The rite concludes with a silent recitation of the Lord's Prayer and the collect used at the day's office (*see* Mario Righetti, *Storia Liturgica*, [2]1955, vol. II, p. 168).

J. D. CRICHTON

Ambo

Also spelt ambon, a Greek term in origin. A structure often approached by a flight of steps and surrounded by a parapet, and made of wood, stone or marble. It was used for the reading of the gospel at the eucharist and was usually larger than the medieval pulpit (q.v.) as its platform not only accommodated the reader of the gospel but also the attendant taperers or candle-bearers. The ambo was used also on the eve of Easter by the deacon who sang the *exsultet* at the blessing of the Paschal candle. In the larger basilicas (q.v.) the ambo was often decorated with carved or tessellated designs, a frequent one being Jonah and the whale, a type of Christ's resurrection (Matt. 12.40).

There were sometimes lesser ambos, as at St Clement's, Rome, from which the other lessons at the eucharist were read. All these structures usually had a desk upon which the liturgical book was placed.

From the steps of the ambo a portion of psalmody was sung by the chanters in between the reading of the epistle and the gospel. Hence this chant came to be known as the *gradual* (q.v.), from the Latin *gradus*, a step. The ambo was not primarily designed as the place from which a sermon was delivered, as this was done by the bishop from his throne or *cathedra* (q.v.). *See* Plate 3.

C. E POCKNEE

Amen

A Hebrew word meaning 'firm' or 'established', and then, as an adverb, 'certainly' or 'assuredly'. It is used often in the OT as an acknowledgment that a saying is valid and binding and constitutes a claim which is accepted. In synagogue worship it served as a community response of assent and confirmation.

In the NT it is frequent on the lips of Jesus, being translated in the AV by 'verily' and in more recent versions by 'truly'. It stands, however, at the beginning and not the end of Jesus' sayings to show that the words are reliable and true and are so because he acknowledges them as his own and hence makes them valid.

Following the example of Jesus and the practice of the synagogue, it was adopted into Christian liturgical usage, and so Paul speaks of the amen of the assembly at the giving of thanks (I Cor. 14.16). According to Justin Martyr the people say amen after prayer and thanksgiving and 'this word

amen answers in the Hebrew language to *genoito*, i.e. so be it'. Cyril of Jerusalem, states that the Lord's Prayer is 'sealed' with an amen.

In the eucharist the amen is especially noticeable as the people's response to the prayer of consecration and, in many liturgies, to the words of administration. It is, however, not only an assent but also a proclamation of faith, for Jesus himself is 'the amen' (Rev. 3.14), i.e. he himself is the response to the divine Yes in him. So the worshippers proclaim their belief that in Christ the faithfulness of God has been vindicated.

TDNT, I, pp. 335-8.   EDITOR

Amice *see* Vestments (1*b*)

Anamnesis *see* Anaphora (7)

Anaphora

A Greek word, meaning 'offering', from the verb *anaphero*, 'I carry up', 'I offer up (in sacrifice)', 'I offer up (to God on high)', which has from a very early date been the normal Greek name for the eucharistic prayer, commonly called in English the prayer of consecration (q.v.), and is universally the name most widely used by liturgical scholars. The oldest name for this

Plate 3   Ambo, thirteenth century, Ravello cathedral, Italy

prayer is probably *eucharistia* (Gk. and thence Lat. 'thanksgiving'); other ancient names are *actio sacrificii* (Lat. 'the act of sacrifice'), *oratio oblationis* (Lat. 'the prayer of offering'), and simply *oratio* or *prex* (Lat. '*the* prayer'). In the Roman rite for many centuries this prayer has been entitled *canon* (q.v.) (Lat. 'rule', the exact sense of which in this application is uncertain); in the revised *Ordo Missae* of 1969 it is entitled *prex eucharistica* (Lat. 'eucharistic prayer').

The common opinion of earlier generations of liturgists, that there was originally a single basic pattern of the eucharistic prayer, has fallen increasingly out of favour in the present century, partly as a result of the greater number of early documents now available, and partly as a result of the more scientific detailed study both of these and of documents previously known, to such an extent that there are some writers who deny that there was even an approximation to such a pattern. This assertion, however, appears to rest upon an inability to see the wood for the trees, as well as, in some cases, speculations belonging to the realm of fantasy rather than to that of sober scientific scholarship, and sometimes involving positive mishandling of the evidence. A serious study of all the available evidence, and of the work done upon it, suggests that the earlier opinion may be right after all, in principle although not in detail.

For the apparently considerable differences between the anaphorae of the historic rites, and between all of them and such primitive evidence as is available, all reveal themselves, when carefully examined, to be the consequence of secondary elements added to the primitive structure or elaborated from it — secondary elements which were added or elaborated in different ways and at different points in the common basic structure. That common basic structure appears to be preserved in the oldest actual text of an anaphora which, so far as is at present known, survives, that in the *Apostolic Tradition* of Hippolytus of Rome, written *c.*215. The integrity of the textual tradition of this document has been disputed, notably by Dix and Ratcliff (in different ways and with different, and mutually incompatible, implications), but it has been established beyond reasonable doubt by the editor of the definitive critical edition, Bernard Botte, who has also vindicated the authorship and date of it.

The eucharistic prayer of the *Apostolic Tradition* may be divided into the following parts (the definition and description of which we leave to a later point): introductory dialogue; thanksgiving; narrative of the institution; anamnesis; epiclesis; concluding doxology. With one exception (apart from certain Hispano-Gallican and Ethiopic documents which are in such a manifest state of textual confusion that no reliance can be placed upon them), there is no known anaphora in any of the historic rites which does not contain, or has not contained at some time, all these parts in this order. The one exception is the mid-fourth-century Egyptian Anaphora of St Serapion, in which the narrative of the institution ·and the anamnesis are conflated; a second apparent exception, the East Syrian Anaphora of the Holy Apostles Addai and Mari, from the existing text of which the institution narrative is missing, has been conclusively proved once to have included it, on both internal and external grounds, by Dom Botte.

Absent from the anaphora of the *Apostolic Tradition* are three elements, two of which are all but universal, and one of which is not uncommon, in the historic anaphorae: the anthem *Sanctus*, which occurs in the course of the thanksgiving or at its close in almost every other complete anaphora at present known, with the single significant exception of that in a fourth-century (?) Syrian document, the *Testament of our Lord Jesus Christ*, closely dependent on the *Apostolic Tradition*; the intercessory prayers technically called the diptychs (q.v.), which occur in every other anaphora but those of the ancient Hispano-Gallican rites, where they are placed between the offertory (q.v.) and the anaphora; and a preliminary epiclesis before the institution narrative, which occurs in the Alexandrine and Roman rites. The varying arrangement of these elements, in itself a strong indication of their addition to an original common structure which did not include them, is the principal means by which the anaphorae of the historic rites are classified, and the great liturgical families distinguished one from another.

In order to clarify the issue, we will first enumerate the possible component parts of a developed anaphora of classical structure, and then examine their disposition in the anaphorae of the great liturgical families. The possible component parts are as follows: (1) introductory dialogue; (2) preface (q.v.)

or first part of the thanksgiving; (3) *Sanctus*; (4) post-*Sanctus* or second part of the thanksgiving; (5) preliminary epiclesis (alternative or additional post-*Sanctus*); (6) narrative of the institution; (7) anamnesis; (8) epiclesis; (9) diptychs or intercessions, which may be divided; (10) concluding doxology.

The expansion of the postulated original common structure in the anaphorae of the Antiochene or West Syrian family of liturgies (which includes the second most widespread of the great historic rites, the Byzantine, commonly called, through the anachronistic application of denominational labels to the ancient liturgies, 'Orthodox') is clear from a comparison of the anaphora in the *Apostolic Tradition*, that in the *Testament of our Lord*, and those of the developed Antiochene type. The order of the first of these is: 1 2 6 7 8 10. The order of the second is: 1 2 6 7 8 9 10. All the developed anaphorae of this family follow the order: 1 2 3 4 6 7 8 9 10. (Some of them conclude 8 10 9 10, a variant which clearly reveals the way in which 9 was added to an existing complete structure.) The distinguishing features of the Antiochene anaphora are (*a*) the absence of any preliminary epiclesis (5), together with the continuation of the thanksgiving, often indeed the greater part of it, in the post-*Sanctus* (4), and (*b*) the insertion of the diptychs between the epiclesis and the doxology.

The anaphorae of the East Syrian family follow the order: 1 2 3 4 6 (absent, as already noted, from the existing text of one of them, but undoubtedly originally present) 7 9 8 10.

The anaphorae of the Alexandrine family exhibit a number of internal variants (although many of these are due to the textual confusion of the Ethiopic anaphorae, which constitute the majority of the family). The normal order appears to be that found in the Liturgy of St Mark, the principal liturgy of the family: 1 2a 9 2b 3 5 6 7 8 10. This exhibits the principal distinctive features of this type of anaphora: (*a*) the insertion of the diptychs (9) in the middle of the thanksgiving, and (*b*) the presence of a preliminary epiclesis (5) before the institution narrative, together with the absence of any further thanksgiving (4) after the *Sanctus*. Certain variants deserve notice. The conflation of the institution narrative and the anamnesis in the Anaphora of St Serapion has already been noted; the same anaphora has no intercessory insertion in the preface, but a brief one after the epiclesis, in

the position characteristic of the Antiochene type. Some liturgists suggest, on fragmentary evidence and technical grounds, that originally the Alexandrine diptychs may have been divided, like those of the Roman rite (*see below*). A feature common to a number of the Ethiopic anaphorae is the substitution of a post-*Sanctus* thanksgiving (4) for a post-*Sanctus* preliminary epiclesis (5), but this probably originated in direct borrowing from Antiochene liturgies; one ancient Alexandrine liturgical fragment, however, has a post-*Sanctus* succinctly combining 4 and 5. ·

The surviving texts of the ancient Hispano-Gallican liturgies of the West are in a state of evident confusion similar to that of the Ethiopic texts in the East. It is, however, possible to reconstruct from them a normal form of their anaphora (which was almost entirely composed of variable prayers appropriate to the day or season). The diptychs (9) were recited between the offertory and the anaphora, and the structure of the latter appears to have originally been that of the *Apostolic Tradition* with the sole addition of the *Sanctus* with a post-*Sanctus* continuation of the thanksgiving: 1 2 3 4 6 7 8 10; in the extant texts the anamnesis (7) is often reduced to a minimal form and combined with the epiclesis (8).

The most distinctive feature of the historic Roman canon is the division of the diptychs, half being placed before and half after the central prayers. Its order is as follows: 1 2 3 9a 5 6 7 8 9b 10. The new eucharistic prayers of the Roman rite abandon this particular distinctive feature, being structured thus: 1 2 3 4 5 6 7 8 9 10. Like the Roman canon itself, therefore, their structure falls midway between those of the Antiochene and Alexandrine types, although they have moved a stage nearer the former.

From this consideration of the structure of the anaphorae in the primitive and historic liturgies, we pass to a more detailed examination of its component parts.

1. *The Introductory Dialogue.* Like the Jewish forms of thanksgiving from which it is derived, the Christian thanksgiving begins with a dialogue inviting the participants to remembrance of God and thanksgiving for his mercies. That still in use in the Roman rite and its derivatives is the basic form, closely resembling that preserved in the *Apostolic Tradition* of Hippolytus; most of the Eastern

rites elaborate it to a greater or lesser extent, as did the ancient Hispano-Gallican rites in the West. But in all the Christian forms the basic content remains the same: mutual greeting; an invitation to lift up the heart to God, with a response declarative of doing so; an invitation to give thanks, with a response declaring the propriety and duty of doing so. It is the third versicle, 'Let us give thanks', and response, which explain the universality and necessity of the dialogue: before he may proceed with the thanksgiving, the president of the assembly must receive the assembly's authority to do so in the name of all, and its assent to what he is about to say. (This is even more clearly marked in the otherwise very different Jewish forms of the dialogue.)

2. *The Preface or (First Part of the) Thanksgiving*. The significance of the word 'preface' in this context is explained elsewhere (*see* **Preface**). The thanksgiving is the foundation of all that follows it in the anaphora: the church gives thanks for God's mighty works in the past, in creation and redemption, and thereby proclaims its faith in their continuance in the future, the faith which is the source and spring of the prayers which follow.

During the formative centuries of the liturgy a clear distinction arose between two types of this thanksgiving: the one variable, stressing from day to day one part or aspect after another of the saving work of Christ, and the other fixed, longer, and presenting a general view of the whole history of salvation at each celebration of the eucharist. The first type came to predominate in the West, and the second in the East. Each has its advantages and disadvantages: the variable thanksgiving, or 'proper preface', makes it possible to think more deeply and appositely of the mystery appropriate to the day or season than does the invariable type, while the latter enables thanksgiving to be made at one eucharist for the whole action of God in creation and redemption more fully than does the variable type. The proper preface has the advantage of comparative brevity, the invariable thanksgiving that of maintaining a better balance between thanksgiving and prayer in the anaphora. It is perfectly possible to have both types of thanksgiving in one rite, either by providing a full general thanksgiving into which proper clauses or paragraphs can be inserted when appropriate, or by including one or more such general thanksgivings among a full range of proper prefaces, for use either on certain occasions or at will. It is also possible to have a number of alternative forms of the full internally invariable thanksgiving, as is common in the Eastern rites.

The content of the preface is also affected by the insertion of the anthems *Sanctus* and *Benedictus* in the anaphorae of all the historic liturgies. In certain rites, notably the Roman, these anthems conclude the thanksgiving; in others, including most of the great Eastern liturgies, they divide the thanksgiving, and in the latter case it is common either for the preface to be essentially no more than a formal ascription of praise, the detailed thanksgiving for the works of creation and redemption being postponed until after the *Sanctus* (*see below*), or alternatively for the greater part of the thanksgiving to be made in the preface, leaving only, e.g., a specific reference to Christ's passion to be made after the *Sanctus*, as an introduction to the institution narrative. Other divisions of the thanksgiving matter are also found, and in some anaphorae there is a considerable amount of repetition. Further reference to this question will be found below, in the consideration of the post-*Sanctus*.

3. *The Sanctus*. In all the great historic liturgies the preface ends with the singing or saying of the anthem *Sanctus*, to which is added in all but the Alexandrine anaphorae the anthem *Benedictus qui venit*. In the oldest surviving texts these anthems are either missing or evidently interpolated. This interpolation, while it provides for the congregation to join vocally in the climax of the thanksgiving, has not been an unmixed blessing: it has done as much as anything to confuse the clarity of structure which ought to be apparent in the anaphora. Whether, as in most rites, the thanksgiving originally led directly to the narrative of the institution as the account of the divinely-given means of making the thanksgiving truly effective, or, as in the Roman and Alexandrine rites, to a prayer for the acceptance or hallowing of the offerings within which the narrative was set, the transition from the thanksgiving by word to the thanksgiving by act was clear: we thank God . . . and therefore we *offer*. Once the *Sanctus* and *Benedictus* are interpolated, this sequence is obscured: it is all too easy for the thanksgiving (especially the first part of it,

when it is divided) to be seen as a mere preliminary, concluding with these anthems – we thank God . . . and therefore we *sing* . . .

For these reasons some have suggested the suppression of these anthems in contemporary liturgical revision. This, however, is unnecessary; it is perfectly possible so to integrate them into the thanksgiving that the sequence of thought is clear and uninterrupted. It is also undesirable; they provide a valuable opportunity for the whole assembly to join its voice with that of the celebrant at this climactic point. Moreover, the question of the date and circumstances of their introduction into the anaphora is a far from simple one, and those who argue that in some places they may have formed part of it from the beginning are not without evidence which may reasonably be held to support their thesis, not least the presence of markedly similar passages in certain Jewish thanksgivings of this type. Nor is there sufficient reason for dividing them, or suppressing the *Benedictus*, or transferring *Sanctus* and *Benedictus*, or *Benedictus* alone, to the end of the anaphora: the arguments which have been put forward for these courses all rest on debatable hypotheses based on evidence carefully selected and interpreted for the purpose, and while they may be of great interest to liturgical scholars, they are not an adequate foundation for practical liturgical reform.

4, 5. *The Post-*Sanctus *and Preliminary Epiclesis.* Whether the *Sanctus* was inserted in the middle or at the end of the thanksgiving, its insertion necessitated the provision of a passage linking it with what follows. It has already been noted that the post-*Sanctus* may take one of two forms, so far as its content is concerned: it may be either a continuation of the thanksgiving, or a prayer consequent upon the thanksgiving called for convenience the preliminary epiclesis; it may comprise both, as in the new Roman anaphorae. In most of the historic liturgies in which it is a continuation of the thanksgiving, it is linked to the *Sanctus* by the device of opening it with some such phrase as 'Holy in truth and blessed in truth . . .', thus taking up the themes of the divine holiness and blessedness from the *Sanctus* and *Benedictus* respectively. In the Alexandrine anaphorae, in which the post-*Sanctus* takes the form of a preliminary epiclesis, the theme of fullness is taken up from the preceding anthem, the prayer asking

that as the heaven and earth are full of God's glory, so the gifts now offered in sacrifice may be filled with his blessing, or some equivalent petition. Only in the historic Roman canon is any link of this kind all but absent, and the sequence of thought obscured by the insertion of the diptychs of the living at this point.

In liturgical revision, the form and content of the post-*Sanctus* should be determined by two principal considerations: first, the content and structure of the thanksgiving, and in particular by whether the preface is variable (in which case an invariable thanksgiving is desirable in the post-*Sanctus* making mention of the whole economy of creation and thanksgiving, however briefly) or invariable (with or without variable insertions, in which case the post-*Sanctus* needs to be so worded as to make a smooth transition from the verbal thanksgiving to the ritual thanksgiving with the bread and cup); second, the theology of consecration which the rite is intended to embody, a preliminary epiclesis being required in the post-*Sanctus* if the theory of consecration by the recitation of the words of institution is held, although the presence of a preliminary epiclesis does not necessarily imply such a theory of consecration. This issue will be considered further in connection with the epiclesis.

6. *The Narrative of the Institution.* The recital of the narrative of the institution of the eucharist at the Last Supper is universal in the primitive and historic anaphorae (the one apparent exception being, as already remarked, due to demonstrable textual corruption). It appears always to have been held necessary, whether or not the recitation of our Lord's words in it is regarded (as in the West from quite early in the Middle Ages) as itself constituting the whole consecration. In almost every anaphora the narrative is elaborated to a greater or lesser extent; in many, congregational responses are provided in the course of it or at the close of it, an enrichment which has been introduced into the new eucharistic prayers of the Roman rite, the historic Roman canon having none. Theologically, in those traditions which do not regard the recitation of the words of institution as by themselves operating the consecration, their essentiality is understood in the sense that they are the authority for proceeding to the anamnesis and the epiclesis, an authority which must be invoked in order that the

anamnesis and epiclesis may be effectual.

7. *The Anamnesis.* A Greek word expressing a Semitic concept, *anamnesis* is all but untranslatable into English. Memorial, commemoration, remembrance – all these suggest that the person or deed commemorated is past and absent, whereas anamnesis signifies exactly the opposite: it is an objective act, in and by which the person or event commemorated is actually made present, is brought into the realm of the here and now. And the eucharist, as the early church understood it, is 'the "re-calling" before God of the one sacrifice of Christ in all its accomplished fullness so that it is here and now operative by its effects in the souls of the redeemed' (Dix, *Shape of the Liturgy*, p. 243: so far as the doctrine of the early church is concerned, he ought to have written 'bodies and souls').

As a liturgical term, then, the anamnesis signifies that part of the anaphora in which it is explicitly stated that the church is offering the bread and cup with this meaning and for this purpose, in obedience to Christ's command so to do. The normal form of the anamnesis, which is all but universal in the primitive and historic liturgies, comprises a statement of the memorial and a statement of the offering, inseparably linked by making the former grammatically dependent on and relative to the latter. The former always mentions at least the passion, resurrection and ascension of our Lord; other aspects of the mystery of redemption, such as the incarnation, the burial, and the mediation of the ascended Christ at the right hand of the Father are added in some anamneses, and most contain also a reference to the second coming which sets the eucharist in its eschatological perspective. The statement of offering in the ancient liturgies always explicitly offers the bread and cup, either using those words or some elaborated equivalent; certain anaphorae, notably those of the Byzantine rite and the historic Roman canon, contain clauses emphasizing that in this offering the whole of the created order is representatively offered, but all make it clear that the offering is dependent upon its identification, in virtue of Christ's institution, with his own offering of himself. The anamneses in the new eucharistic prayers III and IV of the Roman rite carry this to lengths unprecedented in expression although not in content in the ancient anaphorae, a con-

sequence of the formal embodiment in these prayers of the medieval and post-medieval Western doctrine that the consecration is effected solely by the recitation of the words of institution.

8. *The Epiclesis.* Though the Greek word *epiclesis* simply means 'invocation', it has long been commonly used only of the prayer for the consecration of the bread and cup in the anaphora, and it is usually restricted to that form of it which asks the Father to send the Holy Spirit upon them to change them into the body and blood of Christ. This restriction appears, when the evidence is examined with care and without *a priori* presuppositions, to have little or no historical or theological justification, and to be partly the result of, and partly responsible for, the unfortunate controversies which have raged about this prayer, notably that which arose between East and West in the Middle Ages concerning the 'moment of consecration'.

A prayer at this point in the anaphora is universal, and the essential content of it, as distinct from its formulation and elaboration of the content, is also universal: it asks for the divine response to the church's obedience to Christ's command in the preceding anamnesis. The epiclesis in the anaphora of the *Apostolic Tradition* comprises a petition for the descent of the Holy Spirit on the elements and a statement of the ends for which this is sought, the fruits of communion. It does not specify the change of bread and cup into body and blood (although this is clearly implied throughout the prayer), and has therefore been called by some a 'communion epiclesis' as distinct from a 'consecration epiclesis'. This distinction is anachronistic, in that it implies a later and more sophisticated theology of the eucharistic action. It is also inaccurate, in so far as it is the prayer for the descent of the Spirit which is the actual petition for consecration in later and more elaborate Spirit-epicleses, the specification of the effect of this descent as the change of bread and cup into body and blood being essentially no more than a descriptive elaboration of it. The first certain evidence for the fuller form is the Greek Alexandrine Anaphora of St Basil, the basis of the Byzantine Anaphora of St Basil (which has been proved to be the work of Basil), and a document which cannot date from later than the first half of the fourth century and may well be older. From the middle of the fourth century the fuller form, comprising (1) the petition for the operation of the Spirit, (2) the description of the effects of this operation as the change of the bread and cup into the body and blood of Christ, and (3) the statement of the ends for which this is sought, the fruits of communion, has been universal in the Eastern liturgies. The Anaphora of St Serapion has an epiclesis asking for the descent of the Logos or Word instead of that of the Spirit, but this is an isolated theological variant, as there is evidence of an epiclesis of the Spirit in Egypt before it as well as after it. Some Eastern epicleses ask for the descent of the Spirit on the people as well as on the elements, a prayer clearly related to that for the fruits of communion with which they conclude.

In the West the epiclesis asking for the descent of the Spirit to effect the consecration appears to have been common in the ancient Hispano-Gallican rites. It has commonly been asserted that the historic Roman canon contains no epiclesis, but this assertion is based on the *a priori* presupposition that the epiclesis must ask for the descent of the Spirit, and specify the effect of this as the change of the elements, in so many words. In fact, so far from not containing an epiclesis at all the Roman canon contains one of an unusually rich and elaborate kind: it comprises two paragraphs (not one as in most anaphorae), the first (*supra quae . . .*) praying for the acceptance of the gifts, with profound typological scriptural references, and the second (*supplices te . . .*) asking for their translation to the heavenly altar (i.e. Christ himself), followed by the statement of the ends for which this is sought. A more explicit, or theologically more precise, petition for consecration than the latter of these two prayers would be difficult to conceive.

The issue has been confused both by the development in the West of the doctrine of consecration by the recitation of the words of institution and by the presence of the clause describing the change of the elements in a preliminary epiclesis (*quam oblationem*). The Alexandrine anaphorae, as previously noted, also have such a preliminary epiclesis, the division of the epicletic material between this and the epiclesis after the anamnesis varying somewhat from one anaphora to another, and in some involving considerable repetition. The origin of this division or duplication of the epiclesis is by no means clear, for there is

no adequate evidence for supposing that either is a later interpolation in those anaphorae in which they occur.

In the new eucharistic prayers of the Roman rite the preliminary epiclesis is definitely 'consecratory' in content, introducing the institution narrative, while the second epiclesis is specifically a prayer for the fruits of the eucharist: the operation of the Spirit is invoked in both. This arrangement is clearly designed to embody a particular doctrine of the moment of consecration; and this is true of the arrangement of the epicletic material in most modern eucharistic prayers. But it would be anachronistic to regard the double epicleses of the ancient Roman and Alexandrine traditions as the result of considerations of this kind. On the other hand, it is not now possible to eliminate them from the mind in the work of contemporary liturgical revision; given that the issue of a 'moment of consecration' has been raised, even the attempt to abandon such a concept by saying that the whole prayer consecrates merely results, in practice, in regarding the conclusion of the prayer as that moment.

In the Antiochene tradition, which has no preliminary epiclesis, as well as in the Alexandrine tradition which has, the conclusion of the epiclesis after the anamnesis has from a very early date been regarded as 'the moment of consecration'. This should not, however, be understood as an exact parallel to the developed Western doctrine of consecration by the recitation of the words of institution, although in controversy some Eastern writers have themselves tended so to regard it; the classical Eastern position is that the epiclesis is necessary to the consecration, and therefore that its conclusion is the moment when the latter is complete, but this insistence on the necessity of the epiclesis is not exclusive – the narrative of the institution and the anamnesis are equally so.

9. *The Diptychs.* The origins of the diptychs (q.v.), or eucharistic intercessions, in the historic anaphorae are considered in the article devoted to them, and it has been pointed out both in that and earlier in the present article that their insertion at different points in the prayer is one of the principal structural distinctions between the anaphorae of different traditions. A word must be added on the theological rationale of intercessory prayers in the anaphora, in view of the current

tendency in some quarters to eliminate such prayers from the eucharist proper altogether, which appears to owe more to liturgical archaeologizing (and that on a rather slender basis) than to serious theological and pastoral consideration. To remove all intercessory prayer from the memorial of Christ's one all-sufficient sacrifice cannot but obscure the fact that we can offer this, like any other prayer, only as members of Christ, redeemed through that sacrifice, and in the power of that sacrifice. Nothing can make this clearer, nor more effectively express the co-inherence of all redeemed humanity in Christ, than placing the intercessions in the anaphora, in the context of the offering of the eucharistic sacrifice, and of the prayer for the supreme gift of God which we ask for ourselves and for all men, the fruits of unity with Christ in communion. This is most clearly apparent when the intercessions are placed, as in the Antiochene anaphorae and the new Roman eucharistic prayers, after the central prayers of the anaphora as a continuance of the prayer for the fruits of communion. In the words of Alexander Schmemann:

... before we partake of the heavenly food there remains one last, essential and necessary, act: the *intercession*. To be in Christ means to be like him, to make ours the very movement of his life. And as he 'ever liveth to make intercession' for all 'that come unto God by him' (Heb. 7.25), so we cannot help accepting his intercession as our own. The Church is not a society for escape – corporately or individually – from this world to taste of the mystical bliss of eternity. Communion is not a 'mystical experience': we drink of the chalice of Christ, and he gave himself for the life of the world. The bread on the paten and the wine in the chalice are to remind us of the incarnation of the Son of God, of the cross and death. And thus it is the very joy of the Kingdom that makes us *remember* the world and pray for it. It is the very communion with the Holy Spirit that enables us to love the world with the love of Christ. The Eucharist is the sacrament of unity and the *moment of truth*: here we see the world in Christ, as it really is, and not from our particular and therefore limited and partial points of view. Intercession begins here, in the glory of the messianic banquet, and this is the only true beginning for the

Church's mission. It is when, 'having put aside all earthly care', we seem to have left *this world*, that we, in fact, recover it in all its reality. Intercession constitutes, thus, the only real preparation for communion (*The World as Sacrament* [1966], p. 53).

10. *The Doxology*. The anaphora ends as it begins with praise and thanksgiving, all but universally in the form of a particularly solemn Trinitarian doxology (q.v.). The concluding *amen* by the people is of equal importance with their responses to the introductory dialogue, expressing their assent to, and participation in, all that the president has said in their name.

Further reading: So many works have been devoted to this subject that it is impossible to recommend even an adequate representative selection, and any less adequate selection would tend to reflect the personal preferences of the present writer to an undesirable extent. Two books should, however, be mentioned: the first, *Prex Eucharistica*, by A. Hänggi and I. Pahl (1968), contains the most complete documentation of the subject available, together with an extensive bibliography; the second, *On the Epiclesis of the Eucharistic Liturgy and in the Consecration of the Font*, by E. G. C. F. Atchley (1935), is the most fully documented treatment of the epiclesis.

W. JARDINE GRISBROOKE

Anglican Worship

Anglican worship was a unique product of the Reformation, in that it is a development from the traditional Western Christian cultus and not merely another variant of continental Protestantism. Its base was a liturgy whose use was obligatory and whose contents conformed to what was believed in the sixteenth century to be a truly primitive pattern. Its principles were set out in the 1549 *BCP* in the preface and in the tract entitled *Of Ceremonies*.

First, instead of a series of local variations of the medieval Roman rite, there was now to be a single 'use' for the whole country. Furthermore, the ceremonies connected with it were essential to the rite and conducive to order, reverence and intelligibility. Secondly, all services were to be in English instead of Latin, in the interests of intelligibility and lay participation. Thirdly, there was an emphasis on edification, particularly through scripture, whereby men might profit in the knowledge of God and 'be the more inflamed with the love of his true religion'. To this end there was a daily office of morning and evening prayer – a unique Anglican feature among the worship of the Reformed Churches – involving the systematic recitation of the psalter and the reading of the Bible in accordance with a drastically simplified calendar. Fourthly, the central act of public worship was to be the eucharist, to be celebrated at least on Sundays and holy days, and possibly even daily. Finally, the liturgy was to be loyal to scripture and loyal to tradition – it was to contain nothing repugnant to the word of God and was to be expressive of the mind and purpose of the early fathers.

With the passage of time these basic principles have been modified, either by law or by common consent. Strict uniformity is no longer recognized as tenable: a church as comprehensive as the Church of England must make provision for differing attitudes – the sacramental and the prophetic, the corporate and the individual, simple austerity and rich splendour, the other-worldly and the this-worldly. It now attempts to have 'a tendency to conservatism in respect of the past; a passion for freedom in respect of the present; a reverence for the institution which incorporates its life; and an inveterate individualism in living that life'. Anglican worship has therefore moved away from a rigid and universal adherence to a single 'use' towards a conformity to a general pattern within fairly wide but nevertheless prescribed limits. This was recognized in the report of the Royal Commission on Ecclesiastical Discipline in 1906: 'The *law* of public worship in the Church of England is too narrow for the religious life of the present generation.' The report therefore recommended that this law should be modified in the light of the comprehensiveness of the Church of England and its existing needs. A great part of the twentieth century has been occupied in attempting to implement that recommendation, and the operation still continues.

Secondly, although English is still the language of liturgy, it has remained unchanged since 1662; in consequence it is now increasingly thought to be irrelevant and unintelligible. Only in the present day has the task of creating a truly contemporary liturgical language been undertaken, and this task is far from completion.

Thirdly, the system of public daily worship shared by both clergy and laity has never really worked, because the practising Christian layman has never been more than a Sunday worshipper. Broadly speaking, corporate worship of the entire community of clergy and laity is now a weekly event, while the daily round of worship is largely maintained by clergy and the members of certain institutions – religious communities, theological colleges, college chapels and cathedrals. But this in itself has produced another element in worship which is unique in the Church of England, the choral daily office, and around this has developed a corpus of church music such as no other church possesses.

Fourthly, it is now recognized that worship cannot be static; it is affected not only by developments in theology but also by the changing pattern of life in the world. The church today cannot be committed to the precise doctrinal positions of Anglican reformers and revisers of the sixteenth and seventeenth centuries. It can only be committed to their general appeal to scripture and the early church, and it must take into account fresh and contemporary understanding of the gospel. It is true that the ideal of the eucharist as the basic act of public worship has become generally accepted, but the way in which that rite is celebrated and the circumstances in which it is celebrated are beginning to change. Anglican worship has begun to combine with the sense of order and tradition a greater degree of freedom and spontaneity, largely under the influence of the Ecumenical and Liturgical Movements (q.v.). This is particularly evident in those acts of worship which now take place outside the traditional church building. There is a growing recognition of the connection between worship and the mission (q.v.) of the church, and of the need to relate worship to a variety of situations.

Nowhere has this been seen more clearly than in the developing worship of the Anglican Church overseas. Until the twentieth century, with relatively few exceptions, the 1662 prayer book was the basis of all public worship throughout the whole Anglican Communion. But the Lambeth Conference of 1920 sounded the note of reform with the assertion that the development of self-conscious and 'indigenous churches had created a demand for new forms of worship and for local adaptations of the prayer book. The principle of uniformity as expressed in the preface to the prayer book was not applicable to Anglican churches overseas, nor was it necessary as a bond of union between churches which possessed a unity of faith. This note was repeated by the Lambeth Conferences of 1930 and 1948, while the Conference of 1958 urged that each part of the Anglican Communion must be free to order its worship in ways which were real and meaningful in its own area. Anglican worship is therefore now beginning to assume different forms in different parts of the world, although the basic appeal to scripture, to the primitive church and to reason is maintained.

F. E. Brightman, *The English Rite*, 1915; Church of England Liturgical Commission, *Prayer Book Revision in the Church of England*, 1957; P. Dearmer, *The Parson's Handbook* (revised by C. Pocknee, 1966); C. Dunlop, *Anglican Public Worship*, 1953; E. Underhill, *Worship*, 1936.

R. C. D. JASPER

Anniversary

An annual celebration in the life of a church. A church or chapel anniversary is the Free Church equivalent of what others call a dedication festival (q.v.). It usually commemorates so many years of worship in the building, but sometimes the continuous history of a congregation, even though the building is not that which was used originally. Particular departments of church life also have anniversaries, e.g. choir anniversary, sisterhood anniversary. Anniversaries are often divorced from the original starting-date of the department; they are simply annual festivals. The chief of these is the Sunday school anniversary usually held in the spring. At these services Sunday school scholars sing hymns and anthems during the services. Sunday school anniversaries have been held, especially in Methodist churches, since at least the early part of the nineteenth century. Many local customs attached themselves to them, e.g. the building of a special platform for the scholars, the wearing of white dresses, the holding in the afternoon of a 'demonstration' of the work of the Sunday school. They were for long the best-attended services of the year. They are still held, but are not as popular as formerly.

A. RAYMOND GEORGE

Annunciation
see Mariological Feasts

Ante-communion

The *BCP* provides that 'if there is no communion' the communion service shall be said to the end of the prayer for the church and concluded with a collect and the blessing. Such a service is known as ante-communion, and this name was preserved in the Series 2 experimental Order of Holy Communion in the Church of England for that part of the service which included the introduction, the ministry of the word, and the intercessions. The name is a relatively recent innovation. From the seventeenth century until the nineteenth both the communion service and the ante-communion were commonly called the second service; during this period of infrequent communion the ante-communion was more frequently observed for the second service. It was 'second' in relation to mattins (q.v.) and the litany (q.v.) which came before it, since the strict observance of the Act of Uniformity required mattins, litany, and holy communion every Sunday morning.

This service is comparable to the mass of the catechumens of the patristic age, when catechumens (q.v.) were dismissed after the lessons and sermon (but before the prayers of the faithful), and also to the dry mass of the Middle Ages, which consisted at the least of the epistle, gospel, Lord's Prayer and blessing, and at the most of the whole rite of the mass except the canon and the use and presence of the elements and their vessels. The dry mass came to be associated with superstitious notions and practices, and came to be regarded as quasi-sacramental in character, and so incurred the disapproval of the reformers. Another name for the dry mass was *memoria*, and it is noteworthy that Archbishop Grindal and others described the ante-communion as 'a commemoration of the holy communion'.

The position from which the priest read the ante-communion was a matter of contention in the seventeenth century. The Puritans read it from the reading desk, and their 'exceptions' included a demand that the rubric should require it. The high churchmen read it from the altar, 'the church thereby keeping her ground, visibly minding us of what she desires and labours towards, our more frequent access to that Holy Table' (Sparrow, *Rationale*). It was one of the charges against

Laud at his trial that he 'read the Second Service at the Communion Table or Altar'.

W. E. Scudamore, *Notitia Eucharistica,* 1876, pp. 814 ff.

E. C. WHITAKER

Anthem

Although various alternative derivations for the term anthem have been suggested, it is almost certainly an anglicization of the word antiphon (q.v.). Traditionally a musical setting of words drawn from the psalms or from scripture, the anthem may be regarded as a vernacular equivalent of the Latin motet (q.v.), authority for its place in the liturgy being conferred by the rubric in the *BCP: In choirs and places where they sing, here followeth the anthem.* Regarded in that light, to justify its place in a service, an anthem should be chosen not only for its musical excellence but as making a valuable and relevant contribution to an act of worship. When selected on a seasonal or *de tempore* basis, and when the words are made known to the listening congregation, that result becomes possible; but the precarious performance of an anthem beyond the choir's abilities must inevitably cause distraction to the listener, thus contradicting its true function.

Anthems may be accompanied or unaccompanied, for 'single' or 'double' choir, and with or without soloists, a particular type in which the full choir is employed alternately with a soloist or group of soloists being known as a 'verse anthem'. The wide repertoire is perhaps best considered chronologically:

1. *Tudor, Elizabethan and Jacobean.* Tallis and Tye, who were active as composers both before and after the Reformation, provide a direct link between motet and anthem, the Latin or English of their texts, rather than questions of musical style, frequently marking the distinction. Other representative composers of the period are Tomkins, Byrd, Farrant, Morley, Mundy, Weelkes, Orlando Gibbons, Bevin and Batten. Characteristic of the period is a general absence of independent organ accompaniment – though many sixteenth-century anthems sung unaccompanied today probably received light organ support in contemporary performance.

2. *Restoration.* The type of anthem written for the Chapel Royal under Charles II was influenced by the French idiom made familiar to the monarch during his exile at Versailles. Accompanied by a string band and organ, such anthems were often lightly rhythmic and contained solo passages and sections in recitative. Perhaps most familiar in Purcell's 'Bell Anthem' (Rejoice in the Lord alway), the style was first introduced by Pelham Humphrey, to be continued by Blow, Wise and Turner – all of whom, like Purcell himself, had been Chapel Royal choristers.

3. *Hanoverian.* Representative of the English Baroque manner, and recalling Handelian conventions, the anthems of Boyce, Croft, Greene, Battishill, and Handel himself are marked by a dignity which sometimes approaches ponderousness; but which fades into dullness with Nares and Kent.

4. *Late Georgian and Early Victorian.* Sometimes influenced by Mozart and Mendelssohn, the best anthems of Crotch, Attwood, Goss and Walmisley yet preserve an integrity of their own. Those of S. S. Wesley introduce a new emotional content coloured by the chromaticism of Spohr, but avoiding excess. S. S. Wesley and Walmisley were the first to write the important independent organ accompaniments at this time which became a feature of most later anthems.

5. *Later Victorian and Edwardian.* Few of the multitude of anthems produced during the age of 'fashionable' church-going have earned a lasting place in the repertoire, the emotionalism and lack of dignity of much of Stainer, Sullivan, Barnby, and their successors proving unacceptable to modern tastes. Recovery began with Stanford, whose anthems include several masterpieces, and Parry, whose coronation anthem, 'I was glad', in particular, affords luxurious harmonies and sonorities without offending propriety. Charles Wood continued the new tradition to produce several rich anthems which still satisfy.

6. After the founding of the Motett Society in 1841, the anthem repertoire was further widened and enriched by the inclusion of works by Catholic composers such as Palestrina, Victoria, and their successors, often with an English paraphrase of the original texts. In the present century, the

advent of radio brought about a general rise in musical awareness which stimulated the revival after 1920 of many sixteenth-century compositions hitherto regarded as merely archaic. The same development encouraged a new astringency in composers as diverse as Vaughan Williams and John Joubert. There is today no shortage of modern anthems written by English composers of international standing who have managed to discipline their writing successfully so as to avoid making impossible demands upon the church choirs anxious to perform their works. It is perhaps in that direction that the biggest challenge to the modern anthem composer is presented.

C. Dearnley, *English Church Music, 1650-1750*, 1970; E. H. Fellowes, *English Cathedral Music*, rev. Westrup, 1969; M. B. Foster, *Anthems and Anthem Composers*, 1901; P. le Huray, *Music and the Reformation in England*, 1967; C. H. Phillips, *The Singing Church*, rev. Hutchings, 1968; E. Routley, *The Church and Music*, 1970.

BERNARR RAINBOW

Antidoron

Antidoron (Gk lit. 'instead of the gift') is the name given to the blessed bread which is distributed to the congregation after the eucharistic liturgy in the Byzantine rite.

The purpose of this distribution is threefold: (1) to consume what remains of the bread offered by the faithful for the eucharist but not used for it (*see* **Prothesis; Oblation**), (2) to provide immediate sustenance for communicants who have been fasting at least since midnight, and (3) to provide an additional element of participation in the service for non-communicants. It is from the third of these that the name 'antidoron' is derived: for non-communicants it to some extent takes the place of *the* gift, the eucharistic elements themselves. In recent years, with the spread of ecumenical contacts, this third purpose of the antidoron has been extended to provide an additional element of participation, and of fellowship with the congregation, for non-Orthodox visitors.

Similar usages have existed, and in some places still exist, outside the Byzantine rite: the distribution of blessed bread after the liturgy is a feature also of the Armenian and Syrian rites in the East, and it was once common in many parts of the West as well,

surviving in France until recent years and still in certain parts of that country.

W. JARDINE GRISBROOKE

Antiphon

This word has several liturgical meanings. The most familiar is the ancient practice of antiphonal singing, that is the two sides of the choir alternately singing in psalms or canticles. This is the Christian adoption of the Greek word *antiphonos*. The term antiphon was, however, applied later on to texts taken either from the psalms or from scriptural or other sources. Such antiphons were sung before and after the psalms or canticles of the divine office (q.v.) and provided matter relevant to the Sunday or feast day, or feria. The mode of the antiphon determined which of the psalm tones should follow, and so the final of the mode is to be sought in the concluding note of the antiphon, not of the psalm tone. Another use of the term applies to the four songs addressed to Mary, known as Marian antiphons, and also to other chants, as at the blessing of the palms on Palm Sunday and the exquisite 'In Paradisum' in the absolution after the mass for the dead.

ALEC ROBERTSON

Apse

An architectural term denoting a semicircular structure roofed with a half dome. It was the standard form of the sanctuary in the early Christian basilica (q.v.), and could either project beyond the east end, as in the Latin or Roman type, or be enclosed by a wall, thus providing side chambers, as in the Hellenistic form found in Syria.

EDITOR

Architectural Setting

The nature of Christian worship is such that it does not of itself require any particular architectural setting. It does not centre in a cult object, such as an image, that has to be protected within a shrine. It does not require a large item of liturgical furniture, such as a stone altar (q.v.), that has to be housed in a special way. It can be and has been celebrated in a dining room, a hospital ward or an open field. Nevertheless, throughout the centuries, it has had an architectural setting, which has expressed the Christian understanding of worship. Hence the study of worship historically cannot be divorced from a knowledge of the buildings in which it was conducted.

Fig. 1 Basilica of St John of Studion, Constantinople, Turkey

Yet, it has to be recognized that the minutiae of liturgical change can have little architectural effect. The addition of a prayer here or a petition there is not reflected in the buildings. New ideas only produce alterations if they are related to (1) new concepts of the nature of worship and of the church; (2) movement; (3) different ways of doing things. The development of Christian architecture in its connection with the liturgy is in part an account of the operation of these three 'laws'.

Primitive Christian worship, centring in the eucharist (q.v.), was essentially domestic and so was celebrated in the private house. The shape and location of these house-churches differed therefore according to the several forms of domestic architecture throughout the empire. In the east, where one-family buildings up to four storeys high were the norm, worship took place in the dining room which was usually on the top floor. In Rome, on the other hand, tenement dwellings were general, with apartments horizontally across them, and not necessarily having a dining room, so that the largest chamber available would have been used.

In time, houses were bought by or given to the church and these were then specially adapted to the needs of the cult. So the one at Dura Europos, built shortly after 200, had two rooms made into one, by removing a wall, and a dais was set up, while, to the right of the entrance, a small chamber was transformed into a baptistery, complete with font and wall decorations.

After the victory of Constantine, with Christianity replacing the pagan cults as the state religion, worship ceased to be a family gathering and became a public occasion. Its architecture accordingly was made to correspond with civic and imperial forms, and so the basilica became general in both east and west. The basilica (q.v.) was a large meeting hall, belonging to a recognizable class of public buildings, with nave (q.v.) and aisles (q.v.), possibly galleries (q.v.) and clerestories. These pagan forms were given religious overtones by the presence of the emperor's image. The Christian basilica was a similar monumental place of public gathering with religious associations, devotion to God as emperor of heaven being substituted for the imperial cult. Here, then, is an example of the operation of 'law' (1) above, i.e. a new concept of worship, public instead of private, being embodied in fresh architectural forms. Since the genus basilica did not have a uniform plan, the early Christian examples differed, but by the end of the fourth century they had assumed a recognizable identity.

Its general aspect was that of a single room, its horizontal perspective being emphasized by parallel colonnades which seemed to converge on the altar standing towards one end on the middle axis. This was the focal point of the building, and around it priesthood and laity gathered for the celebration of the liturgy, each section having its prescribed place. In the centre of the semi-circular apse (q.v.), roofed by a half-dome, the bishop had his throne, on either side of which were the seats of the presbyters. The superior clergy were separated from the rest of the congregation by the altar (q.v.) around which

Plate 4   The Christian basilica, Abbey of Pomposa, Italy

the deacons were grouped. It could stand on the chord of the apse or even in the body of the church, well down the central nave. The rectangular hall was divided by parallel rows of columns into areas of which there was always an odd number. The centre one, the nave, corresponded to the apse in width and was equivalent to the sum of the side aisles. Its walls rose above them and were pierced with windows to form a clerestory and allow the access of light (*see* Fig. 1 and Plate 4).

In the eighth and ninth centuries in western Europe, the operation of 'law' (2) above, i.e. movement, produced a new type of church, known as the porch-church or *Vollwestwerk*. In effect this was still a basilica but with its west end completely transformed and composed of two elements: a crypt at ground level and, above it, an upper church with aisles and galleries. Externally this was provided with a central tower and two smaller ones on each side gave access to the upper church. This porch-church was in fact to provide for the services of Holy Week and was modelled in part on the Holy Sepulchre complex at Jerusalem; it allowed for the many processions, i.e. movement, as well

as for the celebration of the eucharist, the adoration of the cross, etc. The first examples, from *c*.775, include St Riquier near Abbeville. In the tenth century there was a change in liturgical observance – the operation of (1) above – which immediately had an architectural effect. Whereas in the heyday of the porch-church, worship was something in which all actively participated, it gradually became a spectacle at which the people were passive onlookers. This meant that the plan could be simplified, circulation space being no longer required, and so the porch-church steadily atrophied, first losing its crypt, as in St Pantaleon, Cologne, then being transformed into a western apse, e.g. the cathedral of Paderborn, and finally only surviving as a decorative feature of the western facade, as in the triple towers of Maria-Laach in the twelfth century or the twin towers which appear on the front of so many Gothic buildings (*see* Plate 5).

The passivity of the congregation, which played so important a part in the decline of the porch-church, had, as its obverse, the increasing importance of the clergy who now ceased to conduct the liturgy 'on behalf of'

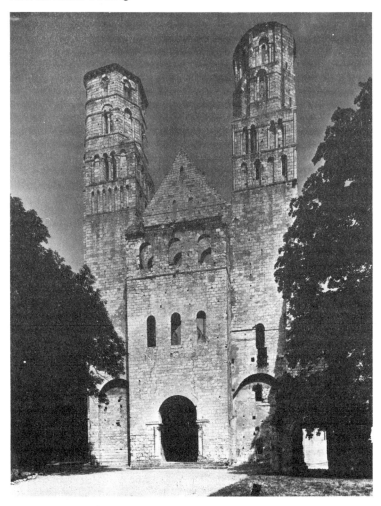

Plate 5 The porch-church, Jumièges, France

and celebrated it 'instead of' the congregation. The architectural result of this was that the place of the clergy, which had usually occupied the east end of the nave together with the apse, was removed out of the body of the church to create a second room (*see* Fig. 2). Hence the two-room plan of the Middle Ages – the sanctuary (q.v.) being for the ordained ministers, the nave for the laity (*see* Plate 6). In terms of the eucharist, this had involved a shift of emphasis from the communion to the consecration with the elevation as its climax – all that was needed therefore, since non-communicating attendance was widespread, was a distant view of the raised host, dimly glimpsed through the chancel screen beneath the rood at the far end of the choir. The priest had also moved from facing the people across the altar to standing with his back to them and so looking towards the east – here 'law' (3) is in operation.

The medieval church plan was not only the product of a different concept of worship – primarily a sacrifice in the presence of an audience – and of the church – an hieratically structured institution rather than an organism with interdependent functions – nor just of a new concept of the eucharist – centred in the consecration – but also of the developed cult of the saints. For this we have to go back to the fifth century and to recognize the existence of a building type other than the basilica.

Fig. 2   St Laurence, Bradford-on-Avon,
England

With the cessation of persecution, the period of the martyrs came to be looked upon as a golden age with the martyrs themselves as the heroes of the faith. Christians then began to enclose their remains in *martyria* (q.v.). These copied the form of pagan tombs and were roofed with domes, the symbol of heaven and the bliss of eternal life. The domes were supported by round or octagonal structures and in some cases abutted at all four points of the compass to pro-

duce the shape of a cross (*see* Plate 7). This so-called centralized architecture was in origin a type of funerary monument and it provided for the cult of the saints side by side with the Jesus-cult in the congregational basilicas. The fusion of the two cults in the east brought the two building types into relation and the result was a new form which perpetuated that of the *martyria* but modified it, sometimes by the addition of a basilican east end, to create centralized churches. This became the standard plan for Eastern Orthodoxy. One had only to add side chambers to the apse and an iconostasis (q.v.) with its doors, and the type which has remained traditional to the present day had been created (*see* Fig. 3). In this instance a developed understanding of the eucharist – 'law' (1) – relating it to the intercession of the saints, has had long lasting architectural effects. In the West, however, this cult did not have the same result; there the relics were placed in direct association with the main altar, either enclosed therein or connected by a shaft. Nevertheless the translation of relics did leave its mark on the internal arrangement of churches in Western Christendom, in so far

Plate 6   Two-roomed medieval plan, Heath chapel, Shropshire, England

Plate 7   Centralized cruciform church, Djivari, Georgia, USSR

as each and every relic had its own altar. This, together with the practice of votive masses and the belief that every priest must celebrate every day – further instances of 'law' (1) – led to the multiplication of altars which was such a feature of the medieval cathedrals and, to a lesser degree, of the parish churches.

The Reformation inevitably marked a watershed in the architectural setting of worship, since the Protestants had their own ideas about the cult, which differed radically from those embodied in the medieval buildings. Within the Roman Catholic Church, however, there was no such break with the immediate past, although the Renaissance initiated a new phase in church design. The Renaissance was a rebirth of classical culture, based upon a careful study of the writings and ruins of ancient Rome coupled with an imaginative re-creation of that past era as a golden age in which consolation and refreshment could be sought. For centuries a

Fig. 3   Typical Eastern Orthodox plan, Djivari, Georgia, USSR

Fig. 4   Centralized Renaissance plan,
S. Sebastiano, Mantua, Italy

church had been regarded as a sacred edifice, and the effect of this concept within the Renaissance context was to equate churches and temples, and so the temples of pagan Rome served as models for Christian buildings. The result was twofold: first, a centralized plan (q.v.) was favoured, e.g. S. Sebastiano, Mantua; and, second, aisles were suppressed, since these had no place in pagan temples, and were replaced by side chapels (*see* Fig. 4 and Plate 8).

Out of Renaissance classicism grew the baroque – an exuberant proclamation of the triumph of the Counter-Reformation. Here the prototype was no longer the temple but the theatre which, through the opera, had become the cultural focus of the period. Churches were now erected to provide distant vistas, with a scenic progression along

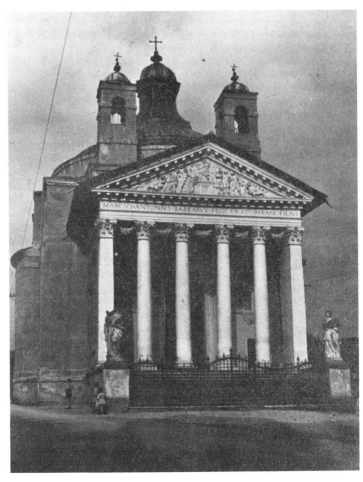

Plate 8
The Renaissance
temple, Maser, Italy

the horizontal axis. The church was now a place for an occasion, similar to a *soirée* at court complete with a *divertissement* by Lully. The focal point of worship became the exposition (q.v.) of the reserved sacrament – 'law' (1) above was operative – and in this divine presence a kind of heavenly grand opera was performed, with the high altar, profusely decorated and housing the sacrament, providing the centre piece (*see* Fig. 5 and Plate 9).

The further operation of 'law' (1) is nowhere better to be observed than in the churches of Protestantism. Many of the Reformers rejected the sacrificial interpretation of the mass and emphasized its communion aspect; they laid stress on the ministry of the word and denied a rigid dichotomy of ordained and lay. The circumstances of the time – wars, religious strife – precluded any large-scale new building programme, and consequently Protestants re-used or re-ordered the existing medieval churches that they had taken over. Anglicans may serve as an example of the first and Calvinists of the second.

The Church of England authorities re-

Fig. 5   Baroque theatrical architecture,
Die Wies, Germany

cognized that the medieval plan did indeed consist of two rooms; it was therefore decided to use them as such for different functions. So the nave was the place for the ministry of the word and the sanctuary became the scene for the celebration of the eucharist, the altar (q.v.) being moved forward into the middle of the choir and the worshippers arranging themselves around it. This was a different way of doing things – 'law' (3) – under the influence of new concepts of worship and of the church – 'law' (1).

The Calvinists replanned the interior of their churches, as illustrated by St Pierre, Geneva. The medieval building, oblong with

Plate 9   Baroque theatrical architecture, Wallfahrtskirche, Innen, Germany

transepts, had the bishop's throne in the eastern apse, the altar in the choir and the pulpit at the same level as the rood screen separating the priest from the congregation. In 1541 rood screen and choir were demolished; the pulpit was moved to the first pillar on the left and the congregation was arranged in the form of a star at the front of the nave, in the transepts and the ancient choir. A table was brought in only on communion days and baptism was administered from a basin.

Within Anglicanism 'law' (1) continued to operate during the seventeenth century and is particularly noticeable during the Laudian controversy. The mobility of the altar under the Elizabethan settlement – being carried forward into the centre of the choir – led on occasion to its being treated with lack of reverence and even profaned. To prevent this, William Laud initiated a policy of protecting it with rails and fixing it permanently against the east wall. Although the archbishop's ideal was repudiated by the Puritans, it came back into favour at the Restoration and by the end of the century the majority of churchmen were shocked when they found an altar not so placed and fenced in. Laud and his later imitators had to deal with the two-room plan, but with Sir Christopher Wren a new type was introduced, usually referred to as the auditory church, and this was in effect a one room design. Wren was convinced that Anglicanism, unlike Catholicism, required its worship to be both visible and audible. His stress therefore was not only on the sermon but on the services as a whole. This involved, according to his calculations, small churches with galleries to seat not more than 2000 people. He suppressed the projecting chancels, dispensed with the screens, and produced a single volume with three liturgical centres instead of well-defined places. So he sited the font by the door; he installed pulpit and reading-pew, and finally the altar (*see* Fig. 6).

A similar concern to stress the importance of both the auditory and visual aspects of worship resulted within Lutheranism in the *Prinzipalstück*. The declared ideal was that of an oblong building, minus Gothic chancel, with a single space at the east end in which were combined all the principal liturgical acts. Altar, font and pulpit (q.v.) were thus assembled together – 'law' (3) operating under the influence of (1). This concept was first advocated by Joseph Fürttenbach, writing in 1649, and was taken up by L. C.

Fig. 6   The Wren auditory church, Christ Church, Newgate Street, London

Sturm in two works of 1712 and 1718. Influenced by the plan of the classical theatre, Sturm supported the adoption of the *Zentralbau*, or centralized auditorium, with *Prinzipalstück*.

A somewhat similar concept of the place of assembly as an auditorium, with the emphasis on the sermon – 'law' (1) – was embodied in the chapels built by the English Nonconformists, first licensed after the Declaration of Indulgence of 1671-72. Most of these were of a modest and domestic nature, without spires or obvious ecclesiastical features on the exterior. The design was rectangular, without chancel or transepts. Galleries (q.v.) were introduced into the larger buildings, mainly to provide greater accommodation, and the pulpit was big and prominent.

There was, therefore, a general tendency within the Protestant church to affirm both the visual and auditive elements in worship, to favour a single room design and even, especially within Calvinism, to adopt a centralized plan. This tendency was completely reversed by the Gothic Revival which was to affect all Christian communions.

To the adherents of the Gothic Revival each religion produces its own supreme architectural form that best expresses its ethos and spirit. Renaissance architecture, in so far as it sought inspiration from the heathen temples of ancient Rome, was to be dismissed as pagan. Only Gothic represented the full flowering and ideal embodiment of the Christian faith. The pioneers of this movement within Anglicanism were influenced to no small degree by the Tractarians, whose teaching about the church and the sacraments was meant to be both biblical and patristic but frequently did not achieve more than an echo of the medieval understanding. The same ideas were shared on the Catholic side by another great leader of the movement,

Plate 10   Gothic revival, two-roomed plan,
St Chad, Nicholas Square, London

Fig. 7   Gothic revival, two-roomed plan,
Privett church, England

A.W.N. Pugin. 'Law' (1) now came into its own. The emphasis upon the nature of the ministry and the sacrificial character of the eucharist required the two-room plan which had originally expressed these same ideas. The ecclesiologists therefore advocated and secured the all but universal adoption of the medieval church design with elongated chancel; the tyranny of an architectural orthodoxy was imposed (*see* Plate 10 and Fig. 7).

Wherever British influence extended, thither the Gothic plan and elevation was exported, so that churches of the period, whether in the USA, in Australia or even in India, followed the same revivalist norm. No church escaped this mixture of antiquarianism and romanticism. Roman Catholic buildings were frequently indistinguishable from Anglican, apart from certain details of the furnishings. Even the Free Churches submitted themselves to the prevailing fashion, but more under the pressure of social considerations than of theological ideas. Anxious to demonstrate that they were as socially respectable as the Established Church, Methodists, Congregationalists, Baptists, all vied with one another in adopting the full medieval plan with nave, aisles, transepts and chancels. For a hundred years, from approximately 1850 to 1950, revivalism dominated church

design and it was only when the Liturgical Movement (q.v.) had sufficiently come of age and had wedded itself to the modern movement in architecture that any liberation from the dead hand of the past was achieved and new forms began to emerge. These embodied new concepts of the nature of worship (e.g. that it is corporate), and of the church (e.g. that it is an organic whole with interdependent functions), different movements (e.g. offertory processions) and different ways of doing things (e.g. celebration facing the people) – so 'laws' (1), (2), and (3) were once again stimulating a development of Christian architecture in relation to the liturgy (*see also* **Architectural Setting [Modern] and the Liturgical Movement**).

G. W. O. Addleshaw and F. Etchells, *The Architectural Setting of Anglican Worship*, 1948; A. Biéler, *Architecture in Worship*, 1965; J. G. Davies, *The Secular Use of Church Buildings*, 1968; C. Heitz, *Recherches sur les rapports entre architecture et liturgie à l'époque carolingienne*, 1963; R. Krautheimer, *Early Christian and Byzantine Architecture*, 1965; T. F. Mathews, *The Early Churches of Constantinople: Architecture and Liturgy*, 1971.   EDITOR

Architectural Setting (Modern) and the Liturgical Movement

To guide us amidst the stupendous and almost chaotic diversity of forms and structures which are characteristic of modern church architecture, we have two main criteria: the human consistency of the architectural setting, and its intrinsic relation to the needs of the Christian community, in other words, hospitality and celebration.

Modern architecture and the Liturgical Movement (q.v.) are very complex phenomena. Their parallel evolution, and in our case their interaction, depend upon a great variety of factors. To avoid overcomplication, we shall concentrate upon a few particularly significant examples. They alone are able to give us insight into the principles (theological, liturgical, functional, etc.) which inspired the evolution of modern church-building. These architectural facts cover a period of almost half a century of continual change, stretching from approximately 1925 to the present day.

1. *From 1925 to 1945.* Many authors take as the starting point for modern church architecture the church at Le Raincy near Paris, by A. Perret (1923), both for its thoroughly honest reinforced-concrete structure and for its one-room plan, which foreshadows in a measure the liturgical spaces of the German and Swiss churches of the following decade. But Le Raincy had only a slight influence upon subsequent church building, and one has to remember that the Liturgical Movement was still almost non-existent in France at that time.

Therefore it is preferable to start with something more decisive, a real and living *centre* of liturgical and architectural renewal.

Fig. 8   The main hall, Schloss Rothenfels, Germany

The obvious choice is Schloss Rothenfels-am-Main, the castle which served as headquarters to the Catholic Youth movement in Germany between 1927 and the Second World War. (Other centres, like Maria-Laach or Klosterneuburg, had only slight contact with modern architecture.)

Castle Rothenfels was remodelled in 1928 under the direction of its chaplain, the already famous liturgist Romano Guardini, and of the architect Rudolf Schwarz, who was to become later one of the greatest church

builders in Europe. It possessed a regular chapel, but the most interesting feature was the main hall, occasionally used for the eucharist.

This hall was a large rectangular space, with pure white walls, deep windows and a stone pavement. It was void of decoration. The only furniture was a hundred little black cuboid stools. The disposition of these stools could be easily changed according to the different functions of the room and the nature of the assembly. For example, it was different for a discussion, a recital, a conference, or for a festive occasion. On the days of liturgical celebration, a provisional altar was set up in the hall and the faithful surrounded it on three sides. On the fourth side, facing them from behind the altar, the celebrant closed the circle. In the autobiographical book which Schwarz wrote many years later about his own churches, we find a description of these celebrations and a record of the extraordinary climate of active unity which characterized them (R. Schwarz, *Kirchenbau*, 1960, pp. 37-46). Rothenfels was frequented by an *élite*. Its influence on the Liturgical Movement in Germany and in Switzerland has been enormous, even if we

Plate 11   S. Christophorus, Köln-Niehl, Germany

Plate 12   Corpus Christi, Aachen, Germany

metrical strictness. It unites in a single space the space for the altar and that for the faithful. But this space is still a *Langbau*, i.e. a narrow rectangle at the end of which the altar remains somewhat isolated. The architect has clearly concentrated on *visual* participation, and thus primarily on the visibility of the altar, which dominates the room with almost dictatorial power. It has almost no connection with the pulpit (q.v.) situated at the centre of the nave (q.v.). Schwarz insisted on the fact that his church was not 'christocentric' (as the hall at Rothenfels) but 'theocentric' and even 'trinitarian', having, so to speak, three 'regions': first the area of the faithful with its black pavement and long rows of benches, image of this earth, realm of the Holy Spirit; then the space of transition with the steps leading to the altar, region of Jesus Christ, the Mediator; finally the great white void of the back wall, image of heaven, the region of the Eternal and Invisible Father, and of the glorified Lord.

There is no doubt that, notwithstanding its concentration on essentials and its functional honesty, the lofty, over elevated interior of Corpus Christi still kept a strong symbolic expressivity (which was to be carried even farther in the great post-war 'theological' churches of Rudolf Schwarz). It is interesting to note that this symbolism was explicitly sanctioned by Romano Guardini, who related it to the 'theocentric' movement of liturgical prayer itself.

The influence of Corpus Christi was instrumental in the planning of some of the best churches of the early thirties, particularly the church at Norderney by Dominikus Böhm (1930), St Theresa at Zürich by Fritz Metzger (1932) and the delightful little country church of Leversbach by Schwarz himself (1932). The first two look literally like smaller 'sisters' of the great geometrical church of Aachen. At the same time, their more human scale points already (and this is even more true of Leversbach) towards the *domus ecclesiae*, i.e. a church building considered primarily as the 'house' of the local community.

The two leading Swiss architects in Switzerland, Metzger and Baur, had been in direct contact with Schwarz, Guardini and the Rothenfels movement. This was to prove a very happy circumstance. The coming to power of Hitler put an end to almost any further development of church building in Germany. From now on, and at least until

had to wait almost thirty years to find a really consistent application of its principles to parish churches. We can say that the liturgical arrangement at Schloss Rothenfels was probably 'optimal', the best possible solution for an active participation of the faithful in word and sacrament. The liturgy was celebrated and understood as a totally corporate affair, to be expressed with the greatest possible simplicity and flexibility. This included celebration facing the people, a free grouping of the faithful and an overall interpretation of the place of worship where the interior symbol (the living community itself) took precedence over the exterior, the world of persons over that of objects, and hospitality (the pluri-functional room) over monumentality.

Some of these principles were refounded in a measure in the first parish church planned by Schwarz, Böhm and Guardini shortly after Rothenfels: Corpus Christi at Aachen (1928–30) (*see* Plate 11). Aesthetically, its relation to the *Bauhaus* is unmistakable. The plain cubic exterior fits perfectly into its industrial surrounding. The interior, with its white walls and colourless windows, is a rectangular space of absolute geo-

1945, the new spirit was, so to speak, a Swiss responsibility. Northern Switzerland became the only place in Europe where one could find authentically modern churches. Most of them were one-room, rectangular spaces, well lighted, and in some cases, of beautiful human proportions. But they kept, as a rule, the over-elevated altar at the far end of their elongated plan. One hesitates to speak here of 'free-standing' altars, because in all these churches, the altar remains rather away from the people, hardly detached from the back wall and much too broad or too monumental to allow the assistants any kind of enveloping movement. Even the most progressive liturgists of that time still considered the church as a building to house primarily an altar and only secondarily the community. Therefore, the altar *had to be* a big static object, the visual and monumental focus of the whole space.

A memorable exception to this situation was provided by three projects for a diaspora church by the German architect Emil Steffann. They show us: (*a*) exteriors which are much closer to a barn, a farm house or a simple family house than to a religious building in the then accepted meaning of the word; (*b*) an organization of the area of celebration which (at least for projects 1 and 3) is that of the main hall at Rothenfels, i.e. a free-standing altar surrounded on three sides by the faithful; (*c*) an extension of the function of the church to other needs of the community than mere worship. (The drawings were published in *Die Schildgenossen*, 1938, pp. 279–81. *See* Fig. 9.)

These plans, however, could not be realized at the moment. The first one foreshadows the famous barn church arranged by Steffann at Bust near Thionville (1942–45). The third is a very close anticipation of one of the most interesting churches of the late fifties: Maria-in-den-Benden at Düsseldorf-Wersten (1958), an almost perfect example of a *domus ecclesiae*. .

Before closing this short review of the pre-war period, we must remember that the really authentic modern churches of that time were an extremely small minority. Between 1925 and 1945, the concept of the church remained by and large the old traditional and monumental concept, or at best a compromise between this concept and the new vision of things. All the examples given above are Roman Catholic. This does not mean that the Reformation did not sponsor any good church buildings before 1945. The experiments of Otto Bartning (project for the 'Star church' in 1924; 'Steel church' in 1928; 'Round church' at Essen in 1930), and later, in the Swiss context, the *Johanneskirche* at Basel by Egender and Burckhardt (1936) or the beautiful church of Zürich-Altstetten by Werner Moser (1941), had a real influence on contemporary religious architecture. But their liturgical inspiration remained somewhat ambiguous. One of the reasons for this limitation is that the Reformed theology of the first part of the century pointed less in the direction of a more active participation of the congregation in the liturgy than towards a re-integration of the symbolic values of the church building itself ('The Evangelical place of worship is not only a meeting-place, it is a "Word in stone" – "*ein gebautes Wort*"', Paul Girkon). One may add that the churches at Basel and Altstetten were too close to the

Fig. 9   Project for a church in the diaspora (Steffan)

A Porch   F School
B Baptistery   G Sacristy
C Sanctuary   H Presbytery
D Choir gallery J Chapel
E Patio

Fig. 10 S. Maria-in-den-Benden, Düsseldorf- Wersten, Germany

passive *auditorium* to be representative of the Liturgical Movement.

2. *From 1945 to 1963.* After the interruption of the war, a new period opened and stretched from 1945 (or rather 1950) to Vatican II, i.e. at least until 1963.

The main characteristic of this new period was the progressive abandonment of the rectangular plan and of the traditional symmetry. This process was realized by two very different, and almost opposite, groups of churches.

The best examples of the first group present in general a very rational vision of space, an interior which is simple, functional, of human scale and of good proportions. Their plan is most of the time based on the *square* (or on a broad rectangle), where the assembly has a real chance to approach the altar and to surround it on three sides. This is not yet the case in the Illinois Institute of Technology chapel of Chicago, by Mies van der Rohe (1952), nor in the church of Maria Königin at Köln, the last work of Dominikus Böhm (1954), two classical examples of the early fifties. But we find this arrangement fully realized (with even the presidential seat and the possibility of celebrating the eucharist facing the people) in a remarkable series of churches by Emil Steffann: St Laurentius at München (1955), St Elisabeth at Opladen (1957), St Maria-in-den-Benden at Düsseldorf-Wersten (1958) (*see* Fig. 10) and St Laurentius at Köln-Lindenthal (1962). Their architecture is not pointedly modern (some

critics call them heavy and slightly 'archaeological') but they have a deep human quality and their liturgical synthesis, with the accent on the living community, is probably the best of the whole period, better even than that proposed as 'ideal' in a famous text of the German Liturgical Commission, the 'Guiding Principles for the design of churches according to the spirit of the Roman liturgy' (1947 and 1955). Together with excellent proposals, this text remains somewhat prone to exalt monumentality. It speaks of objects more than of persons and still insists, in the case of large churches, on a distinct sanctuary (two-room building).

To these churches, we must add some other sober, hospitable, liturgically very sound buildings, for instance, the lovely little Episcopalian church of St James the Fisherman at Cape Cod, Connecticut, by Olav Hammerstrom and the then priest-in-charge, James A. Pike. In this wooden structure, the central, square altar is entirely surrounded by *four* groups of pews – an arrangement which would probably be dangerous in a big church, but which works perfectly in a fifty-eight feet square space. As other good examples, we may recall here St Paul at Bow Common, by Maguire and Murray (1960), the prefabricated churches of Rainer Senn in Eastern France, the churches of Le Donné at Marienau (1955), Mulhouse (1956), Vitry-sur-Seine (1964), and the last churches by Rudolf Schwarz, particularly St Christophorus at Köln-Niehl (1962). In drastic contrast with the 'theological' schemes developed in his book *Vom Bau der Kirche*, Schwarz allowed this small, unassuming church no other symbolism than the fundamental one of the *domus ecclesiae*. Its climate of simplicity, of tranquil harmony, of plain and radiant humanity, is the very kind of architectural setting which points towards the future of the liturgy. (*See* Plate 12.)

The second, very different direction taken by church-building after 1950 is by way of a much more organic vision of space and symbol. The typical examples, here, are of course strongly individualized. Their forms become more and more lyric. All the elements of architecture: walls, ceilings, floors, etc., become parts of each other. Continuity is everywhere, in the materials and the furnishing as well as in the functions. Applied to the space of worship, this organic character becomes the symbol of the organic, hierarchized body of the faithful.

One of the first experiments in this direction is the church of St Franziskus at Basel-Riehen, by Fritz Metzger (1950) (*see* Plate 13). Its sanctuary and the nave (an ellipse and trapezium) blend in one symbolic form, whose meaning is to express, and at the same time to activate, the participation in the celebration. The floor of the nave follows a slight declivity, where the benches are disposed in a segment of a circle. Everything is organically concentrated on the sanctuary and particularly on the altar. This kind of direct, quasi-physical symbolism is always dangerous in architecture. We must admit that in the case of Riehen, it remained rather discreet.

But directly after 1955, the impact of Le Corbusier's chapel at Ronchamp accelerated the normal pace of the evolution to the point of almost changing its nature. It led to a complete break away from the axial symmetry and other rules which had governed Christian churches since Constantine. Not a bad thing in itself, this liberation unfortunately resulted in the attempt to infuse into every new country church the lyrical creativity of Ronchamp. Many German and practically all Swiss architects were intoxicated by this. It is evident that in this unhealthy, competitive atmosphere, it was difficult to avoid overdoing things, and to escape a touch of

Plate 13   S. Franziskus, Basel-Riehen, Switzerland

megalomania. And what is true of the Swiss churches could be repeated of a large number of 'organic' churches designed between 1955 and 1965 all over the world. From our point of view in the 1970s, we realize that there was little more in this movement than a new metamorphosis of the old temptation to monumentality – a climate in which the liturgical functions were either swallowed up in the *décor* (the form of the space, the dazzling rhythm of the lighting, the heavy fixation of the liturgical poles, etc.) or stressed in a one-sided way.

One has to remember that Ronchamp, the most famous of all 'modern' churches, had been the embodiment of a very special programme (a pilgrimage chapel at the top of a hill). It had only little to do with normal, everyday worship. It had almost no connection with the Liturgical Movement in France, which had become at that time the thinking and living *milieu* which laid the basis for the liturgical revolution of Vatican II.

This does not mean that the organic direction in church building is necessarily to be condemned. It is not lyricism as such which is wrong, but lack of coherence, of human scale, of ecclesiastical and functional fitness. However, when trying to point out the churches which really anticipated the 'post-conciliar' church, we see that the examples are generally found in the other group, illustrated by the works of Steffann, Le Donné, etc. They are the best churches liturgically, and also architecturally, in so far as they unite strictness with poetry, and architectural seriousness with a sufficient amount of creative liberty.

3. *From 1963 to 1970*. We have now reached the period of Vatican II. Its importance in the realm of church building does not depend only upon the 'Constitution on the Sacred Liturgy' (1963), but also upon other later texts and statements such as the 'Constitution on the Church and the World' (1965) and the 'Declaration on Religious Liberty' (1965). Even more important was the general climate of freedom, research and the need for authenticity.

Strictly speaking, the 'Constitution on the Liturgy' did not do much more than 'officialize' the major tenets of the Liturgical Movement of the post-war period, particularly the principle of *assembly* worship (considered as the living sign of the universal body of the faithful) and the close link which unites liturgy and mission. But this was enough to suggest a new image of the church building, completely at the 'service' of the assembly. It meant a break with the image still familiar to the great majority of Christians, the 'monumental' image which came from the beginning of the Middle Ages and remained ours even – as we have seen – in the most recent metamorphoses of organic architecture. This break could not be achieved in a single day.

It seemed easier to start from the *functional* modifications implied by the new liturgy and to comply with the demands of the Constitution by a simple readjustment of the poles of celebration.

Before the Council, many liturgists still arranged everything in church in strict subordination to *one pole*: the altar. The new emphases on the liturgy of the word, celebration facing the people and concelebration (q.v.), obliged them now to give prominence also to the chair of the celebrant and to the pulpit, i.e. to the two poles of the liturgy of the word, and to find a distinct location for the tabernacle (for example, against the wall or on a pillar). These three or four poles have to be at the same time clearly differentiated and formed into a living synthesis. The liturgical arrangements of the years immediately following 1963 display an extraordinary variety of solutions. But these arrangements have one thing in common: the *fixity* of all the liturgical furniture. Chair, pulpit, and altar remain firmly bound in stone, concrete and marble. In the organic climate of the Swiss churches, for example, one is confronted with a sanctuary full of huge stones, themselves over-activated by the talent of the sculptor. We are still very far from the place of *interpersonal* communion supposed by the new liturgy of word and eucharist.

The same is true for the liturgy of baptism. In the earlier stages of the Liturgical Movement, the baptismal font (q.v.) was still located in its traditional chapel, or elsewhere near the entrance area. A special stress was thus given to the initial rite of entry into the church. But the act of incorporation into the community, which is the *living* image of the church, is far more important. Therefore, some liturgists looked for other solutions. They located, for instance, the font in one of the lateral spaces of the church, largely open to the assembly (*see* **Baptistery**). We find examples of this arrangement in some churches by Rudolf Schwarz, like St Anna at Düren (1955) and St Christophorus at Köln-Niehl (1962) (*see* Plate 12).

Other liturgists think that baptism should normally be celebrated facing the assembly; thus the best position for the baptismal font is in a symmetrical relation to the ambo (q.v.). Apart from its communal value, this position emphasizes the close tie that binds baptism to the liturgy of the word and to the eucharist. The danger of this new location is of overcrowding the area of celebration, and this is exactly what happened in the Swiss churches mentioned above (*see* Plate 14). The baptismal font added one huge stone to others.

Real progress in the general arrangement of the church and especially of the sanctuary was to be found by way of more suppleness, simplicity and movement. Paradoxically, this was first realized in countries like Austria or Belgium, where the movement of modern churches had remained, at least up to 1960, practically sterile. It is these countries, too, which offered the first truly post-conciliar churches – completely and uncompromisingly so.

The idea coming to life in these churches can be summed up in one phrase: the serving of the assembled community in the simplest possible form. Beyond the limited perspective of pure liturgical functionalism, this means humility, limpidity, and above all a great opening to a living dialogue. But dialogue excludes any kind of rigid confrontation between the celebrant and the faithful, and thus also rigidity in the form, material and location of the liturgical objects. The Belgian architect Marc Dessauvage was probably the first to accept this evolution and to draw the consequences. In the parish churches he built after 1963, the altar, the pulpit, the chair and the font are generally *mobile* (*see* Plate 15).

An even more important change, introduced by the Austrian architect Ottokar Uhl, was the possibility of movement for the assembly itself. In his students' chapel of the Peter Jordanstrasse at Vienna (1965), the single space is divided into two distinct areas. The first is furnished by benches and occupied by the assembly during the liturgy of the word. The second is an open, free space for the eucharist. The faithful enter this space after the sermon and stand in a semi-circle around the altar. Provision for movement is carried even farther in another chapel by Uhl, arranged at the Benedictine abbey of Melk (1967) (*see* Plate 16).

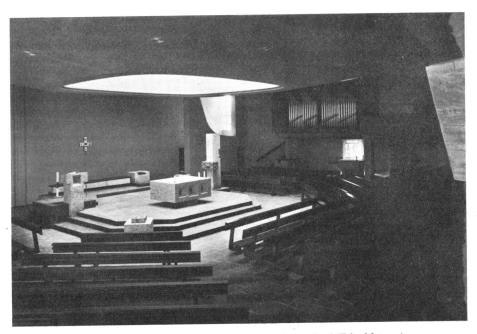

Plate 14   S. Pankratius, Oberkirch, Lucerne, Switzerland (Fritz Metzger)

The question of movement in church is related to the question of number and to other fundamental problems. At the New York Congress on Religion, Architecture and the Visual Arts (1967), which is another major milestone in the evolution of modern church building, the main theme in discussion was not any more the liturgical fitness of the church, but the very question of still building churches in a situation of acute mobility, anonymity, urbanization and secularization. The parochial system, i.e. the frame of Christian life and worship which the faithful had known for centuries, and until a very recent time, appeared now clearly to be in the process of crumbling away. The question was: how to replace it? In the conclusions of the Congress, Prof. Houtart demonstrated the need to develop the new solutions on three levels: the small group (a homogeneous meeting of no more than twenty people), the congregation (a flexible, not strictly territorial adaptation of the parochial assembly) and the large community (an occasional grouping of many hundreds or even thousands of faithful). These three levels of ecclesial belonging and expression have to be simultaneously ordered for several functions: not only the liturgy, but also communication, social action, etc. (*Revolution, Place and Symbol*. Journal of the New York Congress, 1969, pp. 57-9).

The small group is characterized by the openness and simplicity of its contacts, and, in the liturgy, by the reduction of external rites. It does not need any specialized space for worship. Because the centres of life and worship coincide, everything can normally take place in the homes of individuals. For the large community, there is no architectural problem either: it will use great, pre-existing spaces (a cathedral, a theatre, a cultural centre, a stadium, etc.). Only the group called 'congregation' will still need and ask for specialized church buildings.

The problem is to adapt these buildings fully to the new situation. It is evident that the majority of the churches built between 1967 and 1970 do not differ very much from the churches of the early 'sixties. In a few cases, however, we find a real attempt to integrate the new values. Good examples are the Church of St Paul at Waterloo, Belgium

Plate 15   S. Rochur, Aarschot, Belgium

Plate 16   Chapel for students, Melk, Austria

(1968) and the church at Neuville near Liège (1970), both by Jean Cosse. In the second of these buildings, especially, which has a demountable podium and movable furniture, the space for worship is occasionally used for conferences, concerts, etc. It can be extended towards the reception room (with open fire-hearth, adjacent kitchen, cloak room and other facilities). The dominant character of the main space remains thus that of a place of worship, but it is flexible enough to accom-modate other functions. Although at least 150 people take part in worship, the liturgy in this church has a real family climate: it is a *domestic* liturgy, thanks to the very hos-pitable setting. (*See* Fig. 11.)

Neuville is thus a kind of multi-purpose church. This new concept, elaborated between 1965 and 1967, will certainly gain more and more attention and probably dominate the church building of the 'seventies. It supposes

Fig. 11   Church at Neuville, Liège, Belgium

a real synthesis, and not only a juxtaposition, of the liturgical and the secular functions. In his important book on *The Secular Use of Church Buildings* (1968), Prof. J. G. Davies has demonstrated that the union of liturgical and secular functions is deeply traditional and corresponds to the very nature of Christianity. In the modern context, the experiments of multi-purpose churches point towards a plurality of solutions. The church at Neuville is a timid, but quite acceptable one. Another possibility is to keep a *fixed* sanctuary, and to screen it off when using the nave for other purposes. This solution is best known, probably because it is the easiest to put into practice, but its future is very uncertain if only because it is not really honest, and is better defined as dual-purpose rather than multi-purpose.

The Institute for the Study of Worship and Religious Architecture of the University of Birmingham, and Prof. Davies himself, have inspired multi-purpose churches of another type, where the worship area includes a fixed and defined space for the sanctuary, choir

and the font, but without any screen to shield them during secular use (*see* Fig. 12). This enables the unity of the functions 'to be demonstrated and to be lived' (*The Secular Use of Church Buildings*, pp. 243-8).

A fourth kind could be illustrated by the new pastoral centre at Kessel-Loo near Louvain, in Belgium, by Dessauvage (1970). The very flexible main space, which offers pluri-dimensional possibilities, serves for worship on Sundays and feast days only, and has no permanent liturgical furniture. Normally, it is used for secular purposes (like the hall at Rothenfels). However, in the quietest part of the centre, a much smaller room, liturgically fully equipped, is reserved for daily worship and personal meditation. This could seem a regressive arrangement. But in 1970, 'secularization' is no longer the only problem. One has to take into account the rediscovery of meditation and intense personal prayer. The same can be said of the need for new and vital forms of festivity and celebration. The Liturgical Movement will have to integrate better these two, almost opposite, forms of

0 10 20 30 40 50
Scale in feet

1 Entrance
2 Baptistry
3 Congregational space
4 Sanctuary
5 Choir
6 Stage/playroom
7 Workshop/changing/store
8 Stores

9 Stage control/projection
10 Organ
11 Garden of rest
12 Quiet room
13 Choir vestry/workroom
14 Lavatory
15 Clergy vestry/office
16 Lounge
17 Reading room
18 Kitchen
19 Coffee bar/foyer
20 Games hall

21 Coats
22 Control
23 Youth leader
24 Committee room
25 Powder room
26 Showers
27 Plant room
28 Gallery
29 Group room
30 Snug
31 Outdoor areas
32 Parsonage

Fig. 12 St Philip and St James, Hodge Hill, Birmingham, England worship; and so will the church building, if it is to remain faithful to its never-ending quest for adaptation and authenticity.

F. Debuyst, *Modern Architecture and Christian Celebration*, 1968; P. Hammond, *Liturgy and Architecture*, 1960; R. Maguire and K. Murray, *Modern Churches of the World*, 1965.

F. DEBUYST

Ascension Day

The commemoration of the ascension of Christ on the fortieth day after Easter (q.v.). Late in the fourth century, Etheria's description of worship at Jerusalem includes an account of a service held in the Church of the Nativity at Bethlehem on the fortieth day after Easter, the preaching being related to the place and the occasion. At first sight it seems that this can hardly be other than a festival of the Ascension. But when we consider the sense of appropriateness which was so characteristic of the worship of the Jerusalem church, it seems incredible that there would be a celebration of Ascension Day at Bethlehem. Further, Etheria immediately goes on to speak of the arrangements for the Day of Pentecost, which was a unitive festival commemorating the ascension of the Lord and the descent of the Holy Spirit. The unitive commemoration was still in existence at Jerusalem early in the eighth century. The problem disappears when we examine the ancient lectionary of the Jerusalem church preserved in the *Rituale Armenorum*. The entry preceding that for Whitsunday runs – 'May 18, in holy Bethlehem, of the children slain by King Herod' (F. C. Conybeare, *Rituale Armenorum*, 1905, p. 525). One of the passages read was Matt. 2. 16-18, which recounts the massacre of the innocents. This is clearly the commemoration to which Etheria refers, held appropriately at Bethlehem, in the Church of the Nativity. It must be emphasized that Etheria does not testify to a festival of the Ascension on the fortieth day after Easter. In the *Apostolic Constitutions*, deriving from the region of Antioch towards the end of the fourth century, the festival is definitely prescribed in the context of regulations concerning the liturgical year. It may be stated that the evolution of Ascension and Pentecost was probably taking place during the last quarter of the fourth century, and that in all likelihood the theatre of this evolution was the region Constantinople-Asia Minor-Antioch.

A. A. McArthur, *The Evolution of the Christian Year*, 1953.

A. A. MCARTHUR

Ash Wednesday

At Rome in the middle of the fifth century the Station days of Wednesday and Friday, in the week preceding the first Sunday in Lent, were transformed into full liturgical days with their own services. Then the Thursday and Saturday would be included in a preliminary penitential period. As Lent came to be more rigidly observed, so the difference between Sundays and fasting days became more marked, and it was noted that only thirty-six days were actually fasted. But already it was customary for the Church to keep a preliminary fast of four days beginning on the Wednesday. The Quadragesima was reconstituted by the incorporation of these four days. This was the situation early in the eighth century. The emergence of Wednesday as the commencement of the Quadragesima was a deformation of the original Lent. (*See also* **Commination**.)

A. A. MCARTHUR

Ashes

Ashes are a symbol of (1) purification (*cf.* Num. 19.9, 17f.; Heb. 9.13); (2) penitence (*cf.* Judith 9.1; Jonah 3.6; Luke 10.13; Matt. 11.21).

The former symbolism is seen in the consecration of a church (q.v.) according to the Roman rite. Water, called Gregorian water, is mingled with wine, salt and ashes, and with this mixture the bishop sprinkles the altar and the walls of the church in different places. It is an exorcistic rite intended to purify the building before it is consecrated by the anointing with chrism (*see* **Chrismatory**).

The latter symbolism, common to many religions and part of the common stock of OT and NT religion (*cf.* texts quoted), is to be found in the rite of the imposition of ashes on Ash Wednesday. In the earlier centuries of the church, when the discipline of public penitence was in force, penitents sometimes sprinkled ashes on their heads or alternatively received from the bishop a rough garment on which ashes had been sprinkled. In the tenth to eleventh century when the primitive discipline had become obsolete, Christians generally associated themselves with the modified discipline and came to church on the Wednesday before the first Sunday in Lent (subsequently called Ash Wednesday) to have blessed ashes (made of the palm branches of the previous year) put on their foreheads (*see* **Commination**). The prayer(s) used indicate that the rite is a penitential one and one formula used for the imposition of the ashes suggests the necessary abasement before God if forgiveness is to be achieved: 'Remember, man, that you are dust and into dust you shall return' (*cf.* Gen. 3.19).

Formerly the rite took place before the mass. Since 1970 it takes place within it, after the homily.

J. D. CRICHTON

Asperges

The word comes from Ps. 50.9 in the Vulgate Psalter: 'Thou shalt *sprinkle* me with hyssop and I shall be cleansed: thou shalt wash me and I shall be made whiter than snow', which in the Roman rite is recited when holy water is sprinkled over the people, before mass, when holy communion is given in the home and on some other occasions. Formerly other verses of the psalm were sung or said during the sprinkling, which took place usually in a procession of celebrant, ministers and servers around the church before the principal mass on Sunday. The rite (now to be performed after the entrance chant) is no longer of obligation in parish churches.

Originally, it would seem, an exorcistic rite (though there is a reference to sprinkling of the people in the ancient prayer of the blessing of baptismal water of the Paschal Vigil [q.v.]) for the cleansing of a building or place where a liturgical service was to take place, and also more strictly so when fields were sprinkled, it has become in the course of centuries connected with baptism. It is seen both as a reminder of baptism and as a means of renewing its grace. This is indicated both by the sprinkling of the people after the renewal of their baptismal promises at the Paschal Vigil and by the change of text for the Sunday sprinkling in Paschal time. The *Asperges* is replaced by a text based on Ezek. 47.1,8,9: 'I saw water coming out from the temple on the right side and all whom this water touched were saved.'

The rite of the Sunday *Asperges* probably had its origin in the monastic custom of sprinkling the monastery on that day. In the Middle Ages in some parts of Europe the procession for the sprinkling with holy water went through the whole village.

In modern Roman Catholic churches the rite is replaced for ordinary masses by the custom of taking holy water from stoups placed at the entrance to the church. The people are supposed to recite the *Asperges* while doing so.

J. D. CRICHTON

Assemblies of God Churches' Worship

The Assemblies of God, with international headquarters in Springfield, Missouri, was organized in 1914, and ten years later the Assemblies of God, Great Britain and Ireland was constituted by about seventy independent Assemblies agreeing to form a recognized fellowship. It is one of the denominations brought into existence as a result of the Pentecostal (q.v.) revival of the late nineteenth and early twentieth centuries. In addition to being a church of the evangelical tradition, the Assemblies of God is known for an emphasis on the manifestation of the gifts of the Holy Spirit as described in I Cor. 12-14.

In many ways the architecture of Assemblies of God churches is similar to that of other non-liturgical churches. Almost invariably the pulpit (q.v.) is in the centre of the platform, indicating the emphasis placed on the centrality and authority of the scriptures. Ordinarily a communion table is directly in front of the pulpit at the level of the congregation; altar rails (q.v.) or benches are either made a part of the platform or placed between the congregation and the platform, symbolizing the direct access man has to God through Jesus Christ. A baptistery (q.v.) is usually located behind the platform.

The Assemblies of God considers the mission of the church to be threefold. The ministry of the church towards God involves worship and obedience (Acts 13.2). Its ministry towards its members provides for edification and maturation (Eph. 4.11-16). Its ministry towards unbelievers emphasizes the need of personal regeneration (John 3.3). The Assemblies of God ministry to unbelievers includes a missionary programme built on indigenous principles which reaches around the world.

Assemblies of God services are informal and non-liturgical. Vestments (q.v.) are not worn by officiating clergy. In expression of the threefold mission of the church, regular services may have one of three major emphases. The Sunday morning service usually emphasizes worship, but it is also designed for the edification of the worshippers. The Sunday evening service usually emphasizes the need of regeneration and is intended to bring unbelievers to a personal commitment to Christ. A mid-week service is most often thought of as a time for Bible study and prayer. Special services of the local congregation include evangelistic meetings, Bible conferences, mission conventions, and training courses. Because the Assemblies of God has a basic congregational polity, there are variations of the emphases mentioned, and the degree of informality varies.

The order of the services usually includes congregational singing of hymns and gospel songs, often accompanied by a variety of musical instruments, public prayer, ministry of music by a choir and/or individuals, receiving of tithes and offerings, and the ministry of the word. Quite often opportunities are given for members of the congregation to share personal testimonies concerning scripture portions which have been especially meaningful to them or experiences in which they feel God has helped them in a special way. The testimonies may be interspersed with the singing of choruses by the congregation. Enthusiastic congregational participation is an important aspect of worship in Assemblies of God churches.

Ways in which an Assemblies of God service differs from other non-liturgical evangelical services include times of united audible prayer and worship; manifestations of the gifts of the Holy Spirit, such as speaking in tongues, interpretation of tongues, and prophecy; and prayer for the sick, including anointing with oil. In many instances, especially in smaller congregations, opportunity is given in a service for members of the congregation to mention needs which they feel should be remembered during public prayer. Most services end with an invitation for those present to kneel at the altar rail or at their seats for a time of prayer.

The Assemblies of God recognizes two ordinances and considers both symbolic rather than being inherently efficacious.

Baptism (q.v.) by total submersion is considered essential as an act of obedience and outward sign of the believer's identification with Christ in his death, burial, and resurrection. Baptism is administered only on profession of faith in Christ, and for this reason infants are dedicated to God rather than baptized. Baptismal services are conducted either in a church baptistery or in an outside natural body of water.

The Lord's Supper (q.v.), usually celebrated monthly, is considered a memorial of Christ's substitutionary death and a reminder of Christ's second coming. Faith in Christ, rather than membership in an Assemblies of God church, is the basis upon which worshippers are invited to participate in this ordinance. Communicants partake of both elements, usually at their seats, served by laymen.

The churches of the Assemblies of God without exception accept the Bible as the infallible and authoritative rule of faith and conduct.

                                   THOMAS F. ZIMMERMAN

Assumption
see Mariological Feasts

Atrium

The entrance or fore-court of a basilica (q.v.). It was usually open in the centre and surrounded by covered colonnades.

                                   EDITOR

Aumbry

A cupboard or recess in the wall of a church or the sacristy (q.v.) in which the sacred vessels and books, and sometimes also reliquaries, were kept. Aumbries were also used to house the three oils used in certain sacramental rites; these were stored in a chrismatory (q.v.). They were also used with a locked door for the reservation (q.v.) of the blessed sacrament usually in a wall near the altar, but sometimes in the sacristy. This method of reserving the consecrated elements has been revived in the Church of England during the last hundred years, and the door and surround of the aumbry sometimes have elaborate decoration, as we can see in the examples at St Mary-le-Bow, London, and St Philip and St James, Oxford. But an even longer standing tradition for this method of reservation exists in the Scottish Episcopal Church, to which reference is made in the 1929 Scottish prayer book as 'the long standing custom in the Scottish Church'; this custom is to be traced back to the Liturgies of the Nonjurors in the eighteenth century, where we are told 'that some of the consecrated Elements be constantly reserved in the vestry or some other convenient place in the church under a safe lock'.

While the wall-aumbry does not appear to have been used very much in medieval English churches as the place of reservation, it was undoubtedly employed in pre-Reformation Scottish churches. The wall-aumbry was also in use for reservation in Sweden, Germany and Italy. With the post-Tridentine legislation in the sixteenth century the use of such cupboards was abandoned in Italy and some of these were converted to housing the oil for the sick, as at St Egidio, Florence, by having the legend *Oleum Infirmorum* inscribed on the plinth; but the original sculpture displays a chalice and host with adoring angels.

The wall-aumbry was also termed 'sacrament house' in Germany; but there and in the Low Countries this term came to be applied at the end of the Middle Ages to a large spire-like structure standing on a pedestal in which the reserved sacrament was housed.

A. A. King and C. E. Pocknee, *Eucharistic Reservation in the Western Church*, 1965; E. Maffei, *La Réservation Eucharistique jusqu'à la Renaissance*, 1942.

C. E. POCKNEE

Baldachin

Also spelt balddachino, baldachinum or baldaquin. This term is often used rather loosely to describe any kind of canopy over an altar (q.v.), but it should only be applied to a canopy of woven fabric and not to wooden, stone or metal canopies. Baldachin is derived from the Italian *Baldacco*, meaning Baghdad, where woven textiles of silk woof and metal thread were first made. Canopies made from such textiles first appear in the Renaissance period, and particularly where the altar was near or attached to a wall or screen. Fabric canopies known as baldachins were also placed over the thrones of kings and princes. A canopy resting directly on four columns and made of wood, stone or metal is more correctly described as a ciborium (q.v.). Sometimes the reserved sacrament was suspended in a pyx (q.v.) hanging from under the canopy.

In the return to the more cube-shaped altar that is now being made under modern liturgical reforms, such an altar tends to appear insignificant and the provision of a ciborium over the holy table will give an emphasis that is likely to be otherwise lacking in the focal point of Christian worship.

C. E. Pocknee, *The Christian Altar*, 1963.

C. E. POCKNEE

Baptism

The rite whereby a person is made a member of the church. From the Greek *baptizo*, to dip, baptism has especial reference to the water rite, but it can be used of Christian initiation as a whole and may therefore, on occasion, include both the water rite and confirmation (q.v.).

1. *Patristic*. The principal authorities for the patristic rite of baptism are: in Africa, Tertullian, Cyprian and Augustine; in Rome, Hippolytus and John the Deacon; in North Italy, Ambrose; in Spain, Isidore and Hildephonsus; in the East, Cyril of Jerusalem, Chrysostom, Theodore of Mopsuestia and Pseudo-Dionysius Areopagiticus.

In the West baptism was normally administered at Easter, Pentecost being an alternative season. The font (q.v.) was blessed by the bishop with a prayer invoking the Holy Spirit upon the water so that baptism should not be a mere physical washing. Anointed with the oil of exorcism (q.v.), the candidates renounced Satan. Asked successively whether they believed in the Father, the Son and the Holy Spirit, they replied in the affirmative to each question and were dipped in the water, this threefold series of question, answer and dipping constituting baptism in the name of the Trinity. Emerging from the font, they were anointed on the head by a presbyter to signify their incorporation into the royal and priestly body of Christ. During this period it became customary for them to be vested in white robes after their baptism. From the privacy of the baptistery (q.v.) they were led into the church, where all the faithful were assembled with the bishop, who then prayed over them, invoking the sevenfold Spirit upon them, laid his hand upon them and signed them with chrism on the forehead. Finally, regenerated by water and the Spirit and sealed with the Spirit of adoption, they took part in the corporate prayers and received communion for the first time, never before having been allowed to see the last part of the eucharist, or even know what happened at it. There was no strict uniformity throughout the West, the African church, for instance, having only one unction (q.v.) after baptism and placing more emphasis on the episcopal hand-laying, and the Gallican churches including the ceremony of washing the candidates' feet.

In the East there were some notable differences. The negative renunciation of Satan was followed by a positive declaration of adhesion to Christ. The Trinitarian formula of baptism, 'N. is baptized in the name . . .', goes back at least to Chrysostom's time, thus anticipating by several centuries the appearance of the formula 'N., I baptize thee in the name . . .' in the West. There was only one anointing after baptism, a sealing with chrism not only of the forehead, as in the West, but also of the breast and organs of sense. At an early date hand-laying disappeared from Eastern usage. In some Syrian rites from the third to the seventh centuries the gift of the Holy Spirit was associated with the unction before baptism, in the opinion of some scholars the original sequence of events.

The rite was essentially corporate, presided over by the bishop (q.v.), assisted by his clergy, and with all the faithful involved. Candidates might be of any age from infancy upwards, the rite itself, though not the catechumenate, remaining unchanged long after infant candidates began to outnumber all others. There was as yet no question of infants being prevented by their age from receiving the grace conveyed by one part of the rite as opposed to another. Liturgically and theologically the patristic rite possessed far more unity than modern Western students can easily appreciate. Everything from the renunciation of Satan to the final episcopal unction could be covered by the word *baptisma*, Tertullian describing baptism, anointing and hand-laying under the heading *De Baptismo*. The episcopal unction was the moment when the candidates received the Pentecostal gift of the Spirit, and were anointed with chrism, or christened with the same Spirit with whom Christ, the anointed One, was endowed at his baptism. What is now called confirmation (q.v.) was that part of baptism which signified and conferred the baptismal gift of the Holy Spirit.

The rite could be administered in its entirety only if a bishop were present. This was impossible in the case of adult catechumens (q.v.) suddenly taken ill, or newborn infants not expected to survive, as soon as it became generally accepted that they must not be allowed to die unbaptized. While the Eastern Church solved this problem by delegating the whole rite to presbyters when a bishop was not available, in the West the rule was gradually established that the post-baptismal unction and hand-laying must be reserved to the episcopate, a decision for which scriptural justification was claimed in the apostolic laying on of hands in Acts 8.17. Consequently, where this rule was in force and baptism was required in haste, presbyters, being instantly available, gave baptism and communion, hand-laying and anointing being, in the case of those who recovered, deferred until the next episcopal visitation.

Thus, while the Eastern Church has been able to keep the unity of the patristic rite of initiation intact even to the present day, the Western Church allowed it gradually to be divided into the seemingly independent rites of baptism and confirmation. So arose the need to define the activity of the Holy Spirit in each of these rites. A sermon preached by Faustus of Riez in the late fifth century, in which he said that the Holy Spirit restores to innocence at the font and in confirmation confers an increase in grace, was one of the main sources on which medieval theologians based their solution of this theological problem.

J. D. C. FISHER

2. *Orthodox*. More correctly, Byzantine. The baptismal service of the historic rites, like those of the other Byzantine rites, is a conflation of a number of short services designed to be spread over a period of time – originally Lent (q.v.), leading to baptism at Easter – but now celebrated together, one after another. Its shape and content have changed remarkably little for at least eleven hundred years, and probably very much longer, even to the extent that although it is, and has been throughout that time, used far more often for the baptism of infants than for that of adults, the rubrics for the most part still seem to presuppose the latter.

The service falls into two halves, the order for the making of a catechumen (q.v.), and the order of holy baptism, and this division is still clearly retained in the service-books, the two halves being printed separately, each with its own title.

The order for the making of a catechumen comprises four separate acts: (*a*) the prayer for the admission of a catechumen; (*b*) the exorcisms; (*c*) the renunciations; (*d*) the profession of faith.

The prayer for the admission of a catechumen asks for the deliverance of the candidate from error, and the bestowal upon him of the gifts of faith, hope and love, that he may come to know God, to follow his commandments, and to be united to God's flock, that in him God's name may be glorified; it is preceded by a triple breathing upon the candidate by the priest (*see* **Insufflation**), and a triple signing of him with the sign of the cross (q.v.) on brow and breast, and commences with a laying-on of hands in the name of the Trinity.

The exorcisms (q.v.), four in number (although the modern Greek books print the third and fourth together), all beseech the expulsion from the catechumen of all evil spirits and their influence, while the fourth beseeches also the gift of the guardian angel. Each was originally accompanied by the laying on of hands, but this is no longer customary now that they are all said together immediately after the admission of the catechumen, with the laying on of hands at the beginning; at an appropriate point in the fourth the priest breathes upon the brow, mouth and breast of the catechumen.

The renunciations follow the exorcisms. The catechumen, turned towards the west, and with arms upraised, three times renounces Satan, all his works, all his angels, all his worship, and all his pomp; confirms the renunciation; and then blows and spits as an expression of his contempt for all that he has renounced.

The profession of faith follows at once; its inclusion in the order for the making of a catechumen rather than in that of holy baptism may occasion surprise, in the light of the intimate connection between the profession and the baptism in the early liturgy, but it is probably due to an historical accident in the arrangement of the books, an issue too involved to go into here, consequent upon the conflation of the several baptismal rites into one service and their celebration at times other than Easter. The essential element of the profession of faith, to which are added various decorative questions and answers, is the recitation of the Nicene-Constantinopolitan Creed, the candidate facing east. The order for the making of a catechumen is then concluded with a prayer for the grace of baptismal renewal and enlightenment.

The order of holy baptism comprises: (*a*) the hallowing of the baptismal water; (*b*) the pre-baptismal anointing: (*c*) the baptism itself.

The hallowing of the font (q.v.) is introduced by a litany, based on the common greater litany (*see* **Litany**) with several appropriate additional petitions – for the hallowing of the water by the coming of the Holy Spirit, for the descent upon it of the grace of redemption, for illumination by the power of the Holy Spirit, for the averting of every device of evil spirits, and six petitions for the candidate, that he may truly acquire all the benefits of baptism. During this litany, sung by the deacon, the celebrant prays secretly for the divine assistance in the administration of the sacrament. The litany concluded, he proceeds to bless the font, with a very lengthy prayer, following the pattern of the eucharistic prayer or anaphora (q.v.), commencing with a thanksgiving for God's manifestations of himself in creation and redemption, continuing with a prayer for the hallowing of the water by the descent of the Holy Spirit, and concluding with a petition for the effects of this hallowing to be operative in him who is to be baptized, with a closing doxology. The ceremonial accompanying this prayer is of the simplest, the essential act being a triple breathing on the water in the form of the cross at an appropriate point.

The pre-baptismal anointing is preceded by the blessing of the 'oil of gladness' corresponding to the Western 'oil of catechumens', and a triple signing of the water with this oil – a typical early medieval addition to the blessing of the water, paralleled in the other historic rites, which adds nothing to the clarity of the liturgical structure of the rite. The candidate is then anointed on brow, breast and back (*see* **Unction**).

The baptism itself then follows immediately. Orthodox theology and canon law require total immersion, except in emergency; the candidate is held upright in the font, with his face towards the east, and is immersed three times, at the naming of each person of the Trinity, with the formula: 'The servant of God N. is baptized in the Name of the Father, Amen; and of the Son, Amen; and of the

Holy Spirit, Amen.' Psalm 31 (32) is then sung (while the newly-baptized is dried), after which the new white clothing is put on the newly-baptized, with appropriate formulae.

The administration of the sacrament of chrismation (the Byzantine name of what is called confirmätion in the West) follows at once, for infants as well as adults. The administration, like that of baptism and the eucharist, is of course delegated to the priest, although he uses episcopally consecrated (in modern practice patriarchally or·primatially consecrated) chrism (*see* **Unction**). The celebrant says a prayer giving thanks for baptism, beseeching the gifts of the seal of the Holy Spirit and participation in the eucharist (which anciently also followed without a break). He then anoints the newly-baptized with the chrism, making the sign of the cross on the brow, the eyes, the nostrils, the mouth, the ears, the breast, the hands and the feet, saying at each anointing 'The seal of the gift of the Holy Spirit, Amen.'

The baptismal rites are concluded by a brief form of the synaxis (q.v.) with an appropriate epistle and gospel; originally, of course, this was the synaxis of the baptismal eucharist. It is still the custom in many Greek churches, unless the celebration of the eucharist is to follow shortly, to give the newly-baptized and confirmed (especially if he is an infant) communion from the reserved sacrament at the end. With the spread of liturgical reform it is reasonable to hope that before long the restoration of the baptismal eucharist will be achieved at least in some places, in which case the Byzantine baptismal liturgy will again manifest the integrity of the rites of Christian initiation as they were celebrated in the early church; as it is, it has for many centuries done so more fully than has any of its Western counterparts.

W. JARDINE GRISBROOKE

3. *Medieval and Roman Catholic.* In Rome from the sixth century, since adult baptism had become rare, the custom of baptizing infants became general. The *ritual* of the catechumenate (q.v.) was retained and even elaborated, but the adult catechumenate became obsolete.

The child was necessarily passive, and, as it were to compensate for this, the scrutinies (examinations) were increased to seven; since instruction could not be given to unconscious children, a rite of the 'tradition' of the gospels was substituted for it. The questions about faith formerly put to the candidate during the action of baptism were now anticipated and addressed to the parents and godparents. The formula, said by the priest, 'I baptize you, in the name of the Father, etc.', is attested in eighth-century Rome. Gradually, too, the traditional liturgical days of scrutiny and the giving back (*redditio*) of the Lord's Prayer and the creed (q.v.) were separated from the traditional days of Lent when these acts had taken place. By the eighth century there were only two assemblies in church, the first for the enrolment and giving of salt (indicating that the child was now a catechumen) and the 'tradition' of the gospels which consisted of no more than the reading of the first phrases of each of the four gospels. Neither of these observances required the response of the candidate. With the compilation of the Romano-German pontifical of the tenth century, the ceremony of the giving of the white garment was accompanied with a prayer giving its sense, a prayer that passed into the Roman rite of baptism of a later age, and the giving of the lighted candle, a symbol of Christ the light of the world, was added. This, too, has survived in the Roman rite. Later still, in the fourteenth century, baptism by 'infusion', the pouring of the water on the head, replaced the ancient custom of immersion, though immersion was still known in the thirteenth century (witness Thomas Aquinas, *Summa Theologica*, III,66.7) and the practice of baptism by immersion has never been forbidden in the Roman Catholic Church.

All traces of a catechumenate as a separate ceremony were finally wiped out by the ever more prevalent custom of baptizing infants as soon after birth as possible, a custom that became general from the tenth century onwards. By the thirteenth century all the pre-baptismal ceremonies of catechumenate, renunciation of Satan and the anointing with the oil of catechumens had been combined into one service which is first found in the *Ordo ad cathecumium* (sic) *faciendum* of the Pontifical of the Roman Curia of the same century. The books of the local churches, e.g. the *Manuale* of Salisbury, merely endorsed this situation. But local usages remained, and in the post-Tridentine period, it became necessary to introduce order into the administration of baptism. The *Rituale Romanum*, issued by Pope Paul V in 1614, tidied up the situation and this book remained in force until the new order of baptism of 1969. Unfortunately, it was no more than a work of compilation. No effort was made to construct an order of infant baptism that would meet the changed conditions of the church. The compiler merely took two orders found in the tradition, one longer and one shorter: the longer, which comprises all the ancient rites of the catechumenate in one service, was destined for adults and the other, shorter, for infants.

The new order for the baptism of infants was promulgated on 15 May 1969 and came into force on 8 September of the same year.

It was issued with two introductions, one on baptism in general and the second on the baptism of infants. This order, then, is part of a fuller document, still awaited, which will contain the rites of the (restored) catechumenate and of adult baptism. Both introductions are documents of considerable theological importance, a summary of which would, however, take up a good deal of space. It may be noted, however, that the faith of the parents, who play a central role in the service, is the crucial factor in accepting infants for baptism. They, with the gathered community, profess the faith of the church which they represent, a faith they are required to communicate to the child as it grows up.

A brief description of the rite. Baptisms are to be celebrated normally on Sundays in the presence of the local community whether at mass or at some other time of the day.

The celebrant welcomes the baptismal party at the church door and asks the first questions establishing the willingness of the parents to bring their child up in the Christian faith. He then signs the child on the forehead with the cross and the parents and godparents are invited to do likewise. This is a relic of the ancient enrolment ceremony.

There follows 'the celebration of God's word', consisting of one or two passages from scripture, a homily, intercessions for the child, the family and all baptized persons.

There is a single prayer of exorcism (q.v.) and the anointing on the breast (only) with the oil of catechumens. Local conferences of bishops may allow, for good reasons, the omission of the whole of this rite.

'The celebration of the sacrament' follows with the blessing of the water (three forms provided, to be used at choice), the parents'

renunciation of evil (two forms given) and profession of faith with the gathered community, the act of baptism (either by immersion or affusion), the anointing with chrism, the giving of the white garment, and of the candle.

The service concludes before the altar where a blessing is given to the mother (replacing churching), to the father and the assembled congregation.

The new order is both new and traditional. It is adapted to circumstances of infant baptism, it addresses itself to the parents and their friends and it requires a genuine commitment. Traditional elements will be found in the ministry of the word, parallel to the ancient vigil, the anointings and the ceremonies after the act of baptism. In one respect it fails to keep the ancient order: the renunciation of evil is separated from the exorcism (q.v.).

J. D. CRICHTON

4. *Anglican.* After it had separated from the Roman Communion, the teaching and practice of the Church of England in respect to the sacrament of baptism remained largely those which had become commonly accepted in Western Catholicism. The attention of the English Reformers was occupied chiefly with the presentation of a strong apologetic for continuing the practice of infant baptism, the provision of instructional material, and the revision of the baptismal service. The order for baptism in the first English *BCP* of 1549 was a combination of materials drawn from the pre-Reformation Latin service and early Lutheran sources. It followed closely the structure of the Latin rite, but abridged the catechumenal introduction which had become prefixed to the baptismal rite in the Middle Ages. The traditional ceremonies of signing with the cross, exorcism, unction (qq.v.), and bestowal of the white baptismal dress were all retained. Many of the words translated or paraphrased the Latin. There were a number of new compositions, chiefly prayers and exhortations; in these the influence of the Reformation is the most apparent. Reformed influences, however, were much more evident in the second *BCP* of 1552. The baptismal order in this book reduced the introductory section still more, made a number of changes in the words of the service, and added a thanksgiving section. With the exception of signing with the cross, which was transferred

to follow the baptism, all the traditional ceremonies were omitted. Without significant alteration, the 1552 baptismal rite passed eventually into the 1662 *BCP*. All of the orders for baptism in the various Anglican prayer books derive from the 1662 order, and all follow it closely, while differing from it and each other in details.

The Anglican baptismal rite begins with an introductory section consisting of prayers, addresses, and a reading from the gospel. The baptismal vows or promises follow. These are made personally in the case of adult candidates, by sponsors in the case of infants. The promises are in the form of a series of questions and answers involving a set of renunciations, a promise of adherence to the Christian faith as stated in the Apostles' Creed, and a promise to follow the Christian way of life. The baptismal water is then consecrated according to a form adapted from that prescribed for monthly use in the first *BCP*. The baptism then takes place. Water is poured upon the candidate or he is dipped into water – the latter rarely in actual practice – while the Trinitarian baptismal formula is recited. The newly-baptized are then signed with the cross and declared received into the church. A thanksgiving and address to the sponsors or a blessing concludes the service. The Anglican prayer books design baptism as a public liturgy, and make provision for the insertion of the baptismal service into the regular services of worship. However, in common practice, baptisms have been more generally held before or after regular services or at specially arranged times, with only those immediately concerned present.

Anglican teaching about baptism has changed but little since the Reformation, and is very much the same in all of the churches which make up the Anglican Communion. Most of its baptismal doctrine Anglicans hold in common with other parts of the Christian church, and it is difficult to discern anything distinctively Anglican about it. Anglicans have always regarded baptism as a sacrament instituted by Christ and, except in the presence of most unusual conditions, necessary for salvation. The sacramental sign is water, poured upon an unbaptized person, or into which he is dipped. The form of words which must accompany this action are: 'N., I baptize thee in the Name of the Father, and of the Son, and of the Holy Ghost.' Any baptism carried out by means of this sign and formula Anglicans regard as true baptism, and all persons thus baptized are accounted members of the Christian church. While it is baptism which Anglicans hold to be necessary for admission into the Christian church, the Anglican churches have generally required confirmation (q.v.) as well as baptism for admission to communion and full participating membership in the church, thus in effect regarding baptism by itself as incomplete; some Anglicans have taught that this is the case. The spiritual gifts of baptism may be summed up in the words: 'A death unto sin, and a new birth unto righteousness'. Repentance and faith are the necessary requirements for the effective reception of the sacrament. Baptism is to Anglicans a mystical washing away of sin both original and actual. It is a sharing in the death and resurrection of Christ, a rebirth into the saving community of the church. By means of it one is incorporated into Christ's mystical body, made a child of God, and an inheritor of the Kingdom of Heaven. While Anglicanism has always taught that the baptism is of water and of the Spirit, and that the Holy Spirit is active and in some way given in baptism, it has never clearly defined the activity and gift of the Spirit in baptism in relation to those in confirmation. Everywhere in Anglicanism, from the Reformation to the present day, infant baptism has continued to be defended and to be the norm of practice.

During the last three decades there has been a debate about baptism which has gathered force and has spread to all parts of the Anglican Communion. The present pastoral situation, insights gained from the Liturgical Movement (q.v.), and increasing ecumenism have all combined to produce a growing dissatisfaction with traditional Anglican teaching and practice. A Baptismal Reform Movement has been started and is doing much to further investigation of baptism in relation to the modern situation of the church and to awaken the church to the needs for change and revision. A major point in the discussion has been the practice of baptizing all infants presented for baptism, and the relevance of infant baptism in the contemporary pastoral scene. It is also evident that the rites of baptism in use at present are but one part of Christian initiation; a re-integration of baptism, confirmation, and first communion into a single rite of

Christian initiation is necessary to a full appreciation of the meaning of the sacrament in the life of the church. At the present time there are before the Anglican churches a number of proposed revisions of the baptismal rites which attempt this re-integration. There is also a deep need for a re-statement of the traditional theology in a manner understandable by our contemporary world. The debate is by no means resolved, and will doubtless increase as Anglicans examine more deeply their mission in the present-day world.

H. ELLSWORTH CHANDLEE

5. *Baptist.* The use of the title *Baptist* may account for the belief, now widespread, that the baptism of believers by immersion is the basic principle of that denomination. It is, in fact, secondary and derivative. Believers' baptism rests on three primary convictions about authority, faith, and the church. The source of authority is God manifest in Christ, and the medium of his authority is scripture. The only baptism found in the NT is the baptism of believers. On the authority of scripture, baptism is administered only to those who have professed repentance towards God and faith in Jesus Christ. Conversion must precede baptism. This personal response to the activity of the Holy Spirit is essential for membership in the body of Christ. For the Christian society consists of those who have heard the gospel with faith; it is the fellowship of believers. It follows from these three convictions that it is not the *mode* but the *subject* of baptism which is of primary importance. The mode is immersion; the subject is the believer. The Anabaptists and the early English Baptists baptized by affusion or pouring. When circumstances, such as sickness or extreme age, make it advisable, baptism is occasionally administered in that way today. It was to exhibit the full meaning of the rite that immersion was eventually adopted. The actions of going down into, of being buried beneath, and raised up from the water, proclaim the death, burial, and resurrection of Christ. The mode has importance because of what it signifies, but what really matters is *who* is baptized, not *how* the rite is administered. The emphasis on personal response is characteristic of the teaching and practice of all Baptists. The candidate is said to be following the example and obeying the command of Christ, making a confession of

faith in him, pledging allegiance to him. This stress on the human response has been and is accompanied by a widespread tendency to ignore or deny the activity of God, not prior to, but in the sacrament. To many Baptists, baptism is represented as a purely symbolic rite, a dramatic portrayal of what has already taken place in the experience of the candidate. It would be misleading to generalize on this matter, and among Baptists today, as in the past, there are marked differences of teaching. Recent Baptist scholarship has emphasized the relationship between baptism, the Holy Spirit, and the church. On the question of when baptism should be administered to a believer, there are two conflicting points of view. On the one hand, since conversion and baptism belong together, there is a desire to minimize the period between the initial response and the administration. On the other hand, especially on the mission field, the need for an adequate period of preparation is recognized. Candidates are usually, though not always, taught before baptism. Baptists have no prescribed liturgy, but administer the rite in the threefold context of the fellowship, the word, and the prayers. Baptism is not regarded as a private or domestic occasion, but is administered in the setting of the congregation at worship, and of the reading and preaching of the word. There is a marked evangelistic quality about the service. The candidates bear witness, sometimes verbally, and always in the act of baptism, and it is expected that this witness, together with the preaching of the gospel, will be used to make disciples from among those present. Baptism is regarded as a converting ordinance, and the service often concludes with an appeal for others also to respond. After the preaching it is the usual, though not invariable custom, to put questions to the candidates. Typical answers include a confession of faith in the Holy Trinity, the acceptance of Jesus Christ as Lord and Saviour, and a pledge to follow and serve him. The occasion is often preceded by prayer meetings, and in the service itself a prayer for the candidates precedes or follows the questions and answers. In the baptistery, the names of the candidate, and words indicative of personal response, often precede the traditional Trinitarian formula. 'N., on thy profession of repentance towards God and of faith in our Lord Jesus Christ, I baptize thee in the name of the Father, and of the Son, and of the Holy Spirit.' Immersion takes place in one of three ways. The candidate stands in the water, and is lowered backwards into it until submerged, and is then lifted up again. The candidate may kneel in the baptistery, and then be immersed forwards. When the rite is administered in a river or pool, as often in Africa, Asia, or Latin America, the candidate is led out into the water until it reaches the neck, and then, after the formula, the head is pressed under. In many churches, the Aaronic blessing (q.v.) is said or sung after each immersion. The baptisms may be followed by an appeal for decisions; the service then concludes with a hymn and the blessing. In some churches, the laying on of hands after baptism, practised by the early General Baptists of Britain, and always adhered to by a small minority of Baptist communities, has been restored. The practice of baptizing at the Lord's Supper is also on the increase. The desire to enrol the candidates as members of the church at the baptismal service itself is one outcome of the new emphasis upon baptism as initiation into the body of Christ.

S. WINWARD

6. *Christian Church (Disciples of Christ)*. Although the major founders of the Christian Church (Disciples of Christ) stood in the Reformed tradition, they early set aside the practice of infant baptism in favour of the baptism of believers by immersion. Alexander Campbell (1788-1866) took the lead in the examination of the NT that led to the conclusion that the 'one baptism' mentioned in scripture required a specific action, upon certain candidates, with a particular meaning. The action was defined as immersion, to the exclusion of other modes, and that mode was single immersion as contrasted with trine immersion practised by people in the various Brethren churches. The proper candidate was a penitent believer. The meaning ascribed to the act was phrased in this way by Campbell: 'Baptism is, then, designed to introduce the subjects of it into the participation of the blessings of the death and resurrection of Christ.'

In his writings Campbell regularly translated the Greek terms into immerse and related words instead of into baptize and its related words. Yet his discourses clearly indicate that he was talking about the Christian sacrament of baptism rather than merely a water rite. Furthermore, his views constituted a high doctrine of baptism. He claimed that regeneration and conversion were both equivalent terms to immersion (by which he meant the sacrament of baptism). Therefore wherever the scripture discusses regeneration or conversion that teaching must be applied to baptism. The scripture, said Campbell, calls for 'an actual coming' to the Lord Jesus. But 'Where shall we find him? Where shall we meet him? Nowhere on earth but in his institutions, the first of which is the institution for remission of sins – the sacrament of baptism.'

It is clear in early writings of the Disciples that salvation was seen as the free gift of God; in this way they stood firmly in orthodox Christianity as interpreted by the churches of the Reformation. The new element in their view was the emphasis upon man's active participation. Faith was considered to be a requisite of baptism, faith understood as trust in Christ and therefore an act of complete obedience to Christ. Repentance was to follow from faith and was understood to be a complete turning around of life. Then would come immersion, death and resurrection with Christ, the first act signifying complete surrender to Christ's will. The result was that a person was changed to a new relationship with God.

This careful synthesis has suffered from abuse through the years since it was first articulated. Some have stressed the active participation of the baptizand to the degree that the free gift of God has been compromised. Some have stressed the idea of obedience to the degree that divine grace and the imperative to lead a new life have been neglected. Some have emphasized the mode of the act so much that the equivalence of regeneration, conversion, and baptism has not been recognized.

At first Disciples admitted only persons immersed as penitent believers into membership in their churches. If there had been previous baptism in some other mode, baptism by immersion would be administered anew, under the rubric of 'completing one's obedience to Christ'. The severity of this closed membership policy has been moderated by open admission to communion, so that persons from other denominations may share freely in the liturgical and congregational life of a Disciple church even when not admitted to formal membership because of irregular baptism. An increasing number of congregations have, since about 1900, received by transfer of membership Christians from churches who baptize by other modes. Furthermore, there is a growing resistance in the denomination to what is now widely recognized to be rebaptism.

There has been a widespread custom in Disciple congregations for a simple act of blessing and dedication to be ministered shortly after a baby is born into one of the families of the church. This rite has sometimes included the naming of the child. More characteristic has been the practice of asking parents to pledge that they will rear the child in the Christian faith. The congregation is asked to share in this responsibility and a prayer of dedication concludes the service.

The baptismal rite, as commonly practised, has two parts which may be separated in time and place. The first is called *confession of faith* and always takes place in a regular service of worship. During an *invitation hymn*, usually following a sermon, the believer walks to the front of the church where he is met by the minister. The minister, usually drawing upon Peter's confession in Matt. 16, asks him: 'Do you believe that Jesus is the Christ, the son of the Living God; and do you accept him as your Lord and Saviour?' The person answers affirmatively, after which the minister speaks a brief word of commendation, usually drawing upon some appropriate passage of scripture. At some later date, again at a regular service of worship, the baptism takes place. Although the rite is occasionally performed in running water, it is ordinarily administered in a baptistery constructed so as to be visible to people in the main worship room of the church. The minister may read a passage of scripture dealing with baptism. Then he pronounces: 'By the authority of our Lord Jesus Christ, in whom you have confessed your faith, I baptize you (N) in the name of the Father and of the Son and of the Holy Spirit. Amen.' Single immersion, the baptizand leaned backwards into the water, then takes place.

Current discussions among Disciples indicate that the theological position first developed continues to be widely supported. There is somewhat less emphasis now upon the absolute necessity of immersion, although that mode continues to be the only one practised. There is ambivalence about the appropriate age of baptism. As a general rule children from church families are received for instruction and baptism at about the age of twelve; only then are they received at the communion table.

KEITH WATKINS

7. *Congregationalist.* The early Congregationalists (or Independents, as they were then known) held the same views about baptism as the English Presbyterians. Both groups dissented from three characteristics of the Anglican administration of the sacrament according to the *BCP*. First, they objected to signation with the cross as an additional ceremony for which there was no biblical warrant. Secondly, they disliked the godparents taking the role of the parents in making the promises that the child should be brought up as a Christian, since this was the duty of the parents. Thirdly, they objected to private baptism. In their view baptism was a sacrament of the gospel, giving assurance of forgiveness of sins and of eternal life, which ought to be celebrated in the church.

John Cotton's *The True Constitution of a Particular Visible Church* (1642) describes the classical Independent administration of baptism:

> As for Baptism, it is to be dispensed by a Minister of the Word unto a Believer professing his Repentance, and his Faith, being a member of the same Church Body as also unto his seed, presented by the Parent unto the Lord and his Church at which time the Minister in God's roome calleth upon the Parent to renew his Covenant with God for himselfe and his seed and calleth upon God as the nature of the Ordinance requireth, for the pardon of originall sinne, and for the sin of the Parents and for a blessing upon the Sacrament and Infant and then calling the Childe by the name, which the Parent hath given it for his owne edification, and the Childes, he baptizeth it either by dipping or sprinkling into the name of the Father, the Son, and the Holy Ghost (pp. 6f.).

Plainly, early Congregational baptism was the claiming of the covenant promise of God to be with his children and his children's children, a solemn inclusion of the child of believing parents within the company of the elect, by baptism in the triune name, and accompanied by the parental promise to bring up the child in the nurture and admonition of the Lord, until this promise should be honoured by the child when he reaches physical and spiritual maturity. The only point of difference between Independent and Presbyterian usage was that the latter used to require the parent to recite the Apostles' Creed as a test of orthodoxy in belief, whereas the Independents insisted that a covenant (or affirmation of loyalty) was more appropriate than a creed, which was a historical summary which could be recited with 'the top of the mind'.

In the early and middle part of the twentieth century, when theology had become increasingly more immanental, there was a tendency for baptismal orders of worship to stress the human profession of faith rather than the divine initiative in baptism. This meant that baptism came to look increasingly like infant dedication. *A Manual for Ministers* (1936) in its baptismal order affirms that there are three purposes in baptism: to acknowledge God as the source of all good; to affirm the divine fatherhood of all children; and that 'we solemnly re-dedicate ourselves in the presence of God, and ask for His help worthily to fulfil these new and sacred duties' (p. 73).

A richer theological exposition of the meaning of baptism will be found in the 'Order for the Baptism of Children' in *A Book of Public Worship* (1948). It reads:

This Sacrament is a sign and seal of the covenant of grace, of union with Christ in his body, of remission of sins in his blood, of resurrection unto eternal life through him, and of our calling and engagement to be his for ever. It declares that the children of Christian parents belong, with us who believe, to the membership of the Church; and that Christ claims them as his own . . . (p. 159).

Surveying contemporary Congregational baptismal practice in Britain and the USA, it could be stated with confidence that a typical administration of baptism would comprise the following elements, though not necessarily in the order given:

1. Warrant for baptism (usually Matt. 28.18-20; occasionally Mark 10.13-16).
2. Exhortation on the meaning of baptism.
3. Questions to the parents to elicit solemn promises from them.

4. Prayers for the sanctification of the child to be baptized.
5. The act of baptism by sprinkling of water on the child's head, mentioning the child's name, and saying, 'N., I baptize thee in the name of the Father, and of the Son, and of the Holy Ghost.' The Aaronic blessing (q.v.) follows.
6. A declaration by the minister, with the congregation as witnesses, that the child is now received into the congregation of 'Christ's flock.
7. A concluding prayer for the child, parents and congregation, that they may be protected and guided by God to fulfil their vows and to recall their own baptism, and finally attain to everlasting life.

A similar service, with the necessary adaptation, is used for the baptism of believers.

In recent times Congregationalists, like other Christians, have been disturbed by the relatively small percentage of infants baptized who come to confirmation or full church membership at maturity. They have attempted to meet this problem in two ways. They have made the explanatory section of the rite fuller and more clear. In England they have made considerable use of the Rev. H. A. Hamilton's book *The Family Church*, which is an attempt to cross the abyss between church and Sunday school (which previously had met in different buildings). He insisted on including children in the beginning of common worship in the sanctuary on Sundays and throughout the service for the four major festivals of the year. He also advocated the provision of 'church friends' with whom the children might sit if their own parents took no interest in their spiritual progress. Imaginative as this suggestion is, the problem is still of major proportions.

HORTON DAVIES

8. *Jehovah's Witnesses*. (*a*) Water baptism marks the initiate's entry into the family of God, with consequential privileges and responsibilities, including ordination to public Christian ministry.

Water does not wash away sins: 'The blood of Jesus [God's] Son cleanses us from all sin' (I John 1.7). However, baptism performed in faith is with the consciousness of God's forgiveness, and is therefore a 'request made to God for a good conscience'. It is also 'now saving you' since withdrawal from the world's course, presupposed to be antagonistic to God's righteousness, has necessarily preceded it (I Peter 3.21-4.6).

Jehovah's Witnesses have always practised total immersion (*Zion's Watch Tower*, 15 June 1893). Not only do the lexicographers show *baptizo* to mean 'to dip in or under water' (Liddell and Scott), but scriptural usage demands total immersion. Jesus, baptized in Jordan River, came 'up out of the water'; Philip and the Ethiopian 'went down into the water' (Mark 1.10; Acts 8.38).

Only adults are baptized. The Lord's command was to baptize 'disciples'; 'teach all the nations, making them your pupils' (K. S. Wuest's translation), and *then* baptize them (Matt. 28.19, 20). They were old enough to be 'pupils'. Acts 10.48; 18.8 and others speak of whole households being baptized, but only 'those hearing the word' (Acts 10.44) and 'believer(s) in the Lord' (18.8), hence at an age of understanding.

A preparatory course, usually at least six months long, is undertaken by each candidate. He should consider what he is doing soberly and with a clear mind (Eccles. 5.2-6). The 190-page Bible study aid *The Truth That Leads to Eternal Life* is currently being used for this pre-baptismal course. It summarizes fundamental Bible doctrine and practice in uncompromising terms. Worldwide Jehovah's Witnesses immersed 434,906 adults in the period 1969–71, a substantially increased rate over previous years.

(*b*) John's baptism (Acts 19.3) was 'in symbol of repentance for forgiveness of sins' against the Mosaic law covenant (Luke 3.3). Jesus was baptized, not in repentance over sins (I Peter 2.22), but as 'presenting himself to his Father Jehovah to do his Father's "will"' (*Aid to Bible Understanding*, 'Baptism'; Heb. 10.5-7). Christ's disciples are baptized similarly, hence not with John's baptism, superseded by (a) and (c).

(*c*) A baptism which can be performed only by Jehovah God is that by holy spirit into Christ and his death (Rom. 6.3). Christ understood he was to be plunged into death but raised out of it on the third day, and he likened the experience to a baptism into death (Luke 12.50). His disciples were to experience a like baptism (Mark 10.39; Col. 3.3,4). At their anointing by holy spirit, Christ's footstep followers and joint heirs become united to him, their Head (I Cor.

12.12, 13). They belong to him. Baptism 'into his death' is climaxed by a willing sacrificial death like his and the reward of unity with him in resurrected heavenly glory.

(*d*) The baptism 'with fire' of Matt. 3.11 is understood to refer to Jerusalem's destruction in AD 70 (vv. 10-12).

A. HELEY

9. *Lutheran.* Baptism, according to the Lutheran confessional writings, is an ordinance commanded by God and instituted by Jesus Christ, through which a special promise of inward grace, regeneration and incorporation into Christ's body the church, is offered in conjunction with an outward material sign, water. It is therefore one of the true sacraments and normally necessary for salvation (*Large Catechism* IV; *Apol. der Conf. Aug* XIII, 3 ff., *Smalcaldic Articles* III, 4; *Augsburg Confession* = *CA* IX). It summons the baptized to lifelong trust and obedience and the expectation of perfect renewal at the last day.

The Lutheran doctrine of baptism developed during the Reformation period both as a reform of the Roman Catholic view and as a defence against more radical teachings, e.g. those of the Anabaptists.

The main points emphasized were:

1. That the effective working of baptism is *by faith*, not by the objective performance of the rite. Faith is not just an outward profession but is the fruit of God's grace growing within man until it is manifested outwardly. Faith is not proved empirically (*CA* IV, 57).

2. That since baptism is God's act, infant baptism is the clearest demonstration of this (Luther, *Werke*, Weimar, 1883 ff. = WA 26, 157; American edition, 1958 ff., 40,244). Luther held that baptism calls forth faith in infants, though he agreed that we do not understand how (WA 26,157; Amer. ed. 40,243). Child faith is inferred from child baptism, not vice versa.

3. The relationship of baptism to sin. Baptism is seen as a continuing work of God, preparing a Christian for the last day. The entire Christian life with its struggle against sin is a constant return to one's baptism. This eschatalogically oriented view of baptism helps to establish a tone of trust and prayerful responsibility and offers a key to the Christian quest for sanctification.

4. The responsibility of all who are baptized to the word of God and to the people of

God.

5. The exaltation of the baptismal vow of faithfulness to Christ in all walks of life.

Luther's interpretation generally set the pattern for the Lutheran church. Lutheran orthodoxy, however, as it developed in the sixteenth or seventeenth centuries transformed Luther's flexible, paradoxical view into a more fixed and institutionalized conception. In the background was what eventually became a complex and rigid analysis of the 'order of salvation' with a sharp distinction between justification and sanctification. The rise of rigid state-church systems also helped to externalize baptism.

The rite. At the Reformation, Luther conservatively simplified the traditional rite and laid the emphasis on earnest prayer for the child (WA 12,38 ff.). In the *Taufbüchlein* of 1523 he retained the medieval practices. In his revised order of 1526, which attained great popularity in Germany, he made some editorial revisions and omitted a number of symbolic features, such as the two anointings (*see* sections 1–3 above, and **Unction**). His positive contribution was a collect known as the 'Flood prayer'. For the mode of baptism he preferred immersion as more adequate to signify the drowning of sin, but he did not insist on this mode. Lutherans have agreed that immersion is not essential; pouring and sprinkling have become the most common modes in Lutheran churches.

During the eras of pietism and rationalism exorcism (q.v.) and renunciation generally dropped out of the Lutheran rite, though the latter has returned in many orders.

In Scandinavia the admonition to the sponsors and the salutation were added to the liturgy. In many of the churches the custom of signing the child with a cross (*see* **Cross, Sign of**) was retained or has reappeared. The renunciation of the devil is retained in most liturgies except that of the Church of Sweden.

The German churches experienced a proliferation of baptismal liturgies, basically on the lines of either Luther's rite of 1526 or Bugenhagen's of 1535. Since 1961 they all have a common one which closely follows Luther's.

In view of Luther's doctrine of the priesthood of all believers any Christian may in an emergency perform baptism according to the order laid down for such situations. Such a baptism, which is to be reported to the auth-

orities of the church, is considered a proper function of the church (WA 12,181; 31,211).

The place of baptism in the worship of the church is less prominent in Europe, where the practice of private baptism in homes or at the church after public worship has developed, than in the American tradition, where there is a strong tendency to administer baptism at a public service to emphasize the communal significance of the sacrament.

E. J. R. H. S. VON SICARD

10. *Methodist.* John Wesley's *Sunday Service of the Methodists in North America*, 1784, is the foundation for subsequent initiation rites in Methodism. Its baptismal services were adopted from the *BCP*, 1662, of the Church of England, but with some drastic alterations.

The private baptism of infants was omitted. All references to godparents were omitted, though the 'Friends of the Child' were asked to give the name; consequently the vows of renunciation, belief and obedience in the name of the infant were omitted. In 1784 two references to regeneration were removed, but that in the prayer 'Almighty and Immortal God' was retained, as was the phrase 'that he may be born again' in the prayer 'Almighty and Everlasting God, Heavenly Father'. These prayers were both omitted, among other changes, in 1786; the prayer for the sanctification of the water was then still retained, but the central petition was in some editions modified and in the others wholly omitted. In 1784 Wesley added to the modes of baptism 'or sprinkle', but omitted the possibility of pouring water. A few of the 1784 copies retained the signing with the cross and the reception, but the others omitted them. Other changes were aimed at shortening the service.

In Great Britain there were further changes in the Wesleyan Church in 1846, 1864 and 1882 (in *Public Prayers and Services*), as well as in very different services produced in the non-Wesleyan Churches. After the union, *The Book of Offices*, 1936, produced a further revision, in which a leading feature of the service was the promises made by the parents.

In America the Methodist Episcopal Church (MEC) in 1864 and the Methodist Episcopal Church South (MECS) in 1866 added reference to others than parents, and the term 'sponsors' appeared in MEC in 1916 and is retained in the *Book of Worship (BW)*,

1964. The prayer for the sanctification of the water lasted till 1858 in MECS and 1916 in MEC. The 1792 *Discipline* allowed sprinkling, pouring or immersing, all of which are provided for in the 1964 rite, though sprinkling is almost always used.

In American Methodism today baptism is almost always performed in the presence of a congregation. Baptized children are regarded as 'preparatory members' in the United Methodist Church. The current rite has moved away from mention of OT precedents, from reference to washing from sin, and neglects the sense of incorporation into the church evident in Wesley. It stresses more the vows the parents or sponsors take for themselves in promising to rear the child as a Christian. The congregation also joins in this. The service is very brief, because of its insertion in the midst of the Sunday service.

An office for the 'Baptism of Children and Youth' appeared in 1914 (MECS) and remained till 1964.

Wesley's treatment of the ministration of baptism to such as are of 'riper years' was, in general, similar to his treatment of infant baptism. Several references to baptismal regeneration disappeared, rubrics and exhortations were dropped, and, in this case, the sign of the cross was definitely omitted in all editions of the Sunday service. The renunciation, creed and vow of obedience were retained, though the 1786 editions dropped the phrase in the creed (put interrogatively): 'that he went down into hell', and the same editions dropped the petition for the sanctification of the water. The British books made various changes, in the same years as for infants, though the changes did not always correspond. In America, Wesley's version remained remarkably intact until twentieth century revisions began pushing in the direction of brevity. Alternate gospel lessons were provided, four choices appearing in the *BW*, 1944. The American service of 1964 for baptism of 'youth and adults' remains brief, but represents a move away from the watering down of sacramental doctrine of the recent past with more emphasis on remission of sins and the reception of the Holy Spirit.

Wesley's most significant change was the omission of a confirmation rite (q.v.). Not till 1864 did MEC add an office for the reception of members and MECS followed in 1870. In 1886 MECS added a rubric to adult baptism to allow the minister to 'lay his hands on the subject . . . with suitable invocation'. Today baptism of youth and adults is often (but not always) followed by confirmation, though as yet most United Methodists are more familiar with the designation of this rite as 'reception into the church'. In Britain the Wesleyan Conference did not adopt a service for the 'Public Recognition of New Members' till 1894. There was a new form in 1936.

In general, the black Methodist churches have done less pruning of the Wesleyan services than the predominantly white churches, though the African Methodist Episcopal and the Christian Methodist Episcopal churches have alternate brief orders for infant baptism.

The British Conference of 1967 authorized a booklet 'Entry into the Church' for experimental use. The service for the baptism of infants has an entirely fresh structure: gospel, homily, the great prayer of baptism, promises by the congregation, the parents, the sponsors (the sponsors are optional), Apostles' Creed, presentation of the child by the parents, baptism, signation, reception, Aaronic blessing, final prayers, grace. The booklet then contains 'Public Reception into Full Membership, or Confirmation'; and then finally 'The Baptism of those who are able to answer for themselves with the Public Reception into Full Membership, or Confirmation'. This proceeds as follows: hymn, prayer, OT lesson, epistle, hymn, gospel, sermon, hymn, homily, the great prayer of baptism, promises by the congregation and the candidates, Apostles' Creed, further question to the candidates, baptism, homily when there are others to be confirmed who have been baptized previously, confirmation and reception, prayer, hymn, Lord's Supper, with alternative ending 'if, in exceptional circumstances and for good reason, Confirmation does not immediately follow the baptism of those who are able to answer for themselves'.

A. RAYMOND GEORGE
JAMES F. WHITE

11. *Old Catholic*. The teaching of the Old Catholic churches of the Utrecht Union on baptism is that of holy scripture and the catholic church. Baptism is administered with water 'in the name of the Father and of the Son and of the Holy Spirit', usually by affusion. The baptismal water is blessed in the liturgy of Easter night and kept in the

font. Infant baptism is generally practised.

Grace received at baptism is completed and developed by the sacrament of confirmation (q.v.), bestowed on children by the bishop, after the children have received instruction in the Christian faith. In the Old Catholic Church of the Netherlands confirmation is brought into closer connection with baptism by the renewal of baptismal vows. In other countries, this takes place on receiving first communion. In the Polish National Catholic Church in America, baptism and confirmation together are regarded as a single sacrament: 'The Word of God, heard and preached', is regarded as the seventh (or second) sacrament.

The baptismal rite of the Old Catholic churches is based on the *Ordo Baptismi Parvulorum* of the *Rituale Romanum* of Paul V; it is partly an exact translation and partly a free revision. In the German and Swiss rites of baptism there is a clear concern to explain the sacred actions by accompanying words.

Taking over the order of baptism from the old *Rituale Romanum* raises a number of difficult problems: (1) This rite is not made for infant baptism, but is an abbreviation of the rite for adult baptism. In some Old Catholic rites of baptism, therefore, attempts have long been made to adapt the content of the prayers to the normal situation (infant baptism!), for example, with the addition of the reading of the 'children's gospel' (Mark 10.13-16). On the rare occasions when adults are baptized, John 3.1-21 or Rom. 6.3-11 are substituted. Mark 10.13-16 (for adults, John 3.1-8) together with the command to baptize (Matt. 28.18-20) stand at the beginning of the Swiss rite as a biblical foundation for baptism and especially infant baptism. (2) The first part of the earlier Roman, and so also Old Catholic, baptismal rite contains the rites of the catechumenate (q.v.), which were originally spread over a considerable length of time; here, however, they are compressed into a single celebration. The significance of some of these rites is no longer immediately recognizable, as they are no longer connected with their original situation. (3) Individual rites seem strange and incomprehensible to men of today, e.g. touching the candidate's ears and nose (*cf.* Mark 7.34) with spittle to the accompaniment of the word 'ephphatha'. In the Old Catholic rites, however, this has long been replaced by a simple touching (without spittle) of mouth and ears. The repeated exorcisms (q.v.), too, have a distressing effect at the baptism of small children and seem unjustified. They are therefore either omitted from the ritual of Old Catholic churches or replaced by other texts. The custom of breathing on the person baptized is retained in part, but more stress is laid on the idea of insufflation (q.v.), i.e. the breathing in of the Holy Spirit, than on the 'exsufflation' (the breathing out of evil spirits).

In the context of liturgical renewal which is also taking place in Old Catholic churches, new formulae for baptism, too, are being worked out, in which the difficulties of the earlier rite, mentioned above, are taken into account.

In the Netherlands, baptism was administered in Dutch as early as the eighteenth century, according to formulae which were a complete literal translation of the *ordo baptismi parvulorum* from the *Rituale Romanum*. In 1902 the bishops introduced a revised text. Though they kept to the old Roman pattern for the most part, the exsufflation and the exorcisms disappeared. After the threefold renunciation of Satan the promise 'to love the Lord your God with all your heart and with all your soul, and with all your strength, and with all your mind, and your neighbour as yourself' is required. At the first anointing a prayer for Christ's grace was added, for strength to fight the good fight.

Between World War I and World War II it became the practice more and more to baptize the child in the presence of the mother, and therefore after a few weeks rather than immediately after birth, as the strict Dutch practice had been before. Also, increasingly, baptism took place immediately after the eucharist, in the presence of the congregation. For the past few years there has been a tendency to baptize during the eucharist, after the gospel and the sermon.

As an example of an Old Catholic order of baptism, there follows here a short description of baptism in the Old Catholic Church in Germany. After an address, the priest assures himself of the willingness of the sponsors or the person to be baptized, and informs him of the chief commandment (Luke 10.27). The *exsufflatio* is hardly used any more. The exorcisms have been replaced by a single formula, entirely in accord with the spirit of the Bible. Thereupon the priest signs the person to be baptized on the forehead and chest with the sign of the cross, and salt, which has previously been blessed, is placed on his lips. The reading of a passage from the gospels (Mark 10.13-16 or John 3.1-21) has been taken from the ritual of Cologne, but it has its roots in the *traditio evangeliorum* from earliest times.

The repetition of the creed and Lord's Prayer no longer has its original form of question and answer, but the two are said together. The renunciation of Satan, which occurs in the earliest baptismal formulae of East and West, and has also been preserved in Anglican and Protestant forms of service, is summed up in a single clear question. There follows the anointing of the breast with oil. After a threefold question about belief, the priest pours the baptismal water three times on the head of the person to be baptized, in the form of a cross, and says, 'N, I baptize you in the name of the Father and of the Son and of the Holy Spirit.'

The baptism is followed by the anointing of the head with chrism (see **Unction**), the bestowal of a white baptismal garment and a lighted candle. The priest dismisses the person baptized and his sponsors with the blessing.

KURT PURSCH
A. E. RÜTHY
C. TOL

12. *Pentecostal*. In classical Pentecostalism (*cf.* **Pentecostal Worship**), many churches have no given rite of baptism but improvise a a ceremony according, as it is said, to the movement of the Spirit. A rite of baptism which the author observed in the Bahama Islands consisted of a procession from the church to the sea, accompanied with singing, hand clapping, ejaculatory prayers. On the beach the pastor addressed the faithful, admonishing them to repent of their sins and to accept Christ as their personal Saviour. Baptism was by immersion. The spontaneity of the people and deep sense of prayer and celebration made it evident that the participants were not going through a prescribed rite, but were deeply involved in prayer. In many classical Pentecostal groups the baptismal rite is accompanied with tongues, prophecies, and in one African church, the rite is accompanied with a prayer for healing. In the Church of the Twelve Apostles (Nackabah), an African church, the baptismal candidates are properly soaped and bathed (W. Hollenweger, *The Pentecostals*, 1971, p.391). Within classical Pentecostalism one can also find baptismal rites written down and printed in a disciplinary book or a minister's manual. These would include prayers, exhortations, and either the Trinitarian baptismal formula or a formula mentioning only the name of Jesus. These rites would be used with great freedom by the ministers.

Most classical Pentecostals (e.g. Assemblies of God) follow a Baptist conception of baptism, that is, for adults who have made a personal commitment to Christ. But there is a sizeable minority of classical Pentecostals who use sprinkling: the majority of Chilean Pentecostals, the largest of the German churches, a Yugoslav group, and in the beginning, the Finnish and Norwegian movements (Hollenweger, *The Pentecostals*, p.392). Often the pastor dips his hand in a bowl of water and rubs the head of the candidate. One American directory says that 'the candidate shall have the right to choose whatever mode of baptism he prefers' (*Discipline of the Pentecostal Holiness Church*, 1961, p.78). The Quaker Pentecostals think the whole baptismal controversy peripheral. Both a Chilean and a German church allow adult baptism *and* infant baptism and therefore have baptism by immersion or sprinkling. In addition to these groups, all of which are Trinitarian, there are the Pentecostal modalists, or 'Jesus only' groups, which take Acts 2.38 to mean that the Trinitarian formula is not to be used, but rather candidates should be baptized only in the name of Jesus. Among some of the Churches of God (USA) there are groups which baptize only in the name of the Father (E. Clark, *The Small Sects in America*, 1949, p.105).

Neo-Pentecostals (*cf.* **Pentecostal Worship**) would tend to follow the rite of their respective churches. Some Lutheran Pentecostals have taken over the patterns of classical Pentecostals and have been re-baptized by immersion, not necessarily because their baptism by pouring was thought invalid. When a Catholic priest who is involved in the charismatic renewal baptizes a child of a Catholic neo-Pentecostal couple, the rite of the Roman Catholic Church would be followed but there can, in addition, be quiet praying in tongues, interpretation, prophecy, and free prayer.

In Chile men and women admitted that they were deeply moved the first time they attended a Pentecostal service: 'Not because of the beauty of the ceremonial – oh, no, it is not as beautiful as with Catholics – but because people spoke to me, the pastor shook my hand, and I was able to sing and pray with them' (C. Lalive d'Epinay, *Haven of the Masses*, 1969, p. 49).

At their worst, Pentecostal baptismal liturgies can be theologically impoverished and too subjectivistic. At their best, Pentecostal baptismal liturgies are successful because each individual is a participant, because their liturgies are essentially oral rather than printed (and usually oral even when printed), because they are simple, direct, and personal, because baptism is more immediately a prayer act than an external ritual, because whether dealing with a pre-literate or post-literate culture they know how to elicit a personal commitment through involvement in an experience which is self-explanatory, because the baptismal rite is itself an instrument of evangelization.

Finally, their rites are not techniques and are not separable from their spirituality, which is fullness of life in the Spirit and the exercise of the gifts of the Spirit. (For bibliography *see under* **Pentecostal Worship**.)

KILIAN MCDONNELL

13. *Plymouth Brethren*. The Open Brethren almost without exception practise the baptism of believers only, on personal confession of faith, and the accepted mode is, almost invariably, total immersion. If immersion is impracticable for reasons of health or age, such token baptisms as affusion or sprinkling are not employed; the will is simply accepted for the deed. In these respects they closely resemble the Baptists; they do not, however, treat their baptismal doctrine and practice as so essential a feature of their church life that they could properly be described as Baptists.

Baptism is commonly understood among them as an act of public confession and Christian obedience, not as a vehicle of grace or as necessary to salvation. Probably the majority of those baptized among them are young people who have either grown up in the fellowship with their families or have become attached to it through various departments of its youth work; but one finds people

of all age-groups asking for it and receiving it. It is normally administered before a congregation; most of the Open Brethren's meeting-places have suitable baptisteries sunk in the floor and boarded over when not in use.

Open Brethren do not, for the most part, treat baptism as an indispensable condition for admission to the communion table or to church membership; this would unfairly exclude Christians who have been baptized in infancy and cannot conscientiously recognize any obligation to receive 'responsible' baptism. But the baptismal teaching given at their meetings is uniformly that connected with believers' baptism.

Among the Exclusive Brethren the situation is much less uniform. Those who adhere most closely to the Darbyite tradition follow J. N. Darby in baptizing the infant children of their church members; this practice is commonly called 'household' baptism' (on the basis of Acts 16.15, 31-34; I Cor. 1.16, etc.). In the Taylorite connection such baptized children are regularly admitted to church fellowship at the age of twelve, if not earlier. Some of Darby's closest associates who disagreed with infant baptism found it expedient not to press their views: when an argumentative lady once asked him what his principal lieutenant, George Vicesimus Wigram (1805-1879), held about baptism, he is said to have replied, 'Madam, he holds his tongue.' And when the first major division took place within the Exclusive ranks (1881), although the issue had nothing to do with baptism, practically all those who held 'Baptist' views seceded with William Kelly (1820-1906), while the paedobaptists went 'nearly solid' for Darby (W. B. Neatby, *A History of the Plymouth Brethren*, 1901, pp. 237f.).

An interesting situation arises when reunions take place (as they happily do from time to time) between groups or congregations which have incidentally differed from each other in baptismal doctrine or practice; there proves in practice to be no obstacle to the peaceful coexistence of the two ways (believers' baptism and infants' baptism). Tension is perhaps prevented by the fact that among the paedobaptist Exclusives infants are in any case baptized at home whereas Open Brethren and others who baptize believers do so in public.

F. F. BRUCE

14. *Reformed.* The baptismal rites in the Western church at the eve of the Reformation show that many ceremonies had been added to the practice of the early church, but these were not essential to the sacrament and their omission in cases of emergency did not affect its validity. This led to revision. In 1523, Luther published his *Das Taufbüchlein verdeutscht* (*Works*, Weimar XII, 42-48), which with minor alterations was a German translation of the medieval order in use at Wittenberg. When Diebold Schwarz translated the order in use at Strasbourg in 1524, he drew heavily on this. This was revised in 1525 (Hubert, *Die Stras. lit.,* 37-52), but it was now more than a translation, for the whole rite was re-cast. Under the influence of Bucer, further revisions were carried out during the years 1525-33, and it was on these Farel based his *La Manière et façon.* To Farel and Bucer, Calvin was much indebted for his Strasbourg rite. This later was simplified for use in Geneva (*Op.,* VI, 184-191) and became the determining influence in the *Form of Prayers* (*FP*, 1556) of the English exiles there and the Scottish *Book of Common Order* (*BCO*, 1564).

Calvin's Strasbourg order, as found in the 1545 edition published by Paul Garnier, is:

1. Scripture sentence (Ps. 124.8).
2. Question: Do you present this child to be baptized, earnestly desiring that he may be engrafted in the mystical body of Christ?
3. Long exposition and exhortation.
4. Prayer for grace and reception of the child into the Kingdom of Christ.
5. The Lord's Prayer.
6. Question: Do you wish this child baptized in the name of the Father and of the Son, and of the Holy Spirit?
7. Apostles' Creed, said by parents.
8. Exhortation to parents.
9. Baptism with water in the triune name.
10. Declaration that the child is a member of Christ's church.

In *FP* and *BCO* the order is altered to 2 3 7 4 5 9 and a concluding prayer of thanksgiving and for the blessing of the Holy Spirit.

In the Reformed Church baptism was always placed in the setting of the worship of the people of God, the rite following the reading and preaching of the word. It was to be administered only 'in the face of the congregation'. Baptism, being a sacrament of the gospel, could only be administered by a minister of the word. For this reason also, the font (q.v.) was removed from the church-door and placed near the pulpit.

The Reformed Church sought to remove all non-scriptural elements from the rite and to make it relevant to the baptism of infants. Whereas some other traditions superimpose a baptismal order upon the existing medieval rite, which was designed in the first place for the baptism of adult believers, in Reformed rites no vicarious profession of faith is required of the parents or godparents, the children being admitted to baptism on the grounds of the covenant of grace. For this reason also, exorcisms (q.v.) and renunciations are laid aside as being inappropriate to the baptism of children of Christian parents. The Creed is repeated by the parents as the faith which they themselves believe as members of the church of Christ and into which they wish their children baptized, they taking a vow to bring them up therein. While there is no objection to godparents, the chief sponsor is, generally speaking, the father of the child.

In the early Reformed rites there is no epiclesis in the baptismal prayer. The reason for this could be that in the medieval church the consecration of the font had become a separate rite, or perhaps it was held that the declaration of intention of baptism was sufficient. Baptism is normally by affusion, but nothing is prescribed as to whether it should be single or triple. The latter has always been the practice of the Reformed churches in France, Switzerland, Germany and Hungary.

The order in *FP* (1556) and *BCO* (1564) remained the practice in the Reformed churches in Britain until it was replaced by that in the Westminster *Directory for the Public Worship of God* in 1645. Its order is:

Exhortation.
Prayer, including epiclesis.
Inquiry as to name.
Baptism with water in the triune name.
Prayer of thanksgiving and for the blessing of the Holy Spirit.

Here no profession of faith is required of the sponsors, but the adopting Act of the General Assembly of the Church of Scotland shows that the same requirement was continued. This is also true of Irish Presbyterianism. The

Directory, being really only one extended rubric, resulted in a period of decadence. Renewal did not begin until the Church Service Society published the first edition of its *Euchologion* in 1867.

(*a*) *Rites in English*. The editors of *Euchologion* (1867) said concerning the baptismal order: 'The following Service is based upon the Baptismal Service in John Knox's *Book of Common Order*. It is condensed and considerably curtailed; but may be regarded as presenting the original and genuine doctrine of the Scottish Church regarding the sacrament of Baptism.' Several revisions followed, and the fifth (1884) may be said to have become normative. It is:

Scripture sentence (Ps. 124.8).
Scripture readings: Matt. 28.18-20; Mark 10.13-16; Acts 2.38-39.
Vows: Apostles' Creed, or alternative, answered by parents; upbringing of child.
Prayer: based on Greek, *BCP* and Catholic Apostolic rites with epiclesis from Westminster *Directory*.
Baptism with water in the triune name.
Apostolic or Aaronic blessing (optional).
Declaration that the child is received into the church: from 'Savoy Liturgy' (1661).
Prayer: from *BCO* (1564) and 'Larger Catechism'.
The Lord's Prayer.
Apostolic benediction.

This rite won its way into most of the English Reformed rites, and became almost universally accepted, remaining substantially unaltered in the Scottish *BCO* (1940) and American *Book of Common Worship* (*BCW*, 1946). In recent years, however, revision has taken place as a result of continental, Scottish and Irish research.

The Irish *Book of Public Worship* (*BPW*, 1965) may be taken as representing a transitional stage between the old and the new, (1) having references in the scripture readings to God's covenant with Abraham and the baptism of Jesus, (2) requiring the congregation to take a specific vow; and (3) departing from the traditional wording of the parents' vow to bring up the child in the Christian faith by adopting the form in *BCW* of the Church of South India.

Good examples of the new rites are *BCO* (Presbyterian Church, Canada, 1964), *Public Service Book* (*PSB*, England and Wales, 1968)

and the Scottish 'Order for Holy Baptism' (1969). While there are variations in these orders the last may be outlined. It is:

Liturgy of the word.
Scripture readings: Matt. 28.18-20 (reference to baptism of Jesus), Acts 2.38-39 (statement on end of baptism), Mark 10.13-16.
Vows of parents, added first in Calvin's rite.
Congregation accepts responsibility by reciting Apostles' Creed.
Prayer: *Sursum corda*, adoration, epiclesis.
Baptism with water in the triune name.
Aaronic blessing.
Declaration that the child is received into the church.
Matt. 18.5, 6, 10 may be read.
Prayer: supplication and intercession.
The Lord's Prayer.
Psalm or hymn.
Benediction: 'The peace of God . . .'

The English-Welsh and Canadian rites both open with Ps. 124.8. In the former the reference to the baptism of Jesus is omitted, but in the latter Mark 1.9-11 is read. In both the Apostles' Creed is said by the congregation before the parents take their vows. The Scottish rite, in 1963, re-introduced Calvin's first question to the parents. The other two do not do so. The English-Welsh rite adds a vow for godparents, if there are any. In the baptismal prayer the *Sursum corda* is omitted by both, the Canadian also omitting the epiclesis. Both conclude with the apostolic benediction.

While theologically these rites add nothing new to what was always the doctrine of baptism in the Reformed Church, they do give fuller expression to it.

The Presbyterian Churches in America used the 1788 revision of the Westminster *Directory*, and this practice, apart from the experiments of individuals, continued until the formation of a Church Service Society, on the Scottish model, in 1897. Its instigators and leaders were Henry van Dyke and Louis Benson. This led eventually to the *BCW: Prepared by the Committee of the General Assembly of the Presbyterian Church in the USA for Voluntary Use* (1906), in which the baptismal rite was firmly based on a 'covenant theology', but rather defective structurally. This was revised in 1932, when it was also adopted by the Southern Presbyterians 'for the optional and selective use of our ministers'. The impetus for a third edition came from the publication of the *BCO* (1940) by the Church of Scotland, and this appeared in 1946. The new baptismal rite was considerably influenced by the Scottish and it reveals a more careful handling of the theological implications of baptism.

In 1955, the Presbyterian Church in the USA set up a committee to revise the *BCW*, and in this work three things are of note: (1) the United Presbyterian Church of North America and the Presbyterian Church in the United States (Southern) decided to participate together in the project; (2) in 1961 a revision of the old *Directory* was published setting out basic principles; and (3) before issuing a revised *BCW*, a *BCW: Provisional Services* (1966) was prepared for use and report. This is the baptismal rite now in use, and is noteworthy for three distinctive features: (1) 'the service is designed to be used both for the baptism of adults and for the baptism of infants'; (2) opportunity is provided for an elder representing the session to take a part in the service; and (3) 'the service includes opportunity for the whole congregation to renew baptismal vows in a unison prayer'.

(*b*) *Rites in French.* The liturgical movement in the Reformed Church in France begins with *La Liturgie d'Eugène Bersier* (1874). This work was destined to exercise a wide influence not only in France but in French-speaking Switzerland and elsewhere. The result of this movement may be illustrated by the Genevan rite (1945):

Scripture sentence: (Ps. 124.8).
Declaration of intention.
Scripture readings: Ezek. 36.25-28; Matt. 28.18-20; Acts 2.38-39.
Baptismal instruction.
Vows.
Exhortation to parents.
Baptism with water in the triune name.
Prayer of supplication and intercession.
The Lord's Prayer.
Benediction (Phil. 4.7; Rom. 15.33).

Here, as in the English-speaking rites, recent research has exercised a great influence. While they differ structurally, good examples of the new rites are those in the Canton de Vaud (1962) and in France (1963). The order for the latter is:

Welcome based on Mark 10.13 and Ezek.
36.24-27.
Invocation and adoration.
Apostles' Creed said by congregation.
Institution: Matt. 28.18-20.
Prayer.
Baptismal instruction.
Exhortation to parents.
Desire of parents.
Involvement of congregation.
Baptism with water in the triune name.
Vows of parents, may be placed before baptism.

The rite for Vaud adds Mark 1.9-11 and Acts 2.38-39 to the readings, which are followed by the creed and a prayer based on Geneva (1542) and *La Liturgie des Églises du Pays de Vaud* (1725). Then come the vows, institution, and a prayer from the Roman rite. Neither rite contains an epiclesis, although the Vaud rite has a petition that the child may be 'baptized with water and the Spirit'. The baptismal instruction (omitted in Vaud) is based on Strasbourg (1536) and Geneva (1542). In the French rite the vows are presented as laid upon the parents by the church, which itself is a 'witness' to the baptism and required to take upon itself 'responsibility' for the baptized. Baptism is always with water 'in the name of the Father, and of the Son, and of the Holy Spirit'. The concluding prayer is based upon Genevan, French or Vaudoise sources. The Vaud rite ends with a declaration, 'We receive you into the family of God, the church of Jesus Christ.'

(*c*) *Rites in German.* The baptismal order in the German rites, broadly speaking, is:

Scripture readings: Matt. 28.18-20, Mark 10.13-16.
Baptismal instruction.
Prayer: supplication and intercession.
Apostles' Creed, sometimes said by the congregation.
Vows of parents and godparents.
Baptism with water in the triune name.
Exhortation to parents and congregation.
Prayer of thanksgiving.

This may be taken as representative, even though some service-books in addition include the form in *Der Taufordnung der Pfälzischen Kirchenordnung* (1563).

The scripture readings from Matthew and Mark are always included as the warrant for baptism. The baptismal instruction is drawn from many sources – Strasbourg (1524), a'Lasco (1550), Geneva (1542), Pfalz (1563) and Basle (1572), as are the questions to the parents. The words introducing the Apostles' Creed are drawn from Micronius (1554), Pfalz (1563), or Basle (1572). Baptism is with water 'in the name of the Father, and of the Son, and of the Holy Spirit'. The exhortation is based on Zurich (1529) and Pfalz (1563). The supplications and intercessions have a common content but vary considerably in different rites, according to whether or not they are derived from Zurich (1525), Strasbourg (1536), Geneva (1542), a'Lasco (1550), Scottish *BCO* (1564), Basle (1572), Bern (1598), Cassel (1657), or St Gallen (1699). None includes an epiclesis. Generally speaking several thanksgivings are provided, but they almost always include a'Lasco (1550) and Pfalz (1563).

(*d*) *Confirmation, Baptism of the Sick, Baptism of Believers*. All these rites contain an order for confirmation (*see* **Confirmation**). In cases of sickness and emergency, private baptism is permitted. The liturgy of the Reformed Church in France provides a separate rite for this, and others contain special prayers. Here it might be worth making into a universal practice the decision of the Perth Assembly (1618):

> That the minister shall the next Lord's day after such private baptism declare in the church that the infant was so baptized, and therefore ought to be received as one of the true flock of Christ's fold.

The early Reformed liturgies and the Westminster *Directory* make no provision for the baptism of adult believers. The first such rite was prepared by the Dutch Reformed Church in 1604. The first in English is in the third edition of *Euchologion* (1874). The latter casts the rite as baptism-confirmation, for the baptism is followed by prayer 'with imposition of hands'. This theological position remains basic in all the rites, and the changes taking place are parallel to those in the rites for the children of believers.

(*e*) *Theology*. Baptism is a gift of God to men through his church, in which he 'presents' and 'seals' Christ to them, admitting them to the fellowship of the church and demanding from them the response of faith and a life of godliness through the power of the Holy Spirit. All these rites do set forth clearly the Reformed doctrine of 'the grace of baptism'. At the same time, two questions require to be raised: (1) If in a sacrament God, through the 'visible sign', 'presents and seals Christ', should the prayer before the act of baptism not always include a petition that the 'visible sign' may fulfil God's purpose? (2) Does the eschatological significance of baptism always receive adequate expression?

JOHN M. BARKLEY

15. *Seventh-day Adventist*. Seventh-day Adventists believe that baptism is the ceremony of initiation into the Christian church, and is therefore a solemn ordinance, the proper form of which is to be administered by immersion. Baptism is the antitype of the Genesis flood, which prefigured the freely accepted 'reduced flood'. It 'typifies the death, burial, and resurrection of Christ, and openly expresses faith in His saving grace' (*Church Manual*, 1967, p. 58). As such it is a condition of entrance into church membership. In addition to the etymological argument stemming from the basic meaning of the Greek word *baptizo* ('to dip', 'to plunge', 'to overwhelm'), Seventh-day Adventists hold that the soundest argument for baptism by immersion is the theological one derived from Paul's symbolism (Rom. 6.1-11) of baptism as representing death, burial and resurrection. Baptism signifies death to sin, moral resurrection in this life and corporal resurrection in the life to come. The practice of another mode of baptism by the apostolic church would have rendered meaningless the significance of the symbolic character Paul gave to the baptismal ceremony.

In harmony with other followers of the Baptist tradition, Seventh-day Adventists reject infant baptism, believing that there is no biblical support for this custom. Accordingly they practice believer's baptism, administering it only to those who have reached accountability and meet the prerequisite of active faith.

Baptism is not just a momentary act, but should be a continuous sign witnessing to the believer's acceptance of Jesus Christ as his personal Saviour. Persons joining the SDAC, who have already been baptized by immersion, are not rebaptized, except when they desire rebaptism. Seventh-day Adventists who have apostatized and have publicly violated the faith and principles of the SDAC, thus nullifying the sign and witness of baptism, are in the case of reconversion asked to enter the church as in the beginning, namely by baptism (*Church Manual*, 1967, p. 72).

Adventists do not view baptism as a ritual washing with some kind of supernatural power or magical cleansing of sin *per se* without true repentance. In common with their Protestant heritage, they therefore reject the sacramentalist view of baptism as imparting grace *ex opere operato*, that is, as an act or sign that, in and of itself, imparts grace and effects salvation. Though baptism does not automatically convey grace, it is intended to be a public sign of grace that comes through incorporation into the family of God.

Baptismal candidates are thoroughly instructed in the Christian faith, and prior to baptism an examination takes place either before the church board or at the baptismal service itself, when they are asked to affirm publicly their assent to the teachings of the SDAC. Baptism is usually administered by an ordained minister, but 'in his absence the local church elder may officiate' (*Manual for Ministers*, 1954, p. 84) after making proper arrangements with the conference or mission president.

A typical baptismal service is preceded by a hymn, prayer and short discourse on the meaning of baptism. As each candidate is immersed, the congregation often sings a stanza of some appropriate hymn. Where the local church does not have a baptistery, a stream, lake or other aquatic facility is used.

Before the candidate is immersed, the minister performing the baptism raises his right hand and pronounces the following formula (or a very similar one): 'My brother, upon the profession of your faith in Jesus Christ as your personal Saviour, I now baptize you into the name of the Father, and of the Son, and of the Holy Spirit. Amen' (*Manual for Ministers*, 1954, p. 88).

B. B. BEACH

Baptism and Confirmation, Prayer Book Studies I, 1952; *Baptism and Confirmation,* Report of the Church of England Liturgical Commission, 1959; *Baptism and Confirmation Today,* Report of the Joint Committees on Baptism, Confirmation and the Holy Communion of the Convocations of Canterbury and York, 1955; J. Baillie, *Baptism and Conversion,* 1964; *Le Baptême dans l'Église Réformée par un groupe de pasteurs,* 1954;

J. M. Barkley, *Worship of the Reformed Church,* 1966; G. W. Bromiley, *Baptism and the Anglican Reformers,* 1953; J. D. Benoit, *Initiation à la liturgie de l'Église Réformée de France,* 1956; R. L. Child, *A Conversation about Baptism,* 1963; Church of Scotland, *Biblical Doctrine of Baptism,* 1958; N. Cryer, *By What Rite?* 1969; J. G. Davies, *The Spirit, the Church, and the Sacraments,* 1954; W. Elert, *The Structure of Lutheranism,* 1962; J. D. C. Fisher, *Christians Initiations – the Reformation Period,* 1970; W. Jetter, *Die Taufe beim jungen Luther,* 1954; R. Josefson, *Luthers tära omdepet,* 1944; U. Kury, *Die altkatholische Kirche* (Die Kirchen der Welt II), 1966, pp. 185-187 (Old Catholic); G. W. H. Lampe, *The Seal of the Spirit,* 1967; G. W. H. Lampe and D. M. Paton, eds., *One Lord, One Baptism,* Studies in Ministry and Worship 17, 1960; M. Luther, *The Holy and Blessed Sacrament of Baptism* (*Works,* American ed., vol. 35), 1960; *Manual for Ministers,* 1965 (Seventh-day Adventist); A. J. Mason, *The Relation of Confirmation to Baptism.* 1893; B. S. Moss, ed., *Crisis for Baptism,* 1965; K. F. Müller and W. Blankenburg, eds., *Liturgia. Handbuch des evangelischen Gottesdienstes,* 5. Taufe, Konfirmation, 1952; Don F. Neufeld, *Seventh-day Adventist Encyclopedia,* 1966, pp. 102 ff.; C. E. Pocknee, *The Rites of Christian Initiation,* 1962; A. Segond, *Le Baptême Chrétien,* 1954; *Seventh-day Adventist Church Manual,* 1967; G. Wainwright, *Christian Initiation,* Ecumenical Studies in History, No. 10, 1969; J. Warns, *Baptism,* ET, 1957; E. C. Whitaker, *Documents of the Baptismal Liturgy,* 1960.

Baptist Worship

Baptist worship can only be understood from the Baptist understanding of the church. For Baptists, the chief manifestation of the visible church is the gathered congregation. The gathered or local congregation which is faithful has within it, according to Baptist ecclesiology, the fullness of the church visible. It is made up of persons who have committed themselves to Jesus Christ and his church and upon profession of faith have been baptized and received into church membership. Such a congregation 'gathers' for worship. Worship is celebration of the gospel, i.e. the good news in Jesus Christ. Thus worship for Baptists is primarily a time of praise and thanksgiving, but it is also marked by private and corporate confession, by petition and intercession. The worshipper seeks a living presence of Christ and that spiritual renewal which will enable him to live as a Christian in the world. Congregational worship can take place where two or three are gathered together in the name of the Lord, and he is in the midst of them. Robert Browning's recollection of his Christmas visit to a nonconformist chapel describes well Baptist worship at its heart:

> I remember, he did say
> Doubtless that, to this world's end,
> Two or three should meet and pray,
> He would be in the midst, their friend;
> Certainly he was there with them!
> (Robert Browning, *Christmas Eve and Easter Day*)

The modern Baptist movement had its beginnings in the early years of the seventeenth century as a part of English separatism. It manifested itself first in a congregation of separatists which had fled persecution in England and settled in Holland. Under the leadership of John Smyth this group in the first decade of the seventeenth century separated from the parent congregation over the question of believer's baptism. Smyth's group felt that a local congregation (church) should be made up of those who were baptized after they had made their personal professions of faith. Such 'gathered' congregations met regularly for worship, yet little is known of the form and content of their worship. No manuals of worship have come down to us, for they did not exist. For these early Baptists, such books would have been hindrances to spiritual worship. Smyth himself left a few directions which doubtless reflect the way in which the Baptist congregation of Amsterdam worshipped. He wrote:

1. We hold that the worship of the New Testament properly so called is spiritual proceeding originally from the heart: and that reading out of a book (though it is a lawful ecclesiastical action) is no part of spiritual worship, but rather the invention of the man of sin, it being substituted for a part of spiritual worship.
2. We hold that seeing prophesying is a part of spiritual worship: therefore in time of prophesying it is unlawful to have the book (i.e. the Bible) as a help before the eye.
3. We hold that seeing singing a psalm is a

part of spiritual worship: therefore it is unlawful to have the book before the eye in time of singing a psalm (John Smyth, *The Differences of the Churches of the Separation: Contayning a Description of the Leitourgie and Ministerie of the Visible Church*, 1609, in W. T. Whitley, *The Works of John Smyth*, 1915, p, 273).

According to a contemporary description, the Sunday service in Smyth's church would begin at 8 a.m. with a reading from the Bible. The book would then be set aside. Sermons up to five in number, as time would permit, would be preached on the text. These would be interspersed with prayers (from the heart); psalms from memory would be sung. At 12 noon the service would be concluded with prayer. Another service following the same pattern would begin at 2 p.m. and go on until 5 or 6 o'clock.

Smyth's worship pointed to the centrality of the remembered and experienced word and the freedom of the Spirit in worship. In these points he made a permanent contribution to Baptist liturgy. When the refugee congregations returned in part to England and the Baptist movement began to grow, the main stream of Baptist church life that developed took on the worship patterns of its Presbyterian and Congregational counterparts. The typical worship of these churches consisted of the reading and proclamation of the word preceded and followed by scripture sentences, prayers and the singing of psalms, particularly at communion services. Later, hymns came into general usage.

With the Congregationalists and others, Baptists became a part of the Free Church Movement. While the term 'free', when used in relation to the church, has a variety of meanings, such as freedom from clerical control, freedom from the state, freedom to organize and maintain churches, freedom of worship, etc., in relation to worship it means primarily freedom from prescribed liturgical forms. Thus the Baptists, as other Free Churches, have no one required form of worship such as the divine liturgy of the Orthodox churches, the Roman mass, or the forms of worship of the Anglican *BCP*.

To say that Baptists have no required orders for public worship does not mean that Baptists believe that worship should be disordered. Worship that is careless and undisciplined is an offence to God and may be the means of destroying rather than of building the faith of a congregation. Baptists frequently quote Paul's well-known words on spiritual gifts. He urged that 'all things should be done decently and in order' (I Cor. 14.40). He further directed the Corinthian congregation: 'When you come together, each one has a hymn, a lesson, a revelation, a tongue, or an interpretation. Let all things be done for edification ... For you can all prophesy one by one, so that all may learn and all may be encouraged . . . For God is not a God of confusion but of peace' (I Cor. 14.26,31,33). Baptists believe in ordered worship but not required ordered worship. For them, as for others, word and table are the two basic points for the ordering of Christian worship, for here the primary foci of God's revelation are presented. The believer responds to this revelation by acts of adoration, repentance, thanksgiving, petition, dedication, and intercession. His response comes in the forms of prayers, litanies, doxologies, *Glorias*, sung psalms and hymns, the spoken word, and the breaking of bread and drinking of wine.

In a Baptist church, the responsibility for public worship lies with the congregation. No hierarchy hands down forms and materials for worship. This means that great variety characterizes Baptist worship. Some Baptist churches, particularly those that have been influenced by the movement for liturgical renewal, have formal services. They use set prayers which are read from printed orders distributed to the congregation beforehand. Choirs and clergy are robed, and church buildings are often neo-Gothic in architecture. In such churches one can find present lamps, candles and crosses, often set upon altars backed by a reredos and decked out in seasonal liturgical colours. On the other hand, Baptist worship may be completely informal and spontaneous. Such informality and spontaneity would characterize most Black church worship in America. While Black church worship does have a structure or pattern, the structure is not allowed to interfere with the free flow of the spirit. The congregation gathers to find joy in the Lord and it feels that such joy can only be hindered by set forms. In between the highly formalized and the completely informal, most Baptists worship according to a pattern generally developed over a period of time by the congregation and yet sufficiently free to allow for considerable spontaneity.

Baptist worship has been largely conditioned by the culture in which it has found itself. Reference was made above to the informality and spontaneity of Black church worship. This spirit goes back to the days when the Black man was a slave and the church was the only place where he could express his human freedom. Thus in the church he turned himself loose and lived, at least during the time of worship, as a man free in the sight of God. On the American frontier the characteristic Baptist service was the revival meeting. Here lively singing, testimonies as to the freedom and forgiveness which has come in Christ, and spontaneous prayer characterized the first part of the revival service. These 'preliminaries' prepared the congregation for the reading and the preaching of the word and the call to repentance, followed by the response of the sinner or 'backslider'. When these revival services resulted in churches, the people who formed them had become used to the style of the revival meeting and the services of worship tended to be planned as a repetition of the revival service. In Germany and the Scandinavian countries where Baptists arose out of the pietistic ferment of past centuries, worship still has strong overtones of pietistic devotional life. Bible reading and meditation, spontaneous prayer and introspective hymns tend to characterize such services. In England as well as New England, Baptist worship has been strongly influenced by the plain and decorous character of the chapel service.

Historically, Baptists have been strong exponents of the Reformation doctrine of *sola scriptura*. Nothing is to be done that is unscriptural and everything that is done is to be done in accordance with the scriptures. Reading and proclamation of the word have occupied a central place in Baptist worship. The Baptist stress upon the importance of preaching has produced a striking number of 'great' preachers. From John Bunyan to Charles Haddon Spurgeon, Harry Emerson Fosdick and Billy Graham, Baptist preachers have gained hearings far beyond their own churches and denomination. So central is preaching to worship for Baptists that most Baptists when asked to evaluate worship will immediately turn to the sermon, and the success or failure of a given worship service will stand upon the fact as to whether or not the sermon is good or bad. In some areas Baptists tend to distinguish or to separate worship and preaching. The morning service is called a service of 'worship *and* preaching'. Or the worship segments are characterized as 'preliminaries'. The *pièce de résistance* is invariably the sermon. In most Baptist worship it occupies the concluding and climactic point of the service. It is often followed by a hymn of invitation in which an opportunity is offered for non-believers to give themselves to Christ and for believers to rededicate themselves to the Christian life. This self-offering is doubtless related to what has been called the offertory in the traditional liturgy.

While the Lord's Supper is regarded highly by Baptists, it is not frequently practised. Relatively few churches observe weekly communion. Most churches will hold communion on a monthly or a quarterly basis. Formerly communion was often separated from the preaching service. At the conclusion of the preaching service the congregation would be dismissed and only those who were members of the local congregation would remain for the Lord's Supper. For those who were included, communion was indeed a high and holy time in which the congregation remembered in deep solemnity the life and passion of their Lord, and renewed their hope in his return in power and glory. Today the services of word and table are generally one service.

Baptists differ on the issue of open and closed communion. Many churches invite all who believe in Jesus Christ to participate. Others seek to restrict communion to Baptists and in some places reserve communion to those who are members of the local congregation. The pastor of the congregation generally presides at the communion service, but if no pastor is available, a layman can be designated by the congregation to officiate. Baptism, as well as other elements of worship, can be performed by a layman if no ordained minister is available or present. Such lay leadership is done by licensing. The congregation votes to designate one or more of its members to serve its needs.

The communion service is primarily a memorial meal. Any 'real presence' comes as the individual believer renews his faith and fellowship in Jesus Christ. In most Baptist churches today, the elements of bread and wine are distributed by the deacons to the congregation as they sit in their places. They eat the bread simultaneously as the leader repeats the words of Jesus, 'Take, eat. This is my body which is broken for you. Do this in remembrance of me.' Then, as the minister says, 'Drink of it, all of you; for this is my blood of the covenant, which is poured out for many for the forgiveness of sins,' the congregation drinks the wine (*see* **Communion**).

The structure of the Sunday morning preaching service in a Baptist church is relatively simple. The service generally begins with a scripture sentence followed by a prayer of invocation and a hymn of praise. A responsive reading, usually from the psalms, is read, followed by the singing of the *Gloria*. Then comes the pastoral prayer which covers such elements as adoration, confession, thanksgiving, and intercession. Following the prayer, church announcements are made and the offering is received with the singing of the doxology. A hymn may then be sung followed by the reading of the scripture and the sermon. After the sermon a hymn of dedication and invitation is sung and the benediction is pronounced. If a choir is present, suitable anthems come at various places in the service and responses, introits, etc. provide introductions and conclusions to the spoken parts of the service.

Baptists have no official manuals of worship or books of common prayer. In Britain Ernest A. Payne and Stephen F. Winward compiled *Orders and Prayers for Church Worship*, and in the USA John E. Skoglund published a *Manual of Worship*. While books like these have no official endorsement, they have received denominational encouragement. The orders which are included in the books are not in any way required of the congregations, but are intended to provide guide lines for worship done 'decently and in order'.

Baptists have not been at the centre of the movement for liturgical renewal. Individuals have participated in liturgical conferences and have written on the issues of worship, but for the most part church life has not been greatly influenced. The freedom allowed in worship in Baptist congregations has afforded opportunities for a number of experiments. Baptist worship can be readily adapted to such informal gatherings as house-churches, to services with high lay participation, and to other experimental forms. In this Baptists may make in the future a significant contribution to liturgical renewal.

Winthrop S. Hudson and Norman H. Maring, *A Baptist Manual of Polity and Practice*, 1963; Ernest A. Payne, *The Fellowship of Believers*, 1952; Ernest A. Payne and Stephen F. Winward, *Orders and Prayers for Church Worship*, 1960; John E. Skoglund, *A Manual of Worship*, 1968; John E. Skoglund, *Worship in the Free Churches*, 1965; *Stephen F. Winward, The Reformation of Our Worship*, 1965.

JOHN E. SKOGLUND

Baptistery

Baptism does not of itself require any particular building type or indeed any building at all, any more than does any other form of Christian worship (*see* **Architectural Setting**). Nevertheless to study Christian initiation upon a textual basis alone is to indulge in something of an abstraction, for the rites need to be considered in their setting, which was both architectural and iconographical. In such a context the documents assume a deeper and more real meaning, and conversely the conjunction of text and monument illuminates the latter, which tends to be no more than an empty shell if there is ignorance of what took place within it.

The story of the baptistery does not begin until the opening decades of the third century. Baptisteries may have existed before then, but of these no literary evidence survives and no archaeological traces have been discovered. In the apostolic age and during the second century, baptism was administered in rivers and pools, while the gatherings for eucharistic worship were held in private houses. When at length special architectural provision was made for the latter, we may assume that it would embrace the former, so that as accommodation was created for the liturgical assembly of the church, it was also set aside for the sacrament of initiation into the church.

The earliest baptisteries of the third and fourth centuries were square or rectangular with or without an apse at one end. This type persisted in such areas as Greece, Palestine and North Africa until the seventh century. In other parts of the empire, notably France and Italy, the quadrilateral was superseded from the middle of the fifth century by round or octagonal designs. In many provinces these baptisteries were either detached from or loosely attached to the main building for worship, but in Greece they frequently formed part of the church, being an adjoining room opening off the narthex (q.v.).

The adoption of the quadrilateral in the first instance was the outcome of three factors. First, when baptism ceased to be administered out of doors and a baptistery was arranged in the house-church, it naturally had the shape of an ordinary room, i.e. it was quadrilateral, and as such is to be found at Dura Europos. Second, since the baptismal rite had affinities with bathing, the *frigidarium* of the Roman baths, often a square or rectangle, had its influence. Third, from NT times baptism was understood in terms of a death and resurrection with Christ; the baptistery was therefore a kind of tomb, and since many pagan funerary monuments were domed quadrilaterals it was natural to reproduce this design. Its persistence in certain areas is explicable because it was in precisely the same provinces that the square tomb was and continued to be the norm.

This last factor provides the clue to the reason for the adoption of other shapes in Italy and in those countries under her direct influence. Here there was a transition from the square to the circle and also to the hexagon and octagon. The circular plan with ambulatory was the plan of many tombs and this funerary association was also expressed through the six- and eight-sided design. The symbolism of the hexagon refers to the sixth day of the week, i.e. Friday, upon which Christ was crucified and buried, so it declared the baptismal co-death with the redeemer. The octagon represented the day of Christ's resurrection, i.e. the first day of the new week, and so it served to emphasize co-resurrection with Christ in baptism and the dawn of the Age to Come.

Other less widespread forms derived from the same association of ideas. Thus trefoil and quatrefoil baptisteries reproduced the designs of tombs and martyria (q.v.), and the few cruciform examples relate directly to the manner of Christ's death. The iconographical scheme of baptisteries is further evidence of the close connection in belief between baptism and death, for the mosaics which decorated many of them reproduced the same themes as sepulchral art, e.g. the Good Shepherd who lays down his life for the sheep, the star-studded domes which represent heaven and eternal life.

Baptism (q.v.) itself was gradually elaborated into a complex rite which included the disrobing of candidates, their affirmation of faith, their entry into the water, their anointing, their clothing in white robes and their procession to the main building for the eucharist. In planning their baptisteries, Christians could have produced a series of rooms, each corresponding to one element in the rite as a whole. Indeed this is what took place, and although, probably due to lack of material resources, some were no more than a single room, others had two or more adjoining the one in which the font (q.v.) was placed. As an example we may take the complex opening out of the north end of the narthex of Basilica A at Philippi (see Fig. 13).

Fig. 13   Basilica A, Philippi, Macedonia

There are three rooms: the first cannot be anything other than vestibule; the second is the baptismal area with font, and beyond that is a third with an apse in one of its walls. There is every reason to suppose that the apse was constructed with a specific purpose in view, namely to enshrine the episcopal throne. This permits the identification of the room as a *chrismarion*, i.e. the place where the bishop administered the chrism which completed the rite of initiation. Sometimes, in default of other rooms, 'confirmation' (q.v.) could take place in the area of the font, and where there is an apse (q.v.), such as the one at Tropaeum Traiani, this was almost certainly to provide a space for the *cathedra* (q.v.).

Whether simple or complex, baptisteries were at first erected only in episcopal cities, since it was the bishop's office to confirm and since baptism and confirmation were for centuries united. The occasional baptisteries in non-episcopal centres existed to spare candidates too long a journey. In the East, where priests were eventually allowed to confirm in place of the bishop, using for the

Fig. 14   Baptistery, Florence, Italy

purpose oil that had been episcopally blessed, baptisteries became more numerous, and were therefore not confined to episcopal centres. In parts of Syria in the sixth century, each town had its baptistery, not infrequently two and sometimes three. In the West, on the other hand, where the bishop did not delegate this authority, it was not until baptism and confirmation were finally separated that each parish came to possess its own.

From the seventh to the fourteenth centuries, detached baptisteries (see Plate 17), after the model of the early Christian ones and with the same plan and ideological content, continued to be erected, of which the ones at Florence (see Fig. 14) and Pisa are perhaps the most well known. But the later Middle Ages witnessed a complete transformation of the architectural setting of baptism in so far as the detached type ceased to be built and the font was placed within the church itself. The factors that contributed to this result were all different aspects of the situation that obtained when the whole population of a country had become nominally Christian. The virtual cessation of adult initiation and the corresponding preponderance of infant baptism meant that provision for undressing and privacy for the nude were no longer required. The public nature of baptism, with all present accepting the Christian faith, meant that a separate building was no longer necessary. Hence there was no reason why a simple font should not be introduced into the nave, usually by the main door to indicate that baptism is the means of entrance into the church. The result of this movement was that baptism ceased to have an architectural setting properly so called. However, in a number of churches a

Plate 17 Detached baptistery, Parma, Italy

ATLANTIC BAPTIST COLLEGE
MONCTON, N. B.

Fig. 15   Dodford Church, England

baldachin or ciborium (qq.v.) was erected over the font and occasionally a low wooden railing surrounded it, thus defining a space and dignifying the celebration of the first gospel sacrament.

Within the Roman Catholic Church this practice was fostered by Charles Borromeo who issued directions for his diocese of Milan in 1559. In legislating for parish churches, Borromeo ordained that 'an oratory or chapel should be built, inside close to the chief doorway and on the gospel side, and it should be alike to the other lateral chapels erected to contain altars'. So he advocated the creation of a defined space which was to be enclosed by iron or wooden railings, with the font sunk in the centre to the depth of several steps. Being of a practical turn of mind, he had to acknowledge that there were some buildings in which even this would not be feasible, and so he was prepared to allow the font to stand alone at the rear of the church in the medieval fashion, but this was clearly not his ideal, and this ideal, formulated in great detail, has continued to have its effect upon the architectural setting of baptism within Roman Catholic churches right down to the present.

Within Protestant churches the baptistery proper ceased to exist. Anglicans were content with a font by the church door, following the medieval practice. Calvinists used shallow basins placed either on the holy table or in brackets fixed to the pulpit. The Lutherans eventually adopted the *Prinzipalstück* (*see* **Architectural Setting**) and located the font close to the table and pulpit at the east end.

With the Gothic Revival the medieval precedent continued to be observed, but about the middle of the nineteenth century influences were at work to produce exceptions to this norm and ultimately to issue in a new approach to the architectural setting of baptism and indeed in the restoration of the baptistery. The first of these influences was a growing awareness of the detached baptisteries still standing in Italy. As more and more architects made the grand tour, ignorance of the baptistery proper was no longer possible. The second influence was the contemporary Roman Catholic practice. Pugin argued forcibly that the font should be given prominence by an enclosing chancel and in several of the churches he designed he did create a baptistery at the west end. Architects working for Anglican patrons began to adopt the same concept and they were further affected by the gradual re-use of the many chapels and chantries in the English cathedrals for weekday services; this suggested that one of them could house the font, so creating a baptistery. In existing buildings, where the font had been an isolated object, baptisteries were introduced by defining the space with rails. In some new churches western apses were deliberately planned as baptisteries (*see* Fig. 15).

In the twentieth century this movement has continued. Architects and their clients began to think no longer in terms simply of a font but in spatial categories. It was thought that the rite required not only certain necessary items of furniture but a defined space suitable

Plate 18   Macgregor Chapel, Afikpo Teacher Training College, Eastern Nigeria

quently the practice increased of creating baptisteries within existing churches and making provision for them within those that were rebuilt after damage or destruction during the Second World War.

In the majority of modern Roman Catholic churches the idea of a separate baptistery, apart from the main assembly hall for worship, has predominated. The baptistery may project from the western facade; it may be located to one side of the church, usually the north; it may be contained within the entrance hall or narthex. Other denominations represent a greater variety, with no one concept entirely to the fore. In some modern Anglican churches the medieval disposition continues; in others the baptistery is combined with the porch, while in others again the idea of the *Prinzipalstück* is being reproduced with the font inside or close to the sanctuary (*see* Plate 18). This last arrangement, which was for centuries the Lutheran norm, has now commended itself to many Calvinists and is frequent in Holland, but in some recent Lutheran designs the font is

actually at the rear of the congregation in
medieval style and occasionally within its
own baptistery (*see* Plate 19 and Fig. 16).
Within the Free Churches the *Prinzipalstück*
has been widely accepted, while the Baptists
necessarily give prominence to the font, to
which they apply the term baptistery, by
placing it at the sanctuary end, although
since it is for submersion and so below floor
level, it is covered and so lost to sight except
when actually in use.

As we look to the future, it may be said
that past history and the understanding of
the nature of baptism suggests three principles to be observed. These are (1) the need
to make provision for congregational participation; (2) the need to give the setting a
visual importance that accords with the
celebration of the first gospel sacrament; (3)
the need to devise a shape and décor that
conveys some of the meaning of the rite.
Clearly these can be applied in a variety of
ways and no one can say that there is any
single correct solution.

J. G. Davies, *The Architectural Setting of
Baptism*, 1962; A. Khatchatrian, *Les bap-
tistères paléochrétiens*, 1962.   EDITOR

Plate 19
St Andrew, Malmö, Sweden

Fig. 16
Siegburg S. Joseph, Germany

Basilica

The basilica is an early form of church building derived from pagan prototypes (*see* **Architectural Setting**). Although initially there were many varieties, from the late fourth century four main types may be distinguished.

1. *Roman or Latin.* Its main characteristics were: (*a*) a projecting apse (q.v.); (*b*) an architrave or continuous beam supported on the abacus of each column; (*c*) a covered porch; (*d*) an atrium; (*e*) a transept (q.v.) – although this is also found in the second type.

2. *Hellenistic.* Its main characteristics were: (*a*) the apse was polygonal on the outside or was flanked by side chambers which, especially in Syria, were contained within one wall to preserve the rectangular shape; (*b*) archivolts, i.e. arches linking the columns; (*c*) galleries over the aisles for the women; (*d*) there was often but not invariably an atrium; (*e*) transepts were included in Greece and the adjoining lands, but in North Africa no examples are known and only one in Palestine and one in Syria; (*f*) a narthex (q.v.) was attached (*see* Fig. 17).

3. *Oriental,* also known as the barn or hall church (*Hallenkirche*), originating in Mesopotamia and found in Anatolia, Armenia, Crete, Cyprus and Greece. In plan, it is indistinguishable from the previous one (*see* Fig. 17), but it differed in elevation, in that the walls of the nave were not carried up above the roofs of the aisles to form a clerestory. Hence its characteristics are: (*a*) a blind nave; (*b*) windows in the apse and aisles; (*c*) no atrium; (*d*) a narthex; (*e*) it was usually vaulted.

4. *Transverse.* This is a primitive Mesopotamian form found in Armenia, Cappadocia, the Hauran and the Tur Abdin. It consisted of a single nave at right angles to the line connecting the entrance door with the apse.

Under the impact of the modern Liturgical Movement (q.v.) in its somewhat archaeological phase, a number of churches were built in the twentieth century which reproduce the basilica plan.

EDITOR

Basilican Position
see Postures (1*c*)

Bells

Gregory of Tours (*c.* 585) is the first person to mention their considerable use in Christian worship with any certainty. The story that they were first introduced into Christian worship by Paulinus of Nola, Campania, is doubtful. But it has given us two Latin words for a bell, *campana* and *nola*. It may be that the story was invented to account for the origin of the words. Bells were much used in the British Isles from the sixth century. From the eighth century they came into widespread use and were blessed by a bishop with holy water and chrism and they were 'named' and bore inscriptions. They were not only used to summon people to worship but also a bell was rung at the death of a parishioner. Small bells were used at the altar and in some instances a special small bell in the belfry at the elevation of the host. Bells are used in the Eastern Orthodox rite not only to summon people to worship but also during the liturgy and offices to mark certain points in the services.

H. B. Walters, *The Church Bells of England*, 1913 (with extensive bibliography).

C. E. POCKNEE

Fig. 17   Church no. 4, Bin Bir Kilisse, Turkey

Benediction

The word has a wider and a narrower use in liturgy. For the wider use *see* **Blessing**. In the narrower use, Benediction is a rite which springs from two distinct sources, Marian and eucharistic.

A litany or hymn to the Blessed Virgin, which often follows the rosary (q.v.), is derived from evening canticles, originating in Italy under the name of *laude*, in the thirteenth century. The custom spread throughout Europe. Later, it became the practice to expose the sacrament in a monstrance (q.v.) during these canticles and, finally, to give a blessing with the sacrament before the congregation dispersed.

Marian devotion and eucharistic devotion were thus joined for an afternoon or evening service, which in England goes by the name of Benediction. It was very popular from the seventeenth century until the recent introduction of evening mass, but it was seldom, if ever, seen in the British Isles until Catholic emancipation in 1829, except, possibly, in the chapels of the foreign embassies. The rite is begun, normally, by placing the monstrance (q.v.) on a throne elevated above the altar. After the devotions, which are optional, the hymn *Tantum ergo* ('Therefore we, before him bending' *Hymns Ancient and Modern, Revised*, 1950, no. 383, part 2) is sung and the sacrament is censed. Then, after a prayer, the priest takes the monstrance from the throne and, at the altar, makes a cross with it over the kneeling congregation. A bishop or an abbot makes a threefold sign of the cross (q.v.).

Benediction can also be given with the host enclosed in a ciborium (q.v.), but for the use of a monstrance the express permission of the bishop is necessary.

The rite expresses for Roman Catholics a lively and practical sentiment of the real and perpetual presence of Christ in the holy eucharist.

A. A. King and C. E. Pocknee, *Eucharistic Reservation in the Western Church*, 1965.
A. A. KING

Benedictus

see Anaphora, Canticles

Bible Services

In the Roman Catholic Church these services are the fruit of the Liturgical Movement (q.v.)

and the biblical revival of more recent years and they received official recognition in the *Constitution on the Liturgy* (35,[4]) of Vatican II.

They remain a free form of service, may be conducted by a lay person, though where, for want of an ordained minister they replace the mass, it is recommended that they follow the order of the ministry of the word in the new *Ordo Missae.*

They consist of three main elements, the reading of God's word, homily or homilies on it, the response of the people by word, song or silence and intercessions or other forms of prayer.

The Council saw them as a useful means of giving the people a deeper appreciation of holy scripture and strongly urged that the clergy should organize such services especially during the great seasons of the year, such as Lent and Advent, and as vigils of preparation before the greater feasts.

These services are much used in informal groups of laity, and in those parts of the church where there is a lack of ordained ministers they are used (and must be used) as a preparation before communion from the reserved sacrament.

Constitution on the Liturgy (as above); *Instruction for Implementing the Liturgical Constitution* (37-39); commentary 'Bible Services' by Edmund Jones, OSB, in *The Liturgy and the Future*, ed. J. D. Crichton, 1966.
J. D. CRICHTON

Bible, Use of in Worship

The Bible of the early church was the OT in its Septuagint or Greek version. Passages from it were read out in the course of Christian worship, following the practice in the synagogues, and indeed this, with the sermon, formed part of the first half of the eucharist, known variously as the ministry of the word, the synaxis and the mass of the catechumens (qq.v.). To lections from the Jewish sacred book were soon added others from documents believed to be of apostolic authorship, so that by the middle of the second century, according to Justin Martyr, 'the memoirs of the apostles or the writings of the prophets are read as long as time permits' (*Apol.* 1.67). The portions of scripture assigned for worship were eventually collected in several books, the gospels in the *evangelarium*, the epistles in the *epistolarium*, the psalms in the *psalterium* and the OT lections in the *lectionarium*. Even after the production, in the sixth century, of pandects, i.e. manuscript copies of the entire. Bible, the separate volumes were in use for convenience.

This practice was not greatly altered by the invention of printing and the publication of more manageable complete Bibles, so that to the present day the Orthodox Churches still have several volumes, while the Roman Church has grouped the mass lections in the missal and the office readings in the breviary. Similarly the churches of the Anglican Communion print the epistle and gospel in full but provide only tables of lessons for morning and evening prayer. Other churches give tables for all lections, so that the complete Bible is regularly in use, e.g. by the Church of Scotland, the Church of South India, the Methodists and the Presbyterian Churches of England and Wales.

In the Church of England the Bible remains permanently on the lectern or is placed there immediately before a service, although in the seventeenth and eighteenth centuries it was common for copies of the Bible and the *BCP* to stand upright at the back of the altar. In the French Reformed Church it lies open continually on the holy table. In the Church of Scotland it is carried in at the beginning of a service. As a liturgical object, the Bible is also used in the gospel procession, the little entrance (q.v.) and in ordination (q.v.), it being the almost universal practice to present a NT or complete Bible to the candidates.

EDITOR

Bidding Prayer

The element of intercession (q.v.) in the eucharistic rites of the Western church has been variable. The Good Friday *orationes solemnes* of the Roman rite survive as the only example of the earliest known form of the prayers of the faithful at the beginning of the mass of the faithful. In the sixth century their place was taken by a litany (q.v.) of Eastern origin, found among the introductory material in the rite, and the *kyries* survive as a relic of this litany. When the litany fell out of use after about a century, the element of intercession virtually disappeared from the Western liturgy, apart for the brief prayers for the living and the dead in the canon of the mass, until the bidding of the bedes appeared in the unofficial vernacular element in the Latin

rite known as the prone. The prone is an example of a measure of pastoral concern in the Middle Ages, and was a vernacular passage in the course of the mass consisting of a sermon, which was preceded or followed by the bidding of the bedes, notices, and instruction in the Decalogue, the Lord's Prayer, and similar formularies. The word 'bid' in Anglo-Saxon means 'pray', and the 'bidding of the bedes' means the 'praying of the prayers': *cf.* 'Ye shulle stonde up and bydde your bedys...' in a fourteenth-century example of the bidding prayer which was used at Worcester. In its earlier and better examples the prayer covered the full range of matters for intercession, the church, the state, the departed, and all men in their various callings: it was flexible and gave scope to the initiative of the celebrant. With the passage of time it became formalized, and at the time of the Reformation, when such freedom was not acceptable, precise forms were laid down, as appears in Canon 55 of 1604. The canon lays down that the bidding prayer shall be said before sermons, although so far as the sermon at the eucharist is concerned this seems pointless, since the prayer book since 1549 has restored the provision for intercession which the old rite lacked. Canon B 19 of 1967 leaves the bidding prayer optional. The association between the sermon and the intercessions which is found in the liturgical forms of some of the Reformed churches is probably derived from their association in the prone.

F. E. Brightman, *The English Rite*, 1921; H. O. C(oxe), *Forms of Bidding Prayer*, 1840.

E. C. WHITAKER

Bishop

The highest order in the traditional pattern of the ministry, though there was a medieval view that bishops are not to be reckoned as an order entirely separate and distinct from the priesthood but are merely priests with additional powers and functions. This view arose from contemporary eucharistic theology which stressed the importance of the sacrament as a sacrifice and made it difficult to imagine an order of ministry higher than the priesthood. NT evidence is not entirely clear, but there are passages which suggest that originally the terms 'bishop' (*episcopos*, overseer) and presbyter (q.v.) were interchangeable (Acts 20.17-28). It has been widely assumed that the early Christian communities were governed by colleges of elders, as Jewish synagogues were, and that in the course of time a monarchial episcopate developed. Disagreement about when and how this happened is notorious. It is possible that the need to have a liturgical president (like the ruler of the synagogue) may have contributed to the process. By the time of Ignatius of Antioch it was possible to claim that the presence of the bishop or his authorized representative was essential for the eucharist, and in Cyprian's writings the same argument is further developed. But by this later date the process of delegation had had to be taken further. In earlier days the presbyters had been associated with the bishop in his liturgical as well as his governmental function. They had a place if not a separate liturgical activity and were gathered round the bishop as he celebrated. But by the middle of the third century it was evidently no longer possible for the Christian community in the larger centres to assemble in a single congregation. Presbyters were given authority to take charge of separate districts and there to preside over celebrations of the eucharist. There is evidence for this in Rome and Carthage and in rural areas. But the bishop remained in theory the chief minister in all sacramental acts. Ordination and confirmation (qq.v.) remained in some sense the bishop's special prerogative, though not in quite the absolute sense that has sometimes been suggested. There is some evidence that persons not in episcopal orders have on rare and extraordinary occasions been authorized by the papacy to ordain. And in the East confirmation is administered by the priest at the same time as baptism, using chrism that has been blessed by the bishop.

At the Reformation the office of bishop was retained by Anglicans and some Lutherans. In some cases it was the intention to retain the historic succession (e.g. in England and Sweden), in other cases it was deliberately not so (e.g. in Denmark). The *Unitas Fratrum* (Moravians) also preserved the episcopal order and claim an unbroken succession through the Bohemian Brethren, but they have not always regarded the laying on of the bishop's hands as necessary for ordination. In some parts of the Methodist Church the title is used, particularly in America where Thomas Coke introduced it, having been set apart by John Wesley as superintendent of Methodist work there. Methodist bishops have the power of appointing ministers and exercise a pastoral and disciplinary oversight over them. They also perform all ordinations but not confirmations. In the third decade of the twentieth century German Lutherans adopted the title for the majority of those ministers who had been called superintendents up to that date. In the Church of South India bishops have been part of the ministry since that church came into existence by the reunion of separate Christian denominations in 1947. All ordinations are performed by them, though confirmation is not necessarily an episcopal act. The schemes proposed for united Churches of North India, of Pakistan and of Ceylon also make provision for an episcopal ministry as do most other reunion proposals.

K. M. Carey, ed., *The Historic Episcopate*, 1954; R. P. Johnson, *The Bishop in the Church*, 1966; K. E. Kirk, *The Apostolic Ministry*, 1946; G. Simon, *Bishops*, 1961; W. Telfer, *The Office of a Bishop*, 1962.

P. HINCHLIFF

Blessing

1. A blessing is an authoritative declaration of divine favour addressed to persons. It is used liturgically: (*a*) Immediately before the act of communion. Although not primitive, this was customary in all eucharistic rites by the end of the fourth century, being an encouragement and preparation for those about to communicate. It assumed elaborate forms in the Gallican rite and survives in the ritual of the Church of Lyons. It was omitted from the Roman rite *c.* 500, and no post-Reformation order has retained it. (*b*) At the end of the eucharist. Although not prescribed in the missals, this became customary in the late Middle Ages, and probably derived from the blessing by the bishop of his flock as he went out. This medieval feature has been perpetuated in most reformed rites (except the Zwinglian), with the Aaronic form (Num. 6.24-26) appearing in the Lutheran, Calvinist and derived orders, and Phil. 4.7, with the medieval episcopal blessing as the second half, in the Anglican and most British churches. (*c*) During the eucharist and other services, e.g. the blessing of the deacon who is to sing the gospel and of the penitent about to make confession. (*d*)

Frequently at the end of other services, e.g. the Sunday services of the Free Churches, confirmation in the *BCP*, etc.

2. A blessing can also be a verbal formula for the sanctification of objects, which include the water at baptism, oil for exorcism or for the anointing of the sick (*see* **Unction**), the Paschal Candle (q.v.), etc.

EDITOR

Books, Liturgical

Liturgical books are those used in the performance of church services. Both in manuscript and printed form they are an essential source of information for the worshipping practice of any group of believers.

1. *The Early Church.* Since liturgical prayer was largely extempore until the early third century, the only books required were rolls of the scriptures. In time, however, there were produced the church orders, a series of documents, claiming apostolic authority, which contained both liturgical prescriptions and also rules for the life of the congregation. The earliest extant example is the *Didache* or *Teaching of the Twelve Apostles*, probably a product of the second century. There followed the *Apostolic Tradition* of Hippolytus, *c*.217, the *Didascalia*, *c*.250, the *Apostolic Church Order*, *c*.250, the *Apostolic Constitutions*, *c*.375, and the *Testament of Our Lord*, *c*.400.

In addition to these general handbooks, individual bishops made their own compilations, e.g. the prayer book of Serapion of Thmuis, *c*.350, containing prayers for the eucharist, baptism, ordination (qq.v.), the blessing of oils and a commendation of the dead. With the elaboration of the liturgy and the acceptance of stereotyped forms, numerous service-books eventually became necessary.

EDITOR

2. *Orthodox.* (More properly, Byzantine.) The service books at present in use in the Byzantine rite are as follows:

(*a*) *The Euchologion* (Greek, 'book of prayers') contains those parts of the sacraments and other services, together with many occasional offices and blessings, which are required by the officiating ministers (bishop, priest and deacon). It exists in two forms, in addition to which excerpts from it are often printed separately, individually or in combination.

The Great Euchologion (Greek, *euchologion to mega*) normally contains:

(i) The fixed parts, or ordinary, of vespers, mattins, the eucharistic liturgy, and the liturgy of the presanctified (q.v.), the priest's part being given in full, and those of deacon, reader and singers usually in an abbreviated form.

(ii) The six remaining sacraments, namely: baptism, with a number of related offices; chrismation or confirmation (which forms an integral part of the baptismal rites); ordination; confession; marriage; and the anointing of the sick. A more complete text of these is provided in most editions, the deacon's, reader's and singers' parts not being so readily available elsewhere as those of the services in the preceding group.

(iii) Other occasional offices, some of them what in the West would be called sacramentals (although the Byzantine books do not distinguish liturgically between sacraments and sacramentals so rigidly as do those of the West), such as the various services connected with monastic profession, the consecration of a church, the greater and lesser blessings of holy water, and so forth; and others such as the various rites connected with the burial of the dead.

(iv) A large number of offices for the particular blessing of persons and things.

The Small Euchologion (Greek, *mikron euchologion*, or *agiasmatarion*, 'book of blessings') omits the whole of the first group of services listed above, and also those rites, such as ordination and the consecration of a church, which appertain specifically to the bishop; it contains the five remaining sacraments, the funeral offices, and those occasional offices and blessings most commonly required. Some editions do add the priest's part of the major daily offices and the liturgy.

The Liturgikon (Greek, 'book of the liturgy') or *Hieratikon* or *Hierotelestikon* (Greek, 'book for the priest') is an altar book, containing the priest's, and in some editions also the deacon's, part at vespers, mattins and the liturgy, together with related supplementary matter, the extent and arrangement of which differ from one edition to another.

The Archieratikon (Greek, 'book for the bishop') corresponds to the Western pontifical, and contains services and blessings either reserved to or most commonly performed by the bishop. Some editions use *Hieratikon* as the title of this book and not of that considered in the preceding note.

The next group of books, seven in number, is concerned principally, although not exclusively, with the divine office.

(*b*) *The Horologion* (Greek, 'book of hours') is a book for the use of readers and singers, just as the *Euchologion* is for the use of priest and deacon. Its fuller form, the *Great Horologion* (Greek, *horologion to mega*) includes:

(i) The ordinary, or fixed part, of the daily offices, namely, nocturns, mattins, the lesser hours (prime, terce, sext, none), vespers and compline (qq.v.), together with graces before and after meals. The reader's and singers' parts are given in full; most of the priest's and deacon's parts are omitted.

(ii) A list of feasts and saints' days throughout the year, for each of which a short account of the feast or the life of the saint is given, together with certain of the principal anthems appointed for the day.

(iii) A similar section, covering Sundays and movable feasts, within the periods of the *Triodion* and *Pentekostarion* (see below).

(iv) The common principal anthems for the days of the week.

(v) A miscellany of other services related to the divine office and in frequent use.

All the lesser hours can be recited in full from the *Great Horologion*. But a number of other books are required for vespers and mattins, books containing the proper texts which change from day to day. These volumes contain the material of the three cycles which together constitute the Byzantine liturgical year: (i) the weekly cycle, contained in the *Oktoechos*; (ii) the annual cycle of movable feasts, contained in the *Triodion* and *Pentekostarion*; (iii) the annual cycle of fixed feasts, contained in the *Menaia*.

(*c*) *The Oktoechos* (Greek, 'book of the eight tones'), also known as the *Parakletike* (Greek, 'book of supplication'), contains the variable parts of the daily offices through the week. Eight series of offices are provided, one for each of the eight tones of Byzantine chant, and each series comprises seven sets of services, one for each day of the week. The eight tones are used in sequence, week by week, through the year, beginning with the first tone on the Sunday after Easter. The texts contained in the *Oktoechos* are

combined, when appropriate, with those for fixed feasts contained in the *Menaia*. The *Oktoechos* is used in Lent only on Saturdays and Sundays, and it is not used at all from the Saturday preceding Palm Sunday until the Sunday after Pentecost, any material from it which is used during these seasons being repeated in full in the proper seasonal books. An edition of the *Oktoechos* for Sundays only also exists.

(*d*) *The Triodion* (Greek, 'book of the three odes', from the circumstance that for most days it provides only three proper odes or canticles for mattins) contains the propers for Lent.

(*e*) *The Pentekostarion* (Greek, 'book of the fifty days') contains the services proper to Eastertide and Pentecost.

(*f*) *The Menaia* (Greek, 'books of the months') contain the propers of fixed feasts throughout the year; most editions are divided into twelve volumes, one for each month. Various combinations of excerpts from the *Menaia* are also published.

(*g*) *The Eirmologion* (Greek, 'book of the *eirmoi*') contains the texts of the anthems known as *eirmoi* which are sung at the beginnings of the odes or canticles of mattins. The major books listed above commonly give only the opening words of these, assuming, apparently, that the reader will know them by heart; hence the need for the *Eirmologion*.

The next group of books comprises three volumes, the *Evangelion*, the *Apostolos*, and the *Psalterion*.

(*h*) *The Evangelion* (Greek, 'book of the gospels') contains the text of the four gospels; in some editions the text is printed continuously, the lessons to be read on particular days being noted in the margins, or in some similar way, while in others the text is arranged in the order required for liturgical use, the latter being the more common arrangement. The *evangelion* is treated with great reverence: it is usually bound in a cover decorated with silver or gold, often indeed actually made of silver or gold; when not in use it is usually kept on the altar; it is carried in procession and venerated by the congregation when there is a gospel lesson at mattins, and on certain other occasions.

(*i*) *The Apostolos* (Greek, 'book of the apostle') contains the lessons from the Acts of the Apostles and the epistles, together with the *prokeimena* or graduals (q.v.) which are sung before the epistle at the liturgy, and the alleluias which are sung after it.

(*j*) *The Psalterion* (Greek, 'book of psalms') contains the psalms, arranged according to their normal liturgical use, together with the necessary canticles from the OT and NT.

The lessons from the OT are normally included in the appropriate choir book for the day in question – *Triodion, Pentekostarion*, or *Menaion*; some editions, however, do include a separate book containing them.

(*k*) *The Synaxarion* (Greek, 'book of the assembly') or *Menologion* (Greek, 'book of remembrance') contains brief lives of the saints, and brief accounts of the mysteries of redemption celebrated on particular days, and is an exact counterpart of the Western martyrology (*see* 3[2] below).

(*l*) *The Typikon* (Greek, 'book of the ordinances') corresponds to the Western *ordo* (in the older sense of a permanent book, not the more recent one of an annual one), and contains the rules and rubrics governing the celebration of services throughout the year. The history of the *Typikon* is extremely involved: that now in use represents a crystallization of liturgical practice in the high Middle Ages, and includes elements of two originally very distinct liturgical traditions within the Byzantine rite, the 'monastic' and the 'cathedral' (*see* **Cathedral Office**), which were fused during that period; the Greek-speaking churches now follow a redaction of this *Typikon* dating from no earlier than 1888, and many aspects of modern Russian usage do not antedate the seventeenth century.

From the preceding remarks on the *Typikon* the reader will realise that the Byzantine rite liturgical books described here embody an order of service which is essentially medieval, although many of its parts are very much older. It will also have been noticed, however, that whereas in the West the whole division and arrangement of the service-books was changed in the medieval period, in the Byzantine East the old division and arrangement of the books was retained, notwithstanding the considerable changes of content. There is unfortunately no book in English

which deals in detail with either the pre-medieval or the post-medieval books.

                                        W. JARDINE GRISBROOKE

3. *Medieval and Roman Catholic.* (1) *Medieval.* This section is concerned with the books used in liturgical worship during the Middle Ages, a period running roughly from the sixth to the thirteenth centuries. Today, the books used for worship in the Roman rite may be numbered as seven: the missal, the breviary, the gradual, the antiphonal, the pontifical, the ritual and the martyrology. In medieval times this was not so. The books used in worship were many and complex. C. Vogel has counted as many as a hundred. The reasons for this number and diversity are to be sought in the facts of history. The Middle Ages knew no principles of uniformity in matters liturgical, despite the attempts of pope and emperor. Each ecclesiastical province, each diocese, each monastery had its own liturgical books and rites. Before the thirteenth century, and even as late as the *incunabula* of the fifteenth century, this diversity was widespread. A further reason for this is to be found in the fact that each minister or celebrant had his own book, and often enough a special book for each rite or ceremony. In the following pages we can treat only the main liturgical books of the period. This may be done under two headings: the mass and the divine office.

(*a*) *The mass*

(i) *The sacramentary.* This was the celebrant's book. It contained all the texts needed for the celebration of the eucharist, the administration of the sacraments, the formularies of blessing, the rites of ordination. Its history is obscure, but it would seem that from the sixth century onwards the compilation of a sacramentary was part and parcel of a bishop's charge. Already in the times of Augustine collections of euchological formularies were being drawn up in Africa and authorized for official use by the local bishop's synod. This was a countermeasure to the many such productions emanating from heretical sects. The sacramentary was preceded by small collections of euchological texts, to which the name *libelli missarum* has been given. The earliest collection of such books would seem to have been gathered together to form the well known sacramentary preserved in the chapter library of Verona, the *Sacramentarium Vero-nense*. Other official sacramentaries have come down to us under the names of Gelasius and Gregory the Great. By the thirteenth century each see, each church, each mona-stery had its own collection of sacramen-taries, until the process ended with the production of the missal.

(ii) *The antiphonale missarum*. In origin this book developed from the antiphonal. This latter was a book containing all the sung portions of both the office and the mass. In time the collection became voluminous and the portions were divided into two distinct parts. The material to be used in celebrating the eucharist was called the *antiphonale missarum* or the *graduale*. Ehrens-berger divides the book used at mass into *gradualia*, *troparia* and *rotuli paschales*. Ban-nister added a further division into *kyrialia* and *sequentiaria*. Historically such divisions are justified. Manuscripts of these books are rare, and their contents are found in the graduals.

(iii) *The lectionary*. This book contained the epistles and gospels read at mass. It is found in several forms during its history. Its most perfect form is the *lectionarium missae* containing in full the liturgical pericopes read at mass throughout the liturgical year. In origin this book consisted of a list of references to the Bible. Each reference began with the first and last words of the passage to be read. Such lists were known by differ-ent names: *capitulare epistolarum* or *evan-geliorum*; *comes* or *liber comitis* or *comicus*. Over the past sixty years the Roman lection-ary system has been studied by such scholars as Beissel, Godu, Frere, Herbert, Klauser, Wilmart, Chavasse, and Gamber.

(iv) *The missal*. This is a book which resulted from the fusion of the above three distinct volumes into one. This fusion, how-ever, was gradual. Its history is not clear, but the book itself appears in MSS from the end of the tenth to the middle of the thirteenth centuries. The evolution seems to have begun with small collections of complete mass formularies within the compass of one volume. This type of book seems to have been a link between the sacramentary and the later *missale plenum*. The Vatican library contains some forty interesting examples.

(b) *The divine office*
   (i) *The psalter*. At the origins of Christian

worship the Bible itself was sufficient for the essential prayer of the church. Once the period of improvisation was over, and the liturgy was celebrated within the bounds of set forms, various books for use in the celebration of the divine office came into being. One of the earliest books to be formed was the psalter. This was a distribution of the psalms for liturgical use over the period of a week or according to feasts. Little by little these psalters attracted additions. From the twelfth century onwards, antiphons and versicles are found written in the margins or between the lines of the psalms. Later other elements of the office were added: invita-tories, responds, the opening words of hymns, etc. By the fourteenth century it became the practice to group certain psalms according to the offices celebrated during the day or the week. Thus evolved the liturgical psalter described by V. Leroquais and P. Salmon.

(ii) *The antiphonal*. This book contained the antiphons and responds of the divine office. There are two types, a monastic type, easily recognized by the number of responds for the celebration of mattins (twelve), and the Roman type, containing only nine re-sponds. Normally this book contains the chant for the antiphons and responds, but there are exceptions.

(iii) *The hymnal*. The collection of hymns, used at the celebration of the office, was often combined with the psalter, but there are many MSS which contain the hymns alone.

(iv) *The breviary*. Like the missal, the breviary is the result of the fusion into one volume of the above elements. Like the missal also it was the product of an evolution. Towards the eighth/ninth centuries, the col-lects used at the office became separated from the sacramentaries, and formed a book of their own, called a *collectarium*. From the eleventh century onwards other elements of the office were added to this book: the calendar, the antiphons, responds, hymns. Later still a description of the office and its celebration was added under the title *Bre-viarium sive ordo officiorum per totam anni decursionem*. It was only a step to the forma-tion of the breviary. The result of this evolu-tion, and the fusion of four or five distinct books into one volume, was a shortening of the elements of the office, hence the name *breviarium*. The biblical and patristic lessons were no longer read from the Bible or the great tomes of the patristic authors. This was one of the results of the reform begun during the eleventh and twelfth centuries, and ended with that of the office of the Curia under Innocent III. The composition of these breviaries, especially those of the eleventh to twelfth centuries, is highly diverse, and often run into several volumes.

HENRY ASHWORTH OSB

(2) *Roman Catholic.* By the end of the Middle Ages both liturgical observance and the liturgical books were in a state of disarray. Reform had become necessary; the Council of Trent decreed it and committed the task to the papacy. A small commission, of whose work little is known, produced the liturgical books that were in use until recently. The *Missale Romanium,* 1570, was substantially the same as the first printed missal of 1474, containing the Roman rite as celebrated in the papal chapel in the thirteenth century and as propagated throughout Europe by the Franciscans. Like the *missalia plenaria* of the earlier Middle Ages, it contained the order of mass, the propers (q.v.) and the lessons to be read at the eucharist. It was prefaced by a long document, *Ritus Servandus,* giving minute directions about the celebration of the mass.

The *Breviarium Romanum,* 1568, giving the offices of the night and day (mattins, lauds, prime, terce, sext, none, vespers, and compline [qq.v.]), represented a conservative reform. The offices were long and the form monastic.

To these must be added the *Pontificale Romanum,* 1596, giving the rites celebrated only by a bishop, and the *Rituale Romanum,* 1614, for the administration of baptism, marriage and a great variety of other rites.

Apart from the breviary, which received a newly arranged psalter in 1911, these books remained substantially the same throughout the centuries. New feasts required new propers and there were one or two revisions, notably that of the liturgy of Holy Week in 1955.

The reform of the liturgy decreed by the Second Vatican Council (1963-1965) necessitated a complete revision of all the liturgical books. At the time of writing they are:

Missale Romanum, 1970, containing the order of mass with the four eucharistic prayers, the prefaces (82) and the collects with their corresponding prayers over the offerings and after communion and the entrance and communion verses.

Lectionarium, 1969, containing the course of scripture readings for Sundays (three-year cycle) and weekdays with the responsorial psalms and other texts used in the ministry of the word.

The *Breviary,* now called *The Liturgy of the Hours,* 1971, is a radical revision of the divine office and is intended for use both by the pastoral clergy and the people.

The *Pontificale Romanum* underwent partial revision in 1961 and a further revision (the rites of ordination) in 1968 and 1971.

Parts of the new *Rituale Romanum,* the Orders of Baptism (Infants, 1969), Marriage (1969), Confirmation (1971), have appeared and the revision of the other rites is proceeding.

Other book used in the Roman Rite are the *Martyrology* (last edition, 1956), a list with brief biographies, of the saints recognized by the Roman Catholic Church; the *Graduale Romanum* (1907), giving the plain-chant propers for the eucharist for the year, and the *Antiphonale* giving the plain-chant texts for the day hours of the divine office. The *Caeremoniale Episcoporum* (1600) gives the rubrical directives for episcopal ceremonies and like the foregoing books is in need of revision.

J. D. CRICHTON

4. *Anglican.* The book with the best claim to be called the first Anglican service-book is the *Litany* of 1544, which was published under the auspices of 'the King's Majesty and his clergy'. It was followed by *The King's Primer* (1545), *The Book of Homilies* (1547), and *The Order of the Communion* (1548). Each of these, however, presupposed the continuance of the traditional Latin services, and the first book to provide a complete range of reformed services in English was the *BCP* of 1549. This was a translation and abridgement of the Sarum rite with a strong admixture of Reformed ideas, owing much to the services of the continental Reformers, notably Luther and Bucer. It covers the ground formerly occupied by the breviary, the missal, the manual, and the processional, and was supplemented in 1550 by a set of ordination services, replacing the pontifical. The saying of the daily office requires in addition the use of a Bible, as the psalms and lessons are not printed in full. The other services are self-contained. A music edition

by John Merbecke appeared in 1550, and a French translation for use in the Channel Islands and a very inaccurate translation into Latin.

A revised version was issued in 1552, of a much more definitely Reformed character, though the main outlines of 1549 are retained. Zwingli is now the influential figure. It was followed by a similarly reformed *Primer*, but the two books had a life of only a few months before the Roman allegiance was restored under Mary.

On Elizabeth I's accession the book of 1552 was reissued with minor alterations designed to make it slightly less Protestant. The Edwardine *Primer* reappeared, together with three new books of devotion which attempted to reintroduce traditional forms (*Primer*, 1559; *Orarium*, 1560; *Preces Privatae*, 1564). A new Latin translation of the *BCP* appeared in 1560, followed by a more accurate rendering in 1571; and a Welsh translation was issued in 1567. A second *Book of Homilies* followed in 1563. From 1578 onwards unofficial editions appeared, conforming the book to Puritan ideas.

The accession of James I resulted in further minor changes, this time with an eye to the Puritans. This version appeared in Irish in 1608. Charles I commissioned a book of devotions for the ladies of the court from John Cosin, who took the *Orarium* of 1560 as his model. In 1637 a prayer book was printed for use in Scotland, which reintroduced many of the ideas of 1549 that had been discarded in 1552. Not surprisingly, the book proved completely unacceptable. In 1645 the *BCP* was banned and was only restored with the return of Charles II in 1660. Despite vigorous demands for revision from both wings of the church, Laudian and Puritan, the book eventually annexed to the Act of Uniformity of 1662 was substantially the book of 1552 with minor ceremonial additions. There were, however, numerous small improvements in the text, and some additional services.

It will be convenient at this point to list the contents of the book, which remained almost unchanged for 300 years. After three prefaces, tables of psalms and lessons, and much calendrical matter, the services included are:

Morning and evening prayer
The litany, prayers, and thanksgivings
Collects, epistles and gospels
Holy communion
Baptism (public, private, and for those of riper years)
Catechism and confirmation
Matrimony
Visitation and communion of the sick
Burial of the dead
Churching of women
Commination
The psalms
Ordination services (deacons, priests and bishops)
Forms of prayer for use at sea
State services

The Psalter, either in the translation of the Great Bible (Coverdale) or in metrical form (Sternhold and Hopkins), had often been bound up with the *BCP*, but now became an integral part of it; and the same is true of the ordinal. The state services added in 1662 were withdrawn in 1859; an accession service was a normal part of the book from Queen Anne onwards. The Thirty-Nine Articles, though customarily printed at the end of the book, have never formed part of it. There has never been an official music edition; pointed psalters, chant-books and hymnals have been left to private enterprise, though the metrical psalter of Tate and Brady (1696) was so widely used in the eighteenth century that it acquired a virtually official status.

The 1662 *BCP* was translated into French (1662), Greek and Welsh (both 1665), and Latin (1670). With the spread of missionary enterprise in the nineteenth century, the number of languages in which the *BCP* was available had reached a total of 140 by 1970. Editions of the book for use in Ireland from 1666 onwards contained supplementary services such as consecration of churches and visitation of prisoners. The disestablished Episcopalians in Scotland produced a series of 'wee bookies' containing a communion service based on primitive liturgies, which reached its definitive form in the communion office of 1764. This was taken as a model by the infant Protestant Episcopal Church of the USA, which produced an entire prayer book in 1790. During the eighteenth century various bodies in the process of secession from the Church of England made their own revisions of the prayer book, notably the Non-jurors, the Unitarians, and the Methodists. The disestablishment of the Irish Church in 1871 led to the issue of a conservative revision in

1877, while the Americans revised their own book in 1892.

From the beginning of the twentieth century revision took different forms. In England it was unhappily seen as a means of enforcing uniformity, especially upon Anglo-Catholics. Others, especially overseas, saw it as an opportunity of 'enrichment', usually from medieval sources. A considerable encouragement was given to the process of revision by the Lambeth Conference in 1908. This was soon reflected by draft proposals in Scotland, Canada, and South Africa, and later in the USA and Ireland. Each of these drafts is closely related to the others and to the English book of 1928, the product of twenty years' drafting. The latter book, intended as an alternative to 1662, was rejected by Parliament, though it subsequently came into wide, if unofficial, use. It departed sufficiently from the doctrinal standards of the Thirty-Nine Articles to alarm the Evangelicals, but without appealing to many Anglo-Catholics. In other parts of the world there was no need for parliamentary sanction, and the revisions duly appeared in their final forms as follows: 1922, Canada; 1926, Ireland; 1928, America; 1929, Scotland and South Africa. Of these, the first two are Evangelical in churchmanship, the others Anglo-Catholic. The South African is perhaps the most thorough and satisfactory.

In 1947 the archbishops of Canterbury and York issued an abridged version of the prayer book incorporating the more popular proposals of 1928. These were reintroduced in 1966 in a modified form entitled *Alternative Services: First Series*. Interest in liturgy had become much keener since the Second World War, and in 1955 the archbishops set up a Liturgical Commission to prepare new alternative services. At the time of going to press it had produced services of morning and evening prayer (1966, revised 1970), holy communion (1967), and baptism and confirmation (1958, revised 1967-8); other services were in preparation.

The pace continued to quicken: 1959 saw the adoption of new revisions in Canada, Japan, and the West Indies, and 1960 in the Church of India, Pakistan, Burma, and Ceylon. In the 1960s Scotland, Ireland and America resumed the work of revision; Wales, Australia and New Zealand entered the field for the first time. Experimentation was also proceeding in East Africa, Nigeria,

Brazil, Chile, Iran and Hong Kong. The last twelve countries were concerned with individual services rather than service-books; and it seems that the 'omnibus' volume containing all the occasional offices as well as the normal Sunday services, to say nothing of psalms, epistles, and gospels, is obsolescent, if not already obsolete. Future service-books will probably consist only of the eucharist and the daily office, the other services being printed in booklets or on cards. *The Revised Psalter Pointed* (1966) is a semi-official psalter, but there is no sign of an official hymn-book.

G. J. CUMING

5, *Baptist*. The use of liturgical books was regarded by John Smyth, the founder of the General Baptists, as 'the invention of the man of sin'. It was incompatible with the spiritual worship of the NT proceeding from the heart. The Separatists rejected not only prescribed liturgies but also the use of books of any kind in worship. As books were excluded prayers could not be said or praises sung by all together. During the course of the seventeenth century, the singing of metrical psalms, paraphrases, and hymns was introduced, and by the eighteenth century congregational singing had become general among Baptists. Many collections of praise material were made by individuals, the most notable of which, after revision by a committee of ministers, was published in 1858 under the title *Psalms and Hymns*. The publication of *The Baptist Church Hymnal* (1900, revised 1933) was a landmark, for in addition to hymns and metrical psalms, it contained the traditional canticles, a selection of prose psalms for chanting, and anthems. *The Baptist Hymn Book* (1962) is now widely used throughout Britain and by English speaking Baptists overseas. It contains hymns, canticles, prose psalms, a few prayers, and passages of scripture for alternate reading. Responsive readings are also a feature of American hymnals. It should be understood that the hymnal is *the* liturgical book of the Baptists, in comparison with which all other service-books are of secondary importance. Concerning the latter, there are three facts to be emphasized. First, since each Baptist church is autonomous there is no prescribed liturgy, and a service-book may be used much, occasionally, little, or not at all. Secondly, the service-books have been prepared for the pulpit, not the pew; they are manuals for ministers, not congregational prayer books. Thirdly, they have been compiled by individual initiative, not by representatives commissioned by the denomination. In Britain, a small book of services for special occasions was compiled by Dr M. E. Aubrey, General Secretary of the Baptist Union (*A Minister's Manual*, 1927). The current service-book, in widespread use throughout Britain, is a comprehensive book of common order (Ernest A. Payne and Stephen F. Winward, *Orders and Prayers for Church Worship*, 1960, revised 1965, adapted for use in the USA by James W. Cox under the title *Minister's Worship Manual*, 1969). A second comprehensive service-book has been produced in the USA (John Skoglund, *A Manual of Worship*, 1968). While these, together with the service-books of other communions, are now used by many ministers and lay preachers, the hymnal is the only liturgical book used by the congregation in all Baptist churches.

S. WINWARD

6. *Christian Church.* In its century and a half of history the Christian Church (Disciples of Christ) has made the congregation, with its minister and elders, responsible for ordering worship. One result of this policy has been to avoid the publication of official liturgical books. Not until 1953, with the publication of *Christian Worship: A Service Book*, did the denomination produce an authorized book, and this was for voluntary use only. This volume was largely the work of Professor G. Edwin Osborn (1897-1965), who for a third of a century was the denomination's acknowledged authority in liturgics. Educated at the University of Edinburgh, Osborn was an advocate of a psychological basis for worship. He represented a liberal attitude, holding that a service should be planned by the minister around a theme that he had chosen.

The book included recommended liturgies for the several rites of the church, a lectionary and some 400 pages of biblical materials and prayers for use by ministers and congregations. Although the book enjoyed only modest sales, it remained in print for some two decades and greatly influenced Disciple liturgical practice. Prior to the publication of this volume there were other books of lesser quality developed by pastors and

published for wider use.

Throughout their history Disciples have published hymnals. A hymnal first published by Alexander Campbell in 1834 was in widespread use throughout the several decades that followed. Other hymnals were developed under unauthorized auspices, including *Hymns of the United Church* co-edited by C. C. Morrison, editor of *The Christian Century*, and published in 1924.

In 1941 a new hymnal was published by the denomination's publishing house in co-operation with publishers for the American Baptist Convention. In 1970 a successor was published in similar fashion. Each one is representative of mainstream Protestant hymnals. The 1941 book, while superior to many other hymnals also in use among Disciples, was less highly regarded by musicians than were other leading hymnals, such as the *Hymnal 1940* of the Episcopal Church. The 1970 volume was superior to the earlier hymnal in two ways: it contained fewer of the sentimental revival songs of the late nineteenth century and it included a sizeable collection of modern hymns.

KEITH WATKINS

7. *Congregationalist.* Since the first Congregationalists believed in free prayers, not in a liturgy, there are no early Congregational prayer books. There is, however, an influential manual for ministers in the Westminster *Directory for Public Worship* (1644), which was the joint work of Presbyterians and Congregationalists. This became the standard for English-speaking Calvinist churches (Congregational, Baptist, and Presbyterian) for 250 years.

In the nineteenth century and after, some influential Congregational ministers compiled their own service-books. The two most famous were John Hunter's *Devotional Services for Public Worship* (1882) and W. E. Orchard's *Divine Service* (1919), the former being a liturgical expression of the social gospel, the latter being more traditional and Catholic in character.

The twentieth century sees the publication of denominational service-books. In England the first was *The Book of Congregational Worship* (1920), strongly imitative of the *BCP*. No attempt was made to return to the biblical or Reformation sources of worship. The same is even more decidedly true of its successor, *A Manual for Ministers* (1936).

An important but unofficial service-book which did return to the scriptures and original Calvinism was *A Book of Public Worship Compiled for the Use of Congregationalists* (1948) by John Huxtable, John Marsh, Romilly Micklem, and James Todd. A companion volume was the latter's *Prayers and Services for Christian Festivals* (1951). 1959 saw the publication of another official English Congregational manual of worship, *A Book of Services and Prayers*, the chairman of the compilers being W. Gordon Robinson. The eucharistic theology shows a notable advance from the book of 1920 by the following of the traditional structure of the Western prayer of consecration, with the addition of an epiclesis.

On the American side two important denominational service-books have appeared. *A Book of Worship for Free Churches* (1948) was prepared under the direction of the General Council of the Congregational Christian Churches, Boynton Merrill being the chairman of the compilers. It has many alternative orders, uses ecumenical resources, and stresses the importance of symbolism.

The United Church of Christ, which came into being with the union of the Congregational Christian Churches and the Evangelical and Reformed Church in 1950, necessitated the provision of new orders of worship. The new commission on worship, under the leadership of Louis H. Gunnemann, produced as its first fruits *The Lord's Day Service* (1964). Two years later the commission published *Services of Word and Sacrament*, and the two orders have exactly the same structure stressing the unity of word and sacrament, but the first uses traditional and the second contemporary language. Recognizing the transitional character of modern liturgical productions, the commission has committed its successive works to paperback publication, thus combining realism with modesty and tentativeness.

Modern Congregational liturgical books seem to be based upon five liturgical principles: (1) the reaffirmation of the biblical basis and content of Christian worship; (2) the importance of claiming our ecumenical inheritance; (3) the combination of a firm order of liturgy with a place for free prayers and silent prayer; (4) the provision of many alternatives to provide variety and flexibility within order; and (5) the inclusion

of both classical and contemporary prayers.

There are three current hymn-books in use. The English Congregational hymnal is *Congregational Praise* (*see* E. R. Routley and K. L. Parry, *Companion to Congregational Praise,* 1953). The United Church of Christ in the USA is in the process of compiling a new hymnal, but the pre-union hymnals are still being used. The ex-Congregationalists use *The Pilgrim Hymnal,* while former members of the Evangelical and Reformed Church use *The Hymnal Containing Complete Orders of Worship* (1941).

HORTON DAVIES

8. *Jehovah's Witnesses.* The society of Jehovah's Witnesses is Bible-orientated, and the Bible is the one book consistently to the foreground in all meetings.

Until the 1950s the translation generally used was the Authorized Version, supplemented by the American Standard Version, Weymouth's, Moffatt's and others. In 1950 the Watch Tower Bible and Tract Society published the first volume of the *New World Translation of the Christian Greek Scriptures* (i.e. NT). By 1960 the entire Bible had been translated and published and by 1970 was available in English, Spanish, Portuguese, Dutch, Italian, and (Matthew to Revelation only) French and German.

The translation has played an important part in the meetings of Jehovah's Witnesses; not so much in development of basic theology, where its effect has been peripheral – Witnesses had established a framework of Bible teaching long before 1960 – as in that analytical Bible study which is the groundwork of all Kingdom Hall meetings.

The translation's aim is to be as literal as possible, 'where a literal rendition does not for any clumsiness hide the thought' (Foreword). Each major word is assigned one meaning 'as far as the context permits', the object being to make for good cross-reference work and 'a more reliable comparison of related texts or verses'. This method restricts diction but is helpful in research. The result is an intelligible and highly practical work for the Bible analyst.

One stage further, 1969 saw published in English *The Kingdom Interlinear Translation of the Greek Scriptures,* a word-for-word translation beneath Westcott and Hort's Greek text, with the above modern-English translation in a right-hand column. A feature of the interlinear is its analysis of the Greek's particles and compound words, the aim being to help the reader determine what the 'koine Greek basically or literally says'. Its use is now a feature of Witness meetings.

Other set books for use in congregation worship include: a song-book (latest edition 1966; all the [anonymous] songs written and composed by Witnesses); 'Your Word Is a Lamp to My Foot', a Bible-based guide to the Society's structure; Qualified to Be Ministers, a textbook for the public ministry; and The Watchtower, the Society's official semi-monthly magazine (monthly circulation, 15,250,000 in January 1972).

The place of The Watchtower in congregational instruction is important. Through it scriptural exegesis is presented. 'The Watchtower is no inspired prophet, but it follows and explains a Book of prophecy the predictions in which have proved to be unerring and unfailing till now' (title-page). Much is said about family life, promotion of the public Christian ministry, moral cleanness, and adoption of missionary service by Witness youths.

Where new congregations of Witnesses are formed, the first meeting arranged is the weekly Watchtower Bible study. The Bible, in whatever translation, is central to the worship of Jehovah's Witnesses; The Watchtower encourages and promotes its study.

A. HELEY

9. Lutheran

(1) European. Lutheran liturgical books have their starting point in two orders of service outlined by Luther, the Formula Missae of 1523 and the Deutsche Messe (German mass) of 1526. These in turn followed the pattern of the Roman mass, which was altered to follow the perspectives of the Reformation.

(a) Germany. Because of the territorial divisions of Lutheranism, there was no single service book used by all the German-speaking Lutheran churches in common, as was the case with Luther's translation of the Bible, his catechism and his hymns. Indeed, appeals to article VII of the Augsburg Confession even prevented energetic efforts at such a book. Nevertheless, a series of common liturgical features are to be found within the various 'church orders' that appeared. The North German orders, in which Luther's friend Johannes Bugenhagen played a substantial part, come close to the type of the Deutsche Messe. Their freedom in shaping the eucharist is striking. Similar influence was exercised by the Brandenburg-Nürnberg church order of 1533, which continued the conservative line prefigured in the Formula Missae. In South-West German Lutheranism, a liturgy going back to the medieval Dominican pattern was used.

The Reformation orders of service were preserved down to the period of pietism, when the traditional liturgical forms rapidly began to break up. Their place was taken by private forms of service, newly-constructed artificial orders in the spirit of rationalism. A restoration counter-movement began in the nineteenth century. In Prussia, where in 1817 a union had been brought about between the Lutherans (numerically, by far in the majority) and the Reformed, a 'church order' (with fundamentally a Lutheran structure) worked out by king Friedrich Wilhelm III was introduced. The great Lutheran churches of Bavaria, Hanover, Mecklenburg and Saxony similarly took upon themselves regulative orders, which were based on the sixteenth-century forms of service. They also set the pattern for the smaller district churches. The formation of the United Evangelical Lutheran Church of Germany (VELKD) in 1948 led to the creation of a great four-volume work which for the first time in the history of German Lutheranism provided a common basis for liturgical action. The main liturgy has the structure of the 'evangelical mass', from which the sacramental part can be excluded. Lutheran churches which belong to the United Evangelical Church also have the possibility, after the new service book of 1959, of using the main Lutheran liturgy as well as the preaching service and the eucharist following the Reformed pattern. So far, the separation of the organizations of the Lutheran churches in East and West Germany has not led to any sacrifice of liturgical uniformity.

In many places, the demand for new, contemporary forms of service alongside those forms of service shaped by traditional patterns has led to modern attempts at liturgies. Such experiments are not, however, given fixed forms in service books. Suggestions and models are published in 'work books', which do not have any official standing. The tendency to avoid the constricting pressures of a service book is at present stronger than ever.

(b) *Northern Europe.* The *Swedish* service books similarly begin from Luther's reform of the mass. However, from 1560 onwards, a predilection for richer liturgical forms is perceptible, though intensive efforts to restore the liturgy of the ancient church (Liturgy of king Johann III) were rejected as being too 'catholic'. With the service book of 1693, the particularism of the episcopal sees was broken and a national church uniformity was introduced throughout Sweden, with the full support of Lutheran orthodoxy. Orders of service maintained a much purer form than in Germany through the period of the Enlightenment. The church books of the nineteenth century, stamped with the spirit of the age, were replaced by the new service book of 1942. This is characterized by a far-reaching reform of the lectionary of the ancient church.

Until the separation of Finland from the Swedish communion of churches in 1809, the *Finnish* liturgy was closely connected with developments in Sweden. After two service books of 1886 and 1913, a new liturgy was adopted in 1969.

Bugenhagen was also an influence on the *Danish* mass of 1539. Even now, the 'Church Ritual' of 1685 is the basis of the Danish liturgy. An 'Experimental Book of Ritual' which appeared in 1963 is intended once again to make greater room for sung liturgical prose.

The most recent order of the *Norwegian* church, which received its church ritual in 1683, is the Norwegian mass of 1920. Since 1969, a new experimental service book has been introduced, which seeks to pioneer new liturgical music.

(c) *The rest of Europe.* The minority Lutheran churches have mostly adopted new service books since the Second World War, following the line laid down in the great book of the VELKD (e.g. France 1953, Czechoslovakia 1954, Poland 1955).

F. KALB

(2) *United States.* Lutheran settlers in the USA brought with them their own vernacular liturgies and it was not until 1748 that the foundation was laid for an American liturgy, when H. M. Mühlenberg devised an order in German which was adopted by the Ministerium of Pennsylvania; the same body adopted an English liturgy in 1860 and eight years later the General Council approved a revision. The General Synod and the United Synod of the South then joined with the Council to produce the *Common Service* of 1888, and a complete book, the *Common Service Book*, was published in 1917 to coincide with the foundation of the United Lutheran Church of America. In 1957 there was issued a *Service Book and Hymnal* which contains forms for the eucharist, mattins, vespers, baptism, confirmation, confession, burial and matrimony (qq.v.).

EDITOR

10. *Methodist.* The first Methodist liturgical book, as distinct from collections of prayers and hymns, was *The Sunday Service of the Methodists in America, With Other Occasional Services*, 1784, an abridgement, with some amendments, mostly of a Puritan character, of the *BCP*, 1662, of the Church of England. There were many subsequent editions, two at least for Methodists in the USA, one for Methodists in His Majesty's Dominions, and the rest simply for Methodists. The Americans did not view it with much favour and soon discarded it, but they incorporated some parts of it in their *Discipline* under the title 'Sacramental Services, etc.'; the title was subsequently changed to 'The Ritual'. There were extensive revisions in 1864, 1916 and 1932 in the Methodist Episcopal Church and from 1854 to 1870 and in 1910 in the Methodist Episcopal Church South. The *Methodist Hymnal*, 1935, incorporated some orders of service for optional use which were not part of 'The Ritual' but had come to be printed with 'The Ritual' in the *Discipline*. The *Book of Worship for Church and Home*, 1944, was an innovation, and contained 'The Ritual' and much else, though many people in the pew used only the material in the *Methodist Hymnal*. All these books were revised in 1964 and *The Book of Worship for Church and Home*, 1964, included orders and offices for the official rites of the church and all the other liturgical material, except hymns, which were needed in this church. It has now united under the title of the United Methodist Church with the Evangelical United Brethren, whose *Book of Ritual*, 1959, is recognized together with the books previously mentioned.

In England *The Sunday Service* went through many editions until 1910. Between 1839 and 1881 a shorter version, containing only certain services, *Order of Administration of the Sacraments*, also went through many editions. There were revisions in 1846 and 1864. The Wesleyan conference of 1882 produced a modified version of it known as *The Book of Public Prayers and Services*, which was intended to safeguard the principles of evangelical Protestantism; at several points, however, it restored portions of the *BCP* which Wesley had omitted. It is curious that this also had a shorter version with the same title as its predecessor, *Order of Administration of the Sacraments*, and that *The Sunday Service* continued to be published for many years after it had been officially superseded. The non-Wesleyan branches of Methodism also produced service-books, which were very much simpler and less Anglican than the Wesleyan books and also were probably much less used.

After the union of the Wesleyan Methodists, the Primitive Methodists and the United Methodists in Britain in 1932, the conference in 1936 published *The Book of Offices*, being the orders of service authorized for use in the Methodist Church, together with *The Order for Morning Prayer*. This book, though it had the characteristically liberal Protestant tone of that period, is still recognizably indebted to the *BCP*. It is still the official book, though various supplementary services are published, to some extent under the control of the Conference.

Liturgical books do not have the same binding authority in Methodism which they have in some other churches. The services in them are authorized and generally followed (at ordinations invariably); but other forms are not prohibited. As the order for morning prayer is not widely used, the preaching service can and usually does proceed in Britain without any reference to the book. A book, *Divine Worship*, 1935, intended for such services, is not widely used.

It has often been said that the true liturgy of Methodism is to be found in its hymns, and this is reflected by the fact that its hymn-books are authorized by its Conferences. The Wesleys published many hymn-books; the definitive edition was that of 1780. British Methodism currently uses *The Methodist Hymn-Book*, 1933, together with a recent supplement *Hymns and Songs*, 1969.

The lectionary is also an official publication of the Conference. This has frequently been changed in recent years. The British Conference of 1969 authorized a new lectionary incorporated in *Collects, Lessons and Psalms* based on *The Calendar and Lectionary*, 1967, of the Joint Liturgical Group. Parts of *Collects, Lessons and Psalms* are authorized for experimental use, but the lectionary itself is authorized fully.

The British Conference has undertaken the revision of *The Book of Offices*, and certain portions of it have been authorized for experimental use, notably *The Sunday Service*, 1968. These services represent a considerable revision, adopting many of the insights of the Liturgical Movement and thus showing considerable resemBlance to the liturgies of the churches which have been similarly influenced. When the work of revision is complete, the main services are likely to be gathered in a volume probably to be called 'Services and Sacraments'; the other services will have the same authority, but will probably be published as separate pamphlets.

There are many Methodist churches in other parts of the world, but they all stem originally from either British or American Methodism, and their service-books are usually adaptations, sometimes indeed abbreviations, of the English or American books, often translated into other languages.

A. RAYMOND GEORGE

11. *Old Catholic*. Each of the Old Catholic churches belonging to the Utrecht Union has its own liturgical books. The *jus liturgicum* (i.e. the right of ordering the liturgy in the church) belongs to the bishops of each church; they also have the duty of supervising the versions of the liturgical books.

The basis of the liturgical books of the Old Catholic churches is the books of the Roman Catholic rite. As the liturgy has long been celebrated in the vernacular, these books have had to be translated into various languages. Sometimes they are almost literal translations; sometimes they are free revisions. Corresponding to the geographical spread of the Old Catholic church, there are liturgical books in the following languages: German for Germany, Austria and the German-speaking parts of Switzerland; French for the French-speaking part of Switzerland and France; Italian, Croatian, Dutch, Polish (and also English for the Polish National Church in the USA and Canada), and Czech.

The following is a list of the more important liturgical books of the Old Catholic churches as far as they are known to the authors of this article.

(*a*) *Altar books and mass books for the congregation*: Germany has the *Altarbuch für die Feier der heiligen Eucharistie im Katholischen Bistum der Alt-Katholiken in Deutschland*, Bonn 1959; Austria has the *Altkatholisches Altar-Buch*, Vienna 1933. For the ordinary of the mass it has now been replaced by the *Ordnung des Heiligen Amtes der Gemeinde*; the proper is still to come. The volume *Das heilige Amt für die Gemeinde, II Ordnung*, provides alternative texts for the eucharistic prayer as experimental forms.

Switzerland has the *Messliturgie der Christkatholischen Kirche der Schweiz*, Bern [2]1905. The French edition (1910 is its most recent date) is at present out of print. In 1971 a completely revised text of the ordinary of the mass has been published (*Nouvel Ordinaire de la Messe*); a new proper will follow. Italy has the *Messalino e piccolo Catechismo, Chiesa Cattolica Antica*, no date.

Holland has the *Misbook ten dienste van de Oud-Katholieke Kerk van Nederland*, 1909. The edition in a small format for the congregation last appeared in 1960 in a fourth edition (with some alterations); in addition an experimental *Tweede Misorde* (second order) appeared in 1968. The order of mass for the Polish National Catholic Church is to be found in *A Book of Devotions and Prayers according to the use of the Polish National Church in Polish and English*, Scranton, Pa, 1951.

(*b*) *Books of ritual*, containing the rites for the celebration of the sacraments, burials, blessings, etc., are as follows: *Katholisches Rituale der alt-katholischen Kirche des Deutschen Reiches*, Bonn 1876, abbreviated edition 1933. A thorough revision is planned. *Das österreichische Rituale* of 1929 is out of print; a new edition is being prepared. There was a completely revised second edition of the *Rituale der Christkatholischen Kirche der Schweiz*, Bern 1940. For the Netherlands, *Gebed en Sacrament* has gone through a number of editions since 1935; it also contains private devotions and the order of the mass. *Rytual Kosciola Polskokatolickiego* for the Polish Catholic Church appeared in Warsaw in 1961. It also contains the Holy Week liturgy and a number of benedictions, liturgies and hymns.

(*c*) *Prayer books* for congregational use corresponding approximately to the English *BCP* usually contain the order of the mass, morning and evening prayer and the sacraments, as well as private prayers, especially for the sick; some also have a hymn-book. One is the *Katholisches Gebet- und Gesangbuch für die Alt-Katholiken in Deutschland*, Bonn [2]1965. It also contains the special liturgies for Good Friday and Easter Even. *Unser Beten* is the prayer book for the Old Catholic Church of Austria, Vienna [2]1962. The *Gebetbuch der Christkatholischen Kirche der Schweiz*, Allschwil [11]1968, is bound up with a hymn-book (*see* [*d*] below); it also contains all the propers of the mass. *Prières liturgiques en usage dans l'Eglise Catholique-Chrétienne de la Suisse* (the last full edition, Soleure 1910) is about to appear in a considerably altered new impression (1971). For Holland *see* (*b*) above, *Gebed en Sacrament*. For the Polish National Catholic Church *see* (*a*) above, *A Book of Devotions . . .* and (*b*) *Rytual . . .*

(*d*) *Hymn-books*. These contain truly liturgical hymns and above all the congregational hymns which are much loved in Old Catholic churches.

For Germany, *see* (*c*) above. The *Gesangbuch der Christkatholischen Kirche der Schweiz* is combined with the prayer book (*see* [*c*] above). A new and enlarged edition of the French hymn-book, now out of print, is in preparation (1971). There are three hymn-books for the church of the Netherlands: *Misgezangen* (mass hymns), new edition, 1949; *Vesperboek*, several editions since 1909; *Gesangboek ten dienste van de Oud-Katholieke Kerk*, enlarged edition, 1942.

(*e*) *The rites for the consecration of priests* (major and minor orders) were produced in German at the request of the Conference of Old Catholic Bishops in a free rendering that followed the *Pontificale Romanum*, Bern 1899. This was translated into Dutch in 1900 and Polish (in *Rytual . . .*), *see* (*b*) above. In addition there are formulae for the consecration of a bishop and for the consecration of churches, altars and bells.

New editions of most of the Old Catholic liturgical books are being produced in the course of the movement for liturgical renewal.

KURT PURSCH
A. E. RÜTHY
C. TOL

12. *Pentecostal*. E. Leonard called attention

to the oral, non-literary character of classical Pentecostalism (*L'illuminisme dans un protestantisme de constitution récente*, 1953, p. 99). Since classical Pentecostalism (*see* **Pentecostal Worship**) represents a pre-literary culture whose tools of socialization are the story, the parable, a witness, a prophecy, a song, and face-to-face encounter, since the Pentecostal ethos is experience-oriented and leader-dominated, since their liturgical presuppositions are the actuality and immediacy of God's presence ('He is real; the really real'), and since all is under the guidance and prompting of the Holy Spirit, there are many classical Pentecostals who look upon a written liturgy and liturgical paraphernalia as a quenching of the Spirit. However, in South Africa the Apostolic Jerusalem Church in Sabbath has taken over the office of bishop together with copes, capes, mitres, acolytes or deacons (qq.v.). In Chile certain denominations have developed a ritual of entrance for the pastor. 'Like the bishop who enters only after the ceremony has begun, he (the pastor) comes with hat on head and a cape on his shoulders, three councillors following him, one carrying a Bible. When they reach the platform, an elder takes the hat, one the cape, and the third hands the Bible to the bishop, who then takes his seat' (C. Lalive d'Epinay, *Haven of the Masses*, 1969, p. 52). Though such rituals might never be reduced to print – indeed to do so might in some cases be a scandal – yet rubrical observance might be as rigorous as in any of the high liturgical churches.

Some of the tendencies towards ritual are motivated by desire for social respectability. In South America norms of social acceptability are determined by the mores of Catholic practice. To disassociate their churches from the image of the culturally disinherited, Pentecostal churches conform to the socio-cultural patterns of the more respectable churches, i.e. the liturgical practices of Catholicism.

Those churches which have lost some of their prophetic character and become more or less centralized and bureaucratized also tend to move away from the oral and non-literary culture of classical Pentecostalism. These groups have published manuals with ceremonies for the reception of members, Lord's Supper, baptism, marriage, burial, dedication of churches and children (*Discipline of Pentecostal Holiness Church*, 1961;

Ministers' Manual, 1965). When these manuals are used it is as a servant rather than a master. An Assemblies of God pastor wrote: 'I believe that the Holy Spirit should be able to break in at any time he chooses. When we lose this – we've lost everything' (F. Masserano, *A Study of Worship Forms in the Assemblies of God Denomination*, Master's Thesis, Princeton, 1966, p. 70).

Classical Pentecostals are not at their best when composing liturgical texts, even in those churches which have moved beyond an oral, pre-literary culture to a literary culture. Their liturgical experience is, even in these cases, determined by their pre-literary origins. This can be deceptive. A classical Pentecostal eucharistic service the author attended in Minneapolis, Minnesota, was a liturgical success; but if it were reduced to the printed page it would look impoverished. Also, the rite is not understandable apart from spirituality of which it is an expression.

Neo-Pentecostals tend to follow the liturgical books of their own churches but with a freedom which allows for the exercise of charismatic gifts. In some Lutheran neo-Pentecostal groups (e.g. Arnold Bittlinger, Schloss Craheim, Germany; Larry Christenson, Trinity Lutheran Church, San Pedro, California), the charismatic element has been integrated into the total Lutheran approach. Instead of an aggressive self-conscious Pentecostal message, there is the quiet availability of the Pentecostal dimension within the Lutheran framework. Roman Catholic Pentecostals follow the liturgical order with greater fidelity than the underground churches, but with moments within the eucharistic action for community participation through the exercise of the gifts.

The weaknesses of the classical Pentecostal liturgical practice (e.g. excessive subjectivism, restricted theological horizon, ritualization of impoverished patterns, want of theological penetration) indicate that for the liturgical churches to abandon their tradition of printed texts would be an ill-advised move. But the strengths of the Pentecostal tradition would indicate that to concentrate on a purely literary tradition is to ignore those elements of the non-rational, pre-literary in the theological and liturgical traditions of the early church (O. Cullmann, *Early Christian Worship*, 1953, p. 20; E. Schweizer, *Church Order in the New Testament*, 1961, p. 221) and also to ignore the experience orientation of much of contemporary culture with its sensitivity sessions, T-groups, drug addiction, hippy movement, and participatory theatre. The classical Pentecostals have been especially productive and successful in creating new worship forms. A negro preacher from the Dominican Republic sang his worship service to a Chilean congregation. It was a free rhythmed spontaneous composition of high musical quality (film *Gloria a Dios, Pfingstkirchen in Chile*, Zweites Deutsche Fernsehen, directed by Fritz Puhl). From the Pentecostals the historic churches can learn how to maintain a more immediate contact between cultural patterns and liturgical forms, a contact which is established in an oral, pre-literary mode. What Ernst Troeltsch wrote of the social ethics of the churches is in a measure also true in the area of liturgical renewal:

> It is the lower classes which do the really creative work, forming communities on a genuinely religious basis. They alone unite imagination and simplicity of feeling with a non-reflective habit of mind, a primitive energy, and an urgent sense of need. On such a foundation alone is it possible to build up an unconditional authoritative faith in a divine revelation with simplicity of surrender and unshaken certainty. (*The Social Teaching of the Christian Churches*, ET, 1931, I, p. 44).

Though classical Pentecostalism can no longer be identified without qualification with the lower strata, it is from this level that its liturgical creativity still comes. (For bibliography *see under* **Pentecostal Worship**.)

KILIAN MCDONNELL

13. *Plymouth Brethren*. The Brethren have no liturgical books in the ordinary sense. Traditionally they interpret the freedom of the Spirit as ruling out such 'aids' to public worship. If this interpretation were pressed to its logical conclusion, it would rule out the use of hymn-books, but in fact liberal use is made of hymn-books in their worship. The selection of appropriate hymns for various services, and especially for the successive stages of the communion service, will sometimes be regarded as a mark of spiritual intelligence.

Among the Exclusive Brethren the standard hymn-book since 1856 has been *Hymns for the Little Flock*, compiled in that

year by G. V. Wigram, revised in 1881 by J. N. Darby and subsequently issued in several further revisions for the use of the various Exclusive bodies. In the body led by the late James Taylor, Jr, successive revisions (by T. H. Reynolds in 1903, James Taylor, Sr, in 1932 and A. E. Myles in 1951) have increasingly made this collection a handbook to the liturgy (*see* **Liturgies** 13: Plymouth Brethren). It accurately reflects some notable features of this body's doctrine and practice, as in the avoidance of any reference to the eternity of Christ's relation as Son to the Father and in the absence of any note of confession of sin (which is not, however, a sign of antinomianism).

Among the Open Brethren a variety of hymn-books is in use. The most widely used in Great Britain and Ireland are *The Believer's Hymn Book* (1884; enlarged with a supplement, 1959), *Hymns of Light and Love* (1900) and *Hymns for Christian Worship and Service* (1909). Some of their churches prefer to use interdenominational collections, such as *Christian Praise* (1957) or *Hymns of Faith* (1964). To the latter of these the Brethren at Mitchley Hill Chapel, Sanderstead, Surrey, have provided an excellent supplement of hymns specially suitable for use at the communion service.

Apart from its use as the basis for expository ministry, the Bible serves in some degree as a liturgical book. At the communion service in particular, one or another of the worshippers may read (with or without brief comment) a scripture bearing on the purpose of the meeting – for example, a suitable passage from the NT or a 'messianic' psalm or prophecy from the OT calculated to promote the spirit of worship and anamnesis. As with the selection of suitable hymns, use and wont have established a feeling for what scripture lessons are appropriate for this purpose, so that the reading of passages that are deemed inappropriate may be put down to lack of spiritual intelligence. Departure from the accepted though unwritten liturgical pattern may be the result of inexperience or of mature and deliberate breaking with tradition.

F. F. BRUCE

14. *Reformed*. The Protestant Reformation brought changes in service books for use in worship as in other things. The replacement of Latin by the vernacular was a far-reaching change adopted by all the reformers, which

enabled the worshipper to understand the service. But on other points the reformers adopted differing policies. In the *Book of Common Prayer* (*BCP*) the text had to be strictly adhered to. But in other books there were specific points where variation was permitted. Thus in Calvin's *Forme des prieres* (1542) one rubric says, 'on use de cette action de graces ou semblable', and in the Scottish *Book of Common Order* (*BCO*) 1564, at a few places the rubrics permit the minister to pray 'either in these words following or the like in effect'. Another change was that the books were used by all the worshippers. Indeed in the case of *BCO* an Act of Assembly of 26 December 1564 ordered 'every minister, exhorter and reader to possess a copy' and use it, and an Act of Parliament of 1579 decreed that every person of a certain rank and class had to have copy. Possession of a copy by the worshipper was required because it contained metrical psalms for singing. Calvin's *La Forme* of 1542 contained thirty-five psalms with music and others were added in later editions. *BCO* of 1564 for the first time provided metrical versions of all the psalms. How widely used the various editions of *BCO* were is shown by the condition of most surviving copies, the beginning and the end being usually defective, leaves missing or heavily finger-marked and dirty.

Out of the many Reformed liturgical books that have been produced, the following deserve special mention. The story begins with Zwingli, who produced two forms, both for the Lord's Supper. The first in 1523, *De Canone Missae Epicheiresis,* was an attack on the Canon of the Mass and indicated his ideas for the service. The second, two years later, entitled *Action oder Bruch des Nachtmals*, was more radical, but it became the guiding rule for Zwinglian worship. Next to be noted is Farel's *La manyere et fasson qu'on tient es lieux que Dieu de sa grace a visites,* dated 1533, prepared for the use in Strasbourg of the Zwinglian Reformed congregation. This was Zwinglian in tone and had little influence on other rites, though Calvin adopted the marriage rite almost as it stood.

Strasbourg had already seen the important first reformed German Mass, arranged by Diebold Schwartz in 1524, and frequently revised, more and more under the influence of Bucer. When John Calvin came to Strasbourg in 1538 he made a Latin version of the Schwartz form; this was later translated into French as *La manyere de faire prieres aux eglises francoyses* and used by the Strasbourg French congregation. A later edition was printed in Geneva in 1542. This contained thirty-five psalms with melody, the creed, the Lord's Prayer, and an order of service for Sunday morning with the addition necessary when the eucharist was celebrated, the marriage service, and a section for the visitation of the sick. Some revisions of this were issued in succeeding years. A Latin translation was issued in Geneva in 1552, and one in English, by William Huycke, in London in 1550. Other editions continued to appear, a very important one being that printed in Geneva in 1556, under the title, *The forme of Prayers and ministration of the sacraments as used in the English Congregation at Geneva.*

This was John Knox's *Genevan Service Book*. There was also a Latin translation, *Ratio et Forma*. An edition similar to that of 1556, but containing additional prayers and the Genevan Confession of Faith, was issued in Geneva in 1561. The next edition takes us to Scotland where in 1562 Robert Lekprewick printed *The Forme of Prayers and Ministration of the Sacraments* at the order of the General Assembly, which gave him a grant towards his expenses. This was adopted for use in the Church of Scotland under the title *The Book of Common Order*.

La Forme des prieres continued to exert great influence both in Switzerland and in France. Many of the Swiss Cantons, such as Geneva, Vaud and Neuchâtel produced their own books, based on the great original though with many local accents. A notable attempt at revision was that of Jean-Frédéric Osterwald, who published a liturgy in 1713 which showed the influence of *BCP*, but had little influence on further Swiss books, except that of Vaud in 1725, but, translated and revised, it became the book of the Huguenot congregation in Charleston, South Carolina, 1853. Recent Swiss revisions include those of Vaud (1945) and Geneva (1946).

In France liturgical books were issued from time to time, and there were many attempts to revise and enrich the content. One important attempt was that of Eugène Bersier who in 1876 issued a *Projet de revision* and in 1888 a liturgy. Here was evidenced a moving towards a new spirit of worship. Its influence is seen in the recent *Liturgie de l'Église Réformée de France* of 1963, the result of the prolonged work of a Commission de liturgie.

The German and Dutch Reformed Churches gave much attention to the problems of the liturgy, and issued various service-books. The majority of the German Reformed churches joined with Lutheran churches in 1817. But in the Dutch Reformed Church there was a liturgical revival with the foundation in 1920 of the *Liturgische Kring* and in 1938 of the *Kring Eeredienst* which published its *Kanselboek* in 1944.

Now we return to consider the liturgical books of the churches which came to be known as Presbyterian. The original of these was *BCO*, popularly known as the Psalm-book. From 1564 to 1644 fully seventy editions appeared. The contents of these editions varied very considerably, but usually included the calendar; the psalter with music; scripture songs or hymns, i.e., metrical versions of the Ten Commandments, the Lord's Prayer and the Veni Creator, etc.; the catechism (Calvin's up to 1611, the Palatinate or Heidelberg in 1615); the order of baptism, the Lord's supper, marriage, visitation of the sick, the order of burial. Much other material appeared in some editions. This book was widely used, though not without some criticism at times, but its use ceased in 1645, when the General Assembly adopted the *Westminster Directory*.

The *Directory* was not a liturgical book. It did not provide prayers or forms of prayer, but detailed subjects for prayer. It completely superseded *BCO*, but itself soon came to be much neglected, and worship reached a low level. But by the end of the eighteenth century many ministers grew tired of the baldness and poverty of the services, and not a few published orders especially for holy communion. The Church Service Society of the Church of Scotland was formed in 1865 and its influence, especially through the issue of *Euchologion*, gradually led to much improvement. Other Societies, with the same intention, were formed in the United Presbyterian and Free Churches in Scotland, and they also published service-books. The United Free Church after 1900 followed the same course, leading to the issue in 1928 of the *Book of Common Order, 1928*. Similar movements were taking place within the Church of Scotland, an influential book, *Prayers for Divine Service*, appearing in 1923, revised in 1929. The reunited Church produced the *Book of Common Order, 1940*, which was revised in 1952, and is now under detailed revision. This book has greatly influenced the books of other Presbyterian churches throughout the world. These churches, in England, Canada, Australia, New Zealand and South Africa, have all issued service-books and have all revised them. In the USA three Presbyterian churches produced their own books, but have recently joined in the publication of a new book for all – *The Worship-Book* (Philadelphia 1970). In spite of many differences in detail, these all show some evidence of their derivation from Calvinist sources. Yet in many services, especially in the eucharist, many of the ancient forms, such as *Sursum Corda* and *Agnus Dei*, have been adopted, thus enriching them and adding to their value.

JOHN A. LAMB

15. *Seventh-day Adventist*. The Seventh-day Adventist Church, in the tradition of Evangelical Protestantism, does not use special liturgical books for its worship services. Various publications are drawn upon for guidance in worship, but they are not authorized or used as service-books.

The early leaders of the Seventh-day Adventist Church emphasized the blessedness of genuine worship, as opposed to what they called the evil of formal worship. Adventists still generally keep to the relative informality of early years and do not worship according to a prescribed ritual with fixed words and formalized prayers. In recent years form consciousness in the regular services for worship has become more pronounced. *The Seventh-day Adventist Church Manual* (1967 ed.) states: 'We do not prescribe a set form or order for public worship' (p. 109). Nevertheless, the *Manual* does suggest a longer and shorter order of worship and offers considerable guidance regarding the Sabbath worship service.

The Church Hymnal (USA, Australia, etc.) and the *New Advent Hymnal* (Britain, some West African countries) are the two most widely used hymn-books in English-speaking Adventist churches. *The Church Hymnal* also contains a selection of responsive scriptural readings. A series of special devotional readings is prepared annually for use in all Seventh-day Adventist churches around the world during the yearly Week of Prayer in November.

The Manual for Ministers contains suggested services and prescribes certain ritual forms for special occasions, such as ordinations, burials, church dedications and marriage ceremonies. In addition, various Seventh-day Adventist publishing houses issue every year quite a number of new books and inspirational readings for private and corporate devotions.

B. B. BEACH

J. S. Andrews, 'Brethren Hymnology', *Evangelical Quarterly* 28, 1956, pp. 208-29; J. C. Bowmer, *The Sacrament of the Lord's Supper in Early Methodism*, 1951; F. E. Brightman, *The English Rite*, 1915, 2 vols., esp. pp. xlix-ccxxx (Anglican); C. O. Buchanan, *Modern Anglican Liturgies, 1958-1968,* 1968; Horton Davies, *The Worship of the English Puritans* 1948; Horton Davies, *Worship and Theology in England, 1900-1965*, 1965, ch.x; Jean Deshusses. *Le Sacramentaire Gregorien. Ses principales formes d'après les plus anciens manuscrits*, 1971; K. Gamber, *Codices Liturgici Latini Antiquiores*, 1963; A. R. George, 'The People called Methodist – 4. The Means of Grace' in *A History of the Methodist Church in Great Britain*, ed. S. R. Davies and G. Rupp, 1965, pp.259-73; N. B. Harmon, Jr, *The Rites and Ritual of Episcopal Methodism*, 1926; W. K. Lowther Clarke, ed., *Liturgy and Worship*, 1932; A. G. Matthews, 'Puritan Worship' in *Christian Worship*, ed. N. Micklem, 1935, reissued 1955; Pierre Salmon, *Les Manuscrits liturgiques latins de la Bibliotheque Vaticane*, Vols. I,. II, 1968, 1969; Cyrille Vogel, *Introduction aux Sources de l'Histoire du Culte Chrétien au Moyen Age,* 1965; B. J. Wigan, *The Liturgy in English*, 1964 (Anglican).

Bowing *see* Postures (2*a*)

Buddhist Worship

Buddhist worship is a peculiarly delicate topic, in a religion or ethic which has been called atheistic and appears to emphasize meditation rather than prayer. Buddhism began as a reform movement within Hinduism; and its religious objects may be compared with those which feature in Hindu worship (q.v.). Some of the Hindu gods remain in Buddhism, so that it is not atheistic but perhaps 'transtheistic', since the gods Indra and Brahmā which figure in Buddhist texts are subordinate to the Buddha. To this day many, perhaps all, Buddhist temples in Ceylon have images of at least two Hindu gods, usually Vishnu and Indra (Sakka), though they are often behind curtains. But Kataragama (or Skanda), second son of the great Hindu deity Shiva, is the most popular god of the Hindus of Ceylon and his temples are visited by Buddhists to pay reverence and make vows.

In Buddhism it is the Buddha or Buddhas who are pre-eminent, even in the conservative Theravāda Buddhism of South-east Asia. The gods exist, as part of the world of beings, above most men except monks, but the Buddha is supreme, 'the teacher of gods and men' and the 'god above the gods', as the texts call him. Although in monkish theory the Buddha was a man, who is now dead, and only one in a series of Buddhas, yet in practice from olden times till now he is the supreme object of worship. It was the first lay convert, therefore about 500-400 B C, who is said to have invoked the Threefold Refuge, or the Three Jewels, which are still the daily expression of Theravāda Buddhist devotion: 'I go to the Buddha for refuge, I go to the Doctrine (*dharma*) for refuge, I go to the Order (*sangha*) for refuge.'

The earliest centres of Buddhist devotion were probably small *stūpas*, relic-holders, containing some fragment of the Buddha's body or an object associated with him or his disciples. Already at the cremation of Gautama the Buddha, eight cities are said to have shared his relics. Buddhism was established in Ceylon by the arrival of the collar-bone and begging-bowl of the Buddha, and a shoot of the Bo-tree under which he had been enlightened. Relics not only show the teacher to have been historical, but even more convey his power. All great temples claim some outstanding relic, and one was brought to England in 1964 by the Prime Minister of Ceylon to hallow a new Buddhist temple in Chiswick. In Ceylon the relic-holders have developed into dome-shaped buildings, *dāgobas*, which are called pagodas in Burma and beyond. Some great *dāgobas* are over a hundred feet high and made of brick. The relic is enshrined in the depths, but unseen by most visitors who lay their gifts of flowers, incense and money in small shrine rooms full of images. Burmese pagodas and Thai wats have spires above the images and wide courtyards for worshippers.

Images are of the Buddha in various postures, meditating, teaching or passing into ultimate Nirvāna. In making the images, great care is devoted to painting in the eyes, a dangerous operation which reveals the power of the being represented. In front of these images, monks and laymen meditate and repeat sacred texts from the extensive Buddhist scriptures. But prayers are also offered. One widely known prayer in Ceylon, in the Pāli liturgical language, is used daily at the Temple of the Tooth, the greatest relic in the town of Kandy: 'Forgive me my transgression committed through careless-ness by body, word or thought, O Tathāgata (Buddha) of great wisdom' (R. F. Gom-brich, *Precept and Practice*, 1971, p. 140). The significance of such a prayer is that it not only reveals religious worship, but contains an appeal to cancel sin which in theory might be held to depend on the individual's own efforts in conquering Karma.

Although there have been and will be other Buddhas, yet Theravāda texts say that there can only be one Buddha in this present long world-eon, and in practice he holds the centre of worship in monotheistic fashion. In Northern Mahāyāna Buddhism, however, in Tibet, China, Japan, Korea and Vietnam, there are countless Buddhas and Bodhi-sattvas, 'beings of enlightenment', to whom men pray for help and salvation. Amitābha or Amida, Buddha of 'infinite light', rules in the Buddha-fields or Western Paradise to which he guides the faithful over the sea of sorrows. Avalokita, who 'looks down', be-comes Kwanyin and Kwannon in China and Japan, not a goddess but a gracious Bodhi-sattva who 'hears the cry' and gives children. Maitreya, the Buddha to come, is the fat jolly figure depicted with money-bags and giving fortune.

Tibet has been noted for its prayer and praising wheels, prayer flags, prayer walls, and common invocation: *Om mani padme hum*, 'Hail to the jewel in the lotus', the doctrine in the scripture. In China and Japan, the Pure Land schools repeat the names of Amida endlessly on great rosaries and their prayer is adoration rather than petition. In Japan also, great Buddhist temples were built for regular congregational worship com-parable to that of Western religions.

Much Buddhist worship is individual and occasional, with invocations at home and visits to pagodas when time permits. But great festivals are held on anniversaries of events in the lives of the Buddha or Buddhas, and at ancient national ceremonies such as

the famous Perahera festival in Ceylon in August, where processions of four gods join up with that of the sacred Tooth. There are also important feasts for the dead, to ensure their rest and blessing, since although Nirvāna is the goal, it is far distant. In China, where many temples have been destroyed or turned into museums, ceremonies for the departed remain and Buddhist texts are used.

The Sangha, the church and monastic order, is not a priesthood, though monks have been teachers and leaders of the religion in Theravāda lands. In Mahāyāna countries there are Buddhist priests, often married, who officiate in temples, while monks may also participate or meditate and teach in monas-teries. But for monks and laity Buddhism is not merely an ethic but a religion of devotion and salvation.

S. Dutt, *Buddhist Monks and Monasteries of India*, 1962; C. Eliot, *Hinduism and Buddhism*, 1921; R. F. Gombrich, *Precept and Practice*, 1971; K. W. Morgan, ed., *The Path of the Buddha*, 1956; E. G. Parrinder, ed., *Man and His Gods*, 1971; E. G. Parrinder, *Worship in the World's Religions*, 1961; K. L. Reichelt, *Meditation and Piety in the Far East*, 1953; M. E. Spiro, *Buddhism and Society*, 1971.

GEOFFREY PARRINDER

Burial

The solemn interment of the dead is a practice found in almost all the great religions. Christian funeral rites express the church's care for the departed, its belief in the resurrec-tion and its reverence for the body as sharing in redemption.

1. *The Early Church*. Funeral rites consisted of five main items, of which certain were in pointed contrast to contemporary pagan customs. (*a*) Prayer in the house – the corpse was washed and anointed and swathed in white linen to the accompaniment of prayers. (*b*) Procession – whereas the Romans chose night for interment because of a belief that a funeral was of evil omen, the Christians chose the daytime, and, wearing white garments, sang psalms of hope and alleluias of victory. Palm leaves were carried, together with lights, and incense was burned – all expressing the idea of triumph over death. (*c*) Office – a short service of praise and thanksgiving, around the body, including Bible readings and psalms. (*d*) Eucharist – the celebration

expressed the belief in the communion that still exists between the living and the dead. The kiss of peace (q.v.) was given to the corpse. (e) Interment – the corpse was placed in the grave with feet towards the east as a sign of hope in the coming of the Sun of Righteousness (see **Orientation**).

An agape (q.v.) often followed, and on the third, ninth and fortieth days afterwards friends and relatives met to join in psalms, hymns and prayers. The procedure was not immediately stereotyped and differences are to be noted depending upon whether the procession went to the church or directly from the house to the cemetery. The whole was characterized by the note of peace and hope, confidence in the felicity of the departed and the certainty that death had erected no real barrier.

EDITOR

2. *Orthodox.* 'Death is swallowed up in victory' (I Cor. 15.54). Christ is risen! (Orthodox Christians exchange this greeting with one another for the entire forty days between Easter and Ascension Day.) This fact, the central point of the Christian 'Good News' (see in particular Acts 2-4, or I Cor. 15.3-7, the resurrection of Christ was the central point of the apostolic proclamation after Pentecost), is the cardinal preoccupation of the worship of the Orthodox Church. All of Orthodox liturgy is permeated by the celebration of the resurrection of Christ from the dead. 'If Christ has not been raised, then our preaching is in vain and your faith is in vain' (I Cor. 15.14). Around this inner pattern, the whole liturgical life of the Orthodox Church unfolds.

In this scheme of things the Orthodox rite of burial is no exception. While the burial service imparts the whole of the Orthodox view concerning anthropology, i.e. paradise and man's original beauty and calling before God, the fall and its destructive effect on man, the full reality of death, the incarnation, the power of Christ's own death and resurrection, and the eschaton, all is reduced to the basic questions of death or life. Is there ultimately tragedy or victory, death or resurrection? During the course of the Orthodox rite of burial these questions are both posed and answered.

The character of death is exposed in all its realism. The Orthodox burial rite does not avoid the fact of death, brush it casually aside

in the 'joy' of the resurrection, or poetically explain it away. It is the final enemy and the greatest tragedy to confront man. Not forgotten in the inner reasoning of the service are the moments when Christ himself, the 'Resurrection and the Life' (John 11.25), wept before the tomb of his dead friend, Lazarus (John 11.35), and later prayed in Gethsemane that the cup of his own passion and death might be removed (Luke 22.39-44). John Damascene unflinchingly describes the reality of death in one of the hymns which he composed for the burial service: 'I weep and I lament, when I contemplate death, and see our beauty, fashioned after the image of God, lying in the tomb disfigured, dishonoured, bereft of form' ('The Order for the Burial of the Dead' in I. F. Hapgood, *Service Book of the Holy Orthodox-Catholic Apostolic Church,* [3]1956).

During the burial service the deceased lies in the centre of the church facing the altar. The coffin is generally open so that the body is in full view. The 'disfigured, dishonoured, bereft' form spoken of in the above anthem, however, is not just man's body (this is especially true in view of the funeral practices which really beautify the corpse). 'It is the whole of man. Here the ultimate tragedy of death is revealed. Death destroys man, not just man's body. Man is the unity of soul and body. Death separates the two and ontologically mutilates man. It makes man's body a corpse and his soul a ghost. In effecting this breakdown of man as man created by God, death is the greatest sign of man's separation from God' (Georges Florovsky). Such are the sober and realistic categories in which the Orthodox burial service reveals the character of death.

The open evaluation of death leads to the true appreciation of Christ's resurrection. The great tragedy is overcome by an even greater victory. Christ shatters death by entering into its very depth, by 'trampling down death by death' (*Troparion*, or main hymn, of the Easter liturgical cycle). He who rises is he who was within the tomb. Thus, during the rite of the burial of the dead the light of the resurrection begins to shine forth. The order of the service is that of mattins, the same resurrectional type used on Sundays (Sunday is the weekly day of commemorating the resurrection in the liturgical cycle of the Orthodox Church) throughout the year as well as on Great and Holy Saturday, when

Christ reposed in the tomb. The clergy wear light-coloured vestments (q.v.). Liturgical expressions typically used by the Orthodox Church as signs of the victorious presence of the risen Christ, e.g. an abundance of lights, burning candles and incense, dominate the external actions of the service. The body of the deceased in particular is repeatedly censed as a sign that in it, 'the redemption of our bodies' (Rom. 8.23) has already begun. The deceased is a baptized, chrismated and communing member of the body of Christ. Sacramentally, his whole substance is permeated by him who, having risen, is 'the first fruits of all those who have fallen asleep' (I Cor. 15.20).

A large portion of the text of the service is occupied by Ps. 119, the praise of the law of God. The love of this law is the love and obedience to him in whom it is fulfilled – Christ. As the gospel section (John 5.24-30) read at the service says: 'He who hears my word and believes in him who sent me has eternal life' (John 5.24).

The epistle section (I Thess. 4.13-17) strongly emphasizes the hope engendered through Christ's resurrection: '. . . that you may not grieve as others do who have no hope' (I Thess. 4.13). The 'funeral dirge' of the service is the singing of 'alleluia', that ecstatic Hebrew word used in this case to glorify the presence of Christ – even in death ('The Order for the Burial of the Dead' in Hapgood, p. 383).

In the same experiential way that the Orthodox Church understands Christ's resurrection, i.e. as the gradual yet shattering overcoming of death from within death, the Orthodox burial service reveals the destiny of each member of the church. He comes to death in all its reality, but already has the token of his deliverance through his sacramental unity with the abundance of life, Christ himself. The inner pattern for the whole of Orthodox liturgy remains the hymn of Easter:

Christ is risen from the dead,
trampling down death by death
and upon those in the tombs bestowing life.

(The rite described in this essay is that used for the burial of laymen. The Orthodox Church also has special rites to be used for the burial of clergy and children, along with variations to be applied during Easter Week.)

PAUL LAZOR

3. *Medieval and Roman Catholic.* This topic requires a threefold division: the Middle Ages, the *Rituale Romanum* of 1614 and the 1969 *Ordo Exequiarum.*

(*a*) *The Middle Ages.* In the early Middle Ages the funeral liturgy consisted essentially of the preparation of the body for burial, accompanied by psalms and prayers, the procession with the body from home to church, a period of prayer for the dead person which might include the eucharist, and finally the procession from the church to the grave and the interment. By this time the ancient custom of continuous psalmody for the dead person had become ritualized in the form of the office of the dead, consisting of vespers, mattins and lauds (qq.v.) This office was sung daily in addition to the normal office of the day. The word *Dirige*, beginning the first antiphon of mattins, gives us the English 'dirge'.

Later the preparation of the body for burial is accomplished in private, without liturgical accompaniment, and the eucharist becomes a normal part of the funeral liturgy. It is followed by responsories, prayers of absolution and the incensation and aspersion of the corpse. These rites indicate an increased stress on need for forgiveness and fear of judgment, and also the value attached to the priest's prayer of absolution, an extension of his power to absolve the living.

These developments find excellent expression in the *Dies irae* chant, composed in the twelfth or thirteenth century, and they modify somewhat the atmosphere of joy and hope so characteristic of the ancient funeral liturgy, which looked forward to the resurrection of the body and entrance into God's kingdom. The medieval liturgy is conscious rather of sin and death, purgatory and judgment, thinking of the soul's destiny rather than the body's.

(*b*) *The Rituale Romanum of 1614.* Our sources for the medieval burial rites are mainly monastic, but the Roman ritual's burial rite is a simplified version of the medieval one, designed for use in parishes. While permitting local adaptation it remains the first official and universal funeral rite.

It begins with the processional transfer of the body from home to church, accompanied with psalmody. After the reception of the body into church the office of the dead follows, in whole or in part, though it is acknowledged that circumstances may prevent this. Mass is followed by a single absolution, after which the body is taken out to burial, the traditional antiphons *In paradisum* and *Chorus angelorum* being sung. Interment is preceded by the canticle (q.v.) *Benedictus*, versicles and a prayer. The rite retains some of the best of the ancient burial chants and prayers which stress welcome into paradise and bodily resurrection, yet the medieval emphasis on the need for forgiveness and fear of judgment remains.

(c) *The Ordo Exequiarum of 1969.* The Second Vatican Council's Liturgy Constitution called for the revision of funeral rites to express the Paschal character of Christian death, while taking account of local customs. Accordingly, the new funeral rite envisages three types of service, the traditional one with prayers at home, in church and at the graveside, a second form in the cemetery chapel and at the graveside, more in line with German custom, and a third form taking place entirely in the home, in accordance with conditions in Africa and elsewhere. The rite is extremely flexible, with great scope for local variations.

Provision is made for funeral vigil in the home, and it is no longer presumed that the eucharist will always be celebrated as part of the burial rite. The absolution after mass is transformed into a final farewell to the deceased. There is a wide choice of readings, prayers and chants, prayers for the mourners are included, and the whole rite expresses Christian hope in our share in Christ's resurrection and enjoyment of God's presence in his kingdom.

It may be noted that cremation has been permitted for Roman Catholics since 1963.

BRIAN NEWNS

4. *Anglican.* In medieval England, burial rites had two distinguishing features, their complicated and drawn-out structure and their purgatorial theology. Thus when Cranmer put the service into English in 1549 he simplified its structure and assimilated material from the previous vespers and mattins into the 'office'. The rite began with the churchyard procession, and this 'office' in church might come before or after the committal. Finally came proper introit, collect, epistle and gospel for the (presumably optional) eucharist. In doctrine, cautious petitions for the departed were retained, but with the excision of mass-sacrifice (let alone the earlier confiscation of chantries) votive masses for the dead ceased. The atmosphere now reflected a new emphasis on rest in Christ and resurrection to life. The service was generally directed to giving hope to the living, rather than indicating the deliverance from sufferings of the departed.

1552 worked out the logic of 1549 more exactly. The service was further truncated, and was performed wholly at the graveside. The procession to the grave led almost immediately to the committal, and to an 'office' consisting solely of the reading from I Cor. 15, lesser litany, Lord's Prayer and two other prayers, one of which was the 1549 eucharistic collect (there was now no eucharist). Petitions for the departed disappeared. For the living there was prayer that they should be joined with the departed in the general resurrection to life. (The 1552 communion service dropped all mention of the departed.) Petitions for the departed (though perhaps theoretically a possible private practice) were now contrary to the policy of the Church of England for public worship. They escaped condemnation in the 1571 Articles, but the Homily on Prayer discountenanced them as lacking commandment in scripture, and as devoid of rationale once purgatory is rejected.

The 1552 rite, revived in 1559, remained unchanged till 1645 (though the 1637 Scottish eucharist reintroduced remembrance of the departed). Then the Puritan Westminster *Directory of Public Worship* forbade all burial services, and bodies were to be interred without ceremony, prayer, scripture or preaching.

At the 1661 Savoy Conference the Puritans objected that the 1552 rite was too assured about the state of the departed. They gained the addition of a 'the' to the committal – thus giving to the living hope not specifically of the deceased person's resurrection to life, but more objectively in *the* (general) resurrection of all at the last day. A new rubric disallowed use of the rite over the unbaptized, the excommunicate and suicides.

Other additions were made. The service could now be read in church and psalmody preceded the reading of I Cor. 15 straight after the procession. The committal followed, and the 1552 'office' (except the reading, but including 'The Grace . . . etc.') completed the service.

The hundred years since 1870 have seen great changes in the ecclesiastical and social context within which burials are conducted, and the following in particular have inevitably affected the liturgical evolution not only in England, but also in the Anglican Communion around the world.

First, the gulf between church and society has broadened visibly and continues to do so. Yet the great bulk of society still expects a Christian burial, and this has set up a tension for the church (and particularly for the Church of England).

Secondly, the church building has been slowly but surely set aside from the majority of funerals in England. Until the second part of the last century parish churches generally had their own churchyards attached, and the committal would take place under the walls of the church building. Then, as churchyards filled and were closed under the pressures of fast-increasing population, corporation cemeteries, divorced from the churches and boasting their own chapels, slowly took their place. In recent decades these in turn have given way to crematoria, and cremation appears to be the almost invariable future practice. Curiously, in a crematorium chapel, the 1662 sequence can once again be followed, as the 'committal' can come naturally before the prayers, which is difficult when a service is split between church and graveside. However, the practice of cremation calls in question the suitability of a committal 'to the ground' and 'earth to earth'. The wording has to be amended.

Thirdly, the practice of the last century has seen a growing flexibility introduced. Clergy who have treated the requirements of the Act of Uniformity fairly loosely in their Sunday services are hardly likely to take it very seriously in the cemetery or crematorium chapel on a weekday. The pastoral situation has often cried out for more relevant liturgical material (e.g. at the funeral of a child). And liturgical revision has inevitably followed what was already being done without controversy. Thus the 1928 rite (now authorized as the Church of England's *First Series* rite) provided other psalms, alternative readings, prayers for the bereaved and other occasional material. Overseas revisions have gone the same way, and there is often renewed provision for communion services at funerals.

Fourthly, there has been a reintroduction of petitions for the departed. Partly this arose through the doctrinal convictions of the 'Catholic Revivalists' of the last century,

partly through a growing national sentiment (e.g. in the First World War) that wished to say *something* about the departed, while being hesitant to state they were undoubtedly in bliss. The petitions have usually had a rationale which excluded belief in purgatory, and with that exclusion have some show of primitive, and possibly even Anglican, precedent. In Scotland, America and other 'Catholic' provinces the reintroduction has usually gone unchallenged. But Evangelicals have always contested the move. Thus the Church of England's *First Series* rite only just secured the requisite two-thirds majority in the House of Laity in 1966, and the Liturgical Commission's *Second Series* rite (which also raised the problem of petitions for the *un*faithful departed) was never put to the final vote in the same House in 1968. The dialogue necessitated by such controversies led to a more satisfactory 'remembrance' of the departed in *Second Series* communion. In January 1971 the Archbishops' Commission on Christian Doctrine published their Report *Prayer and the Departed*. The intention of the recommendation here was to produce cautious and unitive proposals in which the whole Church of England could agree. The Liturgical Commission's *Third Series* burial rite has been drawn in accordance with these proposals at the doctrinally sensitive points.

C. O. BUCHANAN

5. *Baptist*. No common practice prevails in Baptist memorial, including burial, services. Local custom usually dictates the time, place and form. Also, Baptist services tend to be similar to those in the other free churches.

Generally the service is in two parts: the first in the church or funeral chapel and the second at the graveside or crematorium. An ordained minister generally conducts the service, but if no ordained minister is available a lay minister, designated by the congregation, may conduct the service.

The service at the church or funeral chapel begins with the minister saying a number of suitable scriptural texts, followed by a hymn, choral or solo musical number. After a prayer the scripture lessons are read. These may be followed with the *Gloria Patri*, a doxology or a hymn of affirmation. The minister then usually interprets a scripture passage dealing with Christ's victory over death. He follows this with a prayer and a blessing. Occasionally a eulogy will be included.

The service of committal at the grave or crematorium begins after the people have assembled with several scripture sentences followed by the words of committal, a prayer and a benediction.

Increasingly Baptists along with others are moving away from the 'funeral' service with the body present to memorial services in which family and friends gather to remember with thanksgiving the life of the one who has departed. For such a service the setting may be a home with an informal service of readings, prayers and words of remembrance. Or a more formal service is held as part of the regular Lord's Day service and incorporated as an act of thanksgiving and remembrance for 'the saint (or saints) who from their labours rest'. When such a service is held, then a family memorial usually takes place at the time of death.

Present-day Baptists generally have no special places of burial such as 'Baptist cemeteries'. They generally use the common grounds provided by the community or a burial association.

JOHN E. SKOGLUND

6. *Congregationalist.* In their earliest days the Independents had deep doubts about the propriety of burial services, partly because they led to superstition and partly because they were · the occasion of hypocritical eulogies.

In modern days these dangers are overcome by services that avoid elaborate eulogies, or, in many cases, have no eulogy at all, and by keeping strictly to the biblical promises. The emphasis in 'burial' services (English) or 'funeral' services (American) is on scriptural readings and prayers that reiterate the promises of the risen Christ, the enduring covenant love of the divine Father, and the comfort of Christian friends in the hope of the gospel, with a solemn reminder of the transitoriness and accountability of human life.

· According to the most recent English Congregational service-book, *A Book of Services and Prayers* (1959), provision is made for three separate but related burial services. There is first a short, simple, and intimate family service in the home. This consists of the reading of declarations of notable divine promises and affirmations of faith from the scriptures, including Ps. 23, and

of prayers for faith and hope and comfort, concluding with the Lord's Prayer. The minister usually offers one or more extempore prayers.

The second service, no longer restricted to family and close friends, but now including former associates in many walks of life, takes place either at the church or cemetery chapel. It may well include a hymn (frequently the favourite hymn of the deceased), and a short address, especially if the deceased were a pillar of the church and community. It will include scripture lessons and prayers which will normally include thanksgiving for our hope and assurance of eternal life through the gospel; a prayer of grateful memories; supplication for the mourners; and a petition for grace to live the life of faith (*ibid.*, p. 78).

The third service is held either at the graveside or in the crematorium. The form of committal is that of the *BCP* 'For as much as it hath pleased Almighty God of his great mercy to take unto himself the soul of our dear *brother* here departed, we therefore commit *his* body to the ground: earth to earth, ashes to ashes, dust to dust; in sure and certain hope of resurrection to everlasting life through our Lord Jesus Christ . . .' At a cremation the wording of the committal is changed to read, 'we therefore commit *his* body to the elements . . .'

The same service-book also provides two very moving alternatives for use on special occasions. The one is for the burial of a child. The other is 'A Service for use in Circumstances of Deep Distress', including the burial of a suicide. Each is as compassionate as is appropriate.

HORTON DAVIES

7. *Jehovah's Witnesses.* Burial services by Witnesses are simple and restrained. They are designed to give comfort to the bereaved and explain the Bible's hope for the dead.

Since the congregation has no separate clergy, any suitable male speaker may be invited to take the service. In March 1888, *Zion's Watch Tower* carried the article 'How Shall We Bury Our Dead?' (pp. 7, 8) with suggestions for a funeral discourse. Nowadays a printed outline is provided. The most recent (January 1966) has five sub-headings: God's purpose in creating man; why man dies; condition of the dead; hope for the dead; and, Kingdom will accomplish God's purpose towards man. The speaker, of course, varies the outline as he chooses. The discourse does not exceed thirty minutes in length.

Witnesses do not believe the Bible teaches inherent immortality of the soul (Ezek. 18.4; I Cor. 15.6; etc.). They have hope in a resurrection for the unconscious dead (Acts 24.15). Those dead whom God holds in his memory will be restored to life. They are in 'memorial tombs' (mnemeion, e.g. John 5.28; cogn. mimnesko, mneia, remind, remembrance, etc.). It is scripturally proper to speak of a 'dead soul' (e.g. Num. 19.13 [Heb.]; Rev. 16.3 [Gk]). Mourners look to the dead soul's resurrection.

The restraint mentioned above extends to clothing worn and to mourning. In the spirit of Matt. 6.16-18 mourners do not normally wear black. Of extended mourning, The Watchtower (15 September 1958, p. 575) said: 'It would seem, therefore, that a Christian who has advanced to a mature appreciation of these things [Christ's resurrection, his enthronement, and the resurrection hope] would not feel called upon to carry on mourning along with the wearing of special types of clothing as an outward show . . . [However,] it is his own personal conscience that must guide the course he takes (I Thess. 4.13, 14).'

Cremation is left to the individual conscience. 'As to how the dead body shall be disposed of is a matter of no consequence to the dead, but the proper disposal of the remains of our departed friends is a mark of our respect and affection' (Zion's Watch Tower, March 1888). And more recently, 'So whether a body returns to the elements by decaying in the ground or is burned to ashes does not in any way affect God's ability to resurrect the person . . . it remains a matter for personal decision' (The Watchtower, 1 July 1965, p. 416).

No special burial grounds are used. 'The Christian will not be as concerned about the place of burial as he is about the prospect of a resurrection' (Awake!, 22 September 1965, p. 7).

Rather than elaborate ritual, the death of a Witness is followed by practical consideration for the deceased's family, who are much comforted in the hope of the resurrection.

A. HELEY

8. *Lutheran.* Luther and the Reformers had more criticisms to make of the Roman Catholic rite of burial than of any of the other traditional offices of the church. As early as the writing 'To the Christian Nobility of the German Nation' (1520; *Martin Luthers Werke*, Weimar, 1883 ff. = WA 6,444 f.), Luther vigorously attacked masses for the dead and vigils. In a late writing, a collection of Christian hymns for funerals, he regards vigils, requiems, funeral pomp and purgatory as 'papistical abominations' which must be completely rejected because they contradict scripture, especially in the fact that their help is enlisted to influence the fate of the dead (1542; WA 35,478; *cf. Apolog. der Conf. Aug.* 24, 89 ff.). On the Reformed side this radical rejection of traditional rites meant that for a long time burial was left to the personal initiative of the members of the family, the guilds or the authorities; the church did not co-operate. The same tendency can also be found, to begin with, in Lutheran areas. But very soon a criticism of this attitude makes itself felt: having laid aside 'superstitious pomp of the dead', people treat them 'quite bestially' (Strasbourg 1533). However, for some decades there is no liturgical formulary to lay down the details of a funeral. Luther produced manuals for baptism and marriage, but no order for funeral services; he was content – as has been said – to publish a few German and Latin chorales for this purpose. The lack of an order of service authorized by Luther is presumably the reason why there is a confusing number and variety of forms and orders for burial in individual Lutheran churches and areas. This position has only been changed in the last few decades.

Nevertheless, some common principles and even some basic structures for funerals can be found in the sixteenth century. According to Luther, a funeral should serve to 'strengthen our faith and encourage the people to true devotion. For it is right and fitting that a funeral should be performed honourably, to the praise and honour of the joyful article of our faith, the resurrection of the dead' (WA 35, 479). Accordingly, from now on (a) the focal point is no longer to be the dead body but faith in the resurrection, which is to be expressed in hymn, prayer and sermon. In addition, (b) even in early times, burial was regarded as an act of love by the congregation towards the dead man and his family. 'For the dead are still our brothers, and have not fallen from our community by death; we still remain members of a single body'; therefore it is one of the duties of 'civic neighbourliness' to accompany the dead to the grave (Church order of Schwäbisch Hall 1526; Richter I, 47). Finally, (c) burial is to remind us of our own deaths and to cause us to lead an appropriate way of life (for these three points see Württemberg 1536; Richter I, 273).

Traditional features retained are the ringing of the church bells, either at the moment of death or at the burial, and the walk to the grave. The church ordinances of the sixteenth century prohibit 'secret burials'. Pastor, verger, teacher, school children and as far as possible one person from each house in the community are to join the family in accompanying the body to the grave, usually in a strictly prescribed order. On the way to and at the grave, hymns are to be sung by the congregation or at least by the children, 'not mourning hymns nor sorrowful, but comforting hymns about the forgiveness of sins, rest, sleep, the life and resurrection of departed Christians' (Luther, WA 35, 478 f.). It seems that at the beginning people were content simply to sing hymns at the burial. This expressed the fact that it was the congregation that bore the body to the grave and confessed its faith in the resurrection. Prayers and a sermon were added relatively soon; there is not always explicit mention of either, but in the course of time they will have become the rule, though with exceptions.

According to Schulz, some forty-five funeral prayers have been preserved from the sixteenth century; they have a christological basis and express faith in the resurrection, ask for a strengthening of faith in earthly life and give thanks for the life of the departed. At first there are only hints of a prayer for the departed at the burial itself (e.g. Württemberg 1536, Richter I, 273); they occur occasionally later (e.g. Hessen 1566 and 1574; Sehling 8, 336 and 450). The coffin or body is at first lowered into the grave to the singing of a hymn. Only later are affirmations made, e.g. 'Earth thou art . . .' (following Gen. 3.19; Dessau 1532, Sehling 1.2, 541), Rev. 14.13 (Pfalz-Neuburg 1543, Sehling 13, 90) or, as earth is thrown three times: 'Of dust thou art made and to dust must thou return. May the Lord Jesus Christ raise thy body and soul (!) that thou mayest rise again with the righteous on the Last Day. Amen' (Waldeck 1556; Richter II, 171).

To begin with, a sermon was only preached in the case of people of standing (princes and other notables), usually not at the burial itself but as a memorial sermon some time afterwards. Generally speaking, if there was a sermon at all, short admonitions were thought to be sufficient, often in connection with the readings I Thess. 4.13-18 and John 11.21-27. In the course of time the sermon became an essential part of the funeral; thus the *Kursächsische Kirchenordnung* of 1580 contains four funeral sermons, two each for adults and young people, which are to be read in the church after the burial (Sehling I, 1, 371 ff.). At this particular point, however, ominous differences arise at an early stage. According to the *Wittenberger Kirchenordnung* of 1533, 'common men' are to be buried without bells, 'citizens of middle degree' with the singing of school children, and 'honourable people' with a procession and the sound of the great bells (Sehling I, 1, 195). As early as 1540 it is mentioned on many occasions that differing fees are exacted for the different forms of funeral. This is related above all to the sermon: 'funeral sermons' or 'eulogies' are delivered only on the payment of an appropriate fee; otherwise, people have to be content with a brief 'dismissal' or a mere 'blessing'. This shameful classification of funerals lasted right down to the beginning of our century; it involved not only the sermon, but the whole form of the funeral.

Leaving aside new hymns and prayers for funerals, the structure of the funeral service hardly altered over the next two centuries, down to the time of the Enlightenment. This was not, however, the case with funeral sermons, where they were required and given. In the sixteenth century the preaching was predominantly biblical and christological, but in the seventeenth century a strong personal element was added, among other things by the inclusion of a *curriculum vitae*; at the same time, funeral sermons took on a learned tone, used allegory and often occupied an intolerable amount of time. A culogy of the dead person took precedence over what were originally the main themes of funeral sermons (the proclamation of the last things, preparation for a happy death) (E. Winkler). At the time of the Enlightenment the biblical orientation of the funeral sermon disappeared still more; at its centre stood the life of the dead person and the parting from him, both presented in the baroque and sentimental style of the time.

In many places there was no funeral sermon at all. This was connected with an extremely strange development. Silent 'interments', once provided for suicides, notorious sinners, etc. took the place of public funerals. It became the custom to inter the dead at a late hour of the evening or at midnight, by torchlight, with only family and friends present, and usually without any participation by the pastor. The place of the funeral sermon was taken by the 'eulogy' of a friend at the graveside. The funeral service of the congregation in many cases, particularly in towns, became a family gathering. In addition, under the influence of the numerous private forms of service published and used, the hymns, prayers and words of committal were adapted to the language of the time. For example, one committal takes the following form: 'Take this body, mother earth, into thy protection under the oversight of almighty God! The day will surely come again when death must return even this its prey' (1802, according to P. Graff, II, 275).

Contradictory intentions arise with the movement for liturgical reform in the middle of the nineteenth century. Using portions of church orders from the sixteenth century, W. Löhe and others propose complete funeral services for the first time; their characteristics are that a number of passages are proposed as readings, and a large number of collects and prayers, especially the committal from King Edward VI's prayer book of 1552 (with a few alterations), are suggested. Most local churches in Germany shaped their funeral services along these lines about 1900. Usually the funeral begins – often after a biblical sentence – with Ps. 130 or another psalm; one or two lessons, for which a number of passages are suggested, are followed by the sermon (which has become a permanent feature) and a prayer, for which a few models are provided. At the graveside, the coffin is lowered with the committal from the prayer book, occasionally (as in Prussia, 1895) with the additional words: 'From the earth thou art taken, to the earth thou shalt return. Jesus Christ, our Redeemer, will raise you on the Last Day.' Here, too, a lesson and prayers are provided for. The service can begin at the grave and be continued in the church (or cemetery chapel) or vice versa. There is singing by the con-

gregation or a choir at appropriate places.

Some private forms of service have had an influence on the further shaping of the funeral by providing different psalms, scripture readings (sometimes made up of isolated verses from the Bible) and prayers depending on the life, status, age and sex of the dead person. Newer official forms, which have appeared since 1960, take up this suggestion; they offer a considerable number of introit psalms, readings, prayers, hymns and committal prayers to suit individual cases. The prayers aim at a modern form of expression, without always being successful. One leading funeral service is that in the *Agende für Evangelisch-Lutherische Kirchen und Gemeinden* (vol. III, 1964, pp. 155-222). First of all it has the ordinary forms for different places: (*a*) house of mourning or undertaker's chapel (greeting, collect, hymn, invitation to proceed to the cemetery); (*b*) cemetery chapel or church (introit hymn, biblical sentence, Ps. 130 or another, scriptural reading, hymn, sermon, possibly with *curriculum vitae*, hymn, prayer, invitation to proceed to the grave with Ps. 121.8); (*c*) at the grave (hymn, greeting, biblical sentence, committal ['Since it has pleased almighty God to call from this life our brother N., we lay his body in God's earth, that he may become again the earth from which he is taken: earth to earth, ashes to ashes, dust to dust. We commend our brother N. into God's hand. Jesus Christ will raise him on the last day. May he be gracious to him in judgment and assist him to his everlasting kingdom'], scripture reading I Cor. 15.42-44, 55-57; I Thess. 4.13-18; Rom. 14.7-9 or Rev. 21.1-5a, possibly an anthem; Lord's Prayer, a collect, possible Apostles' Creed, hymn and trinitarian blessing); the forms also contain suggestions for cremation and the committal of ashes. This is followed by a proper of about ten psalms, thirty readings (all from the New Testament) and about the same number of prayers, mostly with indications of individual usage.

The new forms produced by the Pfalz (1963), the Union Church (1964), Hessen and Nassau (1967), Baden (outline 1967) and Kurhessen-Waldeck (1970) are similar; some have alterations and a different and larger selection of psalms, readings and prayers. However, criticisms are already being voiced, especially of the antiquated language of the prayers and the committal sentences. Kurhessen-Waldeck form B (1970) presents a modern, very brief proposal, but it is not always adequate theologically. As always, the funeral sermon remains a problem; it has as many dangers as possibilities. (For full references to the authors cited above *see* the bibliography below.)

ALFRED NIEBERGALL

9. *Methodist*. John Wesley, in the Preface attached to some copies of *The Sunday Service of the Methodists*, 1784, said that he had omitted some sentences in the office for the burial of the dead. He had in fact omitted Ps. 39, the committal, and the prayer 'Almighty God, with whom we live, etc.'. These changes were largely in harmony with Puritan objections. In other respects Wesley followed almost exactly the *BCP*, 1662, of the Church of England. Methodist funerals were marked by a strong note of joy, as was shown by the use of such hymns as:

Rejoice for a brother deceased,
Our loss is his infinite gain.

In the following century these omitted passages were for the most part restored, often with some alterations, in the service books, both in America and in Britain. In England, Methodists in country districts are often buried in the Anglican parish churchyard, and the service was thus the Anglican service performed by an Anglican clergyman until a change in the law in 1880 made it permissible for burials to take place in such churchyards without the Church of England service and thus by a non-conformist minister.

In the present century there have been further changes. The current form for the United Methodist Church in America is in *The Book of Worship*, 1964; the British form is in *The Book of Offices*, 1936, but we describe rather the form authorized for experimental use in 1968. Both the American and the British forms have sentences, prayers (an addition to Anglican use), psalm(s), lesson(s) (parts of Ps. 90 and of I Cor. 15 being retained among a wider selection), optional sermon, prayers to conclude the service in church (an addition; the old custom was that the service had prayers only at the graveside). The British service has a further new feature designed to make the service in church more complete, namely a commendation of the deceased to God's mercy and wisdom. This was suggested by a similar Anglican proposal.

Both services have the optional use of the Apostles' Creed, but at different points. At the grave or in the crematorium, both services have sentences, committal (both services have variant forms to provide for different circumstances), Rev. 14.13, prayers. Both services have unambiguous prayers for the dead; they are, however, optional. Both services make special provision for the burial of a child. Funerals are much influenced by local customs. In practice the whole of the first part of the service is sometimes said in the home rather than the church.

A. RAYMOND GEORGE

10. *Old Catholic*. Rites for the burial of the dead differ in detail in the Old Catholic churches, and in addition, liturgical practice is influenced by regional and local customs. Nevertheless, some common features can be established. These, in essentials, are: blessing of the corpse and the grave, the recitation of appropriate psalms, intercessions for the dead and the bereaved, thanksgiving for God's grace towards the dead and through them to us. A eucharist often accompanies the funeral. All Souls' Day (q.v.) (2 November) is celebrated as a day of remembrance for all the departed.

As an example, we give a brief description of the form of funeral to be found in the Old Catholic Church of Germany.

The service opens with a prayer for blessing on the departed, after which the priest says an appropriate psalm. Then he delivers an address to the congregation. The Lord's Prayer, said together, follows the *Kyries*, and finally comes another prayer. At that point the coffin is sprinkled with holy water. The congregation then moves to the graveside, which is first blessed. The coffin is lowered, and the priest says Ps. 130, followed by the promise of the resurrection, 'I am the resurrection and the life' (John 11.25f.). Then follows the Lord's Prayer and another prayer. The priest sprinkles the grave with holy water, and in some places also censes it. Then he throws the first handful of earth into the grave. Once again he makes the sign of the cross over it, and then says a prayer for all the departed who lie in the cemetery and for the one whom God will next call home.

There are some alterations to this rite when the ceremony takes place in a crematorium, and at the burial of children. For a long time it has not been possible, in cities, to let the dead lie at home or to take them into church. Funerals are therefore usually held in the cemetery chapel.

In the Old Catholic Church in the Netherlands, it is in some places the custom to have a prayer-meeting with scripture reading, prayers and hymns selected by the officiating clergyman, on the eve of the burial. The official rite is made up of the requiem mass and burial prayers. The requiem mass is an almost literal translation from the Roman missal. As it was forbidden in the Netherlands to practise the Old Catholic faith openly between the beginning of the Reformation and 1800, and as it was only possible to do so secretly and in hidden churches, the different elements of the funeral are still gathered up into one continuous whole: bringing the body to the church, prayers in connection with the absolution after the mass and the ritual in the burial ground. This is usually said in the church building after the requiem mass (in former times, more often in the home of the dead person). After a month and after a year (and, if required, monthly and annually), the departed is remembered during the mass.

KURT PURSCH
A. E. RÜTHY
C. TOL

11. *Plymouth Brethren.* There is no distinctive order for the burial of the dead among the Brethren. Frequently, when a member of the fellowship dies, a service is held at his home or at the meeting-place which he attended, before the departure of the funeral procession for the ceremony, and a short committal service is held at the graveside. These services may be conducted by elders of his church or by friends of himself or of his family who are able to say what is appropriate for such an occasion. At these services emphasis is customarily laid on the faith in which the departed lived and died, and reference will be made to features of their Christian life, service and witness which can be commended as an example to others. It will be made clear that their friends' assurance of their eternal bliss is based not on their record or merit but on the faithfulness of God, in whom they had put their trust. Sometimes one or two suitable hymns of confidence and hope will be sung. Scriptures read will probably make mention of the immediate and present well-being of departed believers

as being 'absent from the body and at home with the Lord' (II Cor. 5.8) and of the coming day of resurrection and reunion at the Second Advent. Prayers for the dead are never heard, for it is not doubted that the dead in Christ do rest in peace; interesting situations arise, however, when an informal service is conducted jointly by (say) the vicar of the parish and a member of the Brethren; it is not unknown for the former to pray for the soul of the departed and the latter (presumably for the sake of Christian unity) to add a loud Amen.

Where the deceased has lived to a good age, or has been released from long illness and pain, this atmosphere of confidence and hope can make a burial service a remarkably joyful occasion. The confidence and hope will still be present, but the feeling and language will be different, at the burial of a child or young person, or of someone whose life has been tragically or suddenly cut short; yet the comfort of the scriptures will send the mourners away greatly strengthened in heart. Where the departed person is a known unbeliever, the character of the service will be perceptibly modified, but it will be emphasized that the only hope for eternal life lies in the Saviour who died and rose again.

In some areas (e.g. in the north of Scotland) it is taken for granted that a funeral service will be the occasion for a full-blown proclamation of the gospel, but this is not confined to one denomination.

Cremation is chosen only exceptionally, though probably in a larger proportion of instances over the years.

F. F. BRUCE

12. *Reformed.* In the early Reformed Church the procedure at burial was influenced by the medieval background and reaction against it so that in some places no service was held at the grave. This appears to have been the practice at Strasbourg to, at least, 1533, when at the first Synod of Strasbourg the Kirchenpfleger protested against the custom for its irreverence, citing the OT patriarchs and early Christian usage (*Arch. S. Thos*, 45.1, fol. 87). It was ordered that a pastor should be present at burial, but no order for burial was drawn up until 1537. It consisted of scripture reading, exhortation, silent or free prayer, collect and almsgiving (Hubert, *Die stras. lit. Ordnungen*, pp. 128-130).

This would have been Bucer's practice, and he makes similar provision in the *Con-*

sultatio he prepared for Cologne in 1543 (*Con.* fol. ccxliv). Calvin would have known it, but no such provision is made in either his Strasbourg or Genevan liturgies (*Op.* vi, 172-208). The Genevan *Ordonnances ecclesiastiques* (1541) simply says:

> The dead are to be buried decently in the place appointed. The attendance and company are left to each man's discretion. It will be good that the carriers be warned by us to discourage all superstitions contrary to the Word of God . . .

Calvin approved an 'appropriate sermon' being given 'in the churchyard' (*Letter to Farel*, 1543), and considered 'the Spirit no less attentive to the burial rites . . . than to the chief mysteries of the Faith' (*Inst.* III. xxv. 8), so his practice may not have been so severe as in the *Ordonannces* but have approximated to Pullain's *Liturgia Sacra*:

> The corpse shall be carried by trusty men from the city to the cemetery. The whole church shall follow with great modesty, the pastor or other minister leading. When it is come to the place where the body is to be placed in the ground, a brief address concerning death and the resurrection of the dead is given, with commendation of the deceased, if he has any virtues from which to edify the church. Prayer shall be made for the church that as God gives us this transient life so we may pass through death into his Kingdom, and that he will raise all through Christ at the last day to immortality. The people shall be dismissed with an admonition that they give an offering for the relief of the poor.

The *Form of Prayers* (1556) of the English congregation in Geneva ordered:

> The corpse is reverently brought to the grave, accompanied with the congregation, without any further ceremonies, which being buried, the minister goeth to the church, if it be not far off, and maketh some comfortable exhortation to the people, touching death and resurrection.

This was incorporated into the Scottish *Book of Common Order* (*BCO*, 1564), adding after 'minister' the words 'if he be present and required'. This leaves the question of a service open, as had the first *Book of Discipline* in 1560, although the General Assembly in 1562 had enacted:

> That one uniform order shall be taken or kept in ministration of the Sacraments, and solemnization of the Marriages and Burial of the Dead, according to the Kirk of Geneva.

Funeral services were not uncommon in Scotland, although in some places there were none, until with the growth of Brownism the Glasgow Assembly in 1638 decided 'to discharge funeral sermons, as savouring of superstition'. In England, the *BCP* contained a burial office, but among the Puritans there is evidence for 'sermon' only or 'singing of a psalm' only, and no service at all.

The debate on burial in the Westminster Assembly show the Scots to be opposed to 'sermons', but that the opinion of the divines was that there should be liberty concerning whether 'something might be said at the very interment of the body' and that the clause 'without any ceremony' did not prevent a minister 'at putting the body in the ground' saying, 'We commit the body to the ground, etc.' (Lightfoot, *Works*, xiii, p. 340). The text of the Westminster *Directory of Public Worship* adopts the extreme Puritan position, but tries to keep open the door for the 'positive' approach demanded by Palmer, Whitaker and Marshall:

> When any person departeth this life, let the dead body, upon the day of burial, be decently attended from the house to the place appointed for public burial, and there immediately interred, without any ceremony. . . .
>
> For that, praying, reading both in going to, and at the grave, have been grossly abused, are no way beneficial to the dead, and have proved many ways hurtful to the living, therefore let all such things be laid aside.
>
> Howbeit, we judge it very convenient, that the Christian friends, which accompany the dead body to the place appointed for public burial, do apply themselves to meditations and conferences suitable to the occasion; and that the minister, as upon other occasions, so at this time, if he be present, may put them in remembrance of their duty.

This, together with the triumph of Independency during the Commonwealth, resulted in a position where it was possible to write in 1867 of Scotland (equally true of

Ireland and England):

In many, if not most, parts of the country, the religious observance at present consists of prayer alone . . . the solemn reading of the pure Word of God, without which no Protestant Service is true to its character, or complete – is generally omitted . . . The religious Service at funerals . . . is, as a general rule, confined to the house of mourning, except on the occasion of the death of ministers, and of others who have filled positions of special prominence, when sometimes a Service is held at the Church or the place of interment.

In the renewal of English rites the main influence was the Church Service Society, who in the first edition of *Euchologion* (1867) included a 'Manual for the Burial of the Dead' based on the American 'Manual of Devotional Services' and the Dutch and German Reformed rites.

American Presbyterianism followed the 1788 revision of the Westminster *Directory of Public Worship*, and, if anything, this was even more deficient than the original. Indeed, the deficiency of this aspect of the church's ministry to people was one of the factors leading to liturgical renewal, which resulted in the formation of a Church Society, on the Scottish model, in 1897, and eventually to the *Book of Common Worship* (*BCW*) in 1906, which was revised in 1932 and 1946. In the last and the *BCW: Proposed Services* (1966), the influence of the Scottish *BCO* (1940) is evident.

Modern Rites

English. An examination of modern Reformed burial rites in Scotland, England, Ireland, Wales, Canada, Australia and South Africa reveals a common structure and content, and that they have all been much influenced by the *Euchologion* and *BCP*. All provide for two services, one in church or home, and the other at the graveside. While there are variations in details, the general order of the former is scripture sentences, invocation, psalm, scripture readings, address, prayers of adoration, confession, thanksgiving, supplication, intercession and commemoration of saints, hymn and benediction. At the graveside the order is scripture sentences, committal, prayers and benediction. The prayers are drawn from the Reformers, *BCP*, *Euchologion*, Dutch, German,

Scottish, English and American sources.

American. The rite used in the United Presbyterian Church in the USA and the Presbyterian Church in the US (Southern) provides for two services – one for use in the church, and one for the committal service. No provision is made for worship in the home. Each is entitled 'Witness to the Resurrection'. The church service consists of scripture sentences, prayer, OT and NT lections with a prayer, hymn, sermon (optional), Apostles' Creed, prayer of thanksgiving and intercession, hymn and benediction. The committal service is brief, consisting of scripture sentences, committal, prayer, Lord's Prayer and benediction.

French. Taking the liturgies of France, Geneva and Vaud as representative of French rites, the *Liturgie de L'Église de Genève* and *Liturgie de L'Église Nationale Évangélique Réformée du Canton de Vaud* provide for two services as in the English rites and are similar to them in content. The church or home service is invocation and introduction, scripture texts and psalm, prayer before Bible reading, scripture reading, address, prayer after address and benediction. At the graveside the order is invocation and committal, scripture reading, prayer, conclusion (scripture sentences of exhortation) and benediction.

On the other hand, the *Liturgie de L'Église Réformée de France* provides for three services – home (*levée de corps*), church (*service principal*) and cemetery. The first consists of invocation, declaration (*accueil*), Apostles' Creed, prayer, psalm, scripture reading, address or meditation, chant, prayer, Lord's Prayer and benediction. The third is introduction, prayer, scripture sentences of exhortation and benediction.

German. These rites retain many of the exhortations of the Reformation era against 'abuses' and emphasize the necessity for 'absolute simplicity and common decency'. Structurally they do not differ greatly from the English and French rites, but lay a greater stress on the necessity for 'sermon'. Basic to them all is à Lasco's *Forma ac Ratio*, the Palatinate order for the preaching of the word of God at burial, and the Zurich order for burial (1529).

The prayers in the French and German rites are drawn from Strasbourg (1537), Calvin, *BCP* (1549, 1552), à Lasco, Micronius, Pullain, Cassell (1657) and St Gallen

(1699), adding in the case of the German rites Zurich (1529, 1626) and Pfalz (1563), and of the French Neuchâtel (1713).

Others. As Reformed rites belong to the one family, they contain many common features. The Dutch rites remain closely related to à Lasco and Pullain. The Hungarian and Czechoslovak rites are akin to the German, as are the Waldensian and Belgian to the French. The Portuguese and Brazilian rites (through American influence) and the Spanish (through Irish) have much in common with the English.

Theology

In all these rites the centrality of the life, death and resurrection of Christ is basic. The Strasbourg order (1537) declared: 'It is our task at burial to comfort each other in the Lord and to encourage to Christian endeavour.' All give adequate expression to this. On the other hand, one point appears to receive inadequate expression. With Paul and the Fathers, Calvin could write 'baptism is the seal of our future resurrection (Col. 2.12); no less does the sacred Supper invite us to confidence in it' (*Inst.* III. xxv. 8). Few, if any, of the rites include a specific reference to this.

In all these rites a large selection of lections is provided, some of them numbering over seventy. While recognition must be given to the fullness of scriptural teaching, surely for liturgical purposes this could be reduced considerably.

JOHN M. BARKLEY

13. *Seventh-day Adventist.* The burial service of the Seventh-day Adventist Church does not differ a great deal in its forms from that of most Protestant churches. Since interment customs vary from country to country, there are naturally also some variations in Adventist burial rites in different parts of the world; there are, however, also many constants. It is the generally accepted practice for SDA ministers to charge no fee for conducting funerals. They co-operate closely with the funeral director and endeavour to meet the wishes of the sorrowing family in making arrangements for the funeral service at the home, the funeral parlour or the church.

The doctrinal basis for the SDA funeral service is conditionalism, that is, the belief that immortality or everlasting life is the gift of God through faith in Christ. As condi-

tionalists, Adventists believe that the Bible teaches that man rests in the grave until the resurrection and they therefore consider as unscriptural the doctrine of immortal-soulism, according to which man was created with a soul that has a separate, indefeasibly immortal existence, apart from the body.

A typical church funeral service is opened by a hymn followed by a brief prayer. Then a suitable collection of scriptural passages may be read, taking into consideration the age, life and experience of the deceased. As a rule, the reading includes such Bible passages as Ps. 90.1-4, 10, 12; Job 14.1, 2, 14, 15; I Cor. 15.51, 57. Then a short obituary sketch presenting the life of the deceased is read. There follows a brief homily, not a long doctrinal sermon on the state of the dead, pointing the bereaved to the glorious hope of the resurrection and underlining the power of Christ to deliver from sin and conquer death by bestowing immortality upon the righteous at his second coming – the blessed hope of all ages.

After the homily or address a prayer follows, making thanksgiving for all that God's goodness has done for the departed, for the assurance of the resurrection's restoration, praying for the finishing of the gospel work on earth, and remembering the dear ones left to mourn. Another song may be sung at this point in the service, which closes with the benediction.

At the graveside a quartet or some other group may sing, and as the casket rests above the grave, or is being lowered into the earth, the minister reads appropriate scriptural passages, such as John 11.25; Rev. 1.17, 18; 14.13; 21.3-5; I Thess. 4.13-18.

In some countries the minister or funeral director drops a little earth or flower petals on the casket as the minister repeats the liturgical committal. If a hymn is sung at the graveside it is usually sung at this point. A closing prayer follows together with the benediction.

B. B. BEACH

S. Benko, *The Meaning of Sanctorum Communio*, 1964; B. Bürkli, *Im Herrn entschlafen. Eine historisch-pastoral theologische Studie zur Liturgie des Sterbens und des Begräbnisses*, 1969; G. Cope, ed., *Dying, Death and Disposal*, 1970 (a treatment of pastoral, architectural and theological problems arising in connection with funerary practice today); O. Cullmann, *Immortality of the Soul or Resurrection of the Dead?*, 1958; J. Dowdall, 'The Liturgy of the Dead' in *Studies in Pastoral Liturgy*, I, ed. P. Murray, 1964; L. E. Froom, *The Conditionalist Faith of our Father*, 1966 (Seventh-day Adventist); P. Graff, *Geschichte der Auflösung der alten gottesdienstlichen Formen in der evangelischen Kirche Deutschlands*, ²1937, I, pp. 345-372; II, 272–279; M. Gy, OP, 'La Mort du Chrétien' in *L'Église en Prière*, ed. A. G. Martimort, 1965; B. Jordahn, *Das kirchliche Begräbnis. Grundlegung und Gestaltung*, 1949; T. Kliefoth, *Liturgische Abhandlungen*, I and II, 1869; M. Luther, *Werke*, Weimar 1883 ff.; *La Maison Dieu*, 101; *Manual for Ministers*, 1965 (Seventh-day Adventist); H. Maser, *Die Bestattung*, 1964; R. Mehl, *Notre vie et notre mort*, 1953; K. F. Müller and W. Blankenburg, eds., *Leiturgia. Handbuch des evangelischen Gottesdienstes* (6: Begräbnis, etc.), 1952; *The Prayer Book of Edward VI* (Everyman or other editions; there exists no collection of later Anglican funerary rites); A. L. Richter, *Die evangelischen Kirchenordnungen des 16. Jahrhunderts*, 2 vols, 1846; G. Rietschel-P. Graff, *Lehrbuch der Liturgik*, ²1951, pp. 764-788; M. Righetti, *Storia Liturgica*, II, ²1955; F. Schulz, 'Die Begräbnisgebete des 16. und 17. Jahrhunderts', in *Jahrbuch für Liturgie und Hymnologie*, XI, 1966, pp. 1-44; E. Sehling, *Die evangelischen Kirchenordnungen des XVI Jahrhunderts*, 14 vols, 1962 ff.; *Services Funebres*, 1963 (Reformed); John E. Skoglund, *A Manual of Worship*, 1968 (Baptist); E. Winkler, *Die Leichenpredigt im deutschen Luthertum bis Spener*, 1967.

Calendar

The list of commemorations observed throughout the Christian year. It represents a fusion of a series of christological festivals, such as Christmas, Easter, etc. (qq.v.), together with Mariological feasts (q.v.), e.g. the Purification, and saints' and holy days (q.v.).

EDITOR

Camp Meeting

The origin of the camp meeting lies in the American frontier around 1800. People travelled several miles to reach the place where the preaching took place. They could not leave early enough to return home the same night. Therefore they brought their equipment for camping on the spot. The preaching was soul-searching. People were faced with a choice between God and the devil. Terrible was the description of hell, when a sinner was 'sinking into the liquid, boiling waves of hell, and accursed sinners of Tyre and Sidon, and Sodom and Gomorrah sprang to the right and left and made way for him to pass them and fall lower down even to the deepest cavern in the flaming abyss. Here his consciousness like a never-dying worm stings him and forever gnaws his soul ... Now through the blazing flames of hell he sees that heaven he has lost ... In those pure regions he sees his father, or mother, his sisters or brothers, or those persons who sat under the same means of grace with him, and whom he derided as fools, fanatics, and hypocrites' (J. C. Brauer, *Protestantism in America*, 1965, p. 107). Such preaching led to highly emotional results. Men and women began to cry for mercy. Turning and twisting, wringing their hands, beating their breasts, they struggled to be released from sin and to experience the new birth in Christ.

The camp meeting matched the needs of the frontier: an un- or even anti-intellectual preaching, a personal decision on things which were controllable (sinners were swearing, drinking and dancing; saints abstained from such things; there was no middle way), the possibility of leaving the isolation of every-day life and enjoying fellowship with a crowd.

In the middle of the last century the mainline churches abandoned the camp meeting. Some Christians, longing for revival, gathered together and revived the old customs, which eventually gave birth to the Holiness denominations, with their tangible experience of sanctification, including 'holy laughter', 'holy barking' and 'holy jerks'. At the beginning of the twentieth century the Holiness denominations became more fashionable. The camp meeting tradition was then taken up by the Pentecostal movement.

Today the camp meeting has lost its cruder sides. It is a place where one lives as the forefathers did, assembles around a fire, sleeps in country houses or tents, far away from the jungles of modern cities.

The future of the camp meeting can be just this (or – what is not excluded – a re-awakening of the former emotionalism). But it could also be an exercise in using leisure time intelligently, rediscovering those parts of the person which are suppressed in today's society, through relationship with other persons and nature, through a growing awareness of intuition, through means of art and meditation.

J. C. Brauer, *Protestantism in America*, 1965; W. J. Hollenweger, *Handbuch der Pfingst-bewegung* (02a.02.001), 1965/1967; W. L. Sperry, *Religion in America*, 1948.

W. J. HOLLENWEGER

Candlemas *see* Mariological Feasts

Candles, Lamps and Lights

The use of the term 'lights' in Christian worship refers to the use of candles and lamps not only for the purpose of illumination but also for liturgical observance. The history of the use of such lights is complicated and somewhat obscure. There is some difference of opinion as to how far Christian usage was influenced by the use of such lights in the worship of the Jewish Temple and synagogue.

The reference to the 'many lights' in Acts 20.8 at the celebration of the eucharist at Troas probably implies no precise liturgical use, since this observance was at midnight. The reference to the seven lamps of fire in Rev. 4.5 probably reflects an apocalyptic vision of the heavenly temple rather than current Christian practice. Also the argument that such lights are derived from their use in Christian worship in the catacombs during the early centuries is no longer regarded as valid, and the use of the catacombs for public worship in times of persecution was not normal; they were too confined and too well-known to the Roman authorities.

Tertullian (*c.* AD 200) inveighs against 'the useless lighting of lamps at noonday' (*Apol.* 46); but he is probably referring to their use in pagan worship if we consider his words in their context.

It is most likely that the lighting of candles and lamps in Christian worship is bound up with the vigil service that was held on the Saturday night-Sunday morning, and to which the reference in Acts 20.8 may be early evidence, if it preceded the mass held at dawn. The kindling of light at this service, although probably originally entirely functional, became a liturgical celebration of which the lighting of the Paschal candle (q.v.) is a traditional continuance.

By the fourth century, both lamps and candles were in normal use in Christian worship. The Spanish Christian poet, Prudentius (*c.* 348), in his hymn *Inventor rutili*, says: 'The lamps hang by flexible cords and shine over the ceilings to which they are fixed, and the flame, fed by floating wicks, casts its light through clear glass. You would believe that the heavens were adorned with the twin constellation of the Wain' (*Cath.* V.141). A similar kind of testimony comes to us from Italy in the poems of Paulinus of Nola about the same date. The *Liber Pontificalis* tells of lamps of gold given by Constantine the Great to burn before the altars of the Roman basilicas erected by him. Lamps burnt before the shrine of St Peter, a custom which has continued to the present day not only at Rome but before the shrine of St Francis at Assisi. In the fourth and fifth centuries, the *Liber Pontificalis* records the gifts of bronze and silver candlesticks as well as crowns and candelabra given by popes Damasus, Innocent I and Celestine. While some of these were utilitarian, the suspension of lamps in the form of dolphins from the corners and under the canopy of the altar (*see* **Altar**) must clearly have had a votive and honorific significance.

For over a thousand years it was not the normal custom to stand candlesticks on the altar. Indeed, there is little explicit evidence for this arrangement until the twelfth century. The evidence of Pope Innocent III (*c.* 1198) in his *De Sacro Mysterio* is the most important. In the earlier usage it was the custom to carry lights and incense before the bishop and his assistants at the entry for the mass; and some commentators have derived this from secular custom in which the emperor and other persons of note had such ceremonies accorded them. The bishop came to be regarded as a civil dignitary from the fourth century. *Ordo Romanus Primus*, an eighth-century document, but which reflects the customs of the papal mass in the time of Pope Gregory the Great (d. 604), shows that the papal cortege was preceded by seven acolytes with candlesticks which were set down round the altar and not on it during the mass.

As we have indicated, it is not until the second part of the Middle Ages that the placing of candlesticks on the altar commences; but there was no invariable rule about this matter, and medieval paintings and

illuminated MSS of the fourteenth and fifteenth centuries often depict the mass in
progress with no candlesticks on the altar.
What was regarded as of importance from the
thirteenth century was the holding of a
lighted torch or candle by the parish clerk or
one of the assistant ministers at the elevation
(q.v.) of the host.

Until the sixteenth century there was considerable latitude and freedom of action in
the Latin West as to how candles were employed in the Mass and in the choir offices,
and there were variations as to the number of
candlesticks placed on the altar in the later
Middle Ages. The custom of the Roman
Catholic Church is now to require six lights
on the altar at high mass and seven when a
bishop sings such a mass. This, however, is a
requirement first laid down in the *Caeri-
monale Episcoporum* of 1600 and there is no
explicit evidence for this arrangement before
its mention by Burchard and the writers of the
Counter-Reformation. In France until the
nineteenth century, modern Roman Catholic
ceremonial both in regard to lights and other
customs was widely disregarded. A point that
should be noted is that candlesticks were not
left on the altar as a permanent form of
decoration but were only placed there at the
time of liturgy.

In the Church of England in the nineteenth
century there was considerable litigation and
dispute as to the legality of the use of lights at
the eucharist. But since the Restoration under
Charles II there is continuous evidence for
their use and some of our cathedrals and
greater churches possess altar candlesticks
belonging to the seventeenth century. Up-
holders of Anglican tradition point to the
injunction of Edward VI in 1547 referring to
the retention of 'two lights upon the high
altar, before the sacrament, which for the
signification that Christ is the very true light
of the world, they shall suffer to remain still'.
There is also evidence that during the reign of
Elizabeth I not only were candlesticks in use
in the Queen's Chapel but 'in many cathedral
churches, besides the chapels of divers noble-
men' according to Bishop Cosin in his *Notes
on the Book of Common Prayer* (*c.* 1640).

A matter that has also been disputed is the
question of a continuous light burning before
an aumbry (q.v.) or tabernacle containing the
reserved sacrament. While reservation (q.v.)
can claim a very high antiquity, the custom
of a perpetual light can only be found in the

later Middle Ages. In 1240, Walter de
Cantilupe, bishop of Worcester, ordered that
'a lamp must burn day and night before the
eucharist'. There is little evidence earlier than
this time.

In the Eastern Orthodox Church it is
customary to have a seven-branched candlestick standing on the altar; and the bishop
blesses the people during the liturgy holding
the *dikiri* and the *trikiri* (a two branched
and three-branched candlestick) in either
hand.

D. R. Dendy, *The Use of Lights in Christian
Worship*, 1959; L. Hertling and E. Kirsch-
baum, *The Roman Catacombs and their
Martyrs*, 1960; A. A. King and C. E. Pocknee,
Eucharistic Reservation in the Western Church,
1965; V. Staley, ed., *Hierurgia Anglicana*,
pt. I, 1902.

C. E. POCKNEE

Canon

The Greek word *kanon* means a rule or
measuring rod; it came to be applied to the
consecration prayer in the eucharistic rite of
the West. In some early sacramentary manuscripts the word appears in the heading above
the *Sursum Corda – incipit canon actionis* – indicating that the text from this point was
fixed. The word then came to be used for the
whole prayer. As early as Justin Martyr (*c.* AD
150) this prayer was not regarded as fixed, for
at this point the president prayed 'as he was
able'. By the time of Hippolytus of Rome
(*c.* AD 210) it would appear that a text
existed, but was still not regarded as definitive: it was simply a model to be used as
required. The precise origins of the Western
canon remain obscure: but the basic elements
must have existed by the late fourth century,
for Ambrose in *De Sacramentis* (*c.* AD 378)
quoted portions of a eucharistic canon which
is found in its entirety in manuscripts of the
sixth century. The texts of the canon as they
appear in the Gelasian and Gregorian sacramentaries of the seventh century have remained basically the same until the twentieth
century.

A noteworthy characteristic of the Roman
canon is its small amount of variation
throughout the church's year. In this respect
it resembles the eucharistic prayer or anaphora (q.v.) of the Eastern liturgies rather
than the canon of the non-Roman Western or
Gallican rites, which was simply a collection

of constantly changing elements. The Roman canon is a combination of short prayers lacking any real cohesion; its pattern would suggest that at an early stage in its history the text suffered some dislocation. Its elements are as follows:

Introductory dialogue – *Sursum Corda*

Preface, culminating in *Sanctus* and *Benedictus*

A plea for the acceptance of the offerings

Prayer for the living and departed

Prayer of offering

Narrative of the institution

Anamnesis – oblation

Prayer for acceptance and fruitful reception

Prayer for the living and departed

Two doxologies

At the Reformation the abolition of the canon was almost an article of faith with the Reformers except for Cranmer. In nearly all Reformed rites it was normally reduced to the narrative of the institution with the possible addition of a prayer for worthy reception. But in the 1549 Anglican prayer book Cranmer retained the main elements of the Roman canon. In 1552, however, these were divided into three distinct prayers at different points in the rite – the prayer for the church militant, the severely truncated prayer of consecration ending with the narrative of the institution, and the prayer of oblation following communion and the Lord's Prayer. Today there is a general movement among both Catholic and Reformed Churches to recover a primitive Trinitarian pattern of canon, in which God is blessed or thanked for his mighty acts of creation, redemption and sanctification, the total redemptive activity of Christ is 'remembered' and proclaimed, and the Holy Spirit is invoked to unite and strengthen the communicants.

J. M. Barkley, *The Worship of the Reformed Church*, 1966; B. Botte, *Le Canon de la Messe*, 1935; F. E. Brightman, *The English Rite*, 1915; W. S. Porter, *The Gallican Rite*, 1958; L. D. Reed, *The Lutheran Liturgy*, 1947; C. Vagaggini, *The Canon of the Mass and Liturgical Reform*, 1967.

R. C. D. JASPER

Canonical Hours

The *canonicae horae* are the times of daily prayer laid down in the Roman Catholic breviary, or the comparable hours of the Eastern Churches and, hence, the services appointed to be recited at these times. The seven hours officially appointed in the Western Church are mattins and lauds (reckoned as one hour), prime, terce, sext, none, vespers and compline. This rota of prayer was already complete in the West probably by the end of the fifth century, but the structure and content of the hours were modified by later reforms of the breviary, notably by the Council of Trent, which led to the issue of the *Breviarium Romanum* in Rome in 1568 under Pius V, by Benedict XIV and by Pius X (1911).

In his Tract No. 75 'On the Roman Breviary', published in 1835-36, J. H. Newman asserted that 'the Jewish observance of the third, sixth, and ninth hours for prayer, was continued by the inspired founders of the Christian Church' (*Tracts for the Times*, III, [2]1837, Tract 75, p. 3). He proceeded: 'Such was the Apostolic worship as far as Scripture happens to have preserved it . . . in subsequent times the Hours of prayer were gradually developed from the three, or (with midnight) the four seasons, above enumerated, to seven, viz. by the addition of Prime (the first hour), Vespers (the evening), and Compline (bed-time); according to the words of the Psalm, "Seven times a day do I praise thee . . ."' (*ibid.*, p. 4).

The origin of the canonical hours, however, is not so simple as Newman supposed. Newman relied on Scripture to prove that the Jews observed the third, sixth and ninth hours for prayer. He cited Daniel who prayed three times a day (Dan. 6.10); at the third hour the Holy Spirit descended at Pentecost (Acts 2.15), at the sixth hour Peter 'went up upon the housetop to pray' (Acts 10.9), and at the ninth hour 'Peter and John went up together into the temple' being 'the hour of prayer' (Acts 3.1). Tertullian had already noted these biblical references, but wisely contented himself with the remark, 'these facts are simply stated without any command about the practice' (*De Orat.* xxv).

A more modern approach to the subject is reflected by Mgr Pierre Salmon who, while recognizing the NT teaching, reiterated by Tertullian, Cyprian and Clement of Alexandria, that the whole Christian life should be one of prayer, sees the origin of the canonical hours in the Roman division of the day into four 'hours' (*prima, tertia, sexta* and *nona*) and the night into four 'watches' – the first in the evening, the second at midnight, the third at cock-crow and the fourth at dawn (P. Salmon, 'La prière des heures' in *L'Église en Prière: Introduction à la Liturgie*, ed. A. G. Martimort, [3]1965, p. 814). The present writer had already drawn attention in 1944 to the fact that Tertullian called the third, sixth and ninth hours 'these common hours, which mark the intervals of the day' (*De Orat.* xxv; *cf. De Jejun.* x); that they were publicly announced (Varro, *De Ling. Lat.* vi. 89); and that it would be natural for Christians to adopt them as hours of prayer, hallowed as they were for them by the events connected with the crucifixion (C. W. Dugmore, *The Influence of the Synagogue upon the Divine Office*, 1944, pp. 66f., repr. Alcuin Club Collections, XLV, 1964). The *Apostolic Tradition* of Hippolytus of Rome (*c.* AD 215), indeed, was already urging prayer at home or 'if thou art elsewhere' at these hours for this specific reason (*Ap. Trad.* xxxvi. 2-6, ed. Gregory Dix, reissued with corrections and preface by H. Chadwick, 1968, pp. 62-64). Lechner rightly regarded the prayers at terce, sext and none in the second century as 'private daily practice', but, like Salmon, he thought the night office and the prayer at dawn were also private-prayer hours (Ludwig Eisenhofer-Joseph Lechner, *The Liturgy of the Roman Rite*, ET edited by H. E. Winstone, 1961, pp. 438f.). Salmon noted that Tertullian described the (older) morning and evening prayers as *legitimae orationes* (Salmon, *op. cit.*, p. 815; *cf.* C. W. Dugmore, *op. cit.*, pp. 47, 60) but failed to give the context or to point out that the prayers at dawn and at dusk (*ingressu lucis et noctis*) derive, through the hours of prayer in the Synagogue, from the hours of sacrifice in the Jerusalem Temple. Tertullian was supporting the new rota of private prayer at the third, sixth and ninth hours, introduced by the ascetics in North Africa – but these must, he said, be in addition to the regular hours of public prayer, on Sundays and weekdays, *quae sine admonitione debentur ingressu lucis et noctis* (*De Orat.* xxv; *cf.* Cyprian, *De Orat. Domin.* xxxv). The morning prayers, consisting of the four elements of synagogue worship (namely prayer, psalmody, scripture lections, and a sermon expounding the lections), formed the first part of the Sabbath and Sunday service of the eucharist. The evening prayers were probably conducted on the same plan, without the sermon, as in the synagogue. We have the evidence of Hippolytus that the *missa catechumenorum* (as this part of the service was later called) was used on weekdays (*Ap. Trad.* xxxi. 2; xxxv. 2), but nothing is said about public assembly in the evening: the *lucernarium* of the Ethiopic version and the *Testamentum Domini* (Dix-Chadwick, *op. cit.*, pp. 49-52) clearly belongs to a service preceding the agape (q.v.) or eucharist, and was therefore, originally not a daily service.

Among the canonical hours, lauds (or mattins) and vespers are the ancient prayers of the church, said at dawn and at sunset. Terce, sext and none have no basis in Jewish usage, except that none (3 p.m.) was the hour at which the 'evening sacrifice' was offered in the Herodian Temple (*cf.* Acts 3.1). There is no evidence of Jewish worship, either in temple or synagogue, at noon (the sixth hour) and the prescription that Christians should say the Lord's Prayer thrice daily (*Didache* viii. 3) makes no mention of the time of prayer. The hours of terce, sext and none were first observed as times of private prayer by the specially devout (the ascetics) and later were incorporated with the older lauds/mattins and vespers into the cycle of daily prayer developed by the monks. Jerome wrote in the fourth century, in a letter to the virgin Eustochium: 'Prayers, as everyone knows, ought to be said at the third, sixth and ninth hours, at dawn and at evening' (*Ep.* xxii. 37). Cassian tells us that it was at Bethlehem (where Jerome ruled the men's monastery from *c.* 386) that prime was introduced, at the first hour, to put an end to the laxity of the monks *c.* 382 (Cassian, *De Coenob. Instit.* iii. 4). Compline, consisting of Ps. 90, is mentioned by Basil, but was probably not introduced to the West as part of the regular cycle of daily prayer before Benedict (P. Batiffol, *History of the Roman Breviary*, ET by A.M.Y. Baylay, p. 28). Thus the 'seven times a day do I praise thee' referred to by Newman were complete.

It has been noted above that the earliest Christian daily public prayer was at dawn and at sunset (*ingressu lucis et noctis*, to use Tertullian's phrase), and that these times of prayer were basic to the canonical hours observed by the ascetics and the later monks. There is no problem concerning the evening prayer (vespers), but the relationship between mattins and the nocturnal offices has been the subject of much discussion among liturgical scholars. Mgr Salmon has remarked that 'it is difficult to know what were the night offices' (*op. cit.*, p.816). Anton Baumstark, the author of a famous study entitled *Comparative Liturgy* (revised by B. Botte, ET by F. L. Cross, 1958) maintained in his *Nocturna Laus* (ed. Odilo Heiming, 1957) that the Christian nocturnal hours of prayer were modelled on those of the Graeco-Roman world – the Dionysian rites (*Nyktelia, Nyktophylaxia*), the *Bacchanalia*, known at Rome about 168 BC, the *Pannychis* of the cult of Aphrodite, and so forth. In his view the Christians imitated, or took over, non-Christian custom, and the origin of the nocturnal hours is to be found in the early Christian night-time vigils. But there is no evidence of any nightly vigil, except the Easter Vigil, before the time of Tertullian and Cyprian. Baumstark was apparently not acquainted with the work of J. M. Hanssen (*Nature et Genèse de l'Office des Matines*, Analecta Gregoriana, LVII [Series Facultatis Theologicae, Sect. A No. 7], Rome 1952), who rightly saw that the dawn office is the oldest (though he did not trace its origin to Temple and synagogue) and rejected the hypothesis of an origin derived from pagan nocturnal acts of worship. Hanssen argued critically, with reference to the various liturgical texts, the case for the three possible hypotheses concerning the origin of mattins. He utterly rejected, first, the theory that it was partly a nocturnal and partly a dawn office, on the grounds that the 'midnight office' was purely a later monastic invention (despite Paul and Silas, Acts 16.25); secondly, the theory that mattins resulted from the juxtaposition of two offices (nocturns and lauds), previously recited separately, the one in the night and the other at dawn. He concluded that mattins as it was later known was the result of the amplification of the primitive mattins, or lauds, augmented by the addition of a pre-mattins, or prime. The use of the psalms is the key. The recitation of one or more chosen psalms and the recitation of the psalter itself are two totally different modes of psalmody: the first characterizes a well-defined office to be celebrated at a precise hour, the second provides the means of occupying piously a more or less long space of time, such as was the vigil. The office of mattins consisted of specified psalms, hymns and prayers. The earliest documents mention Pss. 50; 66; 117; and especially Pss. 148-150, called *laudes*.

The first text which describes in any detail a regular cycle of prayer comparable to the later canonical hours is to be found in the journal of a woman pilgrim, named Egeria (or Etheria), who visited Jerusalem about 385-88. In the *Peregrinatio Egeriae* there is a description of a service at the tenth hour ('called here [Jerusalem] *licinicon*, which we [in the West] call *lucernare*') and another at dawn. The services of the hours are obviously of a monastic nature, attended by ascetics and nuns, but at the evening and morning services (*vespers* and *mattins*) the laity were also present in the church of the Anastasis.

But it was in the monasteries that the hours found their natural home. Some Eastern features were introduced at Milan by Ambrose and in Gaul by John Cassian, who had spent the early years of his life in a monastery at Bethlehem and had studied the monastic systems of Egypt. But the greatest influence on the development of monasticism in the West was Benedict of Nursia, who was probably the first to give a permanent place in the hours to compline (*completorium*), as a last office in the evening before retiring to rest. According to Professor David Knowles, at Monte Cassino in St Benedict's day the following would seem to have been the skeleton time-table.

In winter, on 1 November

2.00 a.m.	rise for nocturns (the modern mattins)
2.10-3.30	nocturns
3.30-5.00	reading
5.00-5.45	lauds
5.45-8.15	reading, including prime (20 mins.)
8.15-2.30	work, broken by terce, sext and none (10 mins. each)
2.30-3.15	dinner
3.15-4.15	reading
4.15-4.45	vespers, collation (reading), compline
5.15	in bed

In summer, say 30 June

1.00-2.00 a.m.	nocturns
2.15-3.00	lauds
3.00-4.30	reading
4.30-9.15	prime and work
9.30-11.30	reading
11.45-12.30	dinner
12.30-2.00	siesta
2.00-6.30	work
6.30-7.00	vespers

7.00-7.30   supper and collation
7.30-8.00   compline and bed

The most remarkable thing, to us in the twentieth century, about this daily programme is the early rising and early end of the day, but in central Italy darkness fell about 5 p.m. at the winter solstice and about 7.45 p.m. at midsummer. (The author wishes to thank Prof. Knowles for permission to reproduce these tables and facts from his *Christian Monasticism* [World Christian Library], 1969, pp. 213f.) Candles (q.v.) or olive oil lamps would suffice for reciting the hours at the beginning of the day and for reading, but work could only be done in daylight, and if the day began at 1 or 2 a.m. it was reasonable to retire at nightfall. In more northern climes the hours of daylight were different and five centuries after St Benedict the *horarium* of the English monastery of Christ Church, Canterbury, began in winter at 2.30 a.m. and ended at 6.30 p.m., but the scheme drawn up by Lanfranc differed greatly from that of St Benedict. 'Of the time, roughly fourteen hours, available after the hours of sleep, meals and toilet have been deducted, no less than eight are occupied in religious services in church, while reading has less than three hours and work three at most . . . What, we may ask, had made the change? Above all, two weighty additions. The first was the two masses daily attended by the whole community – perhaps three, if the priest's private mass was taken out of reading or work time. The second was the large quantity of psalms, prayers, litanies and minor offices. Besides these, both office and mass had been lengthened by the chant [q.v.], which was now far more elaborate than in St Benedict's day' (*ibid.*, pp. 218-20).

In the later Middle Ages the divine office became so elaborate that reform of it was almost continuous from the time of Gregory VII to the Council of Trent. The Gregorian Reform and the twelfth-century Renaissance did not immediately produce changes in the *Ordo Romanus* of the office, which Gregory VII confirmed against those who wished to reduce the psalmody of mattins to three psalms. Indeed, he extended to all Christendom the obligation of observing the festivals of martyr popes and, while he ordered that on Easter Day and the six week-days following, as on Pentecost and the six days following, the nocturnal office should have only

three psalms, three lessons and three responds, for the rest of the year, the nocturnal office for festivals was to have nine psalms, nine lessons and nine responds; the ferial office twelve, three and three; and the Sunday office eighteen, nine and nine. Gregory VII suppressed the Mozarabic rites in favour of the *Ordo Romanus* – an illustration of the Holy See's new interest in the canonical hours, which was part of the progressive assertion of the Roman primacy in the field of liturgy, as elsewhere. Attempts by the clergy, through laziness, to reduce the office to one nocturn of three psalms and three lessons were thwarted by Gregory VII. But the offices were too long for the changed circumstances of the twelfth century, when travel became more frequent, many beneficed clerks frequented the universities and non-residence increased. Thus the *modernum officium*, used by the pope and the curia in the papal chapel, came into use during the twelfth century. This modified the calendar, abbreviated the lectionary and adopted the monastic hymnal (which had been gradually making its way into the monastic hours, despite Roman disapproval, since the time of Ambrose). It also added the *Quincunque vult*, the daily office of the Blessed Virgin Mary (a brief office in honour of the Virgin modelled on the divine office [q.v.] and containing the usual canonical hours) and the office of the dead (*see* **Burial** 3) as supplements to the canonical office, together with commemorations (*Memoriae*) of the saints, always comprising an antiphon, versicle and response, appended to lauds and vespers.

The *modernum officium* was shorter than the old *Ordo Romanus* and it was adopted by the Franciscans in 1223, but they needed an office still shorter; thus, their general, Haymo of Faversham, undertook a revision of the *Breviarium Romanae Curiae* which was approved by Gregory IX in 1241. Already in 1227 a Council of Trier obliged all priests to possess a breviary which would permit them to recite the hours when travelling. The Franciscans, because of their itinerant and apostolic way of life, could not always recite the solemn office in choir: they often had to recite it privately. Thus, in the thirteenth century a profound change occurred, not so much in the structure of the canonical hours as in the manner of their observance. The scripture lessons were further reduced, the number of festivals was increased; the Franciscans did not celebrate the double office still maintained in the Roman basilicas, but recited only the office of the festival, omitting that of the day. Thus the recitation of the breviary office became a succession of festival observances, and the old office of the day or season fell largely into disuse. This, in turn, resulted in the introduction of lessons from mythical and spurious 'lives' of the saints. By the fifteenth century the structure of the earlier canonical hours, based on regular recital of the psalms and scripture lections, had become so overlaid by later accretions that council after council vied with one another 'in deploring the coldness with which the clergy perform their duty of reciting the canonical office, even in choir' (P. Batiffol, *History of the Roman Breviary*, ET 1912, p. 173). The offices were now almost entirely the concern of the clergy and there was little attendance by the laity, except at mattins sung before mass and vespers on Sundays and festivals. It is interesting to observe here the continuity of tradition, despite all the medieval changes, with the observance of the hours of morning and evening (originally sunrise and sunset) by the laity in the early church. We noted above that these hours of prayer, taken over by the church from the synagogue, were observed in the period before Tertullian in North Africa and Hippolytus in Rome, as well as in Jerusalem in the late fourth century. They were destined to survive the sixteenth century Reformation.

By the sixteenth century the *modernum officium*, with its complicated service due to the multiplication of festivals, the frequent recitation of the office of the Blessed Virgin Mary and of that of the dead, and of the gradual and penitential psalms, was felt to be burdensome, unedifying and far removed from the canonical hours of the early church as they had been enshrined in the old *Ordo Romanus*. Two attempts to remedy the situation were made under Clement VII (1523-34). He first approved the plan of Carafa, General of the Theatine Order and later Pope Paul IV, to revise the office and also the missal for the use of his order. Nothing came of this. More important, in 1529 Clement issued a commission to Cardinal Francisco de Quiñones, General of the Franciscans, to prepare a new breviary which would simplify the divine office by a return to the practice of the fathers of the church and so attract the

clergy to discharge their canonical duty of reciting it (as laid down by Innocent III in 1215). Quiñones's *Breviarium Romanum nuper reformatum* was published in 1535 (modern ed. by J. Wickham Legg, 1888). 'The reform was drastic: antiphons, responds, chapters and preces are abolished. The Psalter is redistributed, three Psalms being assigned to each office throughout the week, except in so far that the *Venite* is added at Mattins, and the Old Testament canticle of each day serves as the third Psalm in Lauds' (F. E. Brightman, *The English Rite*, 1915, I, xxvi, where further details of the reform may be found). In July 1535 the Sorbonne condemned these innovations and Cardinal Quiñones produced a further revision in July 1536 (*The Second Recension of the Quignon Breviary*, 1908). This restored the antiphons to the psalms in all the offices, and some other features which had become traditional, but it was abandoned by the Council of Trent and suppressed by Paul IV in 1558. Eventually a new reformed breviary was issued by Pius V by the bull *Quod a nobis* of 15 July 1568, which abolished that of Quiñones and all other Roman breviaries of less than 200 years' standing.

Meanwhile, reform of the canonical hours which comprised the breviary had been urged by Hermann von Wied, archbishop-elector of Cologne, in 1536. By 1543 he had become a Lutheran; he invited Martin Bucer from Strasbourg, Philip Melanchthon from Wittenberg and others to help in carrying through his reform. The resulting Church Order, in which Bucer was mainly responsible for the liturgical parts, was issued in a Latin version, known as the *Simplex ac pia deliberatio* in 1545 (ET entitled *A Simple and Religious Consultation* published in 1547 and 1548). This made use of several Lutheran German Church Orders, but chiefly Osiander's Brandenburg-Nürnberg order of 1533.

Since Thomas Cranmer was certainly in Nuremberg in 1532, where he married Margaret, niece of Osiander's wife, it is inconceivable that he was unaware of the existence and content of the last-named Church Order. It does not follow from his contacts with Lutherans that he himself became a Lutheran, either now or later. The important point in the present context is that he was acquainted with the Lutheran revisions of the canonical hours to form two vernacular services of morning and evening prayer. Within the year he became Archbishop of Canterbury (30 March 1533).

There is in the British Museum a manuscript (MS Royal, 7.B.iv) which contains two draft schemes for the reform of the Latin daily office (best edition in J. Wickham Legg, *Cranmer's Liturgical Projects*, I, 1915). 'The handwriting of a part of the manuscript is that of Cranmer's secretary, Ralph Morice. The additions and corrections are in Cranmer's own hand. The manuscript undoubtedly once belonged to Cranmer. We need not hesitate in attributing the authorship of these schemes to him' (E. C. Ratcliff, 'The Liturgical Work of Archbishop Cranmer' in *Journal of Ecclesiastical History*, 7 [1956], p.190). As Ratcliff pointed out (*ibid.*, p.194), Cranmer had the choice of two methods of revision. Either he could follow Quiñones and preserve the traditional cycle of eight canonical hours of the breviary, or he could follow the Lutheran church orders and reduce the daily services to two. In the British Museum MS, Scheme I is Lutheran in type: Scheme II is Quiñonian. Since the later *BCP* is closer to Scheme I, in the matter of two daily services (mattins and evensong), the monthly recitation of the psalms and the system of lessons, Gasquet and Bishop concluded that this Scheme was nearer in date to the *BCP* and that Scheme II was earlier. This theory was accepted by Frere and Brightman, but C. H. Smyth and E. C. Ratcliff have concluded that the reverse is the truth. In Ratcliff's words: 'Scheme I, therefore, may be assigned to 1538, the year in which Thomas Cromwell was conducting Henry VIII's last and abortive negotiations with the Lutherans . . . Scheme II, on the other hand, belongs to the period between 1543 and 1546 when, more conservative ideas having regained ascendancy, Cranmer was obliged to conform his liturgical projects with the prevailing mood' (*ibid.*). Both Schemes were in Latin and, therefore, could only concern the clergy. In the next reign, when a vernacular *BCP* became possible, an English translation of Scheme I provided the basis for mattins and evensong.

The prayer book of 1549 and the services of mattins and evensong which it contained were, nevertheless, no mere English reproduction of a Lutheran liturgical book or rite. The Preface to the *BCP* was modelled on that of Quiñones's *Breviarium Romanum nuper*

reformatum (1535), but the order for mattins and evensong was derived directly from the Sarum breviary. Cranmer's innate conservatism, as also his creative skill, may be seen in the fact that, while the Lutheran church order of Calenberg-Göttingen (1542) provided an ingenious fusion of the old services of mattins and lauds for use on Sundays and festivals, Cranmer drew upon mattins, lauds and prime for his English mattins, and where the Lutheran order depended on vespers alone, Cranmer no less ingeniously fused vespers and compline to form his English evensong. Thus the two offices retained by the English church represented in their contents five out of the eight medieval offices. The result was as follows:

English Mattins

Lord's Prayer	
Versicles	
Gloria (Alleluia)	
Venite	⎱ From Sarum Mattins
Psalms with Gloria	
Lesson from OT	
Te Deum	
Lesson from NT	⎱ From Sarum Lauds
Benedictus	
Kyrie	
Creed	⎱ From Sarum Prime
Lord's Prayer	
Preces	
Collect for the Day	⎱ From Sarum Lauds
Collect for Peace	
Collect for Grace	From Sarum Prime

English Evensong

Lord's Prayer	
Versicles	
Gloria (Alleluia)	⎱ From Sarum Evensong
Psalms with Gloria	
Lesson from OT	
Magnificat	
Lesson from NT	⎱ From Sarum Compline
Nunc Dimittis	
Kyrie	
Creed	
Lord's Prayer	⎱ From Sarum Evensong
Preces	
Collect for the Day	
Collect for Peace	
Collect for Aid	From Sarum Compline

The sixteenth-century Englishman was not entirely unfamiliar with regular liturgical prayer. For a hundred years the educated layman had been accustomed to use the psalms, prayers and litanies (q.v.) of the Prymer, and the early years of the sixteenth century saw the publication of various Prymers in English. Now the Tudor Englishman had a more truly catholic as well as more scriptural form of liturgical service for use on Sundays and week-days. For the clergy there was provided a less complicated and more easily discharged form of daily devotion, much more suited to the needs of the parish priest now that monastic communities had ceased to exist. Moreover, the congregational services held in the early church at dawn and at dusk were restored to the laity as mattins and evensong, while the terce, sext and none of the ascetics, together with the night offices of the later monks, ceased with their demise. Quite naturally, they were revived in the Anglican Communion with the re-establishment of religious orders in the nineteenth and twentieth centuries. But for four centuries the mattins and evensong of the 1549 *BCP* (with small additions in the revisions of 1552 and 1662) remained the chief services on Sundays and festivals in the English-speaking world, since weekly communion was almost unknown before the Evangelical and Tractarian revivals of the nineteenth century.

Attempts at further reform of the prayer book in the eighteenth and nineteenth centuries concentrated mainly on the communion office, and although they bore fruit outside the Church of England they had little impact within it (*see* A. Elliott Peaston, *The Prayer Book Reform Movement in the XVIIIth Century*, 1940; R. C. D. Jasper, *Prayer Book Revision in England 1800-1900*, 1954). The proposed prayer book of 1928 which was rejected by Parliament made only minor alterations in mattins and evensong, apart from a revised lectionary and calendar (qq.v.) (for details *see* W. K. Lowther Clarke, *The Prayer Book of 1928 Reconsidered*, 1943). Between 1929 and 1965 the climate of opinion in Parliament and in the country underwent a change and the Prayer Book (Alternative and Other Services) Measure 1965 was passed by Parliament, received the Royal Assent in March 1965, and came into force on 1 May 1966. Under the provisions of this Measure, morning and evening prayer in *Alternative Services: First Series* were authorized for permissive use in the Church of England for seven years from 10 June 1966.

These were basically 1662 with the amendments and additions proposed in 1928, together with a new 'Table of Psalms' for Sundays and certain other days and ordering the holy scriptures to be read either in accordance with the lectionary of 1871, or that of 1922 (as revised in 1928), or that revised by the Convocations of Canterbury and York and authorized by them in May 1961. *Alternative Services: Second Series*, which began 'The Order for Morning Prayer, commonly called Mattins' – similarly 'Evensong' – at 'O Lord, open thou our lips', making the introductory scriptural sentences and penitential introduction voluntary, even on Sundays, was authorized for experimental use for three years from 16 February 1968. The *Second Series (Revised)* 'Morning and Evening Prayer' was laid before the new General Synod of the Church of England in November 1970 and was approved in February 1971 for experimental use for four years from 28 November 1971. This departs still further from the *BCP*, both in the penitential introduction by providing alternative forms, and in the services themselves, by introducing as alternative canticles at mattins, a shortened form of *Benedicite*, *Salvator Mundi*, and *Gloria in Excelsis*, and at evensong Psalm 134, 'Hail, gladdening Light', 'Great and wonderful' (Rev. 15.3b-4) and 'Worthy art thou' (Rev. 4.11; etc.). Provision is thus made both for Sunday and weekday use of the daily offices, and an alternative lectionary is provided for weekdays.

The canonical hours in the Orthodox Church are virtually the same as in the Latin rite of the old *Ordo Romanus*. There are eight hours, beginning with vespers, since the day starts at sundown as among the Jews (Gen. 1.5; Lev. 23.5; *cf*. II Cor. 11.25). They are vespers (*esperinos*), compline (*mikron apodeipnon*), mattins (*mesonuktikon*), lauds (*orthros*), together with the minor hours (*mikrai horai*) of prime, terce, sext, and none. During certain periods of fasting each of the hours is followed by an intermediate office, or inter-hour (*mesorion*). The offices consist principally of liturgical compositions – hymns and chanted prayers – but the whole Psalter is read each week, divided into twenty parts (*kathismata*), each comprising seven or eight psalms. These services are to be found in the *Horologion*, which corresponds to the *Breviarium* of the Western (Latin) Church.

The discussions in the Second Vatican

Council reflected a widespread desire for the reform of the Roman breviary. The breviary had its roots in the monastic choral office and the Council had no intention of rejecting this tradition. At the same time it was desired to make it easier to pray at least some of the canonical hours with a congregation in church. Thus, since 1965, over eighty experts from various parts of the world, divided into twelve study groups, have been working on the revision of the Latin Roman breviary. When the *editio typica* appears, English, French, German, etc. official translations will be authorized for use by the pope and the hierarchy in each country. In the meantime, an 'Interim Version of the New Roman Breviary', entitled *The Prayer of the Church* was issued in London and Dublin in 1970, authorized for interim optional use in England and Wales by the Bishops' Conference of 9 April 1970 and confirmed by the Sacred Congregation for Divine Worship (in Rome) on 15 April 1970. Experimental use of the new office is proceeding in the houses of the various religious orders, but the introduction to *The Prayer of the Church* (Geoffrey Chapman, 1970) asserts that 'one of the main aims of the new Breviary is that its riches should not be reserved to priests and religious, but that it should also be a prayer book which many of the faithful could use whether in church or on their own. This holds especially for the Morning and Evensong Prayers' (p. xviii). The general structure of the new office presents us with 'two major hours: Morning Prayer (Lauds) and Evening Prayer (Vespers); an Office of Readings (Mattins) which may be said at whatever time of the day is found most suitable, or as a Vigil; a Midday Prayer (Little Hour); a Night Prayer (Compline)' (p. xix). A French version of *The Prayer of the Church* was published in Paris in 1969. In the words of the Constitution on the Liturgy (art. 89a): 'Lauds as morning prayer and Vespers as evening prayer are the two hinges on which the daily Office turns: hence they are to be considered as the chief hours and are to be celebrated as such.' As we have seen, this return to the usage of the early church, together with the participation of the laity, was achieved by Cranmer for the Church of England in 1549. The present series of interim (or experimental) rites in the Roman Church is paralleled in the Anglican Church, and *The Prayer of the Church* provides a revised lectionary over a period of two

years similar to, but not identical with, the Anglican two-year cycle of lections. As in the morning and evening prayers of the Anglican *Alternative Services: Second Series*, in the new arrangement of the breviary the day begins with 'O Lord open my lips': in the evening prayer, the office starts with the second suffrage of the Anglican office – 'O God, come to my assistance. Lord, make haste to help me.' This is followed in the morning by Ps. 94 and then a hymn, which is always found at the beginning of the other hours. Among the other principal changes are the redistribution of the psalms over a four-week period; the psalter includes fourteen new biblical canticles for the morning office and seven from the NT (Paul or the Apocalypse) for the evening office; the short lections of each hour are much more varied than in the past; the intercessory aspect of prayer, restored to morning and evening prayer, permits the expression of the needs of the church and of the world in the chief prayers of the daily office. Times of silence are indicated in the actual structure of the hours. In the interim rite 'different texts for Terce, Sext and None are not given, but only a *Midday Prayer*. In the *editio typica* provision will be made for those who want to say only one Hour and for those who want to say all three of the Little Hours' (*The Prayer of the Church*, p. xxi). The common offices and prayer for the dead conclude the main book, but there are supplements containing the propers (q.v.) of the seasonal cycles and those of saints' days. All this suggests that eventually there will be a revised breviary for the monks, whose chief duty is to sing the full office in choir, and a shortened version based on the present interim rite for the use of parish priests and the devout laity.

C. W. DUGMORE

Canticles

From the Latin *canticulum*, a little song. Canticles are songs from the Bible other than from the book of Psalms. The four canticles most used in Christian worship are the *Benedictus* (Luke 1.68-79) (not to be confused with the *Benedictus qui venit*, which in most eucharistic liturgies follows the *Sanctus* [q.v.]), the *Benedicite* (vv. 35-66a of the Song of the Three Holy Children in the Apocrypha), the *Nunc Dimittis* (Luke 2.29-32) and the *Magnificat* (Luke 1.46-55). The title is also applied to the *Te Deum* and, in the Roman Breviary, to several songs derived from the OT, namely, two songs of Moses (Ex. 15.1-18; Deut. 32.1-43); the song of Hannah (I Sam. 2.1-10); of Isaiah (Isa. 12); of Hezekiah (Isa. 38.10-20); and of Habbakuk (Hab. 3.2-19).

EDITOR

Cantor

The person, clerical or lay, who sets the pitch and leads the singing – especially unaccompanied singing. In synagogue worship the cantor is a minister of considerable importance and the office existed early in both Eastern and Western Christendom. With the elaboration of psalmody and its accompanying antiphons in the monastic and cathedral services of the medieval West, the cantor became essential for the proper performance of the liturgy and offices. Elaborate rules were laid down to govern the number of cantors proper to the various feasts and seasons. The titles of precentor and succentor borne by clergymen in cathedral and collegiate churches are derived from the term, as is the custom of describing the northern side of the choir as 'cantoris'.

P. HINCHLIFF

Carol

In common use, the name given to a type of simple, traditional, essentially rhythmic song, particularly one whose words concern the Nativity. Obscure in origin, the term has been conclusively traced only so far as the Old French form *carole*; but ultimate derivations have been claimed from the Latin *corolla*, Greek *choros*, and even *kyrie eleison*. Continental equivalents of the Christmas carol are the French *Noël* and German *Wiegenlied*.

In England, from their first appearance in the fourteenth century, carols were marked by a characteristic *refrain* or *burden* intended for dancing. The opening words of one of the earliest surviving burdens (*c.* 1350) describe the singers joining hands in a ring-dance: 'Honnd by honnd we schulle us take . . .' Early use (1470) of the term carol for 'a ring of standing stones' (OED) reflects this implicit meaning. There is thus a clear distinction between a carol and a Christmas hymn.

During the fifteenth century, the carol developed as an art-form, both words and music being produced at the hands of learned ecclesiastics, not semi-literate minstrels. Pre-

served in manuscript form rather than by popular tradition, the 'art-carol' of the fifteenth century differed from the 'folk-carol' in a number of respects. First, its text had a highly organized fixed form closely related to the stanza-pattern of the French *virelai* and the Italian *ballata*. Secondly, it was not necessarily composed in the vernacular; many surviving examples are in Latin while others are *macaronic* – having alternate lines in English and Latin throughout. Thirdly, unlike the folk-carol sung by a soloist or a chorus in unison, the art-carol was set for a group of singers in two or three contrapuntal parts. However, such sophisticated examples retained the pronouncedly rhythmic character of the popular carol – though their association with physical movement was likely to have been limited to processional use. In recent years a full study of the fifteenth-century art-carol has been made (*see* bibliography); but the most familiar ancient carols in modern use are folk-carols, handed down by oral tradition until their collection and publication after 1820.

The medieval carol may be seen as the result of a desire to introduce a more jovial element into particular acts of worship – both in and out of church – than the sober traditional melodies of plainchant could afford. The Christmas crib introduced by St Francis of Assisi, and the miracle and mystery plays of the thirteenth century, forecast that desire, doubtless later providing some of the first occasions for carol-singing.

The great age of the English carol was the fifteenth century – the age of humanism and the emergence of the ballad. Subjects treated include many beside the Nativity. Some are purely secular – the *Agincourt Song* is an example. Others are intended to celebrate particular seasons of the year, particularly from Advent to Candlemas. A third type retells in many-versed form a Christian legend (*The Cherry Tree*) or propounds a homily (*Remember, O thou man*). Akin, though hardly to be considered a true carol, is the *Wassail Song* – pagan in origin, but made respectable by its commendation of the virtue of hospitality.

The impact of the Reformation and the consequent growth of Puritanism in this country changed the nature of the English carol, without causing its disappearance. After the ban imposed upon Christmas festivity during the Commonwealth was lifted, the singing of folk-carols was revived, to last in dwindling popularity throughout the eighteenth century.

In 1822, two amateurs independently remarked the imminent disappearance of the carol; and each attempted to 'rescue from oblivion some carol melodies which in a few years will be heard no more'. William Hone's article *Christmas Carols* and Davies Gilbert's *Some Ancient Christmas Carols* were the first printed collections of modern times. Their appearance heralded the rebirth of carol-singing. Other more important collections were to follow: W. Sandys, *Christmas Carols, Ancient & Modern* (1833); E. F. Rimbault, *Little Book of Carols* (1846); Neale and Helmore, *Carols for Christmas-tide* (1853) and *Carols for Easter-tide* (1854); and Edmund Sedding, *Ancient Christmas Carols* (1864) marked the first stage. Stainer and Bramley, *Christmas Carols New and Old* (1871), brought the carol into every pew.

During the last quarter of the nineteenth century a flood of so-called carols issued from the pens of an army of would-be composers, some of whose effusions are still unfortunately current. A first attempt at redress came with G. R. Woodward's *Cowley Carol Book* (1901); and in 1928 the appearance of the *Oxford Book of Carols*, edited by Percy Dearmer, R. Vaughan Williams and Martin Shaw, presented a model carol collection of authentic character. Since that book became available, popular standards of taste and awareness have been strengthened, and carols have recovered something of the health and vitality which was theirs during the fifteenth century. Modern composers have shown that they are able to present the simplicity, strength and honesty requisite in a true carol; but the modern commercialization of Christmas has also encouraged the production of a repertoire of spurious carols of a type as sickly, sentimental and inappropriate as anything produced during the decadence of a century ago.

P. Dearmer, Preface to *The Oxford Book of Carols*, 1928; R. L. Greene, *Early English Carols*, 1953; E. Routley, *The English Carol*, 1958; J. Stevens, *Medieval Carols: Musica Britannica*, Vol. IV, 1952.

BERNARR RAINBOW

Cassock

see Vestments (2*b*)

Catechumen, Catechumenate

An organized preparation for baptism (q.v.) came into being in the second century. Under the heading of the Two Ways the *Didache*, a Syrian document, included moral teaching to be given to catechumens. Justin Martyr in Rome briefly alluded to a moral and doctrinal preparation, which included also prayers and fasting. Tertullian in Carthage mentioned frequent praying, fasts and all night vigils before baptism. Much fuller information is given in Hippolytus' *Apostolic Tradition*, where the catechumenate is divided into two parts, the long-term preparation or catechumenate proper, lasting up to three years, when the candidates were trained in Christian doctrine and morals, and the final intensive preparation, when those accepted for baptism were exorcised daily, fasted on the two days before Easter, kept an all-night vigil consisting in the reading of scripture and instruction, and were finally baptized on Easter morning. A very thorough preparation such as this was possible during the age of persecution when inquirers were comparatively few.

After the peace of the church, however, converts were so numerous that this long and meticulous preparation could not be maintained. Much valuable information concerning the catechumenate in this period is found scattered among the writings of Augustine, in the sermons of Ambrose on the sacraments, in John the Deacon's letter to Senarius, the Pilgrimage of Etheria and the catechetical lectures of Cyril of Jerusalem. Those catechumens who wished for baptism and were approved by the church were enrolled at the beginning of Lent, during which they met frequently for prayer, exorcism (q.v.) and instruction, being taught the creed (q.v.) (*traditio symboli*), and repeating it from memory (*redditio symboli*) shortly before their baptism at Easter. Catechumens who were taken ill could be baptized in haste. Although they attended the first part of the eucharist, they were dismissed before the eucharist proper began, never being allowed to see the communion of the faithful until they were themselves eligible by baptism to communicate.

As infant baptism prevailed the long term preparation necessarily disappeared. All the time that infants were reserved for baptism at Easter or Pentecost they were enrolled as catechumens half way through Lent and were brought to a number of scrutinies which consisted in prayer and exorcism, instruction being now out of the question. But when in the late Middle Ages it was deemed necessary to baptize all infants within a week of birth for fear that they might die unbaptized and consequently be deprived of salvation, the ceremonies of the catechumenate became compressed into a rite, based on the old order for the making of a catechumen, which took place at the church door immediately before baptism. In England this practice is seen in the Latin Sarum manual and in the first English prayer book of 1549. In response to Bucer's criticism, this rite at the church door was abolished in 1552, everything henceforward taking place around the font. So ended the last trace of a catechumenate before baptism.

J. D. C. Fisher, *Christian Initiation: Baptism in the Medieval West*, 1965; E. C. Whitaker, *Documents of the Baptismal Liturgy*, 1960.

J. D. C. FISHER

Cathedra

From Greek, meaning 'a thing sat upon', with particular reference to the official seat or throne of the bishop. Hence the church in which this seat is placed is known as the cathedral church. This is undoubtedly the oldest insignia of a bishop's authority, and many centuries before bishops assumed the wearing of mitres, rings or even the carrying of pastoral staves and croziers, they were enseated in their throne or *cathedra* on the day of their consecration to the episcopate as the sign that they were invested with authority to preside over the church in their diocese. Thus the writer of the fourth-century *Apostolic Constitutions* (8.5) says: 'And early in the morning let him be placed in this throne in a place set apart for him among the bishops, they all giving him the kiss in the Lord.'

In the earlier centuries the bishop's throne was normally placed in the centre of the apse (q.v.) behind the altar; on either side there were lesser seats for his presbyters. It was from this seat that the bishop presided at the eucharist and also preached the sermon.

In the later Middle Ages the consecration of a bishop tended to take place in the church of the archbishop or metropolitan, and thus the enseatment of the new bishop in his own cathedral took place in a separate ceremony on another day. The lawyers discovered that by this means they could ask for two fees in connection with the consecration and enthronement of a new bishop.

In northern Europe in the later Middle Ages the east ends of cathedral churches were developed into a series of chapels and so the bishop's *cathedra* had to be brought round to one side of the sanctuary (q.v.) before the high altar, but the idea that this throne was always on the north side is not correct. In Norwich Cathedral we can see the restored bishop's throne today behind the altar (*see* Plate 20).

In East Syria an entirely different arrangement prevailed, where the bishop's throne was placed half-way down the nave inside a horseshoe-shaped chancel facing east. Thus the bishop sat in his *cathedra* with his back to the congregation and his presbyters on

Plate 20   The restored bishop's cathedra or throne behind the high altar, Norwich Cathedral, England

either side. This arrangement was the apsidal arrangement in reverse. In the first part of the East Syrian liturgy the bishop sat facing east; but at the offertory (q.v.) he advanced to the altar with his assistants and stood facing east as the altar was right against the east wall.

F. Cabrol-H. Leclercq, *Dictionnaire d'archéologie chrétienne et de liturgie,* 1907ff., Tome 3, 19-75 and Tome 15, 1866-1884.

C. E. POCKNEE

Cathedral

A church in which the bishop's *cathedra* (q.v.) is located. All other churches, from the fourth century onwards, were in a sense pro-cathedrals, in that the presbyters who presided and taught there did so as the delegates of the bishop; these buildings were so many extensions of the cathedral necessitated by the growth in the number of Christians and by the fact that the bishop could not be in more than one place at once.

Functionally these buildings were not just centres of worship alone, and it is historically incorrect to visualize them as large liturgical halls with baptisteries attached and with no other accommodation whatsoever. On the contrary, the space for worship was only one of a number of interrelated rooms which made the bishop's church a real service-centre for the Christian community. Living quarters for the clergy, libraries, guest chambers and even bath installations were common. The main hall itself was not exclusively reserved for worship and could be, and was, used for a host of secular activities, among which were included living and sleeping, eating and drinking, dancing, the storage and sale of goods, meetings of all kinds and legal proceedings.

Architecturally, cathedrals began to diverge from parish churches under the influence of four factors. (1) The monastic movement. In the Middle Ages many cathedrals, especially in England, were under the direction of monks, and for the saying of their offices an almost self-contained sanctuary and choir (qq.v.) were fitted into the building. (2) The cult of the saints led to the increase of side altars, containing relics of the saints, and these were also required for votive masses and for the daily celebration of mass by each and every priest. (3) The elaboration of ceremonial. The increase in processions etc. required provision of circulation space, which was also needed for (4) pilgrimages.

The function of the cathedral has been differently conceived throughout the ages. Initially it was the church of the bishop and a centre of mission. In the Middle Ages each one existed mainly to provide intercessions for deceased benefactors. After the Reformation, cathedrals were regarded as providing for (1) worship; (2) theological education; (3) the care of the poor and aged; (4) the upkeep of the surrounding area. In the nineteenth century their role was much discussed but little new thinking emerged. At the present day a whole host of possible fresh uses is under consideration.

G. Cope, ed., *Cathedral and Mission,* 1969.

EDITOR

Cathedral Office

Liturgical scholars are becoming increasingly interested in an important aspect of liturgical history in the late patristic and early medieval periods: the disappearance, more or less complete over a large part of Christendom, and everywhere to some extent, of what is for convenience called the 'cathedral office', the regular public services of the church, other than the eucharist itself, in their original form, and the forms which developed from it, and their replacement by other forms which originated in the private worship of monastic communities in the fourth century.

The original public worship of the church, apart from the eucharist, comprised only two regular gatherings, evening and morning – vespers and mattins; on the eves of Sundays and great feasts a third, a vigil or night office, was added. But the same fourth century which saw the definitive establishment of this pattern – derived ultimately from the synagogue, and in respect of the vigil from the Paschal vigil (q.v.) of the early church – saw also the growth of the movement which was destined to overthrow it, organized cenobitic monasticism. In a very short time monastic ideals and spirituality were dominant, and it was inevitable that the consequent monasticizing of the church's life should extend to its worship. From the beginning the monastic movement had developed a way of worship of its own, which was naturally very different from the public worship of 'secular' churches. In some places, where monastic establishments were attached at an early stage to the public churches, a liturgical compromise grew up between the old way – the 'cathedral office' – and the new way of the monks. The latter was marked, first, by an increase in the number of daily services from two or three to seven or eight (*see* **Canonical Hours**), and second, the structuring of these services round the continuous reading of the scriptures in a given period, and the continuous recitation of the psalter in another given period (in most places, a week), together with the virtual elimination of most other elements of public prayer. Ultimately the monastic round and structure of the office conquered nearly everywhere. In some places the cathedral office disappeared almost completely: at Rome, for example, where monastic clergy were early placed in charge of the great basilicas, the disappearance was so fast and so complete that so far it has proved impossible to reconstruct the Roman cathedral office at all. The Roman breviary offices are purely monastic in structure, and the differences between the 'secular' and 'monastic' breviaries are no more than minor variants within one essentially monastic rite. Elsewhere in the West, elements of the cathedral office survived, and continue to survive, at Milan, and to a much greater extent in the books, although less in actual use, at Toledo. In the East the Chaldean rite preserves more of the structure and content of its original cathedral office than does any other rite in Christendom; the Byzantine rite has preserved far more elements of its cathedral rite than has its Roman counterpart – the persistence of these side by side with the monastic elements is the principal cause of the often excessive length of Byzantine services. (An essentially cathedral office survived at Constantinople, although with some monastic additions, down to the Latin conquest in 1204.)

The principle of *lectio continua* (continuous reading of the scriptures and recitation of the psalter, with little reference to the church's year), which makes the divine office less an act of liturgical worship in the strict sense than a corporate occasion of individual meditation, has dominated attempts at reform or renewal of the office in the West from the early Middle Ages to the present day. In England, Cranmer may have reduced the number of daily services to two in the *BCP*, but the structure and content of those two

services are based on a purely monastic *concept* of the office; and this is true, to a large extent, of the recent *Daily Office* published by the inter-denominational Joint Liturgical Group. It does not seem to have occurred to the authors of this and similar attempts at producing a divine office suitable for modern use that the fundamental principle on which their work is based is itself highly questionable both theologically and pastorally, and is itself part and parcel of a spirituality which, whatever its virtues (and they are many), no longer provides a viable foundation for public devotion. Such a foundation can only be found in a return to the principles of the cathedral office, and an imaginative application of them to the contemporary situation, by which a form of divine office may be produced which is truly integrated with the eucharist, with the church's year, and with the pattern of everyday life.

At the time of writing it is impossible to suggest further reading, as the little that has so far been written on the subject is of a highly technical character, and for the most part hidden in the pages of learned journals in languages other than English.

W. JARDINE GRISBROOKE

Celebrant

The principal minister at the eucharist. Originally Christian worship, like its synagogue equivalent, was probably directed by a liturgical president and there is some evidence to suggest that in the early church the celebrant was actually called 'the president'. When the office of bishop (q.v.) was fully developed, he was the normal celebrant at the eucharist for so long as it was possible for the greater part of the Christian community in each city to worship as a single congregation. Presbyters (q.v.) later became the normal celebrant at the eucharist. By an ironical twist in the meaning of the terms, the bishop when present was said to 'preside' but not to 'celebrate', i.e. the bishop sat in his throne and performed certain actions such as blessings, but a priest at the altar actually celebrated. For various reasons it became the custom, in the medieval West, for the number of celebrations to be multiplied and for the celebrant to recite almost the whole of the service himself. In the East this has never happened and there are certain parts of the rite that can only be recited by another minister, e.g. a deacon (q.v.). The Liturgical Movement (q.v.) has tended to revive the practice of participation by several ministers (ordained or lay) in the taking of the service, and there is a new interest in 'concelebration' (q.v.) (several clergymen sharing together as joint celebrants). The position of the celebrant (whether he should face east, west or south) has also attracted a good deal of attention (*see* **Postures**). In most churches the celebrant is required to be an ordained person, but the Congregational tradition maintains the rights of laymen to preside at the eucharist and in the Methodist Church it is possible for a layman to be specially authorized to celebrate the sacraments.

G. Dix, *The Shape of the Liturgy*, 1945; A. A. King, *Concelebration in the Christian Church*, 1966; B. Minchin, *Every Man in his Ministry*, 1960.

P. HINCHLIFF

Centralized Building

By the central type of architecture no one uniform plan is indicated but the general principle of eurhythmic disposition around a central vertical axis. The buildings for liturgical use to which this classification applies did not develop from the basilica (q.v.) but existed side by side and independently from the beginnings of Christian architecture. Centralized buildings are of three types: (1) *martyria* (q.v.); (2) baptisteries (q.v.); (3) congregational churches (*see* **Architectural Setting**).

EDITOR

Ceremonial

According to strict ecclesiastical usage, ceremonial refers to the prescribed and formal actions that constitute worship. It is therefore to be distinguished from ritual (q.v.), which refers to the prescribed form of words. Hence the use of incense falls within the category of ceremonial, while the canon is within that of ritual. However, the two terms are often used interchangeably and this may lead to some confusion. The Royal Commission, which was established in 1867 to inquire into the differences of ceremonial practice in the Church of England, was known as the Ritual Commission and within its purview it included vestments, incense and lights (qq.v.). In fact, vestments are neither an essential part

of ceremonial nor of ritual but are rather to be classified as ornaments, while lights may be no more than a necessary source of illumination. Lights only come under ceremonial when their use is an integral part of the service, as, for example, at Tenebrae (q.v.).

If this strict sense of ceremonial is adhered to, it includes such actions as the kiss of peace, the fraction, elevation (qq.v.), the pouring of water in baptism, the laying on of hands in ordination (q.v.), etc.

EDITOR

Chairman of District

In the Methodist Church circuits, which are under a superintendent (q.v.), are grouped in districts under a chairman who presides over the district synod and may exercise certain pastoral and disciplinary functions in relation to other ministers. No special liturgical position is reserved to him though, in practice, he may officiate at ordinations. In America the corresponding office is that of the superintendent of the district under the bishop.

P. HINCHLIFF

Chaldean Church *see* East Syrian Worship

Chalice and Paten

The term 'chalice' is an anglicized form of the Latin *calix*, meaning cup. The vessel used by Jesus for the wine at the institution of the eucharist may reasonably be supposed to have been one of the ordinary two handled cups of that period. The cathedral at Valencia, Spain, has in its treasury what has been claimed to be this identical cup. It is a circular cup nearly four inches in diameter, hollowed out from a single hair-brown sardonyx, with a plain stone moulding round the lip. Its style shows it to be of antique Roman origin. While it is not actually impossible that this vessel was used at the Last Supper, modern archaeologists feel that the evidence does not satisfy all the requirements of historical criticism.

In tracing the history of the use of the chalice in Western Christendom and its evolution, two historical facts need to be borne in mind: (1) the recognition of Christianity by the emperor Constantine the Great in the early fourth century; (2) the gradual withdrawal of the chalice from the laity, begun in the twelfth century, which was officially confirmed by the Council of Constance in 1415.

Chalices of precious metal were not unknown in the early days of the church, nor were cups made from large jewels that had been hollowed out. But cups of glass and base metal such as pewter or lead were also used. The official recognition of Christianity gave a considerable impetus to the use of chalices of gold and silver decorated with precious stones. But Boniface, the English missionary to Germany, was not unfamiliar with wooden chalices in the eighth century. Among religious communities there were ascetic objections to the use of any appearance of luxury in worship which chalices of precious metal encouraged.

Prior to the withdrawal of the cup from the laity in the West, two kinds of chalices were in common use at the eucharist, the chalice used by the celebrant on the altar for the consecration, and the ministerial chalice used for the communion of the congregation, known as the *scyphus*. The latter was furnished with two handles for convenience when carrying (*see* Plate 21). The ministerial chalice was filled with wine at the time of the offertory and held by one of the deacons or acolytes. In *Ordo Romanus Primus* we are told, 'when . . . the lay folk are to be communicated, the archdeacon pours a little of the consecrated chalice into the ministerial chalice, the contents of which are

Plate 21   The Gourdon Chalice and Paten, gold and enamel, c. 527, France

supplied by the offering of the faithful'. It was the teaching of the church in the earlier centuries that the addition of a small quantity of the consecrated species to another chalice was enough to extend the virtue of consecration to the whole contents of the second chalice. The consecration chalice was usually smaller than the ministerial chalice. In the larger churches several ministerial chalices were used at one eucharist.

The communicants imbibed the consecrated wine through a gold or silver tube or reed known by a variety of names such as *fistula*, *pipa* or *calamus*, rather like the modern lemonade straw in form. As late as 1269 an inventory of St Paul's Cathedral mentions 'two calami'. The pope at Rome still receives the chalice in this manner. The reception of both sacred species by the congregation was made standing and not kneeling. After the twelfth century with the withdrawal of the cup from the laity the chalice became smaller, since only the celebrant communicated from it; and it assumed the form with which we are now familiar, being composed of three distinct parts or members, the bowl, the knop, and the foot (*see* Plate 22).

The Reformation brought about the restoration of the chalice to the laity in the Church of England. The late medieval form of chalice was then found to be too small and was replaced by the 'fayre', 'decent' or 'comely' communion cup, a vessel of German form, but lacking the grace of the pre-Reformation chalice. In some instances the foot and knop of a pre-Reformation vessel were brazed to a new and larger bowl. But in the seventeenth and eighteenth centuries some magnificent cups of silver-gilt were produced in England. Under Archbishop

Plate 22   A modern chalice and paten

Laud in the middle of the seventeenth century a number of chalices based on a modified form of the pre-Reformation chalice were brought into use.

Since the Oxford Movement in the nineteenth century, there has been the tendency, as in other matters, to revert to pre-Reformation forms of the chalice.

In the Roman Catholic Church in the seventeenth and eighteenth centuries the design of the chalice was considerably affected by the liberal art of the Renaissance. The chalice tended to assume a greater height and the bowl passed from a conical to a bell-shaped form and the decoration assumed secularized motifs.

In Eastern Christendom, where the chalice has never been withdrawn from the laity, it has remained larger in form. In the Eastern Orthodox rite communicants are given both species together, the bishop or priest dipping the consecrated bread into the chalice and then conveying the bread thus intincted on a spoon into the mouth of the communicant.

The Paten. According to tradition, the church of St Lorenzo, Genoa, possesses the dish used by Jesus at the Last Supper for the consecrated bread. It is a shallow glass bowl, hexagonal in form, with two small handles, deep green in colour and was at one time thought to be an emerald. As with the chalice, it is much more likely that Jesus used an ordinary domestic vessel of the time.

Furthermore, as with the chalice it is likely that the paten may have had more than one form and use for many centuries: (1) the dish or paten used by the celebrant at the altar; (2) the ministerial paten for use in distributing the consecrated species. It should be understood that throughout the whole of Christendom for the first millennium the use of leavened bread was more usual. Only in the Latin West did wafer-bread gradually replace leavened bread from the end of the ninth century onwards. Consequently the ministerial paten, used probably for collecting the offerings of bread from the people, and subsequently used also for the administration of the consecrated loaves, was more like the modern tea-tray in form, being made of gold or silver and decorated round its borders with precious stones and filigree design.

The consecrating paten was circular in form and this remained in use after the introduction of wafer-bread in the West. The

later medieval forms usually fitted into the top of the chalice bowl by having a 'well' sunk in them.

In the post-Reformation era in England, when leavened bread was reintroduced the cover of the communion cup often served as a paten when reversed. It was usually surmounted by a disc on which the date was frequently engraved. Towards the end of the eighteenth century the paten took the form of a circular dish of considerable size known as a 'tazza' standing on a raised foot. The Eastern Orthodox rite employs a paten of this type. With a revived use of wafer-bread, under the second phase of the Oxford Movement and the Catholic Revival in the nineteenth century, the late medieval form of paten has also been reintroduced.

J. Gilchrist, *Anglican Church Plate*, 1967; J. A. Jungmann, *The Mass of the Roman Rite*, 2 vols., 1951, 1955; E. Mercenier, *La Prière des Églises de Rite Byzantin*, I, 1947; C. Oman, *English Medieval Base Metal Church Plate*, 1964; W. W. Watts, *A Catalogue of Chalices*, 1922.

C. E. POCKNEE

Chancel

The term chancel is derived from the Latin *cancellus* or balustrade and originally referred to that part of a church which was reserved for the officiating clergy and was divided from the rest of the building by low screens. In this sense it was synonymous with the first meaning of the word sanctuary (q.v.).

In the medieval two-room plan (*see* **Architectural Setting**), chancel continued to be used of the whole space east of the nave, demarcated by the chancel screen, but now it was understood to comprise two sections: the sanctuary, in its second sense, i.e. the limited area immediately around the altar, and the space between it and the screen (q.v.).

In popular parlance, the intervening area from the chancel steps up to but not including the sanctuary is often called the chancel, and therefore corresponds to the restricted sense of choir (q.v.). As with the term sanctuary, this dual usage can lead to ambiguity, since the same word refers both to the whole of an area and to a subdivision of the same area.

EDITOR

Chants

For the purpose of this article chanting may

be defined as the recitation of prose – as opposed to verse – to a melodic formula. Thus, the rhythm of chanting reflects the irregular stresses of speech rather than the regular rhythmic flow of simple melody. The prose psalms provide the main occasion for congregational chanting today, but different systems have been employed for chanting the psalms over the centuries.

Throughout the Middle Ages the psalms were chanted in unison to a series of short plainsong melodies known as tones (*see* **Psalm Tones**).

As their technical competence increased, composers began to 'harmonize' the psalm tones by adding parts for higher and lower voices above and below the original plainsong. These ornamental versions, known as *faux-bourdons*, were sung alternately verse by verse with the unison tones.

From these faux-bourdon settings emerged the Anglican chant. One of the earliest surviving examples of the Anglican chant is given below. Dating from the sixteenth century and sometimes attributed to Adrian Batten, its tenor part comprises the first Psalm tone:

Several other early examples to be found in most modern chant books similarly include one of the tones in their tenor parts.

During the Commonwealth, psalm-chanting was suppressed in England and thus tradition was broken. Efforts to revive the choral service at the Restoration (1660) encouraged the writing of new Anglican chants, both 'single' and 'double', in which the melodic interest of the treble part – rather than the presence of a psalm tone in the tenor – became the main feature. Because of their own independent rhythmic character, such chants lent themselves less readily to the prose of the psalms; and it has frequently been remarked that such 'tuneful' chants, with melodies designed for boys' voices, tend to discourage congregational participation. These characteristics were to be responsible for later attempts to supplant the Anglican chant.

Until the nineteenth century, the psalms were customarily chanted *extempore* from the Prayer Book – the length of the recitation in each half-verse being decided according to the 'Rule of Three and Five', whereby the third and fifth syllable from the end of each half-verse were made to correspond with a change of note in the chant. The standard of chanting, even in cathedrals, was therefore extremely haphazard. Pointed psalters were prepared in an attempt to achieve unanimity, the first example to appear being that of Robert Janes, organist of Ely cathedral, published in 1837. It was followed by those of Stimpson (1840), S. S. Wesley (1843), and Hullah (1844); but the age of congregational chanting of the prose psalms cannot be said to have begun until the publication of Mercer's *Church Psalter and Hymn Book* (1854).

Dissatisfaction with the 'jaunty' character of the Anglican chant led to various attempts to re-introduce the use of Gregorian tones to the Anglican service. The first plainsong psalter with English text was *Laudes Diurnae*, produced by a leading Tractarian, Frederick Oakeley, and his organist Richard Redhead, in 1843. In spite of its faulty pointing the book enjoyed considerable use among Tractarians, until the appearance of Thomas Helmore's more practical *Psalter Noted* in 1849. Thereafter, the use of 'Gregorians' for the psalms tended to be regarded as the prerogative of High Anglicans.

More recently, continuing dissatisfaction with the Anglican chant has encouraged the use of 'Gelineau' psalms in many churches. Originally produced for Roman Catholic use in France in 1953 by Joseph Gelineau, sj, new translations from the Hebrew gave to the words a regular pattern of stress designed to be readily reconcilable with the simple rhythmic tunes provided. These new versions of the psalms have since been prepared in English translations and adopted for occasional use in many churches – without, however, achieving universal acceptance.

Chanting of the prose psalms and canticles necessarily presents much greater technical challenge than the singing of hymns; and most congregations find themselves at a disadvantage in these parts of the service. The metrical psalms (q.v.) introduced by Calvin in the sixteenth century were an attempt to overcome the problem. Yet the beauty of the prose psalms in English is such that few churchmen would be prepared to dispense with their use. In recent times, many attempts have been made to provide pointed psalters edited to enable the psalms to be sung with the 'speech-rhythm' which they require. Perhaps the most widely adopted of these has been Nicholson's *Parish Psalter*, which the Royal School of Church Music has made familiar throughout the English-speaking world.

P. le Huray, *Music and the Reformation in England*, 1967; C. H. Phillips, *The Singing Chruch*, rev. ed. 1968.

BERNARR RAINBOW

The Chants of the Proper of the Mass

The texts of the proper (q.v.) determine the forms of the music set to them. The introit, offertory and communion are processional texts consisting of an antiphon and as many verses of the particular psalm as may be necessary for the procession of the celebrant and his retinue to reach the altar at the introit, to accompany the offering of the bread and wine, and the procession of the faithful to receive Holy Communion. The gradual has a responsorial text in which the congregation, as described by Augustine, originally responded to the verses of the psalm with a brief interjection, such as alleluia, or a verse of the psalm itself. The usual form of the alleluia is threefold – alleluia, verse of a psalm or other text, repeat of alleluia – but in Paschal time two alleluias are sung, the first one supplanting the gradual responsory and having the same form as above, the second having no repeat after the verse. The tract and sequence are *sui generis*, and will be explained in the notes on these various pieces below.

Introit. Only one verse of the psalm is found in the Roman gradual and the antiphon is repeated only after the *Gloria Patri*. This may well have been the practice long before in ordinary parish churches, which did not employ elaborate ceremonial. The descriptions of ritual found in the *Ordines Romani* or the *Ceremoniale Episcoporum* always refer to a high mass celebrated by pope or prelates.

Gradual. This became a virtuoso piece, in the literal sense, and tempted the deacons who sang it to exercise their skill for their own glory. In a decree of 5 July 595, Gregory forbade them to sing it for the good of their souls! Both gradual and alleluia are sung when no action takes place in the sanctuary and all attention is fixed on the choir. The verse is customarily sung by one or two cantors or by treble voices only.

Alleluia. An interesting feature of this piece is the repetition of the *jubilus*, that is, the vocalized final vowel of the alleluia, at the end of the verse and so before the formal repeat of the whole of the opening section. It is quite wrong to regard the alleluia as part of the gradual. They are two separate chants.

Tract. This penitential chant is sung between Septuagesima and Easter when the alleluia is silenced. Its melodies are extremely old and venerable monuments of the chant of the Latin church and were sung by a solo voice. The texts consisted of either a part of or, more rarely, a whole psalm.

Sequence. One result of the new creative impulse to add to existing Gregorian chant that arose in the eighth century was the sequence. It was an addition to the alleluia, either of melody or text, or both, and came about because of the difficulty in memorizing the florid vocalizations of the alleluia. It owes much to Notker Babulus, a monk of St Gall, whose master instructed him to set every note of the *jubilus* to a separate syllable; this shows that Notker did not invent the form. A very large number of sequences was composed, all but four of which were discarded by the Council of Trent. The remaining ones, of which *Dies irae, dies illa* is the best known, are very beautiful, but many others might well be revived, at least by choral groups who almost alone in the present situation can keep plainsong alive.

Offertory. The complete form of this chant dates from Gregory. It consisted at the start of psalms sung between the two sides of the choir. This responsorial treatment ceased when the antiphon alone remained without any psalm verses and so it then became an antiphonal chant, psalm verses only finding a place now in the requiem mass. These chants of the offertory are alone in having repetition of the words. The plainsong of the discarded verses was published by Carlus Ott in 1935. These form superb motets.

Communion. The musical form of this chant was the same as that of the introit, but the major proportion of the words of the antiphon were taken from other parts of the Bible than the psalter, those of the verses being taken from the latter source. It is, as in the case of the offertory, the antiphon that survives in the gradual.

ALEC ROBERTSON

Chapel

From the *cappella* or cloak of St Martin, the term was applied to the sanctuary in which it was preserved and ultimately to any building for worship not being a church. It is now used of: (1) public places of worship in many Christian traditions; (2) a private place of worship, as in a college or school, or belonging to an individual, in which case it is known as a proprietary chapel; (3) part of a large church or cathedral with its own separate altar.

EDITOR

Chasuble *see* Vestments (1*f*)

Choir (Architectural)

Originally that part of the church which contained the clergy, i.e. it referred to the chancel (q.v.) or the sanctuary (q.v.) as a whole, situated at the east end of the building. A church therefore had two interrelated parts, the choir and the nave (q.v.).

In the medieval plan these two were separated to form two rooms (*see* **Architectural Setting**) and the choir itself was further subdivided into the sanctuary, containing the altar, and the place of the clergy, the term choir now being restricted to the latter. So what was once a designation of the whole came to be applied to a part of the whole. The size of the choir, in the narrower sense, was much increased and often equalled in length a half or two-thirds of the nave. This enlargement was to provide space, particularly in monastic establishments, for the staff of clerics. So a tripartite division was created, consisting of: (1) the nave, which constituted one room; (2) the choir, with (3) the altar precincts together forming the second room.

An exception to this separation of the laity from the altar, common to most European countries, is to be noted in Spain. There the short eastern apse containing the altar was retained, and the choir or *coro*, enclosed on the north, west and south sides, was placed at the west end of the nave. The laity therefore had their place between the sanctuary and the choir and were not separated from the former by the latter.

After the Reformation the choir was used in England for the celebration of the eucharist, the communicants coming from the nave to gather round the altar (q.v.), which was brought forward from the east wall. By the nineteenth century this practice had tended to lapse and the choir was pressed into use for the singers. Two men in particular were responsible for this innovation, J. Jebb and W. F. Hook, who adopted the expedient in the newly built parish church of Leeds immediately after its consecration in 1841. They placed the musical choir, robed in surplices, in the architectural choir, and this practice has become widespread in all denominations. As a tradition it has not had a very long history, and at the present day many question the rightness of this separation of the congregation from the altar.

G. W. O. Addleshaw and F. Etchells, *The Architectural Setting of Anglican Worship*, 1948.

EDITOR

Choir (Musical)

The presence of a white-robed assembly of the sons of Kohath 'cunning in song' is the subject of frequent reference in Old Testament accounts of worship both before and after the dedication of Solomon's Temple. Under Asaph, Heman and Jeduthun the Temple choir was divided into sections which undertook their ministry 'by course'. The tradition was preserved until the destruction of the Temple in AD 70, at which time Rabbi Joshua ben Hananiah, a member of the Temple Levitical choir, recorded that the Temple choristers were accustomed to sing as a body both in the Temple itself and in the synagogue. Thus may be traced the pre-Christian ancestry of those choirs which formed a constant element in Christian worship once the days of active persecution were over. A concrete link between the two traditions is provided by the psalms and by the antiphonal mode of singing which they suggest. Another is found in the insistence, both in Judaism and the early Christian church, that skill and training were requisite in those to whom was entrusted the ministry of song. The Council of Laodicea (c. 360) even forbade all others to sing in church beside the canonical singers. That inflexibility was not, happily, to survive; but the need to ensure the worthiness of the music offered in worship which it emphasized is noteworthy.

With the evolution of the Gregorian repertory, by the year 600 clear principles had emerged governing the respective contributions of choir and people in the music of the liturgy. The congregation was given simple melodies and refrains within their competence to perform; the choir was allotted more elaborate melodies, some of which called for skilled solo cantors. The same principle was to govern the situation as the art of musical composition developed to make available the splendid polyphony of the fifteenth and sixteenth centuries as an accessory to heighten worship – so long as trained singers competent to perform such music were available.

It is a fallacy that at the Reformation choirs were abolished, so as to allow the people themselves to sing. This was by no means the case. Luther certainly introduced the chorale with the intention of encouraging the congregation to take an active musical part in the service; but his musical understanding prevented him from robbing the Reformed service of those devotional elements which a trained choir could provide. Calvin, too, introduced the metrical psalm (q.v.) as the people's song; but though his fear of a possible abuse of music's emotional power made him destroy the organs at Geneva, Calvin yet preserved, even developed, the choir as an agent to lead corporate singing. We thus find that, after the Reformation, Protestant choirs assumed a new role. In addition to their former function as performers of music beyond the capacity of the general congregation, they were now required to lead the voices of the people. That situation still exists today – the relative importance attached to one or other aspect varying according to the liturgical ideal observed.

In English cathedrals the choirs are endowed. Thus, apart from an interruption during the Commonwealth (1649–1660), choral services of some elaboration and competence have been performed there daily since their foundation. In English parochial churches, during the seventeenth and eighteenth centuries, the custom arose of introducing 'cock and hen' choirs of men and women into west-gallery singing pews. In urban churches at this time a choir was often provided by Charity Children – pupils from the local charity school. The result was seldom devotional; and in neither case was it usual to find congregational singing stimulated by the development. As a result, with the growth of the Oxford Movement, consistent attempts were made from 1839 onward to introduce surpliced choirs of men and boys into Anglican churches. The avowed intention was to encourage the people to take up again their responsibility as a *singing* congregation; to provide a choir which should lead the people in singing the psalms and chanting their responses, and where possible to add the singing of a simple anthem as a stimulus to devotion. The eventual success of this movement to develop surpliced parochial choirs provided the Anglican church with a feature unique in Christendom.

Like any other institution, the parochial choir proved capable of misuse. And before the end of the nineteenth century, many instances occurred where, perhaps through the use of unworthy music, or because the choir was allowed to monopolize the service, the original role of the parochial choir was forgotten. Under the leadership of the Royal School of Church Music, the situation has been considerably improved during the present century. Certain principles govern choral worship: (1) The music should be subservient to the words. (2) The music should be good, as music. (3) The music should be in keeping with the spirit of the liturgy. (4) The music should contribute to a corporate act of worship, not be addressed to the congregation. (5) The performers should sublimate their own personalities. Current trends in church music frequently fall short of these ideals, and reversal of ancient practice does not necessarily constitute progress or enhance worship. Writers as diverse as St Chrysostom, Calvin and Robert Bridges have emphasized the necessity to distinguish between secular and sacred musical styles. A present trend toward equating them risks reducing the dignity of worship and introduces hazards otherwise easily avoided.

L. Dakers, *Church Music at the Crossroads*, 1969; S. Nicholson, *Quires and Places where they Sing*, 1942; C. H. Phillips, *The Singing Church*, rev. ed. 1968; B. Rainbow, *The Choral Revival in the Anglican Church*, 1970; E. A. Wienandt, *Choral Music of the Church*, 1965.

BERNARR RAINBOW

Chrismatory

A metal receptacle or casket of precious metal, such as silver, but more frequently of latten or brass, designed to hold the three sacramental oils that have been in use since at least the second century: (1) the oil of the catechumens (q.v.), for the pre-baptismal rites; (2) the oil for the sick used in the anointing of the infirm. Both of these were composed of olive oil. But the chrismatory gets its name from (3) the third oil, chrism, which was rather a cream or ointment composed of olive oil and balm, and used in the rite of confirmation (q.v.) and in the anointing of sovereigns at their coronation. All three oils were blessed by the bishop on Maundy Thursday. (*See* **Unction**.)

J. Gilchrist, *Anglican Church Plate*, 1967.
C. E. POCKNEE

Christian Church (Disciples of Christ) Worship

The Christian Church (Disciples of Christ) began in the USA in the early nineteenth century when a loose alliance of independent congregations was drawn together by the leadership of Barton W. Stone (1772-1844), Thomas Campbell (1763-1854), his son Alexander Campbell (1788-1866), and other frontier preachers. This movement now includes three American denominations – Christian Church (Disciples of Christ), the Churches of Christ (using only vocal music), and the Christian Churches (affiliated with the North American Christian Convention) – and denominations in other countries. Worship in all of these denominations is characterized by these practices: (1) the regular act of congregational worship, celebrated each Sunday, is a service that includes preaching and the Lord's Supper; (2) their liturgical practice is in the family of Reformed-type worship, as distinguished from the modified-mass type or the Spirit-filled type; (3) they have entrusted the care of congregations and administration of the sacraments to local elders who ordinarily have not studied theology nor receive salary for their ecclesiastical work; (4) baptism is by complete immersion or submersion and limited to those old enough to answer for themselves; (5) the normal practice has been to use extempore prayer even for the eucharistic prayers.

This liturgical practice emerged in one of the most interesting periods of American intellectual life. Beginning in New England in the early eighteenth century, and spreading through the populated eastern seaboard, a powerful surge of religious revival transformed the American spirit, effectively severing its ties with Europe and the scholasticism of the Middle Ages. Under the most eminent of its theologians, Jonathan Edwards, this Great Awakening re-established a passionate Calvinist theology and created a new social striving for the creation of the Kingdom of God in North America. The American Revolution and Jeffersonian republicanism both resulted.

One last episode in the Great Awakening was the Kentucky Revival of 1800-01. The celebration of the Lord's Supper proved to be one of the chief stimulants of glossolalia and related phenomena. One reporter stated: 'The greatest work was on sacramental occasions.' With the dying of revivalism, the new frontier churches – notably Baptist and Methodist – came to depend more upon preaching services than upon the Lord's Supper as the focus for Sunday worship.

In contrast, the newly emerging Disciples of Christ built their congregational life around the Lord's Supper as the major act of worship. Furthermore, they avoided the emotionalism that had been associated with the revival. Indeed, their approach to things increasingly emphasized reason in religion. In this way they were very much like the anti-revival party during the eighteenth-century awakening, a party made up mostly of 'old side' Presbyterians and Episcopalians. Yet their liturgical practice differed from others of the enlightenment, especially Episcopalians. Like most other Protestants on the frontier, Disciples rejected the use of imposed liturgies. Instead, following the lead of Alexander Campbell, they sought to find a basis for their worship, and everything else in church life, in the 'clear' teaching of the NT. This principle had two implications: everything should be discarded from faith and practice which 'is not found written in the New Testament of the Lord and Saviour', and 'whatever is there enjoined' is to be believed and practised. In order to further the study of scripture by the people, Alexander Campbell prepared a modern speech translation of the NT, first published in 1826 under the title *The Living Oracles*. Probably the best English version then available, it was used widely by Disciple preachers through much of the nineteenth century and was in many congregations the one translation generally read and studied.

Their examination of the scriptures led them to conclude that the Lord's Supper is the significant act of Christian public worship. Their restorationist approach to the Bible led to a tendency towards legalism, that is towards the tendency to minister communion because Christ commanded it. Yet, their understanding of the meaning of 'the breaking of bread' suggests a more profound grasp of this sacrament. When each disciple receives the bread and cup, Campbell wrote, Christ says to him, 'For *you* my body was wounded; for *you* my life was taken.' When he receives these elements, the disciple says, 'Lord I believe it. My life sprung from thy suffering; my joy from thy sorrows; and my hope of glory everlasting from thy humiliation and abasement even to death.'

Interpretation of the meaning of the Lord's Supper has moved in two directions since that time. Formal theological discourse has tended towards commemoration, with very little effort to explain that term. Under the influence of liberal theology, especially in the first third of the twentieth century, this interpretation was drained of the content suggested by related terms in NT Greek. Despite this academic thinning out of meaning, a second trend persisted, the insistence that 'Christ is the unseen host at this table'. Consequently, the piety of church people and the devotional homilies at the table have maintained a seriousness of tone that is felt rather than defined. A theology of the eucharist based on these sources would be closer to Calvin than to Zwingli.

In the mid-twentieth century two reform movements have affected the shape and sense of Disciple worship. The first revolved around G. Edwin Osborn (1897-1965), for long a Professor of Worship at Phillips University in Oklahoma. His doctoral dissertation granted by the University of Edinburgh in 1935 dealt with the psychology of Christian public worship. His work culminated in *Christian Worship: A Service Book*, published in 1953, where he presented a rationale and materials for worship that are biblically rich and ecumenical.

During this same period the Disciples shared with most branches of American Protestantism the trend towards aestheticism in worship. One evidence was the erection of

Romanesque and Gothic churches, with the largest number built after 1925, especially under the influence of A. F. Wickes (1880-1958), for a long time architectural consultant to the denomination.

The second influence began when William Robinson (1888-1963), British Disciple theologian, came to teach at Christian Theological Seminary in Indianapolis. He helped a new generation of students discover what had become obscured during the previous decades – that the Lord's Supper is the very principle of Sunday worship rather than something added on. He opened the doorway to serious theological engagement with classical Christian theology, especially as represented by P. T. Forsyth. Similar lessons have been learned by the Disciples in their extensive activities in ecumenical and union negotiations, most notably the Consultation on Church Union.

At this time, one major question continues: will the Disciples remain 'rigidly Protestant', as one interpreter terms their former stance, or will they move fully into the new ecumenical scheme? There is reason to believe that the latter will be the case and that the one Protestant denomination experienced in the practice of extempore prayer in a service of preaching and the Lord's Supper held every Sunday will bring this experience into the fuller service of Christ's church.

Alexander Campbell, *The Christian System*, 1843; W. E. Garrison and A. T. DeGroot, *The Disciples of Christ: A History*, 1948; G. Edwin Osborn, *The Glory of Christian Worship*, 1959; Keith Watkins, *The Breaking of Bread*, 1966.

KEITH WATKINS

Christmas

In Egypt in 1996 BC the calendar recorded the winter solstice as being on 6 January, but by the time Alexandria was founded in 331 BC the inaccuracy of the calendar meant that the solstice was on 25 December. The dates of the Christian festivals of Christmas and Epiphany (q.v.) are *both* linked with the winter solstice, transmuting celebrations of the pagan world. It is at Rome in the early fourth century that we find the first evidence for Christmas. In the year 274, the emperor Aurelian introduced in the imperial capital the festival of the Invincible Sun, *Natalis Solis Invicti*, on 25 December. At some point before

336 the church must have established on this date the commemoration of the incarnation, the birth of the Sun of Righteousness.

' The evidence is contained in a martyrology written by Philocalus in 354 containing two lists of anniversaries, the one detailing the burial days of Roman bishops and the other those of martyrs. Both lists are set out in the order of the months, and it is highly significant that the opening date in the first is 27 December, and in the second 25 December, where the entry makes reference to the Nativity. The evidence of both lists is that by 354 Christmas was in existence at Rome, and was the beginning of the liturgical year.

But an analysis of the first list makes it possible to carry the evidence further back. If the last two insertions are omitted, the list begins on 27 December and ends on 8 December, thus running within the limits of a liturgical year which started at Christmas. The historical period covered is from 255 to 335, from Lucius to Silvester. The two names appended to this series are those of Marcus, who died on 7 October 336, and Julius, who died in 352. Philocalus evidently made use of an earlier list, completing it with the names of the two bishops who had died between 335 and 354. The initial list must therefore have been compiled after the death of Silvester on 31 December 335, but before that of Marcus on 7 October 336. It may be concluded that by 336 the Christian year at Rome began with Christmas, and it would be reasonable to affirm that Christmas originated in Rome in the early part of the fourth century.

B. Botte, *Les Origines de la Noël et de l'Épiphanie*, 1932; O. Cullmann, *Weihnachten in der alten Kirche*, 1947; A. A. McArthur, *The Evolution of the Christian Year*, 1953.

A. A. MCARTHUR

Church of South India Worship

The Church of South India (CSI) is a union of Anglicans, Presbyterians, Congregationalists and Methodists which was inaugurated in 1947. Initially it was assumed that its congregations would continue to use the service-books to which they were accustomed before union, with occasional united worship as directed by Synod. The rite of ordination (q.v.), prepared before union and inspired mainly by Anglican models in its first edition, was alone obligatory on the whole church.

At an early date, however, the need was felt for new forms to be used when the heirs of the different heritages met together for worship. Priority was given to orders for the Lord's Supper and confirmation (q.v.). The ready acceptance of these prompted the production of others covering all the normal requirements of worship. These were each revised after a period of experimental use before being brought together in *The Book of Common Worship Supplement* (1967). Though the old service-books, not least Anglican *BCP*, are still in use, it is increasingly regarded as old-fashioned to adhere to these pre-union traditions.

The Synod Liturgy Committee, though indebted in its compilations to the rites of the uniting churches, has eschewed any mere amalgam of them. Its intention has been threefold: (1) to return in some measure to the classical heritage of liturgy; here it has been guided by studies emanating from the Liturgical Movement (q.v.); (2) to give value to the insights of the Reformation which were the common heritage of the uniting churches; (3) to take account of South India's own cultural *milieu* and to produce forms of worship which, while treasuring the church's universal legacy of worship, would nevertheless be expressive of India's own religious genius and relevant to the needs of her people.

This third intention may not always be apparent in English, the *lingua franca* which had to be used for the original compositions. In fact the Indian ethos of CSI worship can only be fully appreciated where hymns composed by Indian poets in Tamil, Telugu, Malayalam or Canarese are sung to Carnatic *ragas*, and psalms, canticles, the *Gloria in excelsis*, *Sanctus*, etc. are rendered poetically and sung in the same way. Such Indian musical settings are still in an experimental stage, but are becoming increasingly popular.

Points of particular interest in the several orders are:

1. *The Lord's Supper or Holy Eucharist*. This is on the classical pattern with a preparatory section of adoration and confession, a liturgy of the word and a liturgy of the sacrament. Variability of collects, lections and prefaces, derived from the ancient Western and the Anglican traditions, has been retained. The greeting of peace in its Kerala Syrian form of handclasp (*see* **Gestures 4**) may be passed throughout the congregation at

the point before the offertory (q.v.). Responses derived from the Eastern liturgies are said or sung after the narrative of institution and the anamnesis. The offertory sentences and the epiclesis (which is of a Hippolytean rather than later Eastern type) both stress the theme of congregational corporateness and Christian unity. As in all CSI worship, value is given to congregational participation.

2. *Morning and Evening Worship.* Three alternative orders are specified: (*a*) Antecommunion (q.v.) with adaptations for noneucharistic worship. (*b*) An order modelled on Anglican mattins and evensong. In this the *Trisagion*, or *Kauma*, to give it its Syrian name, may be said or sung as an initial adoration of the Trinity. The *Benedictus* comes between OT and NT lections as belonging between the Testaments, and the *Te Deum* after the NT lection as expressive of the faith of the church which has heard the gospel. The canticles (q.v.) traditionally linked with mattins and evensong respectively may be sung at either of them. More elasticity than in the Anglican tradition is permitted in the concluding prayers. (*c*) A simpler and 'freer' order with 'responsive readings' of scriptural verses and permission to sing either hymns, psalms or canticles between the lections, but with some encouragement to use at the discretion of the minister liturgical pericopae from the other orders.

3. *Baptism and Confirmation.* Appropriately in a church which is in a 'missionary situation', priority in the printed text is given to baptism of believers, with infant baptism taking second place. Baptism by immersion is encouraged, though not obligatory. The fiction of adult promises made 'in the name of the child' in infant baptism has been abandoned in favour of promises made by parents (and godparents if any) to bring up the child in the Christian way. The proleptic character of baptism (q.v.) and of the Christian life as 'becoming what we are' appears in the post-baptismal prayers. Some thought has been given to the relation between baptism and confirmation (q.v.) There is stress in confirmation on the fulfilment of baptism in repentance, profession of faith and self-dedication on the part of the candidates. One petition in the confirmation prayer (which closely follows the Roman/Anglican model)

sums up the meaning of confirmation: 'Establish them in faith . . . by the Holy Spirit . . .', that is, the Spirit is already present and operative in the life of the baptized; but confirmation, which is the occasion for public commitment to the Christian faith and life, is a prayer for and effective sign of the operation of the Spirit in a new way. In baptism there is a brief reception by the congregation of the newly baptized. In confirmation the act of reception is highlighted, and the greeting of peace is given to the newly confirmed for the first time. There is provision in the rubrics for baptism, confirmation and first communion to be linked closely together if desired, as in the ancient tradition of Christian initiation.

4. *The Ordinal.* The radical revision of 1957 was much indebted to the ordinal of the Church of Scotland. At the same time it was warmly commended at its publication by the Anglican liturgist, E. C. Ratcliff, as a model for future revision of ordination services. Some significant amendments were made in it in the ordinal produced in 1965 for the proposed united church in Nigeria. The churches of North India and Pakistan, where union was inaugurated in 1970, have for an experimental period adopted the CSI rites of eucharist and ordination.

5. *The Lectionary and Calendar* have, both in Daily Bible Readings and Propers for Sundays and Special Days, implemented a simplification of the structure of the Christian year, as suggested by A. A. McArthur in *The Evolution of the Christian Year* (1953). Collects and lections have been chosen with a theme for the day in mind.

An alternative Sunday lectionary is in preparation and is expected to be authorized by Synod in 1972. At the same time, synodal authorization is expected for a shorter and simpler order for the Lord's Supper in contemporary English as a prelude to a full-scale revision in this direction of *The Book of Common Worship*, both in its English original and Indian translations.

The Church of South India Book of Common Worship, 1963; *BCW Supplement*, 1967; T. S. Garrett, *Worship in the Church of South India*, ²1965; E. C. Ratcliff, 'The Ordinal of the Church of South India', *Theology*, January 1960. A commentary by several authors on the CSI orders of worship, edited by

E. C. John (title as yet unspecified), is expected to be published in India in 1972.

T. S. GARRETT

Churches of Christ *see* Christian Church (Disciples of Christ) Worship

Churching of Women

The title of the Sarum 'order for the purification of a woman after childbirth before the door of the church' sufficiently indicates the purpose of the rite. Its scriptural authority is to be found in Lev. 12, according to which a woman who has given birth is unclean, and must not 'come into the sanctuary' until she has made a burnt offering and a sin offering, which she brings to the door of the tent of meeting. Luke 2.22 provides an example of compliance with these regulations by the parents of Jesus. The Sarum service was brief, consisting of the lesser litany and Lord's Prayer, Pss. 121 and 128, the *preces* also used in marriage, and a collect; the priest then sprinkled the woman with holy water and led her into church, and the mass followed. The collect gives thanks for deliverance from the dangers of childbirth, and prays that the woman may finish her temporal course faithfully and attain eternal life. A rubric defines the purpose of purification as enabling the woman to enter the church to give thanks. According to ancient custom the woman wore a veil.

The 1549 'Order of the Purification of Women' follows the medieval service quite closely. It is to be held 'nigh unto the quire door' (i.e. the chancel screen). There is no suggestion of ritual impurity barring the woman from entering the church. The priest's opening address states that baptism of the child has already taken place, and puts the emphasis on thanksgiving for safe delivery. Psalm 128 is omitted and the collect is freely paraphrased. The woman is bidden to offer the chrysom (the white robe given to the baby at baptism) and 'other accustomed offerings'. If the holy communion is to follow, it is fitting that she should communicate.

The 1552 *BCP* reflects the change of emphasis by a change of title to 'The Thanksgiving of Women after Childbirth, commonly called the Churching of Women'. The service is now to be held 'nigh unto the place where the table standeth'. The only other alteration is the removal of the reference to the chrysom,

which was no longer given in baptism.

During the seventeenth century, the custom of wearing a veil came under heavy fire from the Puritans, and in many churches special churching-pews were provided in the nave. Laudian bishops in their visitation articles insisted on the retention of the veil and also on the service being said at the altar rail. A rubric proposed in the 'Durham Book' directed that the woman should come 'a month after her delivery . . . decently veiled', but in the 1662 *BCP* this was toned down to 'at the usual time after her delivery . . . decently apparelled', while the place was to be 'as hath been accustomed, or as the Ordinary shall direct'. Psalm 116 with vv. 14-17 omitted was substituted at the suggestion of Robert Sanderson, with Ps. 127 as an alternative.

In the proposed book of 1928 the presence of the woman's husband was encouraged; and a blessing and two optional prayers were added, one dealing with the child's upbringing, the other for use when the child had died. An entirely new service put forward by the Church of England Liturgical Commission in 1965 was rejected by Convocation.

In the current Roman rite, now in process of revision, the old symbolism of kneeling at the church door and admission into church is retained, but the psalm is now 24. The Methodist *Book of Offices* (1936) includes a form for 'The Thanksgiving of Mothers' which is partly derived from the *BCP*.

G. W. O. Addleshaw and F. Etchells, *Architectural Setting of Anglican Worship*, 1948, pp. 84-6; F. E. Brightman, *The English Rite*, 1915, I, pp. cxxviii, clxiv, ccxxii; II, pp. 880-5; A. J. Collins, *Manuale Sarum*, 1960, pp. 43 f.; William Maskell, *Monumenta Ritualia Ecclesiae Anglicanae*, I, 1846, pp. 37 f.

G. J. CUMING

Church Modes

In the eighth or ninth century the Gregorian melodies were classified under one or another of the church modes, a system which postdated the bulk of them, just as did the major-minor diatonic and chromatic system that replaced them from the seventeenth century onwards in modern European music. The pattern of the latter system is invariable: whether you start in the major key on a white or a black note, there will be a series of five whole tones and two semitones always on the same degrees of this scale, and the same is true of the forms of the minor scales.

The modal system is both more complex and more subtle. Each mode has its special melodic flavour: here the tones and semitones occur in each mode on different degrees and there is a complete absence of the characteristic cadence made up of the leading-note rising by a semitone to the key note: e.g. in C major, the semitone B/C. The eight modes can be reduced from eight to four, as each pair shares a portion of the same complete mode.

This explanation can be made clear in the simple diagram below which will avoid the misleading, if picturesque, Greek names, such as Dorian, Lydian, Phyrgian, given them in the textbooks and in use for many years.

		Final (or key note)	Range	Dominant
1	1	d	d – d'	a
	2	d	a – a'	f
2	3	e	e – e'	c
	4	e	b – b'	a
3	5	f	f – f'	c'
	6	f	c – c'	a
4	7	g	g – g'	d
	8	g	d – d'	c'

The even-numbered modes start a fourth below the odd ones. Their dominants are a third below those of the odd modes, but it will be seen that the dominant of the third mode is not the normal fifth note (as in the modern scale), but in no. 3 it is C, not B; in the fourth it is A, not B; in the eighth it is C, not B. The reason for these changes is because the theorists wished to avoid putting the dominant on B so as to avoid the interval F-B, the so-called *diabolus in musica* or, in modern terms, the augmented fourth, consisting of three whole tones. Thus there is an artificiality about the system. Furthermore, the only permitted accidental was B flat, which was another avoidance of the same difficulty. Contemporary scholarship, however, is inclined to be more favourable towards the *diabolus in musica* and in earlier days the avoidance of B was not general.

The beauty of the chant is enhanced by the modal structure of the melodies. Modal writing was not extinguished by the appearance of the modern scale system, but lived on to give welcome variety and contrast to diatonic melody and harmony. It is used in such great works as Bach's B minor and Beethoven's D major masses, and in a large number of church and secular works from the eighteeenth to the twentieth century.

ALEC ROBERTSON

Ciborium

This term is thought to be derived from the Greek *kiborion*, which originally meant the hollow seed-case of the Egyptian water-lily, and the term came to be applied to a drinking-cup because of its resemblance to the seed-case. The use of the word ciborium now applies to two distinct objects in ecclesiastical usage: (1) a canopy of stone, wood or metal supported on four columns over an altar (q.v.); (2) a chalice-like vessel with a cover for holding a large number of wafer-breads. The latter must have developed from a pyx (q.v.) with a stem and foot and this could only have happened when wafer-breads finally replaced the use of leavened bread in the West after the twelfth century. The term was also applied to a little canopy on four columns standing on the altar under which the metal pyx or ciborium containing the reserved sacrament stood. In England some splendid examples of a flat chalice-like vessel with a cover all in silver-gilt and known as the bread cup appeared during the time of the Caroline divines in the middle of the seventeenth century. While the metal ciborium has usually been of silver or silver-gilt, examples of such vessels completely decorated with coloured enamels are known, such as the thirteenth-century Kennet ciborium.

J. Gilchrist, *Anglican Church Plate*, 1967; A. A. King and C. E. Pocknee, *Eucharistic Reservation in the Western Church*, 1965; C. E. Pocknee, *The Christian Altar*, 1963.

C. E. POCKNEE

Class Leader

The class leader is a layman given special pastoral responsibility within the Methodist societies established by John Wesley. One of Wesley's problems was the provision of proper continuing care and discipline for his converts. Part of his solution was to group them in 'classes' under a leader who was responsible for instructing them, developing their devotional life and seeing that they maintained the high moral standards required of all members of the societies. Members of the classes also contributed one penny a week to the funds of the society. At one time the office of class leader was generally regarded as one of great importance and influence. It is still a real ministry in some parts of Methodism, though in others the class system seems to have become vestigial.

P. HINCHLIFF

Collect

(1) A prayer of a distinctive stereotyped form, peculiar to the Western liturgies, although with certain parallels in the Eastern rites, with which the president closes a unit of liturgical worship, or some part of such a unit; (2) one such prayer in particular, namely, that referring to the mystery or person commemorated on a given day, which closes the entrance rite in the eucharistic liturgy; (3) derivatively, any other prayer written in the same form.

In the Roman rite the prayer cited in definition (2) above is called simply *oratio* – 'the prayer'. In some ancient Western liturgical books, however, it is called *collectio*, *collecta*, or *ad collectam*, whence the English name is derived. The meaning of the Latin is not certain: it means literally 'assembly', but it may refer either to a prayer in which preceding devotional themes are assembled, or to a prayer – such as that in definition (2) – which is spoken when the congregation is assembled. These interpretations, however, are complementary, for both throw light on the function of the prayer. In the historic Western liturgies collects are normally preceded, directly or indirectly, by a mutual greeting of president and people and a bidding to prayer, to emphasize the nature of the collect as a solemn summary by the president of the corporate prayer of the assembly.

Ancient examples of the collect after the entrance, of which many survive to this day in the Roman rite, exhibit an all but unvarying structure: (1) an address to God the Father; (2) a reference to some divine attribute or act as a ground for prayer; (3) the prayer proper, short, simple and definite; (4) a concluding doxology, offering the prayer to the Father through the Son and in the Holy Spirit. They also follow a distinctive literary pattern, following the rules of late classical Latin artistic prose. The collects of the Hispano-Gallican rites exhibit much more variation, and are often both theologically and stylistically excessively complicated. Other prayers of the collect type in the historic Western rites, such as those which close the offertory (in the Roman rite called *secreta* or *super oblata*, q.v.) and the communion (in the Roman rite called *postcommunio*), exhibit a theological and literary pattern similar, although with differences according to their function, to those of the collects proper.

The translation of a prayer of this type from Latin into the vernacular presents a considerable problem; the most successful solution of it so far, in its own day, was that of Cranmer in the collects of the *BCP*. The attempts of modern liturgical revisers to translate or compose collects in a more informal style, supposedly more appropriate and intelligible today, have so· far been markedly less successful than those of their sixteenth-century predecessors, and it must be queried whether it is in fact possible to produce prayers of this kind without obeying the conventional rules for their formulation.

J. A. Jungmann, *The Mass of the Roman Rite*, I, 1951, pp. 359-90.

W. JARDINE GRISBROOKE

Colours, Liturgical

The association of particular colours with seasonal worship and personal commemoration has developed for several reasons – some psychological and some historical. It seems 'natural', for instance, to associate red with blood, yellow with energy, white with purity, gold with festivity, purple with dignity, green with growth, light blue with hope, dark blue, violet and black with despair and mourning, and drab earth colours with burial.

The use of colours in connection with Christian worship has had a varied history. For the first millennium the colour of vestments (q.v.) and hangings was without liturgical significance and, save for a preference for white robes, did not differ from what was customary among the Roman middle and upper classes of the empire and of its Byzantine continuation.

Although liturgical vesture remained the same in form as civilian dress, the indications are that the clergy reserved special 'suits' of alb and chasuble for use in church, and also that increasingly these vestments were of white material only. Jerome, in argument with Pelagius (*c.*415), asks what objection could be made if bishop, priest, deacon and the rest of the clergy appeared at the administration of the sacrifice in white array *(candida veste processerit)*. Pseudo-Alcuin in the tenth or eleventh century writes only of white vestments and mentions red stripes on those of the deacons.

Not until the twelfth century is there evidence of correlation between significant colours and the seasonal feasts and fasts of the church's year and the various classes of saints, etc., in the calendar. The Augustinian canons at Jerusalem prepared the first known sequence of liturgical colours and, somewhat surprisingly, this proposed the use of black for Christmas and for festivals of the Blessed Virgin Mary, and blue for Epiphany and Ascension. Presumably the growing wealth of the church had permitted the use of a wider variety and richness of textiles for vestments, hangings and accessories and, understandably, their colours came to be associated with the developed medieval system of annual liturgical observances. At first such sequences were local and informal: they were unavoidably restricted to wealthy cathedrals and abbeys and to rich collegiate and parish churches. A common practice was to wear the newest or most magnificent vestments – virtually irrespective of colour – on the great festivals and to use the older ones on other occasions. Gradually, however, a generally accepted pattern of colour association emerged in the medieval West: Innocent III (1198-1216) outlined the Roman rule based on white for feasts, red for martyrs, black for penitential seasons and green at other times.

A general rule was not formally defined in rubric until 1570 in the reformed missal under Pius V: in brief, the type of sequence which eventually emerged was as follows:

Advent to	
Christmas Eve	Violet / Blue / Black
Christmas to Epiphany	White / Gold
Sundays after Epiphany	Green
Septuagesima to Ash	
Wednesday	Violet / Blue / Black
Throughout Lent	Veiling of colours
Passion Sunday to	
Easter Eve	Red / Rose
Easter	White / Gold
Pentecost	Red
Trinity	White / Gold
Sundays after Trinity	Green
Ordinary weekdays	Green
Blessed Virgin Mary	White / Red
Apostles, evangelists, martyrs	Red

Saints other than martyrs	White/Yellow
Baptisms / confirmation	White / Red
Ordination / marriage	White
Funeral	Violet / Blue / Black
Dedication of a church	White

As the above list indicates, there was latitude in the choice of liturgical colours, especially in the 'mourning' range of violet, dark blue and black: further, distinctions were made in the various shades of red, and in pre-Reformation England, green and yellow were regarded as interchangeable. Regional variation persisted and other colours altogether were sometimes employed, e.g. the brick-red of Sarum for the Sundays after Epiphany. Latin names in medieval inventories include *albus* and *candidus* for white, *rubeus, sub-rubeus* and *coccineus* for various shades of red (including rose), *purpureus* for red-purple and *violaceus* for blue-purple, *viridis* for green and *croceus* for yellow.

The Eastern Orthodox churches use coloured materials in great variety and Eastern churches in communion with the Roman Catholic Church broadly follow the Western customs; they do not, however, regard themselves as bound so strictly to adhere to a colour sequence as did the Roman Catholic Church in the period preceding Vatican II.

The liturgical colours were primarily to be seen in the material of the chasubles and copes and that of altar cloths and textile hangings. The colours were also used in the embellishment of the vestments – orphreys and apparels – and in the material or decoration of the stole and maniple. In this connection it may be noted that the colour of the stole and maniple generally accorded with that of the orphreys and apparels and contrasted with the predominant colour of the chasuble. This custom has been contradicted by the recent practice which is concerned to make everything 'match'.

It is interesting to note that the English Lenten vestments were for the most part *white* (often with a limited amount of red decoration), and that those of passiontide, including Palm Sunday and Good Friday, were *red*.

Many of the Lenten entries include veils (q.v.) and other hangings which were used to cover all pictures and images, and on fast days to curtain off the high altar. The purpose of these hangings was to some extent contradicted when themselves they came to be 'steyned', i.e. painted, with symbols and scenes of the passion. Modern practice is to shroud the coloured adornments of a church with a Lenten array of buff-coloured material sparsely embroidered with red emblems.

In the sixteenth century the Reformed Churches generally rejected colour as an adjunct to worship. Where the Calvinist or the Puritan spirit prevailed, all vestments and coloured textiles were abrogated and the ministers were content merely with a black preaching gown worn over dark civilian clothes. Among other Protestants (especially Lutherans and Anglicans), in sectors where it has been customary to retain or to re-introduce some or all of the traditional vestments and hangings, it has also been usual to observe the 1570 Roman Catholic colour sequence so far as this was possible.

A rubric in the 1549 *BCP* of the Church of England ordered that the parish priest should wear 'a white albe plain, with a vestement or cope', and Canon XXIV (1603-4), based also on the *Advertisements* (1566), curiously ordered that the principal minister at the eucharist in cathedrals and collegiate churches should wear a coloured cope over a plain alb. This perverse practice became quite widespread in the seventeenth century among the so-called Laudian school and, in the early eighteenth century, the high churchmen among the Non-jurors restored the eucharistic vestments in the contemporary Roman Catholic style and sometimes took the liberty of interpreting 'cope' as 'chasuble'. Only in this tenuous way was regard for liturgical colour maintained in the Established Church, for the majority of the clergy obeyed Canon LVIII which prescribed surplice and academic hood or black scarf for the eucharist; there were, however, some clergy who continued to wear a black gown for the celebration as well as for preaching and singing the choir offices until the end of the seventeenth century.

The Catholic sacramental revivalism of the Oxford Movement and the romantic Gothic revivalism of the Cambridge Ecclesiologists converged in the middle of the nineteenth century to focus attention upon Anglican ceremonial, and hence to advocacy of the eucharistic vestments and the liturgical colours for renewed use in the Church of England.

The result of this stimulus was twofold.

On the one hand, Evangelicals denounced the neo-medievalism as 'popery' and refused to wear liturgical vestments other than those prescribed by Canon LVIII, namely surplice and academic hood or black scarf. On the other hand, to meet the growing demand of the high-churchmen of the Church of England and of the clergy of the Roman Catholic Church, Victorian commercial interests were mobilized to supply full sets of vestments and hangings in the 'correct' liturgical colours. It is stated by several writers on the subject that complete standardization of the colours in the Roman Catholic Church was not attempted until the nineteenth century, and this, presumably, is an allusion to the persistence of local uses in France until this time, and to the growing commercial pressures for mass-produced correctness.

Eventually, all but the most extreme of the low-church Evangelicals adopted the strange compromise of wearing a seasonally coloured stole over a surplice for the eucharist, while a different compromise (though with some historical justification) in the form of a complete set of all-white linen vestments was accepted by moderate churchmen.

As a result of the influence of the Liturgical Movement (q.v.), radical changes are taking place in the design and decoration of vestments and the liturgical use of colours. In general it is recognized that there is historical and psychological virtue in the traditional seasonal colours – provided that they are interpreted in terms of mood rather than in conformity to a rigid system of rules. Thus, it is reasonable in penitential periods to use drab materials in the violet-brown-grey range (though avoiding black), to use red-purples and gold to express majesty and high-priesthood, challenging reds for leaders and martyrs, green and yellow to signify renewal, and to employ white and gold (with the whole palette, if desired) for festivals.

In the Roman Catholic Church the post-Vatican II *Ordo Missae* (1969) generally re-affirmed current practice, *white* for Easter, Christmas, feasts of Christ (other than the Passion), of Mary, of angels and of saints (not martyrs), All Saints, John Baptist, John Evangelist, Chair of Peter and Conversion of Paul; *red* for Passion and Palm Sundays, Good Friday, Pentecost, feasts of the Passion of Christ and of martyrs; *violet* for Advent and Lent and possibly for funeral masses in place of *black*; *rose* for Gaudete Sunday

(Advent III) and Laetare Sunday (Lent IV); *green* at other times. It is also recommended that on special occasions more solemn vestments may be used, even if not of the colour of the day.

The combination of a whole range of new materials and colours, together with a fresh understanding of the emotional effect of colours, their optical relationships and their design possibilities, permits a renewed approach to all aspects of their use in worship. For example, especially in new churches, it is possible to integrate all the coloured items – vestments, hangings, carpets, glass, furnishings, timber and other structural materials and finishes – into a total liturgical environment: even in existing churches much can be done to create a meaningful sense of seasonal colour and to refrain from a sterile following of what commercial church furnishers may insist is correct.

___

J. Braun, *Die liturgische Gewandung im Occident und Orient nach Ursprung und Entwicklung, Verwendung und Symbolik*, 1907; P. Dearmer, *The Ornaments of the Ministers*, 1908/1920; W. H. St J. Hope and E. G. C. F. Atchley, *English Liturgical Colours*, 1918; J. W. Legg, *Notes on the History of Liturgical Colours*, 1882; C. E. Pocknee, *Liturgical Vesture*, 1960.

GILBERT COPE

Commination

In pre-Reformation times after Sext on Ash Wednesday, a sermon was preached, and the imposition of ashes followed. The rite consisted of the seven penitential psalms (6, 32, 38, 51, 102, 130 and 143), *preces*, seven collects for penitence and forgiveness, and a solemn absolution; the blessing of the ashes was accompanied by two more collects, and the ashes were applied to the foreheads of the penitents with the words 'Remember, O man, that thou art ashes, and unto ashes shalt thou return'; further antiphons and collects then led into mass.

This ceremony (and by implication the rite accompanying it) was abolished by the Council in January 1548, and there is no reference to ashes in the *BCP* of 1549. Indeed, the name 'Ash Wednesday' is eliminated from the *BCP* of 1552. The occasion is put to a rather different purpose. After mattins, the people are summoned by the ringing of a bell, and the litany is said, in accordance with the injunctions of 1547, 'in the midst of the church . . . before High Mass'. A completely new section follows, which gives the service its name 'commination' (*Oxford English Dictionary*: 'a threatening of punishment'). The priest goes into the pulpit and reads 'a declaration of scripture' consisting chiefly of 'the general sentences of God's cursing against impenitent sinners' (Deut. 27.15-25). This is meant to take the place of the primitive discipline of open penance, and was probably suggested by the medieval rite called the greater excommunication, a denunciation of sinners read three or four times a year. It is followed by a long catena of scriptural texts on judgment and repentance woven together into a continuous sermon.

The priest then returns to the midst of the church, and the rest of the service (described in the title as 'certain prayers') is an abridgment of the Sarum rite, shorn of course of its ceremony. The *BCP* retains only one of the penitential psalms (Ps. 51), the *preces*, the first collect, a collect made up of phrases from four of the Sarum prayers, and one of the antiphons, which leads into the introit psalm (Ps. 6) of holy communion.

The title 'A Commination against Sinners' dates from 1552, and in 1662 Bishop Wren added to it the explanatory phrase 'or Denouncing of God's Anger and Judgments'. The connection with Ash Wednesday, severed in the 1552 *BCP*, was maintained in practice throughout the sixteenth century, and was restored in 1662, with provision for use 'at other times, as the Ordinary shall appoint'. By then the service seems to have become separated from the holy communion, and a blessing was added at the end.

Modern revisions have tried various expedients to keep the service in use. England 1928 substitutes censures based on the Decalogue and abbreviates the catena; Scotland 1929 has the Decalogue itself and the Lucan Beatitudes (6.20-26), while omitting the catena altogether. America 1928 omits the whole of the first part; England 1966, First Series, the whole of the second. Only in India, where penitential discipline is still in force, does Deut. 27 survive; and even here the catena is shortened.

___

F. E. Brightman, *The English Rite*, 1915, I, pp. cxxix, clxiv, ccxxii; II, pp. 886-901; A. J. Collins, *Manuale Sarum*, 1960, pp. 9-12.

G. J. CUMING

Commixture

The commixture is the placing of a particle of the consecrated host in the chalice (q.v.) after the fraction (q.v.) at the eucharist (q.v.). The origins of this ceremonial act are complex. It appears to have derived from the *fermentum*. This was a fragment of bread consecrated at an episcopal celebration and taken to a church where a presbyter was presiding, it being added to the chalice after the fraction as a symbol of unity. This custom died out in the East, probably in the fourth century, but continued in Rome until the eighth or ninth. At that period there was also current the practice of sanctifying extra chalices by adding a piece of the already consecrated host. It would appear that the *fermentum* was transformed into the commixture under this influence. The commixture was further affected by a Syrian symbolic interpretation, to the effect that the words of consecration represent the death of Christ and so the separation of his body and blood, while the bringing together of these two through the commixture shows forth his resurrection. Hence in the Liturgy of St James it is called the *henosis*, i.e. union, while in that of St Chrysostom it is accompanied by the words: 'The fullness of the Holy Spirit' – the Spirit being regarded as the agent of the resurrection.

J. A. Jungmann, *The Mass of the Roman Rite*, rev. ed., 1959, pp. 475-9.

EDITOR

Communion

1. The partaking of the consecrated elements at the eucharist (q.v.), whereby there is a communion or participation (*koinonia*) in Christ and in him with all the members of the congregation. Methods of partaking and of distribution as well as posture have varied throughout the ages and from church to church.

In the patristic period the worshippers received the bread in their hands but do not appear to have touched the chalice. Cyril, or John, of Jerusalem describes the fourth-century practice when he says: 'As you approach then, come not with your wrists extended or your fingers open, but make of your left hand a kind of throne by placing it under your right which is about to receive the King, and in the hollow of your hand receive the body of Christ, replying Amen.

Carefully hallow your eyes with the touch of the holy body, and then partake of it, seeing to it that you lose no particle . . . Then, after the communion of Christ's body, approach also the cup of his blood, not stretching forth your hands, but bending forward in an attitude of adoration and reverence, and saying Amen, be hallowed as well by the reception of the blood of Christ. And while the moisture thereof is still on your lips, touch it with your hands and hallow both your eyes and brow and other senses' (*Catech.* 5.21 f.).

Before the end of the sixth century women were forbidden to receive the bread on the naked hand and the *Ordo Romanus VI* (? c. 900) only allows this for bishops, priests and deacons, apparently from a desire to protect that which is holy from profane or superstitious uses. This practice was also required by the 1549 *BCP* but was thereafter omitted. By the thirteenth century communicating under the species of wine had almost universally disappeared in the West, probably to avoid the risk of spilling. Objections to this were raised by the Hussites in Bohemia, and the Reformers insisted that communion in both kinds alone had scriptural warrant. In the Roman Church communion in one kind persists, although since Vatican II there is a move to 'restore the cup to the laity'.

Another method of partaking is by intinction, i.e. the bread is dipped in the wine so that the two kinds can be administered conjointly. This became popular in the seventh century but was condemned in the West in the thirteenth. In Orthodox churches it is the almost universal practice to partake from a spoon containing the bread sprinkled with a few drops of wine. Today this method is sometimes used in the USA for hygienic reasons. Similar motives have also led to the use in many non-episcopal churches of small individual cups.

Distribution of communion has also varied. In the early church the worshippers came up to a balustrade demarcating the sanctuary (q.v.) and this has continued to be the practice in many churches, e.g. Anglican, Orthodox and Roman. An alternative method is to bring the elements to the communicants. This change was instituted by the English Puritans who then influenced Congregationalists, Methodists and Presbyterians. Some Presbyterians, however, particularly in Holland and Westphalia, leave their seats and sit around a table in the nave or sanctuary.

This last statement indicates that for these Christians the posture for communion is sitting. However, in the early church it was usual to stand, and this is still the norm in many Reformed congregations in Alsace, France and Switzerland. Reception kneeling only gained ascendance gradually in the Roman Church between the eleventh and the sixteenth century and remains usual as well as among Anglicans.

2. Communion can also be a translation of the Latin word *communio* which denotes a psalm sung during communion. According to Cyril, Ps. 34 was sung at Jerusalem in the fourth century, and both the *Apostolic Constitutions* and Augustine refer to the practice. The psalm is sometimes replaced by a communion hymn at the present day.

EDITOR

Communion Table

This term has been preferred by those churches that have sprung out of the Protestant Reformation in the sixteenth century rather than the term altar (q.v.), which in the later Middle Ages in the West had become associated with the idea that in the mass Christ was somehow immolated afresh. The Reformers were concerned to rebut such an idea and to assert the unique character of Christ's atoning work on the cross, which could in no sense be repeated. Perhaps those who have taken this position mistakenly supposed that the term 'altar' could only be applied to a structure of stone, while the term 'table' was applied exclusively to a structure of wood.

In the *BCP* the usual term is 'the Lord's table'; but in common parlance in· the Church of England the term 'altar' is in frequent use. Moreover, in the official rite for the coronation of the sovereigns of England the term altar is always used and retained.

We may say that the term 'communion table' underlines an aspect of the eucharist which had become obscured in the later Middle Ages when eucharistic devotion had tended to become too pietistic and highly individualistic. Hence by underlining the corporate aspect of fellowship at the Lord's table this aspect was redressed. Much of the present-day liturgical revival is connected with the idea of the fellowship of the people of God at the holy table.   C. E. POCKNEE

Compline *see* Canonical Hours

Concelebration

Concelebration in the full meaning of the word is a specific rite in which several priests say mass together, consecrating the same bread and wine.

In the first centuries of the church the president alone recited the eucharistic prayer, since there was no fixed formula throughout the Christian communities. The priests, who stood on either side of the bishop, extended their hands over the oblation and prayed, but without saying aloud the consecratory words. This was the rite described in the *Apostolic Tradition* of Hippolytus (*c*.225), for long considered of Roman origin, but now thought by some liturgists to have an Alexandrine provenance. The 'crowns of priests', who in the eighteenth century surrounded the bishop at the altar in the cathedrals of France, seldom said the eucharistic prayer aloud, except on Holy Thursday. The concelebrants in the Greek Orthodox Church are also silent in the prayer, but in the Russian part of the church they recite the prayer with the president.

It is disputed whether a silent concelebration is fully sacramental or merely ceremonial. Pope Pius XII stated in 1956 that if the concelebrants did not say the 'essential words' aloud it was a ceremonial concelebration, but a lack of evidence leaves the question unanswered.

The custom of a verbal concelebration developed in Rome in the seventh century. The concelebrants recited the words of the canon, with the words of the consecration, aloud with the pope: a function which was later confined to certain days in the year. The primary purpose of the rite was a manifestation of unity. Visiting priests were invited to concelebrate out of hospitality and as a sign of communion.

The rite was introduced into other countries by the spread of the Roman service books. There is no evidence for concelebration in England, unless the title of 'cardinal' for two of the clergy of St Paul's Cathedral, London, originated in this way. It would, however, be rash to infer a universal practice of concelebration. By the thirteenth century the traditional rite had ceased in the Western Church, but the practice was defended by Thomas Aquinas (d. 1274).

Some time between the eighth century and the twelfth, concelebration in the ordination of priests and the consecration of bishops was introduced. It is not known with certainty why another form of concelebration appeared at this time. There is, however, a possible explanation. The Germano-Roman pontifical of the tenth century had adopted the practice of handing a chalice and paten to the candidate at his ordination. This 'porrection of the instruments', as it is called, assumed a very disproportionate importance and was regarded by some as the authentic matter of the sacrament. It is possible that concelebration at an ordination was motivated by the desire that the new priests, who had been appointed to offer sacrifice by the reception of the sacred vessels, should immediately exercise this right. The first known witness to this innovation seems to have been Thomas Aquinas, who spoke of 'the custom of some churches for priests newly ordained to co-celebrate with the bishop ordaining them'. Concelebration at the consecration of a bishop was already attested in the pontifical of Apamea (Syria), taken from a Roman model at the end of the twelfth century. The concelebration of priests was not exact as, although the canon including the words of consecration, and the other prayers after the offertory of the mass were said aloud with the bishop, the priests received the sacrament kneeling and in only one kind.

The Codex of Canon Law, issued for the Roman Catholic Church in 1918, affirmed that concelebration in ordinations was the sole form permissible in the Western Church.

The second Vatican Council (1962-3) discussed a revival of traditional concelebration, in which were emphasized some of the important theological and liturgical truths which centuries of individualism had greatly obscured. The debates were lively and hotly contested, but the final voting gave a very substantial majority in favour of the revival. This meant that the hierarchical nature of the church, the unity of the sacrifice of the mass and the collegiate character of the priesthood were once again put into their rightful perspective.

A commission was set up for the implementing of the liturgical decisions, in which an official text for the rite of concelebration was formulated.

The concelebrants may read the lessons in the liturgy of the word, as the first part of the mass is called, but it is not essential. Full concelebration begins at the liturgy of the eucharist. The concelebrants, at the offertory, stand on either side of the president at the altar.

Sacramental concelebration is effected in the eucharistic prayer or canon (q.v.), with the full co-operation of all the priests. The prayer is recited in a distinct and loud voice, with one of the concelebrants saying the memento of the living, *Communicantes* ('In union with the whole church we honour the memory of the saints') and the memento of the dead. The words of consecration are said by all the priests. The president performs the actions and the concelebrants extend their right hands, first towards the bread and then towards the wine.

Changes have been made in the ordination rites to make them authentic concelebrations.

A concelebrated liturgy is, to the whole people of God, a sign of their unity and a sign that helps them to be more aware that 'they are the body of Christ, not many bodies, but one body', as John Chrysostom affirms.

Concelebration is normal in the Orthodox churches of the Byzantine rite. The Syrians have a 'synchronized' form and the Maronites, about the end of the seventeenth century, adopted a rite under the influence of Catholic doctrine.

The rite is not very general in the Anglican Church, but it was started in St Stephen's House at Oxford in 1955. The concelebrants recite the prayers *sotto voce* and unite with the president in the prayer for the church, preface and eucharistic prayer.

Concelebration has also been practised from time to time in recent years in an attempt to overcome the problem of intercommunion. Where two churches are not in communion with each other, a eucharist has been held with, e.g., an Anglican and a Methodist concelebrating. It is difficult to determine how far this is a valid way forward and how far it is a masking of the issues.

A. A. King, *Concelebration in the Christian Church*, 1966.

A. A. KING

Confession *see* Prayer (2)

Confirmation

The earliest attestation of the ceremony which ultimately came to be called 'confirmation'

(Lat. *confirmatio*, Gk, *bebaiōsis*) is to be found in the baptismal rites of Hippolytus' *Apostolic Tradition* (AD 215) and Tertullian's treatise *De Baptismo* (AD 198). Both works attest a ceremony after baptism (q.v.) consisting of a prayer said by the bishop with his hands extended over the candidates, the anointing of the candidates on the forehead, the imposition of the hand on the head of each, and the sign of the cross (q.v.) on the forehead. The precise manner and order in which these elements were combined varied in the subsequent development and they did not always appear in their entirety. Thus according to· the *Ordo Romanus XI* of the late sixth century 'the pontiff makes a prayer over them . . . and when the prayer has been said he makes the sign of the cross with his thumb in chrism on the forehead of each one, saying, "In the name of the Father and the Son and the Holy Spirit. Peace be to thee".' On the eve of the Reformation, the Sarum Manual and the Roman Pontifical differed from this only in so far as the formula which accompanied the anointing had grown longer and the Roman rite specifically preserves a mention of the extension of the bishop's hands over the candidates as he prays for the sevenfold gifts of the Spirit. The *BCP* has abandoned the anointing and the sign of the cross but preserves the imposition of the hand, in the belief that this accords better with the example of the apostles, and has provided a new formula, 'Defend O Lord . . .', to accompany it. The *BCP* order retains also the prayer for the sevenfold gifts of the Spirit from the Sarum rite, but does not provide any more than the Sarum rite for the extension of the bishop's hands over the candidates while it is said. This prayer is broadly the same as that which appears in the early sixth-century Gelasian Sacramentary and has formed a constant feature of the Roman rite ever since that date. It is believed to be first attested by Ambrose in his treatise *De Sacramentis*, and is almost certainly quoted by some of his Roman contemporaries.

Originally no distinction was made between infants and adults in the use of this post-baptismal ceremony. When infants were baptized they were also anointed and hands were laid on them. But the requirement of the Roman and African churches that the anointing and imposition of the hand must be reserved to the bishop came to result in their separation from baptism, for infants and adults alike. In cases of emergency baptism, administered by a priest, or when bishops were no longer able to preside over all baptisms, the post-baptismal ceremony was inevitably delayed until the candidates could appear before a bishop. This separation between baptism and confirmation, which was originally imposed on the church by practical necessity, came ultimately to be regarded as the normal practice, and led to a situation in which baptism was thought to be appropriate to infancy and confirmation to later years.

Although in the Roman rite this ceremony was associated with the gift of ·the Holy Spirit, it is not clear that this was the case with the other rites of the Latin West. These provide for a simple post-baptismal anointing of the forehead, which in Gaul and Spain was performed by the priest who baptized, with oil which had been consecrated by the bishop. But in rites which were unaffected by Roman influence there is nothing to indicate that the bestowal of the Spirit was understood to be the purpose of the anointing.

In the early Syrian church no post-baptismal ceremony corresponding to the Western anointing and imposition of the hand intervened between the baptismal washing and the holy communion. Although some scholars have claimed that the pre-baptismal anointing in this rite must therefore have been for the bestowal of the Spirit, it seems more probable that this anointing served the same apotropaic purpose as it did in the West and that the Syrian church recognized no sign other than water by which the Spirit was imparted in Christian initiation. If this is correct, it carries with it the important implication that a second sign other than water in Christian initiation was not a matter of universal observance in the early church.·

The earliest Syrian attestations of a post-baptismal anointing are to be found in the *Apostolic Constitutions* (*c.* AD 375) and the *Catecheses* of Cyril of Jerusalem, and these most probably represent an importation from the ·churches of the West. By degrees this anointing after baptism was adopted throughout the churches of the East, where it is now accepted as a sacrament, although the Nestorian rite to this day has no such anointing. The rite consists of a chrismation made in the sign of the cross to the forehead and other parts of the body, but not the imposition of the hand. The formula varies, but the formula of the ancient Byzantine rite is still used in the Orthodox Church, 'The seal of the gift of the Holy Spirit'. This chrismation is performed by the priest who baptizes and has therefore retained its original connection with baptism and is administered to infants.

1. *Origins*. The significance and origin of this post-baptismal ceremony is a matter of controversy. According to the Council of Trent, confirmation is one of seven sacraments instituted by Christ. Roman Catholic theologians define the matter of the sacrament variously as chrism, the imposition of the hand, or the combination of both. The form used throughout the Roman Catholic Church is as follows: '*I sign thee with the sign of the cross, and I confirm thee with the chrism of salvation, in the name of the Father and of the Son and of the Holy Spirit. Amen.*' A distinction is commonly made between the grace of baptism and that of confirmation: in baptism the Holy Spirit is given for pardon and new birth, in confirmation for strength to preach the gospel and to live the adult Christian life. Such a distinction does not seem tenable in the context of infant confirmation, and appears to have originated in the Middle Ages as a rationalization of the situation when baptism was administered in infancy and confirmation in later years.

A. J. Mason, followed by Dom. G. Dix and Fr L. S. Thornton, has argued that baptism and confirmation make up one sacrament consisting of two signs, each one conveying its own distinctive grace. In baptism the Holy Spirit operates from the outside to convey pardon and new birth; in confirmation the gift of the indwelling Spirit is bestowed.

The *BCP* states that '*It is certain by God's word, that children which are baptized, dying before they commit actual sin, are undoubtedly saved*, and this appears to imply the view that confirmation is not necessary to salvation. Consistently with this, the Thirty-Nine Articles distinguish confirmation and other ceremonies 'commonly called sacraments' from baptism and holy communion, which are 'sacraments of the gospel'. Since confirmation is not regarded as a sacrament in the strict sense by the Church of England, its form and matter are not defined: but the laying on of hands with prayer are commonly regarded as its necessary features. While the

Church of England has retained inflexibly the ancient rule that only bishops may confirm, the Church of Rome permits bishops to delegate this function on appropriate occasions: and as we have seen, the priest is the normal minister of the sacrament in the Eastern churches.

In the Middle Ages the origin of confirmation was variously traced to the action of our Lord laying his hands on children (Mark .10.16), or in breathing on the apostles (John 20.22) or to his teaching after the resurrection of 'the things pertaining to the kingdom of God' (Acts 1.3). An alternative to these speculations was the view that confirmation was exemplified, if not instituted, by the apostles when they laid hands on the baptized and the Spirit came upon them (Acts 8.15; 19.6). These passages in Acts had been cited by Irenaeus and Tertullian and others of the fathers to show that the apostles regularly laid hands on their converts for the bestowal of the Spirit. But this interpretation has been contested by leaders of the continental Reformation and at the present day notably by G. W. H. Lampe, who claim that the events recounted in the Acts are not to be understood as normative: and the evidence of the Syrian rite to which we have referred above suggests that in fact it was not normative.

The ablutionary customs of the ancient world called for the use of oil as well as water in bathing, and it has therefore been suggested that confirmation may have originated in the oil which would commonly have been used after the baptismal bath. Passages in the NT which have been thought to refer to the use of oil or chrism in initiation include II Cor. 1.21 and I John 2.20, 27; but the anointing to which these texts refer may be nothing more than a metaphor for the gift of the Holy Spirit in baptism.

Another explanation for the origin of confirmation has been sought in the complexity of the Gnostic and mystery religions in which candidates proceeded from one stage in initiation to higher and more advanced stages.

While some of these accounts of the origins of confirmation may seem more probable than others, their variety indicates that there is no certainty on the point, which remains a matter for speculation.

2. *The Age of Confirmation*. The practice of

infant confirmation did not entirely disappear until the end of the Middle Ages, so that it was still possible in 1533 for the Princess Elizabeth to be baptized and confirmed at the age of three days. Nevertheless, over the previous centuries a number of circumstances led to the situation in which confirmation came to be reserved to the 'years of discretion'. First, the difficulty of obtaining confirmation and the sense that baptism itself conveyed the grace of the Holy Spirit and all that was necessary for salvation (which few medieval theologians denied) led to a general neglect of confirmation and a disposition to delay it indefinitely. This neglect was then countered by the teaching that confirmation was necessary in order to become fully Christian, and by the regulation which in England originated with Archbishop Peckham in the thirteenth century, which laid down that no one should be admitted to holy communion until he had been confirmed. Although a number of continental and English councils laid down that children must be confirmed by the age of two, three, or seven, the result of the process was that the age of seven or more became established as the normal age for confirmation. At the same time a theology of baptism and confirmation had been developing to match the facts of the changed situation, teaching that baptism restores innocence and gives new birth and that confirmation gives the strength to live the Christian life and to preach to others. It was in the light of this that the Catechism of Trent laid down seven to twelve years old as the appropriate age for confirmation, and preferred the latter. Since then pastoral considerations have led the Roman Catholic Church to admit children to holy communion some years before their confirmation: but if confirmation is a sacrament of initiation, this seems hard to justify.

In the Church of England today the most suitable age for confirmation is a matter of debate. To some it is determined by the fact that the laying on of hands is associated with the re-affirmation of baptismal vows, which suggests that confirmation should be deferred to an age when candidates can speak from personal conviction. On the other hand, those who regard confirmation as a source of sacramental grace argue for an earlier age. The school-leaving age and modern insights into child psychology are other factors in the debate.

The Reformers regard confirmation as an 'idle ceremony'. In their experience it was administered with oil (which they sometimes chose to call 'grease'), and thus appeared to have no foundation in scripture. Moreover, as we have noted above, many of the Reformers did not accept that the imposition of the apostles' hands described in the Acts was to be taken as an example which the church must necessarily follow. In their view the NT gives no indication that confirmation can be traced to the institution of Christ, nor indeed says anything at all about confirmation. They regarded baptism as the one sacrament of initiation and resented the teaching that before confirmation a man was only half a Christian. At the same time, they perceived the value of an occasion when the child baptized in infancy might make a public profession of his baptismal faith in later years. This matched their convictions about the importance of individual faith and the need to answer the Anabaptists who criticized the practice of infant baptism; and it was supported by their mistaken belief that Christians in the primitive church commonly made such a declaration when they reached maturity. From these premisses there developed in the Reformed churches a rite of 'confirmation' of which the principal element was an examination of the candidates and a declaration of their Christian commitment: and this was followed by the imposition of the pastor's hands, which was understood as a blessing. In the late Middle Ages it had already been required that parents and godparents should teach their children such elements of the faith as the *Paternoster*, *Ave Maria*, and *Credo*, and from this the Reformers quickly developed the system of preparation for confirmation in classes and by catechisms.

Although Calvin would have been content to see the 'restoration' of the laying on of hands when children made a personal confession of faith, on condition that it was understood as a blessing, he did not provide or practise such a rite himself. The churches of the Reformed tradition have varied, some observing a confirmation of this kind and others not Today, in response to pastoral needs, many churches which formerly had no rite of confirmation have now adopted one, which is often associated with admission to holy communion. Thus the Methodist Church has provided a service of 'Public

Reception into Full Membership, or Confirmation'. Services of this kind provide a form of commitment to the Christian faith and life, followed by the laying on of hands in blessing performed by the local minister, and often include a prayer for the strengthening of the Holy Spirit. Sometimes they also provide that the minister or some other member of the church shall extend 'the right hand of fellowship' to the new member.

In many parts of the Anglican Communion the restoration of anointing to accompany the imposition of the hands is under discussion, and has already been adopted in some countries.

3. *The word 'Confirmation'*. To many people today the word connotes the fact that candidates confirm their baptismal vows at confirmation. This interpretation of the word dates only from the Reformation and takes no account of such prayer-book expressions as 'to be confirmed by the bishop', which go back to a higher antiquity. The words *confirmatio, confirmare*, began to be used of the post-baptismal anointing or hand-laying in the early fifth century in the sense that the bishop then ratified or completed what had been begun in baptism. At a later stage, when the church had accepted the doctrine that this rite supplied strength for the adult Christian life, it was natural that the word *confirmation* came to be understood as 'strengthening'.

For confirmation in the Orthodox rite *see* **Baptism** 2.

A. D'Ales, *De Baptismo et Confirmatione*, 1927; J. D. C. Fisher, *Christian Initiation. Baptism in the Medieval West*, 1965; J. D. C. Fisher, *Christian Initiation. The Reformation Period*, 1970; P. J. Jagger, *Christian Initiation, 1552-1969*, 1970; G. W. H. Lampe, *The Seal of the Spirit*, 1951; A. J. Mason, *The Relation of Confirmation to Baptism*, 1893; L. L. Mitchell, *Baptismal Anointing*, 1966; S. L. Ollard, ed., *Confirmation or the Laying on of Hands*, 1926; E. C. Whitaker, *Documents of the Baptismal Liturgy*, [2]1970; J. Ysebaert, *Greek Baptismal Terminology*, 1962.

E. C. WHITAKER

Congregationalist Worship

The earliest worship of the English Congregationalists had affinities with Presbyterianism and with the Society of Friends. It was both biblical in seeking precedents for all its ordinances and for their content and also charismatic in stressing the role of the Holy Spirit in worship. Had it been biblically-based alone, it would have been indistinguishable from the liturgies of the Presbyterian churches, as in Calvin's *La Forme des Prières* or in John Knox's *Genevan Service Book*. Had it been simply Spirit-led, without a consistently biblical basis, it could easily have led to the silent worship of the Quakers. Like Presbyterian worship, early Congregationalist worship insisted upon six ordinances: prayer; praise; preaching; baptism and the Lord's Supper; catechizing; and the exercise of discipline. Its single important difference from the Presbyterians was in the demand that public prayer, following Rom. 8.26, 27, should be 'not in any *prescribed* form of prayer, or *studied* liturgie, but in such manner as the Spirit of grace and of prayer who teacheth all the people of God, what and how to pray . . . helpeth our infirmities, we having respect therein to the necessities of the people, the estate of the times, and the work of Christ in our hands' (John Cotton, *The Way of the Churches of Christ in New England*, 1645, p. 65).

This distinctive emphasis on free prayer was supported by six arguments. The reliance upon liturgy would deprive minister and people of the capacity to pray in their own thoughts and words. It was also argued that set forms could not meet the varied needs of differing congregations and occasions. Further, the implication that God could only be worshipped properly in a set liturgy was idolatry, in that it equated the liturgy with the Bible and infringed Christian liberty. Yet again, the constant use of set prayers would lead to the familiarity that breeds contempt or heedlessness. John Owen, the Puritan Vice-Chancellor of Oxford, accused the imposers of liturgies of bringing persecution into the church – 'Fire and faggot into the Christian religion'. Finally, and most compellingly, the point was made that read prayers utterly contradicted the appropriate approach to a heavenly Father by his children, especially as he had promised to help the infirmities of his children by the Holy Spirit. Liturgies or set forms must be abandoned like crutches that God's people may walk in the power of faith. So persuasively were these arguments presented by the small number of independent ministers (the earlier name for Congregationalists) at the Westminster Assembly of Divines called to provide a national settlement of religion in the Cromwellian era that they compelled the Presbyterians to drop their demand for a more biblically-based Genevan type liturgy and instead provided a manual or *Directory for the Public Worship of God Throughout the Three Kingdoms* (1644).

The importance of this manual of worship, prescribing the order of the items in public worship, but not the words which are to be used, is that it has provided the standard shape of worship for the Calvinistic churches (Presbyterian and Congregational, as well as that of the Particular Baptists) in the English-speaking world for approximately two hundred and fifty years.

The other pioneering contribution made to worship by Congregationalism came from the pen of Isaac Watts; the Baptist Benjamin Keach had preceded him in time, but not in quality. Watts, in *The Psalms of David imitated in the Language of the New Testament*, made the transition from the old covenant to the new, teaching 'my author to speak like a Christian'. It was then only a short step to the hymn of Christian experience; Watts took this in *Hymns and Spiritual Songs*. His most famous paraphrase is of Ps. 90: 'Our God, our help in ages past' and his most famous hymn is 'When I survey the wondrous cross'.

The strength of the Congregationalist and Puritan tradition in worship was fourfold. (1) Its biblical and revelational emphasis gave it an august objectivity, unchallenged until the arrival of the eighteenth-century Deists and the nineteenth-century historical critics of the Bible. (2) Its second quality was its relevance to life, for this worship held in simple scrubbed meeting-houses was the incentive to, never the substitute for, civic duty, and the exercise of ecclesiastical discipline guarded against unworthy recipients of the Lord's Supper. Also, special days of thanksgiving and humiliation, and the keeping of spiritual diaries as moral ledger books, as well as the practice of family and private prayer daily, all kept morality rooted in devotion. (3) This worship also had the merit of flexibility, spontaneity and warmth. (4) Finally, on the positive side, any tendency to eccentricity or subjectivity due to the absence of a set liturgy was corrected by

the biblical authority of the worship, the unity of Calvinistic theology which controlled it, and the standard shape of worship provided by the Westminster *Directory*.

It did, as its later history was to prove, have serious weaknesses. These included the absence of creeds for which covenants were not wholly a satisfactory substitute; the disuse of the red-letter days of the Christian year; the infrequent celebration of the Lord's Supper; the excessive didacticism of the pastoral prayers and prolix sermons; and the depreciation of symbolism and colour in art and architecture, and of ceremony in worship.

In time the Puritan and classical heritage was dissolved through rationalism, moralism, and pietism, and activism replaced adoration, while the warm-hearted fellowship replaced the theocratic community. There ensued a serious revaluation of the tradition in the late nineteenth and early twentieth centuries. The trend was away from spontaneous to pre-composed prayers, and from the combination of forms of prayer and free prayer o the adoption of liturgies. What individual congregations or their ministers of a 'high church' outlook did in the nineteenth century became a permissive option for all congregations in the twentieth century. By 1920 the Congregational Union of England and Wales had published its own denominational service-book, *The Book of Congregational Worship*, the work of a committee that included the theologian P. T. Forsyth. It was a portent of the future. In the USA the Congregational churches produced in 1948 an important book, *A Book of Worship for Free Churches*. The wheel had come full circle. A denomination that had originated in North America because of the dissatisfaction of the Puritans with a nationally-imposed liturgy (*BCP*) was now seeking to unify its people in a liturgy that expressed the ecumenical insights of the century.

Horton Davies, *The Worship of the English Puritans*, 1948; Horton Davies, *Worship and Theology in England, 1900-1965*, 1965, ch.X; A. G. Matthews, 'Puritan Worship' in Nathaniel Micklem, ed., *Christian Worship*, 1935.

HORTON DAVIES

Consecration of Churches

The consecration of churches is the act of solemnly dedicating them to God for the purposes of worship.

Solomon's dedication of the Temple (I Kings 8.63) provided the model for the consecration of churches by Christians, but no special rite was at first devised. The dedication of the cathedral of Tyre in 314, described by Eusebius, simply involved the celebration of the eucharist. As late as the sixth century the saying of mass was still regarded as the essential element and so the Leonine Sacramentary (*c*. 540) has only a proper collect, *oratio super oblata*, preface (qq.v.) and postcommunion. The first special feature to be introduced was the deposition of relics which were brought into the new building and enclosed in the altar (q.v.) immediately before the mass. A second feature, which was adopted in the eighth century, consisted of lustrations. This practice of sprinkling buildings with holy water had been used in relation to pagan temples converted for use as churches and thence became an element in the rite of consecration of a new building. So by the eighth and ninth centuries the Roman form of consecration consisted of the following: (1) the carrying of the relics in procession; (2) the entrance of the bishop and his party to prepare the mortar for sealing the altar stone and to wash the altar with exorcized water; (3) the temporary withdrawal of the clergy; (4) a second entrance, followed by the anointing of the altar and the deposition of the relics; (5) the blessing of the entire building; (6) the mass. The model of this rite is that of a funeral, the central idea being that the tomb-altar of the saint, represented by his relics, is prepared and he is conveyed to it and buried within it.

The Gallican model was based upon a different rationale, that of baptism and confirmation (qq.v.), the church being washed and anointed. The main elements of this form are to be found in the Angoulême Sacramentary (*c*. 800), the material probably dating from the eighth century. They are: (1) arrival of the clergy; (2) blessing of a mixture of wine and water; (3) aspersion of the whole church and then of the altar; (4) the anointing of the altar and then of the whole building; (5) the blessing of the altar linen and vessels; (6) withdrawal to fetch the relics; (7) return and placing of the relics in the altar; (8) the mass. *Ordo* XLI (775-800) adds a further feature to this sequence, the alphabet ceremony which took place immediately upon the first entrance of the clergy.

This consists of inscribing the alphabet twice along the lines of a St Andrew's cross traced on the pavement in ashes or sand. In this way the building was claimed for Christ, represented by the initial of *Christus* in Greek.

The medieval Western rite was the result of the fusion, in the tenth century, of these Roman and Gallican forms. The prominence given by the former to the deposition was retained, but the washing and anointing and alphabet ceremony were preserved from the latter. This rite, with some minor modifications such as the inclusion of the seven penitential psalms (i.e. Pss. 6, 32, 38, 51, 102, 130 and 143), has persisted within Roman Catholicism up to the present day, since the revision of 1961 was largely an abbreviation and simplification by the removal of doublets, leaving the elaborate fundamental structure untouched. The form is therefore: (1) the bishop is met by the clergy and a procession goes to fetch the relics; (2) the procession makes a threefold circuit of the exterior while the bishop sprinkles the walls; (3) the procession enters, after the bishop has knocked on the door, and the alphabet ceremony follows; (4) lustrations and anointings; (5) the relics are placed in the altar, which is censed and anointed; (6) the mass begins.

Although the deposition of relics is a common feature in Eastern Orthodox rites, e.g. in the Byzantine and Syrian, it is not considered to be an essential element. Rather, the focal point is the solemn consecration of the altar, which is washed and anointed and draped with the *antimension* – a square of linen or silk with relics inserted in one corner. Even the aspersion of the walls and their anointing with oil are to be understood as an extension of what is done to the altar. A circuit of the exterior, a series of litanies, the blessing and censing of the iconostasis (q.v.) and finally the celebration of the eucharist bring the rite to its conclusion and reveal certain parallels with Gallican customs.

Consecration rites were not an immediate concern of the Reformers. The number of churches existing in England in the sixteenth century was ample, and so the question of a form of dedication scarcely arose. Similarly in Germany, it was not until after the Thirty Years' War that new Lutheran churches were built in any quantity. The Puritans rejected all idea of consecrating buildings, partly because they would not countenance the continuation of any medieval practice and partly because they could find no reference to consecrated buildings in the NT. It was not until 1620 that the first Anglican rite was produced by Bishop Andrews and this consisted of a perambulation with appropriate prayers at each stopping place – baptistery, pulpit, lectern, etc. – followed by morning prayer and the eucharist, the general concept being that consecration is effected by use. In 1662 and 1663 the convocations discussed the provision of an official form, but none was ever promulgated with authority, and to the present day, in England, there are only diocesan uses, often based on rites by Bishop Wordsworth of 1887 and 1898. Other provinces of the Anglican Communion, however, have authorized forms, frequently included in their prayer books. In 1666 an Irish rite was promulgated; in 1799 one was approved in the USA, and there exist similar orders for South Africa, Canada and Scotland.

The orders in use in Lutheran churches are noticeable for their simplicity. One example will suffice as an illustration. The rite published by the United Evangelical Church in Germany in 1952 consists of four parts: (1) the bishop, clergy, elders, confirmation candidates, builders, etc. all gather in the building that has been in use for worship prior to the erection of the new church. A short service takes place, with address and prayers; (2) procession to the new building to the singing of hymns and blowing of trumpets. One of the confirmation candidates carries the key, while the clergy bear Bible, vessels, etc. A hymn is sung before the door, which is eventually opened; (3) after an introit psalm or hymn, there is prayer and short address, the Lord's Prayer and consecration formula. The vessels, etc. have prayers said over them; (4) the main Sunday service follows, frequently with communion.

Reformed practice is not markedly different. So the consecration service of the French Reformed Church (1955) opens with a procession in which are carried a Bible, the baptismal bowl, the paten and chalice. During the ensuing prayers and lessons, the Bible is placed on the lectern, the bowl on the table, etc. and the whole culminates in a celebration of the eucharist.

Other churches, which have no authorized service-books, have a number of models suggested. The Call to Worship (1956) includes a possible dedication rite for the Baptists. The service begins at the church door which is ceremonially opened. The minister proceeds to the pulpit and leads the congregation in an act of dedication of the church and people to God. A prayer for the dedication of the baptistery is also included, and there is provision for a lesson, hymn and sermon. According to a Congregational form (Services and Prayers, 1959), the presiding minister knocks on the door and, to the accompaniment of verses from the psalms and followed by the choir and congregation, takes his place. Lessons from OT and NT follow and then the act of dedication which is concluded with a blessing. In the Methodist book for optional use (Divine Worship, 1935) there is a form for the dedication of churches which may be adapted for use on anniversaries – it consists of prayers, lections, hymns, sermon and an act of dedication.

At the present day it is particularly the rationale of consecration that needs further exploration and analysis rather than the exact forms it may take. In the past there have been three ways in which consecration has been understood to be effected. First, by the provision of relics (the Roman form) – but this cannot be regarded as a sine qua non of Christian worship, since this was celebrated for decades before any relics existed and is performed to this day in houses, in the open air, etc., apart from any relics of a saint. Second, by being baptized and confirmed – but to treat a building as a human being is hardly more than a pious fiction. Thirdly, by use – but if this were correct the regular celebration of the eucharist in places other than churches would consecrate these too.

Basically consecration is thanksgiving. The rendering of thanks to God upon the opening of a new church is natural and right: this is its consecration. The result is that its God-relatedness is acknowledged, its function is declared and it is dedicated as an instrument of the mission of God.

J. G. Davies, The Secular Use of Church Buildings, 1968; R. W. Muncey, A History of the Consecration of Churches and Churchyards, 1930; G. G. Willis, Further Essays in Early Roman Liturgy, 1968.

EDITOR

Consecration Prayer

One of the many names of the eucharistic prayer or anaphora (q.v.); its currency in

English-speaking countries is due to the use of 'Prayer of Consecration' as the title of this prayer in the English *BCP* of 1662, following the Scottish *Book of Common Prayer* of 1637.

W. JARDINE GRISBROOKE

Cope *see* Vestments (2*a*)

Coptic Worship

The official liturgical language of the Coptic Church is the Bohairic (North Egyptian) dialect of Coptic, although some use of Greek continued for several centuries after the definite separation of the Copts and the Chalcedonians or Greek Orthodox of Alexandria in the sixth century. *Kyrie eleison* and other acclamations are still in that language. The service-books were printed at Rome by Coptic Catholics in 1736 and following; since the mid-nineteenth century, bilingual Coptic-Arabic editions have been produced in Egypt. Arabic was then introduced for a second reading of the lessons, and is now commonly used for the audible parts of the service.

A distinctive feature of the eucharistic liturgy is the series of four lessons, all from the NT. Those from the Pauline and Catholic epistles and Acts precede the gospel, which is commonly read by the senior cleric present. Three eucharistic prayers are in use, though there are traces of others used formerly. The Anaphora (q.v.) of St Cyril represents the ancient Alexandrian liturgy in a somewhat purer form than the Greek St Mark; it is, however, only used occasionally in Lent. The normal Anaphora 'of St Basil' is a shorter form of the Syro-Byzantine type represented by the Greek Basil and Chrysostom. It probably came into Egypt through the influence of Constantinople as the metropolis of the empire in the sixth century. The third Anaphora 'of St Gregory', used at the midnight liturgies of Christmas, Epiphany and Easter, has the unusual feature of being addressed to the Son. In the intercessions there are prayers for blessing on the land in varying forms for the ancient Egyptian seasons of inundation, sowing, and harvest. Other interesting features are the Three Great Prayers – for peace (of the church and the world), for the patriarch and clergy, and for the congregations, which derive from ancient Alexandrian forms – and the priest's moving profession of faith before his communion – 'this is in truth the body and blood

of Emmanuel our God . . .' The eucharistic bread is in small leavened loaves, stamped with a design including the *trisagion* in Greek. Several are presented to the celebrant at the beginning of the liturgy, of which he selects one. The wine is commonly made from the fermented juice of raisins.

Baptismal and other sacramental rites resemble those of the Greek Orthodox. Baptism begins with exorcisms (qq.v.) which assume that the candidates are converts from idolatry, and anointing. Four lessons follow, as in the liturgy, further anointings, and the actual baptism, for which the positive form 'I baptize thee . . .' is used, as in the West; and finally christmation for the gift of the Spirit with the chrism consecrated by the patriarch. Unction of the sick calls for the lighting of seven lamps by seven priests if available. It is often administered as a public healing service on the Friday before Palm Sunday. Funeral offices, varying for adults, children, clergy, and monastics, each consist of a psalm, epistle, gospel, and prayers. Holy Week is marked by long readings from the OT and NT terminating with the Apocalypse and Gospel of John on Easter Eve. An impressive ceremony is the procession of the entombment on Good Friday afternoon. Water is blessed at the Epiphany, and there are footwashing ceremonies on Maundy Thursday and the feast of St Peter and St Paul. The *temporale* is arranged by the ancient Egyptian calendar, with twelve thirty-day months beginning on 29 August and five or six extra days at the end.

There are seven daily offices (q.v.) – midnight, dawn, third, sixth, and ninth hours, vespers and compline, with a final prayer of the curtain for monks. Following ancient monastic practice they provide for daily recitation of the entire psalter, but even in monasteries selections are now used in the morning and evening. A special feature is the morning and evening offering of incense (q.v.) with hymns and prayers, perhaps derived from the customs of ancient Egyptian temples. It precedes the morning and follows the evening offices, and on certain occasions replaces parts of them.

A traditional (medieval) Coptic church has a solid sanctuary screen (q.v.), with a central door flanked by windows and side doors, and lighter screens to mark off the choir and the men's and women's sections of the nave (q.v.). But the latter divisions are now omitted in modern churches, and often removed from old ones. Music has been preserved by oral tradition, but is now also studied formally. The blind are often trained as church singers and ordained as deacons.

O.H.E. Burmester, *The Egyptian or Coptic Church, A Detailed Description of her Liturgical Services*, 1967.

E. R. HARDY

Corporal

A square of linen measuring about twenty inches square which is spread in the middle of the altar-top before or at the time of the offertory (q.v.) (Latin *corpus*, body, referring to the sacramental context). The correct material is linen of good quality, rather than lawn trimmed with lace. The *BCP* in the rubric (q.v.) after the administration of holy communion expects that there will be a

Plate 23   Two corporals, one beneath and one covering the chalice

second corporal to be used to cover the chalice and paten (qq.v.) if they still contain the remains of the consecrated elements of bread and wine. These two corporals are derived from the one very large cloth, known as the *palla corporalis*, which in the earlier centuries was used as a corporal and drawn up over the chalice. Our present custom of having this cloth divided into two parts belongs to the Gothic or late medieval period. When the corporals are not in use they are kept in a case known as the *burse*. *See* Plate 23.

P. Dearmer, *The Linen Ornaments of the Church*, 1929; C. E. Pocknee, ed., *The Parson's Handbook*, rev. ed., 1965.

C. E. POCKNEE

Corpus Christi

This observance on the Thursday after Trinity Sunday is associated with eucharistic devotion. It was established by Rome in the thirteenth century following the advocacy of Juliana of Liège. It is still celebrated in many countries by a procession of the eucharistic host in a monstrance (q.v.).

A. A. MCARTHUR

Covenant Service

The covenant service is, at present, a special Methodist service, usually held on the first Sunday of the year, at which church members rededicate themselves to God.

1. *Beginnings of the Custom.* John Wesley held the first formal covenant service in London on 11 August 1755. He knew the idea of covenanting with God from OT literature (*see* II Kings 23), Anglican devotional writing on baptism, confirmation and communion, and the devotional writings of Puritans and later Free Churchmen (notably Philip Doddridge). He transformed a custom of private devotion into a corporate renewal of dedication.

2. *Development of the Custom.* Introduced by Wesley at main centres of his work (London, Dublin, Bristol, Newcastle), the service spread throughout early Methodism. It was held in London during Wesley's annual visitation around the New Year. Many other societies imitated this, and the covenant service thus came to seem almost essentially a New Year observance. Apparently, Wesley usually linked the service with the communion. This his unordained helpers could not do, but the combination of covenant and communion service became general when the Methodists, after Wesley's death, came to hold their own communions regularly.

The service was most widely observed by Wesleyan Methodists, less regularly in the smaller Methodist denominations (Methodist New Connexion, Primitive Methodism, Bible Christians, United Methodist Free Churches, United Methodism). It is now almost universal in British and related Methodist churches and districts. It is known, but apparently little used, in American and cognate branches of Methodism. Charles Wesley wrote a hymn for the covenant service, 'Come, let us use the grace divine', now incorporated into the official liturgy. Participation, originally limited to Methodists in good standing, is now (in Britain) open to all Christians, as is communion.

Other traditions have shown interest in the covenant service. It has been adapted for use in the Church of South India, and for special occasions in the Church of England. It is frequently used for ecumenical services, especially where occasional intercommunion is possible.

3. *Content and Form of the Service*. Wesley's own service (published 1780) consisted of a long exhortation to make an explicit covenant with God (derived from *Vindiciae Pietatis*, 1663, by the Puritan Richard Alleine), followed by a lengthy prayer of self-dedication composed by Joseph Alleine. The communion apparently went on from the prayer of humble access. Wesleyan Methodism used this service, with only two major revisions (1879, 1897) until Methodist union (1932). Private individuals made unofficial revisions: J. A. MacDonald, 1883; anonymous Minister in Eccles, 1884; G. B. Robson, *c*. 1922. The smaller Methodist denominations each produced one or more forms of the service. After Methodist union, a form based on that of ·G. B. Robson was prepared for the *Book of Offices* (1936). The service begins with Charles Wesley's hymn, the *BCP* collect for purity and *Our Father*. The lesson is John 15.1-8. The first exhortation describes the Christian situation as God's promise (covenant) made to us in Jesus Christ, and our commitment (covenant) to live for God. This commitment is now to be renewed. Three acts of devotion now follow: adoration of the gracious Trinity; thanksgiving for God's faithful generosity to us; and confession of òur unfaithfulness, with absolution. The second exhortation describes the difficulty of the Christian life, in self-abandonment to divine providence and readiness for total self-denial. This leads into the covenant prayer, the former part said by the celebrant, the second by the whole congregation: 'I am no longer my own, but thine. Put me to what thou wilt, rank me with whom thou wilt; put me to doing, put me to suffering; let me be employed for thee or laid aside for thee,

exalted for thee or brought low for thee . . .' The communion goes on with 'Lift up your hearts'.

A slight revision of this service was authorized by the Methodist Conference (1969) for experimental use, in preparation for the new service-book of British Methodism.

4. *Ecumenical Interest of the ·Covenant Service*. The interest lies in the unusually distinct emphasis on Christian self-dedication, congregationally expressed. No other act of worship regularly observed in any tradition does this in the same way (the nearest equivalent is the renewal of baptismal vows, in the Roman rite of Easter Eve). The pursuit of complete dedication to God in the strength of Christ's incarnation and passion and in the power of the Holy Spirit is a concept shared by the great confessions, and sufficiently central to the faith to serve as a major theme of common devotion.

5. *Some Questions of Principle on the Covenant Service*. The reluctance of some Methodists to take part in the service has raised the questions whether its delineation of the Christian life is too intense for regular repetition, or too demanding for most Christians, and therefore whether or not it should be a principal act of worship for the whole church. Various occasions for it have been suggested: the New Year (to consecrate a natural unit of human life), early September (to hallow a new Methodist church year), or Easter (to show our common dependence on the Risen Christ). The existing forms of the service have been accused of being wrongly introspective and man-centred, of paying inadequate attention to the resurrection and the Holy Spirit, and of saying too little of the maturity and liberty promised to the children of God. The custom of renewing the covenant has in itself been deprecated as tending to overshadow sacramental Christian initiation and to usurp the function of the eucharist in the constant renewal of the Christian life, and as being inconsistent with the uniqueness of Christ's mediation of the New Covenant. ·These serious issues, still under discussion, will doubtless affect the future development of the covenant service.

D. H. Tripp, *The Renewal of the Covenant in the Methodist Tradition*, 1969.

DAVID TRIPP

Creed, Creeds

In the earliest Christian church, candidates for baptism were required to confess their personal belief ('I believe') in the presence of the congregation. The earliest confessions of belief were short and simple: e.g. 'Jesus is Lord' (I Cor. 12.3) or 'I believe that Jesus Christ is the Son of God' (Acts 8.37, RV margin only). Eventually such simple baptismal creeds developed into the confession which we know as the Apostles' Creed. Later, another kind of creed, the Conciliar Creed ('We believe') was promulgated with the authority of a council; its purpose was to define the true faith as over against the teaching of heretics. The Nicene Creed (now usually regarded as a product of the Council of Constantinople in 381, but expressing the faith of the preceding Council of Nicea in 325) is the most important and best known of the conciliar creeds of the patristic age. Its use at the eucharist appears to have been introduced by Peter the Fuller at Antioch in 473 to emphasize the adherence of the Monophysites to Nicea as opposed, by them, to Chalcedon. In the early sixth century its use spread to Constantinople and it was adopted in Spain by the third Council of Toledo in 589 as a test for Arians, being recited before the fraction (q.v.); in the Mozarabic rite it still retains this unusual position. It was later favoured by Charlemagne but was not accepted in Rome until 1014 by Benedict VIII under the influence of the emperor Henry II.

But besides these two credal types there was a third form of confessional utterance, viz. the credal hymn. Examples are, in the opinion of the majority of NT scholars, to be found in the NT, and at least some of these date from the apostolic period. The best known is Phil. 2.6-11, in which the preexistence of Christ with God, his taking the form of man (and a slave at that), his death on the cross and his exaltation and universal lordship, are quoted by Paul as if from a liturgical setting which would be well known to the recipients of his letter. Other examples might be I Tim. 3.16; Eph. 4.4-10; and the doxologies in the Apocalypse. O. Cullmann writes: 'The need to confess one's faith according to a fixed text manifested itself in every gathering of the community. The believer wants to confess with the brethren before God what unites them before him. It was so already in the worship of the Syna-gogue, where in pronouncing the Shema, one confessed with all Israel that Yahweh is One. The confession of faith is pronounced within the liturgy at every divine service of the primitive Christian community.' Even more cogently Cullmann might have pointed to the recital of the *Heilsgeschichte* in the liturgy of the Temple (e.g. Pss. 105, 106 and many others).

This credal recital of God's saving acts is indeed an on-going characteristic of biblical-Christian liturgical worship. It arises naturally from the character of the faith as *historical;* it is a spontaneous thanksgiving for the salvation which God has wrought. Thus, many of the hymns which are most popular among Christian congregations today are those which embody the great themes of the proclamation of God's action in Christ 'for us men and for our salvation'. For example, 'At the name of Jesus' is a hymnal paraphrase and exposition of Phil. 2.6-11, and there are countless other examples in the hymn-books of all the churches. And, of course, in the main tradition of Christendom the recitation of the ancient creeds, whether said or sung, is a normal ingredient of liturgical worship. The choral singing of the Nicene Creed, set to the music of Merbecke in the sixteenth century and by many other composers right down to Beaumont in our own times, bears witness to the continuing 'need to confess one's faith according to a fixed text' in liturgical worship.

O. Cullmann, *The Earliest Christian Confessions*, ET, 1949; R.P. Martin, *Carmen Christi: Philippians ii. 5-11 in Recent Interpretation and in the Setting of Early Christian Worship*, 1967; J. T. Sanders, *The New Testament Christological Hymns: their Historical Religious Background*, 1971, which takes the view, not universally accepted, that the NT hymns are modelled on pre-Christian Gnostic forms.

ALAN RICHARDSON

Cross

The history of the use and development of this emblem in Christian worship is a long and complicated one. There was considerable reluctance to depict the crucifixion of Christ in the earlier centuries as that event was regarded by the early Christians from the side of Easter Day rather than Good Friday (qq.v.).

The complete absence of the depiction of the crucifixion in the paintings of the Roman catacombs, and even as late as the fifth century mosaics at Ravenna, should be noted. The cross was certainly used as a decorative symbol of triumph, as we can see in the mosaic in the saucer of the apse of St Apollinare in Classe, Ravenna. The earliest depictions of the cross with a figure are far from realistic and Christ is frequently shown with a diadem on his head and vested in the kingly *colobium*. His eyes are open and his arms outstretched (*see* Plate 24).

It is not until we come to the twelfth and thirteenth centuries under the impetus of the Franciscans, when the cultus of the passion was greatly developed, that realistic crucifixes (i.e. a cross bearing a figure of the crucified Christ) begin to appear, but this development does not reach its zenith until the fifteenth century in such works as those of Matthias Grünewald (d. 1528). (*See* Plate 25).

Processional crosses can be found as early as the fourth century, but the altar cross was introduced much later. In the Middle Ages altars in England seldom had a cross standing upon them since the Crucified was depicted in the middle of the reredos (q.v.). In the case of free-standing altars the processional cross was sometimes placed in a socket behind the altar. But towering crucifixes standing on a shelf behind the altar are a product of the Counter-Reformation in the Roman Catholic Church.

F. Cabrol-H. Leclerq, *Dictionnaire d'Archéologie Chrétienne et de Liturgie*, 1907ff., Tome 3, cols. 3045-3131; C. E. Pocknee, *Cross and Crucifix*, 1962.

C. E. POCKNEE

Plate 25   Grünewald crucifixion, Isenheim altar, Colmar, France

Plate 24 Thirteenth-century crucifix with crowned and vested figure

Cross, Sign of *see* Gestures (1)

Crucifer

The person who carries the processional cross on liturgical or ceremonial occasions.

P. HINCHLIFF

Crucifix

A cross (q.v.) bearing the figure of the cruci-fied Christ.

EDITOR

Cruet

Derived from the medieval French *cruette*, means 'little jug'. A pair of such vessels is used to contain the wine and water for the eucharist; while they are now usually made of glass, sometimes with a lip or mounting of precious metal, they were anciently made of base metal such as pewter, or else of silver or silver-gilt. Some very handsome examples of silver-gilt 'flagons' for holding the wine and water were made during the seventeenth and eighteenth centuries for the churches in the City of London and elsewhere.

J. Gilchrist, *Anglican Church Plate*, 1967.

C. E. POCKNEE

Culture and Worship

'Culture' is derived from the Latin 'colo', i.e. 'I devote, or apply, myself to'. It is concerned with man's attempt to understand himself in relation to his environment, personal and impersonal. Through this confrontation, patterns of culture emerge: language, ritual, forms of art, buildings, structures of time.

Language is a primary activity of inter-personal communication. It also interprets and implies action. Language cannot be divorced from action. Yet, as a medium of rational analysis, with its tendency to separate reason and exalt it above the other human faculties, language can inhibit or prevent fully integrated action. Ritual (q.v.), by stylizing and objectifying basic actions, events and relationships, serves to give them con-tinuity, validity and authority: so with the cosmic myths enacted in ritual drama; the theatre; ritual connected with such basic functions as sex, eating and washing; and worship. But ritual can also become an end in itself, a means of escape. Art makes present, and apprehensible, aspects of reality which may not otherwise be apparent, or cannot be conveyed adequately through other media. Hence the great part played by art in the religious life. Art can also merely imitate, photograph-like, confirming perhaps a tradi-tional pattern or approach to a thing, yet giving no deeper insight into its reality. Buildings may arise from purposeful action by which people are drawn into deeper community: so, ideally, with buildings for worship. But they may, by enclosing people within separate fields of space, inhibit or prevent communication. Time can be the sphere of creative action, and so of freedom and of hope. Yet, as a pre-existing continuum of space into which our activity must be fitted, it can be a restrictive and anxiety-producing phenomenon: the past conditions and limits, the future threatens.

Man makes various judgments as to the value of his environment and the patterns through which he confronts it. First, that the environment as it now stands is the only given frame of reference within which man must discover his position: reality does not extend beyond this. Secondly, that such an environment proves inadequate, deceptive and imprisoning: man must be freed from this, stand outside it, if he is to reach a more genuine apprehension of reality. Thirdly, that this environment does provide the framework within which man must live. But it has definite limitations. The need for ecstasy (standing outside) and revolution is recognized, and this has to happen through cultural patterns within the environment.

Patterns of culture, therefore, can be either creative, or divisive and limiting. They are for the development of understanding and communication. They provide necessary safeguards and frameworks within which man may grow in relationship and knowledge. They help man to position himself in relation to his environment and so reach some idea of his identity, some sense of security. As such they are creative. But these patterns can also limit or prevent understanding and communication. They can divide men through lack of creative interchange between them: undoubtedly this is reinforced by the analytical, compartmentalizing tendency of classical, Western culture, with its stress on the rational. They can become negative safeguards, shields behind which man hides to avoid the pain of exposure to other viewpoints and apprehensions of reality, and the discovery of his own weaknesses. Man comes to find security and identity in the patterns of culture, rather than in the growth towards deeper understanding and communication for which they provide the framework. As such they are divisive and limiting.

Culture essentially is for the formation of man in relationship, primarily with persons, but beyond this with his total environment, so that he may reach authentic knowledge of reality and of his position within this reality. For this to happen two things must be realized. First, that reality is many-levelled, and that, within this, patterns of culture are complementary. Secondly, that whenever such patterns become divisive and limiting there is the need for revolution.

Christian worship is man's expression of the worth of God and of his environment within the dimension of God's action. It is concerned with understanding and communication in the context of the divine. Worship involves the patterns of culture –

language, ritual, art, buildings, time. It is a ritual action for the projection and objectifying of one's position in relation to environment within the divine context. The degree of structure in worship varies between different traditions, according to views as to how far the direction and content of worship must be controlled by definite structure. But the fact that worship is an objective ritual action, leading towards deeper understanding and communication, argues strongly for the importance of regular acts of worship.

Worship has three fundamental dimensions. First, the work of God in Christ towards man and creation, revealed finally and most completely in the ministry, death and resurrection of Jesus Christ: this is an action of total self-giving, reaching out in relationship towards man and creation. Secondly, the life of the church as embodying within itself God's action. Thirdly, the life of the church as representative of the world, where God is active in creation and redemption, and as pointing to this action.

The central act of Christian worship is the eucharist (q.v.). This is the sacrament of eating and drinking in community: it interprets and makes present the self-giving action of God in Christ through the cross and resurrection. In this sacrament the church, by its response, is drawn into God's action: and through the church, all creation. How is this so? In the ministry of the word God communicates his purpose to man and challenges him to respond. Here it is basically through language that man attempts to understand, make present, and respond to the communication of God. In the ministry of the sacrament this divine activity of self-giving communication, and man's response, is confirmed and fully realized. The bread and wine represent Christ's life offered completely for man and, through his self-giving on the cross, transformed into the new life of the resurrection: the bread and wine become the resurrection body and blood of Christ. But they also represent man's life – his work, his culture – and the life of creation: he offers this in self-giving to God, for himself and all creation – but only through Christ. By sharing in Christ's body and blood, that is, his life, we and all that we offer are drawn into this life and so into deeper understanding and communication with one another. We become what we eat and drink.

There are in the eucharist two levels of action. On the one hand it is a thanksgiving for, and celebration of, God's finished work in creation and redemption. The offering of bread and wine affirms and celebrates man's community, his culture and his environment in so far as they realize God's self-giving love. But it is also a penitential action in which man confesses his brokenness and division and that of the world for which he offers. Through the eucharistic action, the fullness of God's work, which is far from being realized in the church's life or that of the rest of the world, is made present: this stands over against man's failure to realize self-giving love, not least in the patterns of culture which divide him and prevent understanding and communication.

Thus the eucharist action is ecstatic and revolutionary, breaking through all the attitudes, the patterns, and images of ourselves, other persons, and environment which divide and limit us. If culture, therefore, is for the formation of man, Christian worship, summed up in the eucharist, is for the transformation of man – the deepening of understanding and communication in relationship through union with Christ. This involves not only the celebration and preservation of existing community and culture, but also the creation of community and even of revolutionary cultural patterns.

There is naturally a strong formation element in worship, since it involves cultural patterns within which man's response to God, and so a transforming encounter between God and man, can take place. Hence the need for a regular, structured pattern of worship, as well as acts of worship more tied to particular situations and cultural patterns. The most pressing problem with regard to such regular, public worship is to determine a recognizable common culture to provide adequate patterns for response, understanding and communication in worship.

Worship is the activity of man in relationship with God. But the eucharist is primarily the action of God, though made present through man's responsive action. This places a big question mark over man's concern as to how he does worship, and what cultural patterns are most adequate and relevant for contemporary worship. All liturgical revision must be seen in the context of the God-man relationship, in which man responds to and realizes the action of God.

This action is outside time, though made present within time. Therefore worship can never become a mere cultural activity within time, conditioned by this or any other cultural patterns.

Worship, because it is both ecstatic and revolutionary, and also celebratory, is open to two dangers. First, it can become an ecstatic activity of the church, divorced from the life and concerns of the world. The church before the fourth century suffered from this. Admittedly it was in an underground situation. But also, to judge from its penitential discipline, it seems in great part to have viewed itself as the redeemed community which has nothing more to do with the world. Secondly, through its effort to meet, work through and transform the life of the world, the church can become accommodated to this life and conditioned by cultural patterns so that it loses the ecstatic and revolutionary dimension inherent in the divine action. The church of the fourth century and following, after Christianity had become the recognized religion of the state, by no means avoided this danger. To keep the necessary balance in its worship, both affirming and yet standing over against culture, is a task which the church has always been hard put to realize.

What of culture and worship today? There are at present two basic trends in culture to be noted. The first is a dissatisfaction with traditional patterns, an exploration into new possibilities, a disintegration of previously settled and monochrome cultures. Together with this there is a meeting of different cultural traditions, and an awareness of the relativity and complementarity of cultural patterns. The second is a deep concern for honest and genuine personal relationship in the face of the challenge from electro-technology, which while on one level it facilitates communication and awareness of concerns and needs on a worldwide scale, also keeps people apart and prevents face-to-face relationships. The church, in meeting and expressing the contemporary situation in its worship, must start primarily, not from any particular cultural tradition, but from the essential fullness of Christian belief and practice. There is much that is positive in the present exploratory climate and the search for meaningful experience outside the given, traditional patterns of culture and structures of society. Here is a search for understanding and communication, which can never rest content in any set of patterns held up as ultimate, but must always be open to new possibilities. The church and its worship has much to learn from this. On the other hand, in being open to the world, the church in its worship cannot afford to become so conditioned by the world that it jeopardizes its ecstatic and revolutionary dimension. The balance is one which is crucially difficult to maintain, and yet it is fundamental to Christian worship.

L. Bouyer, *Rite and Man*, 1963; R. Haughton, *The Transformation of Man*, 1967; M. McLuhan, *Understanding Media*, 1966; B. Wicker, *Culture and Liturgy*, 1963.

P. V. FISHER

Daily Offices *see* Canonical Hours

Dalmatic *see* Vestments (1*g*)

Deacon

The office of deacon is frequently mentioned in the NT though there is no evidence at all to support the tradition that the seven, whose appointment is described in Acts 6, were deacons. The tradition was strong enough, however, to persist over many centuries and to create the feeling that seven was the proper number of deacons, and in Rome the order was for a long time restricted to that number. In the NT the deacon was a minister associated with the presbyter/bishops (q.v.) in the ministry of the local church. They appear in much the same sort of position in the writings of the apostolic fathers. A little later there seems to have been some tension and jealousy between the orders of presbyters and deacons. Deacons are always formally reckoned as the third order and below the presbyters. On the other hand, they were a full-time and professional ministry, with clear liturgical and administrative functions at a time when the presbyters were hardly more than an advisory board. In Rome, especially, the deacons were of considerable importance and were often chosen to occupy the episcopal throne. Evidence for the importance of the deacon is to be found in the leading part played by Felicissimus in the opposition to Cyprian at Carthage, and the schism of Hippolytus may have been partly a result of presbyteral jealousy of the deacon's growing

importance. As presbyters gained a new position as the normal minister in charge of particular districts and congregations, the balance began to swing the other way. In the Middle Ages the parish priest became the local embodiment of the church's life, while the diaconate lost most of its real functions. In the early church the deacon had often exercised real power as the officer responsible for poor relief and, therefore, for administering the church's property. He had also possessed a prominent liturgical role, reading the lessons and especially the gospel, distributing the elements at the eucharist, directing the prayers of the congregation, generally maintaining order in the services, and assisting at baptism. By the end of the medieval period in the West the office of archdeacon, representing the deacon's administrative function, was almost invariably occupied by a priest. The vestigial liturgical functions, chiefly reading the gospel, were also normally performed by a priest. In the modern Anglican and Roman Catholic Churches the diaconate has become a grade through which a candidate for priest's orders passes for a brief period before being ordained to the higher grade. In the Eastern Churches the deacons have remained a quite distinct order with a liturgical function proper to them alone.

John Calvin included the office of deacon (together with pastors, doctors, and elders) in the fourfold ministry which he believed to be most consonant with the pattern of the apostolic church. In the Reformed tradition the deacon remains the officer charged with the care of the sick and the poor. It is a pastoral, charitable and administrative, rather than a liturgical, office. Baptist and Congregational Churches also use the title but the deacon in these traditions has a role in the celebration of the eucharist and distributes the elements.

H. W. Beyer, in *TDNT*, II, pp. 88-93; L. Vischer, ed., *The Ministry of Deacons*, 1965.

P. HINCHLIFF

Deaconess

In the fourth century the general and informal ministry and service of women in the Christian community seems to have been formalized in the office of deaconess. Before that there are many references to the service and devotion of widows and virgins and other Christian women without necessarily implying that they comprised a special order of ministry. By the fourth century, however, the deaconess's duties and functions were clearly defined. She performed many of the duties of a deacon (q.v.) in relation to the care of the sick and the poor, the maintenance of order in church and, particularly, assisting at the baptism (q.v.) of adult women. The office disappeared by the Middle Ages, but has been revived since about the middle of the nineteenth century in the German Lutheran, Anglican, Methodist and Presbyterian Churches. Her duties are usually to act as a general pastoral assistant in the parish or congregation. How far the deaconess is a 'minister' in any technical sense is usually far from clear and in the Anglican Church, for instance, there is considerable disagreement about whether a deaconess can properly be described as part of the 'ordained ministry' or not. Methodist deaconesses are sometimes in pastoral charge of congregations and are authorized to administer the sacraments.

P. HINCHLIFF

Dedication

Dedication is the act of formally making over something or somebody to another, and in Christian usage the other is God. Dedication is related to five liturgical acts.

1. The term has been used interchangeably with consecration, and so to describe the dedication of a church is to outline the rite of consecration (q.v.). A distinction is, however, made in modern English law between the two, dedication being a simple blessing while consecration is regarded as separating the building for ever from unhallowed uses. This differentiation has little or no basis in Christian usage or theological thought.

2. The dedication of a church also refers to the name given to a particular building, e.g. St Paul's or St Mary's. Strictly speaking the church is dedicated to God in honour of a saint or a divine mystery.

3. A dedication festival is the annual commemoration of the day of a church's consecration and is therefore to be distinguished from the patronal festival which is in honour of the patron saint. The first observance of such a feast is recorded by the fourth-century pilgrim Egeria, who describes the practice at Jerusalem in connection with the Church of the Resurrection and the Martyrion. According to her this takes place

on the same day as the dedication of the Jerusalem Temple by Solomon and it would appear to have been observed on 23 September.

The dedication festivals of the four main Roman basilicas were included in the general ecclesiastical calendar: the Lateran (9 November), St Peter and St Paul (18 November), Santa Maria Maggiore (5 August). Gregory the Great ordered the conversion of heathen festivals connected with temples in England into dedication festivals.

In 1536 the English Convocation fixed the first Sunday in October as the universal date. The Scottish and American prayer books provide for the festival, and the 1928 book does also, with the directive that, if the day of consecration is not known, the feast may be observed on the first Sunday in October.

4. Dedication is also used of the blessing or offering of liturgical objects to God. So the Church of Scotland has a series of forms for the dedication of an altar, the font (qq.v.), etc.

5. In churches which do not practise infant baptism, a service of dedication of the child is sometimes held at which the child receives a Christian name.

EDITOR

Dedication Festival
see Dedication (3)

Devotions *see* Benediction; Exposition; Forty Hours' Devotion; Reservation; Rosary; Sacred Heart; Stations of the Cross; Veneration of the Cross

Diptychs

The name diptych is derived from a hinged board, on the two wings of which were anciently written the names of persons, both living and departed, for whom the prayers of the church were specifically desired in the offering of the eucharistic sacrifice.

The diptychs (*see* **Anaphora** 9) appear to go back to the reading by a deacon (q.v.) of the names of those who had brought an offering of bread for the eucharist. Once the custom of making an offering as an act of prayer or thanksgiving on behalf of other individuals was established (which had certainly occurred by the middle of the third century), their names also, by a natural development, were read together with, and in the same way as, those of the offerers themselves. Originally, such vicarious offerings appear to have been made only, or at least normally, on behalf of the departed; hence there was added to the existing list of the names of the (living) offerers a second list containing the names of the (departed) beneficiaries of the offerings. It was not long before a further development took place – that of making offerings for other people still living: early examples of this include the provision of the ancient Roman rite that godparents should offer for their godchildren while the latter are still catechumens (q.v.). Except in cases of this kind, however, for which special provision was made, the names of the living beneficiaries of the offerings appear not to have been read separately, but to have been added to the list of the offerers. Another slightly later development was the addition of yet another list, containing the names – sometimes only the classes – of martyrs (and then other saints as well) for whom it was desired to give thanks, separately from the rest of the departed. The diptychs, then, may be defined for practical purposes as 'intercessions for, or commemorations of, specified persons, living and departed, by name, offered in close and intimate connection with the offering of the eucharist itself'; the name 'diptychs' should not be interpreted too literally, as there are often sub-divisions within the basic divisions of living and departed – the Roman diptychs in the early Middle Ages, for example, may on certain occasions have comprised up to seven lists of names. The actual place in the eucharist at which the diptychs are read in the historic liturgies varies: this variation, indeed, is one of the principal structural distinctions between the eucharistic prayers of different traditions. In the Eastern liturgies of the Antiochene family (including the Byzantine, commonly called 'the Orthodox liturgy') they are placed in the second part of the prayer, after the consecration; in those of the Alexandrine family they are placed in the first part of the prayer, before the consecration; in the West, the historic Roman canon divides the diptychs – the diptych of the living occurs in the former part of the prayer, and that of the dead in the latter part; the ancient Hispano-Gallican liturgies of the West placed the diptychs before the eucharistic prayer, after the offertory (q.v.). Some scholars have said that this was their original position in the Roman rite as well, but the evidence which is cited in favour of this assertion does not, when closely examined, support it.

In the East the diptychs very early came to be expanded into a more general intercession; in the West, except for certain isolated instances, they retained their original character more closely. In East and West alike the practice, dating from the early Middle Ages, of reciting the greater part of the eucharistic prayer in secret (q.v.) inevitably diminished the pastoral effectiveness of diptychs recited in the course of it, and other provision was made to supplement them, e.g. in the Byzantine East in the prothesis (q.v.) and at the great entrance (q.v.), and in the West during the Middle Ages, in the bidding (q.v.) of the bedes. The theological rationale of the diptychs, and any other intercession, in the eucharistic prayer is briefly discussed in connection with the anaphora (q.v.).

W. Jardine Grisbrooke, 'Intercession at the Eucharist', in *Studia Liturgica*, V, 1, 1966, pp. 20-44; *ibid.*, V. 2, 1966, pp. 87-103. For a detailed study of the Roman diptychs, *see* J. A. Jungmann, *The Mass of the Roman Rite*, II, 1955, pp. 152-87, 237-59.

W . JARDINE GRISBROOKE

Disciples of Christ *see* Christian Church (Disciples of Christ) Worship

Dismissal

The act of sending forth the worshippers at the end of a service. In the early church, the catchumens (q.v.) were dismissed after the ministry of the word. By the third century, a prayer for those being dismissed was inserted at the beginning of the community prayer. Then in the next century, they were allowed to stay until the completion of that part of the prayer of the church which was on their behalf. With the disappearance of the catechumenate, the need for these dismissals ceased, but they still survive in the Byzantine rite.

At the conclusion of the whole service, there was a further act of dismissal of the faithful. The Roman form was terse, namely *Ite missa est*, to which was added an introduction and a response: *Dominus vobiscum – Deo gratias*. The Gallican formula, however, seems to have *Benedicamus Domino*. From the eleventh century both were used, the

Roman when there was a *Gloria* and the Gallican on other occasions. At the present day several new formulae are in use to emphasize that the Christians' duty is in the world and that worship is not an isolated incident.

J. A. Jungmann, *The Mass of the Roman Rite,* rev. ed., 1959, pp. 301-4, 535-58.

EDITOR

Disposal of Eucharistic Remains

During the patristic period there was universal agreement that the consecrated elements at the eucharist should be treated with reverence. As early as Tertullian we read: 'We feel pained should any wine or bread, even though our own, be cast upon the ground' (*de Cor.* 3). What was left after communion was carried into the sacristy (q.v.) at the conclusion of the service. There the remains were kept for at least one day following a precept of the Mosaic law in relation to the disposal of certain sacrifices (Lev. 7.16). They were then consumed by the priests or, in certain areas, burned, again following Jewish practice (Lev. 7.17), or given, in Evagrius' phrase, to 'uncorrupted boys' (*Hist. eccl.* 4.36). The practice of having the ablutions (q.v.) immediately after communion meant that in the West the consumption of the remains eventually took place in the church itself before the end of the mass.

In the Eastern Orthodox churches the early practice has continued, i.e. consumption in the sacristy after the service. The Anglican custom is similar to the medieval and modern Roman practice, i.e. what is left is eaten and drunk immediately after all have communicated. In the Lutheran churches the elements remaining are often stored with those that are to serve for future celebrations, but sometimes they are thrown away. The Reformed practice is not uniform, but the bread is sometimes burned. Among Methodists the wine is returned to the bottle and the bread put out for birds or otherwise thrown away.

W. Lockton, *The Treatment of the Remains at the Eucharist after Holy Communion and the Time of the Ablutions,* 1920.

EDITOR

The Divine Office

It is generally only at Christmas, Holy Week and Pentecost, that the average Catholic hears any part of the divine office – to which Benedict in his Rule declared 'nothing should be preferred' by the monks. On these days mattins and lauds are sung, but this is otherwise rare except in monasteries or convents of strict observance, and even there the vernacular said office is becoming the 'in' thing. A revival of participation in the lovely hours of vespers and compline (qq.v.) would be most welcome and in particular would give opportunity for the many fine polyphonic settings of *Magnificat* or *Nunc Dimittis* to be heard where adquate choirs exist. *Tenebrae* (q.v.) ('Darkness'), in structure a variant of mattins, takes its title from the responsory '*Tenebrae factae sunt*' ('There was darkness when they crucified Jesus'). The *Tenebrae* is sung on the three great days of Holy Week, Maundy Thursday, Good Friday and Holy Saturday. The service is divided into three nocturns, each containing three psalms with their antiphons and three 'lessons', each followed by long responsories. Victoria's settings of the latter are to be found in his masterpiece *Officium Hebdomadae Sanctae* (Office of Holy Week). The texts ('lessons') of the first nocturns are taken from the *Lamentations of the Prophet Jeremiah,* of which Palestrina composed four sets. The plainsong settings of all this material are among the finest in the whole *corpus* of the chant.

ALEC ROBERTSON

Doxology

An ascription of praise (Greek *doxologia,* lit. 'words of glory'), usually trinitarian in form, and often beginning with, or including, the word 'glory'.

The 'lesser doxology' (*see* **Anaphora** 10) is composed of the two verses commonly added, in most Christian liturgies, to the end of psalms and canticles: 'Glory be to the Father, and to the Son, and to the Holy Spirit; as it was in the beginning, is now, and ever shall be, world without end. Amen.' In the Eastern liturgies the second verse usually runs: 'both now, and for ever, and world without end. Amen.'

The 'greater doxology' is the hymn *Glory be to God on High,* which exists in a number of versions, and dates from at latest the third quarter of the fourth century. In the fifth-century Codex Alexandrinus it is entitled 'morning hymn', and it features as such in the divine office of a number of the historic liturgies, notably the Byzantine rite, in which it is the climax of the morning office of *orthros* or mattins (q.v.).

The use of this hymn at the eucharist is peculiar to the West. By the beginning of the sixth century it had already an established place in the mass at Rome, although only when a bishop was the president; not till the eleventh century was the present rule finally settled, by which it is used at all masses on Sundays and feasts, although this had already been the custom in many places for some centuries. In the Roman rite, and in other historic Western rites when it has been used at the mass, as well as in the Lutheran liturgy, the *Gloria* has always been sung after the entrance and before the collect (q.v.) of the day, as a preparatory hymn of praise and prayer, for which use it is particularly well suited; its transference to a position after the communion is a peculiarity of the *BCP* and liturgies derived from it.

J. A. Jungmann, *The Mass of the Roman Rite*, I, 1951, pp. 346-59.
W. JARDINE GRISBROOKE

Dry mass *see* Ante-communion

East Syrian Worship

1. *Historical.* The East Syrian Church (known to many as the Nestorian or Chaldean church) is the Syrian Church of Antioch as it developed east of the frontiers of the Roman-Byzantine empire. Its centre was Nisibis, but its distinctiveness as a tradition could be dated from the Synod of Beth Lapat in AD 484, when this church recognized Theodore of Mopsuestia as its official teacher, i.e. his teachings were to be the standard by which the faith of other churches was to be tested. During the seventh and later centuries this church spread to Turkestan (now in the Central Asian republics of the USSR) with bishops in Samarkand, Tashkent, Karakoram and also in Tibet as well as in China and India. Today this church, apart from a part now in the Roman Catholic communion, is limited to small pockets in USA, Iraq, Iran· and India. The patriarch, Mar Shem'un, lives in America.

2. *Liturgical books.* The main eucharistic liturgies are three, which go by the names of (1) Addai and Mari, (2) Theodore of Mopsuestia and (3) Nestorius. In addition to various lectionaries (one for the gospels, a second for the apostle Paul and the *qaryana* which contains the first two lessons for the liturgical office, from the OT and the Acts), they have the *turgame*, which are homilies on the lessons in the form of hymns to be chanted with the aid of the psalter (*Dawida*), consecration of an altar (without chrism), prayers for ferial days, rites of marriage, the ordination manual, etc. The offices are chanted with the aid of the psalter (*Dawida*), the *hudra*, which contains the propers of the office, antiphons, hymns and prayers, the *gazza*, which contains the offices for the feasts of our Lord and the saints (except those that fall on Sundays), and other books for the choirs.

3. *The eucharistic liturgy.* What has astonished many liturgists about the liturgy of Addai and Mari is the absence of the words of institution; this is not unusual in the West Syrian tradition either. (The two other Chaldean anaphorae (q.v.) do have the words of institution.) This is shocking only to those who believe that the recital of the words of institution effect the consecration. There is a form of the Liturgy of the Presanctified (q.v.) for use on Good Friday.

The Liturgy of the Catechumens begins with the *Trisagion*, which is followed by the lections: one from the OT, and a second from either the OT or the Acts of the Apostles. These are supposed to be read from the *bema*, the raised platform in the centre of the church. After the first two lections, as the priest leaves the *bema* to ascend the altar, the *turgama* or the homiletic hymn for the day is sung, interpreting the main point of the lection from the Pauline epistles which follows it. The *turgama* of the gospel comes next, followed by the gospel itself.

The Liturgy of the Faithful begins with a litany of intercession much as in the Byzantine liturgy. The diptychs (q.v.) after the creed and the *lavabo* (q.v.) are also in the form of litanies. Mary is commemorated thus: 'For the memorial of Lady Mary the holy virgin who bare Christ our Lord and our Saviour.' The 318 fathers of Nicea are commemorated, and among the other fathers are mentioned both Theodore and Diodore as well as Nestorius, Flavian, Ambrose and Meletius. Emperor Constantine, his mother Helena, and later Byzantine emperors like Constans and Theodosius are also commemorated.

Even when the words of institution are missing, the epiclesis of the Holy Spirit upon the offering is given in full.

There is a second *lavabo* before the fraction and consignation. The priest censes his hands after the *lavabo* before proceeding to the fraction. The Lord's Prayer precedes the elevation and communion. The deacon who read the apostle is to administer the body from the paten and the deacon who gave the peace to administer the blood from the chalice.

The eucharist is called the *kudasha* or sanctification; the liturgical language is Eastern Syriac, though the vernacular is used in most churches today. Leavened bread is used and communion is generally now in both kinds by intinction.

4. *Offices.* The canonical offices are mainly three: *lelya* (nocturns), *sapra* (mattins) and *ramsha* (vespers) (*see* **Canonical Hours**).

5. *Other liturgies.* The baptismal liturgy is modelled on the eucharistic liturgy, with a pre-anaphora and anaphora for the consecration of the water with the chrism. Confirmation does not exist as a separate rite. Neither penance nor the sacrament of confession is used in this tradition. The anointing of the sick was also unknown until it was borrowed from the West in the sixteenth century. The marriage liturgy includes crowning and common drinking of wine from the same cup, but it is doubtful whether the East Syrians regarded marriage as a sacrament. The ordination practices are similar to those of other Eastern churches.

The text of Addai and Mari is given in ET in F. E. Brightman and C. E. Hammond, *Liturgies Eastern and Western*, vol. I, 1896, pp.247-305; G. P. Badger, *The Nestorians and Their Rituals*, 2 vols., 1852; H. W. Codrington, *Studies of the Syrian Liturgies*, 1952.

PAUL VERGHESE

East, Turning *see* **Postures (1a)**

Easter

The Pascha, the Christian Passover, the transformation of the Jewish Passover, was the great festival of redemption, and was a unitive commemoration of the cross and the resurrection. In the fourth century there was a process of evolution, and with the development of Good Friday as we know it, the Pascha became limited to the theme of the resurrection. So Easter emerged in our understanding of the term.

The gospel narrative makes it abundantly clear that there was no coincidence in the fact that the passion and victory of the Lord took place at the season of the Passover. He chose the place and time of crisis, and with this in his heart he went up to the Holy City. The secrecy of the arrangements for the Last Supper indicate his intense desire to hold this meal with his disciples. The synoptic narrative in its various forms plainly states that the meal was the Passover. Therefore the Jewish day which began at sunset on Thursday was 15 Nisan. It began with the Passover, and before that day had ended at sunset on Friday the Messiah was dead. The Passover commemorated with joyfulness and thanksgiving the central event of the old covenant, the deliverance from Egypt. But in his cross and resurrection, the central events of the new covenant, the Lord Jesus Christ was to accomplish a new and supreme deliverance for all mankind, the redemption from sin and death. The cross and resurrection, seen as a unity, constituted the new exodus.

The Lord had foretold his passion and triumph and, within the context of these events, the Last Supper was of immense significance. The Pascha which was the interpretation of the exodus became on this most sacred night the interpretation of what was now at hand – the entering of the Lord into his kingdom through the gate of suffering and death. This Pascha therefore stands as the decisive frontier between, on the one side, the Jewish Passover of the old covenant and, on the other, both the annual Christian Pascha and the weekly celebration of the Christian eucharist. It is essential to remember that the annual and weekly Christian commemorations were related in the closest possible way. It was a perfectly natural development that the Christian 'Passover' should be an all-night festival, and that it should be divorced from the Jewish liturgical year, that is, from 15 Nisan. Rather, it was linked with the weekly liturgical day of the church, the Sunday, the day of the resurrection. The Christian Pascha began on the Saturday evening, that is, at the commencement of the primitive Sunday, and it culminated at the resurrection dawn with the sacraments of baptism and the eucharist. For it was in the light of the victory of the Lord's Day that the church looked upon the cross. The weekly Lord's Day (*see* **Sunday**) was very like the annual Pascha, for the eucharist was a memorial, not of the death alone, but of the death and the triumph.

The evidence of the third century enables us to see in the baptism at cockcrow, followed at once by the holy communion, the culmination of the Pascha, that is, the rejoicing in the resurrection. So also in the preliminary fast of the Pascha, which normally extended over the Friday as well as the Saturday, although early in the second century it would have been restricted to the Saturday, the dominant note must have been the passion. But the vigil contained the hope of the resurrection, and there would be no rigid distinction. The unity of the passion and victory was what the whole celebration of the Pascha conveyed. The great redeeming action into the benefits of which the candidates were baptized at dawn was the action of the cross and the resurrection. Baptism took place at the point where the sternness of the fast and vigil yielded to the rejoicing of that hour in which, according to tradition, the Lord rose triumphant over death, and into the joy of which the sorrow of the cross was merged. The sacrament of baptism led at once to the first communion of the newly-baptized. It is to be remembered that the sacrament of the Lord's Supper was essentially a recalling before God of the redeeming work of the Lord in his death and resurrection. This fundamental unity of conception must be grasped so that we may understand the full significance both of the primitive Sunday eucharist and the primitive Pascha.

If we wish to appreciate the evidence for the Paschal controversy of the late second century it is necessary to clear away the obstacle produced by the assumption that the Friday before the Pascha in the Christian world outside Asia had the character of the later Good Friday. Nor is there any warrant for assuming that the Pascha of the Asian Christians was different in nature from the Pascha elsewhere, that, in fact, it commemorated only the Passion. In the evidence of Eusebius, 14 Nisan is set over against the Lord's Day as the occasion of the Paschal festival. The identification of these days in terms of contrast and comparison includes

the statement that 14 Nisan in Asia and the Lord's Day elsewhere were the days on which to complete the fast. But the ending of the fast meant the joy of the resurrection. There is no justification for the idea that at this time the Pascha of the church as a whole excluded the passion, nor that the festival of the Asian Christians excluded the resurrection.

The churches in general obviously felt that the festival of the cross and the resurrection, culminating as it did at cockcrow with the conclusion of the fast and the real beginning of the rejoicing in Christ's victory, must coincide with the weekly commemoration of the resurrection, the Lord's Day, and ought therefore to fall on the Sunday after the Passover. On the other hand, the minority group, the Asian churches, must have been impressed by the apparent appropriateness of celebrating the festival of the cross and the resurrection on the ancient day of 14 Nisan, the day when the Paschal lambs were sacrificed, the day of the crucifixion in the Fourth Gospel. Since this liturgical date was determined by a lunar, not a solar, calendar, the Pascha might fall on any day of the week, and the joy of the great annual commemoration of the resurrection would not usually coincide with the Lord's Day. This is strange to our minds, and it was not acceptable to Christians generally in the second century. Asia took a different starting-point from the church as a whole, and it may be said, simply as a statement of fact, that Asia began from the passion whereas the other churches began from the resurrection. But it cannot be said that the different starting-points controlled the whole nature of the festival. Rather, the evidence suggests that everywhere the Pascha, a unitive commemoration, moved through the austerity of the vigil and the memorial of the cross to the end of the fast and the glory of the triumph. The difference consisted, not in the nature of the liturgical celebration, but in the mode of the liturgical calculation.

If the Asian custom had involved the celebration of the Christian festival on 15 Nisan, the date of the Jewish Passover, it could be claimed that in that province there was not the decisive breach with the Jewish liturgical tradition which resulted elsewhere in the alignment of the Christian Pascha with the Lord's Day, the day of the resurrection. In that case it could be said that the Asian Christians were in this matter very conservative and were holding to the old Jewish ways. But the evidence indicates that the Asian festival was not kept on 15 Nisan, the day of the Jewish Pascha. The reference is specifically and plainly to 14 Nisan. It may well be that the Sunday Pascha and the Asian custom were not independent developments from the same source, but that the latter was a secondary form of growth dependent on the Last Supper of the Fourth Gospel, the meal described by the synoptists as the Passover, but which in terms of the Johannine account took place on 14 Nisan. The peculiar features of the Asian Pascha lead to the conclusion that it did not antedate the Fourth Gospel, and that it may be set aside as we look to the first century and the origin of the Pascha. Significantly, the Pascha has always been dependent on a lunar calendar. But during the first century the lunar yielded to a solar calendar except among the Jews and in the Greek cities. Towards the end of the first century the Jewish influence in the church was weakening. The institution of the Pascha must derive from a time when that influence was effective. It may be that the absence of details referring specifically to Passover customs in the Marcan story of the Last Supper indicates that when the narrative was shaped the annual Sunday Pascha and the weekly Sunday eucharist were already part of the established tradition of Christian worship. Certainly it is to the earliest days that we must look for the origin of these transformations of the natal Jewish environment.

G. Dix, *The Shape of the Liturgy*, [2]1945; G. Dix, *The Treatise on the Apostolic Tradition of St Hippolytus of Rome*, I, 1937; A. A. McArthur, *The Evolution of the Christian Year*, 1953.

A. A. MCARTHUR

Easter Garden or Sepulchre

The Easter garden is a model of the holy sepulchre used in the Holy Week (q.v.) services. Its origins are uncertain; it may have arisen, as did the Christmas crib, as a more or less spontaneous act of devotion during the early part of the Middle Ages. It took the form of a simple walled recess, a tomb, a vaulted enclosure, a chapel or a temporary structure. On Good Friday (q.v.), after vespers, it was the practice to place a cross in the sepulchre to represent the burial

of Christ and a candle was lit in front of the shrine. In the thirteenth century, in England and Normandy alone, one of three hosts consecrated at the mass on Maundy Thursday (q.v.) was also placed in the sepulchre. On Easter Day the cross and/or host was removed to represent the resurrection.

EDITOR

Eastward Position
see Postures (1*b*)

Elder

Etymologically the word is simply the Anglo-Saxon equivalent of 'presbyter', though for some curious reason the two terms are thought of as being quite different. 'Presbyter' almost always means an ordained minister: 'elder' refers to an office in the Reformed tradition which is usually described as 'lay' (though there has at times been considerable controversy over whether an elder is ordained or lay). Calvin distinguished between the minister of word and sacrament and the kind of elder who had no such responsibility but was associated with others in the government of the church. This distinction between presbyter/minister and elder has been retained in almost all churches of the Calvinist, Reformed or Presbyterian tradition. The elders belong to the board or session which governs the local congregation. They may have a certain pastoral responsibility for a part of the community and may sit or stand round the minister when he performs his liturgical functions. Representative elders will also be chosen to participate in the higher courts of the church.

J. H. S. Burleigh, *A Church History of Scotland*, 1960; J. Calvin, *Institutes of the Christian Religion*, bk. IV, ch. iii; G. Donaldson, *The Scottish Reformation*, 1960.

P. HINCHLIFF

Elevation *see* Gestures (2)

Ember Days

These are the Wednesday, Friday and Saturday of three (or four) weeks of the year. Probably there were once only three such weeks, with a fourth added later. In any case, the first Ember week of the year is in fact indistinguishable from the Lenten observance.

Ember weeks, like Lent, were times of spiritual renewal – times of prayer, fasting and almsdeeds. Pope Leo the Great used to remind the people of the purpose of Embertide and repeatedly ended his homilies with the words: 'On Wednesday and Friday let us fast; and on Saturday let us all keep vigil at St Peter's.' The Ember vigil was very like the Easter one in having, at different times, either six or twelve lessons – the only days with this arrangement in the old missal.

The Roman Christians chose the times of the agricultural festivals for the Ember weeks – sowing time, the corn harvest and vintage time. The old Ember formularies clearly show this harvest connection.

The ordination of new ministers calls for the united prayer of the whole community and presupposes its spiritual renewal. Lent was such a season of prayer and renewal, and its concluding service, the Easter vigil, was the oldest ordination service. Ember weeks were small-scale Lents and so, at least since Gelasius I (AD 494), the Ember Saturdays have been ordination days. The modern practice of candidates for ordination preparing themselves by prayer and retreat comes from the older custom of the whole community preparing themselves for the ordinations by the Lenten or Ember observances.

                                                      J. CONNELLY

Enarxis

The name commonly given to the preparatory office of prayer and praise which precedes the liturgy of the word and the eucharist in the Byzantine rite (Greek 'opening' or 'beginning'). It comprises an opening blessing of the Trinity, three litanies (q.v.) (the first a general intercession, the second and third very-brief) each concluding with a collect-like prayer, and three anthems (q.v.) (one after each litany) which vary somewhat according to the day, and are usually psalms or based on psalms, with additional material proper to the feast or season. The regulations concerning the use of these anthems vary somewhat from one Orthodox national church to another; the concluding prayers of the litanies have since the later Middle Ages, and probably since a much earlier date, been said secretly, except for their concluding doxologies (q.v.), a practice which deprives the two lesser litanies of their rationale, their function being simply to act

as an introduction to the prayer.

It is difficult to determine the date of the introduction of the enarxis. There appears to be no evidence for it in the sixth century; it was certainly in use by the end of the eighth century, but for a considerable period after this there were many days on which it was omitted, and there are still a few – those when the liturgy is (in theory) celebrated in the evening, and is therefore combined with vespers (q.v.). Nor is it easy to determine exactly how it was originally used, although there are indications that it may well have been a processional rite, and it was certainly not sung, as it is today, with the celebrant in the sanctuary, a practice which makes nonsense of the entrance rite which follows it. *See also* **Liturgies** 2.

H. Holloway, *A Study of the Byzantine Liturgy*, 1933, ch. 11.
                                                      W. JARDINE GRISBROOKE

Entrance, Great

The name now given to the procession of the ministers bringing the gifts of bread and wine to the altar at the beginning of the eucharist proper in the Byzantine rite, together with the rites and ceremonies before and after it. The celebrant and deacon go to the prothesis (q.v.) on the north of the sanctuary, take up the paten and chalice, and preceded by acolytes (q.v.) bearing tapers (and, according to the customs of some, of the Orthodox national churches, cross and censer also), leave through the north door of the screen, proceed down the north aisle and up the nave (but in most Slav churches this longer procession is omitted) and, after certain intercessory commemorations before the holy doors (the central doors of the screen), re-enter the sanctuary through these doors, and place the gifts on the altar. For further details, *see* **Liturgies** 2.

H. Holloway, *A Study of the Byzantine Liturgy*, 1933, pp. 76-79; A. Schmemann, *The World as Sacrament*, 1966, pp. 39-42.
                                                      W. JARDINE GRISBROOKE

Entrance, Little

The name now given to the entrance of the ministers with the book of the gospels at the beginning of the synaxis (q.v.) or liturgy of the word in the Byzantine rite. Originally the beginning of the service, and therefore a real entrance of the ministers through the church and into the sanctuary, the prefixing to it of the enarxis (q.v.), has reduced it to a purely decorative ceremony: the celebrant, already in the sanctuary, together with the deacon, who takes up the book of the gospels, already on the altar, and the acolytes bearing tapers, leaves the sanctuary through the north door of the screen, and re-enters it almost immediately through the central doors, the deacon carrying the book of the gospels before him, and replacing it on the altar.

Inevitably, the ceremony having lost its purpose, far-fetched 'symbolic' meanings have been invented to explain it, despite the fact that they in no way correspond either to the action itself, or to the texts which accompany and follow it. *See also* **Liturgies** 2.

H. Holloway, *A Study of the Byzantine Liturgy*, 1933, pp. 56-59; A Schmemann, *The World as Sacrament*, 1966, pp. 35-37.

W. JARDINE GRISBROOKE

Epiclesis *see* Anaphora 8

Epiphany

In order to understand Epiphany on 6 January and the complicated problem of its relation to Christmas (q.v.) we must free ourselves from the Western tradition which understands the festival in terms of the coming of the Magi. Its significance as 'Epiphany' or 'Manifestation' conveys, primarily and normatively, not the manifestation of Christ to the Gentiles as such, but rather the manifestation, the revelation of God to the world in Jesus Christ.

Nor can the problem be summarized by saying that Christmas on 25 December was the festival of the incarnation in the Western empire while Epiphany on 6 January was its counterpart in the East, and that in the course of the fourth century when, after the cessation of persecution, there was easy communication among the churches of the Mediterranean, there took place an interchange of festivals with some modifications in meaning. This does not explain why, in the West, Epiphany became a kind of doublet of Christmas, whereas in the East it had for its eventual content the baptism of Jesus. A true solution depends on an awareness of the fact that, before Christmas came into existence in the fourth century, there was already, at least in the Eastern empire, an ancient

festival commemorating in unitive fashion the manifestation of God both in the birth and baptism of Jesus Christ. The result of the spread of the festival of 25 December, which fulfilled the function of a reagent, was that in the East the dual significance of the Epiphany resolved itself into its distinct elements. The commemoration of the incarnation was established on 25 December, and that of the baptism alone retained on 6 January. The Western development was somewhat complex in comparison with this logical process of evolution.

It is from Egypt that we obtain unmistakable evidence concerning the unitive nature of the original Epiphany. John Cassian, who was probably a Western, received a monastic training in Bethlehem. But he and his friend Germanus were anxious to go to Egypt, where monasticism had first developed. Between the years 380 and 400 they paid two visits, and they spent a long time in the country. In the *Conferences* Cassian notes that in Egypt the Epiphany was a unitive festival, commemorating both the incarnation and the baptism.

It was during the last quarter of the fourth century that Christmas acted as a reagent on the original Epiphany in the geographical area of Constantinople, Asia Minor and Antioch. Sermons by Gregory of Nazianzus when he was in Constantinople make it clear that by 380 Christmas was being celebrated there, and that it was called the Theophany or the Birthday. The theme was the incarnation, including, of course, the adoration of the Magi. The festival on 6 January was named the Holy Day of the Lights, or the Day of the Holy Lights, and it commemorated the baptism of Jesus. Thus it seems obvious that, before Christmas was introduced, the Church of Constantinople must have had a festival on 6 January commemorating both the birth and the baptism, and called the Theophany, 'Manifestation of God', clearly a synonym for Epiphany. When the primary theme, the incarnation, was transferred to 25 December, the title also was taken. Evidence from Asia Minor is to be found in an Epiphany sermon by Gregory of Nyssa where the situation is obviously the same as in Constantinople. The evidence from Antioch confirms the outline and completes the picture. In a sermon preached on Whitsunday in the year 386, John Chrysostom makes reference to

Epiphany as the first of the Christian festivals, commemorating the appearance of God on earth. But by the end of that year the situation had changed and, manifestly, Christmas was being celebrated for the first time. It is described as the festival upon which all the others depend. Only within the preceding decade had the tradition of Christmas, derived from the West, become known in Antioch. As in Constantinople, the commemoration of the incarnation included the adoration of the Magi. Unlike Gregory of Nazianzus in the metropolis of the East, Chrysostom retains the term 'Theophany' as a synonym for 'Epiphany' and does not apply it to Christmas. There can be no doubt that in Antioch, towards the close of 386 and the beginning of 387, 25 December now signified the birthday and 6 January the baptism.

The *Apostolic Constitutions* show that in the region of Antioch, at some point towards the end of the fourth century, the process of change revealed by the sermons of Chrysostom was complete. The ordered and coherent nature of these developments during the last quarter of the fourth century in the region Constantinople–Asia Minor–Antioch compels us to regard this as the standard process of evolution of Christmas and Epiphany. The simple and brilliant pattern characteristic of the region where the church was most strongly established did not repeat itself in the whole Christian world, and there were elements of confusion. It is possible that fourth-century Jerusalem commemorated in the Epiphany the incarnation alone. At Rome in the middle of the fifth century the Magi formed the only theme of Epiphany, and with the ascendancy in later centuries of the Roman use the Magi-Epiphany became general in the West. The lectionary of Luxeuil has an Epiphany commemorating the baptism, showing us that far in the West, towards the end of the seventh or the beginning of the eighth century, there was preserved the standard process of evolution.

The last two chapters of the *Epistle to Diognetus* constitute a fragment, the end of a sermon by a different writer, to be dated early in the third or late in the second century. It may be suggested, on the basis of the scriptural references, that the fragment was part of a sermon for Epiphany, the manifestation, the appearance of God in Christ, both in the incarnation and in the baptism.

At the beginning of the third century Clement of Alexandria refers in the *Stromata* or *Miscellanies* to the Gnostic heretic Basilides who had taught at Alexandria in the second quarter of the second century. Apparently his followers celebrated a festival of the baptism, and one date to which reference is made is 6 January. If the Epiphany existed in Egypt towards the end of the second century as a unitive commemoration, it is conceivable that the attitude of the Gnostics would be similar to their reaction to the faith. They could not tolerate the doctrine of the incarnation but they could accept the baptism, although, inevitably, they would misrepresent the true understanding of that event. Another point of considerable significance is that the pagan background of 6 January was the festival of the birth of a god. On this date the church may well have established its festival of the manifestation in the incarnation and the baptism. It does not seem at all likely that the Gnostics would initiate a commemoration of the baptism on this date, for the factor of *birth*, which must form the link between the pagan context of 6 January and the heretical worship on that day, is missing. It could be from the unitive festival of the church that the heretics derived their partial commemoration.

B. Botte, *Les Origines de la Noël et de l'Épiphanie*, 1932; O. Cullmann, *Weihnachten in der alten Kirche*, 1947; A. A. McArthur, *The Evolution of the Christian Year*, 1953.

A. A. MCARTHUR

Epistle

The term epistle in its strict sense refers to the liturgical reading in the eucharistic celebration of a pericope from any of the NT epistles. The term is, however, commonly applied to the first reading of the eucharistic celebration where only two readings (the other being the gospel) are proclaimed. In such a case it may in fact be from any scriptural source other than the gospels.

The traditional Roman lectionary draws on the Pauline epistles for the Sundays from Pentecost to Easter, and the Sundays of the year still show traces of the ancient system of continuous reading, from Romans onwards, though this is far from apparent and as a rule the choice of epistle seems purely haphazard and without any connection with the gospel. During Paschaltide the Sunday epistles are chosen from I John, I Peter and James.

The Lenten Sunday epistles are specially chosen, as are those for the feasts and commons of saints, and for votive masses. The OT first readings used on Lenten ferias are specially chosen and accord with the accompanying gospels.

The new Roman *Ordo Lectionum Missae* (1969) has three readings on Sundays and major feasts, the epistle being the second. On Sundays the epistle is unrelated to the other readings, pursuing the continuous reading of the Pauline epistles, with James and Hebrews, in a three-year cycle. I Peter, I John and the Apocalypse are read during Paschaltide. On weekdays the first reading alternates every few weeks between OT and NT books, in a two-year cycle.

BCP; J. A. Jungmann, *The Mass of the Roman Rite*, new rev. ed., 1959; *Missale Romanum; Ordo Lectionum Missae; M.* Righetti, *Storia Liturgica*, III, [3]1966.

BRIAN NEWNS

Ethiopian Worship

1. *Historical.* The Orthodox Church in Ethiopia was organized by Frumentius in the decade immediately following the council of Nicea (AD 325). According to Rufinus' narrative, Frumentius was from Syrian Tyre, and must have had his early education in the Syrian Church. He was consecrated Bishop by Athanasius of Alexandria (c. AD 340), and brought the Alexandrian or Coptic tradition of faith and worship to Ethiopia.

On the foundation of this fully formed Nicene tradition as interpreted by the Church of Alexandria, the nine Syrian monks who came to Ethiopia at the end of the fifth century built a liturgical structure derived from the Coptic and Syrian Orthodox traditions which had rejected the council of Chalcedon (451). During the sixth century the monastic movement spread throughout the country and propagated the faith of the 'Nine Saints'.

A great revival of the Ethiopian Church took place in the fifteenth century under king Zara Yaeqob (1434-68). Many liturgical and theological books were translated from Coptic or Arabic. The sixteenth century Portuguese missions and later Protestant

missions have made the Ethiopian Church somewhat hostile towards Western churches.

In 1959, as a result of the efforts of Emperor Haile Selassie, the Ethiopian Church became autocephalous under Patriarch Baselius, after being for some sixteen centuries an integral part of the see of St Mark in Alexandria. The emperor has introduced the use of the vernacular (q.v.) (Amharic) in a few churches, but most parishes still worship in the ancient classical language (*ge'ez*).

2. *Liturgical books.* The main sources for Ethiopic worship are *Sunodos* (Apostolic Canons), *Mets'hafe – Kidan* (The Testament of our Lord), *Didaskalia, Feteha Negest* (Nomocanon), *Ser'at-we-tezaz* (Ordinances and Instructions), *Mets'hafe Bahr'i* (The Book of Nature), *Te'aqebe Mestir* (Stewardship of the Mystery). The seventeenth-century liturgical revision resulted in four major liturgical books: *Mets'hafe Qeddase* (Missal), *Mets'hafe Nuzaze* (Manual of Penitence), *Mets'hafe Taklil* (Matrimony) and *Mets'hafe Qandil* (Manual of Unction of the Sick). The missal has two parts, one containing sixteen to twenty anaphorae (*Qeddase*) and another with the psalmody for the eucharist (*Zemmare*), often chanted by choirs specially trained.

In addition there are four books for the canonical daily offices: (1) *Deggwa*, or the antiphonal chants for the whole liturgical year except Lent; (2) *Tsomedeggwa*, containing chants for Lent, but not for Holy Week; (3) *Mawase'et*, an alternate form, less frequently used, of the daily offices; (4) *Me'eraf*, the common order for the daily office.

One could also mention paraliturgical works produced in the monasteries like *Wuddase Mariam* (Praises of Mary) and *Anqetse-Berhan* (Gate of Light).

3. *Eucharistic anaphorae* (q.v.). Twenty different anaphorae are known, under the names: (1) The Apostles; (2) Our Lord Jesus Christ; (3) Our Lady Mary (by Cyriacus or Qirqos); (4) St Dioscurus; (5) St John Chrysostom; (6) St John the Evangelist; (7) St James the Brother of our Lord; (8) The Hosanna – Liturgy of St Gregory; (9) The Christmas Liturgy of St Gregory; (10) The Anaphora of our Lady Mary by St Gregory; (11) Another Anaphora of our Lady by St Gregory; (12) The 318 Orthodox Fathers of

Nicea; (13) St Basil; (14) St Athanasius; (15) St Epiphanius; (16) The longer St Cyril; (17) The shorter St Cyril; (18) St James of Sarug; (19) St Mark; and (20) Yet another Anaphora of our Lady Mary. Marcos Daoud, the Egyptian layman who was the first director of the Theological School in Addis Ababa, published in 1954 an English version of the pre-anaphora and fourteen anaphorae (Apostles; Our Lord; St John the Evangelist; St Mary; The 318 Fathers; St Athanasius; St Basil; St Gregory; St Epiphanius; St John Chrysostom; St Cyril; St James of Sarug; St Dioscurus and St Gregory II). The Ethiopic and Amharic texts of these also have been published. Many of the anaphorae indicate a Syrian origin, possibly in the Syrian monastery of the Skete in Egypt. The Liturgy of St Mark is not widely used in Ethiopia; only three of the Ethiopic anaphorae are found in the Coptic Church of Egypt (Cyril, Gregory and Basil). There is no reason to believe therefore that the Ethiopian Church simply copied the Egyptian liturgical practice. Elements of Coptic, Syrian and Byzantine liturgical practices are seen in the Ethiopian tradition, but the latter has a personality of its own.

4. *Structure of eucharistic liturgy.* The Ethiopic liturgy has two main parts: (1) the pre-anaphora, common to all the anaphorae, (2) the anaphora proper. The pre-anaphora, which is unusually long, consists of six psalms (Pss. 25; 61; 102; 103; 130; 131), prayers for the cleansing of the celebrants and the vessels, prayers of vesting, the prothesis of the elements (ending with Ps. 117), the enarxis (the prayers of the oblation, the prayers of the 'wrappings', the prayers for absolution and a long litany of intercession), and then the liturgy of the catechumens (censing of the elements, prayers of intercession for the living and the departed, censing of the priests and people, the three lections from Pauline epistles, Catholic epistles and Acts, the *Trisagion* addressed to Christ and embellished with incarnational epithets; prayers of the gospel, the chanting of an antiphon from the psalms, the blessing of the four quarters of the world, the censing of the gospel, and then the reading of the gospel and a sermon). The pre-anaphora concludes with a long litany of intercession for the church, the catechumens and the people, especially the poor, the dismissal of

the catechumens, a creed or confession of faith in the mystery of the Holy Trinity, in the full deity and humanity of Christ, in the goodness of all that is created, about the undefiled nature of marriage and childbirth, a repudiation of circumcision, etc., followed by the *lavabo*, the prayer of salutation and the kiss of peace.

The Ethiopic anaphorae vary considerably in structure. The basic structure is: (1) eucharistic thanksgiving, parallel to the Western canon (q.v.) up to the words of institution; (2) prayers of intercession and conclusion of the thanksgiving prayer; (3) *Sanctus* (which is missing in one or two anaphorae); (4) institution narrative (replaced by a prayer in James of Sarug); (5) anamnesis, epiclesis; (6) fraction and commixture; (7) Our Father and continuation prayer; (8) inclination of the head and prayer of penitence before communion; (9) elevation of the body and blood for adoration; (10) the communion, during which Ps. 150 is chanted; (11) post-communion thanksgiving and a special prayer called the 'Pilot of the Soul' and (12) the benediction and dismissal with the imposition of the hands of the priest.

5. *Hymnody and music.* Syro-Byzantine and Coptic musical elements must have come to Ethiopia as early as the fifth century. But it was Yared, a disciple of the nine Syrian saints who came in the sixth century, who is the father of the distinctive Ethiopian hymnody and musicology. He is regarded by Ethiopian tradition as the author of all the divine offices, and of the system of Ethiopian chant called *zema*, with its three different chants: *ge'ez*, *'ezl* and *araraye*. Yared is also credited with being the author of the Ethiopian musical notation system, which uses letters of the alphabet written above syllables to indicate the note.

6. *Liturgical year.* The Ethiopian Church follows the Julian calendar. The year is divided into thirteen months – twelve of thirty days each and one of five or six days. The year commences on 1 Maskaam which corresponds to 11 or 12 September in the Gregorian calendar. The year is seven or eight years behind the Western year (AD 1972 would be 1964 or 65 in the Ethiopian calendar). The major feasts are (1) the nine feasts of our Lord – incarnation, passion, resurrection, appearance to Thomas, ascension,

Pentecost, transfiguration, epiphany-baptism, and the miracle of Cana; (2) six secondary feasts – exaltation of the cross, circumcision of the Lord, feeding of five thousand, presentation in the Temple, invention of the cross, and sojourn of Jesus in Egypt; (3) the thirty-two Marian feasts established in the fifteenth century by king Zara Yaeqob; (4) the fifty main feasts of the saints, of the OT and NT, universal and national, including the archangels Michael, Gabriel, and Raphael.

There is also the special peculiarity of the Ethiopian Church – the liturgical *month*, with its eighteen monthly commemorations, four for our Lord, six for Mary and eight for other saints.

7. *Fasting.* The following fasts are observed very strictly in Ethiopia: The great Lent fast (fifty-five days preceding Easter); Advent fast (forty days); the fast of the apostles (from the day after Pentecost till the feast of the Apostles); the fast of Mary; the fast of Nineveh; and Wednesday and Friday each week.

8. *Daily offices.* Forms of the daily offices (q.v.), of Ethiopian origin, follow the traditional structure used in all ancient churches. There are forms of vigil (*Wazema*); offices for Sunday (*Mawaddes*); offices for special feasts of saints (*Kestat'aryam*); offices for Lent (*Za-atswam*); daily mattins (*Sebhate-nage za-zawoter*) and mattins for principal feasts (*Sebhate-nage za-ba'alat 'abiyan*). Each office consists of: (1) scriptural praises – the 150 psalms and 15 biblical hymns of the OT and NT; (2) special prayers for the feasts or for seasons; (3) poetic or hymnic elements (*qene*); (4) readings from the scriptures; (5) prayers and invocations.

The main manual for the daily offices is the *Me'eraf*, which has been studied in detail by Bernard Velat in the *Patrologia Orientalis*, XXXIII (1966).

Marcos Daoud, *The Liturgy of the Ethiopian Church* (text of pre-anaphora and fourteen anaphorae in English), 1954; E. Hammerschmidt, *Studies in the Ethiopic Anaphoras*, 1961; S. Mercer, *The Ethiopic Liturgy*, 1915; Bernard Velat, *Études sur le Me'eraf, Commun de l'office divin Ethiopien, Patrologia Orientalis* XXXIII, 1966.

PAUL VERGHESE

Eucharist

Since the beginning of the second century and possibly in the NT itself (*cf.* I Cor. 14.16), the term 'eucharist', which derives from a Greek word meaning 'thanksgiving', has been used as a title for the service of holy communion. Its appropriateness rests upon the giving of thanks by Jesus at the Last Supper and upon the character of the rite itself which is the supreme act of Christian thanksgiving. In the gospels the verb *eucharistein* is used interchangeably with *eulogein*, meaning 'to bless', since the Jewish *berakah* was in fact a blessing of God by rendering thanks to him for a particular act. So, e.g., the Jewish blessing of bread took the form: 'Blessed art thou, O Lord our God, King of the universe, who bringest forth bread from the earth' – words that almost certainly were used by Jesus at the Last Supper.

This Jewish understanding underlies all primitive liturgies, so, e.g., the consecration prayer in the *Apostolic Tradition* of Hippolytus is essentially one of thanksgiving.

At the present day this term is widely used, not only because it directs attention to one important aspect of the rite as a whole but also because it is free from the doctrinal undertones of other titles.

A full discussion of the eucharistic prayer will be found under **Anaphora**. *See also* **Communion, Liturgies**.

G. A. Michell, *Eucharistic Consecration in the Primitive Church*, 1948.

EDITOR

Eucharistic prayer *see* Anaphora

Evensong *see* Canonical Hours

Exorcism

The practice of exorcism depends on the belief that persons and things may be subject to evil or diabolic power, and that this power may be driven out through the words and actions of the exorcism rite. The ancient Assyrians, Babylonians and Egyptians practised exorcism, and it is also found in late Judaism, *cf.* Tobit 6.8; 8.2; Mark 9.38; Luke 11.19; Acts 19.13. The gospels mention Jesus exorcizing on numerous occasions; he gave his disciples power to exorcize, *cf.* Matt. 10.1, and we find Paul exorcizing in Christ's name in Acts 16.18.

In the Christian church the power to

exorcize was initially seen as a charismatic gift. This view survived in the East until the end of the fourth century at least, but in Rome in the middle of the third century the exorcistate is listed as one of the minor orders. This was the case until recently in the Roman Catholic Church, whose clerics received the order of exorcist on their way to the priesthood, without, however, exercising this order.

Exorcism played an important part in the preparation of catechumens for baptism (qq.v.), besides being used to assist those thought to be possessed by the devil. The water, salt and oil used in the rites of exorcism came to be exorcized themselves, before they were blessed. The rites of exorcism vary greatly in length and content. They usually involve prayers, commands to the devil to leave the afflicted person, and the imposition of the exorcist's hands on the person. Signs of the cross and anointing with oil are also sometimes used, as is aspersion with blessed water, and the imposition of the exorcist's stole.

The Roman Catholic Church retains exorcisms in its rite for adult baptism, but in its new rite for infant baptism (1969) the exorcism is replaced by a prayer for deliverance from original sin, or from the power of darkness. The pre-baptismal anointing with oil remains, but may be omitted in some cases. Exorcisms precede the blessings of oil, salt and water. *Titulus XII* of the *Rituale Romanum* gives the norms and rites for exorcizing those troubled by the devil. Only priests may exorcize, the bishop's permission is required and priests are warned against confusing diabolic possession with psychological ailments. Nowadays this rite is rarely used.

The Orthodox Church uses exorcism in preparation for baptism and where diabolic possession is suspected. In the Church of England's baptismal rite the pre-baptismal exorcism, retained in the first *BCP* of 1549, was omitted in the 1552 *BCP* in response to Bucer's criticism that it implied all unbaptized persons were demoniacs. No other exorcisms were included in the *BCP*, yet the practice survived, for in 1604 Canon 72 forbade Anglican clergy to exorcize without episcopal permission. Exorcism is uncommon in the Church of England today.

Science reveals that many cases once treated by exorcism can now be helped by medical treatment. This development will not disconcert the Christian, who believes that all evil is of malign origin and that all healing comes from God.

---

1. Texts: L. C. Mohlberg, ed., *Liber Sacramentorum Romanae Ecclesiae* (Gelasian Sacramentary), 1960; *Rituale Romanum*, 1st ed., 1614, Titulus XII; C. Vogel, ed., *Le Pontifical Romano-Germanique du dixième siècle*, II, 1963.

2. Studies: J. Forcet, 'Exorcisme', *DTC*, ed., A. Vacant, V, 1913, cols. 1762-80; C. Harris, 'Visitation of the Sick' in *Liturgy and Worship*, ed. W. K. Lowther Clarke, 1932; A. G. Martimort, ed., *Introduction to the Liturgy*, 1968; F. Procter and W. H. Frere, *The History of the Book of Common Prayer*, 1901; M. Righetti, *Storia Liturgica*, IV, [2]1959.

BRIAN NEWNS

Experimental forms of Worship

I recall once when I was at Green Lake, Wisconsin, for a conference, and we had a folk singing in the lobby. Christians were gathering together singing for joy. We sang 'We Shall Overcome', a song that expresses the hope which is part of God's *shalom*. Then we sang about God's drowning the Egyptians, 'Pharaoh's Army Got Drowned', and 'He's Got the Whole World in His Hands'. These songs were very good theology. Then someone said, 'Oh-oh! Time for the worship service.' We all filed out over to the vesper circle, the organ came in with its tremolo, and we sang some songs about our own souls. That was supposed to be 'worship'. But it wasn't!

That is how the Baptist theologian Harvey Cox describes in his *God's Revolution and Man's Responsibility* (1969, p.84) an experience which most Christians have had. There are everyday experiences which have a dimension of worship, and formal worship services which appear to us very ordinary and boring. Yet it is not true that worship is out of favour. What is out is our present way of conducting worship. Worship has ceased to be *une expérience*, as the French understand the word, i.e. an experience which includes the risk of an experiment. That is what is meant by experimental forms of worship. But this is in fact a pleonasm. Worship is either experimental (in the sense of being a real experience and in the sense that in this experiment one never knows what is coming next) or it is not worship at all. The reason for this is that in worship one expects God himself to act. And who would pretend that we can prejudge his actions?

That worship is not rejected can be seen from the fact that even today secular forms of celebration are continually being invented (*see* **Secularization and Worship**). In an enquiry which was made in the autumn of 1968 among the personnel of the Ecumenical Centre in Geneva it became evident that in principle even the critical observers still expect something from the weekly worship service. 'I keep hoping for something better', said one. And another one was 'sad and sometimes irritated because of the verbal impotence'. People asked for fellowship. They wanted to learn to pray, 'but then scarcely anyone knows how to pray in this day and age, and the clergy are as weak in this as anyone'. We have forgotten how to pray! Responsive prayers are 'almost never true reflections of our lives', particularly if they must be read at breath-taking speed. So the prayers on paper prevent the prayers of heart and body, in which one could find and articulate one's own job, sorrows, joys and faith (or the faith of one's church). So the questions remain: How can we pray together without trying to teach each other theology? How can there be an intensive silence full of content from which well up intercession, praise, celebration and mutual care?

People ask – according to this enquiry – for intelligible interpretative information. They are looking for mutual help and tolerance. No question of secularism breaking into the Ecumenical Centre, of the rejection of the gospel, although many of the staff do not attend worship.

Many other enquiries give similar results. Section V of the WCC's Assembly at Uppsala had the task of dealing with worship in a secular age, but it camouflaged the problem by the alliteration: 'Worship, for a Christian, is not a problem but a privilege' (*Drafts for Sections*, p. 97). The hiatus between secular and sacred liturgies – it proposed – should be overcome by education. People should be adapted, conditioned and shaped for the liturgy of the church, so that the church does not need to change. The document adopted at Uppsala is no better than the draft, except that it proposed a Faith and Order Consultation on 'Worship in a Secular Age'. The *status quaestionis* was formulated by Lukas

Vischer as follows:

The main questions were how to worship and how to worship together. The present generation, however, is less concerned with modes and ways. It rather raises the more radical question as to whether it is possible at all. How can we, as men, speak of God and, even more difficult, speak to God? How can we meaningfully pray? All forms of worship are equally challenged by these questions and in the face of these new challenges it is clear that the differences between the various traditions cannot claim more than secondary importance.

(W. Vos, ed., *Worship and Secularization*, p. 1.)

Indeed, one can go a step further, saying that in worship the difference between those who are commonly called believers and those who are commonly called unbelievers becomes secondary. This lesson I learnt from a group of agnostic nuclear researchers. They wanted to organize a worship service with me. The topics which I proposed to them (Faith and Technology, Art and Technology, etc.) did not interest them. They concentrated on one question, saying: 'We do not believe in God. But we want you to teach us to pray.' These are the people who pray, even when they believe they do not believe.

At the Faith and Order consultation mentioned above the Indian theologian Raymond Panikkar stated: 'Only worship can prevent secularization from becoming inhuman, and only secularization can save worship from being meaningless.' 'Probably one of the reasons (effect or cause, I leave it open) of the crisis of the United Nations organization is that it could not or did not know how to develop a really common and thus universal and meaningful liturgy, cult, worship' (W. Vos, ed., *op.cit.*, pp. 28, 53). And the German theologian Will Adam, in describing Jesus' practice of worship, came to the conclusion that he not only broke the social and political taboos of his time, but violated – in order to do the will of God – what at that time people considered to be the will of God. In celebrating communion with people who were excluded from communion, he defined what he considered to be worship. That is experimental worship in the truest sense! Adam even thinks that worship was the most efficient instrument for mission, because it celebrated the overcoming of segregation (between slaves and free people, rich and poor, men and women), which in their society was considered impossible, immoral or both. Nobody can measure the power worship could regain, if we were to take up once more this original experimental dimension, which at the moment we have frozen with memories of past experiences (called agenda).

The literature on experimental forms of worship – particularly in German – is extensive. New forms of worship do not need to justify themselves any more. They are not the hobby of liturgical playboys. But if they relate mainly to jazz attractions as the worm on the church extension hook to draw the fish into the empty ecclesiastical aquarium, then they are just brushed-up varieties of worship, which are wrongly understood as Christian duty or religious matinees, instead of being the worship 'which the world needs as badly as its daily bread' (Adam), 'the reasonable worship' (Paul).

The question is not to change instruments and words, although this is in many cases necessary and overdue. The question is, how to celebrate communion in the face of the real segregations of this world, how to celebrate hope amid despair, instead of creating artificial barriers by confessional frontiers and then trying to overcome them by so-called intercommunion.

The celebration we have in mind cannot happen unless liturgy becomes an event of the whole people of God and even of those who believe they do not believe. The methods and tools for this 'liturgical alphabetization' of the people of God cannot be described in detail here. They can probably be transmitted by literature only very incompletely, just as one cannot learn to make a film, or to produce a play by reading a book on film-making or play-producing. Learning by doing, with the help of people who have some experience in the field, seems to be the most appropriate method (almost a definition of practical theology!).

Instead of theoretical theses on experimental worship, I mention here an example, which in spite of some liturgical weaknesses, articulated and celebrated hope among the real segregations of our time.

As is the custom on a Swiss Thanksgiving Day, the parishioners wore black at the Sunday morning service. But what a strange smell in the church? Surely, it was the smell of freshly-brewed coffee. And there were present Italian and Spanish waiters, greeting every one as they came into the church and offering them a cup of hot coffee.

During the prelude, the *Kyrie* from the *Misa Criolla*, Italian and Spanish waiters, some Swiss participants and a pastor processed through the church. They were carrying bread and wine for the Lord's Supper, but also a big bag of coffee beans, which was emptied on the altar. Then the foreigners led the service in Italian and Spanish, sometimes with a translation for the Swiss congregation.

First came the *coffee*. Every person received a little bag of coffee. The Spanish layman explained to the congregation how much the Brazilian coffee worker was earning for his work; only enough to feed himself and his family during eight months, even if the harvest is good. For the rest of the year he must suffer from hunger. He only survives by begging and by taking odd jobs.

The bread: an Italian read the famous story by Ignazio Silone of the picture of the Lord's Supper. The Christ in the picture of the euchar-ist in the church at Fontamara has a piece of wheat-bread in his hand, not maize-bread such as the poor farmers of Southern Italy have to eat. Maize-bread is for the farmers, for the pig and goats. But Christ has a real piece of bread and says: this – the wheat-bread – this is my body. The one who has wheat-bread has me, he has God. The one who does not eat it, is like the pigs and the goats. And the Italian finished: how could we help thinking of wheat-bread, when we work day and night to produce the wheat-bread of the rich but never eat it?

A Spanish worker told the story of the Roman Catholic bishop of Cuernavaca in Mexico. He had removed all the images of saints from the church, except one of Mary, pointing to the Crucified. Even the tabernacle was removed. In its place a table was brought into the church for the actual celebration of the eucharist, as in Zwingli's liturgy. The body of the Lord is present in Cuernavaca, when the people of God celebrate the Lord's Supper, when the believers are *sola gratia* transformed into the body of the Lord.

The Bishop of Cuernavaca trains the workers and Indians, so that they can understand the revolutionary undertones of the Lord's Supper. That is why they go to their directors and landowners and talk with them about the Lord's Supper: 'How is it that we are equal partners at the Lord's table, but not at the conference table?'

'*The cup* is the new covenant' (Luke 22.20), the new covenant which the Father has created through his Son between himself and men and between men of all classes and nations. The Swiss parishioner who introduced the cup, mentioned the eucharistic hymn by J. C. Lavater which the congregation had just sung. J. C. Lavater knew what he was doing, when he made the new covenant the topic of his eucharistic hymn. He was pastor at St Peter's in Zürich during the French occupation of Switzerland. Lavater had the courage to live the new covenant, because he believed in it. He had to pay for his belief with his own life. He tried to protect a fellow citizen who was persecuted by a French soldier. The bullet which should have hit his fellow-citizen killed him.

Sermon. The pastor preached for five minutes (in a Reformed service!) in French (which was the common language) on Levi. But not many words were necessary after the congregation had introduced themselves and their foreign fellow human beings into the right context. Levi was an outsider in his society. But when Jesus came to him, he organized a feast for his friends and neighbours with Jesus at the centre. The text does not say that Jesus preached at this feast, but he was the occasion for the feast. Such a feast, the pastor said, we are going to celebrate now.

During the distribution of the Lord's Supper the congregation received cards. They were invited to answer the question: what can we do so that the Brazilians may receive more money for their coffee, so that the people from Southern Italy can eat enough bread, so that the outsiders in our society (both Swiss and foreigners) are not put aside? What are the things in our world which the Lord's Supper changes? The comments of the congregation (published later in the church bulletin) were resumed in the final prayer, a real 'collect' and not the usual pre-written prayer which goes by the name of collect. About half of the people did not react to the question given them, but expressed their thoughts on this form of the Lord's Supper. One woman wrote: 'During the whole week we have to hear these foreign languages. Why should they bother us again in church?' Others confessed that for the first time in their life they had experienced the real presence of the Lord. A Spaniard wrote in impossible Spanish orthography: 'I thank the Lord for the privilege of celebrating the Lord's Supper with my Swiss brethren.'

Harvey Cox, *The Feast of Fools: A Theological Essay on Festivity and Fantasy*, 1969; J. G. Davies, *Worship and Mission*, 1966; Wiebe Vos, ed., *Worship and Secularization*, 1970; WCC, Monthly Letter on Evangelism (Geneva).

W. J. HOLLENWEGER

Exposition

The showing and adoration of the host became a devotion of the church when, in the Middle Ages, the doctrine of the real presence of Christ in the eucharist had been developed by theologians and councils.

The first instance of this 'showing' would seem to have been the practice of the elevation (q.v.) of the host, 'so that it can be seen by all', after the consecration in the mass. The elevation was instituted by the bishop of Paris, Eudes de Sully (1196-1208).

In the centuries which immediately followed, communion was rarely received except at Easter, and this 'visual communion' unfortunately resulted in superstition. Some people would only come to church just in time to see the elevation and leave directly afterwards, while at Eton College the boys were encouraged to leave their games or studies for the elevation.

Religion became more real and spiritual as a result of the Tridentine reform, with more frequent communion and better religious education.

The elevation at mass had an effect on the more prolonged form of exposition, which was introduced at the end of the fourteenth century, for which the feast of Corpus Christi (q.v.), with its procession of the sacrament, was largely responsible.

The host was placed in a vessel known as a monstrance (q.v.), with the sacrament visible. The monstrance would then be placed on or above the altar (q.v.) for the adoration and prayers of the faithful to Christ hidden under the sacred species.

Exposition became too frequent, especially in north Germany, to have a spiritual benefit, and provincial councils and synods gave repeated warnings against excess. Many of the sacrament houses were constructed with a grille, in order that the monstrance with the host might be seen at all times.

Strict regulations concerning exposition of the sacrament were embodied in canon law, requiring the express permission of the bishop of the diocese.

Exposition occurs today preceding Benediction (q.v.) in an afternoon or evening service, and in October during the recitation of the rosary (q.v.). On specified occasions, such as the Feast of Christ the King, exposition is permitted for some hours, with at least two of the faithful present.

In this way, the church encourages silent prayer and worship to Christ present in the sacrament.

A. A. King and C. E. Pocknee, *Eucharistic Reservation in the Western Church*, 1965.

A. A. KING

Extempore Prayer

Spontaneous prayer composed at the time of utterance, though possibly with some preparation. The NT implies (e.g. I Cor. 14) that the ability thus to pray is a gift of God. In the early church the eucharistic prayer was often thus composed by those competent to do so, but according to a fixed pattern. The clearest example is in the *Apostolic Tradition* of Hippolytus, X: 'Let each one pray according to his own ability.' But in course of time the formulae became fixed, and the invention of printing favoured uniformity. In traditional liturgies only a few parts survived where some spontaneity was permitted, e.g. the insertion of names into intercessions.

After the Reformation in England, whereas all Puritans disapproved of the imposition of conformity to the *BCP*, some favoured the production of Puritan liturgies, but others were opposed to all set forms, and conducted a considerable polemic against them. Some even argued that the Lord's Prayer was given only as a model, and was not intended for actual repetition. The objection to read prayers was based on Rom. 8.26; the promised help of the Holy Spirit was to be obtained at the moment of utterance. It was also thought that set prayers could not meet the varying needs of congregations, that they quenched a gift of God, and that their use was hypocritical and insincere. In reply it was pointed out that not all ministers have the gift of extempore prayer, that it is not always easy for a congregation to follow extempore prayer, and that many extempore prayers are florid and ostentatious. This controversy,

which incidentally has somewhat distorted the meaning of the word 'liturgical', often taken to mean 'fixed, stereotyped', has never been entirely resolved in the English Free Churches and in the Church of Scotland. Apart from the Society of Friends, they have now not merely directories, but liturgical books, whether official, as among Presbyterians and Methodists, or unofficial, as among Congregationalists and Baptists; yet these books are guides, not rigidly binding. Many ministers judiciously alternate both methods. It is also possible to combine the two methods as by writing a prayer suitable to a particular occasion, or by composing as one utters it a prayer which nevertheless follows a fixed pattern as in the early church. Probably on the whole extempore prayer is declining in the English Free Churches.

Meanwhile the churches with more traditional liturgies are rapidly adopting more flexible methods, especially in the intercessions of the eucharist. The English Anglican *BCP* of 1928 had a rubric: 'Note: that subject to any direction which the Bishop may give, the Minister may, at his discretion, after the conclusion of Morning or Evening Prayer, or of any Service contained in this Book, offer prayer in his own words.' New Roman Catholic services often have many permitted alternatives and often the rubrics attached to homilies contain the phrase 'or in like words'. These are similar tendencies and may encourage extempore prayer. *See also* **Prayer Meeting.**

A. RAYMOND GEORGE

Fan

The use of liturgical fans was at one time very widespread. In a rubric found before the eucharistic prayer in the eighth book of *The Apostolic Constitutions* (fifth century), their use is ordered thus: 'Let two deacons on either side of the altar hold a fan of thin tissues, or of peacock's feathers, and let them gently ward off the small flying creatures, so that they may not approach the cups.'

In the Latin West fans were undoubtedly employed for a similar purpose, as we can see from the rubrics in the liturgical rites of the Dominicans and the Cluniacs. In the present Eastern Orthodox liturgy, fans are waved over the elements during the recitation of the

Nicene Creed and at the commencement of the anaphora (q.v.) or eucharistic prayer. These fans now have a symbolic meaning, since they have a six-winged cherub depicted on them, whence the name hexapterigon (six-winged). They are carried in processions by deacons, acolytes (qq.v.) and choir-boys on either side of the book of the gospels or at the great entrance (q.v.) of the offerings of bread and wine.

F. E. Brightman, *Liturgies Eastern and Western, I: Eastern Liturgies,* 1896; S. Salaville, *An Introduction to the Study of Eastern Liturgies,* 1938.

C. E. POCKNEE

Fast Days

Fasting is recommended by the scriptures and practised by the church as a means of atoning for sin and commending ourselves and our prayers to God. Hence the fast days of the Christian calendar and their connection with times of prayer, such as Lent and Ember weeks (qq.v.) and the eves of great feasts. *See also* **Ethiopian Worship** 7.

J. CONNELLY

Ferial

Christians, like the Jews, designated the days of the week by numbers, not by names. A day was called a *feria* (without the meaning of a day of rest or a feast). Sunday was the first day, *feria prima,* but from earliest times it was called the 'day of the Lord', *dies dominica* (*cf.* Rev. 1.7). Saturday, the seventh day, was called the Sabbath, *Sabbatum.*

In Christian usage, ferial is opposed to dominical. A *feria* or a ferial day is a weekday to which no solemnity or feast is assigned. Some ferial days have a special place in the calendar, namely the weekdays of Lent, 17 to 24 December, the Ember and rogation days (qq.v.); but most ferial days are an extension of the preceding Sunday. As Sunday is the weekly commemoration of the resurrection, the ferial days make the week a reflection of the Easter Octave. 'Ferial', therefore, is not essentially a synonym for penitential or sorrowful.

J. CONNELLY

Font

A receptacle to hold water for the administration of baptism (q.v.), the term deriving from the Latin *fons* meaning 'a spring of water'.

A sufficient number of datable fonts, from the beginning of the third century onwards, is now known to allow the determination of the historical sequence of their shapes. The most primitive form was the quadrilateral; this was succeeded by the hexagon, octagon and the cruciform. Round or oval fonts were next adopted and finally, in the sixth century, the quatrefoil. Apart from the hexagon and octagon in Italy and France, no one shape seems to have been preferred in any one area, although it is possible to affirm that the cruciform and quatrefoil (*see* Plate 26) were Eastern creations and were thence introduced into North Africa.

Each and every one of these shapes had its own ideological content, the form being a symbol to convey some aspect of the meaning of baptism. The initial adoption of the quadrilateral, which is the design of the first extant font from Dura Europos, is explicable on the grounds that it is similar to a sarcophagus; i.e., since in baptism the believer is buried with Christ, the font was made to look like a coffin. So Ambrose refers to 'the font, whose appearance is somewhat like that of a tomb in shape', Numerology provides the clue to the meaning of hexagon and octagon: six refers to the death of Christ on the sixth day of the week and eight to his resurrection (*cf.* Rom. 6.4). So fonts were shaped in the same way and with the same intention as the baptistery (q.v.), and various combinations were possible. As the candidate entered an octagonal building, he was buoyed with hope in the resurrection of Christ; as he entered the hexagonal font, he knew he was to die with Christ, but as he left the font and stood once more in the eight-sided room he also knew he was to walk in newness of life. Alternatively, as he entered an hexagonal building, he knew that the baptismal death awaited him, but as he entered the octagonal font he knew that this was the means of rising again.

The round font, as the circular baptistery, introduces a different aspect of baptism, namely that of rebirth (*cf.* John 3.3ff.), and so this type of font was regarded as a womb whereby the children of God are regenerated and have the church as their mother. The cruciform font, on the other hand, together with the quatrefoil which is no more than a variant, connects once more with the idea of death. So according to John Chrysostom: 'Baptism is a cross. What the cross was to Christ and what his burial was, that baptism was to us.'

One further feature of the arrangement of the font has bearing upon the meaning of the rite and that is the steps with which many were provided, anything from one to four. Their main purpose was not to allow easy access but to emphasize the fact of descent. So Cyril of Jerusalem, or his successor John, comments: 'You descended three times into the water, and ascended again; here also covertly pointing by a figure to the three days' burial of Christ.'

All these fonts were more frequently placed in a decorative setting, with mosaics on the dome, walls and floors, than they were decorated themselves. Some of them, however, were ornamented, either with simple geometrical patterns, as the one at Timgad, or with a multitude of symbols, as the one at Kélibia. The latter depicts an ark, stressing salvation in the church, fish, based on the *ichthus* symbol of Christ (the initials of the Greek word stand for Jesus Christ, Son of God, Saviour), and a cross, affirming that by baptism we share in the victorious death of Christ.

The fonts themselves not only provide evidence of the early Christian understanding of baptism; they also give a clue to the actual method used. Strictly speaking, there are four principal methods of baptizing: (1) submersion, when the candidate goes completely below the surface of the water; (2) immersion, when the head is dipped, with or without the candidate standing in the water; (3) affusion, when water is poured over the head; (4) aspersion, when water is sprinkled on the head. However, method (2) is now rarely used, and the term immersion normally denotes (1). If the dimensions of all the early Christian fonts known are examined, it is evident that the great majority of them were not capable of being used for submersion; in only a few would this have been possible. Hence if baptismal practice were uniform, then it must have been either by immersion or affusion; even in this case the parallelism with burial would not have been lost, since the essential feature of this was the casting of a handful of earth upon the corpse, and affusion does no more than reproduce this action.

From the medieval period a vast number of fonts have survived, and they are so plentiful and diverse that an exact typology is not easy. However, it is possible to make certain general statements which may be taken as usually valid despite exceptions. In the eleventh and twelfth centuries the tub-font was prevalent and this consisted of an unmounted bowl resting on the ground. Over-

Plate 26 'Quatrefoil font', Stobi, Yugoslavia

lapping this in the twelfth century and continuing through the thirteenth, a mounted type came into use and was polypod in form, i.e. the bowl was supported on four or more legs. This was superseded in the fourteenth century by a monopod, i.e. the receptacle was held up on a single central shaft. This last type was tripartite and consisted of bowl, pedestal and base (*see* Plate 27) but there had existed previously a bipartite form which derived from the tub-font. Many examples of the tub have a band or cable-moulding around the middle; a tightening of this girdle contracts the tub in the centre and both elongates it and makes it assume the appearance of a cup – hence the appearance of the bipartite chalice.

Plate 27   Font, Stottesdon, England

This evolution is explicable in the light of two factors. First, the universal practice of infant baptism required the raising of the font so that the celebrant could handle the children with greater ease. Second, submersion had now become the norm and so the bowls had to be fairly large and, if they were to be at a convenient level, supports were required. Nevertheless submersion did not continue in all countries, being eventually replaced by affusion. In France affusion appears to have been widespread by the fourteenth century, in Italy by the fifteenth, but in England it was not adopted until after the Reformation. Where this was the practice, a second receptacle was required to catch the drops of

consecrated water that dripped from the children's heads; hence the presence of secondary bowls by the side of a number of medieval fonts. Hence also the appearance of font covers to prevent the consecrated water from being stolen for the purposes of magic and witchcraft. The earliest covers were simply flat lids, but their decorative possibilities were soon appreciated and the result, from the fourteenth century, was the towering tabernacles of open-tracery work.

Medieval fonts were covered with sculptural ornament and the subjects chosen naturally refer to baptism. Scenes from the life of Christ were not infrequent, in particular his nativity, baptism, crucifixion and resurrection, each therefore affirming either baptismal rebirth or co-death and co-resurrection. But one of the most dominant themes of the early medieval iconography of baptism was not so much death as the struggle against and destruction of the devil and his minions, hence the host of bas-reliefs depicting the powers of evil as toads, serpents, dragons or griffins. In the fifteenth and sixteenth centuries there was a decline in the artistic merit of these decorations, at the same time as the cult of the saints was reaching its zenith. The result of this was the representation of the saints and/or of scenes from their lives, they being regarded as protectors and intercessors, their names given in baptism to the children, whose patrons and models they thereby became.

From the Reformation to the eighteenth century, the history of the font is relatively uninteresting. There were two main types, either those designed on traditional lines and perpetuating the general features of the fifteenth-century examples, or those of Renaissance pattern, which were usually like vases on slender pillars, the diminutive bowl marking the final discontinuance of submersion (*see* Plate 28). The chief decoration was realistic cherubic heads, disposed around the rim; only rarely were any of the subjects of the medieval iconography reproduced. Among the Calvinists, basins were general, while among Roman Catholics a divided font bowl came into use, one part holding the consecrated water and the other collecting the drops from the children's heads. With the Gothic Revival, octagonal fonts of the decorated period were introduced into church after church, often dispossessing the ancient ones *in situ*.

Plate 29   Font, Audincourt, France

Plate 28   Font, Ruabon, Wales

The twentieth century has witnessed the production of a large number of fonts (*see* Plate 29), some of which are no more than bizarre, but the majority are sufficiently similar to those of the medieval period to allow them to be classified in the same way. So there are unmounted fonts, consisting of either tanks or different forms of the tub-font standing on the ground. There are also mounted ones, both monopods and polypods, but their decorative treatment is almost nil. The result is that few really convey the mean-

ing of baptism. Perhaps the time has come when the refined austerity that characterizes so many of them should give way to a little more boldness in experiment and symbolic representation, in the light of what has previously been achieved.

S. Bedard, *The Symbolism of the Baptismal Font in Early Christian Thought*, 1951; F. Bond, *Fonts and Font Covers*, 1908; J. G. Davies, *The Architectural Setting of Baptism*, 1962.

EDITOR

Forty Hours Devotion

The name probably originated in the prayers said before the 'sepulchre', in the Middle Ages from Good Friday until Easter morning (*Triduum Sacrum*), symbolical of the time when our Lord's body rested in the tomb.

The present devotion to the blessed sacrament exposed began in Milan in the Church of the Holy Sepulchre (San Sepolcro), which may be relevant, but any connection there may have been soon faded into the background, and Pius IV in 1560, when granting permission for the devotion, pointed to Christ fasting forty days in the wilderness.

A missioner by the name of John Antony Bellotti in 1527 instituted the Forty Hours Devotion four times in the year, as it was a time of war. Two years later, it was prescribed in the cathedral church of Milan, to pray for rain, and from thence to other churches in the city.

The year 1534 has been assigned to the beginnings of a universal Forty Hours Devotion, through Antony Maria Zaccaria and others of the Clerks Regular of St Paul (Barnabites). It received papal sanction from Paul III in 1539, and about 1550 Philip Neri brought the devotion to Rome. By this time, when exposition was finished in one church it passed to another and Clement VIII in a constitution of 1592 spoke of it as an 'uninterrupted chain of prayer'. From Italy, the devotion spread throughout Latin Christendom and became very popular in the Baroque centuries. It came to England as a regular diocesan devotion after the restoration of the hierarchy in 1850, as a means of stimulating the faithful in prayer and adoration to Christ present in the sacrament.

The present form of the devotion was regulated by Clement XII in 1731 in what has been called the 'Clementine Instruction'. The full time, however, is forty-eight hours, but where the night watch, at which there are only men, is impracticable, the sacrament is replaced in the tabernacle until the following morning.

The devotion begins with a mass of exposition (q.v.) and procession; then on the following day there is a mass for peace, but not at the altar of exposition. The final ceremony is the mass of deposition with a procession and Benediction (q.v.).

During the exposition, the church or chapel may never be left without at least two persons in prayer before the sacrament.

A. A. KING

Fraction

The ceremonial breaking of the eucharistic bread for distribution. It derives from Christ's own action at the Last Supper (Matt. 26.26) and was a sufficiently striking element to make 'the breaking of bread' (Acts 2.42) a title for the eucharist.

In all non-Byzantine Eastern rites and in all non-Roman Western rites, the fraction takes place before the Lord's Prayer. In the Roman mass, since Gregory the Great, it is performed after the Lord's Prayer, as in the Byzantine rite. The rubric in the Roman mass requires the host to be broken into three, and one particle is then placed in the chalice at the commixture (q.v.). The Mozarabic rite prescribes an elaborate ceremonial, the host being broken into nine, and seven of these pieces being arranged in the shape of a cross.

The 1662 *BCP*, in order to emphasize that the fraction is in imitation of Jesus' action at the Last Supper, requires it to take place during the consecration prayer at the words 'he brake', and this is also the practice in the Coptic and Abyssinian rites.

Originally the fraction was entirely utilitarian and so Augustine refers to the bread being 'broken small for distribution' (*Ep.* 149.16). It soon attracted a symbolic interpretation, Paul paving the way with his argument for unity on the grounds that the communicants have all partaken of the fragments broken from a single loaf (I Cor. 10.17) – so it was a sign of the gathering into one of the children of God (*cf. Didache*, 9.4). Later it was thought to symbolize the death of Christ, although this is in contradiction to John 19.36. The Stowe missal accompanies it with a quotation from Luke 24.35 to the effect that the Lord is known in the breaking of the bread.

EDITOR

Frontal

In the earlier centuries the altar was enveloped in a silk cloth on all sides (*see* **Altar Hangings**). But in the second part of the Middle Ages, when altars came to be placed against screens or walls, this cloth had to be adapted to meet this changed setting of the altar. Thus only that side of the altar which was visible to the congregation came to have a flat silk or brocade cloth hung in front of it; this is what is termed the 'frontal' and in the Latin *antependium*. The frontal is suspended on legs that project from the altar. Over the top of the altar there is hung another strip of silk attached to a coarse linen cloth and this has a fringe running along its length and is termed the *frontlet*, sometimes miscalled the 'super-frontal'. Frontals are often made in various colours to agree with the liturgical colour of the season of the church's year. Where an altar is free standing and visible on both sides two 'frontals' are necessary if the throw-over type of cloth is not adopted. *See* Plate 2 (p. 7 above).

Examples of precious metal frontals were not unknown in the Middle Ages; and we may see an outstanding example still in use at the Church of St Ambrose in Milan by a ninth-century goldsmith.

The present cult of naked and unvested altars so that the structure of the table is visible is not only contrary to the new canons of the Church of England but also to the official rules of the Roman Catholic and Eastern Orthodox Churches.

The practical details for the making of altar frontals and other hangings are given in: C. E. Pocknee, *The Parson's Handbook*, rev. ed., 1965, and The Warham Guild, *The Warham Guild Handbook*, rev. ed., 1963

C. E. POCKNEE

Furnishings *see* Altar Hangings; Corporal; Frontal; Pall; Purificator; Veil

Furniture *see* Altar; Altar Rail; Ambo; Baldachin; Cathedra; Communion Table; Cross; Crucifix; Font; Iconostasis; Lectern; Piscina; Pew; Pulpit; Reredos; Rostrum; Screen

Gallery

A gallery is a platform or balcony projecting from the interior wall of a building. Such galleries were not uncommon over the side aisles in pagan basilicas and were included in the fourth-century Christian basilica (q.v.) as well as in the centralized architecture (q.v.) of the East. They served a twofold purpose: (1) They provided space for the worshippers where the nave was largely occupied by the clergy for the performance of the liturgy and (2) they enabled the women, in the East, to be segregated from the men.

In the large churches of the Middle Ages, particularly cathedrals, the gallery persisted as the triforium, which allowed for circulation and for extra accommodation at the great festivals.

In post-Reformation churches galleries were often erected at the west end for the singers. In auditory churches, galleries, occupying three sides, enabled large numbers of worshippers to have places as close as possible to the minister. So-called Free Church architecture has made great use of this feature. It has one drawback, however, and that is its tendency to divide the congregation to such an extent that its unity and sense of corporateness is impaired.

EDITOR

Genuflexion *see* Postures (2*b*)

Gestures

Liturgical gestures and postures (q.v.) are stylized forms of natural movements of the limbs, especially the hands, in the context of corporate worship. These movements are basically instinctive in character and constitute an important non-verbal mode of communication. The invention of written language eventually made possible the separation of words and gesture and, thus, in religious terms, the differentiation between rites and ceremonies, i.e. the written text of the liturgy and the accompanying gestures and movements.

Protestant rejection of liturgical gesture is based on the association of the gestures with doctrines which are held to be objectionable, e.g. the elevation of the eucharistic elements associated with the theory of transubstantiation and with the eastward position (q.v.).

The significance of liturgical gestures and postures is to be understood mainly in terms of the conversion of personal relationships into directional movements. Thus upward and downward movements can express feelings and beliefs about the man-God relationship, while horizontal movements – towards-self and away-from-self – can be employed to communicate social man-man relationships. Significantly, the Eastern Orthodox name for the central part of the eucharist is anaphora (q.v.) – the Greek word for 'lifting up' or 'offering' (Heb. 7.27). Correspondingly, the kiss of peace is a ritual gesture in which the emphasis is upon the human personal relationships within a Christian community.

1. *Cross, Sign of.* One of the earliest references to signing with the cross is found at the end of the second century in some words of Tertullian: 'at every forward step and movement, at every going in and out, when we put on our clothes and shoes . . . in all the ordinary actions of everyday life, we trace the sign [of the cross]' (*de Cor. Mil.* 3). It is impossible to know whether such continuous domestic self-crossing was ever generally observed, but as a liturgical gesture it certainly became customary and eventually was prescribed as a regular ceremonial gesture at many points in the whole cultus.

A sacramental interpretation is clearly expressed by Augustine (354-430): 'Unless the sign of the cross is made on the foreheads of the faithful, as on the water itself wherewith they are regenerated, or on the oil with which they are anointed with chrism, or on the sacrifice with which they are nourished, none of these things is duly performed' (*Tract.* cxviii *in Joan.* xix 24). Augustine's view of the need for the sign of the cross in the 'due performance' of sacramental acts prevailed in the medieval church, and by the eighth century it was customary to incise crosses on altars and churches at the places where they had been manually anointed with the sign of the cross in the course of their consecration (q.v.).

Thus, signing with the cross became an integral part of the *ex opere operato* sacramental theory of the medieval church and, as such, was rejected by Protestant reformers.

Signing with the cross is still extensively used in this sense in the Roman Catholic Church, but in the Anglican *BCP* it is ordered only in baptism and there merely as a custom which 'is no part of the substance of the sacrament' but which may be accounted 'a lawful outward ceremony and honourable badge, whereby the person who has been baptized is dedicated to the service of him that dies upon the Cross' (Canon XXX, 1603).

The *First Prayer Book* of Edward VI (1549) included two signings in the great eucharistic prayer, but these were omitted in 1552 and the sign of the cross has never been reintroduced into any other authorized *BCP* of the Church of England.

It should be noted that the sign of the cross may be made on or over both persons and things, that it may be single or multiple, and that it may be self-administered or directed towards others. Further, this gesture may take several different forms: originally it seems to have been restricted to the forehead and made with the thumb of the right hand. Subsequently (probably at the time of the Arian controversy), the signing became associated with the Trinitarian formula and the crossing was extended from forehead to heart and across the upper chest – now from left to right in the West and from right to left in the East. Alternatively, a number of small thumb-crossings may be made at various parts of the body, customarily as acts of anointing in the course of rites of initiation or sickness. Self-crossing is common in association with the reading of the gospel, and also at the words 'resurrection of the body' in the creed with the implication 'this, my body'.

2. *Elevation.* This gesture is made in the Roman Catholic Church when the 'celebrant' of the mass raises the host so high that all present may look upon it. The origin and significance of this important act are complex matters and, perhaps more than any other liturgical gesture, it serves to focus attention upon a syndrome of essential differences between Catholics and Protestants, in the matter of sacramental theology.

The elevation itself was first formally recognized in 1210 when the bishop of Paris ordered that before the 'consecration' the bread should not be held more than breast-high, and only after the words 'This is my body' should the host be raised high enough for everyone to see.

The theological arguments of the previous centuries had largely turned upon eucharistic change, and involved the concept of a 'consecration-moment' when the offered bread and wine were so transformed through the words of the priest that the real presence of Christ was an event to be recognized. The faithful had been taught that not only was the 'substance' of the bread and wine changed into the 'substance' of the body and blood of Christ, but that the whole Christ, *totus Christus*, was present on the altar – concealed under the appearance of the bread and wine. The sacrament came to be regarded as so holy that it might not readily be received in hands or mouth, so that, correspondingly, for the faithful, it was all-important to *see* the host. The popular impatience to see led to premature reverence when the priest took the bread and cup into his hands *prior* to the 'consecration', and for this reason it was ordered that the elevation should be a distinct gesture indicating to all the achievement of the real presence and the moment for appropriate reverence.

The eucharistic participation of the congregation consisted in observing with adoration the 'realization' of Christ in their midst and, therefore, it became more important to 'see' *him* in the transubstantiated bread and wine than to eat and drink *them* at the communion.

Other factors in the mainstream emphasis on elevation were the proto-Reformation challenges to the feudal structure and ostentatious wealth of the church from the Albigenses, who virtually denied the hierarchy and the sacraments, and the Cathari, who advocated a church of primitive poverty in which the eucharistic body was accepted as pure bread, *purum panem*. Thus, by emphasizing the real presence of Christ in the cultus, the hierarchy defended its own status and, at the same time, defended a particular theory of eucharistic change against what was judged to be heresy. Essentially the same challenges and reaction reached a climax three centuries later at the Reformation and led to the rejection of any elevation in the Protestant churches. Even the 1549 *BCP* directs that the words of the Last Supper are to be said 'without any elevation, or shewing the sacrament to the people'.

The elevation itself is an extension of a modest 'raising' (*anaphora*) of the sacramental elements as the eucharistic president takes the bread and the cup into his hands when he repeats the corresponding words of the institution narrative. Whether or not it is justifiable to develop this ancient custom into a distinct theological gesture is clearly dependent upon particular theories of how 'consecration' is achieved and how the eucharistic presence of Christ is envisaged.

Prior to the eleventh century the church had not concerned itself with speculation about a precise moment when 'consecration' took place, but, during the thirteenth century, the elevation having been established, a natural ceremonial consequence was that reverence should be expressed by bowing or kneeling and subsequently by prostration and genuflexion, by censings, and by ringing of bells. However, the desire to see waned and it became customary to kneel with bowed head at the elevation. A temporary revival of looking occurred after 1907 when Pius X granted an indulgence to all who said 'My Lord and my God' while contemplating the host, but this practice was officially renounced in 1925.

Current celebration of the mass in the vernacular (q.v.) from the basilican position (q.v.) itself tends to reduce the original significance of the elevation and to reproduce the situation of the first millennium of eucharistic worship when such a gesture and the accompanying reverences were entirely unknown.

3. *Elevation, Little.* The so-called little (minor or lesser) elevation is a gesture of raising both host and chalice (q.v.) at the end of the canon (q.v.), after the words *per quem haec omnia, Domine, semper bona creas, sanctificas, vivificas, benedicis et praestas nobis* (through whom, O Lord, all these gifts are ever created as good, sanctified, vivifie blessed and bestowed upon us). Having said this, the priest then uncovers the chalice and takes it into his left hand and makes a threefold sign of the cross over it with the host held in his right hand, saying 'through him +, with him +, and in him +', and continuing with two more signings between the chalice and his breast 'is to thee God the Father + Almighty, in the unity of the Holy + Spirit', and at this point elevating host and chalice, and concluding 'all honour and glory, world without end'.

The paragraph appears to be a twofold doxology (q.v.), the former part referring to divine creativity mediated through Christ as Logos, while the latter is a declaration of praise being offered through Christ 'present' in the bread and wine. The words '*all* these gifts . . .' are really a vestige of a much earlier prayer associated with the custom of 'eucharistizing' other produce (water, milk, honey, oil, cheese, fruits, seeds, wine and bread) at this point in the mass.

The close association of other 'good gifts' with this elevation of the bread and cup has a certain symbolic value, but in the new *Ordo Missae* (1969) it has been minimized and would generally pass unnoticed in the recitation of the words: 'We hope to enjoy for ever the vision of your glory through Christ our Lord, from whom all good things come. Through him, with him, in him, in the unity of the Holy Spirit [*little elevation*], all honour is yours, almighty Father, for ever and ever.'

The little elevation in the Roman Catholic rite corresponds to a similar ceremony in the Eastern liturgies: the priest within the sanctuary says a secret prayer recognizing the invisible presence of Christ and, as he reaches for the holy bread, the deacon (outside the sanctuary doors) says 'Let us give heed', and then the priest elevates the host and says 'Holy things to holy people'.

4. *Kiss of Peace and the Pax.* As a liturgical gesure, the kiss (actual or token) is a mutual salutation of participants in the Western eucharist: it is now initiated by the president shortly before the communion and, in one form or another, the greeting is exchanged by some or all of those present as a sign of

fellowship.

In the NT there are a number of references to a kiss of greeting, e.g. a 'holy kiss' (Rom. 16.16, etc.), and the linking of the gesture with 'peace' occurs thus: 'Greet one another with a kiss of love. Peace to you all who belong to Christ (I Peter 5.14). Liturgically, the gesture accompanies the pax: *Priest*: The peace of the Lord be always with you; *People*: And with thy spirit. According to Hippolytus a liturgical kiss was given at the conclusion of the initiation rite (thus signifying membership in Christ), and also to a newly consecrated bishop.

It seems probable that the eucharistic kiss originally concluded the synaxis (q.v.) and then, in the light of the command of Jesus to make peace before bringing a gift to the altar (Matt. 5.23f.), became more closely associated with the offertory (q.v.). In the second century, Justin Martyr writes in the *Apology*: 'At the conclusion of the prayers we greet one another with a kiss. Then bread and a chalice containing wine mixed with water are presented to the one presiding over the brethren.' In all Eastern Orthodox rites the kiss remains in this position, but in the Latin rite by the beginning of the fifth century it had been moved to the end of the canon, and was subsequently moved into the midst of the communion ritual.

In the first English liturgy, 1549, the pax remained in a comparable position but without rubrics concerning the kiss: the pax disappeared in the 1552 prayer book but has since been re-inserted in several revisions in English. In the 1967 Series II holy communion of the Church of England, the pax appears as an optional salutation at the end of what is called 'The Preparation of the People' and immediately before the placing of the bread and wine on the table: thus, although no rubrics are provided concerning a ceremonial kiss, the opportunity is provided at the original place in the liturgy, namely the offertory (even though this word is not used). In the 1971 Series III, the pax is made mandatory in the same position, namely, at the beginning of 'The Communion' and immediately before 'The taking of the Bread and Wine': again no suggestion is made concerning any gesture which might accompany the salutation. Similar provision is made in other recent rites, and in some there is a rubric indicating how the gesture may be made; e.g. immediately before the offertory

of bread, wine and alms the Church of South India has: 'The "Peace" may be given here. The giver places his right palm against the right palm of the receiver, and each closes his left hand over the other's right hand . . . The Presbyter gives the Peace to those ministering with him, and these in turn give it to the congregation . . .'.

With few exceptions the liturgical kiss has ceased to be a literal touching with the lips of one person by another, and the gesture may be a light embrace, a hand-clasp or a bow. Again the kiss may be restricted to the sanctuary, or it may be general throughout the congregation. In the latter case, the eucharistic president may initiate a kiss which passes in hierarchical order down through the clergy to the laity or, alternatively, each member of the congregation may simultaneously salute his immediate neighbour. The form of the salutation depends much on what kind of greeting is customary on civil occasions in any community: thus, among East Syrians each person clasps the hand of his neighbour and kisses him, while Armenians merely bow. In the Roman Catholic Church the kiss is limited to a formal 'continental' embrace between the clergy and only at high mass: it is not given on Maundy Thursday, Good Friday or Holy Saturday nor in masses for the dead.

5. *Imposition of Hands*. The gesture of laying hands upon (or over) a person or a thing has the multiple significance of blessing, setting apart, consecrating, commissioning, absolving, healing, confirming, declaring, ordaining, and other associated ideas. Underlying the liturgical act is the notion of the transmission of power, *mana*, authority, spiritual grace, etc., from one specially endowed or recognized person in a community of others. Such channelling of unseen 'charisma' is thought of as being achieved through the physical action of touching with the hands – a visible gesture which can also serve to establish the concept of continuity of role in a sequence of persons, e.g. the apostolic succession.

There are descriptions of laying on of hands in a number of biblical passages – both in the sense of blessing, ordaining or healing and in the sense of setting apart for sacrifice – and these form the basis of the liturgical practices of imposition which developed in the church (e.g. Gen. 48; Acts

8.19; 13.3; I Tim. 4.14; Mark 6.5; 16.18; etc.).

Laying on of hands is often closely associated with anointing with oil and, in this way, the spiritual purposes of ordination, consecration and unction (qq.v.) receive additional visible expression. In the Christian cultus, oil has become a symbol of the gifts of the Holy Spirit – the 'Giver of Life' – and is so used in some rites of baptism, confirmation and ordination (qq.v.) along with the imposition of hands. Such ceremonies still form part of the liturgical practice of the Roman Catholic and Eastern Orthodox Churches, but Protestants generally have discontinued the use of unction, while laying on of hands survives only in those Reformed churches where episcopal ordination is the rule.

In the rites of initiation in the early church, water baptism was always accompanied by anointing and invocation of the Holy Spirit and, through this sacramental gesture, the candidate was incorporated into the 'royal priesthood' (I Peter 2.9; cf. Rev. 5.10) and proceeded to participate in the eucharist. These ceremonies are kept together in the Eastern Orthodox rite of infant baptism without any specific laying on of hands by the priest. In the West, however, the imposition of hands (with anointing) developed as the rite of confirmation (q.v.) and, since the late Middle Ages, in the Roman Catholic Church the sacrament is administered by a bishop anointing the forehead, signing with a cross and extending his hands over the candidate's head. In the Church of England the bishop lays his hands on the head of each candidate but there is no anointing.

Laying on of hands is also an essential ceremony in the rites of episcopal ordination. In the Anglican Church, for example, in the 'making' of a deacon the bishop lays his hands on the head of the kneeling ordinand; in the ordering of priests, not only the bishop but other priests present collectively lay their hands on the head of the deacon; at the consecration of a bishop, the archbishop and other bishops lay their hands on the head of the elected priest. Similar ceremonies accompany the rites of other episcopally ordered communions.

E. Beresford-Cooke, *The Sign of the Cross in Western Liturgies*, 1907; F. Cabrol, *Liturgical Prayer*, 1922; *Dictionnaire d'archéo-logie chrétienne et de liturgie*, 1907/1953; G. Dix, *Shape of the Liturgy*, [2]1945; A. Fortescue and J. B. O'Connell, *The Ceremonies of the Roman Rite*, 1917/1937; J. A. Jungmann, *The Mass of the Roman Rite*, rev. ed. 1959; J. A. Jungmann, *Public Worship*, 1957; C. E. Pocknee, *Cross and Crucifix*, 1962.

GILBERT COPE

Girdle *see* Vestments (1*c*)

Good Friday

In the course of the second century we find the development of the religious observance of fasting on certain days of the week. These 'stations' were half-fasts, lasting until 3 p.m. – the word was a military term conveying the idea of the soldiers of Christ on guard. The observance was clearly an application to the Christian life of the Pharisaic custom of fasting on Monday and Thursday, a change being made, however, to Wednesday and Friday, the days of the Lord's betrayal and crucifixion. Although the stations were accepted by the church, they were regarded as matters private and individual. There was a definite feeling that they were innovations, and that the only real time for general Christian fasting was in the period immediately preceding the great annual festival of the Pascha, commemorating the death and resurrection of the Lord. It seems reasonable to affirm that the existence of the weekly Friday station led naturally to the station on the Friday before the Pascha being transformed from a half-fast into a full fast and being integrally linked with the Saturday of the Paschal fast. This may be regarded as the root of the Good Friday of the late fourth century. Early in the third century the Paschal fast normally extended over the Friday and the Saturday, but in cases of necessity the former could be omitted. At this stage there is not the slightest indication of anything in the nature of Good Friday and, indeed, the Friday is less important than the Saturday. Towards the end of the previous century the custom of fasting on Friday as well as Saturday was not by any means universal, although it was obviously not a recent innovation. It may be affirmed that in the early part of the second century the Friday had no place at all in the fast, which must have been limited to the Saturday. The absence of Friday in the earliest period underlines the truth that there was nothing in the primitive Pascha of what we regard as historical realism.

At Jerusalem late in the fourth century it was beginning to be light on Good Friday when, following services throughout Thursday night, the procession from Gethsemane reached the city. At the Sanctuary of the Cross the entire narrative of the trial before Pilate was read and soon after, still before sunrise, all went to pray at the column where Jesus was scourged. After the people had rested in their homes they returned to the Sanctuary of the Cross. A casket containing a relic which was believed to be wood from the cross was placed on a linen-covered table in front of the bishop. The people filed past, bowing, touching the cross and the title with their foreheads and their eyes, and kissing the wood. At noon they assembled in the open courtyard of the Sanctuary, and from that hour until three o'clock the time was entirely occupied with lessons about the passion, from the psalms and the prophets, the epistles or Acts and the gospels, prayers suitable to the day being said between the lessons. At three o'clock the passage from St John's gospel about the death of the Lord on Calvary was read, and soon after the service ended. In the evening the story of the burial was read in the Anastasis, the Sanctuary of the Resurrection, and a vigil was maintained there throughout the night by all who were able to sustain it. A great crowd took part, although some did not begin their watch until midnight.

It was the development of Holy Week (q.v.) at Jerusalem in the late fourth century which transformed the Friday of the Paschal fast into Good Friday as we understand it. The full growth of Good Friday meant that the commemoration of the passion was detached from the unitive Pascha which eventually came to be designate the resurrection alone. But time was required for the evolution of Good Friday and Easter to become the clear pattern for Christendom.

G. Dix, *The Shape of the Liturgy*, [2]1945; G. Dix, *The Treatise on the Apostolic Tradition of St Hippolytus of Rome*, I, 1937; A. A. McArthur, *The Evolution of the Christian Year*, 1953.

A. A. MCARTHUR

Gospel

The reading of a passage from one of the four canonical gospels concludes and forms the climax of the liturgy of the word which precedes the eucharist proper. The gospel-reading is surrounded with much greater ceremony than the other readings; since the fourth century it has been reserved to the deacon (q.v.). It is customary for all to stand while the gospel is read. The gospel book itself is venerated as a symbol of Christ; before the reading of the gospel the book is carried in procession to the lectern (q.v.), accompanied by lights and incense.

As with the other readings, there are basically two systems for determining the choice of texts to be read. Either a gospel is read more or less continuously, or else pericopes particularly appropriate to the occasion are chosen. Examples of the second system abound in the traditional Roman lectionary as contained in the Roman missal, but the remains of an ancient system of continuous reading can also be discerned. Almost all the gospels of the second half of Lent and of Paschaltide are taken from John's gospel.

The new Roman lectionary (*Ordo Lectionum Missae*, 1969), with its three-year Sunday cycle, devotes a year to the continuous reading of each of the synoptic gospels, John's gospel occupying its traditional place in Lent and Paschaltide annually. The weekday lectionary covers all four gospels every year; in addition a wide choice of gospels is provided for votive masses and the commons of saints, though a number of feasts and saints' days retain proper gospels.

BCP; J. A. Jungmann, *The Mass of the Roman Rite*, new rev. ed., 1959; *Missale Romanum*, 1970; *Ordo Lectionum Missae*; M. Righetti, *Storia Liturgica*, III, [3]1966.

BRIAN NEWNS

Gradual *see* Chants of the Proper of the Mass

Gregorian Chant

From the chronological point of view the chant, which is the traditional music of the Roman Church, is inaccurately described as (1) *Cantus Romanus* (Roman chant); (2) *Cantus planus* (plainchant or plainsong); (3) *Cantus Gregorianus* (Gregorian chant). The term *Cantus planus* was first used in the thirteenth century to distinguish the traditional chant from the various kinds of measured polyphonic music that had come into being. Pope Gregory (590-604) may have had some part in the codification of the chants of the mass *Antiphonale Missarum* that bears his name and perhaps in the organization of a *Schola cantorum*, but there is no certain knowledge about the extent of his activities, and his writings rarely mention music. In any case, the early sources of the so-called Gregorian chant lay not only in Rome but in Western Europe, in such centres of liturgical activity as St Gall, Metz, Einsiedeln, Chartres, Laon, etc. This chant, moreover, arose also in the Franco-German empire, and the Frankish clergy stubbornly resisted the efforts of King Pepin and pre-eminently those of his son Charlemagne to establish the Roman liturgy in their lands and did their best to hold fast to their traditional Gallican rites. The result was that in the tenth century the Roman liturgy began to return in force from Franco-Germanic lands to Italy and to Rome, but it was a liturgy which meanwhile had undergone radical changes and a great development. This importation entailed supplanting the local form of the Roman liturgy by its Gallicanized version, even at the very centre of Christendom.

This is, in fact, substantially the liturgy which has been in use up to the radical reforms arising out of the Liturgy Constitution of Pope Paul VI. The two main choir books before this, were (1) the *Graduale*, which contains the proper, or variable parts of the mass, together with the *Kyriale*, containing the ordinary, or invariable part of the mass; (2) the *Antiphonale*, which contains the chants of the divine office with the exception of those used at mattins. These books contain the largest assemblage of monophonic music in existence, totalling about 3000 melodies for cantors, choirs, and congregations and 'recitatives' for priests, and cover every phase of the church's worship from baptism to the blessing of aircraft. Gregorian chant – to use the now generally accepted term – is spiritually, aesthetically, and practically the ideal kind of church music – truly sung-prayer and prayer-song.

W. Apel, *Gregorian Chant*, 1958; G. Reese, *Music in the Middle Ages*, 1941; A. Robertson, *The Interpretation of Plainchant*, 1937; A. Robertson, 'Plainchant' in *The Pelican History of Music*, ed. A. Robertson and D.

Stevens, Vol. I, 1960.

ALEC ROBERTSON

Harvest Thanksgiving

Although the OT prescribes a feast to celebrate the first fruits of the harvest (Pentecost), and another to celebrate the ingathering of the threshing floor and the winepress (Tabernacles: Ex. 23.16; Deut. 16.9, 13), the church does not appear to have observed any such festivals until relatively recent times. The Ember (q.v.) seasons of June, September, and December were agricultural in origin and very probably related to the pagan observances of Rome at the time of sowing and the harvests of corn and wine; but in Christian liturgy these have always been observed as fasts. However, Lammas (loaf mass: August 1) has been observed in England from Saxon times and throughout the Middle Ages with the blessing of bread made from the first ripe corn.

The harvest home was a secular, weekday, observance, but it is to be noted that since the Reformation, in a period when people made their communion only a few times in the year, 'afore and after harvest' was one of the occasions prescribed by George Herbert and others for the purpose. In 1843 when the Rev. R. S. Hawker, Vicar of Morwenstow in Cornwall, revived the Lammas custom (on the first Sunday of October) and used bread made from the first ripe corn for the bread of the sacrament, it was partly his purpose to redeem the secular character of the harvest home.

A special prayer of thanksgiving for an abundant harvest was first officially provided, for use after the General Thanksgiving, in 1796. Similar provision was made at intervals for the next fifty years, whenever the abundance of the harvest seemed to justify it. This led to the belief that such an observance should be made regularly. It was about this period that most of the popular harvest thanksgiving hymns were written, and in 1862 Convocation made official provision for the occasion with proper psalms, lessons, and prayers. With the exception of the *BCP*, all prayer books of the Anglican Communion today make similar provision for the harvest thanksgiving, and the American prayer book has done so since 1790 and the Irish since

1877.

G. Harford and M. Stevenson, eds., *The Prayer Book Dictionary*, 1912. For Ember days (q.v.), *see* G. G. Willis, *Essays in Early Roman Liturgy*, 1964.

E. C. WHITAKER

Hindu Worship

Hinduism is a complex term invented by the West to indicate the majority religion of the Indian sub-continent, but this is a vast area of great religious diversity in which many kinds of worship are practised. There are ancient models, with elaborate scriptural directions, but restricted today to comparatively small circles, and great popular festivals and pilgrimages which attract millions.

The most revered texts are the Vedas ('knowledge'), which were compiled from about 3000 years ago but not written down for many centuries. The most important is the Rig Veda ('praise'), composed of 1028 hymns to the gods of the Aryan tribes of North India. The three other Vedas are the *Sāma* ('chant'), *Yajur* ('sacrifice') and *Atharva*, named after a priest. The Vedas are followed by a series of Brāhmanas, which explain the hymns and their ritual for Brahmin priests, and by philosophical deductions in the Upanishads, which are the 'Veda's end', Ved-ānta.

Vedic religion was priestly and public and it concerned the worship of the gods (*devas*, related to Latin *deus*). These are chiefly ritual and sky gods and nearly all male. Agni (like Latin *ignis*), the god of fire and messenger to the gods, has nearly a quarter of the hymns. Soma, a fermented drink for libations, also has many hymns in the Rig Veda and much of the Sāma Veda. A third most prominent god was Indra, who combined the functions of storm and national warrior deity. There were countless lesser divinities addressed in hymns and sacrifices, but many of these are long forgotten or survive in little-understood texts since the Vedic form of the Sanskrit language has long been obsolete.

The Rig Veda names eight kinds of priest, and in later times double this number might be required. Sacrifices were performed in the open on a brick altar but not in a temple. They centred upon the sacred fire and libation, and other materials were offered, of butter, milk, wine and animal flesh. Priests recited Vedic formulae and these verses were regarded as having sacred and magical power, so that on the one hand Brahmin priests were masters of magic utterance, and on the other the sacred word or power was developed in philosophy to the supreme power of the universe, the cosmic soul or Absolute. There were also great communal sacrifices, royal consecrations and a Horse Sacrifice (*Ashvamedha*) by which kings strengthened and extended their territory.

The chief survivals of Vedic religion today, among high caste Hindus only, are found in marriage and ancestral ceremonies. When a household is established at a wedding the sacred fire is kindled, which is not used for domestic purposes and should never go out, and here three times a day Five Great Sacrifices should be offered. These are to the gods or Supreme Being, the ancestors, living beings including animals, the poor, and wise men through hearing the Vedas. The most elaborate offerings are those made to the ancestors, who receive food and water every day, and gifts of rice-balls (*pinda*) in an open place at each new moon in a Shrāddha ('faithful') ceremony. This begins after the cremation of the dead, and is held to nourish the departed so that they can bless their descendants. This domestic religion is performed by the householder, who has been initiated previously by the conferment of the sacred thread in adolescence which makes him 'twice born'. He also received at that time the sacred verse (*mantra*) which all high caste Hindus recite daily in all rituals: 'Let us meditate on the glorious light of the Sun, may he inspire our minds.'

Most Indians are not high caste males, and even among the latter, many of the Vedic rites have disappeared and popular gods have replaced Aryan deities. Vishnu, Shiva and the Goddess, with hosts of lesser divinities, are the modern objects of worship. Vishnu is for millions the only god, but his transcendental beneficence is coloured by his Avatars (*avatāra*, descent, 'incarnation') who are glamorous personifications. The two most popular Avatars are Krishna, the herdsman and lover, and Rāma, the noble epic king. Shiva is also regarded as the supreme and only real god by his millions of devotees, and many scriptures sing of him in monotheistic terms. His mixed character makes him at once the Lord of the Dance and the Great Ascetic and Yogi, a god of death and destruction and also a gracious teacher who appears in visions to his worshippers. Shiva is the Great God (*Mahā-deva*) whose spouse is the Great Goddess (*Mahādevī*), known to her followers by various names: Shakti, Durgā, Kālī. In the latter form she is the destroyer-goddess who at Calcutta (*Kālī-ghat*, 'Kālī's steps') and in the region still receives animal sacrifices, practices which most Hindus now find abhorrent. Other very popular gods are the elephant-headed Ganesha, son of Shiva and the Goddess, who brings good luck, and Lakshmi the wife of Vishnu, who is celebrated every New Year. To all of these deities offerings and prayers are made at home and in public.

India is noted for its countless temples, many of them in the south of great beauty and covered with lavish stone sculpture which surpasses even that of Gothic cathedrals. Many northern temples were destroyed by Muslim iconoclasts. Temples are not built for regular congregational services but contain a central sanctuary, usually small, surrounded by courtyards and walls which contain great decorated gateways and pillars, and there are large water tanks for ritual washing. Temple worship is the concern of priests whose rites are not normally observed by the laity. Images and symbols are bathed and anointed, to the accompaniment of repeated texts. In home worship also, images of Krishna and other gods are similarly dressed and washed, and receive food, flowers and incense. Laymen crowd to the temple for special occasions, and notably the annual festivals when temple images are taken to a river and bathed, being drawn in temple cars like the Juggernaut (*Jagan-nātha*, 'world-lord', a title of Krishna).

Other annual festivals mark ancient rites: Holi in the spring as a fertility ritual, Dashara in the autumn celebrating both Kālī and Rāma where carnival processions provide entertainment, and Dīvālī for Lakshmi at the New Year. Many temples are famous places of pilgrimage connected with stories of the gods, and Benares (Varanasi, or Kashi) is the holiest city of all, with rather dilapidated shrines but of antique sanctity, where cremations take place and many holy men come to die. There are also occasional pilgrimage festivals, especially Kumbha Mela ('pitcher fair'), held every twelve years or so, at which millions of people and many holy men attend.

J. N. Banerjea, *Development of Hindu Iconography*, 1946; A. L. Basham, *The Wonder that was India*, 1954; A. Daniélou, *Hindu Polytheism*, 1964; E. G. Parrinder, *Worship in the World's Religions*, 1961; B. Rowland, *The Art and Architecture of India*, 1955; M. Singer, ed., *Krishna, Myths, Rites and Attitudes*, 1966; P. Thomas, *Hindu Religion, Customs and Manners*, 1956; H. Zimmer, *Myths and Symbols in Indian Art and Civilization*, 1953.

GEOFFREY PARRINDER

Holy Saturday

In the primitive church the great festival of the Pascha began on Saturday evening and continued through the night, the fast lasting until midnight or dawn. Although the unity of the cross and the resurrection would be more important than differences of emphasis, the cross would be the great motif of the vigil and the resurrection of the vigil's end, with the sacrament of baptism, followed by holy communion, celebrated at the point where the one yielded to the other. It was inevitable that the evolution of the Pascha into Good Friday and Easter day (qq.v.) should modify in due course the relationship to the latter of Saturday in Holy Week.

A. A. MCARTHUR

Holy Week

When Etheria made her pilgrimage to Palestine towards the end of the fourth century, the complex structure of Holy Week services at Jerusalem was clearly something new in the church's worship. There is no evidence elsewhere at the time for anything of this nature. The week before the Pascha had held a unique position in the Christian year since the middle of the previous century, but there is nothing to suggest that observances on the lines of this rich development existed before the latter part of the fourth century. Now for the first time we find Palm Sunday and Good Friday (qq.v.). The essential feature was the attempt to link the culminating events of the ministry with the days of their occurrence and the places where they happened. Jerusalem was the one locale where the process of change could go forward quite naturally. The essential conservatism of Christian worship makes it most unlikely that important transformations will originate in a region or period which, in respect of the particular matter, is a liturgical vacuum. In Constantinople or Carthage or Rome a development of this nature would not have been evolution but revolution. It was otherwise in Jerusalem. In and around the city were the sacred sites themselves. With the ending of persecution and the erection of sanctuaries on the holy places, pilgrims were arriving from every quarter of the Christian world and ascetics were coming to stay in Jerusalem. Thus, for the enrichment of its worship, the church of Jerusalem doubtless evolved the structure of these services in the third quarter of the fourth century.

Holy Week at Jerusalem was intimately and topographically related to the sanctuaries of the holy places. It was entirely natural in the environment. Etheria described the customs in detail because they were novel. The original contribution of the Jerusalem church involved also the introduction of order and cohesion and the sense of advancing movement from Epiphany to Pentecost. The fundamental aim of this whole development, providentially inspired by the environment, was to make the life of Christ more real and contemporary for the worshipper. So the liturgical year led the Christian realistically from place to place in the sacred narrative, from Bethlehem and the Lord's birth to the Mount of Olives and the ascension, and to the coming of the Holy Spirit upon the disciples in the upper room on Zion. No later complexities could obscure this structure. As for Holy Week itself, there was necessarily some modification in the details of the celebrations as they spread beyond Jerusalem, for complete realism was possible only in the Holy City. It must be emphasized how powerfully the dynamism of this profound innovation surged throughout the Christian world. The pulsation of that movement has never ceased to throb with energy through all the Christian centuries. For it is this idea of liturgical realism, this idea that the life of Christ is manifested to the worshipper in the liturgical year, which has not only transformed Holy Week but has also been the motive power behind the mature growth of the Christian year as a whole.

F. Cabrol, *Les Origines Liturgiques*, 1906; J. G. Davies, *Holy Week: A Short History*, 1963; G. Dix, *The Shape of the Liturgy*, [2]1945; A. A. McArthur, *The Evolution of the Christian Year*, 1953; J. W. Tyrer, *Historical Survey of Holy Week*, 1932.

A. A. MCARTHUR

Hood *see* Vestments (2*d*)

Hour Services
see Canonical Hours

Hymns

1. *Latin*

In his commentary on Ps. 148.14, Augustine described a hymn as 'the praise of God in song', adding that praise to God that is not sung is not a hymn. Ambrose (d. 397) is named as the real father of Latin hymnody, and gave his people hymns in iambic rhythm (short-long) that were easy to understand, to remember, and to sing. *Aeterne rerum conditor* (Eternal creator of the world), sung at the Sunday office of lauds and the most beautiful of the Ambrosian hymns, is unfortunately rarely heard now outside monasteries of strict observance – it has thirty verses! – but a number of hymns of later date such as *Veni creator spiritus* (Whitsunday), *Pange lingua gloriosi corporis mysterium* (Corpus Christi) and *Te Deum* are well known and loved.

About 230 hymn texts occur in the various hours of the divine office (q.v.), but the melodies to which they are set that can be read in the manuscripts date from about the twelfth century. The psalms were regarded as hymns and tradition links the great Hallel group (113-118), which was recited or sung at the principal Jewish festivals and so at the Passover, with the hymn sung at the Last Supper by Jesus and his disciples.

Benedict (*c*.480-*c*.550) made provision in his Rule for hymns to be included in all the hours of the divine office, but the Roman Church did not admit them into the secular office until the twelfth century on account of prejudice against importing other than biblical words into the liturgy, and even more because the form was used by heretics for propaganda purposes.

Polyphonic settings of the hymns began in the thirteenth century and were contributed by such great church composers as Dunstable, Dufay, Josquin des Pres, Tallis and Byrd. Palestrina published a fine collection of forty-five, mostly for vespers, founded on the plainsong melodies.

ALEC ROBERTSON

2. *Vernacular*

Perhaps the first appearance of vernacular hymns came with the Italian *Laudi Spirituali*, introduced as part of the revivalist apparatus of the Franciscan movement in the thirteenth century, to grow in number and popularity over the next four centuries. Hymn-singing in the vernacular also formed a feature of the worship of the Bohemian Brethren led by John Huss early in the fifteenth century. With the Lutheran and Calvinist reforms of a century later, and the translation of the liturgy itself, new types of vernacular song were introduced – to exert lasting influence upon congregational music. The Lutheran *chorale*, epitomized in *Ein' Feste Burg* and the *Passion Chorale*, provided a melodic line of great strength familiar today in four-square Bach-type harmonized form. Once evolved, the Lutheran chorale-book was to to be preserved in its integrity – no new tunes being added. Succeeding generations of Lutherans thus inherited an unvarying repertoire of congregational song. In Geneva, Calvin introduced the metrical psalm (q.v.), which was a verse translation by Marot and Béze of the prose psalter. Sung in unison to subtly rhythmic melodies largely composed by Goudimel and Bourgeois, the Genevan model was to be adopted in Dutch, Scottish and English churches.

Metrical psalmody thus became for two centuries the staple of congregational music in England – at first in the *Whole Book of Psalms* of Sternhold and Hopkins (1562) and subsequently in the *New Version* of Tate and Brady (1696). Both collections included a few supplementary hymns; and the appearance of Wither's *Hymnes and Songs of the Church* (1623) and Bishop Ken's *Morning, Evening and Midnight Hymns* (1674) indicates that hymn-singing was not dead in England at this time. The signal for its revival was the publication of John and Charles Wesley's *Hymns and Sacred Poems* (1739). Thereafter, Wesleyan congregations soon became noted for the fervour of their hymn-singing; while Anglican bishops remonstrated with their clergy upon the neglected and apathetic state of parochial psalmody.

Under the influence of the Oxford Movement, efforts were made after 1833 to restore to the Anglican service something of its lost dignity; and although the hymn was at first regarded by Tractarians as too reminiscent of Nonconformity to receive approval, under J. M. Neale's leadership that view changed with the appearance of the *Hymnal*

Noted (1851), a collection of Latin hymns in translation associated with their plainsong tunes. Less 'advanced' churchmen adopted other collections – such as Havergal's *Old Church Psalmody* (1847) and Gauntlett's *Hymn and Tune Book* (1852) – while Maurice's *Choral Harmony* (1854) introduced the German chorale to English congregations.

All these trends were to merge with the appearance of *Hymns, Ancient and Modern* in 1861. Remarkable for its eclecticism, the new book assembled examples of plainsong, psalm-tune, chorale and old church-tune, adding to that traditional element some new tunes of a distinctive type by Dykes, Ouseley and Monk. During the remainder of the nineteenth century *Hymns, A & M* in successive editions was almost to attain the status of an official Anglican hymnal. Later reaction against the quality of some of the words and music in that book, however, was to produce the *English Hymnal* (1906) and *Songs of Praise* (1926), both of which sought to provide a less emotional tone.

The first authorized modern hymnal for Roman Catholic use in England was the *Westminster Hymnal* (1912). Important collections issued for Nonconformist use include *Wesley's Hymns* (1877), the *Congregational Church Hymnal* (1887) and the *Baptist Church Hymnal* (1900). Perhaps the most challenging hymnal to appear in recent years, the *Cambridge Hymnal* (1967), was designed 'to produce a fitting expression of Christian thought and feeling in the twentieth century'. The words which it contains have been chosen to bear study in their own right, while the tunes have been selected for their excellence and include several commissioned from contemporary composers. The ideals lying behind its compilation are no more exalted than the church is entitled to expect.

P. Dearmer, *Songs of Praise Discussed*, 1952; W. H. Frere, Preface to *Hymns, A & M, Historical Edition*, 1909; J. Julian, *Dictionary of Hymnology*, 1892; K. L. Parry and E. Routley, *Companion to Congregational Praise*, 1953; E. Routley, *Hymns and Human Life*, 1959.

BERNARR RAINBOW

Iconostasis

The term is Greek in origin, and means, literally, 'picture-stand'; it refers to the screen (q.v.) separating the altar in Eastern Orthodox churches from the nave where the main body of the worshippers are assembled. The history of the development of this type of screen has, until recently, been misunderstood by writers in Western Christendom; it has been mistakenly assumed that this kind of screen, entirely covered with icons or pictures and made of wood, has always been a prominent feature of the Eastern Orthodox rite. But this is a telescoping of the historical development of the screen in the Orthodox or Byzantine liturgy.

In the earlier centuries the screen in the Orthodox rite was made of stone or marble (*see* Plate 30) and it differed little from the type of screen still to be found in some of the older Roman basilicas, e.g. Santa Maria in Cosmedin. At first, at Constantinople, pictures were hung on the altar screen on festivals and these were rather like large medallions and made of mosaic or painted with a brush; but they were comparatively small. But as time went on these began to multiply and they tended to become a more permanent feature of the screen in the Byzantine rite.

The solid wooden screen or iconostasis proper, with gates and completely covered with large pictures or icons, appears to be a development in Russia in the late fourteenth and early fifteenth centuries under Theophanes the Greek and the Russian Andrei Rublëv; under them the Byzantine screen was raised in height so that it completely hid the altar from the congregation. With this action, the icons themselves were increased in size from half-length to full-length figures. The fact that these later screens are of wood rather than stone indicates that they are Russian in origin, since that country is a land of vast forests, whereas the stone screen with carved panels and columns was a feature of Byzantium and the eastern Mediterranean area.

The usual explanation of the solid iconostasis is that it veils heaven from earth, the altar being heaven and the saints who are depicted on the screen the mediators between the church on earth and the church in heaven. When the celebrant speaks from the altar obscured by the screen it is as the voice of God speaking to his people on earth. When

Plate 30   Sixth-century Byzantine screen and altar, Archaeological Museum, Athens

the gates are opened and the ministers come forth from the altar to the people at the reading of the gospel and the giving of holy communion, it is like the incarnation when Christ came forth from heaven to earth for the salvation of the human race.

In lesser Eastern churches, such as the Armenian and the Coptic, the iconostasis is not employed, but at certain points in the liturgy a veil or curtain may be drawn across the sanctuary.

V. Lasareff, *Russian Icons*, 1962; C. E. Pocknee, *The Christian Altar*, 1963.

C. E. POCKNEE

Immaculate Conception
see Mariological Feasts

Imposition of Hands
see Gestures (5)

Incense

The term incense is used of a number of

woods and resins which, when heated or burned, give off a fragrant smell; 'frank' or pure incense, otherwise known as *olibanum*, is the solidified resin of trees belonging to certain species of *Boswellia*.

The use of incense in divine worship appears to be of great antiquity and is exceedingly widespread. In the pre-Christian cultures of the Middle East and the Mediterranean, seven religious uses of it may be distinguished: (1) as a sacrifice to the god or gods; (2) as a sacrifice to the shades of a deceased human being or beings; (3) as a symbol of honour to a living person or persons; (4) as a demonifuge, to drive away evil spirits, whether from the living or from the departed; (5) as a means of purification or healing (a use not always to be distinguished from the preceding); (6) as a festive accompaniment for processions and similar ceremonies; (7) simply to create a worshipful atmosphere. It was also used on non-cultic as well as cultic occasions for practical purposes; but there is no evidence for, and considerable evidence against, the theory that this is the origin of its religious use.

During the first three centuries of the Christian era there was no ceremonial use of incense in the church's worship, and many writers of this period refer to it, as to most other practices of other religions, in terms of disapprobation. It is not difficult to account for this attitude; on the one hand incense was inevitably associated in the Christian mind with its use in the emperor-worship test; it was also used in the ceremonies of what the Christians regarded as false religions.

Christian writers of the fourth and fifth centuries modify this disapprobation; they condemn only the sacrificial use of incense. And, indeed, from the middle of the fourth century the honorific use of it spread rapidly in the Christian church. By the sixth century there are clear cases of the use of incense as a sacrificial offering, in the sense of an act of adoration in return for which divine blessings are asked, a use which persists to this day in most of the Eastern liturgies. In the West this sacrificial interpretation has almost completely disappeared since the early Middle Ages, being replaced by the offering of incense not in itself, but simply as a symbol of prayer. The use of incense in one way or another has been common to all the historic liturgies since the beginning of the sixth century at the latest, and in most places it is

probably at least a century older.

1. *Incense at the eucharist*. The earliest use of incense at the eucharist was honorific: it was borne before the celebrant at the entrance, and before the book of the gospels before the reading of the gospel. The use of incense in the entrance procession gave rise in the medieval West to a censing of the altar on arrival, a sacrificial or devotional censing, to which was commonly added an honorific censing of the celebrant, and sometimes of others as well. A censing of the altar, or of the book of the gospels on it, came commonly to be prefixed to the bearing of incense in the gospel procession, and in many places a censing of the ministers and the choir was added after the reading of the gospel. From the tenth century a sacrificial or devotional censing was added after the offertory, often with a censing of ministers, choir and people as well. From the thirteenth century, in many places, with the introduction of elevations of host and chalice at the consecration, censing came to be added at this point, as an act of adoration. The detailed arrangements of the censing at any of these points in the service varied widely. According to the revised Roman missal of 1970, incense, when it is used at all, is used in the entrance procession, to cense the altar after the entrance in the gospel procession and during the reading of the gospel; after the offertory, to cense the offerings, the altar, the ministers and the people; and at the elevation of the host and chalice at the consecration.

In the Byzantine as in most other Eastern rites, the eucharist is never celebrated without incense. According to current Byzantine usage, the celebrant or the deacon censes the altar, the offerings on the prothesis (q.v.), the icons, and the people, before the commencement of the service; further censing, the extent and detailed arrangement of which varies from place to place, takes place before the gospel; before, during and after the offertory or great entrance (q.v.); after the consecration; and after the communion.

2. *Incense at the divine office*. Incense is used at the major offices in all the historic rites (in the Roman rite only on Sundays and festivals, in the Eastern rites normally daily). The most characteristic use is a devotional – in origin, and still in some rites, sacrificial – one which is probably a conscious imitation of Jewish Temple practice, at the principal

morning and evening offices (in the Roman rite at the *Te Deum* at mattins, the *Benedictus* at lauds, and the *Magnificat* at vespers; but at the time of writing the Roman office is in the process of considerable re-arrangement). The origin of this use is almost certainly to be traced to the reference to incense in the classic evening psalm, 140 (141).

3. *Incense at other services.* The use of incense in the Eastern rites is extensive, being prescribed in most of them for all major, and many minor, services. Its use in the West is more restricted: its use at funerals (with what original significance is not easy precisely to determine) appears to have been the origin of its use at the consecration of an altar (having been used in the procession of relics to be sealed in the altar), and its use on this occasion is possible itself the origin of other censings of the altar; its use in other processions may also derive from its funeral use, but may be of independent origin; its use, with holy water, at many blessings may originally have been demonifugal.

4. *Incense outside the historic rites.* The non-ceremonial – and occasionally ceremonial – use of incense was common in the Church of England during the seventeenth century; it disappeared in the eighteenth century, to be revived in the later nineteenth century, together with so many other traditional practices, under the influence of the Tractarian movement, in a considerable number of churches. Those Anglican churches which use incense today usually follow the Roman use of it. Incense is also used in a very small number of churches of other Reformed traditions.

E. G. C. F. Atchley, *A History of the Use of Incense in Divine Worship*, 1909.

W. JARDINE GRISBROOKE

Indigenization

The dictionary meaning of the word 'indigene' is 'native'; that of its adjective, 'indigenous', is 'native, belonging naturally (to soil, etc.)'. Indigenization thus presupposes the making, or becoming, indigenous of that which originally is not so. With particular reference to the church, it means that the church in every land should *belong* in its locality in such a way that it will not be seen as a foreign body, an absurd intrusion, or an

engine of a certain ulterior purpose which will be no longer necessary in a free, independent country, or in a society which is claiming to have come of age. It means further, and more significantly, that the church has to be of an intimate, meaningful, and creatively operative relevance by meeting the spiritual and moral needs of the people and thus serving to inform and give guidance to national activities and aspirations.

Placide Tempels writes with perception when he observes, 'It has repeatedly been said that evangelization and catechetical work should be adapted . . . Adapted to what? We can build churches in native architecture, introduce African melodies into the liturgy, use styles of vestments borrowed from Mandarins or Bedouins, but real adaptation consists in the adaptation of our spirits to the spirits of these people' (*Bantu Philosophy*, 1959 p. 18). This statement, made out of sincere, deep concern, raises a few issues which show how delicate is the subject of indigenization. First, the word 'adaptation' must be carefully evaluated with regard to meaning and connotation. It signifies that something is being made to fit into a place or situation where it does not belong naturally or originally. It may involve a deliberate, purposive action, something planned and executed towards a definite end; implied in it is a sense of borrowing and fixing or appropriation. Now, there may be a case for 'adaptation' in this sense as far as the externals of things are concerned; but with the delicate, inner, spiritual aspect, it will more than likely fall short of the proper end: for there will always be those deep things of the body which will not accept a foreign element which has been improperly introduced. Secondly, although Tempels sees clearly that a change of heart is necessary on the part of those who evangelize (or go out to civilize!), he appears not to have seen clearly that God's instruments in evangelism have only a transmissive function. 'Adapting our spirits to the spirits of these people', as he recommends, may lead the agent of evangelism to assume that what is essentially the work of the Spirit is his own work. Here, in fact, is the most delicate point in the process of indigenization. The word itself suggests too much the activity of man with regard to the inauguration and development of the church. And this constant, attending danger has always translated itself into a hybridization or a syncretism, or a structural formalism, which leaves the heart practically untouched.

'The basic principle of evangelism which will result in a true living church in every area of the world is contained in our Lord's enunciation: 'Truly, truly, I say to you, unless a grain of wheat falls into the earth and dies, it remains alone; but if it dies, it bears much fruit' (John 12.24). The evangelist, be he a foreigner or a national, is a person who, by implication, is always working to liquidate himself. He works to make people see more and more of the Lord of the church and less and less of himself until people are led to know the Lord as the only Saviour, and are endued with the indwelling Spirit who will constantly inform the heart about what is of God (John 16.14, 15). John the Baptist was true to this principle when he said, 'he must increase, but I must decrease' (John 3.30).

The theology of the church is a factor of vital importance with regard to indigenization. The root of the predicament and bewilderment of the church today is its lack of bold, clear-cut theology; and that means that it has neglected the cultivation of the presence of God, meditation and prayer. Theology here does not mean anything abstract, merely 'correct', and deliberately and conformingly systematic. It means the saving knowledge of God in the Lord Jesus Christ, which is boldly taught without quibbling and communicated under the guidance of the Holy Spirit to congregations everywhere; the means by which God speaks to the communities of believers and to individual persons in answer to spiritual and moral needs and the ordering of the total life; something, therefore, which brings people into a dynamic, creative, covenant relationship and living communion with the living Head of the Body.

We are beginning to see clearly that this lack of theology is the major handicap in the areas of the world which used to be known as 'mission fields'. We can afford to ignore, for the moment, the fact of the mixed motives of missions and look with unbiased eyes at the honest, genuinely concerned men and women who went out into the 'fields' to preach the gospel and as a result of whose ministry congregations came into being. It is the fact that, almost without exception, these were well-meaning but theologically ill-guided persons. As 'practical' men and women they

set out with their major assets which were their Christian convictions, their lives · of devotion, and a consequent *practical* Christianity: these were used by God to bring about genuine conversions. But, however good the intentions that they brought to the task, they were little more than evangelistic cobblers who more often than not ended as unintentional founders of a Christianity which is heavily diluted with Westernism, and as advocates of a superior culture and new legalism, to all of which they somehow attach more importance than to the inward reality of conversion. Not only is this so, but their concern to preserve and perpetuate what they have planted is such that they feel called upon to be dispensers of paternalism and to act frequently with such a naive kind-heartedness as that of the man who saw a butterfly struggling to free itself from its cocoon, took pity on it, and tried to help it by prizing the cocoon open, with the result that he only succeeded in killing the butterfly!

When Naaman (II Kings 5) decided impulsively, out of gratitude, no doubt, 'that there is no God in all the earth but in Israel', he ordered 'two mules' burden of earth' from the place where he thought that God resided exclusively. 'Two mules' burden of earth' has been the concomitant bane of evangelism all along. It is either the missionaries who decide that it is a *sine qua non* to the local churches in the 'missionary fields', or it is the young congregations who clamour for it. Whichever way its ordering is initiated, plentiful supply of it has never been wanting. And thus, churches throughout most of the world are living, moving, and having their beings, in prefabricated structures, predetermined doctrines and values, and made-in-Europe liturgies – all of which they hardly understand, but which they regard as acceptable because of their foreign 'trade marks which, to them, are of a vital prestige value.

Experience is now showing that, by and large, this method of work is building with hay and stubble. Africa and Asia afford unmistakable illustrations of the predicament of the church in consequence of the shakiness of its position, the questioning of its motives, the indictment of it as a body existing unnecessarily and irrelevantly, and its spiritual and moral paralysis in face of rampant injustice and wrongs.

With the preachers of the early church, the case was different. To the Corinthians, Paul declared his theological position: 'I decided to know nothing among you except Jesus Christ and him crucified . . . that your faith might not rest in the wisdom of men but in the power of God' (I Cor. 2.1-5). He was a herald, with the one aim of presenting Jesus Christ, so that by knowing him the believers might appropriate for themselves and within their own natural contexts the reality of his saviourhood and lordship. Just as education, properly defined and properly conducted, is not a matter of stuffing the mind with ideas, but of 'leading out' or 'bringing out' the best that is in men so that, through discipline and intellectual exercise, the inner man may be liberated to express itself to the fulfilment of personality, so it is with evangelism that is to have real success: it should end in leading congregations of believers to see and discover for themselves that Jesus Christ is the Saviour and the Lord indeed. This is exemplified in John 4: First, as a result of the testimony of the woman, the initial step was taken: 'Many Samaritans from that city believed in him because of the woman's testimony . . .' This may be enough to bring about an organization of people into some form of congregation, but it is not sufficient to achieve a *koinonia*. For that the second step was also necessary: 'They said to the woman, "It is no longer because of your words that we believe, for we have heard for ourselves, and we know that this is indeed the Saviour of the world." '

This brings us to the heart of the matter. The church has to get its Christology right if indigenization is to be realized. A proper understanding of the implications of the incarnation is vital to the life of the church in every age and every context. For the church to have a real sense of *belonging* and direction, each congregation must appreciate the full meaning of 'And the Word became flesh and dwelt among us, full of grace and truth; we beheld his glory, glory as of the only Son of the Father' (John 1.14).

'The Word became flesh and dwelt among us' signifies the relevance and reality of the living Christ to every age and every culture; that is, Christ as the embodiment of the creative, redeeming love of God who in each national or racial situation continues to fulfil the sympathetic, spiritual nurturing of love: 'A bruised reed he will not break, and a dimly burning wick he will not quench; he will faithfully bring forth justice' (Isa. 42.3;

Matt. 12.20). And this is supported by the divine declaration, 'Think not that I come to abolish the law and the prophets; I have come not to abolish them, but to fulfil them' (Matt. 5.17). Thus, the question of what Jesus Christ means to every people in their own home, in their own particular cultural, political, spiritual and moral situations, during their own passages and crises of life, in the celebrations of their joys, in their peculiar weaknesses and temptations, as they 'labour and are heavy-laden', and in the very depths of personal being – what he means in all these must be *personally settled by the people themselves*. And there is no way to bring this about while the 'Jesus' that is being preached and presented is tethered to the confines of the imported 'two mules' burden of earth', wearing a foreign complexion and lacking in the understanding of the day-to-day joys and sorrows and problems of the people. Such a 'Jesus' has always proved inadequate, and those who accept him have always made him only a fashionable addition to the divinity of the traditional culture, which situation has always resulted inevitably in an ambivalent spiritual life.

What we are saying here should be clear. 'Neither theology nor evangelism can be defined in terms of what *we* think *we* want to teach and say to people. They are properly defined as what God is saying through the church to every people in their own native context and in their own circumstances. Theology and evangelism are not directions as to what *we* think that people should be or what *we* want them to be: they are declarations of God and his sovereign will to every race and every nation' (E. Bolaji Idowu, in the Foreword to Kwesi Dickson [ed.], *Biblical Revelation and African Beliefs*, 1969).

This brings us to a still more crucial point – that of the concept of God. In an access of particularity, Paul describes certain people as 'having no hope and without God in the world' (Eph. 2.12). Surely, this should not be taken seriously today? A Jew with a false particularity can say that because he has travelled a long way in his spiritual pilgrimage, forgotten the process by which God in history has led him so far, and is not reckoning with the streams of revelatory knowledge which have merged into the confluence of his current 'developed' concept of God; a modern European can say it of other nations if he is in ignorance of the blend of cultures and beliefs which are upholding his own current culture, or if he will nòt accept the existence of any other cultures and values apart from his own; but only a brainwashed or imbecile African or Asian will accept it categorically of his own race.

The point here is a serious one indeed; for it is this false particularity, wittingly or unwittingly adopted, which has all along bedevilled all efforts to realize the selfhood of the church in most of the world. It is the major sin which has consistently interfered with the course of the gospel. A wrong conception of God inevitably results in false Christology. The consequent situation, then, is not of God – the living God, 'The Lord . . . the everlasting God, the Creator of the ends of the earth' (Isa. 40.28) sending forth his Son 'when the time has fully come' (Gal. 4.4), but of the strange but good Marcionite Supreme God sending his Son who is caught in a conflict with a Marcionite divinity of evil dispositions. Perhaps there would have been no problem if the thoughts of the missionaries had been the thoughts of the people to whom they present the strange God. As the contrary is the case, a stage has always been set for two Gods in the minds of the congregations of converts – 'the indigenous God', ever alive and active in the intimate places of the passages and crises of life, and 'the imported God', useful only in his own sphere of external, fashionable, and sophisticated activities.

We see, then, that indigenization is first and foremost a thing of the heart. It should come out of the response of the whole being to the authentic and *bona fide* knowledge of the Lord of the church. To be genuine, it must be bound up with true conversion and come as an evolution from within before it expresses itself in outward forms. 'Therefore, if any one is in Christ, he is a new creation, the old has passed away, behold the new has come' (II Cor. 5.17). The antinomous law of discontinuity and continuity applies to individual converts as it does to the corporate personality of a church which forms an organic presence of *the Body* in a nation. The essential person and personal gifts are not destroyed by conversion: on the contrary, the personality is charged with a new life and a new vitality, given a new orientation and purposive direction by the living Head of the Body. For God's purpose to be fully effective

in life, he does not use a person deprived of all sense of initiative; he does not employ a cultural imbecile. The individual or corporate personality whom God uses to fulfil his purpose must be addressable and responsible. 'Such was the appearance of the likeness of the glory of the Lord. And when I saw it, I fell upon my face, and I heard the voice of one speaking. And he said to me, "Son of man, stand upon your feet, and I will speak with you." And when he spoke to me, the Spirit entered into me and set me upon my feet; and I heard him speaking to me' (Ezek. 1.28b-2.2). This is significant. And with it goes the new covenant as prophesied by Jeremiah: true worship and service of God consist in a state of intimate covenant relationship whereby God speaks directly to his people and actuates them in their expression and fulfilment of his will and purpose – God will put his 'law within them, and . . . will write it upon their hearts', then 'they shall all know' him, 'from the least of them to the greatest' (Jer. 31. 31-34).

Indigenization is thus not a mere rearrangement, by borrowing or by imposition or by modification, of external things. Essentially, it is not, and cannot be, man-made. It is essentially of God, in consequence of the deep understanding of the basic facts of Christianity both by spiritual discernment and intellectual grasp on the part of man. This does not by any means signify a suspension of judgment; rather it calls for the conscious pressing on 'to make it my own, because Christ Jesus has made me his own' (Phil. 3.12).

We may now illustrate specifically. Indigenization of the church in Africa, for example, will signify a church that has attained, or is in the definite process of attaining, selfhood. It means that Christian Africans have come to the saving knowledge of God and of his Christ in the way that we have outlined above; and that in everything that has to do with the ordering of the life of the church, they can always say consciously and decisively, 'It has seemed good to the Holy Spirit and to us . . .' The point of this is that in the 'indigenous' church, God is worshipped and served 'in spirit and truth' and not in the way prescribed by some ecclesiastical power-that-be who lives somewhere else. The voice that is heard and obeyed will be the voice of God, and the authority that is the rule of the church's life will be that of the living Head of the church, directly and immediately communicated to it. As I have observed elsewhere (*Towards an Indigenous Church*, 1965, p. 13), with particular reference to Nigeria, so it is with the whole of Africa: the absolute lordship of the church and total, undivided allegiance to him is hardly the characteristic of the church. And consequently, he is not as *real* to Christian Africans as he should be if the church were truly indigenous. 'The result is the detrimental fact that it is these over-lords (overseas authorities), and not the Lord of the church, who are "pre-eminent" over the church . . . The authority which must be obeyed is largely that of some "oracle" enshrined in the Vatican, in Canterbury, in Scotland, or elsewhere in the United Kingdom or Europe, or of some "Providence" dispensing dollars from America.' A church still shackled with foreign authorities or with foreign conventions cannot be truly *the* church.

The nature of a truly indigenous church I have also discussed amply (*Towards an Indigenous Church*, pp. 11 ff.). It will constitute, in its own locality, a true presence of the one, holy catholic and apostolic church. 'As an organic cell belonging to the whole Body, it naturally partakes of certain characteristics which belong to that Body and shares in various forms as common heritage with other organic cells. Thus, she maintains not only the "faith once for all delivered to the saints", but also certain inevitable elements which have become in various forms integral marks of the life of the church. We may compare the church to a powerful, living stream which flows into and through the nations, giving of itself to enrich the people and transforming the land, bringing from and depositing in each place something of the chemical wealth of the soils which it encounters on its way, at the same time adapting itself to the shape and features of each locality, taking its colouring from the native soil, while in spite of all these structural adaptations and diversifications its *esse* and its *differentia* are not imperilled but maintained in consequence of the living, ever-replenishing, ever-revitalizing spring which is its source. Thus, the local church everywhere has to live up to a distinctive character and keep up a cherished heritage which runs down the ages.'

In connection with this, we must give a

warning about the relational attitude of churches to one another, especially with reference to the attitude of the older to the younger churches. It is an elementary theological fact that no ecclesiastical authority or church anywhere who *really* understands the nature of the church and God's purpose in the world has any right to disqualify, or refuse to accept, another *bona fide* church as such, simply because it expresses Christianity in its own cultural spirit under the direct authority of Christ and the immediate guidance of the Holy Spirit. And the younger churches have to be aware of their own position as the redeemed of the Lord and ignore anyone who is threatening to excommunicate them or to stop sending in dollars for no other reasons than that they are 'casting out the demons in your name' and they do 'not follow with us'. The attitude of the churches to one another should be such as is exemplified by Paul: 'To the church of God which is at Corinth, to those sanctified in Christ Jesus, called to be saints *together* with all those who in every place call on the name of our Lord Jesus Christ, both their Lord and ours' (I Cor. 1.2). And here is a message for each local church as well as for all churches in general: 'Therefore, holy brethren, who share in a heavenly call, consider Jesus, the apostle and high priest of our confession . . . Let no one disqualify you, insisting on self-abasement and worship of angels . . . and not holding fast to the Head, from whom the whole body, nourished and knit together . . . grows with a growth that is from God' (Heb. 3.1; Col. 2. 18-19).

What is indicated with regard to the 'younger churches' is that the real help which they need with regard to their growth towards selfhood is training in theological leadership. Wherever leaders who are theologically equipped are missing in the church, where the leaders themselves do not understand the nature of the church or the metaphysics of their offices, it will always be the case of the blind leading the blind. The matter of training of the right kind is an urgent necessity. Theologians who are equipped to interpret Christianity, for example, in Africa to Africans, or in Asia to Asians, in their own home and cultural setting, are the only ones qualified to help in this delicate task. The need is, in fact, for Pauls who are at home with regard to the knowledge of their own people and are at the same time adequately equipped with firsthand knowledge of God in Christ as well as of the Christian heritage down the ages. Thus will the indigenous church be able to have a guiding theology and a sense of stewardship which today is detrimentally lacking in the lives of the 'younger churches', and which makes of them grovelling beggars who are left with no other choice than to sing the tune dictated by those whose bread they eat.

With regard to 'vestures and gestures', liturgy in general, hymnody, Bible translations, eradication of the denominationalism concomitant of missionary efforts, the unity of the church, and Christian literature, all these are things that will come naturally, though not without discipline, as things to be added unto the churches when they seek *first* the kingdom of God and his righteousness.

One final word: indigenization is a requirement of all churches everywhere, anywhere, in the world, if they are to be adequate for their witness in contemporary situations. It is a mistake for the older churches to live in the notion that their *oldness* as a status symbol is what gives them the right and authority to be called 'orthodox' churches. Every church needs constant renewal, the periodic 'Pentecost' by which the Holy Spirit gives it the utterance meet for the need of the moment in a world which is constantly changing.

E. A. Ayandele. *Holy Johnson*; C. G. Baeta, ed., *Christianity in Tropical Africa*, 1968; T. A. Beetham, *Christianity and the New Africa*, 1967; Ernest E. Best, *Christian Faith and Cultural Crisis : The Japanese Case*, 1966; Kwesi Dickson, ed., *Biblical Revelations and African Beliefs*; H. H. Farmer, *Revelation and Religion*, 1954; Adrian Hastings, *Church and Mission in Modern Africa*, 1967; E. Bolaji Idowu. *Towards an Indigenous Church*, 1965; H. A. Johnson, *Global Odyssey*, 1963; Stuart Louden, *The True Face of the Kirk*, 1963; C. Michalson, *Japanese Contributions to Christian Theology*, 1960; H. W. Mobley; *The Ghanaian's Image of the Missionary*; Stephen Neill, *Creative Tension*, 1959; J. Akinele Omoyajowo. *Cherubim and Seraphim Church in Nigeria* (Thesis accepted for the degree of Doctor of Philosophy in the University of Ibadan, 1971); W. Stanley Rycroft, *Religion and Faith in Latin America*, 1958; B. G. M. Sundkler, *Bantu Prophets in South Africa*, 1961; John Taylor, *The Growth of the Church in Buganda*, 1958; Harry Thomas, *The New Religions of Japan*; Charles Williams, *The Descent of the Dove*, 1950; S. G. Williamson, *Akan Religion and the Christian Faith*, 1965.

E. BOLAJI IDOWU

Institution Narrative
see Anaphora (6) and Canon

Insufflation

Having the precedent in John 20.22, the church used insufflation to signify the conferring of the Holy Spirit, and also the expulsion of the evil spirit. This ceremony, however, is found not in the rites of ordination but in those of baptism (qq.v.), where it occurs among the preliminaries in Hippolytus' *Apostolic Tradition*, when the bishop exorcized the candidates, breathed on their faces and sealed them with the sign of the cross, in symbolic fashion expelling the evil spirits and barring the door against their return. Cyril of Jerusalem too said that exorcisms (q.v.), infusing fear by a divine breath, made the evil spirit flee. Infants, said Augustine, are exorcized and breathed upon to show that they are delivered from the power of darkness and transferred to the kingdom of Christ. Quodvultdeus explained that it was not the person created by God that was breathed upon but he who holds in his power all who are born in sin.

According to Gennadius of Marseilles, exorcism with insufflation was an ecclesiastical custom universally observed. Other authorities who mentioned it are John the Deacon of Rome (but not the Gelasian Sacramentary or *Ordo Romanus XI*), Isidore of Seville, Hildephonsus of Toledo, the Mozarabic *Liber Ordinum*, the Gallican Bobbio Missal, and in Germany Alcuin, *Ordo Romanus L* and the Sacramentary of Fulda.

The Latin rite of baptism known to the Reformers began with a breathing on the child's face, together with the words, 'Depart from him, unclean spirit, and make room for the Holy Spirit, the Comforter.' In his first *Taufbüchlein*, Luther retained the ceremony while translating the formula into German; three years later he abolished the ceremony but kept the formula. The first services of baptism in the vernacular used in Strasbourg and Zurich included the insufflation; but

Bucer and Zwingli subsequently abolished it. There was no insufflation in Calvin's Genevan or Knox's Scottish rite. In England the prayer book of 1549 ordered the priest to look upon, as opposed to breathe upon, the child, as he said a prayer of exorcism. Thus among the Reformed churches Luther's view prevailed that insufflation was an unnecessary outward ceremony. It has, however, survived in the Roman Catholic Church to the present day.

Insufflation for the purpose of exorcism accompanied the renunciation of Satan in the Byzantine and Coptic rites and the *Effeta* (*see* **Baptism** 11) in the Ambrosian Manual.

In the Gregorian Sacramentary, Sarum Manual, the medieval rites of Gaul, Spain and Germany, and in the Jacobite and Maronite rites, the officiant breathed on the water in the font while reciting the prayer for its consecration. This symbolized the entry of the Holy Spirit into the water, as a result of which the ensuing baptism was a regeneration by water and the Spirit and not a merely physical washing. Timothy of Alexandria and the Coptic rite supply evidence of a breathing on the candidates at the anointing with chrism which concluded the rite of baptism, and which had the purpose of imparting the Holy Spirit to them.

H. Denzinger, *Ritus Orientalium*, 1863; J. D. C. Fisher, *Christian Initiation: The Reformation Period*, 1969; E. C. Whitaker, *Documents of the Baptismal Liturgy*, 1960.

J. D. C. FISHER

Intercession

Intercessory prayer has from the very beginning been given a prominent place in Christian worship. Its earliest formal embodiment in the liturgy appears to have been in the common prayers which concluded the synaxis (q.v.), to which reference is made in the first detailed outline of the eucharistic liturgy, that in the *First Apology* of Justin Martyr; the forms which these prayers have taken in the principal historic rites are briefly considered in the article just cited.

Intercessions in the eucharist proper appear to have been a slightly later development, although it is not possible to assert this categorically; while no conclusion can be drawn from a possibly ambiguous phrase in Justin Martyr, and there are certainly no intercessions in the eucharistic prayer con-

tained in the *Apostolic Tradition* of Hippolytus of Rome, the earliest text of such a prayer which is known to survive, all other ancient liturgies, and those of the historic rites following them, include an intercessory element either in the eucharistic prayer itself (the most common place) or in close connection with it. Assuming that these intercessions are no original part of the prayer, in its earliest forms, it is most likely that they originate in the diptychs (q.v.), especially as in some eucharistic prayers, most notably the historic Roman canon, they retain a marked diptychal formulation. The theological rationale of intercessions in the eucharistic prayer is briefly considered in the article anaphora (q.v.).

From the last quarter of the fourth century at the latest, intercessory prayers have been included in the divine office (q.v.), their form and content, as well as their prominence, varying considerably from one historic rite to another. A similar considerable variation is to be found in the treatment of the intercessions in the liturgies compiled during and after the Reformation and their later revisions, both in eucharistic and in non-eucharistic services.

Contemporary liturgical revision displays a marked trend towards restoring the intercession of the synaxis (q.v.) where this has been dropped over the centuries, and with it, in some circles, to the suppression of any intercessory element in the eucharist proper; the latter tendency appears to owe more to liturgical archaeologizing than to serious theological consideration. A further contemporary trend is towards a more free and flexible form of intercession than has been customary for at least sixteen centuries, a change admirable in theory, but often productive of considerable problems in practice.

W. Jardine Grisbrooke, 'Intercession at the Eucharist' in *Studia Liturgica*, IV, 1965, pp. 129-55; *ibid.*, V, 1966, pp. 20-44, 87-103, and works therein cited.

W. JARDINE GRISBROOKE

Introit *see* Chants of the Proper of the Mass

Invocation

A calling upon God or the saints in prayer or attestation. So the epiclesis (q.v.) is an invocation of God to send down the Holy

Spirit. Prayers before sermons, calling on God to assist the preacher in declaring his word, are similarly invocations.

EDITOR

Islamic Worship

The Muslim's concept of worship is *'ibādat* or 'service' rendered to God by man, the *'abd* or 'servant' of God. *'Ibādat* is traditionally coupled with *mu'āmalāt* or 'works', in order to stress the Islamic view that spiritual and secular duties, duties to God and duties to one's fellow men, belong together.

The duties of worship are summed up in the 'five pillars of the faith': (1) confession of the unity of God and prophethood of Muḥammad (*shahādat*); (2) ritual prayer (*ṣalāt*); (3) almsgiving (*zakāt*); (4) fasting (*ṣawn*); (5) pilgrimage (*hajj*. These are all obligatory (*wājib*) on the capable adult believer, and all have a communal dimension. There are also many additional duties recommended (*sunnat* or *mandūb*) for the believer; these may have a more individualistic flavour, such as intercessory or supplicatory prayer (*du'ā'*) or free-will almsgiving (*ṣadaqāt*).

The central act of Muslims' worship is the ritual prayer. This is offered five times per day by the orthodox Muslim: between dawn and sunrise; after noon; before sunset; after sunset; when night has fallen. These prayers may be offered anywhere, although it is recommended for men that they should be offered in the mosque (women are permitted, though not recommended, to use the mosque). On Friday the midday prayers should be congregational prayers in the mosque, with a sermon preached in addition. The basic furniture of the mosque is simply a niche (*miḥrāb*), directed towards Mecca (the direction [*qiblah*] of all Islamic prayer), and a pulpit or ladder (*minbar*) from which the sermon is preached; small mosques may have nothing more than an indication of the *qiblah*.

The words used in the call-to-prayer (*adhān*), given by the muezzin (*mu'adhdhin*) from the minaret, if there is one, or from the entrance to the mosque, include, with various repetitions: 'God is most great . . . I bear witness that there is no god but God . . . I bear witness that Muḥammad is the prophet of God . . . Come to prayer! . . . Come to the good! . . . (in the early morning) Prayer is better than sleep! . . .' Only in Turkey have there ever been reforms attempted to use a

vernacular for these formulae; otherwise Arabic, the language of Qur'ānic revelation, is used all over the Muslim world for the call-to-prayer and for the liturgical service of *ṣalāt* which follows. After ritual ablution (*wuḍū'*) of the face, hands and feet (assuming that the body and clothes of the worshipper are already clean), the worshippers line up behind the *imām* who is chosen to lead the prayers by virtue of his learning or seniority; every one joins in the prayers both physically and verbally. They stand and recite the prayer of intention (*niyah*) that they may be sincere. With their open palms by their ears and held facing forwards they say, 'God is most great' (this prayer is called the *takbīr*). Standing with downcast eyes and hands folded, they pray a prayer of praise called the *subḥān*, and then the first *sūrah* of the Qur'ān followed by at least one long or two short verses from elsewhere in the Qur'ān. Bowing from the waist, with hands on the knees, the *takbīr* is repeated with another prayer of praise (*tasbīḥ*). Everyone then stands erect, with arms at the side, and after the *imām* has said, 'God hears him who praises him', they reply 'Lord, thou art praised' (if one is alone one recites both sentences). With knees, nose and forehead touching the ground in full prostration the *takbīr* and *tasbīḥ* are repeated; sitting back on the heels with hands on the thighs the *takbīr* is again offered before renewed prostration and *tasbīḥ*. After repeating this rite (from the Qur'ān recitation to the prostration) one or more times (depending on the time of day), the liturgy concludes with the worshipper kneeling and offering prayers of blessing upon the prophet and upon God's righteous servants. Finally the 'peace' (*salām*) is said first to the right and then to the left.

With the completion of this rite of *ṣalāt* the worshipper may go on to offer further more intimate prayers of 'secret whisperings' or 'supplication' (*munajāt* or *du'ā'*); these are offered in a kneeling position with the open palms held together facing the neck. There is a very rich devotional literature in Islam containing such prayers selected from the Qur'ān, the biography of the prophet and the traditional *Ḥadīth* literature of the prophet and the early community of Muslims. To this has been added a wealth of prayers and poetry attributed to famous mystics of Islam, many of whom asserted their influence over their followers by prescribing particular forms of supererogatory prayer. An excellent analysis of their prayer manuals is Constance Padwick, *Muslim Devotions*, 1961.

A famous treatise on the external and the internal aspects of *ṣalāt* and *du‘ā'* is the book on worship in the *Iḥyā'* of al Ghazālī, translated as *Worship in Islam* by E. E. Calverley, 1925.

Special acts of worship are associated with annual feast days (since the lunar year is followed dates must be calculated from tables such as those in G.S.P. Freeman-Grenville, *The Muslim and Christian Calendars*, 1963). The chief festivals are *‘Id al-Fiṭr* at the end of the month of fasting and *‘Id al-Aḍḥā* during the month of pilgrimage. Descriptions of these occasions could be found in T. P. Hughes, *A Dictionary of Islam*, 1885, and further details of the pilgrimage to Mecca are given in A. Kamal, *The Sacred Journey*, 1961.

The discipline and the rhythm of Islamic worship has been a unifying and appealing factor in Islamic history. Without any dependence upon a 'clergy' (which does not properly exist in Islam), the individual, the group or the whole 'people' have demonstrated a pattern of response to God and communion with God which has commended itself to increasing numbers, especially in Asia and Africa. While other aspects of Islamic jurisprudence have undergone modernization, the 'five pillars' remain intact in theory and also in the practice of many Muslims. Few Muslim parents would neglect to instruct their children in matters of worship.

J. TAYLOR

For bibliography see above.

Jacobite Church
see West Syrian Worship

Jehovah's Witnesses' Worship

Jehovah's Christian Witnesses are a body of ministers 'announcing Jehovah's kingdom' and anticipating an early end to the present system of things.

'Jehovah's witnesses are not a sect but are an association of men and women who put God's service first' (*The Watchtower*, 15 April 1970, p. 249). That is to say, they do not follow any man as founder or leader. Abel was 'the first true witness of God' (*ibid.*). 'You are my witnesses,' Jehovah said to

Israel, 'and I am God' (Isa. 43.10-12). Jesus is God's 'faithful witness' (Rev. 1.5). Today's Christian Witnesses believe they continue this ancient line.

A belief that we are in this order's last generation necessarily affects one's worship. Witness meetings reflect this in a sense of urgency and earnestness. All congregations have five weekly meetings, each an hour long, designed (1) to give Bible instruction and (2) to equip the hearers for public ministry.

Foremost is the *Watchtower* Bible study, a question-and-answer discussion of some twenty-five to thirty paragraphs of *The Watchtower*. Subjects reviewed in 1969 included 'Look to the Bible as Our Guide in Life' (on conduct), '' Sounding Down" the Truth into Minds and Hearts of Learners' (*katecheo*, Gal. 6.6). 'Why Almighty God Laughs at the Nations' (Ps. 2.4), and '"Between-the-Lines" Translations of the Bible' (introducing a new interlinear Bible translation).

Generally held mid-week, the Theocratic Ministry School provides training in public speaking and teaching. Men and women, old and young, are encouraged to enrol. A qualified minister gives commendation and offers counsel to the students in turn as they deliver six-minute talks and demonstrations.

The Congregation Book Study, held in private homes, enables a small group to scrutinize Bible topics. The subject might be a year-and-a-half's study on Christian doctrine and practice, or a verse-by-verse analysis of Revelation, two courses which were featured from 1967-1970.

Remaining are the Sunday Public Talk, on general scriptural exposition, and the Service Meeting, where suggestions for the public ministry are offered, particularly how to conduct home Bible studies with interested persons.

A newcomer to the Kingdom Hall would notice the audience participation and variety of presentation. There is little 'preaching' at the audience. Use may be made of a blackboard, charts, diagrams, platform discussion, short demonstrations, and other teaching aids. In time, everyone in the congregation has some share. Witnesses address one another as 'brother' or 'sister'. The presiding minister and his assistants are termed 'servants': congregation servant, *Watchtower* study servant, ministry school servant, etc.

Modern Witness congregations began in

the 1870s when Charles Taze Russell began a Bible-study class with friends in Pittsburgh, USA. An early book, *Three Worlds* (1877), pointed forward to the year 1914 as the time for God's kingdom to be fully established in heaven. Since 1914 the prophecies of Matt. 24, II Tim. 3, Rev. 6, etc. have seen fulfilment. The generation alive in 1914 will see this system end. Then follows the 'restoration of all things' (Luke 21.29-32; Acts 3.20, 21).

Not unrelated to this, Witnesses are conscientiously honest and law-abiding, and cheerful. They acknowledge governments as 'superior authorities' by God's permission (John 19.9-11; Rom. 13) but adopt a course of 'neutrality', political non-involvement, and are conscientious objectors in war-time (John 18.36). As a consequence, totalitarian governments have found them hard to tolerate – Hitler put some ten thousand into concentration camps, and countries like Portugal, Spain and the communist bloc have a history of maltreatment. Thousands were arrested in the democracies from the thirties to the fifties on the non-combatant issue and for public preaching, followed by vigorous litigation by the Witnesses in the highest courts of the lands. (On Rom. 13 and neutrality, *see Life Everlasting – In Freedom of the Sons of God*, chs. 7 and 11.)

From 71,509 ministers in 1939 they had grown to 317,877 by 1949; to 871,737 by 1959; and by 1969 to 1,345,111 in 200 countries. A weekly average of 1,097,237 free home Bible studies were conducted worldwide with non-Witnesses in 1969. To aid in this 'final witness' the New York printing plant alone produced 502,739,345 Bibles, books, magazines and other items of literature in 1969.

Aid to Bible Understanding, 1969; *Jehovah's Witnesses in the Divine Purpose*, 1959; *Make Sure of All Things*, 1965 (all published by the Watchtower Bible and Tract Society).

A. HELEY

Jewish Worship

Prayers are regarded as the service of the heart (*avoda*), which has the same meaning as the Greek word 'liturgy', connoting duty and service. The custom of saying fixed prayers was established long before the Temple of Jerusalem was destroyed in AD 70. In synagogues (assembly-halls) the local communities met for instruction, communal prayers and recitals of biblical texts. Three quotations from the Pentateuch (Deut. 6.4-9; 11.11-21; Num. 15.37-41) form even today the central part of the morning and evening prayers. They declare God's unity (*Sh'ma Israel* – 'Hear, Israel, the Lord our God, the Lord is one') and the duty to love him and to follow his commandments. Before and after these recitals God is praised as the Master of the Universe 'who creates the light' (morning prayer); 'who lets the night follow the day' (evening prayer); who gave his Law to Israel and who is the Redeemer of his people in past and future.

Many more prayers and petitions were added in the course of time, above all the 'Eighteen Prayers' (*sh'mone esre*) which are said three times a day and contain petitions for the granting of knowledge, forgiveness, health and material well-being, as well as the fulfilment of messianic hopes, referring to the rebuilding of Jerusalem, the coming of the Messiah, the restoration of the temple-service in its old place and a prayer for peace. To create the right devotional atmosphere, many psalms and prayers of great teachers, adopted by their disciples, were added. Though the temple-service with its regular sacrifices came to an end with the destruction of the Temple in Jerusalem, the order of the service left its mark on the liturgy of later times. Not only does the Jew say prayers turning in the direction of Jerusalem, the prayer-times were fixed to correspond with the former daily morning and afternoon-sacrifices. Prayers are said at morning, afternoon and evening. On Sabbath, New Moon and Festivals, when extra sacrifices used to be offered, an additional prayer (*mussaf*) is said in the synagogue.

Readings from the Torah ('Five Books of Moses') and the Prophets are an essential part of the service on Sabbath-days and festivals. Two thousand years ago the Hebrew texts were also translated into a language which the ordinary people could understand, Aramaic (Targum) or Greek. The reading of the Torah is divided into weekly portions throughout the year. The religious leaders, the 'Rabbis', added their own interpretations in homiletical sermons.

After the dispersal of the Jews over many countries and their ensuing separation from their homeland, many poets described the religious message of the festivals and other special days of the Jewish calendar in lyrical form *(piyutim)*. Some of them, like the verses by Eleazar Kalir (eighth century), were universally acclaimed and became part of the prayer-book. Further contributions were made by the great Spanish poets Solomon Ibn Gabirol, Yehuda Halevy, Abraham Ibn Ezra and others, who combined mastery of language and beauty of verse-form with deep spiritual thought. They also wrote prayers of supplication *(s'lihot)* to be recited on days of penitence and fasting, particularly during the weeks before and after the Jewish New Year and the Day of Atonement.

The great multitude of prayers caused many communities to make their choice from the abundant literature available. This led to different collections of prayers. Though prayers were not written down in earliest times, the continuing spread of Jewish communities in the Diaspora made it necessary to give guidance on the form and contents of the prayers. The first known prayer books were compiled by the heads of the Babylonian Academies in the ninth and tenth centuries. Other prayer books were written in different European countries, the best known in the twelfth century, the *Mahzor Vitry*. The prayer books not only contain the daily prayers, but are a compendium for the devotions for all days of the year and for all occasions like birth, wedding and mourning.

In spite of the fact that the Jews who lived for centuries in Mediterranean countries *(Sephardim)* differed in their customs from the Jews of Central and Northern Europe *(Ashkenazim)*, the main prayers and the essential mode of worship remained fundamentally the same. Only the additional prayers *(piyutim)* show a variation according to the place of origin. A great unifying force for Jewish worship is the calendar, common to Jews throughout the world.

Prayers in the synagogue are led by a reader *(hazzan)* and the other worshippers respond by saying amen. The reader is no priest, and anyone with the necessary knowledge of the order of service and its content may act in this capacity.

There are no sacramental features in Jewish worship; even weddings and burial ceremonies are no exceptions. The spiritual head of the community is the Rabbi, which means 'teacher'. His contribution to Jewish worship in modern times is the sermon, which nowadays is an important part of the synagogue service and mostly based on the text provided through the weekly readings from the Torah.

A new element in the order of service came with the spread of mysticism among wider circles of the Jewish population in Europe (seventeenth and eighteenth centuries), above all through the Hassidic movement. Many meditations, the origin of which are to be found in cabbalistic works, were introduced into the prayer book, a number of them containing references to heavenly beings, whose intercession is invoked. The desire to modernize the synagogue service was felt strongly in the nineteenth century, at the time when the medieval isolation of the Jews had finally come to an end. In many communities the knowledge of Hebrew had declined and translations of the texts have found their way into the prayer books. The traditional prayers were revised and cleared of obscurities and grammatical errors (Heidenheim). To enhance the beauty of the service, greater care was taken with the vocal part, in particular the recitations by the reader who is now often supported by a choir. In Orthodox synagogues the use of musical instruments is not permitted, as a sign of mourning for the destruction of the Temple, but in Reform synagogues the organ and other instruments are used and many great musicians have contributed compositions for synagogue services. In Reform and Liberal synagogues the overall length of the service has been reduced; also, contrary to traditional usage, women sit with the men, and take an active part in the conduct of the service. Jewish worship is not confined to the synagogue. It is the duty of the individual to say prayers even when he cannot join in corporate worship. Many prayers have their setting in the home, e.g. *kiddush* and *havdallah*, to be recited at the beginning and the conclusion of the Sabbath and festivals. Grace before and after meals and the well-known Passover-service, the *Seder*, are also acts of worship performed in the home.

On all occasions when prayers are to be recited, heads remain covered.

Ismar Elbogen, *Der jüdische Gottesdienst in seiner geschichtlichen Entwicklung*, 3rd ed., 1931; N. H. Glatzer, *Language of Faith*, 1967 (a selection of Jewish prayers of all times); J. H. Hertz, *The Authorised Daily Prayer Book*, rev. ed. with commentary, 1947; A. Z. Idelsohn, *Jewish Liturgy and its Development*,

1967; L. Zunz, *Gottesdienstliche Vorträge der Juden*, 2nd rev. ed., 1892; L. Zunz, *Literaturgeschichte der Synagogalen Poesie*, 1865.

JACOB POSEN

Kiss of Peace *see* Gestures (4)

Kneeling *see* Postures (2*c*)

Kyrie

The invocation *Kyrie eleison* (Greek, 'Lord have mercy') is found in nearly all the historic liturgies, in many of them in the original Greek, whatever the language of the rest of the service, and appears to have been derived both from Jewish and from pagan liturgical formularies. The first definite evidence of its use as the response to the petitions of a litany (q.v.) comes from fourth-century Jerusalem and Antioch, whence both the litany form itself and this response rapidly spread to all parts of the Christian world.

At Rome an intercessory litany of this type was inserted after the introit of the mass in the fifth century, probably during the pontificate of Gelasius (492-6), who was responsible for considerable changes in the Roman liturgy; texts of this and related litanies survive. At the time of Gregory the Great (590-604), and probably at his instance, the petitions of this litany were omitted on ordinary days, the responses being sung alone, as precatory acclamations. By the end of the eighth century the litany had disappeared altogether, and the acclamations were arranged in a way which remained fixed for over eleven hundred years – *Kyrie eleison* three times, the variant *Christe eleison* three times, and finally *Kyrie eleison* again three times. In the revised *Ordo Missae* of 1969, the same order is retained, on those occasions when the *Kyrie* is ordered to be used, but the threefold form has been replaced by a responsorial twofold one. The *Kyrie-Christe-Kyrie* alternation has often been explained in a trinitarian way, the prayer being said to be addressed first to the Father, then to the Son, then to the Holy Spirit. This is historically incorrect: there is no question that the whole prayer was originally addressed to the Son.

Kyrie eleison is still the most common response to litanies in the Eastern rites, although the acclamation alone, in variously numbered groups, is found in them also; the ninefold and sixfold Roman forms, with other variants, are found also in many reformed liturgies in the West.

J. A. Jungmann, *The Mass of the Roman Rite*, I, 1951, pp. 333-46.

W. JARDINE GRISBROOKE

Lammas *see* Harvest Thanksgiving

Lamps *see* Candles

Last Gospel

The reading of the Johannine prologue (John 1.1-14) at the end of mass only became general with the *Missale Romanum* of Pius V, published in 1570. It was suppressed in 1964 as part of the reform of the rite of mass for which Vatican II legislated. In the Middle Ages this gospel was considered to have miraculous efficacy when read; it was used as a blessing for fine weather and was read over the sick. The 1614 *Rituale Romanum* concludes the rite for the visitation of the sick with the reading of this gospel.

It is first found as the conclusion of the mass in the Dominican Mass Ordinary of 1256. It was said in the sacristy (q.v.) by the priest as he took off his vestments (q.v.), or later. From the Dominicans the custom passed to the Armenians, who retained it even after the schism of 1380. At the end of the Middle Ages the last gospel was read, like the gospel of the mass, at the north end of the altar, and the people often joined in its recitation.

Originally it seems likely that the Johannine prologue was read as a blessing; it came of course immediately after the blessing at the end of mass. As time went on, however, the content of this pericope came to be emphasized for its own sake. This trend clearly predominated once it became customary to read as the last gospel the gospel of a second mass formulary merely commemorated in the mass of the day, a practice found from the fifteenth century which originated in the 'dry' mass (q.v.).

J. A. Jungmann, *The Mass of the Roman Rite*, new rev. ed., 1959; A. G. Martimort, ed., *Introduction to the Liturgy*, 1968; M. Righetti, *Storia Liturgica*, III, ³1966.

BRIAN NEWNS

Last Rites see Unction

Lauds see Canonical Hours

Lavabo

Lavabo is the first word of Ps. 26.6: 'I will wash my hands in innocency' – the verse which is recited at the ceremonial washing of the hands in the eucharist. From the patristic period this washing usually accompanied the offertory (q.v.). Cyril of Jerusalem is the first witness, although it was probably practised long before his day. According to him, it is essentially symbolic: 'We do not set out for church with defiled bodies' (*Mystag.* 5.2). In the *Apostolic Constitutions* (8.11f.) the sequence is pax, handwashing, offertory and *Sursum corda*. So the action was not a cleansing of the hands after the reception of the gifts.

In the Ethiopic rite, the priest does not dry his fingers but sprinkles the remaining drops towards the people with a warning that only the pure should approach. The emphasis therefore is not upon hygiene but upon purity symbolized by the ceremonial cleansing.

In the Middle Ages in the Roman rite the symbolism was subordinated to the cleansing – an unusual reversal, since the general rule was for utilitarian actions to be given a symbolic meaning – and the *lavabo* was transferred to a position after the reception of the gifts and the censing. The ancient position is retained only in the Carthusian rite.

Since Carolingian times a preliminary washing of the hands has accompanied the vesting and a similar practice is found in some manuscripts of the Liturgy of St Chrysostom, but it would be incorrect to apply the term *lavabo* to this.

J. A. Jungmann, *The Mass of the Roman Rite*, new ver. ed., 1959, pp. 349-52.

EDITOR

Lay Preacher

This is often a term used simply to describe a lay person who takes services and preaches when there is no minister. In some Baptist, Congregational and Presbyterian churches, however, lay preachers are formally recognized and authorized, after receiving the necessary training, and are often responsible for maintaining services in small congregations who could not support a full-time minister.

P. HINCHLIFF

Laying on of Hands
see Gestures (5)

Lectern

Lectern, as its name implies, means a structure from which lessons are read in public worship. Sometimes the desk for holding the liturgical book or Bible is attached to a pulpit-like structure, known as an ambo (q.v.). But in other instances the lectern is a desk supported on a post or column of wood or metal with feet at the base. Lecterns of this kind were made of wood, bronze and latten

Plate 31 Modern lectern designed by Colin Shewring

in the Middle Ages. Examples of the desk being supported by an eagle or pelican with wings outspread were much in evidence. But other examples of lecterns made of wood and carved in great detail, and sometimes with a double-desk that revolves on the column, came into use in the late Middle Ages, e.g. the one in Shipdam, Norfolk, England. *See* Plate 31.

C. E. POCKNEE

Lectionary

The term is employed in both a wider and a narrower sense. In the wider sense it denotes an ordered system of selected readings ('pericopes') appointed for liturgical use on specific occasions in the church year, thus presupposing a calendar, while in the narrower sense it is used to designate a MS (especially in Greek) with the pericopes thus used written out in full. Lectionaries in this latter sense provide important evidence for the history of the NT text.

The concept of the lectionary in the wider sense evidently goes back to the synagogue, which also had fixed readings from the OT appointed for the Jewish feasts, with pericopes chosen on the principle of *lectio continua* (*l.c.*) for ordinary Sabbaths. But the extent to which the church took over the synagogue system for its OT lessons is unclear, except for Ex. 12, which was used at the Jewish Passover and also for the Christian 'Pascha' (better: 'Passa', so J. Jeremias), as evidenced both in Rome *c.* 200 and among the Quartodecimans (Melito, *c.* 180). The church added gospels and apostolic writings to the OT readings (Justin Martyr, *I Apol.* 67). It has been suggested that the gospel materials were designed for lectionary use in their pre-literary stage, and that the evangelists arranged the pericopes in the order in which they were already used liturgically in the course of the year (P. Carrington), but this theory has found little acceptance. The notes in early manuscripts, αρχ and τελ, denoting the beginning and end of the pericopes, and the assignations of these pericopes to particular days in the church year in marginal notes are indicative only of the later liturgical use of the written gospels, not of their pre-literary use. Specially selected lessons were appointed at first only for Passa and Pentecost, then for other feasts and fasts of the Easter and Christmas cycles and Ember days (qq.v.) and martyrs' days as the calendar

grew. For ordinary Sundays the principle of *l.c.* was used, a book being selected apparently at local discretion and read in successive pericopes until it was finished. Thus in pre-Nicene times there was a more or less fixed lectionary only for major feast days.

During this period there were several lessons, both OT and NT, interspersed with psalms (*see below*). Later, the use of three lessons (OT, epistle or other apostolic writing, gospel) was widely standardized (Armenian, Mozarabic, Milanese, Gallican), but at Constantinople (fifth century) and Rome (from sixth century) the lessons were increasingly reduced to two, which eventually became the norm in both East and West. Usually the two lessons were an epistle and gospel, but sometimes it is the OT lesson rather than the apostolic lesson that survived (e.g. especially in Lent in *Missale Romanum. Missale Romanum* has occasionally preserved a multiplicity of OT and NT lessons (e.g. in Lenten Embertide).

In the West, Alcuin standardized the mass lectionary from existing local provisions (Roman for the gospels, Gallican for the epistles), though the provisions were never quite complete (last Sundays in Epiphany and Pentecost), the combinations of lessons were largely fortuitous, and only the debris of the earlier *l.c.* survived (as can often be seen in the epistles of the Pentecost season). Sarum, the Lutheran orders, *BCP* and *Missale Romanum* represent variations and successive modifications of Alcuin's standardization.

Modern dissatisfaction with the traditional eucharistic lectionary arises from: (1) the minimal use of the OT; (2) the haphazard selections for ferial Sundays; (3) the non-use of many significant parts of scripture; (4) lack of inter-connection between the pericopes on any given occasion.

To meet these deficiencies new lectionaries have been compiled on the following principles: (1) A two- or three-yearly cycle, (the former: German Lutheran 1896, British-Ecumenical 1968; the latter: Roman Catholic 1968 ff., Protestant Episcopal Church of USA [PECUSA], now [1971] in trial use); (2) OT lesson additional to or alternative to the epistle; (3) more *l.c.* in ferial seasons; (4) the designation of one lesson, usually the gospel, as the controlling lesson for the day, the other lessons being selected to go with it. In the breviary of the West, *l.c.* was featured in one office only, namely nocturns or mattins, the scripture readings of the day hours being only a short text (*capitulum*). At nocturns lessons were read in threes or groups of three (*cf.* the tenuous survival in the popular Christmas service of nine lessons and carols). Non-canonical ecclesiastical writings were used. As the preface to *BCP* complains, this system had broken down completely in the later Middle Ages. Following Quiñones, Cranmer sought to restore the ancient *l.c.*, with an OT and NT lesson at his two daily offices (q.v.), and based his lectionary on the civil calendar. The traditional reading of Isaiah in Advent was preserved by beginning that book on 28 November. Recent Anglican revisions of Cranmer have reverted to the church year as the basis, shortened the lessons (especially PECUSA) and restored other traditional features, e.g. the beginning of the Pentateuch in pre-Lent.

Psalmody. At mass, the standardized Western lectionary provided psalms for the introit, gradual, offertory and communion (qq.v.), the gradual being the most ancient. In the Middle Ages the psalms were drastically reduced in length as the music became more elaborate. At the Reformation the Lutheran orders retained the traditional introits and graduals, but dropped the offertories and communions. Cranmer provided a new introit for each mass (1549), comprising a whole psalm. His principle of selection, except for major feasts, is obscure, but was seemingly governed by considerations of length. The introits were dropped in 1552. Psalmody at the eucharist is being recovered in some current Anglican revisions of the eucharistic lectionary, e.g. Canada (1959) and the PECUSA proposals (introit and gradual), the attempt being made to fit the psalmody to the season, to the lessons, or to both.

For his two offices Cranmer provided (1549) a monthly course of continuous recitation of the psalter, following the civil calendar. In 1552 this system was interrupted by the provision of proper psalms (as also lessons) for 'diverse feasts and fasts'. Cranmer's system has been widely replaced in Anglican revisions by a selection of special psalms for each Sunday and major feast, and in some cases (PECUSA 1944 and British-Ecumenical 1968) by a complete system of daily selections based on the church calendar. In Lutheranism the daily offices have never been widely used, although the American Lutheran *Service Book and Hymnal* (1958) provides a lectionary of psalms and lessons.

R. C. D. Jasper, ed., *The Calendar and the Lectionary*, 1967; Standing Liturgical Commission of PECUSA, *The Liturgical Lectionary*, 1950; ibid., *The Church Year*, 1970. *See also* bibliography under **Sermon**.

R. H. FULLER

Lector

The second of the traditional minor orders after the acolyte (q.v.), his function was originally to read liturgical portions of scripture at the eucharist, especially the OT lesson, but also the epistle and in some cases even the gospel. The order of lector continues to exist in both the Roman Catholic and the Eastern Churches, but has tended to be absorbed by the major orders. *See also* **Reader**.

P. HINCHLIFF

Lent

The English word 'Lent' means 'spring', but this does not express the significance of the six-week period of spiritual discipline before Easter as conveyed by the 'forty days' of the Greek *tessaracoste* or the Latin *quadragesima*. For an understanding of the external structure of the season, the essential requirement is the knowledge that, when Lent was developed, Good Friday as a distinct commemoration of the Passion did not exist. Lent was a preparation for the primitive Pascha, the Christian Passover, the nocturnal festival of Saturday-Sunday, the unitive commemoration of the passion and the resurrection. As for the internal character of the season, Lent had a particular reference to the instruction of the candidates for baptism at the great festival of redemption.

Late in the second century Irenaeus said that some people fasted for one day before the Pascha, while others fasted for two days and others again held to a longer period. In addition he mentions that some counted their day as 'forty hours', but this has the appearance of being a special method of calculating a continuous fast extending over the Friday and the Saturday. Early in the third century the custom was to fast for two days. It is not until we reach a point towards the middle of the third century that we encounter unmistakable evidence of a fast extending throughout six days. It is of fundamental importance to note that a distinction is drawn between the additional period from Monday to Thursday and the long-established fast of Friday and Saturday, the latter retaining a special place within the context of development of a six-day Paschal fast.

There is a gap of about three-quarters of a century between this evidence and the earliest information concerning Lent, to which reference is made by the Council of Nicea in 325. We receive the impression that Lent was not a recent innovation but was something familiar. It is in the *Festal Letters* of Athanasius, towards the middle of the fourth century, 'that we first obtain the detailed evidence which enables us to understand the external structure of the season. Athanasius appears to make a distinction between the 'forty days' and the final week, but this simply means that the Holy Week (q.v.) fast formed a specially important part of the inclusive *tessaracoste*, understood as embracing the entire six weeks preceding the Pascha. In the third century the old two-day fast was not quite absorbed in the six days but retained a real independence and a compelling obligation. Similarly, we gain the impression from the *Festal Letters* that, although the one week had been extended to six weeks, yet for Athanasius the first five were not on the same level as the sixth. The innate conservatism of the liturgical tradition ensured that the concluding week kept a distinctive position within the inclusive *tessaracoste*. It is important to note that the rich development of 'Holy Week' as we understand it had not yet been made, and it was not this particular significance – that only in the latter part of the century attached itself to the successive days – which prevented the complete absorption of the sixth week within the 'forty days' in the time of Athanasius.

It is precisely when we bear in mind the natural process of formation whereby an additional period of five weeks was added to an older six-day fast that we can understand why Lent was called the 'forty days'. The fast of the Paschal Week is invariably calculated in the *Festal Letters* as beginning on the Monday. It lasted until the Saturday, the eve of the Pascha, that is, for six days. Although the week began on the Lord's day, there was no question of this being included in the period, since fasting was forbidden on

Sunday. When we consider the extension of the period to six weeks, we are to think of the five weeks as forming a distinct element in the total calculation. Once again the fast is calculated as beginning on a Monday, the Monday of the first week of Lent. There is no reason, however, to think that *within* the five weeks the days of fasting only would be included in the computation. That would be in accordance with the artificial manner of a later period. The whole season was doubtless regarded generally as one of discipline and purification. Reference is made to the first five weeks as a time of continued fasting although the fast was actually suspended on Saturdays and Sundays. If therefore the first five weeks are considered as a group added to the Paschal Week, and if it is remembered that the Monday of the first week is always considered in the *Festal Letters* to be the starting-point of the fast, this period of thirty-four days being added to the six days of the older fast gives the result of exactly forty days. It is to be observed that Athanasius consistently refers to the new beginning of the fast on the Monday of Holy Week and so, within the compassing circle of the *tessaracoste*, sets an inner fence around the Paschal Week. The Sunday of this week was the line which separated the old six-day fast from the additional five weeks. It is the frontier of this Sunday which makes it possible for us to envisage the formation of the *tessaracoste* as the superimposition of five weeks on an older six-day fast, both periods starting on a Monday and combining to make forty days.

The internal character of the season of preparation before the Pascha was governed by the fact that it was the time of training of the candidates for baptism. This may well be the reason for the origin of Lent, the instruction being spread over a period of six weeks and the old six-day fast extended to cover the 'forty days' on the model of our Lord's fast in the wilderness. The object of this arrangement would be to ensure, so far as possible, that only those of real sincerity in their Christian profession were received into the church at the paschal baptism. It is reasonable to suppose that the Lenten fast was meant to apply not only to the candidates but to the church as a whole. But it is in the nature of things unlikely that such a radical change was immediately accepted everywhere in its entirety. It is quite possible that in practice only the candidates, who were under discipline, and also the more devoted members of the church, or at least those most strongly attracted by ascetic practices, observed the whole period of fasting. Others may have fasted for a restricted period. Time was necessary so that the custom could root itself in the devotion of the church generally, and it was important that church members should be encouraged to exercise themselves in the spiritual discipline of the extended season of fasting. Doubtless there were many who regarded the *tessaracoste* as an innovation. The contrast in the *Festal Letters* between the general assumption that Lent is an established season and the occasional exhortations regarding its due observance disappears at once if we understand that the *tessaracoste* was organized primarily as a form of discipline for baptismal candidates, but that church members were also expected to observe it. It is perfectly comprehensible that the secondary purpose could not be realized immediately. Lent was associated with fasting and study, prayer and humility, and it is manifest that the church member was expected to approach the Pascha each year in the way he had done when he himself was solemnly preparing for his baptism.

G. Dix, *The Shape of the Liturgy*, ²1945; A. A. McArthur, *The Evolution of the Christian Year*, 1953.

A. A. MCARTHUR

Lesson

This term refers generally to liturgical readings from the scriptures or elsewhere. Apart from the occasional reading from the *Acta* of the martyrs in Africa, Gaul and Milan in patristic times, readings at the eucharist have always been scriptural. In the divine office at mattins (qq.v.) there are, however, patristic and hagiographic readings. Here we are concerned only with OT readings in the eucharist and with scriptural readings in the office.

1. *The Eucharist*. The church inherited the OT readings from the synagogue service (*see* **Jewish Worship**), supplementing them with NT ones. The East Syrian (q.v.) liturgy accordingly still has lessons from the law and the prophets preceding the epistle and gospel. In the Roman liturgy, the OT readings survived only on Lenten ferias, vigils and in the

commons of saints.

The new Roman Lectionary (1969) restores the OT lesson on Sundays as the first reading, except in Paschaltide when Acts is read. On Sundays *per annum* the lesson is chosen to accord with the gospel; during Advent Isaiah is prominent, while in Lent passages covering the main stages of the history of salvation are read. The lessons are spread over a three-year cycle, include the principal passages of the OT and in relation with the gospels manifest the harmony between the two Testaments.

On the weekdays of Advent and Lent an OT reading precedes the gospel; during the rest of the year, apart from Paschaltide, the OT lessons alternate every few weeks with NT epistles, over a two-year cycle. The Church of England's *Alternative Services: First Series* (1965) includes a table of OT lessons for Sundays and certain feasts to supplement the epistles and gospels of the *BCP*.

2. *The Divine Office*. The Roman office is monastic rather than popular in form, hence its lessons are found only in the night hour of mattins, other hours having only a *capitulum* (*see* **Canonical Hours**). The present system of lessons (1970) goes back to the seventh or eighth century and once covered most of the Bible, but the gradual abbreviation of the lessons means that much is now omitted.

Cardinal Quiñones' reformed breviary (1535), eventually rejected by Rome, influenced Cranmer, whose office lectionary has OT lessons morning and evening, with readings from the gospels and Acts in the morning and from the other NT books in the evening. Unlike the Roman system which began at Septuagesima, Cranmer's lectionary followed the civil year, covering the OT once and the NT three times annually. Cranmer's lectionary has been greatly revised since, and Sundays and feasts now have their own readings.

The new post-conciliar Roman Breviary provides longer scriptural readings for mattins, which will henceforth be known as the *Officium Lectionis*, and much more of the Bible will be covered than at present. The Joint Liturgical Group, made up of representatives of the Church of England and the Free Churches, includes a new lectionary as part of its proposals for morning and evening services.

Alternative Services, First Series, 1967; *BCP*; *Breviarium Romanum*; W. K. Lowther Clarke, 'The Lectionary' in *Liturgy and Worship*, 1932, pp. 296-301; *The First and Second Prayer Books of King Edward VI*; R. C. D. Jasper, ed., *The Daily Office*, 1969; J. A. Jungmann, *The Mass of the Roman Rite*, new rev. ed., 1959; *Missale Romanum; Ordo Lectionum Missae*; F. Proctor and W. H. Frere, *The Book of Common Prayer*, rev. ed., 1901; M. Righetti, *Storia Liturgica*, IV, ²1956; S. P. Salmon, *The Breviary through the centuries*, 1962.

BRIAN NEWNS

Lights *see* Candles

Litany

'A litany is a form of prayer in which fixed responses are made by the people to short biddings or petitions said or sung by deacon, priest, or cantors' (E. C. Ratcliff). Most litanies are precatory, although litanies of adoration or thanksgiving are not unknown; most precatory litanies are either in whole or in part intercessory.

Some early forms of the litany in Christian worship are reminiscent of pagan formularies: 'We need not, therefore, conclude with some scholars that the Christian Litany is borrowed from pagan usage; but it is nevertheless reasonable to think it an adaptation to a new purpose of a form which was traditionally associated with prayer and devotion, and which in the directness and simplicity of its address was intrinsically appropriate to that purpose' (Ratcliff).

The first definite evidence of the use of litanies in Christian worship suggests that the litany originated at Antioch in the second half of the fourth century; by the end of the century a litanic form of intercession was in use at Jerusalem; from Syria the litany travelled to Constantinople, and thence (apparently) it spread rapidly throughout the East. Whether the importation of the litany to the West was originally directly from Syria, or whether it was from Constantinople, is a question which cannot be definitively answered.

Constantinople certainly took to the litany more thoroughly and more enthusiastically than any other of the great liturgical centres, and to this day it is prominent and frequent in the services of the Byzantine rite. The *lesser litany*, a short form of general content, is the normal introduction to any formal prayer by the celebrant, corresponding in function to the mutual greeting and bidding to prayer in the Western rites; the *greater litany*, a more extended form, containing a number of intercessory biddings, occurs, with variations, in a number of services, commonly near the beginning, in what was originally a 'preparatory' or sometimes a 'processional' context. These litanies are mainly composed of biddings; other litanies of the same type are the *morning litany* at mattins and the *evening litany* at vespers, and the litanies preceding the prayer over the offerings and the Lord's Prayer at the eucharistic liturgy. The *litany of fervent prayer*, so called because the response to each petition (and in this case most are direct petitions, not biddings) is tripled, is the main intercessory litany of the Byzantine rite, coming at the end of the liturgy of the word before the eucharist, and as the intercession at mattins and vespers (qq.v.). Other litanies are those for the catechumens after the liturgy of the word, the proper litanies of the baptismal and marriage liturgies, the greater and lesser litanies for the departed, and the processional festal litany which in addition to intercessions includes a lengthy commemoration of the saints.

The earliest surviving text of a Western litany is that of the *Deprecatio Gelasii*, a Roman litany of the late fifth century, which bears a close relationship both in form and in content to the Byzantine litanies, and was almost certainly inserted between the entrance chant and the collect of the day in the Roman mass by Pope Gelasius (492-6), whose name it bears, replacing the older intercessory biddings and prayers after the readings and sermon. Related texts are found in non-Roman Western rites; one of them is still used at Milan on Sundays in Lent, at the same point in the mass.

At Rome this litany was already beginning to fall into disuse in the late sixth century (*see* **Kyrie**), and later litanies in the Roman rite and its variants differ considerably from it both in form and in use. The latter difference is marked by the change of name: Gelasius' litany was called a *deprecatio*, that is, an intercession without further qualification; *litania*, from which 'litany' is derived, and which is the name used for its successors, signifies either a penitential observance, or a procession, or, ultimately, a penitential procession, and is clearly connected with a particular use of this type of litany on the three days preceding Ascension Day, known as the rogations (q.v.), from which use the combination of penitence and intercession found in the later Roman litany originates.

This rogation litany, commonly called, from one of its parts, the litany of the saints, may be divided into six sections: (1) the introductory *kyrie* and invocations of the Persons of the Trinity; (2) the invocations of the saints; (3) the deprecations, or supplications for deliverance; (4) the obsecrations, or appeals for deliverance by virtue of events in Christ's redemptive life; (5) the intercessions; (6) a concluding invocation of Christ as the Lamb of God; a number of other prayers, of Gallican origin, with the Lord's Prayer and a concluding collect or collects, the set differing somewhat from time to time and place to place, are added to these six sections of the litany proper. Different though this form of the litany is from the type to which the Byzantine litanies and the *Deprecatio Gelasii* belong, it appears nevertheless to have originated, as they did, in Antiochene Syria, and to have been imported to the West in the seventh century, probably during the pontificate of Sergius I (687-701), who was himself of Antiochene descent (*see Agnus Dei*).

In medieval England the litany was sung on the rogation days (q.v.), and also daily in Lent and in many places in procession every Sunday before the parish mass. It is hardly a coincidence that Cranmer provided in the *BCP* what is probably the best-known, and certainly the finest, litany to be found in any of the liturgies of the Reformation, the structure of it based on that of the Roman litany, but the contents showing the influence of Luther's litany of 1529, as well as of the Byzantine greater litany, while from 1549 onward all invocations of the saints were omitted. Cranmer's one departure from the Roman structure is in his treatment of the deprecations and obsecrations, where he combines several of the original petitions in each one of his.

A considerable number of litanies have been produced in the course of liturgical revision during the last few years, which lack of space, unfortunately, precludes us from considering further. Of all forms of public prayer, the litany is perhaps the most flexible and the most conducive, when used competently, to effective congregational participation in the liturgy.

W. Jardine Grisbrooke, 'Intercession at the Eucharist', in *Studia Liturgica*, IV, 3, 1965, pp. 129-55; J. A. Jungmann, *The Mass of the Roman Rite*, I, 1955, pp. 333-46; E. C. Ratcliff, 'The Choir Offices: The Litany', in *Liturgy and Worship*, ed. W. K. Lowther Clarke, 1932, pp. 282-7.

W. JARDINE GRISBROOKE

Liturgical Movement, The

This present century has seen an extraordinary recovery and renewal by the Christian church of its worship and the understanding of that worship as central to its life and work. The name usually given to the means by which this recovery and renewal has been brought about is the Liturgical Movement. Its origins are to be found in the Roman Catholic Church in France during the nineteenth century. In the year 1832, Dom Prosper Guéranger refounded the Benedictine Abbey of Solesmes as a monastery dedicated especially to the study and recovery of the authentic Gregorian Chant (q.v.) and the church's liturgical heritage generally. Solesmes became a centre of liturgical worship and life, and its publication *L'Année Liturgique*, the first issue of which appeared in 1841, had a wide influence. The work of Guéranger and the Solesmes monks awakened a new interest in the liturgy. It was a springboard for a revival by the Benedictines of their traditional concern for the liturgy which eventually placed the monks among the pioneers of the Liturgical Movement, and it spurred an investigation into the origins and history of the liturgy in which such scholars as Cabrol and Batiffol provided the foundation for present-day liturgiological study. Guéranger's work has been adversely criticized as being too narrowly medieval, too limited in pastoral concern, and too archaeological. While this criticism may be right from our present point of view, Guéranger's work must be seen in the setting of the church of his day in order to be evaluated justly. Guéranger and the monks of Solesmes were not alone in their medievalism. Their contemporaries were discovering the Middle Ages, and to many these times were the ideal ages, in which had been all that was right and good. This was the time of the Gothic revival, of romanticism in art and literature. To men of the church, the

Middle Ages appeared to be the epitome of Christian life, to be indeed the Christian Ages. In them was to be found an ideal of worship and church life which must be recovered in order to release the church of their own time from its lassitude and sterility. Guéranger was able to recall men in the church of his time to an interest and concern for the liturgy as something to be prayed and lived, and it is interesting to note that most of the major points which the Liturgical Movement has made in recent times were in some way anticipated by Guéranger. He must justly be called the precursor of the Liturgical Movement.

However, the Liturgical Movement itself began to get under way in the opening years of the present century. In 1903, Pope Pius X issued a *Motu Proprio* on church music. He saw in the active participation of the faithful in the liturgy the source of the renewal of the Christian spirit, and called for more active participation in the worship of the church. A few years later the same pope called for a more frequent reception of holy communion. In 1909, a Catholic conference was held in Malines in Belgium; it is this conference which was probably the real inauguration of the Liturgical Movement. The conference saw the liturgy as the fundamental means of the instruction of the people in the Christian faith and life. An active participation by the people in the liturgy was the best means of nourishing and deepening the spiritual life. The conference called for a translation of the Roman missal into the vernacular (q.v.) so that it could more readily serve as the main manual of devotion for the church. It called for a centring of the Christian life in the liturgy of the church, the restoration of Gregorian Chant as a means of helping participation, and it asked for retreats for church people to be held in centres of liturgical worship and life. The outstanding leader in the conference was Dom Lambert Beauduin, of Mont César in Louvain. His book, *La Piété de l'Église*, published in 1914, contained ideas which became fundamental principles in the Liturgical Movement, and is still necessary reading if the purpose of the movement is to be understood. Beauduin saw that a better understanding of the incarnation and its meaning would lead to a deeper understanding and appreciation of the dignity of human life and all life. He pointed out that an understanding of the

nature of the church as the body of Christ would enable the development of a deeper sense of community in both worship and life, and he emphasized that an understanding of the sacrifice of Christ would result in the living out of the eucharistic sacrifice by the people of God and the offering of their lives along with the offering of Christ. Worship, Beauduin stressed, was the common action of the people of the church, an action which involved them all in a sharing in the saving work of Christ in and for the world. The orientation of the Liturgical Movement during these early years was deeply pastoral. While it was not anti-traditionalist and aimed at renewal rather than revolution, it was concerned with the present situation in the church and how that situation might be changed to bring about a better future. It thus sought to reach the ordinary church people rather than the theologian and the intellectual. It sought to recall the members of the church to an active involvement in the liturgy of the church. That liturgy was not to be a resuscitation of the past, nor something to be merely seen and heard, but a living worship in which the whole church should take part actively and with understanding, and the wellspring of a renewal of Christian life and mission. In these years the principal organ of the movement was *Les Questions Liturgiques*, later entitled *Les Questions Liturgiques et Paroissiales*. It was particularly the eucharist which the leaders of the movement saw as the central act of Christian worship, and it was an active participation in this on the part of the 'people in the pews' which the first stage of the Liturgical Movement sought in every way to encourage. The movement sometimes ran counter to the established ideas and practices of the church of the time; hence it aroused considerable opposition. Despite this, the movement began to spread and to become more and more an influence in the thinking and acting of the Roman Catholic Church, especially at the parish level.

In the years between the two world wars, the focus of leadership in the movement shifted from Belgium to Germany, and the second phase in its development got under way. The ideas of worship which the Liturgical Movement actively propagated had come under criticism as being too radical, too much a departure from the tradition of the church. Some felt that the movement was too modernist, and lacked a sound basis in the theology of the Roman Catholic Church, indeed was contrary to it. There was some justification for the criticisms, given the official patterns of worship and the Ultramontane theology in the early decades of this century; further, the earlier phase of the movement had been more concerned with the immediate pastoral needs of the church than with the production of an apologetic for its position. In the second phase of the development of the Liturgical Movement the emphasis was reversed. The work of building a sound theology of worship was spearheaded by the Rhineland Abbey of Maria Laach. The Abbot Ildefons Herwegen and Dom Odo Casel pioneered in this work, and the publication *Ecclesia Orans*, begun in 1918, enjoyed wide circulation and was an important means of dissemination of the new theology. Soon other theologians and church historians were turning their attention to the study of the liturgy. The result has been the production over the past half-century of a huge literature on Christian worship which has not only provided a deep knowledge and understanding of the origins and development of the liturgy, but has also opened up liturgical theology as an important field of theological studies. The list of contributors to this development is too long to give in full; we mention Josef Jungmann, Jean Daniélou, and Louis Bouyer as outstanding. Neither the historical nor the theological investigation shows signs of flagging at the present time; rather, both will doubtless increase in scope as the liturgy is seen in relationship to modern social sciences, psychology, and the like. While Maria Laach spoke primarily to the expert, the Canons of Klausterneuberg, and especially Pius Parsch, gave the same ideas a more popular expression. Klausterneuberg also turned to a study of the biblical basis of the liturgy, and inaugurated a biblical movement which has spread widely in the Roman Catholic Church, made important contributions to biblical theology and hermeneutics, and has served as a link between Roman Catholics and the Ecumenical Movement. In the period immediately before the Second World War and during the early war years the Liturgical Movement was spreading widely outside Europe. By the late twenties, St John's Abbey in Collegeville, Minnesota, was becoming, under the leadership of Dom Virgil

Michel, a major centre of the movement in the USA. The Abbey's periodical *Orate Fratres* (later renamed *Worship*) was addressed especially to the parish clergy and the laity, and became one of the most important means of spreading the movement in America. The Abbey also published a large selection of tracts and service leaflets which have found their way into churches and homes throughout the USA. Liturgical conferences began to be held and were well attended by clergy and laity. A Liturgical Arts Society was organized to find ways of improving the standards and craftsmanship of church art and architecture and for encouraging contemporary expression in liturgical art. Its journal *Liturgical Arts Quarterly* has become one of the finest reviews of the building and decorative arts. By 1940 a series of annual Liturgical Weeks was begun, and these have trained many for the liturgical apostolate and have taken on ecumenical significance. The Liturgical Movement in the USA has always tended to be less strongly intellectual in its appeal than it was in Europe. It took the form of a more grass-roots movement in the Roman Catholic Church. Liturgical theology was by no means neglected, but in the USA especially the Liturgical Movement and the rediscovery of the ministry of the laity were strongly inter-linked.

By the end of the Second World War, the movement had spread widely in the Low Countries, Germany and France. The Centre de Pastorale Liturgique had been founded in Paris in 1940, and its principal publication *La Maison-Dieu* combined the emphases of Maria Laach and Klausterneuberg and went beyond them. In North America generally the movement was affecting deeply the patterns of worship, and bringing about many changes in them. The church in Asia and Africa in the post-war years was faced with the challenge of nascent nationalisms and the resurgent indigenous religions. The Liturgical Movement was beginning to assist the church in searching for expressions of worship and art drawn from the local cultures, and it was in these lands that the missionary implications of a liturgical renewal were being explored. The movement was less widespread in Southern Europe and in the British Isles, and its influence had hardly begun to be felt in large parts of South America and in some parts of Southeast

Asia. But the Liturgical Movement had become a force to be reckoned with in the Roman Catholic Church. It could not be overlooked or disregarded as something passing and unimportant. It was producing a growing revival of worship, and was a major source of the growing ferment within the Roman Catholic Church which resulted eventually in the summoning of Vatican II. The official framework of the liturgy was proving too restrictive and out-dated to meet the needs of the church in the post-war secular society. Demands for reforms in the liturgy were being made from all parts in the Roman Catholic Church and were constantly becoming more insistent. The attempt to carry out in practice the principles which the Liturgical Movement had widely disseminated led to experimentation and to a search for new expressions of worship which would have more meaning for people in the present day. These often began to outrun the official liturgical rules of the church. Some members of the hierarchy, as in the Low Countries, sought to give leadership and encouraged the experimentation; others adopted a negative and restrictive posture and attempted to restrain or forbid it. The situation in respect to the liturgy was tending to became chaotic, and considerable controversy was being aroused by well-meant, but misguided, efforts at liturgical reform.

Concrete evidence that Rome was now at last prepared to give official recognition to the liturgical renewal and to implement at least some of its demands, while placing a guiding and restraining hand on the more radical tendencies, came in the promulgation by Pius XII in the year 1947 of the encyclical *Mediator Dei et Hominum*. This document has been regarded by some as the charter of the Liturgical Movement, and as endorsement of it. The pope praised the liturgy and emphasized that its celebration should be the work of the whole church. He expressed the desire that the faithful should be able to participate fully in the liturgy with understanding, and that they should take an active part in the services. He recalled the church to the need to live the liturgical life which was renewed and strengthened by the liturgy. This encyclical was the first papal encyclical to be devoted wholly to a discussion of the church's liturgy. Positive steps were taken to implement the encyclical in 1951 by the restoration of the Paschal Vigil

(q.v.), and four years later by the decree *Maxima Redemptionis* followed by the *Instructio* reforming and restoring the whole Holy Week celebration. The intention was a recovery of an important part of the tradition which had been lost. As the Paschal mystery was the centre of the liturgical life of the church, so the annual celebration of that mystery should be the centre of the liturgical year. At the same time, the restoration was intensely pastoral in outlook. The restoration of the major rites to evening hours made possible an attendance on the part of working people, and the provision of an up-dated and reformed liturgy for the rites made a more active participation in them possible. Other reforms followed. The pope sought to meet the need of people living in the industrial-urban complex by relaxing the rigour of the eucharistic fast and by permitting evening celebrations of mass. The rubrics (q.v.) governing the conduct of the services were simplified, and a new codification of them undertaken. Pius XII issued another encyclical, *De musica sacra*, in 1955, which laid down guidelines and rules for increased participation of the faithful in the rites of the church. Further indications of reforms to come were given in the pope's address to a congress meeting in Assisi in 1956. Some of the reforms which were undertaken during the pontificate of Pius XII were completed and promulgated by his successor John XXIII, including the new rubrics and the revision of a part of the Roman Pontifical.

But it was in Vatican II that the work of the Liturgical Movement bore fruit, and the extent to which it had aroused the church became fully apparent. There was no doubt from the beginning of the Council that the assembled council fathers had every intention of making the liturgy more responsive to the needs of the contemporary church. A schema had been prepared after some discussion by a representative group, and this was submitted to the Council. Between 22 October and 13 November 1962, the Council devoted fifteen sessions to debate on the proposed constitution, and its text was approved in principle. But the discussion continued and many amendments and additions were proposed. Finally the Constitution *De sacra liturgia* was passed by an overwhelming majority in 1963. It was promulgated by Paul VI on 4 December 1963, the first Constitution to be published by Vatican II. The Constitution on the Sacred Liturgy contains what is probably one of the best and clearest statements of the theology of the liturgy, its meaning and its function in the life of the church which has as yet been made, a statement which is in its approach thoroughly biblical, patristic, and eirenical. At the same time it is a statement which exhibits an intense pastoral awareness of and concern for the needs of the church and its mission in the present-day world. The Constitution unleashes the liturgy, so to speak, and allows it to become the living service of the Christian community in a way which has not been possible since the beginning of the Middle Ages. Of special significance for the Roman Catholic Church was the opening of the gate for the use of the vernacular tongues in the rites of the church. The Constitution might also be said to be the best and most concise statement of the principles and objectives of the Liturgical Movement. Entirely ecumenical in its scope and significance, the Constitution on the Liturgy must be given thorough study by anyone who wishes to understand the liturgy and the importance of the liturgical renewal of the whole Christian Church. Immediate steps were taken to implement the Constitution. Large parts of the Roman rite, and especially that for the celebration of the eucharist, have now been issued in the vernaculars of the different peoples of the church, and have been received with enthusiasm. The rites themselves have been thoroughly revised and updated. The result of all this is that the worship of the Roman Catholic Church is changing and developing in a truly thrilling manner. It is too soon to judge objectively the full impact of Vatican II upon the liturgical life of the Roman Catholic Church. At the present time that life is being revolutionized. The reforms in the liturgy made as a result of Vatican II have been so sweeping and so many that it will take a number of years for them to be assimilated and their significance realized. The work of the Liturgical Movement by no means ended with the publication of the Constitution on the Liturgy; rather, Vatican II opened the door to new opportunities. The movement in the Roman Communion today is part of the vanguard of the ferment in that church which has not been allayed; if anything, it is increasing. We may predict that in the immediate future the activities of the Liturgical Movement will be chiefly along two lines: (1) leadership and encouragement in still more spontaneity and freedom in worship and in finding new and contemporary ways of expressing that worship; (2) leadership in the re-thinking and renewal of mission and Christian action as necessary parts of liturgical renewal, as part of the service which the church offers to God.

But the Liturgical Movement has not been confined to the Roman Communion. Although it first got under way in that church, it has spread particularly during the past thirty years or so to almost every part of the church, and has made an impact upon the worship of most of the Christian communions. At the present time the Liturgical Movement may fairly be said to be part of the Ecumenical Movement, and it is proving more and more instrumental in drawing together the different Christian traditions of worship. In Anglicanism, the preliminary work carried out by Guéranger was in many ways paralleled by the activities of the ritualist wing of the Tractarian Movement. There was much common ground between the French Catholics of the persuasion of Guéranger and the tractarian Anglicans. Both emphasized the centrality of the eucharistic worship in the life of the church, and both were inspired by that worship to self-sacrificing service to the people of God. The Anglicans, like Guéranger and his associates, were unable to get behind the medieval church and accepted it as their ideal. But they did succeed in provoking interest in the liturgy and discussion of it, even if some of it was of a controversial nature. There was evidence on all sides of a growing dissatisfaction with the limitations of the normative Anglican patterns of worship and with the restrictions and limitations of the 1662 *BCP*. This dissatisfaction was not limited to England. Anglican liturgical scholars of the stature of W. H. Frere, Bishop Parsons, and Howard Baldwin St George both prepared the way for the spate of *BCP* revision which swept the Anglican Communion in the late twenties of the present century and made permanent contributions to the rediscovery of the liturgical tradition. But these revisions proved to be a kind of watershed. It was after them that the Liturgical Movement began to influence Anglicanism more and more widely. If there is any one thing to which we might point as the real beginning of the Liturgical

Movement in the Anglican Communion, it is to the publication in 1935 of the book *Liturgy and Society* by Father Gabriel Hebert of the Kelham Fathers. A movement to restore the parish eucharist as the common central act of parish worship got under way, and its effects are to be seen in the ever-increasing number of Anglican parishes where this has taken place. In the USA, the *Associated Parishes* came into being in 1946 to further the movements objectives and to implement them in parish worship. A few years later in England the *Parish and People* movement began its work with the same objectives. The Anglican Liturgical Movement has also produced a large literature, which has influenced the thinking of leaders in the movement in the Roman Communion, just as the works of Roman Catholic scholars greatly influenced Anglican thinking. We can mention here but a few of the most outstanding Anglican contributors to liturgical knowledge: Dom Gregory Dix, E. C. Ratcliff, Massey E. Shepherd, H. B. Porter, and J. G. Davies. The extent to which the Liturgical Movement has become grounded in Anglicanism and is bringing about a deep liturgical renewal in the Anglican churches may be gauged by a comparison of the proposals for revision of the *BCP* which are at present before most of the Anglican churches for evaluation and decision with the revisions of 1927-30. There is a ferment in Anglicanism which in many ways is very like that in the Roman Communion, and which is arousing the churches of the Anglican Communion to the realization that the *BCP* is not the final expression of liturgical worship and does need to be revised and changed, and which is deeply concerned with renewal of worship in the ordinary parishes as part of the much-needed renewal of Christian life and mission.

Among Christians of the Reformed and other traditions also the Liturgical Movement has come of age. The Reformed churches have also had their liturgical pioneers. In the latter part of the past century Eugène Bersier of Paris emphasized the centrality of the worship of the church in Christian life and the need for the Reformed churches to recover liturgical worship. In the liturgy which he produced may be seen the understanding of the worship of the church as a fully corporate action, and a balance between the word and sacraments which was

uncharacteristic of Protestant worship in his time. In Scotland, we may point to the work of the Church Service Society and its *Euchologion*, which was certainly one of the major influences behind the present liturgical renewal in the Scottish church and that church's excellent liturgies, which in so many respects incorporate the insights of the Liturgical Movement. But probably the extent to which the Liturgical Movement has gained ground in the Protestant traditions may be seen in the liturgy of the Church of South India, in which a number of these traditions, including the Anglican, have been brought together and submitted to the normative tradition of the scriptures and the early church which underlies them all. Yet the liturgy of the Church of South India is not an essay in liturgical archaeology; it is a restatement of the essential Christian tradition of worship in a liturgy which is immediately relevant to the life of Christians in South India. The work of the Church of South India has influenced practically all liturgical revision in the Protestant churches, and it is recognized also as an influence upon Vatican II. Or again, we may point to the thrilling work of the Taizé Community, with its emphasis upon the living of a common liturgical life of worship and mission, its deep ecumenical understanding and outreach, and the contributions of such writers as Max Thurian. The Taizé liturgy is undoubtedly among the very finest expressions of the principles of the Liturgical Movement. Yet it is fully ecumenical, and is an excellent illustration of a liturgy which can at one and the same time stand squarely in both the Reformed and Catholic traditions. The same awakening and ferment as that within Romanism and Anglicanism is today evident in Protestantism, and is bringing all parts of the church to a new willingness to submit to self and mutual criticism and to learn from each other. For the churches of the Protestant tradition as well as those of the Catholic, this is meaning a deep renewal of worship and rediscovery of the liturgy. Of special significance for the future is the growing tendency to search for liturgical expressions which will transcend and draw together the different Christian traditions. In this connection we may mention the new proposed ecumenical texts for the creeds, Lord's Prayer, and other common parts of the liturgy, which will undoubtedly serve to make our worship more truly common, the proposals of the Conference on Christian Union in the USA, the work of the Joint Liturgical Group in Great Britain, the establishment of such societies as the Societas Liturgica, and centres for the study of the liturgy on an ecumenical basis. The church as a whole is finding in the Liturgical Movement a new frontier on which, in the words of H. G. Hageman (*Studia Liturgica*, II, 4), 'all the churches, regardless of the rigidity of their liturgical traditions, now find themselves. In the common exploration of what is for all of us, in one way or another, new material, we are bound to reach easier ecumenical conversation. I do not know where these new agreements may take us; I would be suspicious of any attempt to overplay their importance. But the fact remains that the liturgy is the most fruitful area for ecumenical exploration. If that fact is recognised, and, in the best sense of the word, exploited, we shall know what the next step may be.'

The Liturgical Movement is part of the reawakening of the church. It seeks a recovery of those norms of liturgical worship of the Bible and the early church which lie behind Reformation divisions and medieval distortions, and which are fundamental to Christian liturgy in every time and place. It aims, however, not at an attempt to resuscitate the liturgy of the early church in the twentieth century, but at the restatement of the fundamentals in forms and expressions which can enable the liturgy to be the living prayer and work of the church today.

J.-J. von Allmen, *Worship, its Theology and Practice*, 1965; W. Bardin, 'Phases of the Liturgical Movement', in *Studies in Pastoral Liturgy*, II, 1961; L. Beauduin, *Liturgy the Life of the Church*, [2]1929; L. Bouyer, *Liturgical Piety*, 1950 (also published as *Liturgy and Life*, 1958); L. Bouyer, *Rite and Man*, 1963; O. Casel, *The Mystery of Christian Worship and Other Writings*, 1962; I. H. Dalmais, *Introduction to the Liturgy*, 1961; J. G. Davies, *Worship and Mission*, 1966; J. Jungmann, *Pastoral Liturgy*, 1962; A. G. Martimort, ed., *The Church at Prayer*, ET, 1966; J.A.T. Robinson, *Liturgy Coming to Life*, 1963; A. Shands, *The Liturgical Movement and the Local Church*, 1965; M. H. Shepherd, *Liturgy and Education*, 1965; B. Wicker, *Culture and Liturgy*, 1963.
Periodicals and Series: *Ecumenical Studies in Worship*, London, Lutterworth Press; *Studies in Pastoral Liturgy*, Maynooth, Eire, The Farrow Trust; *Studia Liturgica*.

H. ELLSWORTH CHANDLEE

Liturgies

In the singular the word 'liturgy' denotes an act of worship, more specifically the eucharist. Derived from the Greek *leitourgia*, it was used in Hellenistic Greek of an act of public service. In the NT it is employed of an act of service or ministry (e.g. Phil. 2.30). In time it was confined in Christian usage to the idea of service to God and finally, since worship was regarded as the supreme service to God, it was applied to the eucharist. Consequently to study liturgies is to examine the forms which the eucharistic rite has taken throughout the centuries.

1. *Patristic*. The New Testament does not provide a detailed description of the worship of the early church. Because worship was a regular element in the lives of the first Christians, a great deal was taken for granted. Our knowledge of this period is therefore restricted. It is clear, however, that the eucharist was of great importance, in virtue of Jesus' institution at the Last Supper. His followers continued to partake of bread and wine 'in remembrance of him'. Whether the Last Supper was actually the passover meal or not, it was associated with passover ideas, and it must also be seen in connection with the other references to meals in the gospels – particularly the feeding of the five thousand, to which John attached eucharistic teaching. These NT passages would appear to have been influenced by current liturgical practice in the areas in which they were written; and books such as Hebrews and Revelation clearly indicate a knowledge of the eucharist. The tendency to read liturgy into every page of the NT must be treated with reserve, however.

The early Christian eucharist followed the pattern of the Last Supper. Bread was taken, blessed, broken and distributed before a meal; and wine was taken, blessed and distributed after it. For the Jew, thanksgiving and blessing were synonymous, and bread and wine were blessed when God was thanked over them for his mighty acts of creation and redemption. When Paul wrote his first letter to the Corinthians the eucharist and the meal aere apparently still together; but at some early date, precisely when is unknown, the meal disappeared and the rites over bread and wine were brought together and became a single entity.

Forms of thanksgiving used over bread and wine which date from the late first or early second century appear in the *Didache*. Scholars differ as to whether they all apply to the eucharist, but as forms of thanksgiving they may well indicate the kind of prayer which was used at the eucharist. The first writer to give a detailed account of the liturgy is Justin Martyr in his *Apology* to the Emperor Antoninus Pius, written in Rome *c.* A D 150; this is supplemented by further information in his *Dialogue* with the Jew Trypho. The eucharist was celebrated every Sunday. It began with a synagogue type of service – scripture reading, a sermon by the president, and intercessions concluded by the kiss of peace. Bread and a cup of wine and water were then brought to the president, who said a prayer of thanksgiving over them; the congregation said Amen (q.v.). After the administration, there was a collection for the needy and the deacons took the sacrament to those who were absent. The prayer of thanksgiving was Trinitarian in form and extempore: it referred to God's activities of creation and redemption, the bread and wine was described as a memorial of the passion, and there was an odd passage on 'the prayer of the word which is from him', which might apply to Jesus at the Last Supper or to the Logos. Like the *Didache*, Justin also referred to the eucharist as a sacrifice, quoting Malachi 1.11.

Some sixty years later Rome also provided the first eucharistic text to be discovered. The presbyter, Hippolytus, wrote the *Apostolic Tradition* as a guide to church life in the early third century; in describing the consecration of a bishop, he set out the text of the eucharistic prayer. It was neat and compact, and followed the lines described by Justin. The original Greek text has never been found, and we have to rely on an early fifth-century Latin version, together with Coptic, Arabic and Ethiopian translations: and many scholars argued that the text has suffered changes in the process of transmission. But basically it was a prayer of thanksgiving for creation and redemption, an offering of the bread and cup in memory of Christ's death and resurrection, and a prayer for the gift of the Spirit on the communicants – a primitive form of epiclesis (q.v.). Clearly this was not

the Roman rite of the time, but simply a pattern which could be followed; later its influence was felt, not in Rome and the West, but in Egypt and Syria in the East, and not least in the Ethiopic liturgies.

Much of the liturgical material from the East during the second and third centuries is unreliable, for it derives from Gnostic sects. With strange beliefs about creation, the incarnation and the atonement, their prayers do not follow the lines of Justin and Hippolytus: but one interesting feature was a primitive form of invocation, which became an important element in eucharistic prayers of the East by the middle of the fourth century.

Two centres which were influential in the East were Egypt and Antioch. From Egypt in the fourth century comes the prayer book of Bishop Sarapion of Thmuis (*c.* A D 350) a private and untidy collection containing all the main elements of the eucharistic rite. Noteworthy features in its eucharistic prayer were the absence of the phrase 'Do this in remembrance of me' and the presence of two invocations – one before and one after the institution narrative. The second more explicit invocation invoked the Logos and not the Spirit, and it was characteristically Eastern in that it prayed for the consecration of the elements. The prayer ended with intercessions, which probably came during the third or fourth century in both East and West. Sarapion was the precursor of the Alexandrine Greek Liturgy of St Mark, from which in its turn came the Coptic Liturgy of St Mark or St Cyril.

From Antioch in the later fourth century came the so-called Clementine Liturgy in the eighth book of the *Apostolic Constitutions*. It agreed with the descriptions of the rite given in Chrysostom, and textually it owed much to Hippolytus. Its preface was very long; the institution narrative was introduced by the eastern form 'in the night in which he was delivered up'; the anamnesis (q.v.) included the second coming; the epiclesis was of the developed Eastern type; and it was followed by intercessions. From this rite developed the Liturgy of St James and the West Syrian family of rites, and ultimately the orthodox rites of St Basil and St John Chrysostom.

One further Eastern rite to be mentioned is that of SS Addai and Mari from Edessa in East Syria. It was written in Syriac and it lay outside the main influences of Greek-speaking Christendom. The extant text is very late and corrupt, but it may well point to the existence of an independent liturgical tradition as ancient as the third century. The main part of the eucharistic prayer is addressed to Christ, and it contains no institution narrative (q.v.); the epiclesis is of the Hippolytean type. Its users finally became Nestorians, and the rite came to be known as the Nestorian Liturgy.

Just as there were families of rites in the East, so there were families in the West. There was, for example, a North African family. Unfortunately no liturgical texts or treatises survive from this area: and the only evidence is references in the writings of Tertullian, Cyprian, Augustine and Optatus. It would seem, however, that there was borrowing from both East and West. So some churches used an epiclesis and some did not. On the other hand the kiss of peace (q.v.) was in the Roman position before communion, not before the anaphora (q.v.). At some stage freedom of experiment must have been excessive, for the Council of Carthage (397) and the First Council of Milevis (402) forbade uncontrolled freedom and insisted that all prayers should be officially approved.

In Rome the development of the rite was obscure. After Hippolytus there was a gap of some 150 years about which we know almost nothing. The first solid piece of evidence comes from the end of the fourth century with *De Sacramentis*, the lectures of Ambrose of Milan to the newly baptized. Here he made numerous quotations from a eucharistic text which later appeared in its entirety in the Gelasian Sacramentary. Its original form is unknown, but the disjointed text in the Sacramentary makes it clear that it has undergone revision. Ambrose also wrote of the eucharist in another treatise, *De Mysteriis*, and it would appear that in his time Milan used a rite which was fundamentally Roman. It followed the familiar pattern, but with significant features: intercessions came before the institution narrative, which was introduced in the characteristic Western manner – *Qui pridie*; consecration was effected, not by an epiclesis but by Jesus' own words in the institution narrative; and the Lord's Prayer had now found a place in the rite after the canon.

Other parts of the church in the West would also appear to have enjoyed an independent liturgical life in the early centuries, and the later evidence for what are known as the Gallican family of rites would suggest this; but of their origins virtually nothing is known.

It remains to note a few general developments, particularly in the East. First there was in the fourth century a growing attitude of awe towards the sacrament. Cyril of Jerusalem spoke of the 'holy and most dread sacrifice'; and Chrysostom and Theodore of Mopsuestia used similar language. Furthermore, with the imperial toleration and then the imperial establishment of Christianity, worship became more public and formal. So there developed a growing separation between clergy and laity: the corporate aspect of the eucharist faded; non-communicating attendance by the laity grew; the priest celebrated on behalf of the laity; and the most significant parts of the rite were withdrawn from their sight and hearing. In the West, however, changes were less serious. Gradually the canon came to be recited silently, and non-communicating attendance grew: but the priest remained in sight of the people, and no significant changes in dress or ceremonial occurred until after Gregory the Great.

R. C. D. JASPER

2. *Orthodox.* More correctly, Byzantine: what is commonly called the Orthodox liturgy, because by the historical and geographical accidents of subsequent Christian divisions it has come to be that in practice, is the liturgy of the Byzantine rite; that is, the liturgy of those churches which follow the order of service of the patriarchal see of Constantinople or Byzantium. The word 'liturgy' is normally used in the Byzantine rite only of the eucharistic liturgy, and not of the whole of formal public worship as it is in the West.

In the Eastern Orthodox Church today (as in those churches of the Byzantine rite in communion with Rome) the holy eucharist is celebrated according to three liturgies. The *Liturgy of St James the Brother of the Lord* is now used only on the feast of that saint in certain places. The historic liturgy of the Church of Jerusalem, and in its essentials the oldest of the three, it differs considerably from the other two, although its main parts, such as the eucharistic prayer or anaphora (q.v.), follow the same structure. The *Liturgy of St Basil the Great*, the anaphora of which, at least, was written by the father whose name it bears (on the basis of an older form which has in recent years been distinguished), is used on the eves of Christmas and the Epiphany, on the feast of St Basil (1 January), on the Sundays of Lent (except Palm Sunday), and on the Thursday and Saturday of Holy Week (qq.v.). The *Liturgy of St John Chrysostom* (which has little or nothing to do with St John Chrysostom, the ascription to him not being found until at least three hundred years after his death) is now the normal form: it is celebrated on all other days except those on which Byzantine liturgical law forbids the celebration of the eucharist altogether (*see* **Presanctified Mass**). The liturgies of St Basil and St John Chrysostom are identical in their order; they differ only in the texts of the principal prayers, those of the Liturgy of St Basil being much longer and fuller. They may therefore be considered together; further consideration of the Liturgy of St James must perforce be omitted.

Four principal divisions of the liturgy may be distinguished: (1) the preparation of the bread and wine, or prothesis (q.v.), which is performed privately before the service; (2) the introductory office of prayer and praise, or enarxis (q.v.); (3) the synaxis (q.v.), or liturgy of the word, or liturgy of the catechumens; (4) the eucharist proper, or liturgy of the faithful. A full account of the prothesis, and of its history, is given in a separate article.

The enarxis is also considered in a separate article, but a summary of its order and contents here may be useful: (1) opening blessing of the Trinity, by the celebrant; (2) the first (or greater) litany (q.v.) by the deacon, with responses by the people (in most churches in practice these and other responses are sung by the choir), and a concluding prayer (now said, as are most such prayers, silently, apart from its doxology) by the celebrant; (3) the first anthem (variable, usually a psalm, or based on a psalm); (4) the second (short) litany, with its concluding prayer; (5) the second anthem; (6) the third (short) litany, with its concluding prayer. The enarxis is now sung with the celebrant standing in the sanctuary before the holy doors: originally it was certainly sung with all the ministers outside the sanctuary, and possibly in the narthex (q.v.), or in

procession; the present usage removes all meaning from the beginning of the synaxis.

The synaxis comprises three parts: (1) the entrance rite; (2) the readings from the scriptures; (3) the common prayers of the church.

The entrance rite commences with the entrance with the book of the gospels, commonly called the little entrance (q.v.); further details will be found in the article devoted to it. It is followed by censing, during which anthems proper to the day (*troparia*) are sung: the original entrance chant has been shortened to a single verse sung between the last anthem of the enarxis and these *troparia*. The latter are followed by the hymn called the *Trisagion* (q.v.), corresponding here to the the *Gloria in excelsis* (*see* **Doxology**) in the Roman rite, and a lengthy prayer by the celebrant taking up the theme of this hymn (corresponding in function to the collect [q.v.] of the Roman rite), which is now said silently, and often before the hymn itself during the *troparia*.

The readings from the scriptures comprise: (1) the *prokeimenon*, part of a psalm, corresponding to the Roman gradual or responsorial psalm (the OT lesson, to which it was originally a response, has long since disappeared); (2) the epistle; (3) the alleluia (a verse or verses from the psalms, with the response 'Alleluia'); (4) the gospel. The sermon, if there be one, should follow the gospel, but is often postponed to a later point – in Greek churches before the communion (a practice comparable to the Italian *fervorino*), and in Russian churches to the end of the whole service.

The common prayers of the church comprise three litanies: (1) the litany of fervent prayer, so called from its tripled response, and essentially a litany for the living, although a petition for the departed has been added to it; (2) the litany for the departed (often sung only when there are particular departed persons to be prayed for); (3) the litany for the catechumens (q.v.). They end with the dismissal of the catechumens. In Russian churches all these litanies, together with the dismissal, are used, even when there are no catechumens; in Greek churches, on the other hand, they are commonly all omitted. The prayers which conclude each of the litanies are in most churches said silently, apart from their doxologies.

The eucharist proper commences after the

dismissal of the catechumens, and comprises seven parts: (1) the first part of the preparation of the offerers, or 'prayers of the faithful'; (2) the great entrance (q.v.) or entrance with the offerings; (3) the second part of the preparation of the offerers (the kiss of peace and the creed); (4) the eucharistic prayer or anaphora; (5) the breaking of the bread; (6) the communion; (7) the conclusion.

The 'prayers of the faithful' (which should not be confused, in the Byzantine or any other historic liturgy, with the common prayers of the church closing the synaxis) consist of two litanies introducing prayers (now said silently) of preparation for the offering of the eucharist.

The great entrance comprises five acts, the first four of which are covered by the singing of the almost invariable offertory chant, the 'hymn of the cherubim' (cherubikon): (1) a long secret private preparatory prayer of the priest, a typical 'apologetic' interpolation of the early Middle Ages; (2) censing of the altar, prothesis, and the whole church and congregation; (3) the actual 'entrance' itself, in the midst of which the cherubikon is interrupted for certain intercessory commemorations related to the diptychs (q.v.); (4) censing of the offerings now placed on the altar; (5) a litany leading to a prayer over the offerings, the latter exactly parallel to the Roman super oblata (q.v.), but now, confusingly, said secretly under cover of the litany.

The second part of the preparation of the offerers consists of the kiss of peace (which is no longer passed throughout the congregation, and is therefore omitted in practice unless several priests are present), the Niceno-Constantinopolitan Creed, and a brief exhortation by the deacon to reverence and awe in the offering of the eucharistic sacrifice which is about to take place.

The eucharistic prayer or anaphora is of the Antiochene pattern; it is difficult for anyone not well acquainted with the Byzantine liturgy to follow it in a contemporary celebration, due to the long standing custom, still all but universal, by which the celebrant says the greater part of it secretly (see Silent Prayer), while the congregational or choral responses are extended to cover his praying. Its order is:

(1) Introductory dialogue, of the universal pattern with certain minor elaborations.

(2) Preface, or first part of the thanksgiving, basically a brief and simple thanksgiving for creation and redemption in general terms, expanded at some time in the Middle Ages by Trinitarian interpolations which confuse the theme. Each of the two liturgies has its own form, as it has for every part of the prayer, but apart from this the preface, like the rest, is invariable. The preface is now said secretly, while the choir sings the last response of the introductory dialogue; the last clause is sung aloud, to provide a cue for the Sanctus.

(3) Sanctus and Benedictus, sung by the choir; the text is identical with that of the Roman rite, except that it reads 'Lord of Hosts' instead of 'Lord God of Hosts'.

(4) Post-sanctus, being a continuation of the thanksgiving, said secretly while the choir sings the Sanctus. In the Liturgy of St John Chrysostom a brief thanksgiving for the first coming of Christ, introducing the narrative of the institution; in the Liturgy of St Basil an extended and detailed thanksgiving for the whole history of creation and redemption, one of the finest examples of theological writing in the whole corpus of Christian liturgical literature, concluding with the introduction to the institution narrative.

(5) Narrative of the institution. The actual words of institution are sung, each of the two sentences being followed by the response 'Amen' by the choir.

(6) Anamnesis, normal in structure and content (see Anaphora); said secretly under cover of the prolonged closing 'Amen' of the institution narrative, apart from the penultimate clause, which serves as the cue for a choral response which now covers the epiclesis.

(7) Epiclesis, of a normal descendant type in both structure and content.

(8) Diptychs: commemoration of the saints, said secretly apart from one clause, which introduces an anthem, in honour of the Mother of God, which now covers the secret recitation of the next two sections.

(9) Diptychs: commemoration of the departed.

(10) Diptychs: commemoration of the living (one clause, that for the bishop, sung aloud).

(11) Doxology and final Amen (aloud).

The breaking of the bread comprises (1) a blessing of the people by the priest (many Western rites once had a corresponding blessing, which is in origin a preparation for communion); (2) a litany, similar to that after the great entrance, leading to the Lord's Prayer; (3) the breaking of the bread, with various secondary ceremonies, such as an elevation and a commixture, preceded by the original invitation to communion and its response, now purely formal, and covered by the communion hymn of the day, now thus used as a fraction hymn.

The communion comprises (1) the communion of the ministers; (2) the invitation to communion, to which the choir respond with Ps. 117 (118).26-27; (3) preparatory prayers, said aloud, a medieval interpolation; (4) the communion of the people, during which the choir sing appointed anthems; (5) the blessing after communion; (6) the first post-communion anthem. Communion is given in both kinds, administered together with a spoon, the bread having been placed in the chalice after the communion of the ministers; in the accompanying formula the communicant is referred to by name.

The conclusion comprises (1) the second-post-communion anthem; (2) a brief litany of thanksgiving, leading to the post-communion prayer (the latter said secretly); (3) the prayer over the people, or prayer outside the chancel, the original form of blessing; (4) the dismissal anthem, properly Ps. 33 (34) but now usually abbreviated; (5) the blessing and dismissal, with various responses, all of medieval origin.

The Byzantine eucharistic liturgy is unsurpassed in Christendom for clarity and coherence both of liturgical structure and of theological content – virtues which, unfortunately, are almost entirely obliterated by the combination of medieval interpolations and alterations and the current manner of celebration; there is no rite which would benefit more from a comparatively small measure of informed and intelligent reform.

W. JARDINE GRISBROOKE

3. *Medieval and Roman Catholic*

(a) *Medieval liturgies.* The Celtic liturgy, of which little is known before it had received Roman interpolations, was by the time of the Norman Conquest (1066) confined to Scotland and Ireland. It was probably of Gallican origin, and the lingering Celtic practices were suppressed in Scotland by St Margaret in 1069 and in Ireland in the twelfth century.

The Roman rite was introduced into England by the missionaries of St Augustine (d. 605) and the main structure continued throughout the Middle Ages.

After the Conquest, the building of churches, cathedrals and abbeys on a grand scale involved the compilation of a series of liturgical books of what came to be called different uses or even rites, although all were of the Roman rite.

There were extensive borrowings from the books in the Duchy of Normandy, and the process was completed by the thirteenth century. It is impossible to identify any specific 'ancestors' for the English uses, except, probably, Rouen for that of Hereford.

The structure was the same in each of them, but the prayers often differed, especially the preparatory prayers and those at the offertory and before communion.

By the time of the Reformation only three of the uses remained, since those of Bangor and Lincoln were virtually Sarum: Sarum, York and Hereford. All the others had adopted the Sarum liturgy, which became a model for the greater part of England and also for Scotland and Ireland. York had resolutely refused to give up its local use, but over the centuries many Sarum interpolations were accepted by Hereford.

The elaborate ceremonial of the 'Illustrious Church of Sarum' contrasted vividly with the comparative simplicity of liturgical worship in Rome.

The compiler of this English use could not have been St Osmund (d. 1099), although he may have laid a simple foundation. It is much too elaborate for his period. It was in all probability Richard Poore, dean and bishop (1217-28) of Salisbury, in whose time the cathedral was moved from Old Sarum into the city.

The last Sarum missal was printed in 1557 in the reign of Queen Mary.

In all the countries of Europe, diocesan missals appeared in the course of the Middle Ages, but, like the English service-books, they were variants of the Roman rite, with a choice of prayers.

(b) *Liturgy of Trent.* The fathers of the Council of Trent (1545-63) requested the pope to reform the liturgy, as it varied in almost every diocese. The new missal was completed under Pius V in 1570 to be an exemplar for all churches, and the mass was to be followed for all time. It was not until 1964 that it was superseded and then again in 1970. An exception had been made for those churches and religious orders which could show a distinctive use for at least two hundred years. All of them, however, were variants of the Roman rite, with the exception of the Mozarabic in a few churches in Toledo and that of Milan (Ambrosian), if a Gallican origin is maintained.

A few Marian priests in hiding continued their Sarum, York or Hereford mass, but the 'missioners' who came to England in the time of Elizabeth I followed the new Tridentine missal. Ancient sources had been studied in its production, but it preserved without change or verification the elements added in the Franco-German period to the original form of the Roman mass. The number of the feasts of saints was diminished and only four sequences were admitted. Unnecessary accretions were eliminated, such as the added words (tropes) in the *Kyrie* (q.v.) and the Marial fencing in the *Gloria in excelsis*. The time was unpropitious to reintroduce communion under both kinds. In order to answer difficulties in the celebration of mass, Sixtus V in 1588 founded the Congregation of Rites, but it could not change existing rubrics (q.v.) or the text of the prayers. An epoch of stability followed.

It is a mistake to think that this was a virtually silent mass. The rubrics ordered three voices: heard by the faithful, heard by those near to the celebrant, and silent, as in the canon. Above all, the epistle and gospel, the word of God, were for the benefit of the people and were to be read or sung in a clear and distinct voice. There was no justification for the subdeacon to chant the epistle in the sanctuary with his back to the congregation. True, the gospel was read in the vernacular (q.v.) in the pulpit before the sermon, but this was extra-liturgical, not part of the mass.

There were four revisions of the Tridentine liturgy, but the changes brought little modification of the text. The reform of Pius X (1911) affected the calendar: so that 'the very ancient Masses of Sundays throughout the year and of the week days, especially in Lent, might be restored to their proper place'. Clement XI (1721-24) had decreed that the preface of the Holy Trinity should be said on Sundays and Leo XIII (1878-1903) added the prayers after Low Mass. In 1953, the Liturgical Congress of Lugano discussed revolutionary changes in the mass, with the intention of simplifying the rite, removing what was redundant and giving the faithful a

more active part in the liturgy. At that time, some alterations appeared possible, but not the abandonment of the rite which had served the Western Church since the sixteenth century and the substitution of the vernacular for the Latin. A new Easter vigil appeared under Pius XII in 1951, with a change in all the offices of Holy Week in 1956.

The result of the debate on the liturgy in the Second Vatican Council (1962), which had been called by John XXIII, left no doubt that the changes would exceed mere alterations in the Tridentine mass.

(*c*) *Post-conciliar liturgies.* The aim of the post-conciliar commission was to produce a liturgy which should make the mass more alive and meaningful. Life was very different from 1570.

The priest should lead the community in worship, but the congregation must take a more intelligent and active part. 'Participation' is the key-note of the new liturgy, and, in order to effect this, the mass is said in the vernacular, although Latin is not altogether suppressed.

An 'interim' liturgy was ordered as from Advent Sunday 1964, with the people reciting the *Gloria in excelsis* and the creed, as well as responses and the variable 'chants' of the mass. Instructions were given as to when the faithful should stand, sit or kneel. The psalm 'Judge me, O God' in the preparatory prayers and the last gospel at the end of the mass were suppressed. The prayers of the faithful, general petitions linking the world with the eucharist, were introduced after the creed. The prayer after the offertory (q.v.), known hitherto as the 'secret', was said aloud and rightly renamed the prayer over the offerings (gifts). The Roman canon (q.v.) or eucharistic prayer, unaltered since the sixth century, remained the same, although said aloud and with the final doxology in a more solemn form, with the people responding amen. Three new eucharistic prayers, bringing fresh expression of the role of the Holy Spirit, were introduced in 1969. After the consecration, at the words 'mystery of faith', a choice of four acclamations by the faithful was introduced. Before the communion of the priest, 'Lord, I am not worthy' was said by all. The communicant replied 'Amen' after the words of administration: The body of Christ. Finally, the dismissal was transferred until after the blessing.

The ceremonial (q.v.) of the mass had been

greatly reduced, as had the signs of the cross and genuflections. The commission regulated also the rite of concelebration and, for certain occasions, the administration of communion under both kinds. The number of communicants in large churches would make the giving of the chalice at all times very difficult.

The final and normative order of the mass was first said in France, Italy and Spain on Advent Sunday 1969 and in Great Britain on the first Sunday in Lent 1970. Rome had conceded that its use was not compulsory for two years, but it was largely adopted. The various changes in the 'interim' rite have been retained in the new liturgy.

Incense may be used whether the mass is sung or said. The mass begins with an entrance song, which may be either the old introit or a hymn. Then, after a greeting of the people, there is a penitential act with a shortened confession in which the faithful join with the priest. 'Lord have mercy' and 'Glory be to God on high' are followed by the first of the presidential prayers, the collect, of which there is never more than one.

The liturgy of the word, since the council, has a more vital role. The pope has said that 'the treasury of the written word of God should be more generously distributed'. A third lesson, from the OT, is provided for Sundays and feasts, and a new lectionary has been compiled. The four sequences or hymns before the gospel have been retained, but only those of Easter and Pentecost are obligatory. The creed and the prayers of the faithful follow.

The offertory procession, at the beginning of the eucharistic liturgy, linking the gifts of bread and wine with the giving of money, is encouraged where possible. The prayers at the offertory are shorter and have been modelled on the prayer spoken by the father of the family at the beginning of a formal Jewish meal.

Eight new prefaces have been added, making twenty-two in all. The Roman canon, as an alternative to the three eucharistic prayers, has been retained, with a few minor alterations. The list of saints before and after the consecration may be considerably shortened, and what may be called the three false conclusions in the canon suppressed. An acclamation by the faithful has been introduced after the words 'mystery of faith', as in the other prayers. This acclamation highlights Paul in his First Letter to the Christians of Corinth.

The central and vital part of the canon, including the words of consecration, may be sung, as well as the final doxology. The prayer following the Our Father has been simplified and changed at the end, with an acclamation of faith in the glorified Christ.

The 'sign of peace and mutual love', adopted in some countries for the kiss of peace (q.v.), is not normally in use in Britain. The consecrated bread is broken at the threefold *Agnus dei*. After communion, a silence for thanksgiving is prescribed. Notices are given before the blessing. The ablutions may be taken after mass.

The calendar has been simplified. The titles of the three Sundays before Lent have been suppressed. There are fewer feasts of saints, and very many of the commemorations are optional. John the Deacon (872) in his assessment of the work of St Gregory could be writing of the new mass: 'leaving out much, changing little, adding something for the exposition of the lessons of the Gospel'.

J. D. CRICHTON

4. *Anglican*. The roots of Anglican eucharistic liturgy lie in the reforming work of Cranmer in the reign of Edward VI (1547-53). By 1547 he had already come to strong convictions about the *desiderata*, and when Edward, a minor, inherited the throne, Cranmer's Protestantism in theology was reflected in the Council of which he was a member, and the opportunity came to reform the liturgy.

Cranmer's main aims were: a wholly vernacular (q.v.) liturgy, a simplification of ceremonies, participation by the people (including receiving communion regularly and in both kinds), and elimination of transubstantiation, mass-sacrifice, and other unreformed doctrines. His purpose was far more to write a liturgy embodying receptionism than to revive patristic usage. It was not that he lacked scholarship or materials – rather he was not interested in copying patristic use for its own sake anyway. Certainly his developed liturgy was *sui generis* and unlike any earlier production.

Reform came by stages – a method advertised in advance in the Royal Proclamation prefixed to *The Order of the Communion* of 1548. In 1547 the epistle and gospel had been read in English. Now this brief inset into the mass came as the first new eucharistic work in Cranmer's planned programme. Written in English, it implemented reception in both kinds by being inserted after the priest's communion in the mass. It contained a long exhortation to worthy reception, a short exhortation, confession, absolution, 'comfortable words', and the famous 'prayer of humble access' leading into communion in both kinds. A blessing followed, and if the wine were insufficient more was to be consecrated.

In the 1549 *BCP* the whole service was in English. The mass-plus-*Order* shape was followed closely, but the contents were subtly changed. The ante-communion (q.v.) merely lost the priest's preparation and the gradual chant. It gained a sermon or homily after the creed, and the 1548 long exhortation followed that. The offertory (q.v.) – consisting of a collecting of money – concluded the ante-communion. The worshippers left their places to put their alms in a box near the screen, and intending communicants proceeded on to the choir or chancel.

The elements were then made ready and the cunningly altered canon ensued. The Roman intercessions remained, but only prayers, not oblations (q.v.), were offered. The saints were honoured, but not expected to help. Prayer was made for the departed, now grouped with the living. The intercessions broke off, and the sacramental theme began abruptly. God was invoked as having given his Son to make on the cross 'a full, perfect, and sufficient sacrifice, oblation and satisfaction' for sins – words serving devotional, didactic, and polemical purposes. The *quam oblationem* petition then asked God to bless and sanctify the gifts by his 'Holy Spirit and word'. This is sometimes called an epiclesis (q.v.), but occupied the Western position and owed little or nothing to Eastern models. The institution narrative (q.v.) had two manual acts but no other ceremonial. But the anamnesis was the key to Cranmer's step by step reform. The old canon (q.v.) responded to the command 'Do this in remembrance' with 'we offer a pure victim'. Cranmer removed this oblationary terminology, but left the response unexplained. It read 'we . . . celebrate and make . . . the memorial which thy Son hath willed us to make'. In brief, whatever he meant, we mean! The canon continued with self-oblation, petition for fruitful reception, some wisps of the old canon and a doxology. After it came the Lord's Prayer, the peace,

and the whole 1548 *Order* from the short exhortation to communion (including the priest's). After a brief post-communion, rubrics ordered 'something more larger and thicker' wafers, to be divided during distribution. Further consecration was lacking.

Reactions to this service merely paved the way for the next round, which may have been already in preparation. Implementation came in 1552. Now the shape was altered, slightly in the ante-communion, drastically around the anamnesis (q.v.). To the question, 'What do we do in response to our Lord's command?' the 1552 *Order* answered, 'We eat bread and drink wine'. This was incorporated after the institution narrative not by mere verbal assertion, but by *actual eating and drinking*. New words of administration reflected not new doctrine but the new 'anamnesis' role of communion – 'Take and eat this in remembrance . . .'. The 1552 *Order* left no break between reading the Lord's command and obeying it, the table was in the midst and the distribution was immediate.

Further consequences followed. Sacramentally speaking, nothing preceded reception. There was no trace of consecration, whether name or thing. The elements were not mentioned rubrically till distribution, and the minister took the remains home. The *quam oblationem* petition located consecration in reception, and this is the logic of the whole rite. Further consecration was thus impossible.

The promoted administration squeezed considerable 1549 material out of its place. The end of the 1549 canon became an alternative post-communion 'prayer of oblation' (still, oddly, asking for fruitful reception). The Lord's Prayer opened the post-communion. The peace was lost, and the 1548 *Order* began the sacramental half of the service. Cranmer hit on the happy transition from the fourth 'comfortable word' to 'lift up your hearts', but this excluded 'humble access' from the sequence. It, however, replaced the 1549 intercessions after the *Sanctus*. As these had lost their connection with the 'oblations' they no longer belonged in the canon, and went more naturally (and perhaps primitively) at the end of the ante-communion. Thus they were read each week, even when there was no communion. The saints and the departed disappeared and the intercessions were explicitly labelled for the 'church militant here in earth'. Inserting 'humble access' after the *Sanctus* (q.v.) has been thought to break up the canon, but to Cranmer there was a gaping hole there, and a subjective approach to the table suited the progress of the service, to a single climax in reception, far better than the 1549 intercessions could do. Thus the 1552 'canon' was merely the 'one oblation' paragraph, the receptionist *quam oblationem*, and the institution narrative ending in the administration. The post-communion included *Gloria in excelsis*, and the rubrics ordered bread 'usual to be eaten'.

Mary brought back the mass, but Elizabeth in 1559 revived the 1552 *Order*, though she clumsily prefixed 1549 words of administration to the 1552 ones. Jewel's controversy with Harding made it policy to assert that the dominical words in the narrative of institution consecrated the elements, and a Puritan, Robert Johnson, was imprisoned in 1574 for omitting a 'further consecration'. The 1604 canons underlined this new policy.

The ill-fated 1637 Scottish rite was a half-reversion to 1549. After the *Sanctus* 'humble access' fell out, and the 'one oblation' paragraph followed immediately. The 1549 *quam oblationem* returned, manual acts were reintroduced, the 1549 anamnesis dislodged the administration, and the 1552 'prayer of oblation' followed as in 1549. The Lord's Prayer and 'humble access' intervened before communion, but the rest of the 1549 *Order* held its 1552 position. The canon was now called 'the prayer of consecration', and rubrics ordered both further consecration and consumption of consecrated remains.

The 1662 Restoration liturgy kept the 1552 text and structure, but firmly clamped the 1637 'consecration' rubrics upon it. Cranmer's words were to enact Jewel's theology! A discreet (non-petitionary) mention of the departed came into the intercessions, and an amen concluded the 'prayer of consecration'. As, under Laud's influence, tables had already returned to the east wall of the chancel, a break between the institution narrative and distribution had arisen. Thus the amen merely regularized a *de facto* departure from the continuity which Cranmer had planned.

The 1662 *Order* still remains today the official service of the Church of England and of many other Anglican provinces. However, some provinces have superseded it, and most have at least some alternative. Its use is now

more deeply entrenched in vernacular languages (in, say, Africa) than it is in English-speaking communities. These latter show impatience at its antique (but majestic) language, its unique shape, and (sometimes) its Cranmerian theology.

Early variants occurred in eighteenth-century Scotland. A scholarly theory that the *Apostolic Constitutions* were really apostolic led to changes from 1637 to 1764. The 1637 *quam oblationem* was moved to the Eastern position and made into a full-blown epiclesis. The 1549/1637 anamnesis had an explicit oblation of the elements attached. The intercessions were moved to the end of the canon. Finally, the whole 1548 *Order* returned to its 1549 position. The current Scottish rite descends from 1764. The same text was taken to America by Samuel Seabury in 1784, was crossed with the 1662 rite over there, and a hybrid rite emerged in 1790. The 1790 rite lies behind current American and Brazilian use.

In the early twentieth century the Universities' Mission to Central Africa and Korean mission fields went over to near-Roman rites (usually only available then in vernacular tongues). An Eastern-type epiclesis also had its advocates again, and was not only retained in the Scottish and American rites when they were revised, but was also introduced in South Africa (1924), England (1927-8), and in the 1930s in Ceylon, China, Madagascar and elsewhere. Anglo-Catholics led all these revisions, seeking a more primitive pattern for the canon, petitions for the departed, and some form of Godward 'memorial' in the anamnesis. They were divided, however, about the propriety, wording and position of the epiclesis. In England the 1927-8 rite created grave suspicions among Protestants for these very reasons, but it was finally defeated over the (non-liturgical) question of reservation.

In the late 1940s India experimented with a 1928-type rite, and Japan and the West Indies followed in the 1950 on a more 1549-cum-Roman basis. The 1959 Canadian rite stood between 1662 and the Indian rite.

The 1960s brought a new era. Experimental revision started all round the Anglican Communion. G. Dix's *The Shape of the Liturgy* (1945) had focused attention on the *action* and less on the *words*. The first result of this had been the ecumenical South India liturgy of 1950; its principles, embodied in the 1958 Lambeth Report, were worked out for Anglicans in *A Liturgy for Africa* (1964). Offspring of this family includes ecumenical liturgies in East Africa (1966) and Nigeria (1966). They all have a fuller ministry of the word, including the OT. The creed follows the sermon, and the intercessions are litanical. Penitence has moved to the beginning of the rite, so the sacramental section is a simple placing of the elements on the table, a thanksgiving, a breaking of bread, and a sharing of the elements. The thanksgiving 'consecrates', but not by this brief set of words, but by the totality of the action. The thanksgiving includes emphasis on the cross, but makes mention of the other mighty works of God. There are congregational acclamations at intervals in it.

The Church of England's 1967 *Second Series* experimental rite is similar but not dependent. Penitence remains in the 1552 position, special emphasis on the cross has almost disappeared (for there is no link in salvation-history between the Sanctus and the institution narrative), and the anamnesis is a tentative, half-done job, with echoes of 1549. A more modern English form of it occurs in *Modern Liturgical Texts* (1968), and an adaptation of it (suggesting another new family of rites has started) issued from the South African Liturgical Committee in 1969. The next stage on from *Second Series* in England itself is the *Third Series* rite published in September 1971. Here the language has been thoroughly modernized, and the whole service worked over. A richer style of biblical and other imagery returns, and the anamnesis is a far clearer doctrinal statement than before. Congregational acclamations are added in the thanksgiving, a fuller provision is made for the high seasons of the church's year, and a new Sunday eucharistic lectionary is included. At the time of writing *Second Series* will be extended beyond July 1972, and *Third Series* will be amended and should be authorized from a similar date.

C. O. BUCHANAN

5. *Baptists*. While most Baptists would affirm their worship as 'eucharistic' in the sense that it is a time of thanksgiving, they would not use the term 'eucharist' to describe it. Likewise, they generally do not use terms like 'sacrament' or 'holy communion'. They rather prefer the 'Lord's Supper', or the 'breaking of bread' or the 'memorial meal' to designate the central act of Christian worship.

The Lord's Supper is understood as anamnesis (q.v.). The Lord's death is remembered and re-enacted as a memorial 'until he comes'. The bread and wine are symbols of the body and blood of Jesus Christ. The presence of the Lord is a spiritual presence.

Baptists, though having a high regard for the Lord's Supper, do not observe it with great frequency. Daily communion is not practised by Baptists. Weekly communion is only rarely observed, and then usually by congregations which have had some contact with the contemporary movement for liturgical renewal. The general practice among Baptist churches is monthly communion, usually on the first Sunday of the month. Baptist churches in some places observe only four communion Sundays a year.

The administrator of the communion is generally an ordained minister, but if no ordained person is available the congregation may designate a layman as the administrator. He will also be assisted by deacons (q.v.). They serve the elements, pass the peace, and assist in the prayers. The service is generally conducted from behind the table, the minister facing the congregation.

Communion is in two kinds. Formerly a common loaf was broken and distributed to each communicant and a common cup was passed among the congregation. Today communion wafers or small bits of bread and individual cups are in general use, although in some places the common loaf and cup are being reintroduced. Communion is generally received in the pews. The bread is eaten at the same time by the minister and congregation as the minister says: 'Jesus said, "Take eat; this is my body which is broken for you. Do this in remembrance of me."' The cup is drunk simultaneously as the minister says: 'Jesus said, "Drink of it, all of you; for this is my blood of the covenant, which is poured out from many for the forgiveness of sins."'

Communion among the early Baptists was generally reserved for those who were members in good standing of the local congregation or who were members of sister congregations in good standing. That meant that only those who had been baptized 'on profession of faith' as believers were to be communicants. In many places the practice was to hold two services on a communion Sunday. The first, including the sermon, would be for all who came; the second was only for those who were entitled to receive communion. In recent decades this practice has been greatly modified. While some churches still practise 'closed communion', most Baptist churches issue a general invitation to 'all who believe in Christ and who are in love and fellowship with the brethren' to partake in the service. The service of word and table is one, and all, including those who do not communicate, remain.

Each congregation determines the structure of its worship. Thus no one service would be considered typical, but with modifications the following would find acceptance in most Baptist churches.

THE SERVICE FOR THE LORD'S DAY
(with the Lord's Supper)

Affirmation of purpose and entry of scriptures
Adoration
  Scripture sentences
  Hymn
  Prayer
  Ascription
Confession
  Call
  Prayer
  Assurance of forgiveness
  Praise: *Gloria patri, Gloria in excelsis*, or
  hymn

Ministry of the Word

Scripture lessons
Prayer of illumination
Sermon
Affirmation of faith or church covenant

Ministry of the Table

Offertory: gifts, bread and wine, and self
Prayer of dedication
Invitation to communion
Affirmation of unity and peace
  Scripture sentence
  Right hand of fellowship (the peace)
Words of institution
Prayer of thanksgiving
Prayer for the presence of the Holy Spirit
Lord's Prayer
Breaking and distribution of the bread
Eating of the bread
Pouring and distribution of the wine
Drinking the wine
Agnus Dei
Prayers of petition and intercession

Dismissal

Hymn
Benediction

The service generally includes several hymns, an anthem and service music. A choir is used to assist in the service and to offer the special music.

JOHN E. SKOGLUND

6. *Christian Church (Disciples of Christ).* From its earliest days, in the early nineteenth century, the Christian Church (Disciples of Christ) has combined two principles bearing upon the order of worship. First, the regular service of worship has included preaching and the 'breaking of bread'. Second, this church has entrusted decisions about the order and words of the liturgy to each congregation. Although there has been considerable similarity among congregations, it must be said that the practice is neither common order nor common prayer.

The first exposition of this practice was developed by Alexander Campbell (1788-1866) in his writings during the third and fourth decades of the century. After observing that the NT, in contrast to the OT, gives no formal requirements for worship, Campbell concluded that Christians have reached the 'manhood of the religious world', and are therefore 'permitted to exercise their reason, and to act from the principles infused into their minds from the development of the divine philanthropy'. He affirmed that the weekly observance of the Lord's Supper on the Lord's Day is commanded but that the rules are not. Accounts of that period indicate that a typical service began with readings from scripture interspersed with hymns. There followed brief extempore prayers over bread and wine with the distribution of each. Impromptu exhortations or preaching, spiritual songs, and a collection concluded the service.

During the period from 1880 to 1920 this combination of elements was gradually formalized in general practice: opening praise, scripture lessons, pastoral prayer, communion, offering and sermon. The position of the sermon is a vestige of earlier practice when the congregation always ministered the Lord's Supper whether there was a preacher or not. Communion was ordinarily conducted with these sub-sections: a brief homily on the meaning of the act, an extempore prayer over the loaf by one elder, a second prayer over the cup by a second elder, and distribution of both to the congregation. An invitation to confess faith in Christ was regularly extended following the sermon. A number of private service-books was published during this time giving suggestions for pastors for the construction of their services.

Not until after the Second World War did Disciple congregations in large numbers develop an order of worship more closely parallel to that followed in other denominations. By transposing communion and sermon, they overcame their one major disparate practice. By 'enriching' the service with devotional elements previously not used they developed a tone to their services increasingly like that of other denominations.

The use of extempore prayer at the communion table has continued with little change, illustrating positive and negative values in such a practice. Ordinarily these prayers have referred specifically to the bread and the cup and have given thanks for Jesus who gave himself for our sins. Frequently there have been requests for the Holy Spirit to come and for our sins to be forgiven. A common element has been a vow that we will give our lives now to greater service to God. The use of extempore prayers at the table makes possible a directness and immediacy that rarely is present in the language of prescribed eucharistic prayers. At the same time, this practice opens the way for unevenness and irregularity.

Disciples, despite a long-time tendency towards legalism, have never raised questions about the validity of the Lord's Supper, about the 'form' and 'matter' of the eucharist. Consequently, the varied theological content of the eucharistic prayer has not raised for them the problems that would arise in other portions of the church. Adequacy of the rite has been gauged by different criteria: Is the table spread in remembrance of Christ? Has the conducting of the service been according to the congregation's unwritten standards or expectations? Does the combination of music, word, and act communicate a sense of divine presence? On every Sunday the entire congregation present communicates and in this way affirms the integrity of the rite.

KEITH WATKINS

7. *Congregationalist.* As is explained under **Congregationalist Worship**, there is no single official Congregational liturgy. None the less

the structure, order, and content of Congregational services of word and sacrament do not differ greatly between Britain and the USA (for the sources of these services *see* **Books, Liturgical** 7: Congregationalist).

The nearest approach to an archetypal Congregational liturgy, and one which unites the largest number of Congregationalists in the world, is the first recommended service in *Services of Word and Sacrament*, first published in 1966 by the United Church of Christ. It is archetypal yet not monopolistic, since alternatives are provided. It is a firm guide to worship with a coherent theology and careful order, but welcomes the supplementary use of free prayer, silent prayer, and bidding prayers, as long as they do not break the basic order and progression of the service.

The service has two parts, which correspond to the origin of Christian worship in the synagogue and the upper room. The first part is essentially a service of the word; the second part is essentially the service of the Holy Supper or eucharist. The first part consists of praise, prayers, the reading and exposition of scripture, an affirmation of faith, and the response of the people in the offertory – the climax of the service of the word and the beginning of the service of the Lord's Supper.

The second part of the service recalls not only in words, but also in symbolic and prophetic acts, the four actions of the Lord who *took* the bread and wine, *blessed* them by prayer, *broke* or poured them, and *gave* them to his disciples, as the anticipation of his sacrifice on the cross and of his messianic banquet in eternity.

The aims of the entire service are: to stress the unity of word and sacrament; to offset an overly introspective and penitential character in historic Western worship by accenting the elements of adoration and joyful gratitude and the presence of the risen Christ; to make the central eucharistic actions plain; and, finally, to emphasize that the true consecrator is the Holy Spirit. These are not, of course, uniquely Congregational or even Reformed contributions to liturgical theology – they are the common gains of the liturgical and ecumenical movements of our days.

In two respects only has this liturgy made a distinctive contribution, and these are worthy of elaboration. The peril of the exclusively retrospective gaze and of a theological memorialism are minimized by beginning the eucharistic part of the service with Luke's account of the risen Saviour breaking bread with his disciples. Since the Pauline account of the Holy Supper in I Corinthians is by far the commoner usage as a warrant in our tradition, this feature is genuinely innovative.

The second innovation, for which the Church of South India provides a partial precedent, was to provide some new responses for the people in the great prayer of consecration. The most significant response, after the anamnesis and epiclesis (qq.v.), affirms the priesthood of all God's people, in the following words of oblation: 'Here we offer ourselves in obedience to Thee, through the perfect offering of thy Son Jesus Christ, giving Thee thanks that Thou has called us to be a royal priesthood, a holy nation, thine own people . . .' The distinctive Congregational witness has not been lost, but rather recovered in this rich rite which won the approval of the late E. C. Ratcliff as having recovered 'the spirit and emphasis of the Early Church'.

There have been two significant changes incorporated in the more recent Congregational communion services in both Britain and the USA. One has been the increasing appropriation of the historic structure and wording of the consecration prayer of the Western tradition, including the salutation, the *Sursum corda*, the *Sanctus*, the anamnesis, and the oblation.

A second change has been towards a deeper sense of the real presence in the sacrament as evidenced by the requirement of an epiclesis, in contrast to earlier eucharistic theologies which were virtualist at best and memorialist at worst. The evidence for this claim can be found in the most recent service-books of the Congregational Church of England and Wales and the United Church of Christ in the USA.

The theology of the first and second communion orders of *A Manual for Ministers* (1936) is clearly memorialist. Four of the five communion orders in *A Book of Public Worship Compiled for the Use of Congregationalists* (1948) have an explicit epiclesis, and a fourth has an implicit doctrine of the real presence. Both communion orders in *A Book of Services and Prayers* (1959) have an explicit epiclesis.

In the American Congregational publication, *A Book of Worship for Free Churches* (1948), two communion orders include an ambiguous epiclesis in the words: 'We humbly beseech thee to grant thy Holy Spirit and to sanctify this bread and wine, which now we offer unto thee; that they may become unto us symbols of the body that was broken and of the blood that was shed for us . . .' (pp. 108, 115-6). On the other hand, the two communion orders of the United Church of Christ published in *Services of Word and Sacrament* (1966) include the following epiclesis: 'Bless and sanctify by thy Holy Spirit both us and these thy gifts of bread and wine that in this holy communion of the body and blood of Christ we may be made one with him and he with us . . .'

HORTON DAVIES

8. *Jehovah's Witnesses.* Once yearly Jehovah's Witnesses keep the Lord's evening meal, 'the memorial'. The date is 14 Nisan in the ancient Jewish calendar. Christ instituted the celebration on Passover day (Mark 14.12-26). In the Christian calendar the evening meal replaced the Jewish Passover. It is a yearly reminder of the sacrifice of the Lamb of God, held the same day his death occurred.

For similar historical reasons, it is observed after sundown. The Jewish day commenced at sundown: that was when the fourteenth of the month began. Jesus held it after sundown. It is a 'supper', and 'evening' meal (Mark 14.17; I Cor. 11.20, 21).

Jesus passed both unleavened bread and wine to his eleven faithful disciples (Judas apparently having been dismissed before the memorial meal began; compare John 13.26, 27, 30 with Matt. 26.23-25, 26). The wine would have fermented by the time of the spring festival.

Jesus said the meal was to be kept 'in remembrance of me'. He also connected it with two covenants. Those celebrating would be in the 'new covenant' (Luke 22.20). The old (law) covenant was for a 'kingdom of priests' (Ex. 19.6). Likewise, the new covenant is for a kingdom of priests (I Peter 2.9; Rev. 1.6). The other covenant Jesus mentioned was a covenant 'for a kingdom, that you may eat and drink at my table in my kingdom, and sit on thrones to judge the twelve tribes of Israel' (Luke 22.29, 30).

Interestingly, both these covenants had to do with a kingdom. Those entitled to partake of the emblems of bread and wine were those who would 'eat and drink at my table in my kingdom'. This could not include everyone; for these heavenly kings 'sit on thrones to judge' others. This kingdom of priests who 'rule as kings with the Christ for a thousand years' is limited in Rev. 14.1-3 to 144,000 persons. With Christ in his heavenly kingdom, they rule the rest of creation, including obedient mankind (Rev. 20.4-6; 21.2-4).

Thus, although 2,719,860 worldwide gathered with Jehovah's Witnesses on 14 Nisan 1969 at the Lord's evening meal, only 10,368 who felt they had the witness of the spirit that they would be joint heirs with Christ in his kingdom partook of the bread and wine passed to all. The remainder were respectful observers, remembering too that their everlasting life depended on Christ's ransom sacrifice, yet looking forward to being earthly subjects of the kingdom rather than heavenly kings and priests (Heb. 2.5).

The memorial takes the form of an explanatory discourse followed by passing the emblems to all present, with the invitation to those convinced of a heavenly hope to partake. The meeting lasts about one hour.

A. HELEY

9. *Lutheran*. At the time of the Reformation (1517-), liturgical reform among Lutherans had a twofold motivation: theological and didactic. There was no attempt to break the mould of Western Catholic tradition nor to return to liturgical practices of the primitive church. The inherited rites were judged theologically by the Reformation norm: justification by grace through faith. Neither the Roman canon nor offertory prayers were acceptable because their emphasis on sacrifice suggested that the mass is primarily man's service of God. Lutherans insisted on the opposite, that the mass is primarily God's work among men. The need to release people from medieval superstition and expose them to the teaching of the gospel was met by a strong emphasis on preaching and by the use of the vernacular in the liturgy. Preaching was accorded sacramental status as the living voice of the gospel: Christ present and active.

Martin Luther turned his hand to liturgical reform reluctantly, being forced by what he considered ill-advised attempts of others. Because of his prestige, his two major reforms of the mass were widely imitated. The first, *Formula missae et communionis* (*FM*, 1523), was a Latin rite which provided for vernacular hymns and sermon. Only minor changes were made in the *missa catechumenorum*. The

sermon might come either before the introit or following the creed. The excision of offertory and canon resulted in the following order for the *missa fidelium*: preface, words of institution (sung), *Sanctus* (with elevation), Our Father (omitting doxology), pax (interpreted as a public absolution), communion in both kinds (with *Agnus Dei*), collect, *Benedicamus* (replacing *Ite missa est*), Aaronic blessing (qq.v.). Compared with other Reformation rites the *FM* is conservative, but Luther cut out the heart of the medieval mass, i.e. the offertory and canon (q.v.).

Though he realized its inevitability, Luther took the step towards the vernacular with reservations. The Latin rite was imbedded in his piety and he loved its music dearly. He insisted that a German rite must be supplied with 'German music'; he viewed with horror attempts to fit the heavy accents of modern languages to the fluid grace of plainsong. But the pastoral need triumphed and the *Deutsche Messe* (*DM*) was published in 1526. (English versions of *FM* and *DM* are in *Luther's Works*, vol. 53, American edition, 1965. Original texts are in the Weimar edition: *FM*, vol. 12; *DM*, vol. 19.) It was designed especially for village churches and the unlettered majority. It was not intended to supplant the Latin mass in city churches or schools. (Portions of the Latin rite survived in parts of Germany into the eighteenth century.)

The basic structure of the *DM* is traditional though greatly simplified. The prose texts of the Ordinary were put in metrical paraphrase and assigned to the congregation. The popularity of this practice estranged large portions of Continental Lutheranism from the ancient mass texts. Again the *missa fidelium* is most altered: paraphrased Our Father, exhortation to communicants, words of institution and communion. There was an abortive attempt to divide the words of institution and distribute each element after its appropriate blessing. But the *DM* provided the people with a rite admirably suited to their needs and ability. The post-communion collect is one of Luther's finest prayers.

The Lutheran Reformation in Germany was scattered geographically. Since there was no unified church structure, there could be no liturgical equivalent of the *BCP*. Instead there was a proliferation of local *Kirchenordnungen*, most of whose liturgies were modelled after Luther. These church orders fall into two major groups: the Brandenburg-

Nürnberg type (*FM* as model) and the Bugenhagen type (*DM* as model) (original texts in E. Sehling, ed., *Die Evangelischen Kirchenordnungen des XVI. Jahrhunderts*, vols. 1-11). Johann Bugenhagen was one of Luther's emissaries to churches accepting the Reformation stance, and was responsible for the rites of many churches in Northern Germany and the Church of Denmark (1537). Liturgical development in Norway was tied to that in Denmark.

The Swedish liturgical tradition begins with the vernacular rite (1531) of Olavus Petri which follows the *FM* structure. The *Church Order* (1571) of Laurentius Petri was a revision which restored Latin texts in certain parts. After several abortive attempts at both left and right wing reform, the *Prayer Book* of 1614 was authorized. It followed the 1531 rite and established the *FM* tradition for the following three centuries.

By the eighteenth century, Lutherans were firmly established on the eastern seaboard of North America. Their worship reflected the languages and traditions of their various motherlands. But Henry Melchior Muhlenberg, patriarch of American Lutheranism, dreamed of the day when these groups could be united and have a common rite. Towards that end he produced a communion liturgy based upon several German models which was remarkable for its Reformation fullness. This German rite, together with English orders for baptism and marriage (from the *BCP*), constituted the first American liturgy. The first Lutheran communion service in English was not published until the mid-nineteenth century.

Generally, however, the eighteenth century was a time of liturgical decline affecting Lutheran churches everywhere. Pietism, with its anti-liturgical bias, and rationalism, which had little place for cultic action, took their toll. Liturgies were rationalized (employing deistic expressions), then psychologized as a passion for relevance set in. But by the mid-nineteenth century a neo-orthodox movement brought with it the glimmer of liturgical renewal. Wilhelm Löhe, a leader in establishing a female diaconate in the Bavarian church, joined other voices calling for a churchly and sacramental revival which would return the church to its own rich tradition. Because of his connection with mission pastors on the American frontier for whom he prepared a liturgy, Löhe's work was

more directly influential there than in Germany.

The ecumenical Liturgical Movement (q.v.) of the late nineteenth and early twentieth centuries resulted in various 'high church movements' throughout Lutheranism. But its enduring contribution was to stimulate a recovery of pre-eighteenth-century fullness. The various national and provincial churches on the Continent produced service-books which re-established contact with their own Reformation traditions. Several groups in the USA began work on a Common Service which would exemplify the consensus of the 'best liturgies of the sixteenth century'. This service appeared in 1888 and with musical setting formed the nucleus of the complete *Common Service Book* (with hymnal) of 1917. Subsequently the Common Service was incorporated into other North American service-books and became the common rite for a majority of English-speaking Lutherans.

As a result of earlier development and the impetus of the Second World War, the postwar years were marked by greater Lutheran unification and inter-Lutheran co-operation. *The Liturgy of the Church of Sweden* had already appeared in 1942. 1955 saw the publication of *Agenda I* for the Lutheran Churches of Germany. *The Service Book and Hymnal* for about two-thirds of the Lutherans in North America appeared in 1958. Australian Lutherans brought out their *Orders of Service* in 1966, and in 1970 the *High Mass* for the Church of Norway was published. These books mark the culmination of a long period of recovery of the Reformation tradition. They also symbolize the high degree of uniformity within major geographical areas and among them.

Without its having been imposed by ecclesiastical authority, and allowing for different linguistic traditions, world Lutheranism has achieved a remarkable liturgical unity. It is, of course, only part of a larger unity observable throughout Western Christianity. The newer Swedish, German, American and Norwegian rites all include eucharistic prayers, thus showing an openness to Western Catholic tradition antedating the Reformation.

Lutheran participation in the various ecumenical agencies has opened lines of communication with liturgical commissions of other bodies. The increased ecumenical co-operation in liturgical revision growing out of Vatican II has caused the Liturgical Movement to round a corner. Rapid cultural change has opened a wide gap between church and society and dramatized the need for new approaches.

Having reclaimed their liturgical identity, Lutherans are now prepared to step forward creatively beyond their own tradition. A provisional order for holy communion published by the Inter-Lutheran Commission on Worship (North America) in 1970 is one of the first official products of the new mood. In its relocation of corporate confession, abbreviated entrance rite, fuller offertory section, and expanded eucharistic prayer, it departs from the tradition of the sixteenth-century church orders and exhibits similarities to work being done by other Christian churches. This is shown not only in its structure but also in its use of common texts prepared by the International Consultation on English Texts.

EUGENE BRAND

10. *Methodist.* Methodist communion liturgies are based on John Wesley's revision of the 1662 *BCP* rite as published in his *Sunday Service of the Methodists in North America* in 1784. As Wesley said, it was 'a liturgy little differing from that of the church of England'. Wesley is correct in saying that he made 'little alteration' in the book as a whole and especially with regard to the communion service. Most of the holy days were omitted, the word 'priest' was translated as 'elder' throughout, and the pronouns of the prayer of absolution changed from 'you' to 'us'. Service music was not expected and it was indicated that the *Gloria in excelsis* and the *Sanctus* were to be recited. Wesley expected that hymns would be sung and he and his brother, Charles, wrote 165 eucharistic hymns. A few changes were made in the rubrics, while the Nicene Creed, exhortations, and second post-communion prayer were dropped. One collect for the king was eliminated and the other changed to pray for 'the Supreme Rulers of these United States'. Only one word was omitted in the prayer of consecration, a redundant 'one'. Before the final blessing a significant new rubric appeared: 'Then the Elder, if he see it expedient, may put up an Extempore Prayer'.

Wesley, it soon proved, was a poor judge of the 'poor sheep in the wilderness' to whom the *Sunday Service* was directed. The year after his death in 1791 his book was drastically

abbreviated to thirty-seven pages of 'Sacramental Services, &c.' in the 1792 *Discipline*. The men of the frontier had little learning and less love of what seemed to them overly formal types of worship. 'The Order for the Administration of the Lord's Supper' was drastically abbreviated, the whole synaxis disappeared along with the prayer for the church, the comfortable words, the *Sursum corda*, and all proper prefaces. The collect for purity took the place formerly held by the *Sursum corda*. It was even provided that 'if the elder be straitened for time, he may omit any part of the service except the prayer of Consecration'. Actually, the Lord's Supper usually followed a preaching service hence a service of the word could be presumed. And few words in the eucharistic portion had been changed, perhaps none of theological significance.

Only small changes were made in the next half century. In 1844 the Methodist Episcopal Church underwent a major split on the question of slavery, the Methodist Episcopal Church, South, and the Methodist Episcopal Church emerging. An earlier split had produced the Methodist Protestant Church in 1830 which published a communion service in 1831, a curiously scrambled version of the 1792 service. Changes in the communion service appeared in the *Discipline*, published every four years by each of the three main branches of Methodism.

The most important of these changes are mentioned here. The Southern Church remained the most conservative and made minor changes, none of great theological consequence, from what was left of the 1662 *BCP* rite. The Methodist Episcopal Church was less reluctant to change. Many minor changes appeared, especially in 1864 and 1916. The invention of pasteurized grape juice and the temperance movement became apparent in 1876 when 'unfermented juice of the grape' was first recommended in the rubrics (wine had always been used previously). The most important changes occurred in 1932 when a synaxis was recovered. The liberal theology of the time made some radical changes in the prayer of consecration and the prayer of humble access. With the reunion of Methodism in 1939 both the then current Northern and Southern services appeared in *The Methodist Hymnal*, though liturgically and theologically they had become distinct; the Northern service was more traditional liturgically and the Southern more traditional theologically. Both services were in the first (1944) *Book of Worship*.

A major revision occurred in the 1964 *Book of Worship*, currently in use by the United Methodist Church. It is essentially a revision within the Anglican-Methodist tradition. In a sense it returns to the 1549 *BCP* rite, removing some of the quirks of 1552 by eliminating the Decalogue, restoring the *Gloria in excelsis* to a position at the beginning of the rite, and recovering the *Agnus Dei*. Some of the other changes move in the direction of making the service of the word similar to that used in many Methodist churches when the sacrament is not celebrated. Hence the intercessions precede the lections, the Lord's Prayer comes at the beginning of the service, and the creed precedes the sermon. Compromises have been made in the theological language with regard to the presence of Christ in the sacrament. For better or for worse, the service was completed and published just before the new emphasis on contemporary language came to the fore and so sixteenth-century words and phrases dominate. The outline of the service is: prelude, hymn, scripture sentences, salutation, collect for purity, Lord's Prayer, *Gloria in excelsis*, invitation, general confession, prayer for pardon, comfortable words, prayer for the church, epistle, anthem or hymn, gospel, creed and sermon. After the sermon come notices, hymn, offertory, prayer of dedication, *Sursum corda*, preface, *Sanctus*, prayer of consecration, prayer of humble access, *Agnus Dei*, communion of clergy, communion of people, peace, post-communion prayer, hymn, blessing and postlude.

In 1972 the Commission on Worship published an alternative text, 'The Sacrament of the Lord's Supper'. It is in contemporary language and is not simply a revision of Cranmer but an attempt to follow classical and universal patterns.

The communion rites of the black churches have been among the more conservative. The African Methodist Episcopal Church and the Christian Methodist Episcopal Church have retained essentially the 1792 service. Both also contain rubrics for the benefit of those who have scruples about kneeling, similar to those the two large white churches introduced during the nineteenth century but later removed.

In Britain, Wesley's *Sunday Service* went through various editions till the twentieth century. Other service-books appeared as well. The *Book of Offices* of 1936 contains collects, epistles, and gospels for the church year and two orders of service 'For the Administration of the Lord's Supper; or, The Holy Communion'. The first of these is very similar to the 1662 *BCP* rite minus a few rubrics, exhortations, and collects. The second is shorter and has some of the same material rearranged, placing the words of institution after the prayer of humble access.

More recently (1969) a new *Sunday Service* has been published which makes provision for morning worship with or without the sacrament. It represents some major improvements over preceding liturgies, envisioning a wider horizon of revision than simply the Anglican-Methodist pattern. The location of the Nicene Creed between the peace and the offertory is distinctive. The eucharistic prayer contains new items such as a greatly expanded common preface, *Benedictus qui venit*, epiclesis, a distinct oblation, and acclamations of the people. It is followed by a fraction, and after the communion are a new and brief post-communion prayer and a dismissal. In many ways the service is a major step to more ancient and ecumenical forms, a most appropriate move in the present age. Both 'thee' and 'you' forms are published for portions of the service. How long it will be necessary to hop thus on both legs remains to be seen.

JAMES F. WHITE

11. *Old Catholic*. In the Old Catholic churches of the Utrecht Union, the celebration of the eucharist stands at the centre of liturgical life. Alongside that, however, the greatest emphasis is also placed on the proclamation of the word of God in the reading of scripture and in preaching. The celebration of the mass must therefore be supported by the two pillars of the service of the word of God and the liturgy of the sacrament.

In the Old Catholic churches, the whole service has for a long time (in some cases for almost a hundred years) been celebrated in the vernacular. Some of these churches have been content with an accurate translation of the Latin text with very few deviations; this has been the case in the Netherlands and in the Polish National Catholic Church in the USA and in Poland. Elsewhere, however, the Roman model has been treated with rather more freedom, and this has led to some theologically significant alterations; this has been the case above all in Switzerland, but the same thing has also happened in Germany and Austria. Nevertheless, even here the structure of the Roman mass remains clearly recognizable. It should be noted that the basis for the Old Catholic forms of mass is the *Missale Romanum* in its old form, as laid down by Pius V in 1570, and not the liturgy as revised after Vatican II. It can be seen, however, that some alterations were made to Old Catholic liturgies at an early stage which have only been introduced in the Roman Catholic church in the last few years (for the texts and books used today for celebrating mass in the Old Catholic churches *see* **Books, Liturgical** 11 : Old Catholic).

New ways of structuring the liturgy are still being investigated in the Old Catholic churches today. The Old Catholics of Germany received a new missal in 1959. In Austria and Switzerland, attempts are being made with new formulae, especially for the canon of the mass. Even in the Church of the Netherlands, which until recently has been very conservative in liturgical matters, an experiment is now under way with a new 'second order of the mass'.

It is impossible here to indicate all the differences and peculiarities of the Old Catholic liturgies. The following are the most important points:

Service of the Word of God. In the German and Swiss liturgies the selection of biblical readings has been considerably increased. In Switzerland there are now three readings (OT, epistle and gospel) for each mass in a three-year cycle; in Germany there are two (OT or epistle and gospel) in a four-year cycle.

Creed. The Western addition *filioque* is omitted, with particular concern for the close relationships with the Orthodox church.

Prayer of the Faithful. As in the revised Roman liturgy, the general intercessions, which had vanished from the Roman mass on every day except Good Friday, have been restored before the offertory.

Offertory. The prayers of the old Roman missal imply an anticipation of the epiclesis (q.v.) and consecration, elements which only belong in the canon. Even the notion of an offering of the as yet unconsecrated gifts ('*Suscipe . . . hanc immaculatam hostiam, quam . . . offero tibi*') is rejected. The offertory prayers are therefore rightly limited, in one

part of the Old Catholic liturgies, to the notions of the preparation of the gifts and thanksgiving.

Prefaces. The number of variable prefaces (q.v.) has been considerably increased in Old Catholic missals. The Altar Book of the Old Catholic Church of Germany (1959) contains 19 prefaces (Netherland 15, Austria 14).

Canon. The link between the *Sanctus* and the canon in Austria (second order) and in the Swiss outline of 1971 is made by a *Vere. Sanctus* prayer on the Gallican pattern, as in the second and third formulations of the eucharistic prayer in the Roman *Ordo Missae* of 1969.

It is in the Swiss liturgy that the canon has undergone the most significant transformation. Whereas in the Roman canon the account of the institution occupies the central place, here it is brought quite close to the beginning. The words of institution are followed by the anamnesis (q.v.) and the 'sacrificial prayer' (*Unde et memores*) which closes with a petition for a blessed communion (*Supplices te rogamus*). The 'remembrance of the saints' (*Communicantes*), the prayer for the dead (*Memento etiam*) and for the living (*Memento, Domine*) are brought together into a group.

In the Swiss canon, all expressions are avoided which might suggest that the eucharistic sacrifice was a repetition of the sacrifice of the cross or an offering by the priest. On the other hand, the position of Christ as the one high priest is strongly stressed (*see* Bishop Herzog in *IKZ*, 1911, pp. 340ff. and Küry, *Die altkatholische Kirche*, pp. 190-200).

Epiclesis. The Swiss liturgy has an explicit invocation of the Holy Spirit, *before* the institution, as in some of the oldest Egyptian liturgies and in the new texts of the Roman canon. This has partially been taken over into the German liturgy (first order) and the Austrian missal of 1933. On the other hand, in the second Austrian order and the second experimental Swiss order of 1971, the epiclesis follows the account of the institution as in present-day Eastern liturgies. This is also the case in the 'second order' of the Church of the Netherlands, which closely follows the eucharistic prayer of Hippolytus.

Lord's Prayer. In missals in German and French, the Lord's Prayer now appears in the agreed ecumenical text, which also contains the doxology as in the Anglican order of the holy communion.

Breaking of the Bread. According to the German rite of 1959 (second order), this takes place during the singing of the *Agnus Dei.* Instead of the usual sequence of Lord's Prayer, breaking of the bread, kiss of peace, *Agnus Dei*, we have here *Agnus Dei* with breaking of the bread, kiss of peace, Lord's Prayer.

Communion. Whereas earlier the faithful only received communion on a few days in the year, it is now usually given at every mass and indeed in both forms, sometimes also by intinction.

KURT PURSCH
A. E. RÜTHY
C. TOL

12. *Pentecostal.* In open-air meetings, in worship and evangelistic services, classical Pentecostalism follows the pattern of different Protestant traditions (for Neo-Pentecostalism *see* **Pentecostal Worship**). In certain North American Pentecostal denominations, written liturgies have been developed along Protestant lines. Yet the most interesting liturgies in Pentecostalism are those of the eucharistic service, which is celebrated in British Pentecostal churches usually once a week, and in most of the other Pentecostal churches once a month. The eucharistic service has created some difficult problems for Pentecostals. Donald Gee (1891-1966), a British Pentecostal leader, warns against those Pentecostals who want the eucharist to be wholly unstructured. The result of this, he says, 'is to produce meetings so stereotyped that, for all their boasted freedom, they become more barren than the very liturgical services they deprecate – and with less aesthetic appeal' (*Study Hour* 5/2, 15 February 1946, p. 2).

How is the problem solved? On the one hand a minority of Pentecostal churches use written liturgies as indicated above. In the majority of Pentecostal churches, on the other hand, an 'oral liturgy' is followed which consists of the classical liturgical elements: invocation, *Kyrie*, confession, *Gloria in excelsis*, eucharistic canon and blessing (qq.v.). Yet these parts are never so named and for most observers not recognizable as such, since the elements which structure the different parts of the service are the so-called choruses, i.e. short spontaneous songs, known by heart by the whole congregation. Some of the key choruses indicate the transition from one part of the service to the next. They are intoned either by the minister (*see* **Ordination** 14: Pentecostalist) or by members of the congregation. Key choruses vary from one congregation to another, yet everyone in the congregation understands them as signals. During the time of participation of the whole congregation, if someone sings a song of praise in the *Kyrie* part, or gives a prophecy in the invocation part, he will be corrected either by the pastor, or by an elder, or if he persists, by the immediate and spontaneous singing of the whole congregation. Most Pentecostals are not aware of the liturgical function of these choruses, yet they are clearly observable. The Pentecostals thus demonstrate that the alternative to a written liturgy is not chaos, but a flexible oral tradition, which allows for variation within the framework of the whole liturgical structure, similar to the possibilities of variation in a jam session of jazz musicians (*see* **Spirituals**). For bibliography *see under* **Pentecostal Worship**.

W. J. HOLLENWEGER

13. *Plymouth Brethren.* The Brethren's most distinctive meeting is the communion service normally held every Sunday morning. The communion table is frequently placed in the centre, with the congregation seated in rows round three or four sides of it; where it is not convenient to rearrange the seating, the table will be left in front.

The first part of the service is devoted to suitable hymns, prayers of thanksgiving and scripture readings, introduced or carried through by various members. Then the thanksgiving for the bread is followed by its distribution from hand to hand, each communicant breaking off a small piece and eating it. (The bread is usually an entire loaf, which may be broken in two before distribution.) The thanksgiving for the cup is followed by the passing of the common cup from hand to hand, each communicant drinking a little from it. The wine may be fermented or unfermented according to local preference. It is normally senior members of the church who give thanks for the bread and the cup. In the Exclusive tradition the same brother will give thanks for both elements on any one occasion, breaking the bread in two and pouring the wine into the cup before distribution. The practice of Open Brethren is more variable. Open Brethren customarily welcome all Christians present to communicate, in accordance with the Brethren's original policy.

The communion is followed either immediately or after some further exercises by the offering. Those who regard the offering as an integral part of the worship take it up in close proximity to the eucharist.

In many places the eucharist is followed by a short period of expository ministry; elsewhere this may be given in a separate service preceding the communion service.

Among Exclusive Brethren of the late James Taylor's connection the liturgy is much more uniform. R. C. Walls, writing in *Theology* 60 (1957), pp. 265 f.: 'A Visit to the Brethren – A Lesson in Liturgy', indicates the Trinitarian sequence which would have been followed at that time in almost any of their assemblies throughout the world on any Sunday morning. An introductory hymn to the Holy Spirit was followed by a prayer of thanksgiving addressed to him and a lesson from Ephesians. The Son then became the focus of devotion in the eucharist, which was accompanied by a long anamnesis (q.v.) or thanksgiving for his person and work from his incarnation through his passion, triumph and present high-priestly ministry and abiding presence to his parousia. This part of the service was concluded with a hymn of praise to the Son and a reading from the gospels. Then the worshippers claimed access to the Father, to whom a hymn of praise was sung, and after further devotions and silent intervals the service ended with a hymn to the Trinity. (A more recent development has moved the eucharist right to the beginning of the service.)   F. F. BRUCE

14. *Reformed.* Although the Reformed churches have been accused of neglecting the eucharist, their liturgies all stress its importance. The Reformers were unanimous in their aim to provide liturgies suitable to the new views on religion. Thus Zwingli produced two books entitled *De Canone Missae Epicheiresis* (1523) and *Action oder Bruch des Nachtmals* (1525). These were derived from the mass, but with all accretions removed. He provided separate orders for the ordinary preaching service without communion, and for the eucharist, which he regarded as another form of preaching. The order of the eucharist is simple – exhortation and fencing of the table, Lord's prayer,

prayer of humble access, the words of institution, fraction, communion first of the ministers and then of the people, a psalm (said, not sung), post-communion prayer and dismissal. There is no consecration prayer and no intercession. Celebration was only four times in the year. This rite had little influence on later developments.

Another rite with little influence was Farel's *La manyere et fasson* (Neuchâtel, 1533), the first liturgy of the Reformed churches. The eucharist contains a long exhortation, Lord's Prayer, Apostles' Creed, institution narrative, the communion of all, post-communion prayer and dismissal.

The rite of John Calvin, *La forme des prières* (1542), was of much greater importance. It was derived from the Strasbourg Reformed German rite of Diebold Schwartz, which was derived from the mass. It was greatly simplified through the influence of Bucer. For Calvin the correct procedure was a preaching service followed by the eucharist. The full order was as follows: scripture sentence, confession of sins, metrical psalm (sung), prayer for illumination, lesson, sermon; intercessions, Lord's Prayer (an uninspiring paraphrase), preparation of elements, Apostles' Creed, words of institution, exhortation, consecration prayer, fraction and delivery (during communion, psalm sung or read or scripture lesson), read post-communion prayer, Aaronic blessing.

This form was somewhat bare, but Calvin was prevented from carrying out all his desires. Thus he regarded weekly communion as scriptural, and therefore essential, but the Genevan magistrates allowed it only quarterly. However, the form has had great influence on all succeeding Reformed liturgies. Of these there were many varieties in the Reformed Churches in Switzerland, France, Holland and elsewhere. From time to time suggestions for revision were made, and of these two may be noticed.

In 1713, Jean-Frédéric Osterwald published a liturgy. He had already expressed an aversion from Calvinism and his good opinion of Anglicanism, but his proposals, influenced by these feelings, were too radical for general acceptance. The revision proposals of Eugène Bersier (1874) had more influence. He desired to give the eucharist 'the central place which is its due in Christian worship' and thus to 'return to the true primitive teaching of our Reformed Church'.

The eucharist was to follow (as if not an essential part of) the morning service. The minister, after dismissing those who were not to communicate, descends from the pulpit and, standing before the table, addresses the people who group themselves as near the table as possible. Then he goes behind the table, uncovers the bread and wine, and prays. *Sursum corda* and the consecration prayer follow. 'It is verily right, just and salutary . . .' The prayer includes *Sanctus* and *Hosanna* and words suited to the season of the Christian year. There is an epiclesis, followed by the words of institution, fraction, Lord's prayer, the distribution, thanksgiving and dismissal. Much of this has been found acceptable in France, and the liturgy of 1958 follows many points of this form. The consecration prayer includes thanksgiving, *Sanctus*, epiclesis, Lord's Prayer, Apostles' Creed, words of institution, followed by communion, thanksgiving and blessing. A revision of 1963 has a new eucharistic prayer, which shows some dependence on the liturgy of the church of South India.

The Reformed rites of some other countries have been of interest. Several of the Swiss cantons, such as Vaud (1940), Geneva (1946) and Bern (1955), have issued revised liturgies, influenced both by the earlier Reformed rites and by the classic forms. In Germany and Holland there has been much liturgical work. The two Dutch groups, *Liturgische Kring* and *Kring Eeredienst*, have been specially active, and the *Kanselboek* (1949) and *Dienstboek* (1955) express concern for congregational participation in responses and allow many alternatives.

The Genevan rite of 1556, known as *John Knox's Genevan Service Book*, was the first Reformed rite in English. It was adopted, with only slight changes, by the Church of Scotland in 1562 under the title, *The Forme of Prayers and Ministration of the Sacrament*. In 1564 it became *The Form of Prayers or Book of Common Order*, but with some additions, especially in the completion of the metrical psalter. The full eucharistic order here was as follows: confession of sins and prayer for pardon, metrical psalm, prayer for illumination, lesson, sermon, thanksgiving and intercession, Lord's Prayer, Apostles' Creed, offertory, words of institution (i.e., the warrant), exhortation, consecration prayer (including adoration, thanksgiving for creation and redemption, anamnesis and dox-

ology), fraction and delivery (minister's communion followed by the people's), post-communion thanksgiving, Ps. 103, Aaronic or apostolic blessing. This form lacks an epiclesis, but contemporary evidence shows that one was included in the consecration and was regarded by many as essential. This form remained generally in Scottish use from 1564, many editions being published. Some editions were printed in England or on the Continent for the use of English Puritans. *The Book of Common Order* was superseded by the Westminster *Directory* in 1645.

The *Directory*, as a compromise between the Independents and the Scottish and English Presbyterians, was rather unsatisfactory, but it remained and indeed still remains an authority for public worship. There are no prayers, but only lists of subjects for prayer. The eucharistic order is little changed, but an epiclesis is now prescribed. During the eighteenth century the standard of worship in Scotland, as elsewhere, fell very low, with the loss of the creed, Lord's prayer, *Gloria Patri*, and the people's amen.

By the opening of the nineteenth century some clergy had begun to publish books of their own. In 1867 the Church Service Society was formed, and before long produced a service book with the title *Euchologion*, many editions of which appeared. The eucharist here followed the preaching rite for the morning service, the order of which was influenced by *BCP* mattins, with an exhortation (following the prayer after the sermon), the institution warrant, an address on the significance of the sacrament, Nicene Creed, *Agnus Dei*, prayer of the veil, *Sursum corda*, the consecration prayer including thanksgiving for the divine gifts, anamnesis, *Sanctus*, epiclesis, Lord's prayer, fraction, distribution, pax, exhortation, prayer of thanksgiving and self-dedication, intercession for the church, thanksgiving for the church triumphant, hymn, benediction.

Prayers for Divine Service (1923), issued by the Church of Scotland, largely followed *Euchologion*, but a second edition (1929) supplied two eucharistic forms, the additional one being a shortened form with the intercessions in the post-communion prayer. The United Free Church of Scotland issued *The Book of Common Order*, 1928, which was rather less liturgical but of a high standard. Both of these were influential on the next to be noted.

The Book of Common Order (1940), the authorized book of the reunited Church of Scotland, as revised in 1952, contains five orders for the eucharist. The first is regarded as the regular form; the second is slightly shortened; the third is for use at a second table where communicants receive elements previously consecrated; the fourth is an alternative with slightly different order and less liturgical in tone; the fifth is a short order for use in communicating the sick or where a very short order is desirable. These mostly follow the pattern of *Prayers for Divine Service*. The intercessions are in the 'Liturgy of the Word', with which, however, the 'Liturgy of the Faithful' is continuous. This has the offertory, invitation with comfortable words, psalm (while the elements are brought forward), Nicene Creed, unveiling of elements, the offertory prayer, warrant, salutation and *Sursum corda*, prayer of consecration (including preface and prayer for the season, *Sanctus* with *Benedictus qui venit* and *Hosanna*, thanksgiving for redemption, anamnesis, epiclesis, oblation, brief intercession and doxology), Lord's Prayer, words of institution with fraction, *Agnus Dei*, celebrant's communion, people's communion, pax, post-communion thanksgiving and commemoration of the departed, psalm (usually 103.1-5) or hymn, benediction. This service is now being revised and will probably allow for the words of institution to be included in the consecration prayer and the omission of the warrant, and the addition of *Gloria in Excelsis*.

This book has had wide influence on other Presbyterian service-books, as those of England, Wales, Ireland, Canada, Australia and elsewhere. Most of these books have been revised, in some cases more than once.

In the USA there has been much liturgical activity of late. The recent *Worship-book* (Philadelphia, 1970), prepared by a joint committee of three Presbyterian churches, employs 'the straightforward use of words and language in current contemporary use', and therefore the words of some new translations have been employed for scriptural quotations. The book opens with the only form for the eucharist. The 'Liturgy of the Word' includes confession of sin and declaration of pardon, prayer for illumination, lessons, sermon with ascription, Nicene Creed (using 'we'). The 'Liturgy of the Faithful' includes intercessions, pax, the offering, in-

vitation to the table, thanksgiving (with *Sursum corda*, the seasonal preface, *Tersanctus*, Lord's Prayer), fraction, distribution, post-communion prayer, hymn, benediction.

All Presbyterian books are for voluntary use, and even where used there are many variations due to the ideas of individual ministers. In many places books are not used at all, but there is in general a growing sense of the importance of the eucharistic liturgy. This is evidenced by, among other things, the appointment by many Reformed churches of committees with instructions to prepare forms for specific purposes for submission to the assemblies or other governing bodies. Some churches have standing committees, charged with the study of forms of worship and at times with the preparations of specific forms, eucharistic or otherwise. This is becoming so widespread in the churches that on many points ecumenical discussion is required, often with excellent results.

J. A. LAMB

15. *Seventh-day Adventist (Communion Service)*. In the Seventh-day Adventist Church the communion service includes the ordinance of foot-washing or humility and the Lord's Supper. Adventists believe that in washing his disciples' feet Christ instituted a consecrated ordinance, a religious service with a promise of blessedness (John 13.14-17). It is a memorial of Christ's act of self-abasement and a symbol or type of higher cleansing. Like early church fathers such as Origen, pioneer Adventists considered foot-washing a spiritual experience and a symbol of humility. It was sometimes referred to as Christ's 'least commandment' (*Day-Star*, 7.8, 18 August 1845). While baptism is a symbol of justification once and for all, the daily experience of sanctification is represented by foot-washing. 'This ordinance is Christ's appointed preparation for the sacramental service' (E. G. White, *The Desire of Ages*, p. 650). For this reason Adventists often call this ordinance the 'preparatory service'. It is a time for self-examination, confession of sin and reconciling of differences. Two emblems are used: water, symbol of cleansing, and towel, symbol of service. Some regard the ordinance of humility as a 'miniature baptism' (*see* John 13.10).

Adventist churches have a communion table, not an altar (qq.v.). The Lord's Supper is not a mystery but a memorial, not a sacrifice but a sacred service. Its theme is salvation through the sacrifice of Christ on Calvary. It is a memorial of the deliverance from the power of sin and as such is a continual reminder of the atonement. It also has an eschatological orientation pointing forward to the parousia and is designed to keep this hope vivid (Matt. 26.29; I Cor. 11.26).

Adventists believe in the real spiritual presence of Christ at the supper, but not in the elements as such. 'As faith contemplates our Lord's great sacrifice, the soul assimilates the spiritual life of Christ . . . The Service forms a living connection by which the believer is bound up with Christ' (White, op.cit., p. 661).

In most Adventist churches the communion service is held once a quarter. In early Adventist history the Lord's Supper was a regular part of the 'quarterly meeting'. While other aspects of this meeting have largely faded away, communion is still sometimes called in Adventist parlance the 'quarterly service'.

The opening service may be as usual for divine worship, but the sermon is limited to 10-15 minutes and deals with some aspect of the communion service. The congregation then separates for the ordinance of humility, the men in one place and the women in another. Hymns may occasionally be sung during its progress.

After the foot-washing, the congregation reassembles for the Lord's Supper. The minister and elder (or elders) take their places by the table on which the deaconesses have previously placed the unleavened bread and unfermented wine, covered by a white linen cloth (see I Cor. 5.7,8). After a hymn the minister (in some churches the deaconesses) removes and folds the linen covering. Then he reads I Cor. 11.23,24 or a parallel passage from the gospels, after which the blessing of God is asked on the emblem of the bread, representing the body of Christ, while the whole congregation kneels (in some churches only the officiating minister and elders kneel, while the congregation remains seated with bowed heads). Following the breaking of the bread by the officiating minister, the deacons serve the congregation and, after returning, the minister serves them; then in turn one of the deacons, taking the plate, serves the minister. All are seated and silent prayer is offered while they partake of the bread together.

The minister then reads I Cor. 11.25,26 or a similar passage from the gospels. The blessing is asked on the emblem of the wine, representing the shed blood of Christ, and the deacons serve the congregation following a similar procedure as with the bread. For health reasons the recommended and prevailing practice in Seventh-day Adventist churches is to use small, individual communion cups.

The remaining emblems are recovered and after the service the deaconesses clear the table and the deacons dispose of any bread or wine left over, by burning the bread and pouring out the wine.

In the Seventh-day Adventist Church only ordained ministers or ordained local church elders may conduct the communion service. Adventists practise 'open communion', believing that Christ's own example forbids exclusiveness at his table (see Matt. 26.21-25).

B. B. BEACH

K. Amon, 'Das eucharistische Hochgebet in den altkatholischen Kirchen des deutschen Sprachgebiets', Liturgisches Jahrbuch 18, 1968; A Baumstark, Comparative Liturgy, 1958; F. E. Brightman, Liturgies Eastern and Western, 1896; Yngve Brilioth, Eucharistic Faith and Practice, 1930; R. Bruinsma, 'Christ's Commandment of Humility', The Ministry, July 1966, pp. 24-6 (Seventh-day Adventist); C. O. Buchanan, ed., Modern Anglican Liturgies 1958-68, 1968 (a successor to Liturgy in English containing texts subsequent to 1960); R. H. Connolly, The Liturgical Homilies of Narsai, 1909; A. C. Couratin, The Service of Holy Communion 1549-1662, 1963 (a brief but penetrating review of the controlling motives in each successive revision); J. D. Crichton, The Church's Worship. Considerations on the Liturgical Constitution of the Second Vatican Council, 1964; G. J. Cuming, A History of Anglican Liturgy, 1969 (a definitive and authoritative history from 1500 to 1966); G. Dix, The Shape of the Liturgy, [2]1945; Paul Graff, Geschichte des Auflösung der alten gottesdienstlichen Formen in der Evangelischen Kirche Deutschlands, 2 vols. 1921, 1939; A. Hänggi and I. Pahl, Prex Eucharistica, 1968; J. Jungmann, The Mass of the Roman Rite, 2 vols., 1951-55; T. Klauser, A Short History of the Western Liturgy, 1969; U. Küry, Die altkatholische Kirche (Kirchen der Welt, Band III), 1966; M. Luther, 'Liturgy and Hymns', Works, American ed., vol. 53, 1965; Manual for Ministers (Seventh-day Adventist), 1965; G. A. Michell, *Landmarks in Liturgy*, 1961 (a liturgical and theological analysis of each part of the rite in turn, tracing its development from Apostolic times to 1662); C. F. D. Moule, *The Worship of the New Testament*, 1961; Don. F. Neufeld, ed., 'Lord's Supper', 'Foot Washing', *Seventh-day Adventist Encyclopedia*, 1966, pp. 414-6, 720-2; Ernest A. Payne and Stephen F. Winward, *Orders and Prayers for Church Worship*, 1960 (Baptist); N. F. Pease, *And Worship Him*, 1967, pp. 76-8 (Seventh-day Adventist); K. Pursch, 'Das Opfermahl und die Neuordnung seiner Gestalt', *IKZ* 46, 1956; K. Pursch, 'Die Probleme des Offertoriums und Versuche zu ihrer Lösung', *IKZ* 46, 1956; Luther D. Reed, *The Lutheran Liturgy*, rev. ed., 1959; A. E. Rüthy, 'Bemerkingen und Erwägungen zu den altkatholischen Liturgien', a series of articles in *IKZ* 47-60, 1957-70; S. Salaville, *Introduction to the Study of Eastern Liturgies*, 1938; Emil Sehling, ed., *Die Evangelischen Kirchenordnungen des 16. Jahrhunderts*, vols. 1-5, 1902-1913; vols. 6 and 11, 1955-1961; *Seventh-day Adventist Church Manual*, 1967, pp. 115-21; L. Sheppard, ed., *True Worship*, 1963; John E. Skoglund, *A Manual of Worship*, 1968 (Baptist); J. H. Srawley, *The Early History of the Liturgy*, 1947; E. G. White, *The Desire of Ages*, 1946, pp. 642-61 (Seventh-day Adventist); B. J. Wigan, ed., *Liturgy in English*, 1964 (this contains virtually all Anglican eucharistic texts from 1549 to 1960); L. Winterswyl, 'Das eucharistische Hochgebet der altkatholischen Liturgien', *IKZ* 24, 1934.

F. F. BRUCE

Local Preacher

An office (open to both men and women in the Methodist Church) instituted by John Wesley to provide, as the name implies, a local ministry to supplement that of the few itinerant ordained clergymen who joined his movement initially. The ministry is a 'part-time' one, being exercised normally by a layman with a secular job. A local preacher regularly conducts Sunday worship and appears on the preaching plan. He does not normally celebrate the eucharist, though there are cases where a layman may be specially authorized by Conference to do so if a congregation might otherwise be almost totally deprived of the sacrament. Baptism may also be administered by a local preacher or other layman in very exceptional circumstances.   P. HINCHLIFF

Lord's Prayer

Not surprisingly, the Lord's Prayer has come to be used universally and frequently in liturgical worship. It was not always so, however; its use at the eucharist, for example, does not antedate the middle of the fourth century at the earliest, being first clearly attested in the *Mystagogical Catecheses* of Cyril of Jerusalem. From John Chrysostom onwards, liturgical commentators in the East witness to its use after the eucharistic prayer as a preparation for communion; Augustine and Ambrose presuppose its use at the same place and for the same purpose in the West at about the same time. Since about 400 it has been so used in all the historic liturgies, and in many others as well; it is only in some of the post-Reformation Protestant rites that it has been removed from this position and function, and placed elsewhere. Early commentators stress its suitability for this purpose, laying emphasis on the petitions for the forgiveness of sins and, above all, for daily – or, rather, arguing from the alternative reading, heavenly – bread: Ambrose advocates frequent communion on the ground of the relationship between the two texts.

In most of the historic rites the Lord's Prayer is placed after the breaking of the bread which follows the eucharistic prayer; in the two most widespread of them, however, the Roman and the Byzantine, it precedes the breaking of the bread, the Roman usage in this respect being probably a Byzantine importation.

The use of the Lord's Prayer in a quasi-liturgical context outside the eucharistic liturgy probably antedates its use in the latter; certain early writers prescribe it as the essential prayer to be used by the faithful at set hours of prayer. Its use in the divine office, which is universal in the historic rites as well as in most of the post-Reformation liturgies, presumably originates in this prescription.

J. A. Jungmann, *The Mass of the Roman Rite*, II, 1955, pp. 277-93.

W. JARDINE GRISBROOKE

Lord's Supper

1. This title was used in the patristic period of the Last Supper, e.g. by Hippolytus.

2. It was also employed by Paul (I Cor. 11.20) of the central act of Christian worship, which when he was writing would appear to have consisted of a repetition of the Last

Supper in its entirety, i.e. blessing, breaking and distribution of bread, followed by a meal and concluded with the blessing and distribution of wine.

3. In the fourth century, it was the practice on Maundy Thursday (q.v.), in commemoration of the institution of the sacrament on that day, to combine the agape or love feast (q.v.) with the eucharist, and this, too, was known as the Lord's Supper.

4. The separation of eucharist and agape and the discontinuance of the latter led to the title Lord's Supper being applied to the sacrament alone. This use was widespread in the Middle Ages and the Catechism of Trent endorsed it. The Reformers favoured the title because of its scriptural basis and so, e.g. in the 1549 *BCP*, the service is headed: 'The Supper of the Lorde and the Holy Communion, commonly called the Masse'.

EDITOR

Love Feast

There is little doubt that a common meal with at least semi-liturgical features was regularly held by Christians shortly after the death of Jesus, or that it combined observances which were later separated to become on the one hand the agape or love feast, and on the other the eucharist or holy communion. Such meals were a common feature both of pagan and of Jewish circles, and regulations for that observed by the Qumran sect are found in their *Manual of Discipline*. Dom Gregory Dix, in *The Shape of the Liturgy*, makes a strong case for the Christian meal being a variant of a typical *chaburah* or formal fellowship meal of pious Jewish friends. The early Christians seem to have met for this purpose weekly on the evening of 'the Lord's Day'. The term 'Lord's Supper' may well have been applied both to the occasion as a whole and also to its major components, the meal itself and the liturgical commemoration of the Lord's living presence which accompanied it. Both agape and embryonic eucharist emphasized the fact that his followers constituted a community in spiritual fellowship both with each other and with their risen Lord. Associated with the meal was the distribution of food to the needy, especially widows. The technical term eventually reserved for the meal among the Greek-speaking Christians was *agape*, literally 'a love'. In other words it was an occasion for the display and growth of God-centred

Christian love as opposed to merely human *eros* or *philia*. Among the Latin-speaking Christians this became *caritas*, 'charity', a word whose meaning degenerated (as did the love feast itself) from an expression of the purest of emotions to the social activities which normally demonstrated that emotion, but which could too easily be divorced from it and be regarded as self-sufficient.

Unambiguous evidence about the love feast in the NT is scanty. It is quite clear, however, that throughout his ministry Jesus stressed the importance both of meals in general, especially the evening meal, or supper, and the banquet with invited guests – a favourite symbol of his messiahship. He taught his disciples to pray for food. He was even chided for his emphasis upon eating and drinking (Matt. 11.18 f.; *cf*. 9.10-15). Not only the apostles but two anonymous followers who met the risen Lord on the road to Emmaus were apparently familiar with some idiosyncrasy in his prayer and breaking of bread at such meals (Luke 24.30 f.). At one of his last recorded appearances he presided over a meal with seven disciples by the Sea of Galilee, a meal climaxed by a threefold emphasis alike upon *agape* and upon the pastoral feeding of the Christian flock (John 21.1-17). The 'breaking of bread' was linked with the sharing of goods and temple worship as a distinctive feature of the earliest church (Acts 2.41-47).

In Paul's classic description of the eucharist in I Cor. 11.17-34, a common meal either precedes or is inseparably linked with a more liturgical celebration. Paul's words show, however, that already abuses were creeping in, the table-fellowship occasionally being marred by examples of gluttony and drunkenness. The same was true a generation or two later when Jude wrote – the only undoubted use of the term *agape* (in the plural) in the NT: 'These men are a blot on your love feasts, where they eat and drink without reverence' (v. 12, NEB). Without a familiar background of Jewish piety in the *chaburah* such meals could easily become assimilated to the less restrained pagan banquets, and joy in the fellowship of the risen Lord and his followers could deteriorate into unbridled joy in food and wine, with an emphasis upon variety and luxury such as encouraged gluttony, pride and selfishness. It is sadly clear that this indeed happened, even during the apostolic age, and apparently formed the chief reason for separating the liturgical celebration of a commemorative token meal (the eucharist) from a genuine meal (the agape). Overlapping and some mutual influence continued, however. The need was constantly felt to urge moderation even in the separated agape, which gradually developed its own distinctive rituals, differing from area to area.

The *Didache* preserves the prayers associated with the Eastern agape early in the second century, probably in Syria. It contains groups of prayers to be used by the presiding minister before and after the meal, together with congregational responses, which rang the changes on the theme of 'To thee be glory for ever', the final petition being the Aramaic *Maranatha*, 'Our Lord, come!' Tertullian's *Apology* (c. AD 197) reveals the rite as it was practised in Carthage and probably in Rome – a genuine meal, to which the poor were invited, begun and ended with prayer. The meal was followed with scripture reading, spiritual discourse, the singing of hymns, and apparently an opportunity for individual testimonies of some kind. The *Apostolic Tradition* of Hippolytus shows that in Rome by the third century the agape was celebrated in private homes, guests being invited by the host, though a minister was always present to 'say grace' and to offer a spiritual exhortation. The guests were urged to 'eat sufficiently, but so that there may remain something over that your host may send it to whomsoever he wills, as the superfluity of the saints, and he [to whom it is sent] may rejoice with what is left over' (Dix, *op. cit.*, p. 82). The guests were also urged to pray for their host. Strong evidence exists that the agape gradually came to be assimilated with pagan funeral banquets, which were thus transformed both into occasions for feeding the poor and into symbolic representations of the messianic banquet, a foretaste of the joys of heaven. Conciliar rulings show that from the fourth century onwards the possibility and actuality of abuse, combining with a more formal approach to church life, had steadily undermined the ancient fellowship meal, at least as an official element in Western worship. In the Eastern Church the agape lingered on for two or three centuries more.

By the eighth century the agape seems to have been almost universally defunct apart from vestigial remains whose origins were forgotten and occasional survivals in out-of-the-way sects. Vestiges are probably to be seen in the offertory for the poor at holy communion, in the distributions to the poor on Maundy Thursday, and (in Eastern Churches only) in the distribution of pieces of unconsecrated bread after the eucharist. One example of what appears to be a genuine survival (albeit indirect) is to be found among the Christians of St Thomas in Southern India. Another was probably among the Paulicians of Armenia, who may in turn have sown some of the seed which eventually led to the revival of the love feast among the Moravians.

Along with the Protestant Reformation went a somewhat self-conscious attempt among several pietistic sects to reproduce the actual customs as well as the spirit of the primitive church. Although the details and the dimensions of this process are difficult to recover, it appears that this imitation of the early church combined with the vestigial remains of the agape to foster the modern love feast in some western European communities such as the Mennonites, the German Baptist Brethren (or 'Dunkers'), and the Moravians (q.v.), frequently allied with the kiss of peace (q.v.) and the ceremonial washing of feet. Encouraged by Pietism, the love feast flourished especially during the eighteenth century in Germany and the Netherlands, and was imported to America by the more zealous (and therefore the more persecuted) members of those bodies.

Although the ancient agape thus survived or was revived during modern times in various small sects, the mainstream denominations were hardly affected until John Wesley introduced it to his societies. In his own search for spiritual renewal by means of imitating primitive Christianity, Wesley was greatly impressed by the Moravian love feast as he experienced it both as a missionary in Georgia and as a pilgrim to Herrnhut in Germany. In 1738 he transplanted it to British soil. Convinced as he was of the stabilizing and stimulating power of Christian fellowship, he moulded the love feast into a climactic concentration of the more subdued fellowship of the band meeting and (later) the class meeting. The love feast became the occasion par excellence when after the symbolic sharing of a token family meal the assembled members of several classes and possibly of several societies would take turns in testifying to their Christian experience as they were so moved by the

Holy Spirit. New converts especially were encouraged to speak of the change wrought in them, and their testimonies frequently led to further conversions. Charles Wesley put his genius to work in composing special hymns for these occasions, though strangely enough there was never a distinct love feast collection. At first Methodist love feasts were held monthly, but after a time this gave place to a quarterly, and later still to an annual, celebration, which thus tended to become the more momentous. Enthusiastic Methodists assembling from a wide area rarely failed to experience a spiritual blessing, and the love feast became one of the more exciting events in the Methodist year, to which the general public sought entry, out of curiosity if not always from spiritual expectancy. The fact that these were private gatherings, to which admittance was secured by the possession of a current class ticket or a special note from the itinerant preacher, encouraged scurrilous rumours about immoral practices, though these were readily refuted as without foundation.

When Methodists emigrated they took with them (among other practices) their love feast, so that the Methodist variant became familiar in many parts of the British Commonwealth, as in America. The British offshoots of Wesley's Methodism also adapted the observance. During the nineteenth century, however, with the growing church-consciousness of the Methodist societies, and a consequent lessening of the emphasis upon the conversion experience, as also upon the class meeting and the prayer meeting, the spiritual testimonies at the love feasts lost much of their colourful spontaneity, while the more liturgical element was not by itself sufficient to retain popular adherence. Throughout World Methodism the love feast died out except for a few local survivals and an annual observance in some Methodist Conferences.

During the middle years of the twentieth century there has been a revival of interest in and practice of the love feast, both aspects linked closely with the ecumenical movement. The eucharist has proved the chief symbol both of Christian unity and of Christian disunity. Many Christians have therefore favoured experiments in interdenominational fellowship at a meal which like the eucharist had its origin in the Last Supper, yet which because of a different

theological focus and comparative disuse had not become so hedged around with inhibitions and prohibitions.

In *Christian Worship* (1961), T. S. Garrett speaks of modern revivals of the love feast such as 'the parish breakfast following the parish communion', including a Cambridge college occasion when the breaking of pieces from a loaf was accompanied by the recital of a passage from the *Didache*. He also tells of Christian festivals in Tamil villages historically linked with non-Christian festivities yet in fact called 'love feasts' and having genuine spiritual links with the primitive agape (p. 43). There is a sense in which the 'faith tea' of British churches and the 'covered-dish supper' or 'home-coming' meal of American churches may similarly be regarded as modern forms of the love feast.

Much more self-conscious revivals have taken place during recent years, however, with an avowedly ecumenical intention. After lengthy preparations the two denominations represented in the parish of Hilgay, Norfolk, England – Anglicans and Methodists – came together on Maundy Thursday, 1949, and again on Wednesday in Holy Week, 1951, to celebrate a love feast deliberately representing the church both Eastern and Western, both primitive and modern.

The issue was taken up by the Friends of Reunion and discussed in successive issues of their *Bulletin*, arousing correspondence from many parts of the world. The instigator, the Rev. Ian Thomson, claimed that this was 'a serious attempt to break a deadlock that has long existed between separated churches'. The Ecumenical Institute organized at the Château de Bossey in Switzerland by the World Council of Churches has for years treated the last meal of its course there as an agape, when the participants are urged 'to express, by a symbolical act, the reality of our unity'. In more recent years a revival of the agape in Holland has linked Catholics and Protestants in a joint search for unity. From the initial gathering attended by 800 people of all ages and denominations in The Hague on the Friday evening before Pentecost in 1961 the movement has spread to other places, and has been received with such enthusiasm as a 'pre-eucharistic' meal emphasizing the desire and need for fuller Christian unity around the Lord's table that in 1965 the bishops of Holland issued directives about such 'agape celebrations'.

Granted that an undue emphasis upon a revival of the ancient agape in order to bypass the problems presented by joint communions may be fraught with spiritual peril, any such revival should surely be encouraged if it falls within the terms of the Dutch bishops' directive: 'The conscious intention of the agape celebration is to act in the service of that unity of which the eucharist is the decisive sign and the highest sacramental expression.'

Frank Baker, *Methodism and the Love-Feast*, 1957; R. Lee Cole, *Love-Feasts*, 1916; Dom Gregory Dix, *The Shape of the Liturgy*, ²1945; J. F. Keating, *The Agape and the Eucharist in the Early Church*, 1911; G. I. F. Thomson, *An Experiment in Worship*, 1951; *One in Christ*, II, 1 (1966).

FRANK BAKER

Low Sunday

The English designation for the Sunday after Easter may denote its relationship to the great festival of the resurrection.

A. A. MCARTHUR

Lutheran Worship

The Augsburg Confession (1530) sets the tone for the Lutheran Reformation and clearly indicates that the protest is theological. Structures and tradition of the church are valued though they are attacked where authoritarianism has perverted them. The Augsburg Confession purports to be the authentic voice of Western Catholicism, repeatedly citing the church fathers to register its point. Lutheran reformers harboured no romantic notion of re-establishing the primitive church and were, therefore, conservative in liturgical reform.

Our churches are falsely accused of abolishing the Mass. Actually, the Mass is retained among us and is celebrated with the greatest reverence. Almost all the customary ceremonies are also retained . . . the Mass among us is supported by the example of the church as seen from the Scriptures and the Fathers . . . (*Augsburg Confession*, 24).

When the protest did not register and Rome severed ecclesial ties, liturgical reform became a necessity. Because of its prestige, Luther's own work was widely imitated. He purged the inherited rites ruthlessly

where in his view they reflected an anti-biblical theology, but was remarkably conservative in matters of ceremony. Biblical preaching was restored to the mass and also included in mattins and vespers (qq.v.). The fundamental emphasis on preaching grew out of both polemical and didactic concerns: it would free the people from ecclesiastical bondage and teach them the basis of the faith. The same pastoral concerns led to vernacular services.

Lutheran churches share this common liturgical orientation, but have developed three families of rites: Germanic, Scandinavian, North American. (Lutherans in eastern Europe and South America are Germanic in orientation; Australian Lutheranism combines Germanic and North American influences; Lutheran churches of Africa and Asia combine all three influences.)

All the sixteenth-century German *Kirchen-ordnungen* show their affinity to 'justification by grace through faith', the synoptic theology of the Lutheran protest. The Roman canon and offertory (qq.v.) were cut out and, unfortunately, nothing replaced them. Thus the words of institution, stripped of their context of prayer, gained unprecedented prominence which was intended to enhance their proclamatory function. Instead, 'consecration piety' was reinforced and Lutheranism was kept tied to the medieval ethos of the awesome and dread presence. Disputes with the Swiss reformers made such piety even more tenacious.

In spite of heroic efforts to restore frequent communion among the people and thus balance sermon and sacrament, old habits prevailed. Awe of the presence and the need for solemn self-preparation, the individualism resulting from an almost exclusive emphasis on the forgiveness of sins as chief fruit of the sacrament and the strong stress on the importance of preaching all contributed to infrequent celebrations. This did not result, as it did in England, in the ascendency of mattins. Lutherans used ante-communion (*missa catechumenorum*) as their preaching service with the result that, in spite of the infrequency of the eucharist, their devotion remained oriented to the mass.

Dominance of proclamation produced glorious results in church music. Such giants as Heinrich Schütz and J. S. Bach used music in the exposition of the scriptures. Though their music is not liturgical in the usual sense, neither is it autonomous as masses of Mozart and Beethoven tend to be. It was related to lessons and sermon rather than the Ordinary. From the beginning Lutherans fostered the use of vernacular hymns (q.v.), giving impetus to the chorale tradition. These hymns, in turn, generated a superb body of organ literature based on their melodies. Music is one key to the liturgical ethos of the Lutheran churches.

Scandinavian Lutheranism parallels the German development to a great degree. Denmark, especially, has a similar tradition. Norway, long under Danish rule, was late in developing its own style of life. But Norwegian worship bears the imprint of an intense pietism and tends, accordingly, to be individualistic in mood.

The Church of Sweden made the Reformation transition structurally intact. Because Roman influence virtually disappeared and Calvinistic influence was never significant, the Swedish Church has been comparatively free of theological strife. Structurally, Swedish liturgies resemble the German. But in such matters as ceremony and vestments there has been more continuity with Western Catholic tradition. Even so, the Swedish Reformation could not restore frequent communion, and it also became a preaching church.

North American Lutheranism became the heir to the various European traditions. Since their arrival, the numerous immigrant groups have been engaged in the process of merging into one Lutheran tradition which is at home in the new world. This has required learning a new, common language, confronting a Protestantism of Anglo-Saxon origins with its different theological mentality, and adjusting to being a minority among Christians.

American Lutheran liturgies have followed the Reformation models in matters of structure, but have adopted the verbal habits of the *BCP*. Their musical practice has absorbed the Anglo-American tradition of hymnody and other conventions typical of American Protestantism. Ceremony and vestments have increasingly reflected the influence of the Episcopal Church, the Swedish heritage, and the catholicizing tendencies of the Liturgical Movement (q.v.).

The Liturgical Movement has influenced all branches of Lutheranism. Primarily it resulted in a recovery of the fullness of the sixteenth-century heritage after 150 years of decline. New service-books in the decade after the Second World War demonstrate this. Since then a more ecumenical mood has developed as the result of increased knowledge of the pre-medieval church and the conviction that liturgical renewal cannot take place in isolation.

Most recently, Lutherans have been challenged by Vatican II Roman Catholicism. A reformed Roman Church forces Lutherans to ask whether their protest has registered at last and, if so, whether the time for reconciliation has come. The spirit of rapprochement is strongest, at least on a practical level, in North America. The new American Lutheran rite (1970) for holy communion bears striking parallels to the new Roman mass (1969) and also the eucharist of the (pan-Protestant) Consultation on Church Union (1968).

Liturgical renewal among Lutherans shares goals similar to those of other communions: restoration of significant practices of mainstream Western Catholicism, expressing the interrelation of worship and mission, recovering the spirit of joy and celebration in the eucharist, grasping the mystery that God's work and man's work are indistinguishable. But in all this there is a sustained commitment to proclamation as the living voice of God among his people and a pardonable pride in a rich musical heritage to be shared with others.

Peter Brunner, *Worship in the Name of Jesus*, 1968; F. Kalb, *The Theology of Worship in 17th-Century Lutheranism,* 1965; Vilmos Vajta, *Luther on Worship*, 1958.

EUGENE BRAND

Maniple *see* Vestments (1*e*)

Mar Thoma Church Worship

The Mar Thoma Church is unique in the sense that it is at once Eastern and Reformed. This church still maintains aspects of its Eastern Orthodox heritage, but has undergone a thorough reformation along the lines of the English and Continental Reformations.

The church claims historical continuity with the ancient church supposed to have been established by the apostle Thomas in the first century. The Reformation of the nineteenth century, which originated this church as an independent unit, distinct from the Syrian Orthodox Church of which it formed part before that time, was ostensibly an effort to restore the purity of faith and practice of the original apostolic church which had been corrupted by the Syrian Orthodox.

The liturgical tradition of the Mar Thoma Church thus follows very much the patterns set by the Syrian Orthodox tradition. There have been several revisions of the prayers, especially in the eucharistic liturgy, to eliminate certain supposedly wrong teachings, e.g. (1) to take out all intercessions to the saints or the Blessed Virgin Mary since Christ is the only mediator; (2) to take out all prayers for the departed, since there is no biblical teaching that tells us that the dead will be benefited by our prayers; (3) to take out elements in the liturgical prayers which over-emphasize the sacrificial element in the eucharist; (4) to revise prayers which may seem to imply a doctrine of transubstantiation of the bread and wine into the body and blood of our Lord; (5) to revise texts which over-emphasize the powers of the priesthood.

In these reforms the Mar Thoma Church was guided especially by the pattern of the English Reformation as the Church Missionary Society had interpreted it. As in the English *BCP*, sometimes two alternate versions are given of prayers, one of which has a 'high' theology of the sacrament, whereas the second may reflect a 'low' view. In the revisions, the basic allusions of the Orthodox text have been maintained wherever possible. For example, the opening words of the public celebration of the eucharistic liturgy in the Orthodox and Mar Thoma texts are: *Orthodox* – 'Mary who brought Thee forth and John who baptized Thee – these are intercessors on our behalf before Thee – Have mercy upon us.' *Mar Thoma* – 'Our Lord Jesus Christ who took flesh from Holy Mary and received Baptism from John, pour forth Thy blessing upon us.'

The introduction by Metropolitan Yuhanon Mar Thoma, Head of the Mar Thoma Church, to the finally revised (1954) text of the eucharistic liturgy, gives these basic principles of the revision: (1) removal of all prayers addressed to the saints; (2) removal of all prayers for the departed; (3) removal of the prayer (at the time of communion): 'Thee I hold, who holdest the bounds of the world, Thee I grasp, who orderest the depths; Thee, O God, do I place in my mouth . . .'; (4) change of the prayer 'we offer thee this bloodless sacrifice for thy Holy Church throughout the world . . .' to read 'We offer this prayer . . . for the Church'; (5) change of the prayer 'we offer this living sacrifice' to read 'we offer this sacrifice of grace, peace and praise'; (6) removal of the statement 'this eucharist is . . . sacrifice and praise'; (7) removal of the declaration that the Holy Spirit sanctifies the censer; (8) omission of the rubric about blessing the censer; (9) alteration of the epiclesis, giving freedom to say '(may the Holy Spirit sanctify it) to be the body of Christ' or 'to be the fellowship of the Body of Christ'; (10) insistence on communion in both kinds separately; (11) abolition of auricular confession to the priest; (12) prohibition of the celebration of the eucharist when there is no one beside the priest to communicate.

Changes along similar lines were made in all the forms of prayer and administration of sacraments. Since the revision has not yet been carried out in a thorough manner, elements of the Orthodox tradition now co-exist with definite Reformation features.

In the canonical offices, the use of incense has been largely discontinued. The prayers for the offering of incense are retained, however, the word 'incense' being replaced by the word 'service' or 'prayers'. The typical Syrian Orthodox pattern of *proemion* (introductory doxology) followed by a *sedra* (long meditative prayer) is retained, but the invariable reference to the departed at the conclusion of the *sedra* is either omitted or replaced by reference to 'all believing members of the church'.

The Mar Thoma Church remains Eastern in not adding the *fiilioque* to the Nicene Creed, in insisting on the celibacy of bishops, in vestments and church utensils, in full congregational participation in worship, in the use of the mother-tongue in worship, in adding 'O Christ, who was crucified for us, have mercy upon us' in the *Trisagion* and in many other respects.

At the same time there has been a liberal acceptance of and accommodation to Western Protestant or Evangelical forms of worship. The prayer meeting finds a place in the constitution, and each parish is divided into regional groups which meet together for informal group prayer. The eucharistic service is not obligatory on all Sundays, and quite often the priest or presbyter presides over a meeting around the preached word and prayer alone.

Hymns from the Anglican, Presbyterian, Lutheran, Methodist, Baptist and other books are found in the manuals of worship and are frequently used, either in English or in Malayalam. Several litanies and collects have also been similarly adopted.

The traditional seven canonical offices have been reduced to two (morning and evening), following the Reformers at this point. A form for compline has, however, been retained. There are special offices for Sundays and certain feast days, but different forms for the different days of the week are no longer in use.

A special feast called 'Community Day' (*Samudayadinam*) has been added, and a special form of service provided for the day, which coincides with the feast of St Thomas. A special offering is taken on this day for the central treasury of the church.

PAUL VERGHESE

Mariological Feasts

The Christian church has always held Mary the Virgin in special honour. The church's calendar shows clearly the place Mary has in the liturgy, while private devotions as well as the work of artists and poets show the place she has in the minds and thoughts of individuals.

From early times Mary was honoured with the title 'Mother of God', which emphasized the status she enjoyed by virtue of her Son. In addition, however, the continuing devotion of the church to her person over the centuries led to her being given such titles as 'sinless' and 'immaculate'. Consequently two elements may be traced in the feasts in her honour, the vocational and the personal. The Immaculate Conception, for instance, may well be called a personal feast, while the Annunciation is rather to be regarded as a vocational one. These vocational, mother-and-son, feasts are, in a way, twofold celebrations and they become feasts of the mother or the son according to where the emphasis is put. Thus the Annunciation, Lady Day in England, is renamed in the new Roman calendar 'The Annunciation of the Lord' (by the angel to the mother). The

octave day of Christmas has for centuries been called the Feast of the Circumcision, but originally it was a day in honour of the mother of God and in the new calendar it is now called 'The Solemnity of Holy Mary, Mother of God'.

The oldest feasts of our Lady have a local connection with the church at Jerusalem. They also came into being largely because of the Christological controversies of the early church. As the true humanity of our Lord (as well as his divinity) came to be stated in clearer and more emphatic terms, the reality of the status of the Mother of God came to be better appreciated and underlined by feasts in its honour.

The feasts of the Purification, the Annunciation, the Birth and Assumption seem to be the oldest Marian feasts and to have been of Byzantine origin. They are recorded in the Gelasian Sacramentary, and so must have been known at Rome in the seventh or eighth century. To these very many other feasts, especially of local usage, have been added over the centuries. Only a brief mention of the principal feasts is here possible.

The dogma of the *Immaculate Conception* was not defined until 1854, but the feast is very old. A feast was certainly observed in the East in the seventh century, and spread from there to Naples, Ireland, England and so to the continent. It gained a measure of universal observance through the breviary of Pius V, and became a feast of the highest rank for the whole Roman Catholic Church after 1854. Its date is 8 December.

The *Birthday* of our Lady, 8 September, is a very old feast – in origin as much a feast of her parents, Joachim and Anne, as of Mary. No reason can be given for the choice of date.

The *Annunciation* celebrates the incident related in Luke 1.26-38. It is recalled, in the framework of the Advent liturgy, in the Ember Wednesday mass. But from quite early times it was given a special day of its own – 25 March in the Western calendar. The hymn *Ave maris stella* is said to have been first used as a hymn for this feast.

The *Visitation* (Luke 1.39-55) is recalled in the Advent liturgy on Ember Friday. There is an old Eastern feast on 2 July. The Western feast is probably not connected with the Eastern one and dates from the Middle Ages. The new Roman calendar has transferred it from 2 July to 31 May.

The *Purification* of our Lady, as it has long been called by the Western church, is observed in the East as a feast of the Saviour. In the new calendar it is called the 'Presentation of the Lord'. Both names are derived from Luke 2.22. The real significance of the feast is the meeting (*hypapante*) of the old dispensation and the new, of Simeon and Jesus. The day is also known as *Candlemas*, for candles are blessed for liturgical use and also distributed to the faithful on this day. It also marks the end of the Christmas cycle and, through the candles, emphasizes the 'light' motif of the Christmas feasts: 'a light for revelation to the Gentiles, and for glory to thy people Israel'.

The *Assumption* of our Lady, 15 August, commemorates her death. It also celebrates her entrance into heaven. The dogma was not defined until 1950, but the feast is one of the earliest Marian ones.

Other feasts of our Lady have a local origin or are a development, often devotional and subjective, of one of the earlier feasts. The feasts listed above are Christocentric and celebrate Mary's unique honour of being the mother of God and mother of man's Redeemer.

J. CONNELLY

Martyrium

A building enshrining the tomb and/or relics of a martyr. The forms adopted by the church were those already in use for pagan tombs. Almost invariably roofed with a dome to symbolize heaven, they could be, depending upon local customs and prototypes, cuboid, circular, cruciform, octagonal or triconch, or they could combine more than one of these plans, e.g. Church No. 8, Bin Bir Kilisse, which unites the cross with the eight-sided figure (*see* Fig. 18).

A. Grabar, *Martyrium. Recherches sur le culte des reliques religieux et l'art chrétien antique*, 2 vols., 1946.

EDITOR

Mass, High

The term 'high' translates the Latin *sollemnis* and *Missa sollemnis* (or even *sacra sollemnia*) meant a sung mass at which the deacon and subdeacon (qq.v.) assisted the celebrant and performed certain duties that belonged to them alone. Thus it was the deacon who sang the gospel, the subdeacon who sang the epistle, as well as other lessons if there was no lector. In addition, the deacon was the immediate minister of the priest, pouring the wine into the chalice at the offertory (q.v.) and covering and uncovering the chalice during the canon (q.v.). The subdeacon poured the water with which the wine is mingled. The subdeacon held the paten in a humeral veil (q.v.) from the offertory until the end of the Lord's Prayer. This observance, which had its origin in the papal liturgy when the bread was brought to the altar on large platters at the offertory, which were then held by the subdeacons until just before communion, has now been abolished. At the end of mass the deacon sang the dismissal (*Ite, missa est*) before the celebrant gave the blessing.

The ceremonial of high mass was somewhat complicated not only in the sanctuary, where the deacon and subdeacon had to make their movements in concert with acolytes, thurifer and master of ceremonies, but also in the total organization of the rite. Thus the choir sang the introit, the gradual, the Alleluia and its verse (in Lent replaced by the tract), the offertory verse and the communion verse, and the people were supposed to sing the *Kyries*, the *Gloria in excelsis*, the *Sanctus*, the *Benedictus* (until recently sung *after* the consecration) and the *Agnus Dei*. In fact in most places the choir sang all these too. Before a high mass on Sundays there was the rite of the *asperges* (q.v.), although celebrant, ministers, servers and, where there was a

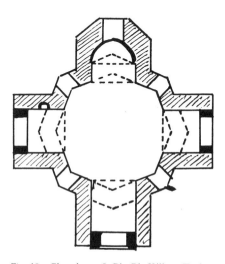

Fig. 18   Church no. 8, Bin Bir Kilisse, Turkey

surpliced choir, the choir had already made their solemn entry. In addition, the celebrant was required to say the prayers of preparation with the ministers in a low voice and to read everything that was sung by anyone else. In cathedrals and parish churches where the gospel was read out in English after its singing in Latin, the gospel was thus recited three times in one mass.

Incense (q.v.) was used (and might only be used at sung masses); the altar was censed after the prayers of preparation and at the offertory, the gospel book before the singing of the gospel and the celebrant on all three occasions. In addition, the ministers and servers were censed at the offertory and the people on the latter occasion only. The blessed sacrament was censed at the two elevations (q.v.) of the consecrated bread and wine.

The whole of this ceremonial was controlled by a rigid corpus of rubrics, elaborated by the ceremonialists whose practical regulations sometimes acquired the force of law.

Its origins are to be found in the Gregorian tradition (the 'Gregorian' sacramentary and the *Ordo Romanus Primus*) of the seventh century, with the elaborations and adaptations of the *Ordines* and pontificals of the following centuries. The 'Gregorian' sacramentary and the *Ordo Romanus Primus* give the ceremonial of the mass when the pope celebrated. North of the Alps this had to be adapted to the conditions of an episcopal celebration and it was the episcopal high mass which, in spite of accretions, gave the best picture of the Roman mass of the seventh century. Then, with the multiplication of churches within a city and outside it, with the spread of monasticism, it was necessary to arrange the rite for celebration by the simple priest. It was shorn of certain ceremonies proper to a bishop (thus the priest did not use a throne but a seat at the side of the sanctuary), and so we get by the thirteenth century the rite known in English-speaking lands as 'high mass'. In spite of the ever increasing prevalence of low mass (q.v.), at least the ceremonialists regarded high mass as the typical rite of the Roman Catholic Church. It had the advantage of indicating that the mass is celebrated not by one man, the priest, but by a community, even if by the eighth century this community had become almost entirely clericalized. The Carolingian reform of the ninth century made attempts to

keep a community spirit alive by enjoining on the people the duty of singing the *Kyries*, the *Gloria*, etc., but apparently without great success. The ceremonial of high mass, as it was known until recently, was finally fixed and imposed as of obligation on the whole church of the Roman rite by the corpus of rubrics called *Ritus servandus* which was inserted into the missal of Pope Pius V in 1570.

The term 'high mass' and much of its ceremonial is now obsolescent or obsolete. The *Ordo Missae* of 1969 has brought a great flexibility to the celebration of the mass. Singing may and should take place at every kind of mass, incense may or may not be used at will, the ceremonial is much simplified, a subdeacon is no longer necessary, but above all, the emphasis is put on the worshipping community and their part in the celebration is considerable. The people are required to sing or say those parts of the rite that properly belong to them, the celebrant never says anything read, said or sung by anyone else, and lay-readers for the first and second lessons are allowed and recommended. The celebration of mass in its simplest or more elaborate form is now once more a paradigm of the Christian community, the church.

J. D. CRICHTON

Mass, Low

The low mass (also called in some languages and places the 'said mass' or the 'read mass' or even 'private mass') is, ceremonially speaking, one that is celebrated by a priest with single server. In practice, for a variety of reasons, it was for hundreds of years the form of mass with which the laymen were most familiar. It was celebrated without song, with a minimum of ceremonial, and the celebrant faced eastwards. The rubrics of the Pius V missal (1570) assumed that the people would be on their knees throughout, occupied with their own devotions and hearing only occasional phrases from the celebrant. On Sundays in parish churches, its rigours were somewhat reduced by the reading of the epistle and gospel in the people's tongue after they had been read in Latin and (usually) by the sermon. In some places vernacular hymns were allowed to form an accompaniment of the rite, notably in Germany. From the eighteenth century, a style of mass that came to be called the *Betsingmesse* (prayer-and-song-mass) was introduced. Here the sung texts were paraphrases (more or less close) of the mass texts and were sung while the Latin text was being read by the celebrant. It was a way of securing some popular participation and became common in the church after the Second World War until the liturgical reform of Vatican II.

The rite of low mass, which the rubrics of the Pius V missal seem to have regarded as typical is the result of a long development. The classical Roman mass of the seventh century (*see* **Mass, High**) was a community celebration. But with the spread of monasticism, the custom of private masses in chapels for special 'intentions' began to come in, and as Christianity spread into the rural parts of Europe, it became impossible to celebrate the mass in country churches with all the ceremonial of the papal-episcopal rite. The sung parts of the mass (introits, etc.) seem to have been omitted, but the priest himself said all the rest, the collect, the epistle, the gospel, etc., and the single minister or server responded for the people. With the changing habits and organization of the papal curia which gave employment to a considerable number of clerics, mostly priests, and with the rise of the new religious orders like the Dominicans and Franciscans who were clerks (in holy orders), the custom of low masses became ever more prevalent. Concelebration, apart from ordinations, was unknown. When in the thirteenth century the Franciscans adopted the papal-curial liturgy and penetrated into every corner of Europe, the Roman rite of low mass became very common. They took over from the Roman books certain prayers provided for the devotion of the priest at the offertory and before communion, and a selection of these prayers was included in the missal of Pius V and were made a matter of obligation.

For this kind of celebration a single book was needed, for it was manifestly impossible for a man to take around with him a small library consisting of sacramentary, collectary, epistle and gospel book and gradual. This the monks had provided by the eleventh century with the so-called *Missale Plenarium*, which contained *all* the texts of the mass whether sung by others or said by the priest. It was this book, reformed in the sixteenth century, that became the *Missale Romanum* and that was the official mass book of the Roman Church until 1969.

Like the term 'high mass' (q.v.), the term 'low mass' is now practically obsolete. The thinking of the *Ordo Missae* of 1969 moves in a quite different direction. It emphasizes the community participation of the people and admits singing at any and every kind of celebration. It does indeed envisage the 'private' mass (a term now frowned on) and provides an order for a priest who has to celebrate in the absence of people. The ritual is slightly adapted, though he is still required to say the entrance text and the communion verse. The server has to make the responses of the people.

J. D. CRICHTON

Matrimony

Matrimony is the rite or action of marriage. Since, according to Western Christian thought, but not according to Eastern Orthodox thinking (*see below*), the actual ministers of the marriage are the bride and groom who marry each other, the liturgical act is not of the essence of marriage and is rather a blessing additional to the primary entering into a contract in front of witnesses.

1. *The Early Church*. A clear distinction was drawn between the betrothal or engagement and the nuptials or marriage ceremony proper, although the former was considered to be as binding as the latter. There remains no full description of the primitive rite, but from scattered allusions it may in part be reconstructed and it can be seen to consist of practices current in paganism.

(*a*) *Betrothal*. According to Ignatius, this must take place with the bishop's cognizance (*ad Poly. 5*). It involved the giving of *arrhae* or earnest money as a pledge that the marriage would eventually take place. Next a ring was given, used for the sealing of household effects, to indicate that the future wife would be in charge of the home. A dowry was then promised and the woman was veiled – the veil being part of the engaged or married woman's normal dress. The couple's hands were joined and a kiss was exchanged (Tertullian, *Apol.*6; *de Virg.Vel.*11). In the course of time some of these elements were transferred to the marriage ceremony itself.

(*b*) *Nuptials*. According to Tertullian this included the celebration of the eucharist and a blessing (*ad Ux.*2.6). From later writers we learn that the man was given a crown, according to Chrysostom 'as a symbol of victory, indicating that he approaches the marriage bed unconquered by pleasure' (*Hom.in I Tim*.9). An agape or love-feast (q.v.) usually followed.

EDITOR

2. *The Orthodox Church.* The Orthodox Church understands marriage as the sacrament whereby two members of the body of Christ become one. Ephesians 5.31, 32 form the root of this understanding:

> For this reason a man shall leave his father and mother and be joined to his wife, and the two shall become one. This is a great mystery, and I take it to mean Christ and the church.

The Orthodox Church sees several fundamental inferences inseparably bound up with this concept:

(*a*) It is Christ who unites the couple in the sacrament of marriage. He is sacramentally present in this great act taking place within his body.

(*b*) The unity accomplished in the sacrament of marriage, just as the unity between Christ and his church, is truly unique and is given the full potential to be total and eternal in character. Therefore, the priest acts as the actual minister of the sacrament.

(*c*) Through the sacrament of marriage the husband and wife are crowned as the king and queen of a family: a small image of the Kingdom of God and a concrete witness to that Kingdom in the world.

The present Orthodox rite of holy matrimony uses symbolic actions and movements to convey these basic, above-mentioned realities concerning marriage to the couple being united as well as to the faithful gathered to witness the event. (The Orthodox rite of holy matrimony has a long history of evolution. A text of its present form may be found in: Father John Meyendorff, *The Sacrament of Holy Matrimony*. A review of the historical evolution of the rite can be found in: Alvian Smirensky, 'The Evolution of the Present Rite of Matrimony and Parallel Canonical Developments' in *St Vladimir's Seminary Quarterly* 8.1 [1964], pp. 38-47.)

The ceremony begins in the vestibule, that part of the church building which represents the world outside the church. In the vestibule marriage, as the world has known it since pagan antiquity, takes place: the promise is made and the rings are exchanged. For a member of the church, however, such a marriage is not sufficient. All the events of his life must be integrated into the saving life of Christ. His birth in Christ is baptism, his food in Christ is the holy eucharist; the inspiring content of his life is the Holy Spirit. His desire for love, companionship and family must likewise be made new, i.e. permeated throughout by the transforming presence of Christ. The marriage of this world must be brought to the church and, through the great mystery of the sacrament, made into the image of the unity existing between Christ and the church.

This movement from the world to the church, from the fallen to the transformed, is symbolized by the first great liturgical action of the marriage rite, the *procession*. The priest leads the couple in procession from the vestibule to the centre of the church building, where the group stops in front of a small lectern or table on which are located the gospel book and cross. The couple hold lighted candles as the sign of their common faith in Christ, the Light of the world. The priest announces the purpose of the gathering by intoning:

> Blessed is the Kingdom, of the Father and of the Son, and of the Holy Spirit, now and ever, and unto ages of ages.

The marital union of the couple is to be integrated into the transformed and eternal life of the Kingdom of God.

The priest then reads three long prayers filled with a multitude of scriptural references. The references point out the interaction between God and man throughout biblical history. They illustrate the way in which God has blessed and fulfilled promises to couples starting from the time of Adam and Eve. The prayers ask that the same blessing be showered upon the couple present.

The *crowning* is the high point of the ceremony. Literally, the priest places crowns or wreaths upon the heads of the couple. The bride and groom are shown to be the king and queen of a little image of the Kingdom of God; they are to increase and multiply, and see their children's children. The crowns also signify the crowns of martyrs and indicate that the newly-joined couple is to be a living witness to Christ in the world. The crowning is concluded by the *prokeimenon*, based on a verse from Ps. 21, which says:

Thou hast set upon their heads crowns of precious stones; they asked life of thee and thou gavest it them.

The epistle section, Eph. 5. 20-33, read following the *prokeimenon*, contains verses used as the basis for this article. The gospel reading, John 2.1-11, tells of the performing by Christ of his first sign – at the marriage feast in Cana of Galilee. At Cana he changed the water into wine, the old into the new. In the sacrament of marriage he changes a union of this world into an eternal unity in his Kingdom.

After the gospel reading and further prayers, the priest presents a *common cup* of wine to the couple. In drinking from the common cup, the couple again realize the nature of their unity in Christ: they drink from one cup, they share one life; they proclaim one source for that life – Christ.

As a conclusion to the service the bride and groom join hands and are led by the priest, who carries a cross indicating the way in which all Christians must walk, in a *triple circling* around the centre table. The circle thus formed is symbolic of the nature of marriage as accomplished in Christ: it has its beginning now in the sacrament, but it has no end.

This is a great mystery, and I take it to mean Christ and the church. (Eph. 5.32).

PAUL LAZOR

3. *Medieval and Roman Catholic.* The marriage liturgy to be found in the early sacramentaries (*Veron., Gelas.* and *Greg.*) was never obligatory and it was not until the social order had broken down (seventh to eighth century) that the church felt it necessary to take cognisance of the matrimonial consent and the conditions attaching to it. This was necessary to protect freedom of consent and to prevent clandestinity. Hence the rite of marriage *in facie ecclesiae*, which meant, literally, at the doors of the church. This is first recorded in Normandy in the early twelfth century. The minister addressed the couple and inquired about the consent. The bride was 'given away', the scrip of the dowry was read, the ring was blessed and put on the right hand of the bride, the bridegroom gave some pieces of gold or silver (according to his wealth) and the priest concluded the rite with a blessing. If there was to be a wedding mass, the spouses (with their party) entered

the church, carrying candles. They made an offering at the offertory, there was the recital of the nuptial blessing (the text being that of the sacramentaries), and at this date and until much later, while the prayer was said, the veil was laid on the head of the bride and on the shoulders of the bridegroom. Thus was preserved the ancient rite of *velatio* which, according to some modern authorities, derives not from the ancient Roman *flammeum* but from the Christian rite of the *velatio virginis*. No formula is supplied in the Norman books, but in other medieval French rituals formulae very much like those of the Sarum rite are to be found.

It is there, however, that the origins of the Sarum rite of marriage are to be found, a rite that was retained by the Roman Catholic Church in England after the Reformation and with a few modifications (e.g. the omission of the blessing of the ring) by the Church of England. In medieval England it is worth noting that the text of the wedding mass was not used; it was replaced with that of the Holy Trinity, often used in England for joyful occasions.

The rite of the Roman Ritual of 1614 derives from the medieval one described above but, as its rubrics remark, since there are many local customs in the celebration of marriage, those countries and regions which have local rites may continue to use them. This is the explanation of the brevity and sheer starkness of the Roman rite of that time. In fact, in Europe there has always been a variety of marriage rites though in the nineteenth century there was a tendency to uniformity.

In recent years, with a developing theology of marriage, it was felt that a more adequate rite was needed. This appeared in 1969. It assumes (but does not order) that marriage is to take place at mass and appoints that it should take place after the ministry of the word where now other sacramental rites like confirmation and ordination are administered. The celebrant greets the couple who are seated in the sanctuary. After the homily he questions them about their willingness to undertake the obligations of marriage and their freedom. It is noteworthy that the English civil form declaring freedom and the matrimonial consent that follows has been incorporated into the rite for use in England. The form of consent has retained most of the phrases of the Sarum rite and these have now become part of the official Roman rite of marriage. After the blessing of the ring (or rings) the bride's is put on her finger with a new formula expressing love and fidelity (the one for the giving of gold and silver has been omitted as being archaic and obscure). In *all* weddings the nuptial blessing is given in one of the three forms that are provided. Bride and bridegroom may receive communion in both kinds if they so wish. The mass (or service) ends with blessings for the bride and bridegroom and for all present.

If there is no mass, the marriage service must be celebrated with a ministry of the word (lessons from the lectionary), including a homily, which may never be omitted. In the case of marriages between Catholics and non-Christians certain adaptations (given in the official texts) are to be made.

Three mass formulae for weddings are provided in the *Missale Romanum* of 1970 with a rich collection of prayers, prefaces and insertions (*Hanc igitur*) into the Roman canon (q.v.).

J. D. CRICHTON

4. *Anglican*. The marriage service is probably closer to its medieval predecessor, and has changed less in the ensuing four hundred years, than any other in *BCP*. The obvious example of this is the vernacular form of vows, which is found in the Sarum and York manuals in almost exactly the same words that are used today. Cranmer keeps the traditional division into two parts (*sponsalia* and *nuptiae*), but allows the espousals to take place in the body of the church, marking the beginning of the second part by the customary procession to the altar.

The service begins with a long address, expanded from the medieval 'banns' with material that was evidently traditional, since Chaucer uses it in *The Parson's Tale* (1387), and much of it is found in the Cologne *Encheiridion* (1538). Marriage was instituted by God in paradise, adorned and beautified by Christ at Cana, and commended by Paul in the Epistle to the Hebrews; it must not be entered upon for the wrong reasons; the right reasons are the procreation of children, continence, and 'mutual society, help and comfort'. The third 'cause' is stressed throughout the service: the medieval promise to love, honour, hold, and keep becomes love, *comfort*, honour, and keep; and the vows now include the duty 'to love and to cherish'.

The introduction of Matt. 19.6 ('those whom God hath joined . . .') and the subsequent declaration of marriage are German customs derived from Luther. The possibility that the woman may be past childbirth is covered by the suggestion of Ps. 67 as an alternative to the traditional Ps. 128 and a rubric before the collect for fruitfulness. This latter reveals a change of emphasis in the second part of the service, which was originally the blessing of the bride. Now there are prayers that 'they may *both* be fruitful' (instead of 'that she may be . . .'), and that 'this man may love his wife' (compare the interpretation of the ring as a token of the '*covenant* betwixt them made'). The attributes of Christian married life include 'quietness, sobriety, and peace' and 'holy love'.

In 1552 the only change of importance was the omission of the 'tokens of spousage' (gold and silver, often bracelets), whose place was taken by the priest's and clerk's fees. The tokens, however, continued to be brought in the North of England well into the seventeenth century. Surprisingly enough, the ring is retained. This became one of the major grievances of the Puritans, on a par with the surplice, the sign of the cross in baptism, and kneeling at the communion. They also objected to the phrase 'with my body I thee worship', but neither objection was successful in 1662.

In 1928 the phrasing of 'the causes for which matrimony was ordained' was modified to suit a more refined taste. The bride was no longer required to promise to obey her husband; and instead of endowing her with all his worldly goods, he was to share them with her. The Puritan criticism of 'worship' was at last met by substituting 'honour'. The prayers in the second part were shortened, chiefly by leaving out allusions to OT figures. No blessing of the ring was provided, though this was done in most other contemporary revisions. The omission was made good in *Alternative Services, First Series* (1966). A eucharistic proper was appointed in which divine love was the chief theme ('Love one another as I have loved you'). The American revision of 1929 omits the second part of the service altogether; the Scottish and South African books provide a form for blessing a civil marriage.

G. J. CUMING

5. *Baptist*. Baptists are found in many parts

of the world, but in no country do they have a prescribed marriage service. These two facts taken together account for a wide diversity of practice. Marriage may be solemnized in a home, or in a church, in a civic hall, or in a registry office. In Britain, since the marriage act of 1863, after the civil preliminaries, it is customary for the ceremony to take place in a Baptist place of worship registered for marriages. The practice of blessing in church a marriage already contracted in a civil registry office, while much less frequent, is on the increase. Civil marriage is obligatory in many countries, but in the USA, where Baptists are most numerous, the church marriage ceremony is recognized by the state. Two convictions are common to Baptists – marriage is not a sacrament of the church, but a divine institution for mankind; believers should enter the marriage covenant in the presence of God and with prayer for his blessing. The persistent opposition of the early Baptists to marriages outside their own communion has disappeared, but unions between believers and unbelievers are still discouraged. A marriage service in church usually includes the singing of hymns, the reading of scriptures, a message, and extemporary or free prayer. The three main parts of the service are the introduction, the covenant, and the word. The ministry of the word sometimes precedes, but more usually follows the marriage covenant. The introduction commonly includes a hymn, a statement of the purposes of marriage, a declaration by the couple that they know of no legal impediment, and a prayer. The marriage covenant is made by the exchange of promises, the joining of hands, and the giving and receiving of a ring or rings. In Baptist manuals, the actual wording of the promises has been profoundly influenced by the service-books of other communions, especially by the *BCP*. The ceremony concludes with the declaration that the couple are now husband and wife, and a blessing. Then the scriptures are read, there is usually a short sermon or address, and prayer(s) for the divine blessing on the marriage contracted. The service ends with a hymn and the benediction. Marriages are solemnized usually on week-days, occasionally on Sundays in the context of the congregation at worship, rarely at the Lord's Supper.

S. WINWARD

6. *Congregationalist*. Traditionally there have been two reasons for Christian marriage. The first is for the avoidance of concupiscence (or, in Pauline words, the choice is 'to marry or burn'). The second is for the procreation and upbringing of children. The third emphasis was added by the Puritan predecessors of the modern Congregationalists: for companionship through life. This also has biblical authority for God is said to have created Eve for Adam 'because it is not good for man to be alone'. This is the dominant emphasis in modern Congregational marriage services, often called 'solemnizations of marriage' because they are regarded as ecclesiastical blessings of civil covenants, and in no sense as sacraments. In common with other Christians, Congregationalists recall that Jesus hallowed marriage by his presence at the marriage at Cana in Galilee, and that Paul used marriage as an analogy of the intimate relationship of Christ to his church.

Though there is no single, exclusive and official form of marriage service for Congregationalists, the many services from which a minister can select have a common lineage and common characteristics. If the English Free Churches have borrowed any single ordinance from the Church of England, it is surely the service of holy matrimony. The ceremonies of the giving away of the bride by her father and the giving and receiving of rings, as well as the very words of the solemn promises which bride and groom make to each other in plighting their troth, are all borrowed from the *BCP*. (The exact words are used in *A Book of Public Worship for the Use of Congregationalists*, 1948, p. 174, and there is a revised version in *A Book of Services and Prayers*, 1959, p. 67.)

The essentials of a Congregational marriage service comprise: reminders of the purposes of Christian marriage in an opening exhortation and in NT lessons; the charge that any impediments to the marriage be openly declared; the affirmations of mutual loyalty made by groom and bride; the mutual pledging of their troth and the exchange of rings; the minister's pronouncement in the triune name of God that bride and groom are married; and prayers and hymns for the keeping of the promises made and for the building of a Christian home, with the divine assistance, concluding with the Lord's Prayer and the blessing. Occasionally the service includes a celebration of holy communion in which the bride and groom are the sole communicants, but this is very infrequent.

HORTON DAVIES

7. *Jehovah's Witnesses.* Biblically, wedlock to be valid must have (*a*) recognition by the state, and (*b*) recognition by God.

In the temporal sphere, common-law marriage is not accepted by the congregation. 'Those living together in common-law marriage should have a legal marriage ceremony performed' and 'this should be definitely registered in the registry of the civil government', since common-law marriage 'has such an uncertain position because it is not universally recognized' (for source of quotations, *see below*.) A consentient arrangement is fornication, forbidden by scripture (Heb. 13.4), and deprives the participants of legal protection, contrary to Matt. 22.21.

In the spiritual sphere, the two must be scripturally free to marry: that is, neither of them must be married, legally or scripturally, to another person. It appears that the only scriptural ground for divorce is adultery (Matt. 5.32). Thus a person merely separated from a marriage mate or being in a state of legal divorce on a ground other than adultery would not scripturally be free to remarry. Death severs the marriage bond (Rom. 7.2).

Polygamy is scripturally improper for Christians (Matt. 19.5, 6). In lands where it is practised, the polygamist wishing to become one of Jehovah's Christian Witnesses must first put away all wives except the first, making suitable provision for the secondary wives and his children by them.

Witness children are discouraged from early marriages and are counselled to marry 'only in the Lord', that is, to fellow-believers, with spiritual and practical advantages (I Cor. 7.36, 39).

For 'those who have the gift' (Matt. 19.11) and can cultivate it, singleness is a fine course. It affords greater freedom to serve the Lord, and many young Witnesses postpone marriage for some time while they enjoy full-time ministry or missionary service; others remain single permanently. However, singleness has its price ('because of prevalence of fornication, let each man have his own wife'), celibacy is imposed upon no one (I Tim. 4.3), and the choice should be 'that which is becoming and that which means constant attendance upon the Lord without distraction' (I Cor. 7.2, 35).

The wedding ceremony itself, like most other Witness meetings, is opened and closed with song and prayer. A discourse specially directed to the couple and offering admonition and advice usually includes reference to the Genesis account and the prior creation of man, but also his duty to exercise his headship with understanding and love, while the bride is reminded of her relative subjection to her husband (relative, that is, to the absolute subjection due to God) (Eph. 5.21-33). After about thirty minutes the vows are taken. The wording recommended, with variations where necessary in accordance with the law of the land, is: 'I take you to be my wedded wife [husband], to love and to cherish [the bride adds: 'and deeply respect'] in accordance with the divine law as set forth in the holy scriptures for Christian husbands [wives], for as long as we both shall live together on earth according to God's marital arrangement.' A wedding meal is generally provided after the ceremony, very often paid for and prepared by the local congregation. Frequently considerable numbers will join in the festivities, a wedding reception being one of the very few occasions for large informal gatherings of Witnesses.

Divorce on grounds other than adultery, and separation, are strongly discouraged: a man should 'stick to his wife'; 'Jehovah has hated a divorcing' (Matt. 19.5; Mal. 2.16; I Cor. 7.10, 16). There are, of course, innumerable variations on these problems associated with marriage. Basic principles relating to such matters as the wedding ceremony, paying marriage dues, rearing children, engagement, and singleness have been discussed at length in such issues of *The Watchtower* as 15 September 1956, 15 November 1960, 1 May 1962 and 15 September 1965.

Both Jehovah God (Isa. 54.5, 6) and Christ Jesus (Rev. 19.7) are symbolically represented as 'married', and this in itself elevates the privilege of marriage to the highest level.

A. HELEY

8. *Lutheran.* On the eve of the Reformation, and indeed throughout the sixteenth century, marriage law and forms of marriage were still developing. At this time we find the precepts or customs of Roman, Germanic, canon and imperial law, according to which the mutual agreement of the nuptial pair is the foundation of their marriage (*consensus facit*

nuptias); certain degrees of relationship are given as hindrances to marriage, and to a limited extent it is presupposed that the marriage will be held in public. The involvement of the church authorities in the ceremony (namely, the publication of banns, the wedding itself as the questioning of the nuptial pair before the congregation, and the nuptial mass) will also have been a widespread custom. At the beginning of the sixteenth century, there can be no question of rules which embraced every detail. Responsible authorities, and later both the Roman Catholic and Protestant churches, fought passionately against *clandestina sponsalia* or *matrimonia*, 'secret marriages' or 'hedge marriages', but they were still permissible under the systems of law mentioned above, as they rested on the principle of *consensus facit nuptias*. Despite prohibitions by the church, lay marriage continued for a very long time. There is no mistaking a certain emancipation movement, which not only grants the female partner in the marriage a greater degree of independence but represents a move towards a greater freedom in the formation of individual modes of living. At the same time, the sources continually lament the detrimental effect this has on the sphere of sexual morality; official ordinances seek to rectify this situation even before the Reformation, and still more after it.

In view of this situation, during the sixteenth century, marriage in church becomes increasingly important on both the Roman Catholic and the Protestant side; towards the end of the century it acquires an unprecedented significance on the Roman Catholic side in canon law as a result of the Tridentine *tametsi* and a growing place in civil law on the Protestant side with the rise of regional churches.

Over against Roman Catholic tradition, all Reformed churches are agreed that the conception of marriage as a sacrament and obligatory celibacy are not in accordance either with scripture or with the original Christian tradition. Consequently the association of marriage with the eucharist in the nuptial mass is rejected, and permission for priests, monks and nuns to marry is passionately required. Virginity is no longer regarded as a merit; marriage is seen as a state or calling in which everyone should and must prove himself as a Christian. This fundamentally different conception, reached from

the testimony of scripture, did not exclude the adoption of features of Roman Catholic marriage where they did not conflict with the Reformers' norm of the word of God; instead of marriage being linked with the mass, scriptural statements about marriage were given a greater place in the service.

The history of Lutheran marriage ordinances is further complicated because in the centres of the Lutheran Reformation (Wittenberg, Strasbourg, Nürnberg, etc.) marriage formulae from the liturgies of the respective Roman Catholic dioceses (Brandenburg, Magdeburg, Mainz, etc.) were often taken over. There were also certain differences in the legal conceptions of marriage in the different areas – at any rate, different terms were used.

There is a report of a first 'priest's marriage' from Augsburg in 1523; as the priest concerned was refused entry into church, he had his betrothal, or marriage, confirmed by an already married priest in the presence of 32 witnesses at a marriage feast in an inn. He and his bride made a mutual declaration that they took each other in marriage (E. Sehling, *Die evangelischen Kirchenordnungen des XVI Jahrhunderts*, XII, pp. 33 f.). The first Reformed marriage formula comes from the year 1524; in its original version it is most probably from the city pastor of Wittenberg, Johannes Bugenhagen. After a brief address, based essentially on the relevant statements of Gen. 1-3, the nuptial pair are asked: 'N., will you take N. to be your wedded wife (wedded husband) according to God's ordinance?' etc. After the exchange of rings ('a sign of betrothal'), the pastor says: 'So I give you both in wedlock before the face of God and our Lord Jesus Christ and before this congregation in the name of the Father . . . God our Father and our Lord Jesus Christ be with you. Be fruitful and increase the world.' Principal additions to other versions of this formula are the declaration in Matt. 19.6 and NT readings. The formula spread very rapidly, especially in South Germany. However, in Strasbourg, in the same year 1524, another form of marriage arose (printed in 1525) which largely followed the diocesan liturgy of 1513. It was more extensive than the Wittenberg formula and regarded the 'blessing of the marriage' as 'confirmation'. The Strasbourg order also had a significant influence on the marriage formulae of South German Lutheranism.

It is Luther's *Traubüchlein* (Little Wedding Book) of 1529, however, that had the greatest significance. Here Luther principally follows the order already existing in Wittenberg, but in some places he also takes up Roman Catholic formulae and the tradition of the early church. The service consists of three parts, public announcement, betrothal and blessing. The proclamation of the marriage, which is also a public summons to prayer for the couple, is first followed by the 'betrothal' (*copulatio*) in front of the church door ('bridal door'). The questions run: 'Hans, will you have Grete as your wedded wife? Grete, will you have Hans as your wedded husband?' After the exchange of rings, joining of right hands and the pronunciation of Matt. 19.6b (in the present tense), the pastor says: 'Seeing that Hans N. and Grete N. seek each other in marriage and acknowledge the same publicly before God and the world, and have given each other hands and rings of betrothal, I join them together in marriage in the name of the Father, the Son and the Holy Spirit, Amen.' The 'confirmation' in the church itself, presumably only on the day after the betrothal, essentially consists of scripture reading and prayer. The first lesson, Gen. 2.18, 21-24, is a kind of word of institution. The following three lessons are addressed directly to the bridal pair: 'Because you have both entered into the state of marriage in God's name, hear . . .' The lessons themselves present a systematic approach: Eph. 5.25, 29, 22-24 (God's commandment), Gen. 3.16-19 (the cross) and Gen. 1.27, 28-31 (consolation), together with Prov. 18.22. At the end there follows a prayer taken over from earlier examples, which the pastor is to say over the bridal pair with hands raised: 'Lord God, who has created man and woman and hast ordained the state of marriage, who hast blessed them with the fruit of the body and hast designated therein the sacrament of thy Son Jesus Christ and the church, his bride . . . We pray that thou wilt not allow thy creation (foundation), ordinance and blessing to go astray or to perish in us, but wilt graciously preserve it in us . . .'

In the 'Preface', Luther describes the purpose and conception of the marriage order that he proposes. In other respects no friend of ceremonies and ordinances, he feels it necessary to compose the *Traubüchlein* because of widespread uncertainty and confusion, and in order to educate the people. In Luther's view, marriage is a matter which falls within the competence of the authorities, especially as 'weddings and the state of marriage are a worldly concern', though at the same time marriage is a 'divine state' as well. Luther does not hold that the order he proposes is in any way obligatory; it is there in case a pastor is asked for it – a further indication that final regulations are still to come and that Luther neither wants to stand in the way of the tradition where it does not conflict with the word of God, nor seeks to create new law. Nevertheless, his order of marriage does have a legal character; anyone who submits to it has (after the preceding betrothal in the family circle) fulfilled all the necessary legal conditions for a valid marriage. That Luther felt it necessary to compose the *Traubüchlein* for pastoral reasons also is clear from the writing 'Marriage Matters' (1530, *Martin Luthers Werke* (WA) 30, III, pp. 205 f.) and countless other statements on the questions of marriage, betrothal and divorce.

Luther's *Traubüchlein* has influenced almost all forms or church ordinances and liturgies in North and Central Germany. There are, however, numerous alterations, expansions and re-arrangements. To the scripture readings provided by Luther with which the ceremony now usually begins are sometimes added Matt. 19.3-9; John 2.1-11, etc. The questions are expanded, partly following the Strasbourg order of 1530: 'N., do you acknowledge before this Christian congregation that you have taken (and take) N. as your wedded wife (husband) and promise to love her (him) as your spouse in the Lord and with the help of God never to leave her (him)?' As in the Brandenburg-Nürnberg order of 1533, a declaration by the nuptial pair can also take the place of a question: 'I N. take thee N. as my wedded spouse and plight thee my troth.' The question can be omitted altogether, as in the Augsburg order of 1527 and the Hessen order of 1539. As far as the betrothal formula is concerned, in North Germany Luther's vow is almost always used which 'pronounces' or 'makes' the nuptial pair man and wife. Instead of this, the Strasbourg and Brandenburg-Nürnberg orders have: 'The obligation of marriage, which you have commended to each other before God and his congregation, I confirm at the behest of the Christian congregation in the name of the Father etc.' There is a controversy as to whether there is a material difference between 'pronounce' (constitutive) and 'confirm' (declaratory); towards the end of the sixteenth and in the seventeenth century, there was a clear tendency to see church marriage as the constitutive act, whereas earlier betrothal had had this function. Matthew 19.6, in the present or the perfect, is almost always used in connection with the act of marriage proper. The usual benediction is that of Luther, occasionally in conjunction with a prayer from Hessen dated 1539. A wedding sermon, whether free or with a liturgical formulation, found its way into the service (first at Strasbourg, as did choir and congregational singing (Pss. 128, 127, Te Deum, etc.) or organ music and more elaborate forms. In some places the service was spread over two successive days, first of all the wedding ceremony with questions and 'saying together' or 'confirming'; the following day the entry into the church with sermon and blessing, in some places still called the 'nuptial mass' or 'nuptial office'. With increasing frequency the ceremony was concluded with the Aaronic blessing.

In the sixteenth century, church weddings were still voluntary acts almost everywhere; as before, there were lay weddings. However, there was an increasing recognition that marriage 'is very useful for the improvement of the church' (Württemberg 1553), that the state of marriage is hallowed not only by faith and trust in the word but also by a ceremony which needs particular conditions and has particular consequences. Among the conditions are often to be found a catechetical examination of the nuptial pair, fulfilment of the requirements of the 'marriage ordinances' that arose everywhere, the strict prohibition of secret betrothals and pre-marital intercourse and the introduction of ecclesiastical and civil penalties for 'fallen couples' ('church discipline'). The ceremony, at first a proclamation and act of blessing, acquired increasing legal significance. Towards the end of the sixteenth century official certificates were required, and the authorities stated that no one was legally married without a ceremony in church. The betrothal questions become more imperative: the nuptial pair promise ('swear', Hamburg 1726) love, faithfulness, support to each other in good and bad times, 'until death do you part'; the

formula of marriage becomes weightier: '. . . in God's stead . . ., as an ordained servant of the church of Jesus Christ . . .'

The strong influence of the ecclesiastical lawyer J. H. Boehmer (d. 1749) led to the view that the marriage ceremony, or more accurately the affirmative answers to the marriage questions as a public declaration of the *consensus matrimonialis* and their public confirmation by the pastor, represented the legitimate conclusion of a marriage. Church marriage thus becomes a legal act which the church performs for the state: 'A fully valid marriage is brought about by the marriage ceremony of the church' (*Allgemeines Preussisches Landrecht*, 1794). While in this way the marriage ceremony acquired a clear legal significance, during the Enlightenment it increasingly lost its ecclesiastical character. The service became a family celebration. In many places the tradition was given up in favour of a sentimental, verbose loquaciousness; the address to the bridal couple stood in the foreground. Proposals to this effect are to be found in the private liturgies which now appear, but they also occur in official liturgies as well. The traditional formula is expanded at Württemberg 1809 as follows: 'God's peace be with you. May your hearts and lives be dedicated to him. May your home be a dwelling of contentment, love and blessing. May each of your days until you go down to the grave be a new testimony to the grace of the eternal Father, who rules over you.'

It is a mark of the nineteenth century that in the West an obligatory civil marriage was introduced, in 1848 by the Civil Code in many districts, and in 1875 by national law. The churches at first fought bitterly before accepting the new situation ('Throne and altar'), without of course fundamentally altering the marriage formulae and without being able to solve the problem of the 'double' marriage, the official act and the church ceremony. The local liturgies which arose about 1900 provide either the scriptural readings from Luther's *Traubüchlein* or a formulated address in the form of a biblical paraphrase; the questions are presented in the traditional, verbose form, and the traditional expression 'pronounce' is used in the formula of betrothal. Some private liturgies are freer. Some of them understand marriage as 'ordination to the priesthood of the home' (J. Smend).

It is only the marriage forms that have been

produced in the last decade, above all the *Agende für Evangelisch-Lutherische Kirchen und Gemeinden* (1964, III, pp. 139-154), that draw the consequences from the introduction of obligatory civil marriage. Now the marriage ceremony is regarded as being the concern of the congregation. Accordingly, on the analogy of a congregational service it is introduced with a biblical vow, prayer or psalm, and then followed by the wedding sermon. The scripture readings provided are those from Luther's *Traubüchlein*. The questions now run: 'N., will you love and honour this N., born N., whom God entrusts to you, as your wife, and live a married life with her according to God's command and promise, in good and in bad days, until death parts you? Your answer should be, "Yes, with God's help."' The question to the wife takes the same form. There follow the exchange of rings, the joining of right hands, Matt. 19.6b and the Lord's Prayer. A new principle is that the marriage formula is to be understood as a consequence of the preceding prayer of intercession for the nuptial pair, as recently also in confirmation and ordination. The first formula runs: 'God the Father, Son and Holy Spirit bless your marriage. May he enlighten you by his word and fill you with his grace, so that you may remain in his community and reach everlasting life.' The second formula comes from pre-Reformation times: 'The blessing of the triune God be upon you and remain with you now and always.' A general prayer brings the ceremony to an end. Some other district churches have adopted the same principle of understanding the wedding as a liturgical ceremony directed towards the congregation and developing the marriage formula as a word of encouragement from the intercession for the bridal pair, though they have occasionally used other formulae (e.g. Evangelische Kirche der Union, 1963/64; outline form, Baden 1967; outline form, Kurhessen-Waldeck 1969). Most recently there have been attempts to provide more scriptural readings, to replace the questions by a 'form of assent' and to formulate the marriage formula as a personal wish, following a meditative prayer.

ALFRED NIEBERGALL

9. *Methodist*. The basis for Methodist marriage services is in John Wesley's edition of the 1662 *BCP* which appeared in 1784 as *The Sunday Service of the Methodists in North America*. Wesley's editing of the wedding service was relatively minor. For unexplained reasons he dropped the giving away of the bride. He also changed the phrase 'plight thee my troth' to 'plight thee my Faith', omitted the rubrics on impediments and receiving communion, removed any reference to the giving of the ring (perhaps in deference to Puritan practice), and dropped out the psalms and exhortation (probably for sake of brevity). In 1792 American Methodists abbreviated the service further, deleting the list of the ends of marriage and omitting the versicles and the prayer for childbearing.

The subsequent development of the service, both in Britain and in America, shows remarkable conservatism, though this may be natural in a service which is rooted in the structures of society itself. In America, the banns were dropped by the Methodist Episcopal Church South (MECS) in 1854 and in the Methodist Episcopal Church (MEC) in 1864, but the giving away of the woman was restored in MEC in 1916. The promise on the woman's part to obey was dropped as early as 1864 in the northern church and in 1910 in the second vows of the southern church. In 1864 MEC and in 1866 MECS restored the giving of the ring. Eventually all but one of the concluding prayers were omitted except for the Lord's Prayer.

Changes in the twentieth century have not been drastic and reflect the conservatism perhaps natural to rites of passage. Some indication of changed theological currents is reflected in the omission of such phrases as 'the dreadful day of judgment'. A prayer over the rings appeared in the 1944 *Book of Worship*, but the words of giving the rings did not recover the mention of one's body and worldly goods. Nor have the rest of the concluding prayers been restored. A rubric in the 1964 *Book of Worship* states that the sacrament of the Lord's Supper should be provided (if requested) at another time. Nevertheless, this sacrament seems increasingly to follow the wedding service.

In general the Black Methodist churches have preserved conservative versions of the 1792 service, especially the African Methodist Episcopal Church which retained the banns and concluding prayers. The Christian Methodist Episcopal Church was more prone to brevity and dropped the second vows though adding an optional ring ceremony.

The Book of Offices of the Methodist Church in Britain (1936) has been likewise conservative. Though the banns have disappeared, the basic shape is still that of the 1662 *BCP*. A new opening collect and the Lord's Prayer begin the service, followed by alternative charges. The concerns of civil laws are represented by inquiries as to legal impediments. Psalm 67 has been restored and I Cor. 13.4-8, 13 added, as has been one concluding prayer and another one rewritten. The giving of the rings has reappeared as has the phrase, 'I give thee my troth', a curious linguistic regression.

JAMES F. WHITE

10. *Old Catholic.* In the period after the Council of Trent, the view became widespread in the doctrine and practice of the Roman Catholic Church that it is the bridal couple themselves who mutually celebrate the sacrament of marriage. This view is also held to some degree in the Old Catholic Church. Alongside, however, and with even greater emphasis, the church teaches that according to an earlier and more correct view, the sacrament is bestowed by the priest through blessing and the laying on of hands; this is the case above all in the Netherlands, but also in the Polish National Catholic Church, in whose catechism it is said, 'The *priest* is the minister of the sacrament of matrimony' (Scranton, Pa. 1962, Question 410).

The Old Catholic churches in common recognize the civil betrothal as a legitimate contract of marriage. This is expressed by the fact that when the bridal couple answer 'Yes', there is always a reference to the marriage vows made earlier before the civil authorities. Thus according to the rite of the Old Catholic Church of Germany, the priest says, 'And now repeat before me, as the servant of the Christian church, and before these witnesses, the declaration of your marriage bond which you made before the representatives of the civil law, and receive the blessing of the church.'

The rite takes different forms in individual churches. Everywhere, however, it is composed of the same elements: address, repetition of the word 'Yes', blessing and giving of the rings, mutual joining of hands, blessing of the bridal couple, the Lord's Prayer and other prayers. The ceremony often, though not always, takes place within the framework of a nuptial mass.

In the Old Catholic Church of the Netherlands, there are two different forms of marriage:

(*a*) The sacrament of the blessing of the church. This sacrament is administered when two Old Catholics, or an Old Catholic and a Roman Catholic, get married. Since 1968 this has also been the case if the partner who is not an Old Catholic is a baptized and communicant member of a Protestant church and accepts this sacramental form of blessing. The formulary is taken from the *Rituale Romanum*, but is fairly freely revised.

(*b*) A non-sacramental form of blessing. Here there is no question of a lesser blessing – this is up to God alone – but this rite seeks to meet with the conviction of the partner who is not an Old Catholic if the latter is not a communicant member of any denomination, yet wants to place his marriage under God's blessing. It is a fairly simple form, consisting of readings (Ps. 121 and Eph. 5.22-33), some prayers, and a concluding blessing.

KURT PURSCH
A. E RÜTHY
C. TOL

11. *Plymouth Brethren.* The marriage service among the Open Brethren closely resembles the order followed in other Free Churches. Some variations arise, as in other denominations, because of differences in national law. In England, where a church building must be registered for the solemnization of matrimony, the person who conducts the marriage ceremony does not need to be specially licensed; what is important is the presence of a member of the local registrar's staff or of a member of the church recognized by the Registrar-General as custodian of the church's marriage register. In Scotland, where the place of the ceremony need not be registered, the person conducting the ceremony must be registered for that purpose by the Registrar-General for Scotland. Normally one responsible member of each Open Brethren congregation is so registered. It is his responsibility to see that the marriage certificate is duly completed by the bridal couple and the witnesses, signed by himself and delivered to the local registrar. As a matter of convenience, an office in Glasgow serves as a clearing-house for communication

between the local churches throughout Scotland and the Registrar-General.

The service takes the usual form: introductory words setting forth the divine institution and purpose of marriage and its indissoluble bond, so that the bridal couple and the congregation may understand clearly what Christian marriage involves by way of blessing and responsibility; then the mutual plighting of troth (for which national law may stipulate a minimum form of words), made while the couple clasp each other by the right hand and followed by the giving of the wedding ring. After pronouncing the couple to be husband and wife, the person conducting the ceremony prays for God's blessing on their marriage, and either he or someone else gives a short address appropriate to the occasion. Two or three suitable hymns are usually sung in the course of the service.

Among the Exclusive Brethren it has been customary for the legal part of the marriage to be performed in the registrar's office. This is followed by a service of prayer, thanksgiving and exhortation in the meeting room or other suitable place, which may well be combined with the wedding breakfast. In their way of life there is no line of demarcation between religious and social activities, just as there was none in the early church.

There is no uniform ruling among Brethren on the admission of divorced (more especially, of divorced and remarried) persons to church fellowship. The importance of maintaining Christian standards is recognized by all, but charity is recognized as one of those standards, so that in some places a less rigorist and in others a more rigorist attitude is taken up on this issue. A common attitude would admit them to church fellowship but not to public ministry in the church.

F. F. BRUCE

12. *Reformed.* All Reformed communions rejected the medieval idea that marriage is a sacrament, yet held high views of its importance. According to them the essence of marriage lies in the mutual declaration and promise of fidelity before witnesses, the consequence being that the 'pronouncing-together' by the minister was only a confirmation of the marriage. Yet marriage services appeared in all the service-books. Many changes have taken place from time to time, though there is a clear ancestral line through them all, since they were derived ultimately from the form of Farel.

Farel's *La manière et fasson*, first printed in 1533, was adopted by Calvin in his *La forme des prières* (1542) and in the *Forme of Prayer and Ministration of the Sacraments* (1558, 1561), followed by Knox's *Genevan Service-Book* (1556). *The Form of Prayers and Ministration of the Sacraments* (1562) came from the Genevan *Forme of Prayer* with only few changes. This was followed by the *Forme of Prayers* of 1564/5, printed in Edinburgh, which came to be known as *The Book of Common Order (BCO)*, of which fully seventy editions appeared before 1645. Throughout these the marriage service remained practically the same. The Westminster *Directory* (1644/5) made little change in the order though no prayers were printed. These books have greatly influenced the many service-books issued by English-speaking Presbyterians throughout the world.

Similarly the French and Swiss (Vaud, Geneva, Neuchâtel, etc.) Reformed service-books were derived from Farel through Calvin. We now indicate the form of the marriage service in Calvin and note some of the variations found in later service-books.

The first requirement is the proclamation of banns of marriage, though this was a pre-Reformation custom (as in Sarum). Banns were to be read on 'three several days'; in practice these would normally be Sundays or preaching days during the week, the point being that intimation should be made when the largest proportion of the parishioners would be present in church. The marriage was normally to take place in church before the sermon on Sunday. But later, at least in Scotland, Sunday marriages were prohibited to prevent 'riotous profanation' of the day, (cf. Westminster *Directory*). Modern service-books do not usually specify any particular day.

The service opens with an exhortation based on scripture, preceded in continental books and in modern English forms by the words, 'Our help is in the name of the Lord . . .'. The exhortation is long in early books (*BCO* has some 600 words), but much shorter in modern books. The couple are then challenged to confess any impediment, and the same challenge is made to the congregation. If none is alleged, the minister says, 'Forasmuch as no man speaketh against this thing, you, N., shall protest here before God and his holy congregation, that you have taken and are now content to have N. here present for your lawful wife, promising to keep her . . .' The answer is, 'Even so I take her before God and in the presence of this holy congregation.' The woman is addressed similarly and gives the same reply. (In some forms the two parties say the words of promise, either by repeating them after the minister, or by memory, or by reading them from a book or card.) The minister then addresses the people on the duties of marriage, reading from Matt. 19. The service ends with the blessing. In the early forms there is no declaration that the parties are married. The ring is not mentioned in early forms. But its use was widely customary, though the Westminster *Directory* says the two parties join the right hands during the vows, 'with no further ceremony'. This has been regarded as prohibition of the ring.

Two other points must be made. First, in some modern continental forms (e.g. Geneva, 1946 and Paris, 1963) there are two alternative addresses after the vows, the first being the more instructive, and the second the more intimate in nature. Secondly, some modern books (e.g. *BCO*, 1940) contain not only the marriage service itself but also a form for 'Blessing of a Civil Marriage' (*cf.* the title in some French books for the marriage service, 'Bénédiction du mariage', due to the French law which insists on a civil marriage).

J. A. LAMB

13. *Seventh-day Adventist.* While attributing no sacramental value to the marriage relationship, Seventh-day Adventists believe that marriage, a divine institution established by God himself prior to the fall of man, is the foundation of human society and was designed to be a blessing to mankind. True affection between man and woman is thus ordained by God. 'Central to God's holy plan was the creation of beings made in His image who would multiply and replenish the earth, and live together in purity, harmony, and happiness' (*Seventh-day Adventist Church Manual*, 1967, p. 251). Thus marriage and the family relationship should be the means for ennobling both partners and facilitating the development of mature, unselfish characters in the home. The marriage relationship is highly exalted in scripture, by using it to represent God's relationship to his people, to symbolize the union between Christ and his church, and thus typify the union of humanity

with divinity.

Monogamy (e.g. Gen. 2.21-24; Matt. 19.5) has ever been God's ideal plan, and any existing polygamous situations were simply tolerated. In the light of God's plan that man should have only one living wife, today when the gospel message in certain countries reaches a man living in a state of polygamy, he is upon conversion required to put away all his wives save one before he is eligible for baptism and membership in the SDA Church. In such cases proper provision is required to be made for the future support of the wives put away and of their children, and for their protection from disgrace (*see* General Conference *Working Policy*, 1968, pp. 48, 49).

In harmony with Christ's statement in Matt. 19.3-6, Seventh-day Adventists believe that the marriage relationship is to be indissoluble. The only scriptural ground for divorce is unfaithfulness to the marriage vow, and this rule is to be followed by the church, whether or not the state or prevailing custom allow larger liberty. In the case of adultery and in the event that reconciliation is not effected, 'the innocent spouse has the Biblical right to secure a divorce, and also to remarry. A spouse found guilty of adultery by the church shall be subject to church discipline . . . [He] has not the moral right to marry another while the innocent spouse still lives and remains unmarried and chaste, should he (or she) do so, he (or she), if a member, shall be disfellowshipped' (*Church Manual*, 1967, pp. 253, 254).

In the SDA Church only ordained ministers (*see* **Ordination** 14: Seventh-day Adventist) are authorized to perform the marriage ceremony. Since laws regarding marriage vary a great deal from country to country, the role played by the minister also takes on different forms. In countries where marriage is legally regarded as a state responsibility and purely civil contract, the SDA minister conducts a marriage service that takes the form of a nuptial blessing. Being a world-wide church, the SDA Church has 'no prescribed nuptial liturgy that must be followed' (*Manual for Ministers*, 1954, p. 100). Though customs vary in different countries, there are some well-defined principles adhered to by Adventists. The marriage of believers with unbelievers is expressly contrary to the teachings of the church. Relative simplicity and dignity in decorations and arrangements are recommended and ostentatious display in dress and ceremony should be avoided.

A typical Adventist marriage ceremony would include the wedding march, sermonette, musical item, charge, vows, prayer, and benediction. The SDA *Manual for Ministers* contains suggestions for sermonettes, charges and vows, providing for variation and allowing the minister to choose the form best suited for the occasion. In all cases, however, the ceremony must be kept strictly within the legal requirements.

B. B. BEACH

F. E. Brightman, *The English Rite*, 1915, I, pp.cxxiv, cxxv, clxiii, clxiv, ccxx; II, pp. 800-17; A. J. Collins, *Manuale Sarum*, 1960, pp.44-59; *Constitution, Bylaws and Working Policy of the General Conference of Seventh-day Adventists*, 1968; H. A. Dombois and F. K. Schumann, *Familienrechtsreform. Dokumente und Abhandlungen*, 1955; H. A. Dombois and F. K. Schumann, *Weltliche und kirchliche Eheschliessung. Beiträge zur Frage des Eheschliessungsrechtes*, 1953; P. Graff, *Geschichte der Auflösung der alten gottesdienstlichen Formen in der evangelischen Kirche Deutschlands*, ²1937, I, pp. 331-54; II, pp.260-72; Clifford Howell, SJ, *Companion to the New Order of Marriage*, 1970; P. Jounel, in *L'Eglise en Prière*, 1961, pp.594-605; T. Kliefoth, *Liturgische Abhandlungen*, 1896, I, p.1; U. Küry, *Die alt-katholische Kirche* (Die Kirchen der Welt, III), 1966, pp.212-14; M. Luther, *Werke*, Weimar ed. 1883ff. (WA), 30, III; C. Mahrenholz, *Die Neuordnung der Trauung*, 1959; William Maskell, *Monumenta Ritualia Ecclesiae Anglicanae*, 1846, I, pp.42-64; A. Niebergall, 'Geschichte der evangelischen Trauung in Hessen, Teil I', in *Jahrbuch der hessischen kirchengeschichtlichen Vereinigung*, Vol. 21, 1970; A. L. Richter, *Die evangelischen Kirchenordnungen des 16. Jahrhunderts*, 2 vols., 1846; G. Rietschel-P. Graff, *Lehrbuch der Liturgik*, ²1951, pp.701-56; M. Righetti, *La Storia Liturgica*, 1959, IV, pp. 455-72; A. Rinkel, 'Ehe und Sakrament', *Internationale Kirchliche Zeitschrift*, 31, 1941, pp.1-28; E. Schillebeeckx, *Marriage, Secular Reality and Saving Mystery*, 1965; E. Sehling, *Die evangelischen Kirchenordnungen des XVI Jahrhunderts*, 14 vols., 1902ff.

Mattins *see* **Canonical Hours**

Maundy Thursday

The title for Thursday in Holy Week (q.v.) derives through Old French *mandé* from the Latin *mandatum novum*, 'a new commandment' (John 13.34), associated with the ceremonial of washing of feet, which is still continued in some token form in Rome. The English distribution of Maundy money by the sovereign is a vestigial trace of this

A. A. MCARTHUR

Methodist Worship

1. *Britain.* John Wesley, a presbyter of the Church of England, intended his preachers and his people to follow his own example by attending 'the Church Service', i.e. the services of the parish churches of the Church of England; they were to be supplemented, not superseded, by simple Methodist preaching services at 5 a.m. and 5 p.m. The Methodists were increasingly reluctant to attend the parish churches where indeed they were not always welcomed and, though the custom of attending the parish churches lingered for a long time in country districts, they increasingly established in their chapels a complete pattern of their own Sunday services, which after the Plan of Pacification in 1795 included in nearly all places the Lord's Supper. From this pattern the preaching service at 5 a.m. eventually disappeared, as did evensong in the afternoon; but evening services, usually at 6 p.m. or 6.30 p.m. became very popular. The morning service, usually at 10.30 a.m. or 11 a.m. replaced attendance at the parish church for morning prayer, litany, and antecommunion (qq.v.). In a few chapels in England and a larger number overseas this morning service still consists of morning prayer, either from the *BCP* or from Wesley's version of it in *The Sunday Service*, together with hymns and sermon. But in most churches the service was a simpler preaching service, though not quite as simple as the supplementary 5 a.m. preaching service had been. It consisted of hymns, lessons, extempore prayers and sermon, though occasionally with traces of morning prayer such as a psalm before the OT lesson. The evening service almost always took this simpler form.

The holy communion was usually observed monthly in towns, quarterly in villages, after the morning or evening preaching service. For that service a liturgical book was generally used, at least in the Wesleyan chapels, as also for occasional offices. In the preaching services, liturgical books (q.v.)

were little used except where the custom was retained of saying morning prayer, often called 'the liturgical service'.

These services were enriched, as Methodist worship still is, by the use of hymns, especially those of Charles Wesley, which are in some sense the 'liturgy' of Methodism.

To these services were added not only such 'instituted' means of grace as scripture reading, prayer (private, family, public) and fasting, but also 'prudential' means such as the love feast (q.v.), the watch-night, the covenant service (qq.v.), and the distinctive Methodist forms of fellowship meeting; society meeting, class meeting (q.v.), band meeting. Some of these survive, and they have given a distinctive tone of fellowship to all Methodist worship. There was also open-air preaching. The pattern of Sunday during most of Methodist history also included morning and afternoon sessions of the Sunday school, which in various ways involved many people.

The main pattern still remains, but in recent decades fresh tendencies have appeared. The afternoon session of the Sunday school is tending to disappear, and the morning session is combined with the morning service under such titles as junior church. The children attend the earlier part of the service, and then depart to their own session. The morning service has acquired a greater prominence; the evening service has a declining attendance, and will probably take more experimental forms.

The British Methodist Conference of 1968 authorized for experimental use *The Sunday Service*, a revival of Wesley's title. This seeks to establish, primarily at morning services, a flexible structure, combining fixed and free elements, which may be used whether or not the service culminates in the Lord's Supper. The structure of the preaching service is as follows, optional elements being in brackets: (hymn or psalm), invocation or prayer of adoration, (commandments), confession, (text declaring forgiveness), (*Gloria in excelsis* or other hymn), collect of the day or other prayers, OT lesson or epistle or both, (hymn or psalm), gospel, (dismissal of children), sermon, (hymn), (announcements), (baptism or other ordinances of the church), intercessions, Lord's Prayer, (hymn), (grace). When there is no communion, a prayer of thanksgiving for creation and redemption and of dedication is to be said before or

after the intercessions. Other forms may be substituted for all the prayers except the Lord's Prayer.

The structure of the Lord's Supper, which immediately follows the preaching service or some simpler form of ministry of the word, is as follows: (peace), (Nicene Creed), offertory, (with hymn), the thanksgiving, the breaking of the bread, (prayer of humble access), communion, final prayer, (hymn), dismissal, (blessing). The thanksgiving includes the dialogue, long preface with recital of the mighty acts of God, *Sanctus, Benedictus qui venit*, words of institution, acclamation, anamnesis, modified forms of oblation and epiclesis, prayers for benefits of communion, doxology (qq.v.).

A. RAYMOND GEORGE

2. *USA*. The forms of worship used in American Methodism reflect in many ways the social and cultural situations of American Methodists. These forms of worship often have had more in common with those of other American denominations than with English precedents.

John Wesley remained a priest of the Church of England throughout his lifetime, highly esteeming and utilizing the *BCP* even while supplementing it with other forms. In 1784 he sent his followers in the newly independent USA a book of over three hundred pages, entitled *The Sunday Service of the Methodists in North America with Other Occasional Services*. It was his revision and abridgement of the 1662 *BCP*, not too different from that adopted a few years later by the new Protestant Episcopal Church. Perhaps even more significant, Wesley sent over at the same time a hymn-book.

Wesley was, it turned out, a poor judge of the American situation. Though the *Sunday Service* was reprinted in 1786 and 1790, it hardly survived Wesley as far as American usage was concerned. One year after Wesley's death, the *Sunday Service* was replaced by thirty-seven pages of 'Sacramental Services, &c.' in the 1792 *Discipline*. Gone were morning and evening prayer, the psalms, litany, and the collects, epistles, and gospels for the Lord's Supper. Orders remained for both sacraments, weddings, funerals, and the forms for the ordination of deacons, elders, and bishops. These services appeared thenceforth in the *Disciplines*. After the split of 1844 the Methodist Episcopal Church renamed this section of the *Discipline* 'The Ritual' (1848). The Methodist Episcopal Church, South, dropped the term 'Sacramental Services, &c.' in 1854 in favour of no title and adopted the term 'The Ritual' in 1870. Both churches eventually added services for the reception of new members and various dedications.

'The Ritual', however, was only used on those occasions when the sacraments or occasional offices were celebrated. Methodist worship tended to centre around preaching services. This is especially the case in the evangelization of the west, a process largely contributing to the rapid growth of Methodism from a small sect to the largest Protestant church in America during the nineteenth century. Bishop Francis Asbury (the American John Wesley) and many of his preachers were men of the frontier, preaching and organizing societies wherever they could gather a few individuals. In such frontier situations, worship usually consisted of fervent preaching and hymn-singing. Since many of the frontiersmen were illiterate, a type of hymn involving considerable repetition evolved. These so-called 'gospel songs' were often testimonials to the worshipper's conversion experience.

At yearly intervals, camp meetings (q.v.) were held in which crowds assembled from considerable distances to hear evangelistic preaching. At times the services developed highly emotional reactions. After several days, the camp meeting ended with separate communion services conducted by the various denominations sponsoring the session. In the second third of the nineteenth century, the revival system spread similar techniques to the churches on the more sedate eastern coast, utilizing such practices as preaching for conversions, the sawdust trail, the mourner's bench, and protracted meetings. Much of the historic content and forms of Christian worship were bypassed in favour of a pragmatic spirit that pointed to results calculated in the number of converts.

The period from 1920 to 1970, on the other hand, has been the era of middle-class respectability due to the upward social mobility of most Methodists. A second Gothic revival occurred in Methodism prompted by denominational executives. Choral music, sometimes of high quality, came to be a normal part of worship, often while congregation singing declined. Orders

of worship began to appear in *The Methodist Hymnal* in 1905. In 1944 the Methodist Church published its first *Book of Worship* and another one followed twenty years later.

Beginning about 1966, another tendency appeared in the growth of experimentation with the forms of worship and a refusal to believe that recovery of past forms was the answer to making worship authentic and relevant. Many innovators have looked to new communications media as indicating directions that worship might move, especially in adding non-verbal forms of worship.

In general, the black Methodist churches have been less attracted by the forms of respectability. Their worship has often retained the spontaneity, rhythmic music, and high degree of participation characteristic of the revival system.

In all these changes Methodist worship has reflected profound changes in the people who worship. Perhaps without deliberation, they have often adopted those forms which seemed most natural to them.

JAMES F. WHITE

The Book of Worship, 1964; William F. Dunkle, Jr and Joseph D. Quillian, Jr, eds., *Companion to the Book of Worship*, 1970; H. Grady Hardin, Joseph D. Quillian, Jr, James F. White, *The Celebration of the Gospel*, 1964; *The Methodist Hymnal*, 1964.

Metrical Psalms

The ancestor of the modern hymnal was the metrical psalter, comprising versifications of the psalms with simple strophic tunes designed to fit the metres employed. Perhaps the most familiar example of a metrical psalm is the version of the hundredth psalm in which the original prose, 'O be joyful in the Lord, all ye lands', has become 'All people that on earth do dwell'. Included in almost every modern hymnal, and hence usually thought of as a hymn, those words first appeared in *Fourscore and Seven Psalms of David* published in Geneva in 1561. The tune always associated with them is from the still earlier *Genevan Psalter* of 1551. Thus, both words and music take us back to the same source – the English Protestant exiles who fled to Geneva in 1553 to escape persecution under Queen Mary at home.

First given a formal place in Protestant worship by Calvin, the metrical psalm owed its origin, not to him, but to Clement Marot, a poet at the court of Francis I who had begun to translate the psalms into French verse in 1533. Marot's versions soon began to enjoy great popularity at the Catholic court; but they were quickly taken up in Protestant circles, first by the Huguenots and later by Calvin for use among his 'little flock'.

By coincidence, shortly after Marot had begun to produce his versified psalms, Thomas Sternhold started upon a similar task at the court of Edward VI; and some time before his death in 1549 nineteen of his metrical psalms were published under the title *Certaine Psalmes . . drawen into Englishe metre*. To that nucleus, John Hopkins added several versifications in 1551, certain of the English exiles in Geneva completing the translation of the Psalter between 1556 and 1562. The complete version of the metrical psalter thus produced was first published in the latter year – four years after the accession of Elizabeth I – under the title *The Whole Booke of Psalmes, collected into Englysh metre by T. Starnhold, I. Hopkins and others . . .* The book contained, in addition, a few hymns, metrical versions of the canticles, and a selection of tunes, some of which were drawn from the *Genevan Psalter*. Under the Royal Injunctions of 1559, a hymn was allowed to be sung 'in the beginning or at the end of Common Prayer'; thus legally sanctioned, *The Whole Book of Psalms* became recognized as the chief song book for Anglican worship. Commonly bound up with the Bible and the *BCP*, the collection begun by Sternhold and Hopkins (and invariably referred to by those names) held that authorized position until a *New Version* was published in 1696.

The work of Nahum Tate, the Poet Laureate, and Dr Nicholas Brady, the *New Version* was designed to supplant the 'scandalous doggerel' of Sternhold and Hopkins. It was to become the source of many of the hymns in current use, including 'As pants the hart' – the metrical version of Ps. 42. Authorized for use in churches by an Order in Council of William III, 'Tate and Brady' yet never superseded 'Sternhold and Hopkins', the two collections serving side by side until the advent of the hymn-book ousted them both during the nineteenth century. The best of the contents of both Old and New Versions were then incorporated into the new hymnals where they still serve, together with the fine old tunes

originally associated with them.

M. Frost, *English and Scottish Psalm and Hymn Tunes*, 1953; J. Julian, Preface to *Hymns Ancient and Modern, Historical Edition*, 1909; R. R. Terry, *Calvin's First Psalter*, 1932.

BERNARR RAINBOW

Mission and Worship

The contemporary development of the doctrine of mission (*see* **Mission**, *DCT*), has inevitably raised the question of its relationship to worship. This relationship may be examined in three complementary ways: (1) The precise nature of the relationship may be considered. (2) Specific acts of worship, e.g. the eucharist, may be interpreted in terms of mission. (3) Particular elements in the cultus, e.g. prayer, may be given a missionary dimension. An examination of worship and mission under each of these three heads will illustrate the scope of this subject.

1. A contrast has to be noted between the OT understanding of Israel's vocation and the role that worship has to play within that vocation, and the NT understanding of the vocation of the church and the role that worship has to play within that vocation. Briefly put, Israel's vocation is to be a holy people (Lev. 19.2), i.e. a people whose life is patterned after the very being of its holy God. In so far as this is achieved, Israel then becomes a 'light to the Gentiles'; it is a witness before the nations to Yahweh in order that the nations themselves may come to acknowledge his universal lordship. The function of worship in relation to this vocation is to enable Israel to be holy; it is a means of sanctification for the Chosen People, who are set apart for the worship of Yahweh (Ex. 19.6). The Temple cultus is both the guarantee of the purity of Yahwism and the centre to which the nations are to come (Isa. 2.2 f.). It will be noticed that Israel's vocation is interpreted centripetally; Israel is not sent to the nations; instead they are to come to it, attracted by its life and worship. In exact conformity with this, Israelite worship is understood centripetally; it has its true centre in a single place, namely the Jerusalem Temple, and it is to this that all the nations are to come.

The NT presents the antithesis to this view,

in that this centripetal attitude is replaced by a centrifugal one. The church's vocation is to go out; it is to participate in the divine mission (Matt. 28.19; John 20.21; Acts 1.8). It is to join in God's action in the world as he continues his movement of humanization, assisting man towards that maturity or fullness that is embodied in Christ. The function of worship in relation to this vocation is to celebrate God's action in the world and 'so to proclaim the Lord's death until he come' (I Cor. 11.26), this being involved in the eating of the bread and the drinking of the wine at the eucharist (q.v.). Thus, as the church's vocation is interpreted centrifugally, so is its worship; it does not have a centre in a single place; anywhere is the place of encounter with God in the context of everyday life, and in so far as any temple continues to exist, this is not a building of stone but a community living in the world (II Cor. 6.16). Hence the OT is consistent in understanding both the vocation and the worship of Israel centripetally, while the NT is equally consistent but understands both the vocation and worship of the church centrifugally.

To these concepts must be added a third, namely the contrast between the general understanding of Christians today of their vocation and worship and that which we have just examined in the NT. As a consequence of the great missionary awakening of the eighteenth and nineteenth centuries, many Christians now understand the vocation of the church centrifugally, but they still persist in viewing their cultic acts centripetally. They thus give up the logical consistency that is to be found in both the OT and NT, and attempt to combine the NT centrifugal concept of vocation with the OT centripetal concept of worship in terms of ingathering. Hence the relationship of worship and mission has for decades been defined in terms of gathering and sending. The idea of gathering and sending was prominent in German missiological thought at the end of the last century and it is often re-presented at the present day. According to this, worship is an occasion for the gathering together of the Christian community in order that its members may be strengthened to engage in mission. So cultic acts and missionary activity can be compared to breathing in and breathing out, which are both necessary for life, and hence both worship and mission – gathering and sending – are

essential for the church. The analogy is a plausible one, but is it accurate? In effect it merely associates centripetalism – breathing in – with centrifugalism – breathing out – and therefore fails to resolve the basic tension between them. Moreover, it involves the idea that cultic acts are interruptions in the church's participation in mission. When the church ceases its centrifugal action in mission, for however brief the periods may be, in order to engage in centripetal actions or worship, it is no longer being missionary during those cultic acts – in terms of the analogy, one is breathing either in or out; one cannot do the two at once. Whereas if mission and worship are to be truly united, the cultic assembly must be understood within the context of mission; the coming together takes place in mission and it is not preparatory to mission. The church is the church when it is participating in the mission of God; if it is to fulfil its role constantly, it cannot disengage itself from mission in cultic activity. The church services then must not be conceived as halting places on the way nor as iron rations; they are an essential part of being on the way. So while the gathering and sending analogy does point to a relationship, it is not a relationship of unity, and this is precisely what has to be rediscovered if we are to be true to the NT. Worship then is not a means to mission; nor is it a preparation for mission, since we worship in mission. The inadequacy of the analogy should become more apparent, as we examine what worship means from a centrifugal or missionary perspective.

Worship, as presented in the NT, is the joyful celebration of life in the world; it is the response of man to what God has done and is doing in history. Two examples will serve to illustrate this.

In Luke 17, Jesus is met by ten lepers who ask him to have mercy on them. He accedes to their request and they are made whole. One of them, a Samaritan, recognizes in this the act of God and accordingly he worships – 'praising God with a loud voice, he fell on his face at Jesus' feet, giving him thanks' (17.16). The man does not draw apart from the world in order to worship; the basis of his act of worship is his response to God's action in the world – his restoration to wholeness by Christ – and this takes the form of expressing thanks and giving praise. The Lord's Supper (q.v.) itself, throughout the apostolic age, was also essentially a secular act, since it was an everyday meal, although one which, while not ceasing to be a source of physical nourishment, was at the same time a vehicle of worship. So it can be said that in the NT worship was not defined in terms of what happened at a certain time when and at a certain place where Christians assembled. What happened on those occasions was understood within the context of response to God in their total existence.

Here we have worship interpreted from a centrifugal position. Just as the world is the sphere of mission, so it is of worship which is to be offered in terms of the Christians' total existence. The church of the apostolic age does not withdraw from mission to engage in cultic acts which prepare it for mission; it never ceases to be in mission in the secular world whether it is preaching, serving or worshipping. There can therefore be no great single centre of worship corresponding to the Jerusalem Temple.

2. The two chief Christian liturgical acts, baptism (q.v.) and the eucharist, can themselves be understood in terms of mission. It is possible to indicate this by a series of theses which, in a full treatment, would require considerable expansion:

(a) Baptism is ordination to the royal priesthood and acceptance into the covenant, both priesthood and covenant being understood in terms of mission. The eucharist renews both the ordination and the covenant.

(b) Baptism, with its pattern of life and death, initiates us into mission. The eucharist re-establishes us in this pattern.

(c) Baptism includes us in the obedience of Christ and so in his mission. The eucharist renews our commitment to God and so to mission.

(d) Baptism is an eschatological sacrament and so is the eucharist; both are intimately related in this sense to mission.

3. Of the many specific elements that make up an act of worship, two may be selected to demonstrate their necessary missionary dimension, namely prayer and the dismissal (q.v.).

According to Karl Barth, Christ's 'earthly mission was accepted through his prayers as well as by his preaching and his mighty works'. This means that prayer is a part of mission. Prayer is not something separate from mission nor is it the cause of mission. When the church prays, as when Christ prayed in Galilee, it is engaged in mission; it participates in the divine action for the world. So in Eph. 6.18, prayer is referred to in the context of the weapons of warfare against the alien powers that threaten to dominate men and from which they are to be liberated through mission. Prayer is therefore one aspect of the total missionary outreach.

Next, the dismissal. Although it is now customary to conclude every service with a blessing (q.v.), in the early church the dismissal did not take this form and was very brief. Indeed it is or should be an echo of the missionary command in Matt. 28. Any and every service is most fittingly brought to an end by a dismissal which expresses this outgoing to the world at large. It is therefore not a cosy rounding-off of a cultic act but part of the sending of God's servants in mission.

Within the NT there is a continual emphasis upon the unity of worship and mission. Not only does Paul describe mission in cultic terms and cultic acts in terms of mission (cf. Rom. 12.1; II Cor. 2.15; Phil. 2.17), but the life and work of Jesus are similarly spoken of in terms both of mission and of worship (John 6.51, 57; 12.49; Heb. 3.1). It is this relationship of unity that is gradually being rediscovered at the present day.

J. G. Davies, *Worship and Mission*, 1966; J. Rossell, *Mission in a Dynamic Society*, 1968.

EDITOR

Mitre see Vestments (2*j*)

Mixed Chalice

The reference is to the mingling of water and wine in the cup at the eucharist. This was the invariable practice of the early church (*cf.* Justin, *Apol.* I, 65, 67; Cyprian, *Ep.* 63.13) and was probably what Jesus himself did at the Last Supper, since it was usual for the Jews to mix water with their wine. All the ancient liturgies either contain a direction for the mixing or refer to it in the prayers, e.g. in the *Apostolic Constitutions* (8.12), reading the words of institution, the priest says: 'Likewise also mixing the cup of wine and water and blessing it, he gave it to them.'

Various symbolic meanings have been attached to this. Some have seen it as a sign of the union of the people with Christ, others of the issue of water and blood from his side on the cross, and others again of the union of the two natures in Christ. This latter interpretation has led the Armenians to reject the practice because it conflicts with their monophysitism, i.e. belief in the one nature of Christ.

It was rejected, too, at the Reformation by Luther, who regarded it as symbolizing an impossible participation of the human with the pure work of God. Churches in the Calvinist tradition, e.g. the Church of Scotland and the Reformed Church of France, do not practice it. The 1549 *BCP* ordered it, but the rubric was omitted in 1552. It is customary in the Episcopal Church of Scotland, but was expressly forbidden by canon 37 of the Church of Ireland. It is widespread, but not universal, in the Anglican Communion, having been declared legal in a judgment in the case of the bishop of Lincoln (1891).

In the Liturgy of St Chrysostom *hot* water is added to the chalice at the commixture (q.v.). The origins of this are unknown, but it appears to have been established from at least the sixth century. This *zeon* or living water, as it is called, is said to symbolize the fervency of faith and the descent of the Holy Spirit.

EDITOR

Monstrance

A vessel designed for the purpose of showing the consecrated host to the people came into use from the thirteenth century in the Latin West as a result of the increased cultus of the reserved sacrament that arose in the later Middle Ages. No such cultus has ever existed in the Eastern Orthodox Church or the lesser Eastern Churches. The earliest forms of the monstrance were pyxes (q.v.) standing upon a stem and foot with openings or fenestrations on the sides of the pyx as in the thirteenth-century example preserved in the Church of St Quentin, Hasselt, Limburg. The next stage was to replace the metal sides with a cylinder of glass (*see* Plate 32); then finally it assumed the form of a circular window surrounded by a silver or gold frame with rays. The ceremonies associated with the use of the monstrance arose in the Low Countries and Germany, first in connection with the Feast of Corpus Christi (q.v.), but in the Counter-Reformation era

Plate 32   The Belem Monstrance,
Lisbon, Portugal

the exposition of the host became very much more frequent (*see* **Benediction, Exposition**).

The monstrance and its associated ceremonies have come into use in the Church of England since the Catholic revival, but liturgical reforms now taking place in the Roman Catholic Church are tending to discourage this type of devotion to the blessed sacrament.

A. A. King and C. E. Pocknee, *Eucharistic Reservation in the Western Church*, 1965.

C. E. POCKNEE

Moravian Worship

Moravian worship cannot properly be understood or evaluated without some introduction, however brief, to the history of the church itself.

The Moravian Church came into being in the kingdom of Bohemia (now part of Czechoslovakia) in the year 1457. It consisted at first of a small group of men and women who lived in brotherly fellowship according to the principles of the Sermon on the Mount. They called themselves 'The Unity of Brethren', or in Latin, *Unitas Fratrum*, which is the official name of the Moravian Church. In 1467 they established their own ministry with episcopal orders and withdrew from the Church of Rome.

In 1620 Protestantism was overthrown in Bohemia and the *Unitas Fratrum* ceased to exist as an organized body. But about a century later some survivors from the old *Unitas* fled into Saxony and were allowed to settle on the estates of a Lutheran nobleman, Count Nicolaus Ludwig von Zinzendorf. Other religious refugees joined them and together they founded a new community called Herrnhut. This diverse and often disunited group experienced a 'second Pentecost' at a celebration of the Lord's Supper on 13 August 1727, which marks the birth of the renewed Moravian Church.

One direct result of this renewal was a burning desire to carry the gospel wherever Christ should call, and it was in fulfilment of this task that the renewed church became established in the eighteenth and nineteenth centuries in England, North, Central and South America, the Caribbean, Africa and India.

Moravian worship as it is practised today contains active elements from these three periods of the Church's history – the ancient church, the renewed church and the missionary church.

In the ancient *Unitas Fratrum*, in sharp contrast to the Roman Church, worship was Bible centred and congregation orientated. To provide for this, the first hymnbook of the *Unitas Fratrum* was published in 1501 and was followed a few years later by a translation of the Bible into the Czech language, the Kralitz Bible. The services in this early period were extremely simple and consisted of the singing of a hymn or hymns, a threefold reading of psalm, gospel and epistle, and a sermon. 'Free' prayer was linked with the Bible reading and the sermon, but from about 1566 onwards Luther's 'German litany' was introduced into the Moravian hymn-book. A liturgy retaining elements from these early sources is still used in parts of the Moravian Church.

In the renewed church some of the forms of worship from the ancient *Unitas* were taken over and adapted, but other distinctive services developed to meet particular needs. Of these the following are of special interest in that they are still in use:

1. The love feast (q.v.). The 'agape' of apostolic times was part of the common meal which ended with the Lord's Supper. The spontaneous revival of this custom in the renewed Moravian Church at Herrnhut followed the rich experiences of unity and fellowship in the historic communion service on 13 August 1727. At the close of this service many members were loath to leave the church but continued in prayer, in religious conversation and hymn singing. Hearing of this Count Zinzendorf sent food to the church – 'in order for them to stay undisturbed together'. From this the love feast grew into a recognized service expressing in a special way the fellowship of each member with his brethren and sisters. The Moravian love feast today consists of the singing of hymns and an informal discourse by the minister on the life and work of the church, during which a simple meal is served and partaken of together.

2. The use in public and private worship of the Moravian 'Daily Texts' or 'Watchwords'. Soon after the renewal of the church, the Herrnhut elders went each morning from house to house giving a scriptural 'watchword' for the day as a guide to meditation and conduct. Count Zinzendorf selected these texts and later added to them a few lines from hymns in current use. In 1730 a collection of these 'watchwords' was printed in advance for the year 1731. Moravian family worship usually consists of the reading of the texts for the day followed by Bible reading and prayer. The 'text book' is printed in twenty-six languages with a circulation of over a million copies. It is frequently used in public worship especially in the love feast, which closes with a short homily on the NT text for that particular day.

In the missionary period, with the granting to the provinces and mission fields of the Moravian Church of a greater measure of autonomy, coupled with a diminution in the control and influence formerly exercised by Herrnhut, each province has tended to develop worship forms and usages to suit its own needs. But in the Moravian Church throughout the world there is still a recognizable basic pattern of worship which owes something to the two earlier periods of the ancient and the renewed church. The chief characteristics of this basic pattern are:

1. The use in public worship of liturgical forms of service, and of 'free' services comprising hymns, 'free' prayer, scripture reading(s) and a sermon.

2. Regular observance of the Lord's Supper in which common features are the distribution of the elements to the congregation during the singing of hymns, partaking of the elements together, and the conclusion of the service with a so-called 'covenant hymn' during which the members of the congregation exchange the right hand of fellowship with each other in token of the renewal of their 'covenant' of love and service with Christ and with one another.

3. The use of the love feast as a preparation for the Lord's Supper, or to mark some special church gathering, festival or anniversary.

Congregational singing has always had a major part in Moravian worship. It is therefore not surprising that the Moravian Church has produced down the centuries many famous hymn writers, including Michael Weisse, Count Zinzendorf, John Cennick and James Montgomery, whose works are to be found in most Protestant hymn-books.

J. T. and K. G. Hamilton, *History of the Moravian Church*, 1967; J. E. Hutton, *A History of the Moravian Church*, 1909; A. J. Lewis, *Zinzendorf, The Ecumenical Pioneer*, 1962.

J. H. FOY

Motet

The motet, a part song for two or more voices, usually unaccompanied, derives its name from the French *mot* (word) on account of the upper part in the early medieval motet having a text and music of its own, instead of being a *vocalise* as in twelfth-century *organum* (*see* **Polyphony**).

The medieval motet and its allied forms cover a huge quantity of music, little of which in modern times is sung in church but which can be fairly frequently heard in the concert hall, on the radio and gramophone records, performed by specialist vocal groups. The characteristic features of the thirteenth-century motet were that the text in the upper part (*duplum*) was a paraphrase of the plainsong text in the *tenor* or lower part, and another paraphrase would be added when a third voice (*triplum*) was included. This plan is well shown in the example below:

1. *In. saeculum saeculi, Artifex saeculi*, etc.
2. *In saeculum saeculi, supra mulieres*, etc.
3. *IN SAECULUM* (plainsong *cantus firmus*).

Each part was independent, so that if, in fact, one of the two upper parts was omitted or was sung alone, the music still made sense, but the fragmented plainsong, deprived of its flowing phrase and rhythm, by itself would not.

Polytextuality enabled the clerical poet-musicians to make a kind of musical mosaic in this way but, as prayer, one that could only be appreciated fully by the singers. This inherently attractive scheme became corrupted by the use of polylingual texts, sometimes of purely secular origin; thus a French *chanson* might be in the top part with the liturgical Latin texts below. Among the many developments in succeeding centuries the most important was, at the start of the fifteenth century, free invention replacing the use of plainsong and a contrapuntal treatment in which the parts were equally dependent on one another, often imitating one another's phrases and none being *primus inter pares*. About 1530 the Renaissance-style motet spread throughout Europe, inspiring some of the finest church music in existence, contributed by such great masters as the Flemish Josquin, de Monte, and Lassus, the Roman Palestrina and the Venetian Gabrielis, the Spanish Morales and Victoria, the English William Byrd and Peter Philips.

The motet was always an extra-liturgical piece, that is, it had no necessary place in mass or vespers (qq.v.); the liturgy, strictly speaking, required that if a motet used the text (or a part) of the offertory, the latter had still to be sung in plainsong in its usual place in the mass before the motet was introduced.

Settings of the proper of the mass have been called motets, for example, those in Byrd's *Gradualia*, his greatest work, but in this case they should properly bear their liturgical titles. Palestrina, for example, set the offertory texts for the whole of the church's year and they are published under that title.

ALEC ROBERTSON

Music *see* Anthem, Antiphon, Canticles, Carol, Chants, Chants of the Proper of the Mass, Choir (Musical), Church Modes, Divine Office, Gregorian Chant, Hymns, Metrical Psalms, Motet, Music (Modern), Music in the Mass of the Roman Rite, Notation and Rhythm, Office Hymn, Organ, Polyphony, Psalmody, Psalm Tones, Responsorial Psalms and Responsories, Roman Missal, Spirituals, Tract

Music, Modern

A vague term used to denote the music of the present century or its antecedents in the romantic movement. In the later nineteenth century the Austro-German tradition, and its means of structuring music through tonality or key relationships, was extended by composers within it and challenged by those from outside. Particularly crucial was the work of Arnold Schoenberg and his pupils Anton Webern and Alban Berg, sometimes referred to as the Second Viennese School – a misleading title, as the tradition was continuous, even though Schoenberg's development of twelve-note technique appeared revolutionary at the time. Claude Debussy (France), Bela Bartok (Hungary), Igor Stravinsky (Russia), and Charles Ives (USA) must also be included among the major innovators of the first half of this century.

After the Second World War there emerged a generation less radical than some of their elders and often showing humanitarian or specifically religious commitment: Olivier Messiaen (France), Luigi Dallapiccola (Italy), Michael Tippett and Benjamin Britten (England), Hans Werner Henze (Germany). There is a breadth of popular appeal in much of the work of Aaron Copland (USA) and Dmitri Shostakovitch (Russia). John Cage (USA) is the pioneer of the musical avantgarde where some of the recent work of Karlheinz Stockhausen (Germany) also belongs.

The twentieth century is the age of jazz, which has grown rapidly from Negro folk music into a performing art of great virtuosity and international acclaim. The 1960s have seen a flowering of pop, or rock, and the importance of groups such as The Beatles is recognized by critics and historians as well as fans. The range of musical experience is now greater than ever, thanks to recordings and broadcasting, and electronic resources are increasingly used for musical composition of all kinds.

These developments have resulted in a fragmentation of musical society where separate groups of listeners specialize in jazz, orchestral or avant-garde. There is no longer a common musical language, although there are signs that these categories can interact. A recent example is the *Sinfonia* by Luciano Berio (Italy), which uses the Swingle Singers and quotes from Mahler in the context of Berio's own idiom.

The use of contemporary music in church presents problems which reflect wider debates. On the purely musical level, church choirs find the rhythms and harmonies of a Stravinsky difficult to master and congregations do not always respond to Messiaen's visionary organ music. Stockhausen's electronic *Gesang der Jünglinge* was written in 1956 for a large cathedral but is not often heard in such places. There is a split between the most vital music and the opportunities the church affords. Some composers have specialized in writing music for their liturgy, and some churches have commissioned works from living composers. Some are undistinguished, but there have been many inspiring concert works to sacred texts, such as Stravinsky's *Symphony of Psalms, Canticum Sacrum* and *Threni*; Britten's *War Requiem*; the *St Luke Passion* of Penderecki (Poland), which brings together monody, choral polyphony and avant-garde effects.

Some composers, like Britten, have written church music in an existing tradition which respects the formalities of public worship. But in the search for a means of communication, the church has turned enviously to the success of folk groups and there are now many masses and hymns in popular style. The situation can only be regarded as transitional, a challenge to the future, where a questing and experimental attitude is healthier than the formulae of the past.

William W. Austin, W. W. Norton and J. M. Dent, *Music in the Twentieth Century*, 1966; Wilfred Mellers, *Music in a New Found Land*, 1964; E. Routley, *The Church and Music*,

1967; Eric Salzman, *Twentieth-Century Music – An Introduction*, 1967; H. H. Stuckenschmidt, *Twentieth-Century Music*, 1969.

P. DICKINSON

Music in the Mass of the Roman Rite

The Tridentine *Missale Romanum* of 1570 is frequently spoken of as if it were a creation of the Council of Trent as a result of proceedings concerning it in the session presided over by Pope Pius V. In fact, as Dom David Knowles has pointed out, it was in all essentials a replica of the Roman missal of 1474, and that, in its turn, followed the practice of the church in the reign of Innocent II which itself derived from the usage of the epoch of Gregory the Great and his successors in the seventh century. The 1570 missal was, therefore, essentially traditional, more so, some scholars think, than the reformed missal published in 1971.

It is important to realize that when the present Latin mass is celebrated today (replacing the Tridentine mass) 'the treasury of sacred music', as Pope Paul VI called it, dating from Gregorian chant (q.v.) to the first decade of the seventeenth century when the greatest era of liturgical music came to a close, is available to choirs competent to do justice to it.

The new Roman missal is now imposed on the whole Roman Church and normally only retired priests are allowed to use the Tridentine mass. An English translation of the new missal has not yet been published.

ALEC ROBERTSON

Narthex

The porch or vestibule in the Hellenistic basilica (q.v.), closed to the exterior but opening into the nave. It was the place where people waited before services, and from which the Great Entrance (q.v.), in its original form, began.

EDITOR

Nave

The body of a church, usually separated from the aisles or wings by pillars. The term derives from the Latin *navis* meaning a 'ship'. This comparison of a church building to a ship was made at an early date, so the

Apostolic Constitution (*c*.375) says: 'When thou callest an assembly of the church as one that is the commander of a great ship, appoint the assemblies to be made with all possible skill, charging the deacons as mariners to prepare places for the brethren as for passengers, with all due care and decency. And first, let the building be long, with its head to the east, with its vestries on both sides at the east end, and so it will be like a ship. In the middle let the bishop's throne be placed, and on each side of him let the presbytery sit down; and let the deacons stand near at hand, in close and small girt garments, for they are like the mariners and managers of a ship: with regard to these, let the laity sit on the other side, with all quietness and good order. And let the women sit by themselves, they also keeping silence. In the middle let the reader stand upon some high place' (2.57).

In certain areas during the patristic period the nave was kept free from the laity who were confined to the aisles, either because the altar was placed there, as in North Africa, or because, as in Syria, it was occupied by a large semi-circular construction containing the bishop's throne and seats for the presbyters.

In the Middle Ages, churches were widely used for secular activities, the nave in particular being the scene of dancing, eating, drinking, plays, etc.

EDITOR

Nestorian Church *see* East Syrian Worship

New Fire

The lighting and blessing of the 'new fire' takes place at the opening of the Paschal Vigil (q.v.).

Fire, a most important element to primitive peoples as the source of warmth and light, was added to the rite of the Paschal Vigil most probably under the influence of the Irish monks in Gaul in the eighth century, though its use was known in Spain, too. From Gaul it came eventually (not before the twelfth century) to the Roman liturgy. Roman usage was quite different. Light from the church lamps was preserved from Good Friday (later from Maundy Thursday) until the beginning of the Vigil on Saturday evening. The lamps were brought back into the church, and from them all the other lamps and candles were lighted. The Roman use probably recalls the Jewish custom of the blessing of God for the gift of light on the Sabbath, a custom that was christianized and is witnessed to by Hippolytus in the *Apostolic Tradition* (XXV. 18-27), *c*. 215. This in turn gave rise to the ceremony known as the *Lucernarium*, still preserved in the Ambrosian rite and of which there are echoes in Roman vespers.

Even in the Gallican tradition the significance of the new fire is to be found rather in light than heat. But to understand its use at all, it is necessary to give the background of the whole liturgy of Good Friday and Holy Saturday. The church celebrates the Passover of the Lord in which he suffers, dies and rises again. In the phrase of Tertullian, Good Friday is the day *ubi ablatus est sponsus*: the bride (the church) is bereft of her bridegroom. The church as it were dies and has to be brought back to life again. This is done in symbol through fire and light, and the lighting of the new fire at the beginning of the Paschal Vigil is the first sign that the church is returning to life. The new fire thus had to be kindled from a virgin flame, struck from a kindling stone and steel. Or, as one of the prayers of blessing had it in the rite before 1951 when it was suppressed, Christ is the corner stone which, struck by the rod of the cross, sends forth the light of the Holy Spirit.

However, as the order of the service indicates to this day, the new fire is in fact lighted before the service proper begins and in some places is a great bonfire. It is on account of this that the rite has to take place outside the church; since there are practical difficulties in city and town churches, the procedure may be considerably modified. Once the fire is lit, the celebrant with ministers and servers comes to the place of the fire and after a short address giving the sense of the whole Vigil, blesses the fire with a single prayer. Then, from the fire, light is taken for the lighting of the Paschal Candle. This now becomes the centre of interest, for it is the candle that is the symbol of the Risen Christ. The fire having served its purpose is left to die out.

In many parts of Europe in former ages and perhaps even now, not only were all the lights in church extinguished, but the all-important hearth-fire was allowed to die. From the new fire or the candle people took light with which to re-kindle their fires at home. It is an interesting example of how the liturgy could influence social customs outside the church and in the life of the people.

J. D. CRICHTON

Nocturns *see* Canonical Hours

None *see* Canonical Hours

Notation and Rhythm

Saint Isidore (*c*. 560-636), Archbishop of Seville, says in one of his writings that in his day music was taught and handed down orally, for there was no way of setting down audible sounds on paper. In fact, the Vedic hymns of Southern India had a system of writing down the syllables of the spoken language in which each symbol represented a group of notes; a similar – but very complicated – system was in use in the early Byzantine church. The Greeks used a system derived from the letters of the alphabet and Boethius (d. 524) adapted the Latino-Greek alphabet to the musical scale. The introduction of stave lines by Giulio d'Arezzo (born *c*. 995) was a most important step in fixing accurately the step interval from one note to another. He determined the pitch by the use of coloured lines, yellow for C, red for F, and there prefigured our modern treble and bass clefs.

Neumatic notation will be familiar to those who look even casually at the manuscripts, often beautifully illuminated, of plainsong on show in museums; it is also known in its final stage to choirs who sing plainsong in square notation, from the modern Roman *Graduale* and *Antiphonale*.

The term neumatic is derived from the Greek word *pneuma*, a breath. These signs were developed from grammatical accent-signs said to have been invented by Aristophanes of Byzantium (*c*. 180 BC): they were basically called the *virga*, the acute accent, and the *punctum*, the grave accent. They combined with other 'signs' to form symbols representing melismas, that is, groups of notes sung to one syllable, which were often of considerable length. The earliest surviving manuscripts with neumatic notation probably date from the middle of the eighth century, but the system may well have been in use earlier than this. Before staff lines were invented, the neumes were written in what musicologists call *campo aperto*, 'in the open field', and so showed only a rise or fall of uncertain pitch between one neum and another. As the chant repertoire had to be learned by heart, these signs would have served at least as an *aide-mémoire* to the cantors gathered – as we see them in illuminated manuscripts and later in pictures – round a large choir book on the lectern. In the eleventh century there appeared 'heighted' neums in some Italian manuscripts, in which staff lines had been either imagined or are actually shown. These can be read, unlike the earlier manuscripts. Finally, in the thirteenth century came the quadratic or square notation familiar in the modern chant books today.

In origin the grammatic accents were purely melodic in character and carried no notion of duration or stress. Raising and lowering of pitch could be shown as time went on but, as has been said above, not the actual intervals between notes. When these intervals came to be shown, there remained the question of rhythm, a matter on which the singers must have been agreed. The proof lies in the presence in the earliest 'rhythmic' manuscripts of the tenth century of a whole set of valuable markings which do not appear in the later documents. The researches of the monks of the Abbey of St Pierre, Solesmes – pioneers in the restoration of Gregorian chant – showed that here was to be found the clue to the rhythmic tradition followed. The principal markings, or letters, placed above the notes are 'c.' (*cito* – lightly, quickly) and 't' (*trahere* – holding back, slowing down). There is still a considerable area of disagreement as to the correct interpretation of the rhythm of the chant.

ALEC ROBERTSON

Oblation

A synonym for 'offering', derived from the Latin *oblatio*, and like the latter may refer either to an act of offering, or to the thing offered. Four different Christian uses of the term may be distinguished: (1) the self-offering of Christ in the Last Supper and on the cross for the redemption of the world; (2) the celebration of the eucharist as an anamnesis (q.v.) of this self-offering; (3) its application to the material elements of bread and wine with which this anamnesis is made, according to Christ's command; (4) its appli-

cation to the dispositions of the worshippers which are externalized by (2) and (3).

Other uses, such as the application of the term to monetary offerings in general, would seem to fall outside the legitimate Christian usage of the term. In the Christian dispensation the only offering or oblation which may strictly be so described without qualification is that of Christ himself, the only oblation which is intrinsically acceptable. Its application to the eucharist, which is ancient, and universal until the period of the Reformation, depends upon the doctrine that what the church does in the eucharist is, in virtue of the divine command, and by divine grace, identified with the self-oblation of Christ; its application to the eucharistic elements is further dependent upon that identification, which was anciently and universally held to be effected by the identification of the bread and wine with Christ's body and blood; its application to the dispositions of the worshippers is equally dependent upon it, in that they can only offer themselves *in Christ*, into whose self-offering they are assimilated by participation in the celebration of the eucharist.

The Protestant Reformers denied the legitimacy of describing the eucharist, and *a fortiori* the eucharistic elements, as an oblation, on the ground that to do so denigrated from the uniqueness of Christ's offering, an objection based on a misunderstanding of the doctrine involved, as well as on *a priori* grounds derived from their novel doctrine of justification and grace. Some of them, however, were still prepared to apply it, with qualification, to the dispositions of the worshippers – an application which, outside the context of its application to the celebration of the eucharist itself, would seem to merit their condemnation of the latter.

No other individual issue has so divided Western Christendom since the sixteenth century as the oblatory concept of the eucharist. In recent years, however, there has been a considerable softening of attitudes and drawing together on this subject; at the same time, there has been an increase of emphasis on the offering of the material elements of bread and wine as symbols on the one hand of the natural order, and on the other of the lives and labours of the worshippers, in a way which, valuable as these concepts are in themselves, has tended towards an implicit doctrine of the possibility of oblation other than, or in addition to, that of Christ. Only the doctrine of the identification of the oblation of the church, and of the individual member of it, with the oblation of Christ in the celebration of the eucharist as the divinely-appointed anamnesis of the latter is able to safeguard the uniqueness of Christ's oblation on the one hand, and provide for man's desire and need to offer all that he is and has to God on the other.

W. Jardine Grisbrooke, 'Oblation at the Eucharist' in *Studia Liturgica* III, 4, 1964, pp. 227-39; *ibid.*, IV, 1, 1965, pp. 37-55, and the works therein cited.

W. JARDINE GRISBROOKE

Octave

This reference to the continued commemoration of a festival denotes the *eighth* day, that is, one week later since the calculation is inclusive, or the *eight* days, that is, the week itself.

A. A. MCARTHUR

Offertory

The name given to the oblation rites which come at the beginning of the liturgy of the eucharist (as distinguished from the liturgy of the word). The motif of oblation (q.v.) runs throughout the eucharist, but the offertory is specifically concerned with oblation. The theme of the offertory is that the church must provide the elements for the sacrificial meal. The elements of bread and wine are presented, prepared and formally offered by the presiding priest, who then prays over them. These elements are to be transformed into the one gift that pleases God during the eucharistic prayer which follows the offertory, though their transformation is curiously anticipated, particularly in the Roman offertory. Still, Roman Catholic theologians hold that the offertory is not essential to the sacrifice. However, though the offertory may not be theologically essential, some presentation, preparation and perhaps formal offering of the elements, no matter how simple, seems practically indispensable. It is this presentation, preparation and formal offering of the elements which might be called the function of the offertory and which offers us insight as to the nature of the offertory. The offertory is that part of the mass which is concerned with the fitting oblation of the elements to God for their

consecration.

The theme of offering gifts is as old as religion, and the ancient cults and folk practices were a providential preparation for the Christian offering of gifts for the eucharistic sacrifice and the service of the poor and the otherwise needy. There is reason to believe that the early church had an understanding of the eucharist as a corporate action, with each rank having its special task in relationship to the offering of the gifts. Writing as early as the autumn of AD 96, Clement of Rome reminds the church at Corinth that Christ is the 'high priest of our oblations' (*I Cor.* 36.1) and that he 'commanded us to celebrate oblations and liturgies' (*I Cor.* 40.2). Clement continues: 'Unto the high priest (bishop) his special liturgies have been appointed, and to the priests their special place assigned, and on the levites (deacons) their special ministry; the layman is bound by the ordinances for the laity. Let each of you, brethren, make eucharist to God according to his own order, keeping a good conscience and not transgressing the appointed rule of his own liturgy' (*I Cor.* 40.5-41.1). That Clement was talking about the oblational aspects of liturgy is indicated further on in the letter where he says that it is the bishop's office to 'offer the gifts' (*I Cor.* 44.4). We might conclude from this that every rank in the church had its role to play in the offering of the gifts. This implies that the layman, too, has a role, though his role is in no way spelled out by Clement.

Justin Martyr, in the early years of the second century, is the first to give explicit evidence about the offertory. In the first and fuller reference in his *Apology* (ch. 65), he gives the following order of service: the prayers are concluded; the kiss of peace (q.v.) is given; bread and wine are presented to the one who presides over the assembly; he takes them and over them he pronounces the thanksgiving. Justin, in his *Dialogue with Trypho* (9-13), also seems to reject all oblation of things which might be used for sustenance. But this is in reality a rejection of the material sacrifices of creatures as practised by Jews and pagans. His ideal is the *oblatio rationabilis*, the spiritual sacrifice, which the Greek philosophers declared to be the only veneration worthy of God. He sees that there is no longer any room for bloody sacrifices since the Logos himself, Jesus Christ, is the victim of the spiritual sacrifice which is the eucharist. But emphasis on the spiritual sacrifice gives way to a re-statement of the importance of the material and material sacrifices in the face of Gnosticism in the latter part of the second century. Irenaeus leads the battle against those who would spiritualize the Christian sacrifice out of existence.

The *Apostolic Tradition* of Hippolytus (AD 215-217) offers two descriptions of the eucharistic order of service. In the first account we find one item to add to Justin's description, namely, the deacons (q.v.) are expressly mentioned as offering the oblation. The second account, which is an account of the eucharist in conjunction with baptism, does add something further. On this occasion, milk, honey and water are added to the usual oblations of bread and wine, and these are received by the newly baptized at communion before the consecrated wine. Interestingly, the catechumen (q.v.) is earlier told to bring some offering for the eucharist which will follow his baptism. Hippolytus' accounts therefore give some confirmation to what is much earlier suggested by Clement as to the participation of deacons and laymen in the offertory rite. In North Africa in the same century we have the witness of both Tertullian and Cyprian to lay participation in offering the elements, though the precise time when these elements were presented (before the mass began or at the offertory) is not indicated.

In the fourth and fifth centuries, after peace had come to the church, there was a great growth of the liturgy. In the East during the fourth century, the laity provided the elements for the sacrifice, though, except in the Egyptian rite, the exact time of their offering is not known. It is also generally agreed that during this century whatever presentation of the gifts at the offertory there had ever been in the East died out, and with the beginning of the fifth century we have the evidence of Theodore of Mopsuestia (in his *Catechesis*) that the offertory was moving in the direction of a 'processional' rite as opposed to the Roman 'oblational' rite. The East now substitutes the great entrance (q.v.) for the simpler presentation, preparation and offering of the elements, and the participation of the laity and even the meaning of oblation is more and more obscured in the representational rite of the Byzantine liturgy. The evidence from the West during this two-century middle period is sparse indeed. Except for passing references in Spain and Milan which indicate that the laity in those cities provided the oblations according to a certain ritual, the only important Western evidence we have is from North Africa where Augustine reports that the laity actually offered the elements at the offertory.

If there was ever a real offertory procession of the laity, it occurred during the following centuries at the papal stational liturgy in the city of Rome. *Ordo Romanus Primus* describes in detail the action, but instead of the laity coming up to the altar to hand in their offerings, the pope and his assistants go down to the laity to take up those gifts to be used for the sacrifice and for the needs of the church and those who were in the care of the church. It is the opinion of this author that the formalization of the people's offertory in the Roman stational liturgy dealt the death blow to a sense of liturgical role which until that time the laity had understood themselves as having. During this same period the Gallican rite developed an approach to the offertory which was in spirit closer to the later Eastern practice. Duchesne, describing the Gallican rite in *Christian Worship*, [6]1931, p. 204, states categorically that 'the offering by the people at this point in the mass (i.e. the offertory) is a ceremony of Roman origin, and is incompatible with that of the *processio oblationis*, a custom common to the Gallican and Oriental rite'. Before passing on to the post-developmental period, it is important to note that the secret prayers which we find in the Roman sacramentaries of this period, particularly the Leonine and the Gregorian, reflect a highly developed theology of the offerings as oblations (*see* **Silent Prayer**). One can learn a great deal about the theology of the offertory by a study of these prayers, many of which are still to be found in the Roman missal.

By the year AD 800, the eucharistic liturgy of the Western church, like that of the East, had become more or less uniform and established. Substantially the liturgies of both East and West manifested no important change after this date, though the actual offertory rite was considerably modified in the West, particularly by the addition of prayers full of Gallican symbolism and piety to accompany the simple actions. All of this was made uniform and unchangeable in the West with the publication of the Roman missal in its first edition in 1474. So it remained until the recent missal of Pope Paul VI. In this missal the prayers are considerably simplified or omitted. The offertory is once again restored to a relatively simple, straightforward rite. The gifts are brought up. Bread is offered to the accompaniment of a modified OT blessing. Wine with a little water is taken and similarly offered to the accompaniment of a similar blessing. After hand-washing and an invitation to the gathering to pray that the sacrifice may be acceptable to God, an invitation which evokes a proper corporate response, the ancient secret prayer, re-named the 'prayer over the gifts' (*see* **Super Oblata**), is spoken by the presiding priest. And so ends the present offertory of the Roman mass.

One might argue that even greater simplification would make the offertory rite more effective. More importantly, there is still a great need to find a way to re-awaken in the laity a sense of their having a proper liturgy – probably in connection with the offertory and the heightened sense of the social needs of less fortunate brethren.

A. Clark, 'The Function of the Offertory Rite in the Mass', *Ephem. Liturg.* 64 (1950), pp. 309-344; G. Dix, *The Shape of the Liturgy,* [2]1945; A Hamman, *Vie Liturgique et Vie Sociale,* 1968; J. A. Jungmann, *The Mass of the Roman Rite,* rev. ed., 1959.

THOMAS PHELAN

Office Hymn

A hymn appointed for use at the hour services (q.v.). They were omitted from the *BCP* for lack of English versions, but many have now been translated and find their place in Anglican hymnals. A custom had arisen in some churches of singing such a hymn after the first lesson and before the *Magnificat* at evensong.

EDITOR

Old Catholic Worship

Of the Old Catholic churches, linked together in 1889 in the Union of Utrecht, the church in the Netherlands is by far the oldest. This church was a continuation of the church for which Willibrord was consecrated first archbishop of Utrecht in Rome, in 695, and after the period of the Reformation, which was extremely difficult, it was involved in an increasingly sharp conflict with Rome

in the seventeenth century. In 1703, the archbishop Peter Codde was suspended by Pope Clement XI. From that time onward the episcopal succession was continued in the church as the 'Roman Catholic Church of the old episcopal clergy'. As this was a split for reasons of canon law and not because of dogmatic differences, there was a continual hope that the difficulties might be resolved. During the early period of the split, the old Roman post-Tridentine liturgy was adhered to almost completely.

There was an important turn of the tide after 1870. Vatican I and the development of Old Catholic movements outside the Netherlands not only caused the 'Old Episcopal' clergy to call themselves increasingly 'Old Catholics'; it also induced them to be more closely connected in theological thinking as well. This led to the Union of Utrecht in 1889. The influence of the German and Swiss sister churches was also felt in the liturgy through the spread of the idea of community, the introduction of the vernacular, the rejection of private masses and the renewal of the liturgy. Thus several new liturgical books came out, especially in the period between 1900 and 1910, taking the place of the old Roman formularies (*cf.* **Books, Liturgical** 11: Old Catholic).

Compared to the Old Catholic reforms abroad, those in the Netherlands were on the whole less radical. For instance, in the translation of the liturgy of the mass and especially of the canon dating from 1909, there were very few departures from the Roman missal. The cycle of saints' days was far less restricted than elsewhere. After the Second World War, the voices clamouring for a renewal of the liturgy grew louder and louder. In 1960 a revised liturgy of the mass did in fact come out, but as research had not yet been completed, the alterations were still fairly limited. Under the influence of very lively liturgical renewal movements in the Netherlands, both among Roman Catholics and among Protestants, the desire for radical changes has grown very strongly since. What is specifically aimed at is directness, greater transparency and ecumenical openness. This desire for radically revised formularies has by no means been fulfilled yet. In 1968 there appeared an alternative 'Second Order of the Mass', and here and there new formularies for the administration of the sacraments have been tried out. It looks as if, within a couple of years, tangible results in the shape of official formularies may be expected.

In the Old Catholic churches which separated from Rome because of their rejection of the Vatican dogmas of 1870 (above all in Germany, Austria and Switzerland), powerful reform movements soon became evident, in contrast to the situation in the Netherlands. As a result of their separation from Rome, these churches gained the freedom to carry out reforms which had long been desired in progressive Catholic circles. In those parts of Switzerland and South Germany which had belonged to the See of Constance until 1814 or 1821, the ground for liturgical reform had been prepared by the activity of the Vicar General (later vicegerent of the See), I. H. von Wessenberg. His German ritual served as a model for Old Catholic rituals, and the tradition of German vespers still lives on in the Old Catholic congregations in Switzerland. In Austria, the church reforms of Emperor Joseph II (1741-1790) had a wide influence.

Soon after 1870 the liturgical books were produced in German and French editions. The editors were not, however, content with a translation of the Latin books, as in the Netherlands, but worked over them more freely. Of course, all Old Catholic liturgies are descended from the Roman liturgy, like those of the Anglican and Lutheran churches, though like them they differ to a greater or lesser degree from their ancestor.

A considerable part in the reform of the liturgy was played by Eduard Herzog (1841-1924), the first bishop of the Christian Catholic (Old Catholic) Church of Switzerland, and Adolf Thürlings (1844-1915), Professor of Liturgy in the Christian Catholic theological faculty in Bern (Switzerland), who was also a distinguished musicologist. In the Polish Old Catholic Church in the USA and Canada (founded in 1897), as in Poland itself, the liturgy was translated into Polish, but the translation strictly followed the Roman rite. In America, English has been used to an increasing extent alongside Polish.

In the Old Catholic churches, some of the manifestations of so-called vulgar Catholicism have been rejected, e.g. pilgrimages, reverencing of images, indulgences, the Cult of the Sacred Heart, and so on. The liturgy is meant to be celebrated in a clear and pure form, bringing the Christological element, in particular, to the fore. Thus the Old Catholic

churches play a lively part in the liturgical renewal that is taking place in both Roman Catholic and Protestant churches.

———

For Old Catholicism with particular reference to worship, *see*: K. Algermissen, *Konfessionkunde*, [8]1969; P. Fox, *The Polish National Catholic Church*; U. Kunz, *Viele Glieder – ein Leib*, 1953 (and especially P. Pfister, 'Die altkatholische Kirche'); U. Küry, *Die altkatholische Kirche* (in: *Die Kirchen der Welt*, III), 1966; C. B. Moss, *The Old Catholic Movement*, [2]1964; A. E. Rüthy, 'The Place of the Old Catholic Church in the Liturgical Scene', *Studia Liturgica* II, 1963, pp. 66f.; F. Siegmund-Schultze, ed., *Ekklesia*, III: *Die altkatholische Kirche*, 1935.

KURT PURSCH
A. E. RÜTHY
C. TOL

Open-Air Meeting

The tradition of the open-air meeting was common in Europe among the persecuted minorities of the Middle Ages (Hussites, Waldensians). It was also used by popular preachers like Bernard of Clairvaux and Francis of Assisi. Later the French Protestants held their meetings in woods and fields (*L'église du désert*). In another form this tradition was taken up by Fox, Wesley, the Salvation Army, the Pentecostals in Latin America and many African churches (*see* **Liturgies** 12: Pentecostal). The latter three added to the oral methodology of communication the tradition of folk music. So, the Salvation Army used the folk music of the turn of the century (brass-band!). By now this has become traditional in the Salvation Army, although some attempts are made to use today's folk music.

Of the greatest importance are the open-air meetings of the OT prophets. They did not preach from a pulpit, nor did they usually interpret a written text, though they related themselves critically *and* positively to the tradition of their listeners. They had to formulate their message in short, easily memorized sentences and parables, not unlike the modern commercial spots on television, but very different from today's sermons. The same method was used by Jesus and the apostles. This form of concentrated communication was forgotten in the main-line churches for many centuries. It was replaced by the sermon, which has no precedent in biblical tradition, but has its roots in the cultural background of the early church and the Reformation.

Roughly speaking there are two types of open-air meetings today:

1. *The public religious mass meeting.* With the invention of high-powered loud-speaker systems, it has become possible to address thousands of people in the open air. Billy Graham and the German Kirchentag, Martin Luther King and ecumenical youth gatherings at Taizé, Roman Catholic congresses and ecumenical festivals are public demonstrations which seek to strengthen certain (evangelical, catholic, ecumenical, or pentecostal) beliefs among their followers and friends. In the case of the German Kirchentag this public propaganda is corrected and deepened by controversial public debates and small discussion groups.

2. *The open-air meeting as an encounter with the world* is in certain cultures one of the best schools for the humanization of man. Every one – and not only the pastor – who has the courage and the gift can speak. The speakers realize themselves as persons who have something worthwhile to contribute, a tremendous process of experiencing the value of the human person. One must have seen these people, reduced to silence by political and religious powers through centuries, suddenly discovering that they have something to say, although they do not have much formal education. For this process it is not of the first importance for them to use the ready-made language of their tradition. The main thing is that they discover the possibility of standing up and speaking. In a more sophisticated stage the open-air meeting could offer the chance to rediscover the proclamation of the gospel in the world's agenda, i.e. a proclamation which does not protect itself from any criticism by basing itself on a biblical text; by confining itself to biblical thought patterns and to a religious public which agrees with the preacher's basic assumptions; and by shutting itself in a church building, where counter-arguments are rarely allowed and never expected. Thus, this preaching could be more biblical than the usual sermon, not by basing itself *expressis verbis* on a biblical text, but by risking the biblical method of proclamation, which begins with the listener's questions, with his concrete situation, and accepts his interruptions as a vital means of communicating the gospel.

W. J. HOLLENWEGER

Ordinary

A term of the Roman rite which has had three different, although related, meanings: (1) the unvarying parts of the mass; (2) those unvarying parts of the mass which are rendered chorally, and which compose the 'mass' as a musical work, namely, the *Kyrie, Gloria in excelsis, Credo, Sanctus* and *Benedictus,* and *Agnus Dei*; (3) the unvarying parts of the mass up to the secret prayer or *super oblata* (q.v.), a usage followed in the page headings of the Roman missal of 1570, but abandoned in the *Ordo Missae* of 1969.

W. JARDINE GRISBROOKE

Ordination

Ordination is the act of conferring holy orders and so admitting a candidate into the ministry of the church. Strictly speaking only presbyters or priests undergo ordination, and it is customary to refer to the consecration of bishops, to the making of deacons, and to the admitting of readers, etc., to the minor orders. The central element in ordination is the laying on of hands with prayer, and various NT passages are regarded as the basis for this practice (Acts 6.1-6; 13.1-3; 20.28; I Tim. 4.14; 5.22; II Tim. 1.6).

1. *The Early Church*

(*a*) *Bishops.* They were elected by the people and consecrated by a fellow bishop laying his hands upon them and uttering prayers in the presence of other bishops and the local Christian community. After being saluted with the kiss of peace (q.v.), the new bishop presided at the eucharist, occupying the *cathedra* (q.v.), so consecration can be described as 'being placed in the *cathedra*'. Consecration rites were not greatly elaborated, but by the fourth century deacons held a gospel book over the candidate's head (*Apost. Const.* 8.4) and one of the other bishops present is instructed to 'elevate the sacrifice upon the hands of him that is consecrated' – possibly in imitation of the consecration of the Jewish high priest (Lev. 8.27).

(*b*) *Presbyters.* They were ordained by the laying on of hands with prayer, of both the local bishop and other presbyters.

(*c*) *Deacons.* The bishop alone laid his hands upon them with prayer.

EDITOR

2. *Orthodox*. In Orthodox ecclesiology the sacrament of holy orders is essentially bound with the realization of the church as the body of Christ (I Cor. 12.27; 10.17).The directly implied ecclesial structure of this body is hierarchical, having head and members. The hierarchical order, however, is not to be confused with a power structure. The ministries of the church are those of love and service, not power and domination. All ecclesiastical functions are performed precisely *within* the church – not over and above it. The Holy Spirit, the one source behind all ministerial gifts, resides in the whole church (I Cor. 12.4-11). It does not reside in one member to the exclusion of others. The church taken together is the realization of the body of Christ.

The priestly function is no exception to this rule of corporateness. It is a function ascribed to the whole membership of the church: '. . . you are a chosen race, a royal priesthood, a holy nation . . .' (I Peter 2.9). All church members are called upon to '. . . offer spiritual sacrifices acceptable to God through Jesus Christ' (I Peter 2.5). Orthodox baptismal rites support this view of the priestly function. They are full of liturgical acts and words which point to the ordination of each church member to the royal priesthood. Some signs of this priestly consecration which appear in the present Orthodox liturgy of baptism (q.v.) and chrismation are: the laying on of hands, anointing with oil, the tonsure and the vesting in a white robe. The NT speaks of the *whole church* as the clergy: the lot which God has chosen and separated from the fallen world (Acts 26.18; Eph. 1.11). This wholeness lies at the root of the Orthodox understanding of the specifically ordained functions of bishop, priest and deacon.

The bishop is the 'overseer', which is the meaning of the word from the Greek of the NT. He is specifically consecrated to oversee the total life of the local church. He is the head of the body. He presides at the eucharistic assemblies and literally oversees the entire community of priests, the holy nation, as it makes its offering to God in Christ. The bishop is the archpriest, the first among the whole community of priests, and through his presence the church as an hierarchical organism, the body of Christ, is realized. He is the guardian and first teacher of the apostolic faith and tradition. In this sense, and not in some magical understanding of the

continuity in the laying on of hands, he is consecrated in the apostolic succession. He in turn ordains priests and deacons to their respective ministries and continues to check them in the manner in which they discharge their duties. He is the mouth of the local church before God and the church as a whole; he is the image of God and the link with the church as a whole within the local church. Ignatius of Antioch offers an excellent summary of the function of the bishop in his letter to Smyrnaeans:

Nobody must do anything that has to do with the church without the bishop's approval . . . Where the bishop is present, there let the congregation gather, just as where Jesus Christ is, there is the Catholic Church (*Smyrn*. 8.1 f.).

The ordained priest has a role in the church subordinate to that of the bishop. In the early church each individual community had its own bishop, and the priests, or presbyters as they are called in the NT, served as a council of advisers and assistants around him. The growth of the church expanded the role of the priest. The bishops began to send priests from their councils to lead the life of the new parishes. At an earlier time Ignatius had already commented that a valid eucharist can be celebrated by someone duly authorized by the bishop (*Smyrn*. 8.1). The local church in Orthodoxy has thus come to be a diocese: a specifically defined territory led by a bishop, with the parishes therein attended by duly authorized priests. The role of the parish priest or presbyter is that of an 'elder', the one who leads his parish in the name of the bishop. The essential link between parish, parish priest and bishop is continuously emphasized by the presence of a cloth called an *antimension* on each Orthodox altar table. This cloth is unfolded at each celebration of the holy eucharist and the holy gifts are placed thereon. It bears the signature of the bishop and demonstrates that the realization of the church is dependent upon communion with him.

The function of the diaconate has followed a curve opposite to that of the ordained priest. In the early church the deacon was more active than the priest, but today, practically speaking, he is less active. Properly, he is to perform the 'ministry of Jesus Christ' (Ignatius, *Magnes*. 6.1). He is to 'serve tables' at the eucharistic assemblies by bringing forth and helping to distribute the holy gifts (Acts 6.2-6). In general he acts as the 'right hand' in the assistance he renders to the bishop or priest during the celebration of all liturgical services.

The ordinations of deacons, priests and bishops take place at varying times during the celebration of the holy eucharist. As one who is consecrated to 'serve tables', the deacon is ordained after the consecration of the holy gifts. He is then prepared to perform the high point of his function: the carrying of the eucharistic chalice to the faithful.

The priest is to lead the congregation in the celebration of the eucharist. He is therefore ordained prior to the consecration of the holy gifts.

The manner of ordaining both priests and deacons is very similar. The candidate for ordination in both cases is brought before the bishop, who is seated at the front-left corner of the altar table. He is then led in a triple circling around the altar table and brought to a halt, on his knees, at the front-right corner of the altar table. The bishop rises and, placing his hands upon the head of the candidate, says the prayers appropriate for the ordination. At the conclusion of the prayers the newly-ordained rises, and the bishop gives him the vestments (q.v.) proper to his ministry. All present sing: '*Axios* (worthy)!'

A new bishop is consecrated by a minimum of two other bishops. The corporate character of the consecration is a sign of the full communion which must exist between the respective local churches. As the prime teacher and preserver of the apostolic faith and tradition within the community, the bishop is consecrated just prior to the didactic portion of the eucharistic liturgy. The candidate to be consecrated is brought on his knees before the altar table. The consecrating bishops place an open gospel book, with the writing downward, upon the head of the candidate. They then lay their right hands upon the head of the candidate and, through the saying of the proper prayers by the presiding bishop, complete the consecration. The new bishop is given his vestments and all present sing: '*Axios!*'

In conclusion, the sacrament of holy orders is the vehicle through which the church is provided with its essential, hierarchical order and assured of an objective, sacramental basis for an inner life of unity and harmony.

Hence, I urge you to do everything in godly agreement. Let the bishop preside in God's place, and the presbyters take the place of the apostolic council, and let the deacons . . . be entrusted with the ministry of Jesus Christ who was with the Father from eternity and appeared at the end of the world (Ignatius, *Magnes.* 6.1).

PAUL LAZOR

3. *Medieval and Roman Catholic.* The sober rites of the Roman tradition underwent a considerable change in the ninth and tenth centuries when certain observances, deriving from Gallican and German sources, were added to them to give a rather different picture to holy orders. These observances are found in the Roman-German pontifical (tenth century) which made its way to Rome in the eleventh century and became part of the tradition. By way of the pontifical of Durandus of Mende (d. 1298), who made further additions, they came to form the rite of the Roman pontifical of 1485 which in turn was substantially the pontifical of 1596. These new rites consisted principally of anointings (of the head for a bishop, of the hands for a priest) and of the *porrectio instrumentorum*, the handing over of the symbols of office. The intention was to explicate the meaning of the various orders, but in the process the emphasis was somewhat changed. For instance, the handing of chalice and paten to the priest heavily emphasized that his chief duty was to offer sacrifice. On the other hand, the delivery of the gospel book to the deacon underlined that he was a minister of the word. What was more important is that the *porrectio* overshadowed the ancient rite of the laying on of hands (which always remained) and was generally thought to be necessary for validity. This was corrected by Pius XII, who in the Apostolic Constitution *Sacramentum Ordinis* of 1948 laid down that the laying-on of hands for the three orders of the episcopate, the presbyterate and the diaconate, with certain formulae in the ordination prayers, was all that was necessary for validity.

The minor orders of doorkeeper, reader, exorcist and acolyte with the ceremony of tonsure before them and the subdiaconate (until 1207 ranking as a minor order) also underwent development. These officers were from the third century appointed by a simple blessing with the delivery of the symbols of office. Now the formulae were elaborated and the rites expanded. There was an address, the delivery of the symbol of office with a formula and two prayers of blessing.

Modern. That part of the *Pontificale Romanum* containing the liturgy of ordination to the episcopate, the presbyterate and the diaconate was revised in 1968 and the liturgy of tonsure, the four minor orders and the subdiaconate in 1972 when it appeared that the subdiaconate had been suppressed and the minor orders reduced to two.

The pattern of the services for all three major orders is the same: they are conferred within the eucharist, after the gospel and homily; there follow the questions, prayer (litany of saints), the laying-on of hands (in silence), the prayer of ordination and the delivery of the symbols of office.

For the ordination of a presbyter the bishop lays hands on the candidate first and then all the presbyters present do likewise; the anointing of the hands has been retained with a different formula, charging the presbyter to serve God's people and to offer the eucharist. The paten and chalice and the bread and wine to be used at the eucharist are then delivered to him with a new formula indicating that they are the offerings of the people to be used in the mass.

The texts of the prayers of ordination for diaconate and presbyterate remain those of the (early) Roman tradition, that for the presbyterate being slightly shortened. Noteworthy in the rite for the 'Ordination' (*sic*) of a bishop are that the consecrator and then the assistant consecrators lay hands on him, the book of the gospels is placed on his head and held over it during the consecration prayer by two deacons and the principal part of the prayer is said by all the consecrators together. It is a true con-celebration. The anointing of the head remains as well as the delivery of the gospel book (now in first place), the ring and the staff or crozier. The consecrator puts the mitre on the candidate without formula. The whole service has been much simplified. The prayer of ordination (or consecration) is that found in the (Latin) Verona fragment of the *Apostolic Tradition* of Hippolytus, very slightly revised.

Like the major orders, the minor orders are conferred after the gospel and the homily (or during a service of the word). There is an invitatory, a prayer and the delivery of the symbol of office. Tonsure is replaced by a service of 'Admission to the Clerical State'. The candidates are questioned, admitted by the bishop to the clergy, there are prayers of intercession and the final prayer of the bishop.

J. D. CRICHTON

4. *Anglican.* Services of ordination did not appear in the 1549 *BCP* but were published independently in March 1550. In 1552 they were revised and annexed to the second *BCP*. A third edition appeared in 1559, again as a separate document, and finally a fourth edition was annexed to the *BCP* of 1662.

In the Preface to the 1550 Ordinal, Cranmer and the Reformers stated their intention of continuing the threefold order of bishops, priests and deacons which had existed since apostolic times; they made no provision for the subdiaconate and other minor orders. In an attempt to simplify the obscurities of the medieval Roman rite they retained the eucharist as the frame for ordination and emphasized the essential elements as expressed in the NT and by the early church, namely prayer and the imposition of hands. Thus the basic pattern of the rites in the Roman Pontifical was followed, but a number of individual features were changed, and the influence of Bucer's tract *De Ordinatione* was recognizable. The anointing of bishops and priests and the formal vesting of all three orders was abolished. The delivery of the instruments (*porrectio instrumentorum*) was retained in the case of priests, but the staff was the sole insignia delivered to the bishop. A Bible instead of the gospels was laid on the bishop's neck, a Bible was delivered to priests, and the NT instead of the gospels was delivered to deacons. While it was undoubtedly right for the Reformers to avoid the traditional multiplied and diffused acts of ordination and to concentrate on the central imposition of hands with prayer, it would seem that they were misled over the relation between the form and the matter. Not only did the traditional eucharistic pattern of prayer introduced by the *Sursum corda* disappear, but the ordination prayers which were used were separated from the imposition of hands, and the latter were accompanied by imperative formulae addressed to the candidates and authorizing them to execute the functions of the order which they were receiving.

In 1552 further medieval elements in the rites disappeared. Bishops were no longer invested with the pastoral staff, and the Bible was not laid on their necks but handed to them, although the formulae which had accompanied these two ceremonies in 1550 were retained. The delivery of the instruments was also modified for priests: they too received only the Bible, the delivery of the chalice and the bread being omitted. In 1559 and 1662 no further basic changes were made, but in 1662 an addition was inserted in the formulae accompanying the imposition of hands in the case of bishops and priests. A specific reference was made to the order being conferred, 'for the office and work of a bishop' and 'for the office and work of a priest', thereby meeting the Puritan argument that from the similarity of the earlier formulae there had been no clear distinction between the episcopate and the priesthood.

Throughout the Anglican Communion the 1662 rites have continued with little change until the twentieth century. One improvement was made in the Scottish prayer book of 1929 and in the proposed English prayer book of 1928. A eucharistic type of ordination prayer introduced by the *Sursum corda* was inserted before the imposition of hands in the rite for deacons, while the existing prayers for bishops and priests were remodelled to conform to the same pattern. But the most thorough revision appeared in the Ordinal of the Church of South India in 1958. Here the rites for all three orders followed the same pattern within the framework of the eucharist. Candidates were first presented to the congregation, and the latter was required to express approval or disapproval. Then the ordination followed the ministry of the Word: the examination, the prayer for the Holy Spirit, then the solemn ordination prayer itself during which the imposition of hands occurred. Thus form and matter once again were closely related. This Ordinal has met with widespread approval; and it has provided a model for recent revisions – West Africa 1965-6, Anglican-Methodist in England 1968, and America 1970.

R. C. D. JASPER

5. *Baptist.* Baptist ordination is primarily for ministry in a local congregation; therefore, the service of ordination is an affair of a local congregation, generally the one to which the ordinand will minister. When a congregation determines that one of its members should be 'set apart for the gospel ministry' (be ordained) it sends out a call to its sister congregations, usually the area association, asking that a council meet to examine the candidate's qualifications for the ministry. While such a council is not required by strict Baptist polity, it represents symbolically the unity of the Baptist churches as well as the fact that ordination is mutually recognized by other churches than the one actually doing the ordaining. The council reviews the candidate's educational qualification, hears his statement on his Christian commitment and call to the ministry and examines him on his doctrinal views. If the candidate proves satisfactory on these points the council recommends to the congregation that it proceed with the ordination.

The service of ordination is generally held at a time when representatives of the other churches of the association can attend. It is set within a full service of worship which generally includes the Lord's Supper. The act of ordination takes place as part of the offertory, at which time the ordinand offers himself to be set apart for the gospel ministry (for the outline of the Lord's Day service *see* **Liturgies** 5: Baptist). As the gifts and the bread and wine are brought to the table by the deacons, the chairman of the deacons escorts the ordinand to the table. After a prayer of dedication the chairman of the deacons presents the ordinand to the congregation along with the recommendation of the Council that the church proceed with the ordination of the candidate. After receiving vows from the ordinand, the presiding minister declares that he has responded faithfully to the call of the gospel and is fit through preparation to be ordained at this time. After a blessing upon the ordinand, clergymen, and in many cases representative laymen, are invited to lay hands on the ordinand for the ordination prayer. Following the prayer a charge is given to the candidate, after which a charge is given to the church to which he is to minister. In many ordinations a Bible is given to the newly ordained minister, symbolizing his role as a minister of the word. After the presentation of the Bible the newly ordained minister is led to the communion table by the presiding minister and welcomed into the pastoral ministry of the church of Jesus Christ. He then is invited to begin his ministry among his people by presiding over the Lord's Supper. The new minister takes his place at the table and leads the congregation in the observance of the Lord's Supper according to the manner of the local congregation.

Most Baptists view ordination as an act of recognition on the part of a congregation of a person's call and fitness to ministry. It is not the conferring of some special grace, but rather the recognition of graces already received. He still remains a layman in essence; he is set apart to function in special ways within the congregation. Yet nothing that he does as a minister cannot be done by a layman providing the congregation so designates. This process is generally called licensing and is used when no ordained minister is available or when there is need for the extension of the ministry to other areas.

JOHN E. SKOGLUND

6. *Christian Church (Disciples of Christ)*. The Christian Church (Disciples of Christ) is like other churches in that it sets people apart for the office of ministry by an act of prayer and laying on of hands. Where it has differed from many has been in its understanding of the persons who should receive this rite of the church. From their studies of the NT, Disciple leaders in the early nineteenth century derived three ministerial offices. Evangelists were itinerant proclaimers of the gospel whose chief work was to found and organize churches. Elders were mature men, resident in the community, who would be elected by members of the local church and ordained by them for the overseeing of the church's life. Although they held secular employment, they were to preach – if possessing the necessary skill – and administer baptism and the Lord's Supper, the latter every week. Deacons were also local men and their service was limited to matters more temporal than preaching and praying.

During the course of the last third of the nineteenth century and the first half of the twentieth, Disciples developed an educated, salaried ministry. Until the 1960s such ministers would ordinarily preside over the Sunday service and would preach. Always a part of that service, however, was the Lord's Supper and invariably elders (as described in the above paragraph) would preside over that portion of the service. They offered the eucharistic prayer while the minister sat at his place near the pulpit. In recent years the minister came to share in this service at the table – delivering a homily before the prayer and reciting the words of institution after the prayer.

It is normal practice for such a minister to be ordained. Elders from several congregations, and a small group of other ministers, lay their hands on his head while a prayer of dedication and invocation is offered by one of them. There is divided opinion among Disciples concerning the ordination of the elders. Before the rise of the office of minister, the elders in a congregation were ordained because they were understood to be fulfilling the ministerial functions of teaching and overseeing. In some congregations this practice of ordaining elders continues unabated. In others, however, the service of prayer and laying on of hands has been replaced by installation into a functional office.

It is not yet clear what will happen to the Disciple elder in the coming decades. The current trend seems to be in the direction of continued diminution of his office with the result that ordination would be increasingly inappropriate. This trend continues even though there is growing interest in some quarters of the church for a ministry that is not dependent upon the church for livelihood.

At the present time there is no official definition of ordination. There would be widespread agreement to the definition that ordination is a corporate act by the church in which it appoints certain persons to the work of public ministry. Ministers, as distinguished from elders, are ordained, usually after graduation from seminary.

KEITH WATKINS

7. *Congregationalist*. The classical Congregational theory and practice of ordination is described in *The Savoy Declaration* of 1658:

The way appointed by Christ for the calling of any person, fitted and gifted by the Holy Ghost, unto the Office of Pastor, Teacher, or Elder in a Church, is that he be chosen there unto by the common suffrage of the Church itself, and solemnly set apart by fasting and prayer, with Imposition of Hands of the Eldership of that Church . . .

If exception was taken to the laying on of hands, it could be omitted.

Congregational ordination today is not materially different, except that it is more liable to be preceded by feasting than fasting, and that the moderator of a province (in Britain) or a conference minister (in America) will represent the wider fellowship of Congregational churches. Essentially though, the service is still the solemn recognition that the ordinand has been called by God to the ministry and that he (or she) has the necessary gifts and grace, and is now by the invocation of the Holy Spirit and the laying on of hands set apart for this ministry and invited to be pastor of this local fellowship and congregation of Christ. ·

The order of service for the ordination of a minister in *A Book of Services and Prayers* (1959) is the most recently authorized form for the use of English Congregationalists and will be taken as the model.

After an introduction of sentences of scripture and an invocatory prayer, followed by the reading of appropriate lessons from both Testaments, the presiding minister summarizes the foundation and duties of the church and ministry. Then he calls upon the secretary of the local church to record the steps that have led the congregation to the issuing of the invitation to the ordinand to be their minister. The ordinand is then called upon to make a statement expounding 'his Christian experience; his assurance of his call by God to the holy ministry; (and) his Christian belief' (*ibid.*, p.93). Thereupon the ordinand is required to confess his belief in the Holy Trinity, the lordship of Christ, in the scriptures as containing 'all doctrine required for eternal salvation through faith in Jesus Christ', and to give assurance he is truly called to the ministry, and to promise that he will fulfil the pastoral office with all fidelity. The presiding minister then asks the members of the local church to stand in silent prayer in token that they receive the ordinand as their minister.

After the singing of a hymn of the Holy Spirit or the *Veni Creator*, the ordination prayer follows. During the saying of this prayer ministers and church representatives lay their hands upon the head of the ordinand, while the presiding minister prays for the continuance of the gifts of the Holy Spirit, and for the welfare of pastor and flock, ending with the Lord's Prayer said by all. The presiding minister then says in the name of Christ and of the churches of the Congregational faith and order, 'We declare you to be ordained to this ministry of the gospel in the church of Christ, and to be appointed pastor of this church and congregation.' The minister is then given a Bible as token of his privilege and duty to preach God's word, and he receives the right hand of fellowship from representatives of the local and wider churches.

It is then customary for two invited ministers to preach, one of them reminding the congregation of its privileges and duties, and the other reminding the minister of his. Sometimes a single address covers both aspects. The newly-ordained minister gives the final blessing to the congregation.

HORTON DAVIES

8. *Jehovah's Witnesses.* Jehovah's Witnesses hold to the principle of the general priesthood; that is, to 'the Biblical teaching that every spirit-begotten Christian is a priest' (*The Watchtower*, 1 March 1963, pp.137f.; 1 July 1963, pp.415f.). I Peter 2.5-10 says of the entire Christian congregation: 'You are ... a royal *priesthood*, a holy *nation* ... that you should declare abroad the excellencies of the one that called you.' Here priesthood and nation are identical. There is no division into 'priesthood' and 'people' within that nation. Every member of that nation is a priest.

The word 'priest' is drawn from the Greek *presbyteros*, but *presbyteros* does not mean in itself a sacrificing priest who serves at an altar: it means simply an elder, an older man, whether in physical age or in spiritual growth. It refers, not to an office, but to a state. The presbyters of I Peter 5.1 were spiritually older members of the Christian nation of royal priests of 2.9.

To be ordained means to be invested with ministerial functions, or to be appointed authoritatively. Since the early Christian congregation was a working organization, it was necessary to appoint (ordain) some of the members to special service. To be appointed to such a position of service, one had to be a mature, older man (*presbyteros*). From among the older men, congregation overseers (*episkopoi*) and their assistants or ministerial servants (*diakonoi*) were selected. These were not a special priesthood in contradiction of Peter's statement: they were simply the servants of their Christian brothers (Acts 6.1-7; Matt. 20.25-28).

Offices in Witness congregations are thus scripturally limited to two: overseers and ministerial servants. These terms translate *episkopoi* and *diakonoi*, rather than trans-literate them as bishop and deacon (I Tim. 3.1, 2, 8, 12). Such ordinations or appointments are made through men by the Christian governing body (*The Watchtower*, 1 November 1955, pp. 666 ff.). These special appointments correspond to the laying on of hands in the early church.

However, if all are priests or participate in the principle of the general priesthood, all must be ordained. To all the words apply: 'but with the mouth one makes public declaration for salvation' (Rom. 10.10). This Christian ministry is not limited to a few but is for all. The ordination to such ministry comes from God through his word (II Cor. 3.5, 6; Isa. 61.1, 2).

Jehovah's Witnesses understand, therefore, that following from the principle of the general priesthood, ordinations are made both to an internal and to an external ministry. All Christians are ordained by God to preach the good news in a ministry external to the congregation (Matt. 24.14); and for some among the spiritually older men there is an ordination to special office in the internal ministry of the congregation.

A. HELEY

9. *Lutheran.* The Reformation led to a complete change in the understanding of the ordained ministry. Luther denied the traditional view of the priestly office as having a sacrificial and mediatorial character. He turned against the idea of the clerics as a separate order from that of the laity and the idea of the transfer from the ordinator to the ordinand of a *character indelebilis* which was supposed to give him a sacramental character and enable him to perform the right sacrifice when celebrating the eucharist (*Werke*, Weimar, 1883 ff., = WA 6,562, 567; 12,172,190).

As a support for this view of the ordained ministry, he referred to the biblical office, which he considered instituted by Christ when he chose his apostles and sent them out to preach. The apostles in turn sent others thus continuing the office. He could find no support for the idea that the apostles had transferred the office to an order of bishops (q.v.) separated from the elders (q.v.) (*presbyteroi*) (WA 40, 59; cf. 16, 33). So since a special office of bishop did not exist in NT times, there can be no fundamental division between bishops and priests, and hence a non-

episcopal church cannot be considered less apostolic than one which has the office of bishop. The arrangement may serve the church for practical reasons. According to the Lutheran Confessions, therefore, no other authority was vested in the bishop except to ordain, and this authority was not by virtue of any inherent power in the bishop, but was entrusted to him by the church (WA 6,407). The authority to proclaim the word, administer the sacraments and the power of the keys belongs to everyone ordained, as a trust given for reasons of order by the church. Ordination provides for orderliness but does not constitute an 'order'. This development was dictated by the 'enthusiasts' who claimed only an inner and immediate call from the Holy Spirit (WA 30, 519, 524; 31, 211; 32, 483).

Basically every Christian is in baptism ordained priest (priesthood of all believers) with the duty to proclaim the word to those around him. (WA 8, 423; 11, 413). According to Lutheran teaching the main emphasis lies on *ministerium verbi divini*, in which the office is subordinate to the word. 'The ministry of the word makes ministers, not ministers the ministry' (WA 6, 566; 8, 422).

Ordination bestows the office of a public servant of God in his church (WA 38, 228; 15, 721). The office belongs to the church and ordination to it is to be administered by regularly constituted authorities of the church. It is a function, not a rank of the church.

Necessary to ordination are:

1. The assertion of an inner conviction that God has called a person to the ministry of the Gospel.

2. A public confession of evangelical faith with a pledge of loyalty to the revealed truth and the confession of the church.

3. A specific and regular call received and accepted (WA 11, 40 ff.; 12, 169 ff.).

4. A readiness to give unconditional devotion to the work of the Lord.

The rite. In view of the doctrine outlined above the first change in the Lutheran ordination ritual was the exclusion of anointing considered to be an expression of the new character in traditional teaching. In 1535 Luther produced a Rite for Ordination which has been the base for the rites of most Lutheran churches. It is found in toto in *Kirkeordinansen* of 1539 for Denmark and Norway and in its major features in *Kyrkoord-*

ningen 1571 for Sweden and Finland.

To the one ordained is given both authority and assurance as the instrument of the Holy Spirit in the performance of his duties. The laying on of hands, not instituted by Christ but from the old dispensation, is not decreed as necessary. It is however considered symbolically valuable as an expression of the church's interest and intercession. (*See* **Imposition of Hands**.)

Elements included in the rite of ordination:

1. Confirm the call to a specific task in the church's ministry.

2. Commit to the ordinand the office of public ministry of word and sacrament.

3. Pledge the ordinand to faithful service.

4. Invoke the Holy Spirit on the ordinand.

5. Mark the apostolicity of the office by the laying on of hands.

The order for ordination includes distinctive propers (q.v.), the formal presentation of candidate, reciting the approving actions of the church, a series of pertinent questions calling for answers by the ordinand to bind the ordinand to the confession of the church and a life consonant therewith, the laying on of hands, and the commissioning followed by appropriate prayers. An admonition to the congregation assembled is also included.

The fact that ordination is a responsibility of the church at large is seen in the liturgy by the fact that:

1. It is performed by the appointed head of the church or his appointee.

2. Ordained ministers representing the church at large participate especially in the laying on of hands.

3. It takes place in the context of the main service of the church.

4. Candidates are presented as approved by the regularly constituted council of the church.

In Europe ordination takes place in the diocesan cathedral, while in North America some churches ordain in connection with synodical conventions while others ordain in the congregation where the ordained is to serve. In Germany the Lutheran churches have since 1951 had a common liturgy based on Luther's Ordination Liturgy (WA 38, 401 ff.) The Scandinavian countries vary slightly in their forms, while the American churches have had a common one since 1958.

E. J. R. H. S. VON SICARD

10. *Methodist.* John Wesley in *The Sunday Service*, 1784, in general copied the ordinal of the *BCP*, 1662, of the Church of England, but used the names superintendants (sic), elders, and deacons. There were, however, several changes, of which the most important were the omissions both of John 20.23 in the formula for ordaining an elder and of the gospel containing it in the form for ordaining a superintendant. Coke, a presbyter of the Church of England whom Wesley had set apart as a superintendant, took this book to America, and it passed into the Ritual in the American *Discipline*, where it underwent various changes. The current form of it is in the *Book of Worship*, 1964. 'The Form of Ordaining of a Superintendant' has become 'The Order for the Consecration of Bishops'. The word 'bishop' goes back to 1792. There has been much discussion about the difference between ordination and consecration, but it is difficult to attach much significance to it. The phrase 'Receive the Holy Ghost' is replaced by 'The Lord pour upon thee the Holy Spirit', a change which was effected (except for the change of 'Ghost') in 1792 for elders, though not till later for bishops. The terms 'epistle' and 'gospel' are retained, but there is no mention of the rest of the communion service.

In British Methodism the services of 1784 continued to be printed in the subsequent editions of *The Sunday Service*, very curiously because the British ministry is not divided into superintendants (though the word is used), elders and deacons, and ordination services with the imposition of hands were not often held until the Wesleyan Conference adopted the practice in 1836. But in the edition of 1846 and subsequent editions the three ordinations were replaced by the 'Form for Ordaining Candidates for the Ministry in the Wesleyan-Methodist Connexion', which contained features from all three. This was not greatly altered in the revision of 1882, nor indeed in that of 1936 after the union, though the services of the non-Wesleyan churches had been very much simpler. At this service, which is in current use, the President of the Conference or his representative presides, assisted by other ordained ministers. 'Receive the Holy Ghost' has become 'Mayest thou receive the Holy Spirit'. The link with the first part of the communion service has been lost, but after the ordination there follows the administration of the Lord's Supper, beginning with the prayer of humble access. The charge to the newly ordained ministers comes after the communion.

In 1968 the Anglican-Methodist Unity Commission produced new services for the ordination of deacons, presbyters also called priests, and bishops, with a preface on the doctrine, with important changes from both traditions. Whether or not the unity scheme is adopted, this is likely to influence the next revision.

There are also services for the consecration (America) or ordination (Britain) of deaconesses, and American services for licensing persons to preach, and for admission of ministerial candidates to membership in an annual conference.

A. RAYMOND GEORGE

11. *Old Catholic.* The Old Catholic churches of the Utrecht Union have always attached the utmost importance to maintaining the apostolic succession. This holds even for the earliest of them, the Old Catholic Church of the Netherlands, which, despite its separation from Rome since the beginning of the eighteenth century, has succeeded in maintaining canonically valid episcopal orders. As a result, the Old Catholic churches which arose in protest against the papal dogmas of 1870 were able to carry on the apostolic succession. The validity of Old Catholic episcopal orders has always been recognized, even by Rome.

Because they possess the apostolic succession, the Old Catholic churches have a validly ordained clergy at all stages: the lower orders, the diaconate, priesthood and episcopate. Although the traditional system of lower orders (door-keepers, lectors, exorcists, acolytes) has been felt to be problematical for some time, so far it has been kept on in the Old Catholic churches, with an eye to the mother church of Rome. But now that the problem of these lower orders has been recognized in the Roman church within the framework of liturgical renewal, and a new church order has been sought, the question is being re-examined.

The rites of consecration valid in 1971 have been taken from the *Pontificale Romanum*, and in 1899 were produced in German by order of the Old Catholic Bishops' Conference, and then translated into other languages (*cf.* **Books, Liturgical** 11: Old Catholic). All ordinations take place within the mass, but at different points. 'Clothing in the spiritual state' comes first for the lower orders. Candidates are dressed in a white surplice. There is no tonsure. The lower orders are bestowed in accordance with the traditional rites. The office of exorcist, which is no longer held actively, is now interpreted as the entrusting of the duty of pastoral care. It is still an open question whether the subdiaconate is to be included among the lower or the higher orders.

The most important elements of the rites of consecration are: presentation of the ordinands, address by the bishop (instruction on the meaning and the duties of the order to be bestowed), handing over the *instrumenta* (i.e. the vessels and books necessary for exercising the office in question), the prayer of consecration, and dressing in the garments proper to each order. From the consecration of subdeacons upwards, the litany is added, and from the diaconate upwards the invocation of the Holy Spirit; with priests, the hands are anointed and with bishops, the head. At the consecration of priests, hands are laid on the candidate by the bishop and the other priests present, the Apostles' Creed is recited and a promise of obedience is made to the bishop; at the consecration of bishops there is an examination of faith and the handing over of insignia (cross, staff, ring and mitre). The new presbyters and the newly-consecrated bishop concelebrate with the bishop who consecrated them. Two other bishops, at least, should assist at the consecration of the bishop, and should lay hands on the bishop with the bishop who consecrates him.

The forms of address and prayers are not translated from the Latin completely literally, but have been reshaped in a form that has strongly biblical colouring. The rite as it has been described will presumably soon be replaced by a new and simplified form.

KURT PURSCH
A. E. RÜTHY
C. TOL

12. *Pentecostal.* In younger Pentecostal churches ordination is not the initiation into the ministry but its acknowledgment by the church. A young Pentecostal, therefore, begins (with or without Bible school education) to preach, to lead services, to pray with the sick *before* his ordination. If the church recognizes in him the gifts of a preacher he

will *then* be ordained. This pattern is particularly common in Africa, Latin America and Indonesia, but it was also the rule in USA and Europe thirty years ago. With the establishment of Bible schools this pattern begins to be changed towards a system which approaches that of the main-line Protestant churches. The liturgical formulae for ordination vary. In Santiago I witnessed the ordination of pastors and of a deaconess by the bishop and the superintendents of the Iglesia Metodista Pentecostal according to the Methodist ordination liturgy, including laying on of hands. The only difference from a Methodist ordination service was the highly intense participation of the whole congregation by loud Hallelujahs, shoutings and singing. After the ordination there was the 'kiss of peace' among all the pastors, from which the deaconess was not excepted!

The special gifts for which the congregation tests the candidate for the ministry are not in the first place those of intellect and education – although formal Bible school or theological education are beginning to play a greater part in European and North American Pentecostal denominations. Rather they search to learn whether the future minister is able to lead the Pentecostal liturgy by his sensitivity and his musical ability to intone a chorus (*see* **Liturgies** 12: Pentecostal), so that chaos *and* cold stiffness are alike avoided, and further whether he is a man who is able to articulate what his people feel, what they fear and what they rejoice about. (For bibliography *see* **Pentecostal Worship**.)

W. J. HOLLENWEGER

13. *Reformed.* The Reformed Church holds itself to be part of the one, holy, catholic and apostolic church. It is, says Knox:

a part of that holy Kirk universal, which is grounded upon the doctrine of the prophets and apostles, having the same antiquity that the Kirk of the Apostles has as concerning doctrine, prayers, administration of sacraments and all things requisite to a particular Kirk (Knox, *Works*, VI, p.492).

On the basis of the NT (Acts 20.17-35; I Tim 4.14; Titus 1.5-7; I Peter 5.1-4; etc.) and also of the *communior sententia*, found in Aquinas and the scholastics, that the highest order of the Christian ministry is the presbyterate and that the bishop is only

a presbyter who has been given the episcopal office (Barkley in *The Newman*, IV, 3, pp. 115-31), the Reformed Church accepts the original identity of presbyter and bishop. Presbyterianism means government by presbyters (not presbyteries), just as episcopacy means government by bishops. Ordination is an act of God through presbyters, constitutionally associated, within the people of God. In the words of the Provincial Assembly of London, who carried on the work of the Westminster Assembly,

The power of ordination of ministers exercised for these many hundred years by bishops did belong to them as presbyters and not as bishops (*Jus Divinum Ministerii Evangelici*, II, 20, 33).

The procedure for ordination in the Genevan *Ecclesiastical Ordinances* (1541) was:

It will be good in this connection to follow the order of the ancient Church, for it is the only practice which is shown us in Scripture. The order is that ministers first elect such as ought to hold office; afterwards that he be presented to the Council; and if he is found worthy the Council receive and accept him, giving him certification to produce finally to the people when he preaches, in order that he be received by the common consent of the company of the faithful. . . . As to the manner of introducing him, it is good to use the imposition of hands, which ceremony was observed by the apostles and then in the ancient Church, providing that it take place without superstition and without offence. But because there has been much superstition in the past and scandal might result, it is better to abstain from it because of the infirmity of the times (*Corpus Reformatorum*, X, 15).

These regulations cover (i) the election and examination, and (ii) the act of ordination. The former varied in different places. For example, in the English congregation in Geneva, the congregation nominated several candidates to the ministers and elders, who examined them as to their life and education. The one approved was made known to the congregation, and time provided for them to enquire as to his fitness and character. If nothing was charged against him, a day was appointed for his ordination. The same procedure, in broad outline, was followed in

France and Scotland.

One of the essential elements in ordination is the 'call'. As the Genevan *Ordinances* put it, 'No one ought to intrude himself into this office without a call'. This emphasis is found in Zwingli (*CR*, IV, 425), Calvin (*Inst.* IV, iii, 10), the second *Helvetic* (18) and *Gallican* (31) *Confessions*, as well as in Holland (G. Brandt, *The Reformation in the Low Countries*, 1720, I, p. 318). In Scotland however they preferred to speak of a double call: 'called of God and duly elected by men'. The 'call' of the people was seen as confirming the inward 'call' of God. The Holy Spirit works not only in the aspirant, but also in the electors.

With regard to the ordination, it was by prayer with the laying on of hands in Zurich (H. A. Daniel, *Codex Liturgicus*, III, 1851, 234). This is also true of the first and second *Helvetic Confessions* (H. A. Niemeyer, *Collectio Confessionum*, 1840, pp. 110, 119, 507), of Calvin in Strasbourg, John a'Lasco in Frankfurt (*Forma ac Ratio*, 1556), Valerand Pullain (*Liturgia sacra*, 1551) and in France (J. Quick, *Synodicon*, 1692, I, 3, 62). On the other hand, in Geneva and Holland (Brandt, I, p. 319) the laying on of hands would appear to be an open question. The Scottish first *Book of Discipline* (Knox, *Works*, II, 193) contains wording similar to that in the Genevan *Ordinances*, but this may only refer to those who had formerly been priests in the medieval church. In 1566, the Scottish assembly approved the second *Helvetic Confession*, and in 1581 adopted the second *Book of Discipline* (III, 6), both of which prescribe the laying on of hands. It also was the practice of the English Puritans, as the 1586, 1587, and 1602 editions of the *Form of Prayers* show. In all these rites the essence of ordination is prayer (cf. L. Duchesne, *Christian Worship*, [6]1931, p. 377).

Calvin's ordination service is based on the practice of the early church rather than the medieval ordinals, but the liturgical sections do not appear to go farther back than himself or perhaps Bucer.

In the Scottish *Book of Common Order* (1564) the service is headed *The Form and Order of the Election of the Superintendent which may serve in election of all the Ministers*. It is really the form, drawn up by John Knox in 1560, largely based upon a'Lasco, for the admission of John Spottiswood as Super-

intendent for the Lothians (*BCO*, ed. Sprott, pp. 20-7).

After a sermon, which, as with Calvin, dealt with the office and nature of the ministry, the people were asked if they accepted the minister and would 'obey him as Christ's Minister'. Then a series of questions was put to the minister-elect, and after satisfactory answers had been given the people were again asked whether they would receive him. A short exhortation 'to the nobility' followed, and then came the ordination-prayer ending with the Lord's Prayer. After this the ministers and elders gave the right hand of fellowship. A benediction followed, and then an exhortation to the minister, the final direction being 'Sing the 23rd Psalm'.

Spottiswood was in Anglican Orders, so there is no reference to the laying on of hands. The same applied to priests of the medieval church. They were admitted, not ordained.

> Our reformers did not set up a new Church but did reform the old apostatized Church, so that there needed no new ordination (J. Menzeis, *Roma Mendax*, 1675, pp. 350, 379; *Jus Divinum*, II, 28).

Ordination was a catholic rite, not merely an admission to the ministry of a particular church. The people were given a place in the choice of the ordinand, but he was ordained by those already holding the office. His commission was not from the people, but from God through presbyters, lawfully associated, within the people of God.

In 1570 and 1620 further ordinals were produced in Scotland, and both make prayer and laying on of hands the main portions of the ceremony (*Miscellany of the Wodrow Society*, 1844, pp. 597ff.). In 1645, the Westminster *Form of Presbyterial Church Government* was adopted, and it remains the basic document to the present day in English-speaking Presbyterianism. It states:

> No man ought to take upon him the office of a minister of the word without a lawful calling. . . .
> Every minister of the word is to be ordained by imposition of hands and prayer, with fasting, by those preaching presbyters to whom it doth belong. . . .
> He that is to be ordained minister, must be duly qualified, both for life and mini-

sterial abilities. . . .

He is to be examined and approved by those by whom he is to be ordained.

No man is to be ordained a minister for a particular congregation, if they of that congregation can shew just cause of exception against him.

Preaching presbyters orderly associated . . . are those to whom the imposition of hands doth appertain, for those congregations within their bounds . . . (XVIII 1, 4, 7, 8, 9, 10).

It then sets out *The Directory for the Ordination of Ministers.* The structure of the service is:

Sermon 'concerning the office and duty of ministers of Christ'.

Questions to ordinand concerning his faith in Christ, the truth of reformed religion . . . his sincere intentions, his diligence in praying, reading, meditation, preaching, administration of the sacraments, his willingness to submit to the discipline of the church.

Questions to people 'concerning their willingness to receive and acknowledge him as the minister of Christ' . . . 'to obey him . . .', 'and to maintain, encourage, and assist him in all the parts of his office'.

Prayer of ordination with laying on of hands. Following thanksgiving for the incarnation, atonement and ascension of Christ, the gift of the Holy Spirit, and the Christian ministry comes an epiclesis (q.v.) asking God 'to fit him with his Holy Spirit, to give him (who in his name we thus set apart to this holy service) to fulfil the work of his ministry in all things . . .'.

Charge to minister and people.

Prayer 'commending both him and his flock to the grace of God'.

Psalm.

Dismissal with a blessing (XIX 5-9).

These works contain the basic principles which govern all modern rites.

Following the Westminster Assembly, owing to the rise of Independency and Brownism there was a period of liturgical decadence. Renewal came with the founding of the Church Service Society in 1865. It published the second edition of its *Eucho-logion* in 1869. This included an introductory

article (pp. 294-303) on the ordination service, a table of scripture lessons 'proper for the Service preceding the Ordination of Ministers and their Induction to Office' and 'portions of psalms proper to be sung' (p. 317), as well as a text for the rite (pp. 303-316). Its structure may be seen from the rubrics:

Divine Service shall be celebrated according to the usual order, or to such special order as the Presbytery may judge proper. . . .

After the Sermon, the presiding Minister shall read . . . a Narrative . . . of the proceedings of the Presbytery . . . concluding with these words: All having accordingly been so far done in this matter as is required by the law and usage of the Church, the Presbytery will now proceed to ordain the said A.B. to the Holy Ministry. . . .

Then the Candidate . . . shall answer the questions appointed by the Church to be put to those who are to be ordained. . . .

The presiding Presbyter . . . shall pray as follows . . . It is a prayer of thanksgiving, and at the epiclesis the presiding Presbyter and the other Presbyters standing near lay hands upon the head of the candidate.

The presiding Presbyter . . . shall take him by the right hand, saying, We give you the right hand of fellowship, to take part with us in this ministry.

Thereafter the presiding Presbyter shall give a solemn charge to the new Minister, and . . . to the people present, setting forth their respective duties from the Word of God.

Then shall be offered the following prayer. . . . The Service shall conclude with singing, and the following Benediction: Now the God of Peace. . . .

The liturgical sources for the prayers in this rite are Calvin, Knox, the Westminster *Directory*, and the *Provisional Liturgy* of the German Reformed Church in America, 1850 (*Euchologion*, ed. Sprott, p. 431).

In the *Euchologion*, ordination is treated as an ordinance following the liturgy of the word, and this is still the practice in some places. On the other hand, Scotland, Ireland, England-Wales, Canada, Geneva and Vaud see the rite as a unity and set out the service as consisting of both the liturgy of the word and ordination. All include the order for ordination in their service-book, except the Church of Scotland, the United Church of Canada, and America, where it is published in a separate ordinal. As a result of the *Euchologion* in Scotland, Osterwald in Switzerland, van Dyke in America, Bersier in France, van der Leeuw in Holland, and Albertz in Germany, all modern rites show traces of a more careful handling of the theological implications of ordination. As the various rites, whether in English, French, or German, follow a common pattern it is unnecessary to deal with them in detail. The rite of the Church of Scotland is representative:

Psalm
Scripture sentences
Prayer: confession, pardon, and illumination
Old Testament lection
Psalm
New Testament lections
Apostles' Creed
Prayer: intercession, commemoration of faithful departed
Hymn
Sermon on the holy ministry
Declaration of intention
Prescribed questions to ordinand
Prayer of ordination with laying on of hands and Lord's Prayer
Declaration with right hand of fellowship
Vow of people
Charge to minister and people
Prayer
Psalm or hymn
Benediction, The peace of God . . .

Only a few comments are necessary:
(*a*) The lections set forth the biblical basis for the ministry. The following are those most commonly used:

Old Testament
Exodus 3.1-6   Ireland
     4.11-12   Geneva
     18.18b-20   France
Isaiah 6.1-8   Ireland, Germany, England
     61.1-6   Scotland, England
Jeremiah 1.4-9   France
Ezekiel 1.26-2.5   Canada
     34.11-16   England

Epistle
Acts 1.7-9   Canada

     20.17-35   Ireland
Romans 10.13-17   Geneva, Germany
I Corinthians 12.27-13.13   England, Germany
II Corinthians 4.1-13   England
     5.17-21   France
Ephesians 4.4-8, 11-16   Ireland, France
I Timothy 3.1-3   Vaud, Geneva, England
     6.3-12   England
II Timothy 2.4-6   Geneva, Vaud
     4.1-5   Geneva, Vaud, Canada
Titus 1.1-7   England
I Peter 5.1-4   Scotland, Ireland, England, Germany, Vaud, France, Geneva, Canada, America

Gospel
Matthew 5.1-16   England
     28.17-20   Vaud, Geneva, Germany Ireland, England
Mark 10.42-45   France, Vaud, Geneva
Luke 12.35-38   England
John 10.1-11   Canada, England
     10.11-16   France, England
     20.19-23   France
     21.15-17   Scotland, Ireland, Canada, England, France, Germany.

(*b*) In the Presbyterian church in Canada a Statement on the Ministry may be read instead of the sermon.

(*c*) The prescribed questions differ in each church because they are drawn up by the various assemblies. They always cover: 'call of God', belief in the fundamental doctrines of the Christian faith, acceptance of scripture, obedience 'in the Lord' to the church, and fidelity as a minister of Jesus Christ.

(*d*) Some rites, for example, the Scottish, have the *Sursum corda* before the ordination prayer. Basically all are thanksgivings with an epiclesis and the laying on of hands. Though the words vary they are all identical in substance.
The following may be taken as representative:

France
We pray thee, Father Almighty, to send thy Holy Spirit upon our brother, N . . ., whom we consecrate to thy service and ordain a pastor in thy holy Church to the ministry of the Word and Sacraments.

Lausanne
In the name of the Father, of the Son, and

of the Holy Spirit, we consecrate to the service of Christ our brother by the laying on of hands to the ministry of the Gospel in his Church.

Scotland

Send down thy Holy Spirit upon this thy servant, whom we, in thy name, and in obedience to thy most blessed will, do now, by the laying on of our hands, ordain and appoint to the Office of the Holy Ministry in thy holy Catholic Church, committing unto him authority to minister thy Word and Sacraments, and to bear rule in thy flock.

Canada

Send now the Holy Spirit in power upon thy servant here kneeling, whom we in thy name do by the laying-on of our hands, receive and ordain to the Ministry of thy Word and Sacraments in the Holy Catholic Church. . . .

America

Send down thy Holy Spirit upon this thy servant, whom we, in thy name and in obedience to thy holy will, do now by the laying on of our hands ordain and appoint to the office of the holy ministry in thy Church, committing unto him authority to preach the Word, administer the Sacraments, and to bear rule in thy Church.

Germany

We ordain and ratify you with prayer and the laying on of hands as an ordained minister of the Church and teacher of the Gospel in the name of the Father, and of the Son, and of the Holy Spirit.

(e) Some churches, for example, Scotland, provide a Charge which may be read.

In conclusion, in the Reformed Church, the rite of ordination is an ordinance of the Word and always takes place within the setting of public worship, thus placing the holy ministry within the context of the sovereign grace of the Lord Jesus Christ, sole King and Head of the church. All ministry is ultimately his ministry within the life of his body. The holy ministry is of divine institution and derivation, renewed in every age by Jesus Christ through the creative power of the Holy Spirit, acting through his church when it is faithful to its apostolic institution, practice and doctrine.

JOHN M. BARKLEY

14. *Seventh-Day Adventist.* In the Seventh-day Adventist Church ordination is the liturgical act by which a member of the church is set apart by prayer and the laying on of hands for a special function of service in the church and is authorized to perform this function.

In the very early days of the SDAC there appears to have been little need for ordaining new ministers, because congregations were small and most of the ministers had already been ordained in the churches of their former membership. However, as the need for some clear form of church organization arose, and in order to avoid any tendency towards want of method or lack of co-operation by self-appointed preachers, the leaders of the movement began to practise ordination in the early 1850s. It was not instituted to build up a religious hierarchy or to exalt a clergy to a place of special privilege, but rather to provide for proper church order as the ordained individual receives new responsibilities and consecrates his life to God, the special service of the church, and to the world.

The SDAC ordains three categories of church workers: (a) ministers, (b) local church elders and (c) deacons.

Ordained ministers are full-time, salaried workers of the church, who have completed the requisite academic and theological studies prescribed by the church. Candidates for ministerial ordination have for the most part served as licensed ministers for a minimum of four years (including a two-year ministerial internship). Customarily they are married men; however, marriage is not a prerequisite for ordination. Though the church has taken no stand against the ordination of women, in practice only men have been ordained so far. The General Conference *Working Policy* outlines a careful procedure for authorizing ordination. The usual process is for local conference (or mission) and Union committees to suggest ordinands to the committee on credentials and licences at the triennial conference (or mission) session, on whose favourable report the session delegates make the final decision. Before ordination is carried out, a careful interview of the candidate is held, usually in the presence of his wife. It is conducted by ordained ministers only. There must be evidence of the person's divine call before the church sets him apart by ordination. Seventh-day Adventists reject as without biblical foundation the concept of 'apostolic succession', seeing little guarantee in the physical act of imposition itself. The laying on of hands *per se* adds no new grace or virtual qualification. By this act the church sets its seal upon the work of God.

The ordination service is one of the most solemn of all services of the church. It usually takes place on a Sabbath (Saturday) afternoon and is conducted with a view to exalting the office of the ministry in the eyes of the people and solemnizing the call in the heart of the candidate. For this service all ordained ministers present, if feasible, are invited on to the rostrum. Three ministers are chosen to take the three leading parts in the service: *ordination prayer*, the *charge*, the *welcome*.

After a brief sermon on the high calling and responsibility of the ministry, followed by the presentation of the candidate, the ministers, with the candidate in the centre of the group, kneel for the ordination prayer, while the congregation remains seated with bowed heads. When in the prayer mention is made of the laying on of hands, those kneeling near the candidate place a hand upon his head, continuing thus until the close of the prayer.

Rising from prayer, all the ministers stand while the charge is given. It is largely in the language of scripture, including such passages as Ezek. 33.7-9, 11; Acts 20.28; I Tim. 4.12-16; II Tim. 2.3, 4, 24; 4.1-5; I Peter 5.2-4. Following the charge, words of welcome are spoken, usually by the conference president.

Local church elders and deacons are laymen elected by the local church they serve, in contrast to the ordained minister who serves the world-wide church. Local elders and deacons are usually ordained in a simple ceremony during the divine service on Sabbath, with an ordained minister in charge. After reading a few appropriate passages of scripture (e.g., I Tim. 3.1-7 for elders, and I Tim. 3.8-13 for deacons), the candidate and minister kneel for the consecration prayer and the laying on of hands. After the prayer, the minister clasps the candidate's hand with a word of blessing. A local elder need not be reordained again upon re-election by the same congregation or another local church, or if subsequently elected as a deacon. Likewise a deacon is not reordained; however, if he is elected as an elder, he must be ordained as an elder, since this is an office of a higher degree.

In ordaining ministers, elders and deacons,

Seventh-day Adventists believe they are operating in harmony with the NT custom of having apostles and evangelists (itinerant ministry) to look after the general interests of the church as a whole, elders ('presbyters' or 'bishops') looking after the spiritual welfare, and deacons after the more temporal interests, of their local congregation.

B. B. BEACH

P. Bradshaw, *The Anglican Ordinal: Its History and Development*, 1971; F. E. Brightman, *The English Rite*, 2 vols., 1915; W. Brunnotte, *Das geistliche Sint bei Luther*, 1959; Church of South India, *The Book of Common Worship*, 1963; *Constitution, Bylaws and Working Policy of the General Conference of Seventh-day Adventists*, 1968; P. Edwall, E. Hayman and W. D. Maxwell, eds., *Ways of Worship*: Report of a theological commission of Faith and Order, 1951; W. K. Firminger, 'The Ordinal', in *Liturgy and Worship*, eds. W. K. Lowther Clarke and C. Harris, 1932; T. F. Gulixson, 'The Ministry' in *What Lutherans are Thinking*, ed. E. C. Fendt, 1947; Winthrop S. Hudson and Norman H. Maring, *A Baptist Manual of Polity and Practice*, 1963; B. A. van Kleef, *Geschiedenis van de Oud-Katholieke Kerk van Nederland*, 2nd ed., 1953; U. Küry, *Die altkatholische Kirche (Die Kirchen der Welt)*, 1966; N. Lindroth, *En bok om Kyrkans ämbete*, 1951; M. Luther, *Ordinationsformular*, WA 38, 401 ff.; *Manual for Ministers*, 1965 (Seventh-day Adventist); Don F. Neufeld, ed., *Seventh-day Adventist Encyclopedia*, 1966, pp. 925 ff.; A. Nygren, *This is the Church*, 1952; F. Proctor and W. H. Frere, *A New History of the Book of Common Prayer*, 1949; F. C. Ratcliff, 'The Ordinal of the Church of South India' in *Theology*, 63, January, 1960; *Report on Anglican-Methodist Unity: The Ordinal*, 1968; *The Standing Liturgical Committee of Protestant Episcopal Church in USA (Prayer Book Studies No. 20)*, 1970; V. Vajta, *Luther on Worship: An Interpretation*, 1958.

Organ

A keyboard instrument, which can be traced back to the ancient Greeks, in which wind is blown through pipes by mechanical action or, in modern imitations, tone is produced electronically. Pipe organs vary in size from the medieval portative, which can be carried

Plate 33 Organ, The Lyons Concert Hall, York University, England

than a piano, or even the whole orchestra. The characteristic tone of the organ comes from diapason or principal stops, but flutes and string-toned stops are common, as well as a variety of reeds based on wind and brass instruments. High-pitched stops, called mixtures, reinforce the upper frequencies to create a brilliant sound of high definition.

The glory of the organ is its association with Bach in the Baroque era. The magnificence of his organ music, and that of some of his contemporaries, has caused twentieth-century organ builders to re-create the finest features of the Baroque organ, which had been a lost art. Many composers before Bach made contributions to the literature of the instrument: outstanding among these is Buxtehude, and later on Handel wrote his concertos. The changing ideals of romantic composers are reflected in the works of Mendelssohn, Schumann and Liszt. Cesar Franck and Max Reger wrote extensively for the organ, and many twentieth-century composers have written for the instrument at a time of transition. The only major modern composer to specialize in the organ has been Olivier Messiaen, whose innovations have revealed new possibilities to later generations. Avant-garde examples include György Ligeti's *Volumina* and Mauricio Kagel's *Fantasia for Organ with Obbligati*, which requires an electronic tape. The portative organ and the harmonium have been revived by modern composers, and the electronic organ has a life of its own in certain works of Stockhausen quite apart from extensive use in jazz and pop (rock) music.

Organs and church choirs have long been adjuncts to Christian worship, although the Puritans in England and America distrusted music in church and organs were even destroyed during the English civil war. This was a temporary setback following the golden age of Elizabethan music and succeeded by the Restoration era of Purcell and Blow, both of whom were organists at Westminster Abbey. From the sixteenth to eighteenth centuries much concerted music was written for church use (e.g. Bach's cantatas) with an essential part for the organ. Throughout this period and up to the present day the English cathedral tradition has concerned choir and organ, and most British (and some American) composers have written for these resources. Apart from recital music, such as the Preludes and Fugues of Bach, or the Sym-

about, to modern giants with four, or more, manuals (keyboards) and pedals. The tone of the instrument is varied by the use of different ranks of pipes brought into action by the player through controls called stops. A medium-sized church organ is likely to have three manuals: swell, great and choir. The first of these gets its name through the practice of enclosing its pipes in a box with shutters, so that the swell pedal controls crescendo and diminuendo. Alternative, or further, manuals to be found are: positive, solo and echo. The pedal keyboard is a separate division of the instrument requiring a foot technique only otherwise found in the pedal harpsichord, now obsolete.

The compass of an organ manual is normally five octaves (sixty-one notes), or slightly less, and of the pedals two and a half octaves (thirty-two notes) or a few less. Some organ pipes play at unison, or piano pitch, whereas others sound an octave lower or one, two, or more octaves higher, with various fractions of an octave also available. As a result the instrument has a wider compass phonies of Vierne, there is a quantity of organ music from all periods designed for liturgical use, often based on hymn-tunes, the mass, or passages of scripture.

In times of economic stringency churches find organs an expensive luxury, as a large instrument requires skilled and continuous maintenance, not to mention periodic rebuilding. As a result, small churches have had recourse to cheap electronic organs which, although they have been improving in quality, rarely give satisfaction to musicians. A parallel development among organ builders has been the revival of the chamber organ, a small instrument of almost domestic size consisting of four or five ranks of pipes only, with one or two manuals and pedals. The modern trend in organ building is to retain all features of the historic instrument so that the music of all periods can be performed, and the varying demands of church use be met. After a century of attempting to imitate the orchestra the organ has rediscovered its heritage. *See* Plate 33.

William Leslie Sumner, *The Organ, Its Evolution, Principles of Construction and Use,* ²1955.

P. DICKINSON

Orientation

The siting of a building so that its sanctuary (q.v.) points to the east (Lat. *oriens*) ultimately derives from the early Christian practice of facing the east for prayer. In Judaism, prayer was offered towards the Temple at Jerusalem as the place of the presence of God; the Christian eastward direction could well have begun in conscious contrast to the Jewish custom, but it would also have been influenced by the general pagan understanding of the time that the east is the direction in which the good divine powers are to be found, a view originally connected with sun worship. Moreover, the NT itself suggests that the *parousia* of Christ will be from the east (Matt. 24.27), and since the ascension is a type of the second coming – he 'shall so come in like manner as you beheld him going into heaven' (Acts 1.11) – this, too, was envisaged as taking place in an eastward direction. As primitive Christian prayer was directed towards Christ and particularly towards the coming Christ, it was quite natural for orientation to be adopted.

Patristic teaching on the subject also referred to Jesus as 'the dayspring from on high' (Luke 1.78; *cf.* Clement of Alexandria, *Strom* 7.7) and suggested that in praying to the east the soul is hoping for restoration to its ancient home in Paradise through Christ the Second Adam (Basil, *de Spir. Sanct.* 27).

The Constantinian buildings, however, had their sanctuary at the west end. It is difficult to decide which of three possible explanations of this is correct. It may have been that the direction reflected Constantine's continued devotion to the Unconquered Sun. Again, since the president at the eucharist, adopting the basilican position, faced the congregation across the altar, to have the sanctuary at the west end meant that he and his assistant clergy did in fact look towards the east. Finally, it could be that Constantine and his architects understood their buildings as types of the Jerusalem Temple, of which the holy of holies was itself at the west end (I Kings 6).

From the middle of the fourth century the practice of locating the sanctuary at the east end was adopted and became all but universal, but without complete accuracy in every case; so in Rome St Maria Maggiore is north-west, but both St Sabina and St Agnese are south-east. Throughout the centuries since there has been a basic preference for the east-west orientation, and we find Durandus of Mende (1285-96) listing eight reasons for this: (1) 'The east is the image of Christ who, like the rising sun, lighteth every man that cometh into the world.' (2) 'Our souls be thereby taught to turn themselves to the things that are most desirable.' (3) 'Because those who praise God ought not to turn their backs on him.' (4) 'To show that we seek our country.' (5) 'Christ is the true east.' (6) 'Christians look towards Paradise from whence man has been excluded.' (7) 'Christ on the cross looked towards the east, he ascended thither and will come again from that direction.' (8) 'Daniel prayed towards the temple when he was in captivity' (*Rat. div. off.* 5.2.57).

Nevertheless, despite this array of allegory and symbolism, orientation has never been considered absolutely essential and many churches have been built regardless of it to accommodate them to the site available. Certainly in the twentieth century many modern churches neglect it entirely, the primary consideration having been how best to arrange the building in a given confined area.

EDITOR

Orthodox Worship

(More properly, Orthodox worship of the Byzantine rite.)

> The normal Orthodox lay worshipper, through familiarity from earlier childhood, is entirely at home in church, thoroughly conversant with the audible parts of the Holy Liturgy, and takes part with unconscious and unstudied ease in the action of the rite, to an extent only shared in by the hyper-devout and ecclesiastically-minded in the West (A. Oakley, *The Orthodox Liturgy*, 1958, p. 12).

Orthodox worship is indeed marked by this character of natural corporate participation. But in what does its character consist? In current practice, practice of very long standing, it is certainly not the product of those constituents which are commonly held to be necessary to it in modern Western theology of the liturgical reform school.

Some of these constituents are, of course, present. The worship of the Byzantine rite, in contrast to that of the Roman rite in the West, has never suffered from celebration in a language 'not understanded of the people'; at every stage of its expansion, from the conversion of the Slavs in the ninth and tenth centuries to Russian missionary activity in central and eastern Asia in the nineteenth, it has been taken for granted that one of the first prerequisites is the translation of the scriptures and the service-books into the appropriate language. And today, while Byzantine Greek and Old Slavonic are very different from modern Greek and Russian, in neither case is the language so far removed from its modern counterpart as to be unintelligible to the regular worshipper. Consequently, the clericalization of worship which occurred in the West during the Middle Ages has little counterpart in the Byzantine East: in particular, laymen (readers and cantors) play a far greater part in the conduct of services than they have done in the West until very recent years. Nor is there any Orthodox parallel to the overshadowing of the liturgy by popular devotions, embodying a very different spirituality, such as the Roman Catholic Church has suffered from for some centuries: there is no absence of popular devotions, but they have always been cast in a liturgical mould, and integrated into the liturgy itself, and the latter has in any case always remained *the* popular devotion, the staple diet of the ordinary worshipper.

On the other hand, congregational participation in the sense in which the phrase is usually understood today in the West is in most churches markedly absent. Practically the whole of Byzantine public worship, apart from those prayers recited *secreto* by the celebrant, is sung, and commonly only the choir sing. (This is especially true of Russian churches, in which elaborate harmonized music is used.) The sanctuary is separated from the nave by a solid screen, through the central doorway of which the altar is usually visible only from part of the church. The reception of holy communion by the adult laity is infrequent.

But by far the most important aspect of Orthodox worship is its general ethos, which is succinctly summed up in the words of an eighth-century patriarch of Constantinople, Germanos: 'The church is the earthly heaven in which the heavenly God dwells and moves.' The oneness of the worship of the church on earth with that of the church in heaven, and the consequent participation of the former in the latter, is the fundamental sacramental concept on which Orthodox worship is based. The incarnate Christ himself, in whom divine and human, heavenly and earthly, are joined together, is *the* sacrament; because the church is his body on earth, the extension of the incarnation, the church itself is a sacrament; therefore the church's worship is sacramental – all of it, not only those rites specifically called the sacraments. It was not until the seventeenth century that Orthodox dogmatic theology, under the pressures of Reformation and Counter-Reformation, came definitely to reckon seven sacraments, and to this day the service-books do not normally distinguish between sacraments and what in the West are called sacramentals (*see* **Books, Liturgical,** 2).

Nor is this sacramentality confined to sacraments and sacramentals; it is to be found also in the daily offices and the special observances of the church's year. The extent to which the latter involve the ordinary worshipper is well summed up by an Anglican writer:

Nobody who has lived and worshipped amongst Greek Christians for any length of time but has sensed in some measure the extraordinary hold which the recurring cycle of the Church's liturgy has upon the piety of the common people. Nobody who has kept the Great Lent with the Greek Church, who has shared in the fast which lies heavy upon the whole nation for forty days; who has stood for long hours, one of an innumerable multitude who crowd the tiny Byzantine churches of Athens and overflow into the streets, while the familiar pattern of God's saving economy towards man is re-presented in psalm and prophecy, in lections from the Gospel, and the matchless poetry of the canons; who has known the desolation of the holy and great Friday, when every bell in Greece tolls its lament and the body of the Saviour lies shrouded in flowers in all the village churches throughout the land; who has been present at the kindling of the new fire and tasted of the joy of a world released from the bondage of sin and death – none can have lived through all this and not have realized that for the Greek Christian the Gospel is inseparably linked with the liturgy that is unfolded week by week in his parish church. Not among the Greeks only, but throughout Orthodox Christendom the liturgy has remained at the very heart of the Church's life (P. Hammond, *The Waters of Marah*, 1956, pp. 51-52).

It should not, however, be supposed that the Byzantine rite is not in need of liturgical reform. It has passed through phases of development and decadence parallel to those through which the Roman rite in the West has passed; much of it, in its present form, does not antedate the Middle Ages, and much of its current presentation, especially in the Slav churches, does not antedate a much later period still. So far little has been done, except here and there, to cope with the liturgical needs of the very changed situation of the Orthodox Church in the twentieth century, especially in the churches of the emigration: in particular the problem of language has become acute – for the first time in Orthodox history there are many churches in which the congregation does not understand the language in which the church's worship is celebrated. Whether, in the absence of appropriate measures of

reform and renewal, it will continue to play the part in the lives of future generations which it has played in those of their forebears is a question to which it would be dangerously complacent to return an affirmative answer. Yet, while reform and renewal are necessary, it is equally necessary that they take place within the church's authentic liturgical tradition, and that their value should not be compromised by the kind of distortions which in recent years have come increasingly to compromise it in the West.

W. JARDINE GRISBROOKE

Pall

1. The term is applied to any cloth or covering that envelops or covers some object. The cloth of silk which in the earlier centuries completely enveloped the altar, and which was revived in the Church of England in the seventeenth century, was sometimes termed 'altar-pall' (*see* **Altar Hangings**).

2. It is also used for the cloth of velvet or damask that envelops a coffin when it stands in church at a funeral service. This should reach almost to the ground and cover the bier or trestles as well as the coffin. Most parish churches had such a pall until the middle of the last century and it covered the coffin of all parishioners, rich and poor alike, without distinction.

3. The term is also sometimes applied to the cloth that is hung from the desk of the pulpit (q.v.). At the Reformation period, only persons who had a doctor's degree were permitted to have such a cloth displayed when they preached, and preachers who were merely masters or bachelors of arts had no such cloth.

C. E. Pocknee, ed., *The Parson's Handbook*, 1965; The Warham Guild, *The Warham Guild Handbook*, rev. ed., 1963.

C. E. POCKNEE

Palm Sunday

The origin of Palm Sunday is to be found at Jerusalem in the latter part of the fourth century. On the Sunday with which the Great Week, i.e., Holy Week (q.v.), began, the people went to the Mount of Olives in the early afternoon. About five o'clock the gospel passage telling of the triumphal entry was read, and there was a procession by foot from the summit of the Mount of Olives into the city, children also sharing in the celebration and all carrying branches of palm or olive. In the course of time the observance spread from Jerusalem, but at Rome in the middle of the following century there is no hint that the Sunday bore the special characteristics of Palm Sunday, nor do we hear of Good Friday.

Palm Sunday is still regularly marked in Roman Catholic and Anglican churches by the distribution of palms, which are blessed and often carried in procession.

A. A. MCARTHUR

Papal Rites

The title which is borne by the head of the Catholic Church is that of *pontifex maximus*, which conveys the idea of a great high priest. The solemn performance of the sacerdotal functions of the pope first became practicable after the Emperor Constantine the Great had given peace to the church at the beginning of the fourth century. We can get some idea of what the papal liturgy was like up till the Middle Ages from the ancient sacramentaries and the *Ordines Romani*. The popes officiated in the various basilicas and other churches of Rome, chiefly of course in the Lateran basilica, *mater et caput omnium ecclesiarum urbis et orbis*, beside which they dwelt till their exile in Avignon at the beginning of the fourteenth century. When there, they worshipped in the palace chapel. After they returned to Rome in 1376, they went to live in the Vatican and there they continued the custom, begun in Avignon, of celebrating divine worship in their domestic chapels. For this reason Sixtus IV erected the magnificent Sistine Chapel in 1473, and Paul V the Pauline Chapel in the Quirinal palace in 1616. The Sistine Chapel had its daily divine office and high mass till 1788.

The dynamic Sixtus V (1585-90) made a grand effort to restore the pontifical ceremonies in the Roman basilicas and stational churches, but after his death they ceased again. Nevertheless, a good number of the papal 'chapels' continued to be held both in the Vatican and in the churches of the city. Gaetano Moroni (*Le Cappelle Pontificie*, 1841) enumerates ten days in the year on which the pope assisted at vespers and

thirty-five when he assisted at mass. But after the occupation of Rome by the Italian army in 1870, these solemn liturgical functions were considered to be incompatible with the state of mourning adopted by the holy see. The pope never left the Vatican palace till the Concordat was signed with the Kingdom of Italy in 1929. In the Sistine Chapel were celebrated only the anniversaries of the pope's election and coronation, the anniversary of the death of the late pope and a requiem mass in November for the cardinals deceased during the preceding year. Pius XI also celebrated the rites of Maundy Thursday and Good Friday each year. The late Pope John XXIII pontificated several times in St Peter's. He also assisted at the ceremonies of Palm Sunday, Maundy Thursday and Good Friday in the other papal basilicas. His present Holiness Paul VI also takes part in the Easter Vigil in St Peter's and in the Ash Wednesday rite.

High mass celebrated by the pope. The solemn celebration of the papal high mass (q.v.) is in our day a rare event. Before 1870 the pope used to sing high mass regularly three times a year in St Peter's: on Christmas day, on Easter day, and on the Feast of St Peter and St Paul. But after this date the papal high mass was only celebrated on some extraordinary occasions such as canonizations, certain centenaries and papal coronations. In the early medieval ages, on the contrary, it would seem that the sovereign pontiff sang mass on nearly all the Station days, on various feasts and perhaps on Sundays, but of course the rite was much simpler than it became later on, when it took something like four hours to carry it out. Even so, Gregory the Great complained in a letter to the patriarch of Alexandria that he suffered so much from gout when he had to spend three hours in the celebration of mass on feast days.

The best description of the papal mass in the eighth century is to be found in the *Ordo Romanus I*, of which an English version was published by E. G. C. F. Atchley in 1905. For a later period we have *Le Cérémonial Apostolique avant Innocent VIII* by Joaquim Nabuco, published in Rome in 1966. There is no official book regulating the ceremonies of the papal mass today. In 1516 Christopher Marcellus, archbishop of Corfù, wrote the *Rituun ecclesiasticorum sive sacrarum caeremoniarum sanctae Romanae Ec-*

clesiae libri tres, which ran through several editions till the one edited by Joseph Catalani in 1750. Domenico Giorgi had previously, in 1730, published a treatise *De liturgia Romani Pontificis in celebratione solemni missarum*. Francesco Girolamo Cancellieri, in 1788 and in 1814, published editions of his *Descrizione de' tre pontificali, che si celebrano per le feste di Natale, di Pasqua e di S. Pietro*. In 1841 Gaetano Moroni published an extract on the *Cappelle pontificie* from his *Dizionario di erudizione ecclesiastica*. More recent is the *Caeremoniale missae, quae a Summo Pontifice Ecclesiae universalis ritu solemni celebratur*, by Peter Joseph Rinaldi-Bucci.

But, like the general reorganization and democratization of the church's liturgy, which is proceding today, all the papal rites are under review and a special *Coetus* was erected in the *Concilium ad exsequendam Constitutionem de Sacra Liturgia*, concerned particularly *De Ritibus Cappellae Papalis*.

It is at least certain that the papal mass will never again be celebrated in all its solemnity. The pope celebrates frequently in public, but his masses are more or less like the former 'low masses' (q.v.), sometimes with a certain amount of singing. For a canonization he sings a solemn mass at the high altar of St Peter's, but without the throne formerly erected in the apse (q.v.) of the basilica. A smaller throne was erected on the south side for the singing of terce after the imposing entrance of clergy and dignitaries with the pontiff carried shoulder high on the *sedia gestatoria*. In the hall of benedictions above the portico a band of silver trumpets played the march of Longhi. As well as the usual vestments (q.v.) the pope wore a voluminous white skirt called the *falda* and a mantle or large-sized cope. For the mass itself he wore the *succinctorium*, a girdle from which hung a sort of wide maniple with the *Agnus Dei* embroidered on it, also the fanon, a double cape of silk with stripes of gold, white and amarinth. The pope does not use a crozier, instead of it he carries a ferula, a tall staff surmounted by a cross.

The mass followed the ordinary rules of a pontifical mass with the following special rites. After incensing the altar the pope gave the kiss of peace (q.v.) to the three cardinal deacons at the altar. After the singing of the epistle in Latin it was sung again in Greek by the Greek subdeacon, recalling the time when Greek was commonly used in the liturgy in Rome. At the singing of the Latin gospel the seven acolytes with their candles were in attendance, and at its conclusion the Greek deacon sang the same gospel in Greek. Then the pope read his homily seated on his throne. After the verse *Et incarnatus est* in the creed the deacon and the subdeacon spread over the altar a linen cloth adorned with gold braid and called the *Incarnatus*. For the pregustation the deacon chose two out of three hosts and gave them to the sacrist to consume. On Easter day the two junior cardinals came and stood at either corner of the altar to represent the angels at Christ's tomb. During the elevation (q.v.) the pope turned with the host and the chalice first to the right and then to the left, while the silver trumpets sounded Silveri's harmony from the dome. After the kiss of peace the pope returned to the throne. The paten with the host, covered with the 'asterisk' to keep it in place, and the chalice were carried to the throne. The pope, in former times seated, consumed part of the host and part of the precious blood through a fistula, and then communicated the deacon and the subdeacon and kissed them on the cheek. The ceremony ended with the solemn blessing. The pope then mounted on the *sedia gestatoria* and the tiara was placed on his head. The cardinal archpriest approached and presented him with a purse containing twenty-five 'jules', the stipend for a mass 'well sung'.

Several ceremonies are, or were, peculiar to the papal liturgy, such as the blessing of the wax medallions stamped with the figure of the *Agnus Dei*, of the golden rose, destined to honour some sovereign or some community, of the ducal sword and cape to be sent to a Catholic prince and of the palliums worn by the occupants of metropolitan sees.

The creation of cardinals was always a simple ceremony, but now it has been still more simplified, and even the famous red hat has disappeared from the scene. The canonization of saints is still performed as occasion demands, but with reduced rites. The summoning of and the presiding over an ecumenical council is still a possibility, as we have seen in our own day; so too the opening of the holy door for the year of jubilee and the closing of it at the end of the period.

When the pope died, the Cardinal Camerlengo recognized the body and ordered that the Fisherman's Ring be broken. Presently the body, dressed in red vestments, was carried into St Peter's and exposed for a few days and the Novemdiales began, a series of nine requiem masses sung daily. The traditional place of burial of the popes is the Vatican basilica, *juxta corpus beati Petri*. In fact one hundred and thirty-six popes have been buried there. Pius IX was buried, at his own wish, at St Lorenzo Fuori le Mura, among the poor people of Rome, who lie in the great cemetery of the Camp Verano. Leo XIII has his tomb in St John Lateran, which he did so much to restore. Pope John XXIII also expressed in his will an alternative wish to be buried in his Lateran cathedral, but the commission of cardinals decided to keep his remains in the crypt of St Peter's.

On the fifteenth day after the death of the pope the Sacred College of Cardinals attended a solemn mass of the Holy Ghost, sung by the Dean of St Peter's and a sermon *Pro eligendo Pontifice*, then in the afternoon they entered the conclave. The scrutinies of the votings took place in the Sistine Chapel. Against the walls were seats and tables for the electors. They were surmounted by movable baldachins (q.v.), which after the election were all dropped except that over the new pope, who had to obtain two thirds plus one of the votes. When this was achieved, the Dean approached the elected cardinal and asked him 'Dost thou accept thine election canonically made to the sovereign pontificate?', and if the answer was affirmative, the new pope was asked what name he would take and then in an adjoining cabinet he was dressed in the papal garments. He went to a seat before the altar and received the adoration of the cardinals, while the first cardinal deacon from the balcony over the porch of St Peter's proclaimed the election to the people. Soon afterwards he himself gave his first blessing from the same place. A few days later he was solemnly crowned with the *triregnum* or tiara by the senior deacon saying: 'Receive this tiara adorned with three crowns and know that thou art the father of princes and kings, the ruler of the world, the vicar upon earth of our Saviour Jesus Christ, to whom is honour and glory, world without end. Amen.'

(This item is partly abridged from a series of articles which were published in the Westminster Cathedral Chronicle, whose editor I thank for permission to make use of them.)

RONALD PILKINGTON

Paschal Candle

The lighting of a large and special candle on its own stand or candlestick forms one of the ceremonies in the vigil service on the eve of Easter, all candles and lamps having been extinguished on Maundy Thursday. The rekindling of fire and light, including the lighting of the Paschal candle, symbolize the triumph of the resurrection over darkness and sin. The lighting of the Paschal candle was accompanied by the singing of a special chant known as the *Praeconium* or *Exultet* sung by the deacon from the ambon by the side of which stood the Paschal candlestick. In the words of the *Exultet* there were allusions to the Passover and the crossing of the Red Sea which were types foreshadowing the new Passover effected by Christ's cross and resurrection. It is not possible to say with certainty when and where these ceremonies originated. Jerome in the fourth century complained about the deacon's hyperbole of language as he chanted the *Praeconium*. Also the hymn *Inventor rutili*, composed by Prudentius in the same century, was sung during the Easter vigil service; its allusions leave little doubt about the rekindling of fire and light. In the older Roman and Italian basilicas the Paschal candlestick was of marble or porphyry decorated with tessellated inlay and it stood as a permanent feature either on one side of the chancel (q.v.) or even part-way down the nave (q.v.). The idea that this candlestick could only stand immediately on the north side of the altar (q.v.) is a late medieval innovation.

The Paschal candle is now in use from the eve of Easter until Ascension Day (q.v.); but in earlier days its lighting continued in some rites until Whitsunday (q.v.). In some examples the candle was on a pan or dish suspended by chains instead of on a stand. In the late English medieval rites this candle assumed enormous proportions, that at Salisbury Cathedral being thirty-six feet (eleven metres) high, while that at Westminster Abbey weighed three hundredweight (740 kilograms).

At one time it was customary to insert five grains of incense in this candle signifying the five wounds of Jesus; this has now been discontinued by those who note that it is based on a misreading of the meaning of the term *incensum* in the Latin of the *Exultet*. Prior to its being placed on its stand the candle is used in connection with the blessing of the font, and the date of the year is inscribed on its length.

D. R. Dendy, *The Use of Lights in Christian Worship*, 1959; H. J. Feasey, *Ancient English Holy Week Ceremonial*, 1897; J. W. Tyrer, *Historical Survey of Holy Week*, 1932.

C. E. POCKNEE

Paschal Vigil

The celebration of the *Pascha*, the passion, death and resurrection of the Lord, on the Saturday night and Sunday morning of Easter (q.v.), is the church's oldest liturgical observance with the sole exception of the week-end vigil that was celebrated in NT times and from which the Paschal vigil itself is derived.

The church was conscious that it owed its existence to the saving events of the cross and the resurrection, and there was a vivid sense of the presence of the Lord who was with his people in and through the celebration of these events and who would come again in glory to complete the work of his redemption. The Paschal celebration therefore was not a mere recalling of the past events; it made the power of those events present to the worshippers, who could thus make a renewed encounter with their Lord. The first-century vigil centred upon the eucharist, the passover meal of the Lord, but by the second century, baptism, by which new members were added to the church, was celebrated as part of the Paschal vigil. Possibly the Jewish observance of the lighting of the lamps on the eve of the sabbath influenced the Christian liturgy and so we get the third element, light. In the Johannine tradition, Christ is the light of the world, and out of these two elements, Jewish and Christian, the church gradually evolved the symbolism of the candle which in the fourth century became the centre of interest of the first part of the rite. But the Christian vigil had always included the celebration of God's saving deeds in the word of the scriptures, and with the development of the catechumenate (q.v.), the word-service came to be regarded as the last instruction of the candidates before their baptism. Thus by the end of the fourth century all the elements of the vigil celebration had been assembled, and light, word, water and the bread and wine of the eucharist all became efficacious symbols

conveying the power of the redeeming Christ to the gathered assembly.

The Paschal vigil was the total and unitive celebration of the redeeming work of Christ, and until the end of the third century, Good Friday (except in Asia, where Christians kept the vigil on 14 Nisan instead of the Saturday/Sunday, hence their name Quartodecimans) was observed only by a solemn fast, and Maundy Thursday became a separate celebration only when the historicization of the liturgy was well under way in the fifth century. Yet, the sense of a unitive celebration of Christ's redeeming work was retained for centuries, and it was not until in the seventh century, when the hour of the vigil began to be anticipated, that a tendency set in to break up the pattern. All during the early Middle Ages the vigil was celebrated earlier, until by the late Middle Ages it was celebrated in the morning of Holy Saturday. This was the position consecrated by the missal of Pius V (1570) which *ordered* that the service (hardly any longer to be called a vigil) was not to be celebrated *after* mid-day on Saturday. Yet, with astonishing fidelity, the church retained all the ancient rites and texts (though with some strange accretions) and still sang of the 'holy night' when Christ liberated man from sin. With the gathering momentum of the Liturgical Movement, this anomaly became increasingly obvious and intolerable. In response to requests, Pius XII in 1951 restored the proper hour of the vigil celebration and partly revised the rites and texts. This restoration was at first experimental only, and the definitive reform of the whole of the Holy Week liturgy came in 1955. Since then there has been a further revision in the direction of simplicity, and it is this revision that will be described now.

The church is in darkness and the new fire (q.v.) is lighted. From this light is taken to the Paschal candle. This may be simply lighted and then carried into and through the church by a deacon who sings three times 'Christ our light', the third time in the sanctuary (q.v.). Meanwhile the people's candles are lighted from the Paschal candle. There follows the Easter proclamation (*Exultet*) in which the saving events of the OT and NT are recalled. The word-service now begins, and there are readings from the OT (five, to be used at choice, are provided) and the NT (the epistle). Before the epistle, the *Gloria* is intoned and the bells rung, heralding the arrival of Easter. The gospel and the homily follow, and after these the blessing of the baptismal water and baptism itself if there are candidates. If there are no baptisms, the formula of blessing is shorter. There follows the renewal of baptismal promises and the sprinkling of the people with the newly blessed water. The mass then continues as usual.

Two special observances may be noted. (1) The Paschal candle may be marked by the Alpha and Omega, the sign of the cross and the year of salvation, thus indicating that Christ the redeemer is present among his people. Five incense grains may be inserted into the candle with a formula which interprets the gesture: 'May Christ by his glorious wounds preserve and guard us.' (2) After the epistle the *Alleluia* (q.v.), suppressed at the beginning of Lent, is now solemnly intoned. The vestigial lauds which was attached to the rite in 1955 is now suppressed.

J. D. CRICHTON

Paten *see* Chalice and Paten

Pax *see* Gestures (4)

Pentecost

The day of Pentecost, commonly called Whitsunday, was a unitive festival commemorating both the ascension of Jesus and the descent of the Holy Spirit. In the course of the fourth century it was resolved into two commemorations corresponding to the distinct parts of the primitive celebration, the institution of Ascension Day in the latter part of the century resulting in the limitation of Pentecost to the second theme.

The Greek word 'Pentecost' refers to the *fiftieth* day, defining the time after the season of the Pascha when Pentecost, one of the pilgrim festivals of the old covenant, celebrated the wheat-harvest. In the OT itself this agricultural festival is not identified with the law-giving on Mount Sinai. If the identification had been made in Judaism by the time of the gospel, it would be profoundly significant that on the day of Pentecost the disciples experienced the dynamic power of the Holy Spirit. In that case the event, in the particular sense of the occasion as well as in the general sense of the revelation given, would be the action of the divine purpose. As the old covenant, ratified in the Exodus which the Passover com-

memorated, was completed on Mount Sinai, so the new covenant, ratified in the events which the Christian Pascha commemorated, the cross and the resurrection, was completed on the festival of Pentecost when the power of the Holy Spirit came upon the disciples. Pentecost was the birthday of the church as the New Israel of God. The link between the law-giving and the descent of the Holy Spirit was appreciated by Augustine and Leo the Great. When Paul made his contrast between the law and the Spirit he may have written in the context of a liturgical connection between the Pentecost of the old covenant and that of the new. It is possible that he regarded the law-giving as such, the consecration of the Old Israel, as the work of the Spirit within the time of the old covenant. His emphatic rejection of the legalism of rabbinic Judaism from which he had been delivered by the gospel does not invalidate the comparison which gives point and relevance to the contrast.

At the beginning of the third century Tertullian refers to the day of Pentecost in terms which are consistent with a unitive commemoration, but the evidence does not permit a precise statement. Eusebius, describing the death of the Emperor Constantine in 337, makes specific reference to the festival as the occasion of the ascension of Jesus and the descent of the Holy Spirit. It is unmistakably clear that Ascension Day was not in existence at this time. On the contrary, the liturgical commemoration of the ascension on the day of Pentecost must have been so familiar to Eusebius that he forgets the book of Acts and identifies the event historically with that day. In view of the direct evidence, it cannot be doubted that early in the fourth century the day of Pentecost was a unitive festival, commemorating both the ascension of Jesus and the descent of the Holy Spirit.

Towards the end of the fourth century at Jerusalem, according to Etheria's description, there was a procession on the fiftieth day after Easter to the traditional site of the event of Pentecost, the Church on Mount Zion, where, at 9 a.m., a service was held in the course of which the passage was read concerning the descent of the Holy Spirit. This was a commemoration in the Jerusalem fashion at the proper place and time. Just after midday the people gathered at the sanctuary on the traditional site of the ascension, and the passages about the ascension from the gospel and Acts were read. A great candlelight procession came to the city in the darkness, and it was eventually about midnight when the people returned to their homes. This is the early unitive Pentecost, commemorated, in the way worship was now celebrated in the Holy City, with careful attention to the symbolism of the sacred sites.

In the early period of the church the term 'Pentecost' does not simply indicate the fiftieth day as such, but frequently refers to the entire period of fifty days which would begin with the day of the Pascha. This season, our Eastertide, was regarded as a time of joy and triumph. As every Lord's Day was a commemoration of the glory of the divine kingdom in the resurrection of Christ, so the fifty days of Pentecost echoed to the same trumpet note of victory. Kneeling in prayer and fasting were forbidden on Sundays, and this privilege applied also to the great fifty days.

A. A. McArthur, *The Evolution of the Christian Year*, 1953.

A. A. MCARTHUR

Pentecostal Worship

Following the terminology of K. McDonnell ('Catholic Pentecostalism', *Dialog*, Winter 1969/70, pp.35-54), we must distinguish between Pentecostals within *traditional* churches – Roman Catholic, Anglican, Lutheran, Presbyterian, Methodist, Congregational and Baptist – (called *Neo-Pentecostalism* below) and the different Pentecostal denominations (*classical Pentecostalism*). Clearly the worship of the Neo-Pentecostals either forms part of their traditional worship or is celebrated in prayer-groups within the traditional parishes. One finds interesting combinations, therefore, between a Roman Catholic mass and Pentecostal speaking in tongues, or between an Anglican service and prayer for the sick through laying on of hands. Neo-Pentecostals also celebrate separate 'charismatic services' with all the elements of classical Pentecostalism, yet in a different social and cultural environment, since Neo-Pentecostals belong mostly to the upper middle-class. This phenomenon has shattered the 'economic deprivation theory' which held that spontaneous Pentecostal worship was only to be expected in the so-called 'underprivileged' classes. Yet Neo-Pentecostal prayer-groups –

this applies more to the Roman Catholic than to the Protestant section of Neo-Pentecostalism – are not frequented by the uncritical, but by the critical exegetes, not by the unlearned, but by the intellectuals, not by frustrated Puritans, but by normal Christians. In their prayer meetings they not only sing, but create new hymns, they not only speak in tongues, but discuss theological and political problems, they not only pray, but eat, drink and smoke.

In this context, speaking in tongues plays a great role, because it allows prayer in a non-rational meditative language. This is an important prayer experience for the rationally unskilled as well as for the intellectually over-burdened academician, an experience which made the apostle Paul say: 'He who speaks in a tongue edifies himself' (I Cor. 14.4).

The worship of *classical Pentecostalism*, on the other hand, follows the lines of the Protestant Free Church tradition with hymns, prayers (often with spontaneous participation of the congregation through prayers, and sometimes speaking in tongues and interpretation) and preaching (which in the younger Pentecostal churches is open to everyone, but in the older churches is the duty and privilege of an emergent clergy, (*see* **Ordination** 12; Pentecostal).

The indigenous African churches, of which many belong historically and phenomenologically to the Pentecostal family, have adopted many interesting sacramental or quasi-sacramental rites, such as ritual washings, pilgrimages to places which played a great role in the history of the church (e.g. the Kimbanguists in the Congo). Their ministers, sometimes called prophets, bishops, the spiritual head, priests, apostles, etc., wear colourful garments or stoles and carry staffs.

The following example from personal experience in Chile is not, of course, representative of all Pentecostal churches, but may serve as an introduction to Pentecostal worship. The writer was asked to sit in front of the congregation in the red plush seat reserved for honoured guests. An ocean of faces floated before my eyes, 2000 to 3000 faithful, some with car-tyres on their feet instead of shoes. But as soon as the trumpet blew the first melody, those faces creased with the signs of age-long oppression came to life. They danced slowly in a circle the dances of their Indian ancestors. Those who did not dance stood reverently and clapped their hands slowly. A woman prophesied in a deep, soul-searching voice. All of a sudden there was silence! The whole congregation fell down on their knees in order to thank God for the dance he had given them. Above in the gallery at the left side sat fifty to one hundred *cyclistas* in grey blouses. These are the bicycle-evangelists who cycle into the surrounding villages in order to preach, sing, and heal the sick every Sunday. In the evening they come back and the congregation will greet them with a loud '*Gloria a Dios*'. They will draw behind them a queue of curious people, who will be converted tonight. 'Do you also dance? they ask me. This was the test-question. They wanted to know whether I despised them or not. 'I would like to,' I answered sincerely, 'but I do not know your dances.' They were satisfied with this answer. Their own preachers do not dance either; their duty is not to dance, but to interpret the dances.

The most important element of Pentecostal worship is the active participation of every member of the congregation, even if this amounts to several thousand people (M. de Melo, *Monthly Letter about Evangelism*, February/March 1969, Geneva, wcc), in dancing, singing, pilgrimages, praying individually and collectively (called 'prayer in concert'), playing all kinds of instruments from the hand-harmonica to triangle and drum, from the saxophone to the violin, evaluating and judging the sermon by inspiring shouts or critical remarks and questions.

Yet if one considers the future of Pentecostal worship, there are several possibilities open. *Classical Pentecostalism* can adapt itself to the mainline churches, adopting a fundamentalist theology and a written liturgy. This process is in full swing for most of the European and North American Pentecostal churches. The other possibility is to develop a really post-literary liturgy with all the means of that culture, where the main medium of communication is not the written word but the proverb, not the newspaper but the parable, not the statement but the story, not the Gregorian hymn but the chorus. This liturgy, too, can be adapted to non-proletarian cultures, but its main mission would be in the third world and among the subculture of the younger generation.

Neo-Pentecostalism has also two options. In emphasizing the personal aspect of Christianity it can develop into a spiritual revival movement for higher social classes, which would lead to worship services, refreshing and equipping the individual, but would be relatively unaware of collective sins and evils. The other possibility is that Neo-Pentecostalism might develop its charismatic worship in such a way that – following the Pauline rather than the Lucan pneumatology (*cf.* E. Schweizer, 'Spirit of God', *TDNT*, VI, pp. 389-455) – it would include among the charismata not just those common to classical Pentecostalism, but also charismata in the social, political and artistic field – as the Pentecostal leader D. J. Du Plessis has put it – the charismata of those people who are not generally considered to be Christians. This would be a healthy ecumenical complement to the classical Pentecostal understanding of worship.

N. Bloch-Hoell, *The Pentecostal Movement*, 1964; C. Lalive d' Epinay, *A Study of the Pentecostal Movement in Chile*, 1969; W. J. Hollenweger, *The Pentecostals*, 1972; Research Review by W. J. Hollenweger, *Die Pfingstkirchen*, 1970; J. T. Nichol, *Pentecostalism*, 1966.

W. J. HOLLENWEGER

Petition *see* Prayer (3)

Pew

Seating in the naves of churches was unknown in any degree for many centuries, as the worshippers normally stood during the liturgy. In some instances there were stone ledges round the wall of a church, hence (it is said) there arose the expression, 'the weakest goes to the wall' as the infirm sat on these ledges. In the Eastern churches today seating is still unusual.

In the West, and particularly in northern Europe, seating was gradually introduced in the naves of churches from the thirteeenth century. At first such seats were simply backless benches. But most of the medieval examples in England belong to the fifteenth and sixteenth centuries, when the wood carver's craft reached its climax in skill, as we can see in the remarkable examples in East Anglia and the West Country. These late medieval benches or pews are always constructed in 'islands' of seating and they never crowd right up to the chancel or choke up the west end; there is always room for ordered movement.

After the Reformation, pews tended to increase both in number and in their size and proportion, so that almost the whole nave was crowded with 'box-pews' which screened the occupants from their neighbours. In the nineteenth century many of these high pews were done away; but they were sometimes replaced with benches of poor design with the seats being too narrow. The planning and arranging of seating in churches is an important matter both from the point of the comfort of the worshippers and also in regard to the proportions of the building and the setting of the liturgy.

The Warham Guild, *The Warham Guild Handbook*, rev. ed. 1963.

C. E. POCKNEE

Piscina

A Latin word, meaning literally 'fish-pond' or 'fish-tank'. The term was probably transferred to the baptismal font (q.v.), since the fish was one of the symbols of Christ in primitive Christianity. Tertullian, writing at the end of the second century in his treatise *De Baptismo* (ch. 1), says, 'We, being little fishes, as Jesus Christ is our great Fish, begin our life in the water, and only while we abide in the water are we safe and sound.' Examples are known of the fish being depicted inside the basin of the primitive font, e.g. the one in Kélibia, North Africa.

But the term piscina came to assume another meaning in the Middle Ages, and it was applied to a shallow saucer-like basin in a niche in the wall of the south side of an altar. This basin has a drain attached to it leading into the earth. This arrangement was also termed *lavacrum* and *sacrarium*. The purpose of this type of piscina has been disputed. But as early as the ninth century Pope Leo IV ordered that a receptacle was to be provided near the altar for the disposal of the water that had been used in the ablutions of the hands and the chalice. Until the fourteenth century there was a single drain and piscina attached to any altar; then we get examples of the double piscina, e.g. in Exeter Cathedral, England. It is supposed that one drain was used for the ablutions from the chalice and the other for that of the hands. In the fifteenth century there was a reversion to the single piscina.

F. Bond, *The Chancel of English Churches*, 1916; J. G. Davies, *The Architectural Setting of Baptism*, 1962.

C. E. POCKNEE

Plymouth Brethren Worship

The Plymouth Brethren are so called by others – not by themselves – from the fact that their first congregation in England was established at Plymouth, about 1831. They called one another 'brethren', and when they moved into neighbouring areas they were referred to as 'the brethren from Plymouth' or Plymouth Brethren. Their movement began in Dublin some years earlier, when a few young men came together to take the Lord's Supper informally in an attempt to surmount the denominational barriers which otherwise would have prevented their intercommunion and in the hope that they might thus recapture the simplicity of apostolic times. When they were joined by John Nelson Darby (1800-82), a priest of the Church of Ireland, he quickly dominated the group by his powerful personality and forceful ecclesiology, which aimed at reconstituting the faithful remnant of the end-time. During a visit to Francis William Newman at Oxford in 1830, Darby influenced some other young men there, especially Benjamin Wills Newton (1807-99), Fellow of Exeter College, who returned to his native Plymouth the following year and founded the Brethren congregation in that city. Darby then carried his teaching to the Continent, especially to French Switzerland, where his followers are known to this day as *Darbistes*. On his return to the British Isles his imperious pressing of an exclusive church doctrine and polity occasioned a cleavage (1848), those who followed his lead being thereafter referred to as Exclusive Brethren and the others, by contrast, Open Brethren.

The Open Brethren, because of their evangelistic energy, were profoundly influenced by the Revival of 1858-60. In some parts of the UK (e.g north-east Scotland) there were formed, as a result of that revival, independent congregations which were soon attracted into the Brethren orbit; elsewhere their ethos was recognizably modified by the revival. One symptom of this was the widespread use of the term 'Gospel Hall' to denote their meeting-places (nowadays 'Evangelical Church' is becoming increasingly popular). Among Exclusive Brethren places of worship were more commonly and modestly called 'The Room' or 'The Meeting Room'. The initiated can usually tell from the phraseology on the notice-board which group of Brethren worships in the building.

The Exclusive principle of church fellowship has been summed up in the title of one of J. N. Darby's treatises: 'Separation from evil God's principle of unity' – the separation in question being understood in terms of the Darbyite exegesis of II Tim. 2.19-21, in which the 'great house' is the sum-total of Christendom. By contrast, Open Brethren have generally preferred, with Anthony Norris Groves (1795-1853), to accept 'recognition of Christ alone in my brother, as the Alpha and Omega of terms of communion'. Groves, who has been called the archetypal Open Brother, declared in a letter to Darby in 1836, regarding certain Christians who seemed to him in some respects to be following the wrong path: 'I would infinitely rather bear with all their evils, than separate from their good.' Groves was also the Brethren's first foreign missionary; he led a pioneer band to Baghdad in 1829 and spent the last twenty years of his life in India. The missionary work which he initiated is carried on today by over 1000 missionaries in all five continents, especially in India, Central Africa and South America; this enterprise is commonly designated 'Christian Mission in Many Lands' and its records are published in the monthly periodicals *Echoes of Service*, Bath, England and *The Fields*, New York. Other pioneer Brethren missionaries were the two Scots, Frederick Stanley Arnot (1858-1914), the first European to explore Katanga, and Dan Crawford (1870-1926), who opened up to Western knowledge other uncharted areas of Central Africa.

Groves's brother-in-law, George Müller (1805-98), was the Prussian-born founder of the Bristol orphanage which bears his name. Along with Henry Craik (1805-66), a St Andrews graduate and Hebrew scholar, he was joint-pastor of Bethesda Chapel, Bristol, which took a foremost part in resisting the authoritarian demands of J. N. Darby in 1848 and thus became, among Darby's followers, a by-word for all that is ecclesiastically reprehensible. The Exclusive adoption of separation as the principle of unity, when pressed to its logical conclusion, has led to a diversity of Exclusive divisions, the most 'exclusive' of which is that led until his recent death by

James Taylor, Jr, of New York. Some Exclusive groups, however, are 'exclusive' only in name, in the sense that they stem from the Darbyite side of the 1848 cleavage, but in practice they are as evangelically co-operative as the Open Brethren.

The Brethren accept the doctrines of the historic creeds, except that the Taylorite Exclusives have manifested an Apollinarian tendency and, since about 1929, have denied the eternity of Christ's relation as Son to the Father – this relation, they hold, started with the incarnation, although they believe in his eternal pre-existence. The Brethren are evangelical in doctrine and practice, leaning for the most part towards Calvinism rather than Arminianism. Their most distinctive feature is that (like the Friends) they reject all differentiation between clergy and laity. While several of their members are set apart for an evangelistic, teaching or pastoral ministry, this gives them no special status. They do (unlike the Friends) administer the sacraments of baptism and the Lord's Supper (*see* **Baptism** 13: Plymouth Brethren, **Liturgies** 13: Plymouth Brethren). In polity the Open Brethren are uncompromisingly congregational, their churches being administered by elders; the Exclusive Brethren have centralized control, most stringent of all in the late James Taylor's connection.

The Open Brethren participate freely in interdenominational evangelical activity, e.g. in the Evangelical Alliance, the Inter-Varsity Christian Fellowship, etc. Their closest affinities in England are with evangelical Anglicans. In Great Britain and Ireland the Brethren's numbers are estimated at about 100,000 of whom perhaps two-thirds are Open Brethren.

F. R. Coad, *A History of the Brethren Movement*, 1968; H. H. Rowdon, *The Origins of the Brethren*, 1967; B. R. Wilson, ed., *Patterns of Sectarianism*, 1967.

F. F. BRUCE

Polyphony

Polyphony is the musical term for two or more voices singing individual parts simultaneously, as opposed to monophony, where one part only is sung by one or more voices. Homophony is where the voices in polyphonic music sing the same words at the same time to a succession of chords, the upper voice having the melody, the rest supplying the harmonies below it. It provides an effective contrast to polyphony. In settings of the mass, particularly in the sixteenth century, *Et incarnatus est* is often set homophonically to emphasize the solemnity of the incarnation, and at other times, as so often in the masses of Palestrina, homophony is used for massive effects.

There are many theories as to how polyphony came to be used, about the ninth century, in church music. It existed in a primitive form in secular music; it might have been suggested by chants that lay too high for basses at times and too low for tenors at other times. The medieval polyphony did not involve the invention of melodies. The procedure, at first, was to select a piece of plainchant, called the *cantus firmus*, or 'fixed-song', which was exactly reproduced a fifth lower, or later, with the chant doubled an octave below and above. This simple start soon gave place to various kinds of innovations such as the transference of the *cantus firmus* from the top to the lowest part, where it was known as the *tenor* or holding part, above which one or more voices indulged in the long florid phrases called melismas. The chosen chant, put into long notes, lost its character altogether. The increasing complexity, rhythmically and melodically, of these developments gave composers and singers much enjoyment, no doubt, but cannot have nourished the spirit of corporate prayer; Gregorian chant (q.v.), though still a liturgical necessity, no longer held undisputed pride of place. The notating of exact time values to enable several voices to sing together in a disciplined way, led to measured rhythm and, again, put the free rhythm of the chant in chains.

Gregorian chant found its architectural counterpart in the churches of the Romanesque period, the measured music in the cathedrals of the Gothic period, those mounting prayers in stone and glass that from about 1180 to 1250 were offered by the fervour of Germany, England, Spain and pre-eminently France with Notre-Dame Cathedral, Paris, and Notre Dame at Chartres as prime musical centres.

Leoninus and Perotinus – possibly his pupil – were the two great masters of the developed polyphony (*organum*) of the Notre-Dame school. Perotinus was perhaps the first composer to write for three and four voices in a truly contrapuntal style. Some of his works

were sung by the choir of the Vienna Hofburg in 1927, during the Beethoven centenary, and were described as 'a revelation, a flash of beauty, like the windows of Chartres or of Bourges suddenly illuminated by the sun'.

From the little-known achievements of this period church music moves forward to others in the succeeding centuries, ever enriching the treasury of sacred music, but subject to abuses rebuked by various popes and councils. This greatest epoch of liturgical church music came to an end with the first decade of the seventeenth century.

ALEC ROBERTSON

Postures

1. *Orientation*. The attribution of religious symbolism to direction is basically concerned with sunrise and sunset: eastwards is the direction of light, hope and rebirth and, correspondingly, westwards is the direction of darkness, evil and death. Very early in the belief and custom of the church there developed the notion that the parousia of Christ would be 'like lightning from the east, flashing as far as the west' (Matt. 24.27): this imagery is in accord with a few other biblical expressions, e.g. 'sun of righteousness' (Mal. 4.2), 'dayspring from on high' (Luke 1.78), and 'the morning star' (Rev. 22.16). On this basis some importance came to be attached to turning or facing eastwards in the ceremonies of the church. (*See* **Orientation**.)

(*a*) *Eastward turning*. From the second century it became customary to turn eastwards when praying because, according to Clement of Alexandria: 'the East is an image of the day of birth', while other writers suggest that the rebirth of the soul through the Second Adam will be associated with Paradise 'eastward in Eden'. Such interpretations of orientated prayer are linked with the custom at the beginning of the initiation ceremonies (q.v.) for the candidate to turn first westwards to renounce Satan and then eastwards to profess Christ. A similar symbolic movement was adopted in the Church of England in the seventeenth century, and since then eastward turning has been common for every liturgical recitation of a creed. In the medieval West it was customary for the whole congregation to turn eastwards (i.e. altar-wards) at the *Gloria Patri* and the *Gloria in excelsis*. As with most liturgical gestures, this posture also has been discontinued by many Protestants, especially when, in non-orientated buildings, ministers and elders face the rest of the congregation throughout corporate worship.

(b) *Eastward position*. This term is used to describe the posture of the eucharistic president when he stands before the altar with his back to the people: in church buildings which are literally 'orientated' so that the altar is at the eastern end, the priest also is literally eastward-facing, but the term is generally used irrespective of compass direction.

(c) *Westward position*. This term (identical with basilican position) is used when the liturgical president faces the people across the communion table or altar, no account being taken of actual direction. The first churches to be built under Constantine were in the form of a modified basilica (q.v.) with the apse at the western end, thus enabling the bishop and presbyters to face eastwards over the altar. In the middle of the fourth century the orientation was reversed so that the altar in the apse was at the eastern end, with the consequence that the people faced eastwards and the clergy westwards. In order that they too might face the east (and for other reasons), the clergy in the West eventually abandoned the basilican position in most church buildings and assumed places to the west of the altar. Thus, the eastward position was the norm in the Middle Ages and remained so in the Roman Catholic Church until the second half of the twentieth century. In the medieval period when altars came to be placed very close to the east wall and to be furnished with hangings, pictures or more permanent structures, it became impossible to take the basilican position which (with very few exceptions) had been the norm in the early church.

The Reformed Churches generally reverted to the original disposition of ministers facing the people across the holy table at the eucharist, but deliberately ignored questions of solar orientation in the building. When existing medieval churches continued to be used, the Calvinists usually set up a wooden table in the nave on a north-south axis, whereas Lutherans and Anglicans retained the traditional orientation. Characteristically the English church proceeded by way of compromise: at first the 1549 *BCP* ordered the priest to stand 'afore the middle of the Altar' i.e. in the middle of the long side of the wooden table which replaced the fixed stone altar; then, when this was set up 'table-wise'

in the chancel or the nave, the minister faced south in accordance with the rubric of the 1552/1662 *BCP* 'The Priest standing to the north side of the Table . . .'. When, subsequently, in the seventeenth century, the table was returned to its former position 'altar-wise' along the east wall, this rubric was interpreted by some as requiring the minister to stand at the north *end* (or short side) of the table in order to avoid the eastward position, while others faced east but stood at the northern end of the west side. The inherent ambiguity of the rubric was recognized in the 1637 Scottish prayer book and the presbyter was ordered to stand 'at the north side or end' of the table. The option was tacitly accepted in the Church of England, though the 'north end' eventually became a token of evangelicalism while the middle eastward position (Roman Catholic) came to be favoured by the Oxford Movement. Anglican concern was really that superstition should be avoided and that the manual acts of the priest should not be concealed from the people, hence the 1552/1662 rubric before the consecration prayer which reads: 'When the Priest standing before the Table hath so ordered the Bread and Wine before the people that he may with the more readiness and decency break the Bread before the people and take the Cup in his hands . . .'

All these ambiguities and awkwardnesses are obviated when, as under the influence of the Liturgical Movement (q.v.), a return is made to the westward position: and, since this basilican position is acceptable to virtually all sectors of the church, the ecumenical advantage also is considerable.

2. *Reverence*. Various types and degrees of 'respect' for a person (or an object which is symbolic of a person) can be expressed and communicated by bodily posture. In the animal world, bodily attitudes are powerful means of communicating dominance or submission, the 'pecking order', and in the spectrum of human relationships 'respect' (or lack of it) is easily expressed by postural change, e.g. standing for the magistrate, saluting the flag. Comparable attitudes are naturally to be found in religious observance, from a slight bow of the head to complete prostration, and conventions develop concerning the meaning of each and every posture. However, such liturgical postures cannot be wholly rationalized and personal

or group emotions do, from time to time, break through the most stylized forms in movements of revivalism.

In the Christian religion the duality of belief and faith concerning Jesus – human and divine, servant and lord – may result in a corresponding ambivalence of posture according to whether his liturgical 'presence' is being reverenced in terms of historical person or the second person of the Trinity. In some situations the worshipper may stand to greet one who 'did not prize his equality with God, but made himself nothing . . .' (Phil. 2.6f.), while in other circumstances the same worshipper may feel impelled to kneel before one whom God raised 'to the heights and bestowed upon him the name above all names, that at the name of Jesus every knee should bow . . .' (Phil. 2.9f.).

With this complexity of personality at the heart of devotion it is not surprising that temperamental and cultural differences have produced every possible variation of liturgical posture in the history of the church.

(*a*) *Bowing*. Bowing the head, as a natural gesture of recognition and respect, developed liturgically as a reverence to the bishop (esp. on his throne behind the altar), to the altar (as the 'throne' of Christ, or even as a symbol of Christ), to icons of Christ and the divine persons (esp. the crucifix), and more generally as a mutual salutation between participants in the liturgical action. For more than a thousand years, a simple bow was the only reverence given in the course of the Latin mass: in the medieval period it was customary to bow at the *Gloria Patri*, at the mention of the Holy Spirit in the Nicene Creed, and at the *Sanctus*.

A distinction is sometimes made between a simple reverence, i.e. an inclination of the head and shoulders, and a profound reverence, i.e. a bending forward from the hips. The latter tended to be replaced by genuflexion when the clergy came to have their backs to the people, but in the basilican position the bow is more seemly.

(*b*) *Genuflexion*. This posture consists of a brief kneeling on the right knee with body erect. It is usually associated with the *incarnatus* of the Nicene Creed (from the eleventh century) and with reverence for the blessed sacrament (from fourteenth century). It derives from civil recognition of imperial officials in antiquity and previously had no place in the ceremonial of the Christian eucharist. In the Roman Catholic church it is also commonly used as a reverence towards prelates and to crucifixes.

(*c*) *Kneeling*. In the early church there was for a time a class of penitents who were permitted to be present only for the synaxis (q.v.): they knelt at the west end of the nave and were known as *genuflectentes*. Originally, then, kneeling was not a common posture for prayer of all kinds as it has become in the Roman Catholic and Anglican churches. The primitive posture for prayer was standing (often with arms outstretched – as in the catacomb paintings), and this is still the custom in the Eastern Orthodox churches: in contrast, in most Protestant churches sitting is the preferred posture.

The change from standing to kneeling in the West came about through the omission of a command to rise after a short period appointed for silent kneeling prayer. It became customary in many liturgies after the *Gloria in excelsis* to call the people to prayer with the word *Oremus* and then to summon them to kneel with the words *Flectamus genua* for private devotions; this was then followed by the invitation to stand, *Levate*, for the succeeding collective prayers. By the twelfth century the period for silent prayer had been eliminated and, as the command to stand was no longer given, the people were left kneeling for the collects. From this beginning the penitential posture spread to other parts of the service – at first in the Latin rite and thence into the English rites. Thus in 1662 *BCP* the faithful are ordered to kneel from the opening Lord's Prayer and collect, through the ten commandments, collects and epistle, and to stand only for the gospel and the creed; it is also common for the people to kneel from the offertory onwards through the communion to the blessing since there is no rubric ordering them to stand – not even for the *Gloria in excelsis*!

However, in order to guard against a mistaken inference from the requirement to kneel to receive the sacrament, there was inserted in 1552 *BCP* a Declaration on Kneeling. This statement, which was printed without the authority of Parliament, was to the effect that kneeling did not imply the 'real and essential' presence of Christ, and that no adoration was intended but, rather, that kneeling signified the humility and worthy reception of 'the benefits of Christ'. The 'rubric' was omitted in the 1559 edition, but was re-inserted in the 1662 *BCP* with the alteration of 'real and essential' to 'corporal' in order to avoid gross superstition and yet to maintain the reality of the *sacramental* presence. In the nineteenth century it was customary to print rubrics (q.v.) in red and, in order to indicate that this 'declaration' was not technically a 'rubric', it was printed in black: perversely it became known as the *Black Rubric*.

Under the influence of the Liturgical Movement (q.v.) it is now customary in the Roman Catholic Church in England to stand to receive the sacrament, while the currently authorized experimental Anglican *Second* and *Third Series* give no direction concerning posture at this point in the liturgy.

There is much to be said, in principle, for kneeling only for penitential prayer and for either standing or sitting at other points in the liturgical action – standing for praise in fellowship and sitting to listen to readings, sermons, notices, lengthy musical renderings and for meditation. It is to be remembered, first, that for more than a millennium in Christian churches there were seats only for the officiating ministers and for the aged and the disabled ('the weak must go to the wall', i.e. to the seats by the wall), secondly, that 'Let us pray' is not the same as 'Let us kneel', and thirdly, that crouching between seats is not kneeling.

(*d*) *Sitting*. Liturgical sitting was originally the prerogative of the bishop (or his deputy) who at the eucharist was the enthroned president ('one who sits before'), and of the senior members of the congregation – the presbyters – who had their seats alongside him around the apse. No other seats were provided in churches, except for the elderly and infirm, until monastic choir stalls with misericord seats made their appearance. In the medieval period, in line with increased seating on secular public occasions, some additional seating was provided in church buildings in the form of backless benches (from the twelfth century onwards). But not until the period of the Reformation (with long sermons) and the Counter-Reformation (with long musical settings) did extensive lay seating become general. Eventually, what was once only a convenience came to be regarded as a necessity and, correspondingly, there occurred the curious liturgical inversion which gave the clergy little opportunity to sit down and the laity no occasion to stand up –

except for the singing of popular hymns.

Sitting, like standing or kneeling, should really be reappraised as a positive liturgical posture. The clergy, who have usurped much of the liturgy of the laity, need to sit down more frequently or for longer periods in the course of the action, and so enable the latter to rise to their own liturgical occasions: in this way the people will be less inclined to remain seated in order to 'hear mass' or to 'listen to the Word' in a negative manner but will sit down for definite liturgical reasons.

Finally, it may be noted that there is no virtue in postural uniformity *per se*, and that in corporate worship the guidance of the Spirit is not to be resisted in the matter of standing, sitting or kneeling.

GILBERT COPE

Praise *see* Prayer (4)

Prayer

Prayer is the generic term for all aspects of man's conscious relationship to God, as in 'the life of prayer'. As such it has been held to include liturgical worship, meditation and individual prayer, as well as such other religious duties as fasting and almsgiving. In a more specific sense, it denotes that part of man's relationship which consists of mental and verbal fellowship with God. The word can also refer, in the plural or with the indefinite article, to forms of words addressed to God.

Current writing about prayer is generally concerned to direct attention more to the second sense than to the third, and most of all to the first sense given. There is a widespread quest for forms of contemplation and meditation which attach less importance to the recitation of forms of words. Of late there has also been a growing quest for forms of the spiritual life which do not seem to involve emphasis on withdrawal from secular concerns so much as the discovery of the presence of God within the concerns of daily living. Those who are concerned with specific acts of prayer and times of prayer have therefore to discover a way in which these can form a framework for the constant practice of the presence of God.

The traditional divisions of prayer into adoration or praise, thanksgiving, confession and petition or supplication are relevant to all kinds of spirituality whether they involve specific acts of prayer or not, because they describe essential components of man's relationship to God. This is due to the fact that forms of prayer have been considerably moulded by theological considerations; since prayer is the expression of man's relationship to God, the content of it is closely linked with the nature of that relationship as man has discovered it, and the present discussion of prayer results directly from theological questionings. Forms of prayer which have traditionally been valued now raise very serious questions about how God is conceived and how, if at all, he is thought of as intervening in the life of the world.

1. *Adoration.* This aspect of prayer consists in the contemplation and worship of God as he is in himself. It is the word that most accurately describes the prayers of the mystics, and consists in focusing on and celebrating the qualities of the Godhead as they have been revealed to and experienced by the believer. The forms under which such prayer has occurred are many and various; the vision of heaven recorded in Isa. 6 appears to include an intense visual experience of God, and many of those who have been best known for their constant adoration of God, and who are classified as mystics, have experienced visions of God which have given rise to intense adoration. Much adoration has also included intense emotional expression, with extensive use of erotic imagery as the believer has contemplated with joy the deeply intimate relationship between God and the soul.

Others have been led to adoration by the contemplation of the world around them. The word adoration connotes a 'resting' in the presence of God, and of the forms of prayer described here is the least tied to verbal forms of expression. As such it has a strong contemporary appeal to those who are disillusioned with institutional religion and seek a spirituality which would involve the contemplation of the timeless qualities of God, such as truth, beauty, love and faithfulness. The parallels between the adoration of the mystics and the experiences of many who have used the techniques of Eastern religions or hallucinogenic drugs are easy to draw.

The church's attitude to adoration, especially as practised by the mystics, has been characterized by a certain ambivalence.

On the one hand it has been said that God is to be adored, and indeed the traditional picture of heaven includes the constant adoration of God by the angels and the saints. On the other hand it has been suspected, by some because of the quality of freedom from restraint which characterizes much mystical adoration, and by others for a certain 'other-worldly' sense which pervades adoration. On the whole the tendency has been to commend for most believers the practice of a much more disciplined variety which is tied to more verbal forms of expression and is in fact a combination of praise and thanksgiving related both to the biblical account of God and to the specific experiences of the believer. Adoration remains, however, that which is thought by many to be the highest form of prayer, and the canons of most eucharistic liturgies begin with the *Trisagion* (Holy, holy, holy), the song of heaven recorded in Isaiah's vision.

2. *Confession.* The acknowledgment by the believer of his sin. This occurs under three chief forms, general, personal and sacramental.

General confessions are characteristic of most liturgies. They occur extensively in the Bible (e.g. Ps. 51) and consist of the acknowledgment by the believing community of its unrighteousness before God and of its need of his forgiveness. The forms of such confessions vary greatly, but generally include an expression of sorrow for past transgression, a petition for God's forgiveness and, in some cases, the expression of resolve to amend. Under the influence of the Reformation many of the expressions of sorrow were highly elaborate, and there is a tendency at the present time to modify both the tone and the length of such general confessions.

Personal confession after self-examination has always been a feature of Christian private prayer, and in the past some elaborate lists have been provided of questions with which the believer is asked to face himself at the end of the day or at least as part of his preparation for receiving of holy communion. With the questioning of ethical theories which relied heavily on rules there has also come a questioning of this kind of approach to self-examination. Once again, the extensive discussion about God is raising questions that have implications for self-examination; the issue is whether the shortcomings we need to confess actually consist in the breaking of a series of small rules.

Sacramental confession, or confession before a priest, is a practice enjoined on Orthodox and Roman Catholics, but optional in the Anglican churches and some Protestant denominations. In some cases this form of confession is undertaken at regular intervals as a discipline, and in others as a means of quieting a conscience which is burdened with guilt for some specific offence, though Roman Catholics hold that mortal sin can only be forgiven by this means.

3. *Petition.* This aspect of prayer, known also as supplication or, when it is on behalf of others, intercession, has always been part of prayer, and indeed may be the most common and instinctual prayer which men offer. It is the asking of God for something which is desired. There are records of people of all religions and civilizations asking their gods for rain, for success in war, for the healing of the sick, for the blessing of a new ruler and indeed for the satisfaction of just about every conceivable need. It is in some way or other an almost invariable part of liturgical worship, and some liturgical acts are devoted almost entirely to petitionary prayer, e.g. the litany (q.v.).

There has been a tendency among teachers of the devotional life to regard petitionary prayer as the 'lowest' form of prayer, as something which ought not to occupy too large a place in the life of prayer. This is largely because it is seen as that part of prayer which gives the most opportunity for selfish asking in one's own interest. It remains true, however, that this most basic form of prayer occupies a large place in the life of praying people. It early occurs in the psalms, and formed a part of Jesus' prayers recorded in the gospels, as well as seeming to be a feature of some of the healing miracles. He prayed on behalf of the disciples and, in the Garden of Gethsemane, is recorded as asking that the cup of suffering might pass from him.

Petitionary prayer, probably more than any other form of prayer, has been affected by secular patterns of thinking, and the question of whether and how God answers prayer presents an inescapable dilemma. On the one hand, the abandonment of petitionary prayer altogether would seem to deny a basic part of prayer and also to deny to God the power to change and overrule events. On the other hand a *'deus ex machina'* God, who in response to individual requests does things which would not otherwise happen, becomes less credible as more and more of the life of the world is brought under control or at any rate explained. Various solutions to this dilemma are offered: it is suggested that prayer has its primary effect in attuning the mind of the one who prays to the will of God, increasing and focusing concern in a way which could be effective, without the need of miraculous divine interventions. Jesus' prayer in Gethsemane is cited as an example of the way in which all petitionary prayer has to be modified by the petition 'Thy will be done', and thus negative 'answers' have to be expected.

What does need to be pointed out, however, is that prayer in the biblical tradition has always been presented as an activity which did not limit the freedom of God, that is to say it was not a mechanical, magical procedure which was designed to produce automatic effects; rather it appears to be thought of as communication between the believer and God which accepts the liberty and integrity of both. There can be no doubt that petitionary prayer more than any other depends upon the view of God which undergirds it.

4. *Praise.* The outward expression of the believer's worship and adoration of God, in words, music and ceremonial. The focus of praise is not only upon God himself, as in adoration, but above all on his mighty acts in nature and history. Hymns and acts of praise are a common feature of all liturgy, and frequently the distinction between it and adoration on the one hand and thanksgiving on the other is not clear-cut.

A feature of praise in the Christian tradition, but going back to pre-Christian times, is the recital of the great deeds of God in the past. The reading of the gospel in the liturgy is, for example, answered with the response 'Praise (or thanks) be to thee, O Christ', and the ancient hymn of praise *Te Deum Laudamus* (fifth century) begins with the adoration of God but includes the recollection of the work of Christ as the basis of the praise that is being offered ('When thou tookest upon thee to deliver man, thou didst not abhor the virgin's womb; When thou hadst overcome the sharpness of death, thou didst open the kingdom of heaven to all believers').

In being invited to share in the offering of praise, the believer is asked to share in the life of the whole community of believers through the ages and to join in the praise they gave for their deliverance. He is responding to his own prayer in the Lord's Prayer, 'Hallowed be thy name', by participating in the hallowing of God for that which he has done for the world and for mankind.

5. *Thanksgiving.* A feature of prayer both public and private is that the believers are invited to offer thanks to God for their personal experiences of his goodness. It is natural that it should be closely linked to praise, as in the General Thanksgiving in the *BCP*, where thanks for God's 'loving-kindness to us and to all men' passes on to a recollection of 'his inestimable love in the redemption of the world by our Lord Jesus Christ'. The specific need for thanksgiving, however, is part of what is involved in the believer's relating what he knows of God to his experience in daily living. Once again there are problems about the listing of his experiences at the hand of God, and difficulties about the extent to which, in a secular age, it is appropriate to thank God for things which can be otherwise explained. The possibility of thanksgiving, however, is available if the model of a personal relationship with God can be rediscovered in a contemporary form. (For liturgical prayers, *see Agnus Dei*, **Collect, Consecration Prayer, Doxology, Intercession, *Kyries*, Litany, Lord's Prayer, Ordinary, Preface, Proper, *Sanctus*, Silent Prayer, Suffrages, *Super Oblata, Trisagion*.)**

                                    PETER SELBY

Prayer Meeting

An informal meeting, usually additional to the regular worship of the church, at which those who are present offer spontaneous vocal prayers. Scriptural warrant for such meetings may be found in such passages as Acts 4.24ff.; I Cor. 14; they have sometimes been described as 'the liturgy of the Holy Ghost'.

The English Puritans, in addition to the use of extempore prayer by the minister in the regular services, sometimes held meetings, usually on weekdays, at which members, often without a minister, themselves prayed aloud; and some element of spontaneous prayer often formed a part of the church meeting of the Independents. The

Sunday 'meetings for worship' of the Society of Friends still contain this element, interwoven with silence and exhortation.

Pietism and the evangelical revival gave a fresh impetus to spontaneous prayer, and this no doubt formed a large ingredient in the various kinds of fellowship meeting in early Methodism. In some places, meetings for prayer with appointed leaders were planned as carefully as preaching services. The actual term 'prayer meeting' came into use in evangelical circles in the early part of the nineteenth century. A fresh impetus came from the camp meetings (q.v.) which the Primitive Methodists adopted from America, for, while some preached, they were supported by others in praying bands. In some parts of England the custom became widespread, especially in Methodism, whereby almost every Sunday evening, except when the Lord's Supper was observed, the more devout members of the congregation stayed to a prayer meeting after the service. At such an 'after-meeting', as it was sometimes called, fresh converts were made welcome, and the young could listen to the prayers of others and make their own first efforts at praying aloud spontaneously. Individuals would also strike up well-known hymns and choruses in which the others would join. Sometimes the prayers would have an ecstatic, affectionate quality usually more characteristic of mental than of vocal prayer.

Such meetings, whether on Sunday or on weekdays, were indeed prominent in all the Free Churches. They were also widespread in Evangelical Anglicanism, though naturally not in such close connection with the services of the church. They were also held in undenominational gatherings and conferences of evangelical societies, and were often called for special purposes, as to support evangelistic campaigns.

In recent years prayer meetings, especially those closely linked with the services of the church, have tended to die out. One reason is that intense fervour was difficult to maintain, and some members of congregations, lacking fresh inspiration, tended, perhaps unconsciously, to repeat the prayers which they had uttered on previous occasions, so that the meetings lost their spontaneity. The practice has recently grown in some churches of inviting members of the congregation to suggest topics at the time of the intercession, and this could develop into a kind of prayer meeting. This is perhaps the most suitable form for such congregational participation in close association with the regular worship of the church, but prayer meetings of the older pattern are still held where religious fervour continues or revives in evangelical circles.

A. RAYMOND GEORGE

Preface

A name, originally proper to the Roman rite, for the thanksgiving which opens the eucharistic prayer or anaphora (q.v.). The Latin *praefatio* in this context does not mean a preliminary, but a proclamation. In the ancient Gallican liturgy the word *praefatio* was used differently, of a descriptive invitation or bidding to prayer.

J. A. Jungmann, *The Mass of the Roman Rite*, II, 1955, pp. 115-28.

W. JARDINE GRISBROOKE

Presanctified Mass

Mass or liturgy of the presanctified (i.e. 'of the previously consecrated') is a form of service prescribed in the historic rites for use on certain days when the eucharist is not celebrated, but when it is at the same time necessary or desirable to make provision for communion.

In the early church the eucharist was held to be a festive act, by definition, and it was therefore not celebrated, even when it came generally to be celebrated on weekdays as well as Sundays, on days of penitence. From a very early period, however, daily communion was common, being normally made at home from the reserved sacrament taken from church by the worshippers on the previous Sunday; and when more frequent celebration of the eucharist became widespread after the peace of the church in the fourth century, the desire to provide a public opportunity for the reception of communion on the days when it was, for liturgical reasons, not celebrated, became increasingly felt, even with the decline in frequency of communion which set in at this time. This was the origin of the mass or liturgy of the presanctified. For reasons of space consideration of the service today must be restricted to the provision for it in the two most widespread of the historic rites, the Byzantine and the Roman.

In the Byzantine rite the eucharist is not celebrated on any day in Lent other than Sundays and Saturdays (which like Sundays are not fast days) and the feast of the Annunciation if it falls in the season. On other days the liturgy of the presanctified is used; today there is no communion at all on Good Friday, but this is a medieval innovation, the liturgy of the presanctified having originally been used on that day like all other Lenten weekdays. As in theory it is not permitted on fast days to take any food until after vespers, the office for communion from the reserved sacrament is attached to that office, which exhibits certain variants from its normal order, and this combination forms the liturgy of the presanctified. Today it is celebrated in most churches only on Wednesdays and Fridays, and except in the increasing but still small number of churches to which liturgical reform is beginning to penetrate, it is celebrated by anticipation in the morning, which makes nonsense of a large part of the service.

The reserved sacrament is prepared for communion during the recitation of the psalms of the day in vespers; it is taken from the tabernacle on the altar to the prothesis (q.v.) table, where wine and water are also poured into a chalice. Vespers is cut short at the lessons, after which the altar, and then the whole church and congregation, are solemnly censed, to the singing of Ps. 140 (141). The second part of the service is composed almost entirely of extracts from the eucharistic liturgy: (1) the litanies which close the synaxis (q.v.) and open the eucharist proper, with special closing collects; (2) the great entrance (q.v.), in an especially solemn form, with a proper anthem, as it is a procession with the consecrated, instead of the unconsecrated, gifts; (3) the Lord's Prayer, with the litany which usually introduces it, slightly modified; (4) the elevation of the gifts, the fraction, and the placing of the particles of the broken bread in the (unconsecrated) chalice, the contents of which were anciently regarded, in East and West alike, as consecrated by this commixture (q.v.); (5) communion; (6) the normal concluding rites, although with certain proper texts. For further details of these parts of the normal liturgy, *see* **Liturgies** 2: Orthodox.

In the Roman rite, the mass of the presanctified (no longer called by that name since 1955) is celebrated on only one day in the year – Good Friday. For this reason the service exhibits a number of striking features peculiar to that day, such as the veneration of the cross, but in essence, like the Byzantine service, it is simply part of a normal service followed by communion from the reserved sacrament – the first part of the Roman service being not vespers as in the Byzantine rite, but the pre-eucharistic synaxis, in an unusually primitive and simple form, and concluding after the readings with the full ancient Roman synaxis intercession, somewhat adapted to modern use. (The veneration of the cross is interpolated between the intercession and the communion.) The communion rite is extremely simple: the sacrament reserved overnight from the mass of the Last Supper on Maundy Thursday is brought in by the deacon while three short anthems are sung; the Lord's Prayer, with certain other normal prayers of preparation for communion, is recited; the communion follows, and the service is concluded with three post-communion collects. (There may be minor changes in this service in the new edition of the Roman missal in preparation at the time of writing.)

Since 1955 the Roman mass of the pre-sanctified, which like its Byzantine counterpart was for many centuries anticipated in the morning, has again been celebrated at its proper hour – in this case, three o'clock in the afternoon. It has undergone a number of minor changes since its first introduction, which appears to have been not later than the sixth century (the opinion of some writers that it is of later date is based on a misreading of the evidence; the communion is absent from the Good Friday service in the earliest *papal* books of the urban Roman rite because the papal service was held in the morning, while the *parochial* books include it, the parochial services being held in the afternoon, and many people no doubt going to both).

W. JARDINE GRISBROOKE

Presbyter

The term is derived from the Greek word meaning elder (q.v.), and appears to be used in the NT as interchangeable with the word *episcopos*, from which 'bishop' (q.v.) is derived. It is notorious that there are widely differing views of the way in which the early ministry of the church developed. One view, held by a good many authorities, is that in each Christian centre there was a college of presbyter-bishops from among whom the monarchical bishop emerged in due course. Whatever may be the truth of the matter, it is clear that by the second century the presbyters formed an advisory body associated with the bishop in the pastoral and administrative work of his office and also associated with him (by their physical presence round him) in his liturgical functions. In the third century the presbyter began to be the person to whom the bishop delegated the responsibility for the pastoral oversight of an area and the duty of presiding at celebrations of the eucharist. In due course the medieval concept of the parish priest developed, the man who was almost the personification of the church in the local community, who baptized and said mass and performed all other Christian rites except confirmation and ordination. The English word 'priest', like its equivalents in most Germanic languages, is derived from 'presbyter' and not from the Greek or Latin terms for priesthood. (The Greek and Latin terms are hardly ever used for the Christian ministry in the early church, and then of bishops rather than of presbyters. Thus Cyprian uses *sacerdos* to mean bishop, not presbyter.) After the Reformation, Anglican and some Lutheran churches retained 'priest' for the second order of the ministry, though it became more usual for churches of the Reformation to use the term 'presbyter' or the vaguer term 'minister' to describe the person normally responsible for the preaching of the word and the administration of the sacraments. In most modern schemes for a reunion of the churches, 'presbyter' rather than 'priest' is used for the order next below that of bishop.

G. B. Henderson, *Presbyterianism*, 1954; D. N. Power, *Ministers of Christ and his Church*, 1969; B. H. Streeter, *The Primitive Church*, 1929; A. Prolante, P. Siffrin and E. Josi, in *Enciclopedia Cattolica*, IX, cols, 1961-4.

P. HINCHLIFF

Presbyterian Worship
see Reformed Worship

Prime see Canonical Hours

Procession

A planned movement of a group of people from one place to another for some specific religious purpose. It may be a self-contained, independent act, e.g. a Rogationtide procession around the fields, or an act within a service, e.g. an offertory (q.v.) procession at the eucharist. Early evidence for processions is found in the *Pilgrimage of Egeria* (late fourth century) which describes the pilgrimages to the sacred sites in Jerusalem during the rites of Holy Week. A valuable Western source is *Ordo Romanus Primus*, which describes the seventh century pontifical stational masses of Rome. In the later Middle Ages material for various occasions was collected from such books as the *Missal*, the *Ritual* and the *Pontifical* to form the *Processional*.

A procession could be held for various reasons. It could be an act of Christian witness, an act of penitence or praise, or an act of supplication. Some processions served more than one purpose. The St Mark's Day procession, instituted in Rome in the sixth century, was an act of Christian witness on the same day as the old pagan festival of the Robigalia, when the gods were asked to preserve the crops from mildew; but it was also used as an act of supplication similar to the Rogationtide (q.v.) procession, at which litanies (q.v.) were sung, praying for God's blessing on the crops. Again, the Corpus Christi (q.v.) procession, instituted in the thirteenth century in honour of the blessed sacrament, was combined in Germany with a supplication for God's protection on the countryside. Other processions were held in connection with pilgrimage to shrines, or the transference of relics to a new home, or the dedication of a new church. On such occasions full use was made of external aids to excite devotion – incense, lights (qq.v.), banners, relics and rich vestments (q.v.).

Other processions were integral to particular rites: the procession to the font at baptism; the procession of the bridal party to the altar at matrimony; the procession to the grave at burial; the procession before the eucharist; or the gospel and offertory processions (the lesser and greater entrance, qq.v.). The Reformers in general protested against abuses connected with processions and abandoned, not only the processions themselves, but also – with the exception of Luther and Cranmer – the litanies associated with them. Cranmer and Henry VIII apparently contemplated a new English *Processional*, but the project came to nothing. By a royal injunction of 1545 Cranmer's litany of 1544 became the sole procession in England; and by the royal injunctions of 1547, even the litany could only be used kneeling in church. After a temporary reprieve under Queen Mary, processions were again suppressed under Elizabeth in 1559 except those of Rogationtide. The 1662 BCP, however, sanctioned processions occurring within rites – namely in baptism, matrimony and burial. These, with the gospel and offertory processions at the eucharist, are found in whole or in part in the Roman, Orthodox, Anglican and in some Reformed Churches: and their use is still spreading. The public procession as an act of Christian witness or as a pilgrimage has also revived, and, on occasions such as Good Friday, often has great ecumenical value.

M. Andrieu, *Les Ordines Romani du Haut Moyen Age*, 5 vols., 1931-61; F. E. Brightman, *The English Rite*, 1915; C. Dunlop, *Processions*, 1932; W. H. Frere, *The Principles of Religious Ceremonial*, 1906; W. G. Henderson, *Processionale ad usum Sarum*, 1882; *La Maison Dieu*, no. 43, 1955.

R. C. D. JASPER

Prone *see* Bidding Prayer

Proper

A term of the Roman mass (although applicable to other rites also), having two different but related meanings: (1) those parts of the service which vary according to the day or season; (2) those variable parts of the service which are rendered chorally, principally composed of psalmody, and comprising the introit or entrance chant, the gradual or responsorial psalm (formerly sung after the epistle, but since 1969 before it and after the OT reading), the alleluia (sung between the epistle and the gospel), the offertory chant, and the communion chant. Derivatively, the term may be used of those parts of any service which vary according to the day or season.

W. JARDINE GRISBROOKE

Prothesis

The name prothesis (Greek 'preparation') is used in the Byzantine rite (commonly miscalled the Orthodox liturgy) to designate three different but related things: (1) the rite of preparation before the divine liturgy or eucharist; (2) the chamber to the north of the sanctuary in which the greater part of this rite takes place; (3) the table in that chamber on which the elements, usually referred to in the Byzantine rite as the gifts, are prepared.

The rite of preparation currently in use is elaborate, and falls into two principal parts, the preparation of the ministers and the preparation of the gifts. The former comprises three acts: (1) introductory prayers which are recited by the celebrant and deacon together outside the gates of the sanctuary, with the veneration of the principal images on the iconostasis (q.v.) or sanctuary screen; (2) the vesting of the ministers, the putting on of each garment being accompanied by the recitation of a supposedly appropriate verse from the psalms or some other part of the OT; (3) a washing of their hands by the ministers, with the recitation of Ps. 25 (26).6-12. The second and third of these properly take place in the chamber called the *diakonikon* (Greek lit. 'deaconry', commonly translated 'vestry') on the south of the sanctuary, corresponding to the prothesis on the north, but not every church today has such a chamber, and where it is absent the vesting and washing often take place in the sanctuary itself.

The preparation of the gifts opens with the recitation of an anthem about the passion, after which it falls into four distinguishable parts: (1) the preparation of the bread, (2) the preparation of the chalice, (3) commemorative and intercessory prayers, a kind of anticipated diptychs (q.v.), and (4) veiling and censing of the prepared gifts. The preparation of the bread, which varies somewhat in detail from one Orthodox national church to another, consists principally in the cutting out of a square from a pure wheaten leavened loaf (the square being called the 'lamb', an exact counterpart of the Western 'host'), and placing it on the paten, to the accompaniment of a number of scriptural formulae which relate the cutting of the loaf in a highly literal way to the wounding of our Lord in the passion. The preparation of the chalice is much simpler: it consists simply of blessing wine and water, and pouring them into the chalice. There follows a lengthy and involved commemoration of the saints, and of the living and departed for whom the prayers of the church at the eucharist are particularly desired; a small particle of bread is taken from the loaf or loaves at the mention of each name or group of names, and placed

upon the paten beside the 'lamb', theoretically in an intricately specified order. The commemorations completed, the celebrant blesses incense, covers the vessels with their veils, censing each veil as he does so, and saying appointed formulae, including Ps. 92 (93). He then censes the gifts thus prepared and covered, and says a concluding general prayer, after which he or the deacon censes the altar, the sanctuary, and finally the whole church and congregation.

This rite of preparation has undergone a long development, and the greater part of it dates from a comparatively late period. The preparation of the ministers is entirely absent from the earliest surviving texts, and does not arrive at something like its present form until the thirteenth century; the earliest evidence for the washing of the ministers' hands at this point is in a printed edition of 1526. As for the preparation of the gifts, until the ninth century it was done with the utmost simplicity, with a single prayer; as late as the middle of the eleventh century there are still texts in which it has developed no further; not until the late twelfth century is there definitive evidence for more intricate ceremonial at it, and even then this was performed in silence, with a single prayer before and after; something resembling the present form is found in a text of 1225. The pseudodiptychs first appear in the twelfth century, and become longer and more elaborate during the course of the later Middle Ages, finally achieving their present form (apart from a few minor details) in 1600. The whole rite, in its present form, is an outstanding example of the medieval tendency to confuse the essentials of liturgical action by superimposing on them a mass of secondary, and often theologically inappropriate, detail.

On the other hand, the prothesis still makes provision for the ancient custom of individual offering of the bread and wine for the eucharist, lost for centuries in the West, a provision still largely made use of by the faithful, and unless and until the restoration of the diptychs in the anaphora (q.v.) to their pristine integrity is accomplished, the lengthy intercessory commemorations in the prothesis are necessary in this connection.

H. Holloway, *A Study of the Byzantine Liturgy*, 1933, ch. I.

W. JARDINE GRISBROOKE

Psalmody

From the earliest times the Christian community sang the psalms following the practice of the synagogue, in antiphonal or responsorial forms (qq.v.), and the psalter became basic to the liturgy of mass and office. We learn from the fathers of the church how psalmody spread over the Christian world. Eusebius (260-340), Bishop of Caesarea, paints a vivid picture of the result: 'The command to sing psalms in the name of the Lord was obeyed by everyone in every place: for the command to sing is in force in all churches which exist among the nations, not only the Greeks but also the barbarians throughout the whole world, and in towns, villages and in the fields.' Tertullian speaks of the use of psalms at household prayer and exhorts married Christians to emulate one another in psalm singing.

It is certain that all the people took part in psalm singing in the fourth century when Christians were free of persecution. Certain of the fathers forbade women to take part and others, in the next century, gave grudging permission, since if the women were not allowed to sing they would talk during the service. The fathers exhorted monks and clergy to learn the psalms by heart – a practice which was to last for many centuries, until service-books were available to all. Jerome told the nuns of the Convent of St Paul at Jerusalem 'no sister may remain if she does not know the psalms'. Enthusiasm for the psalms followed from the realization that the psalter – as still to-day – was, in the words of Athanasius (296-373), 'a book that includes the whole life of man, all conditions of the mind and all movements of thought'.

As regards the laity, the number of psalms and canticles they knew by heart cannot have been large, hence the simplicity of the refrains which they contributed to the responsorial psalms (q.v.).

ALEC ROBERTSON

Psalm Tones

The eight tones, or melodic formulae, used in the singing of the psalms, have an obvious relation to the eight church modes of the Roman chant. Each tone begins with an intonation used only at the start of the psalm or canticle, but on major feasts in every verse of the canticles (*Benedictus*, *Magnificat*, *Nunc Dimittis*), so as to give greater solemnity. The intonation leads to the reciting note, on the dominant of the tone, and at the end of the half-verse to a cadence known as the mediant. In medieval times the pause after the half-way cadence was accommodated to the time it took to say 'Ave Maria'. The reciting note is then resumed and leads to the termination.

A ninth tone, the beautiful *Tonus peregrinus* ('stranger tone') has two reciting tones, the second, after the mediant cadence, lying a second lower than the first. It is traditionally associated with Ps. 113 (114), '*In exitu Israel*' ('When Israel went out of Egypt'). Bach uses this tone, in its Lutheran form, at a high pitch on the oboes in the sixth verse of his Latin setting of *Magnificat*. The other tones are most effectively used, with some variations such as the introduction of chromatic notes, in all but one of the five psalms of Monteverdi's *Vespers* of 1610. They exert a stabilizing influence, especially in the decorative florid passages in one part or another. Mozart makes effective quotation of the first tone on the oboes, in his fine *Masonic Funeral March* (K 477) for small orchestra.

During the fifteenth and sixteenth centuries it was a favourite practice of church composers to set the odd verses of the canticles of lauds, vespers, and compline (qq.v.) polyphonically, leaving the even ones to be sung directly to one another of the eight psalm tones.

The codification of the psalm tones as they appear in the *Antiphonale* today dates from about the eleventh century. The notable resemblance between the first psalm tone and the *Tonus peregrinus* and Jewish psalmody discloses a link with the practice of the synagogue, as do the recitatives, or chanting tones, of the priest.

ALEC ROBERTSON

Pulpit

Although in the fifth century BC it is recorded that 'Ezra the scribe stood upon a wooden pulpit which they had made for that purpose' (Neh. 8.4), and though in the early Christian centuries the apostles and fathers of the church delivered sermons, there is little evidence that such sermons were given from a pulpit in the nave or body of the church building. It is thought that such sermons were given by the bishop from his throne or *cathedra* (q.v.) from behind the altar. The pulpit-like structure still found in Roman and other basilicas known as the ambo (q.v.) was mainly employed for the reading of the gospel at the eucharist and not for preaching.

In England, pulpits do not seem to have come into use in parish churches until the twelfth and thirteenth centuries. They were usually placed against the first pier on the north side of the nave west of the chancel step. Most of the medieval pulpits belong to the fifteenth century when the wood carver's craft reached its apogee in East Anglia and the West Country.

The Reformation brought about an increased demand for more adequate teaching and preaching, and many fine wooden pulpits were erected in the seventeenth and eighteenth centuries, often with a sounding-board or tester over them. The necessity of providing a pulpit as part of the furniture of a church was underlined by Canon 83 of 1604, 'a comely and decent pulpit to be seemly kept for the preaching of God's Word'. In the eighteenth century, examples of the three-tier arrangement came into use, known as the 'three-decker' pulpit. In this the parish clerk was in the lowest stage, the officiant read the service from the middle tier, while the pulpit-proper was reserved for the sermon.

In the planning of modern churches two pulpits are sometimes provided which can be used for the reading of the liturgical lessons at the eucharist as well as for preaching.

G. W. O. Addleshaw and F. Etchells, *The Architectural Setting of Anglican Worship*, 1948; F. E. Howard and F. H. Crossley, *English Church Woodwork*, [2]1927.

C. E. POCKNEE

Purification
see Mariological Feasts

Purificator

A towel or napkin that is used to dry the chalice and other vessels after the consumption of the remains of the consecrated elements at the eucharist when the ablutions are taken. Another towel is also used for drying the hands of the celebrant and this is termed the *lavabo* cloth. This cloth is somewhat larger than the purificator.

P. Dearmer, *The Linen Ornaments of the Church*, [2]1950; C. E. Pocknee, ed., *The Parson's Handbook*, 1965; The Warham Guild, *The Warham Guild Handbook*, rev. ed., 1963.

C. E. POCKNEE

Pyx

Also spelt pix. A receptacle used chiefly for housing the consecrated elements of bread, and sometimes wine, when reserved outside the time of the celebration of the liturgy. The custom is of very high antiquity, being mentioned by Justin Martyr (*Apol.* I. 65.) about AD 150. This reservation (q.v.) was chiefly for the sick and those prevented from attending the Sunday eucharist. Also, it was the custom during the first three centuries to permit the faithful to take away from the Sunday eucharist portions of the consecrated bread in order to communicate themselves at home during the week. For this purpose, little boxes of wood, ivory or metal with a cord that could be suspended round the neck were in use. These were known as *arcae* or *arculae*; examples have been found on the breasts of the deceased buried in the Vatican catacombs during the second and third centuries. This custom led to the abuse of the *arcae* and their contents as a charm or talisman, so it was discontinued.

From the fourth century the reserved sacrament was kept in the church or its sacristy (q.v.). But not until the ninth century were precise regulations issued regarding the kind of receptacle to be used for this purpose. Pyxes or containers of ivory and precious metal as well as latten and brass were in use; not infrequently the metal ones were decorated with coloured enamels.

In the second part of the Middle Ages in the Latin West, with the development of the cultus of devotions to the reserved sacrament, pyxes displaying the skill of the silversmith and craftsman came into use. Such pyxes were mounted on a stem and foot (*see* Plate 34). A particular form of pyx that has excited antiquarian interest since the last century is that which came into use in England and France in the later Middle Ages, when the blessed sacrament was reserved in a vessel suspended by a chain over the high altar. Sometimes this pyx was contained in a steeple-like tower; in other instances it was suspended under a trumpet-shaped canopy of silk or fabric. A modern revival of this custom is to be seen in Gloucester and Ely Cathedrals. This whole arrangement including the canopy is frequently referred to as a

Plate 34 Fourteenth-century Italian standing pyx, silver-gilt and enamel, Victoria and Albert Museum, London

'hanging pyx'. A particular form of metal pyx associated with this method of reservation was that made like a dove into which the consecrated hosts were placed by lifting a lid on the back of the 'dove'.

Since the revival of continuous reservation in the Church of England and the churches of the Anglican Communion in the nineteenth century, the use of a pyx has been revived. When a priest takes the holy communion reserved to a sick person it is usually in a circular silver pyx suspended round his neck by a cord. Another form of this receptacle is the so-called 'double-pyx' containing

two sections, one for the element of bread, and the other for the consecrated wine.

W. H. Freestone, *The Sacrament Reserved*, 1917; A. A. King and C. E. Pocknee, *Eucharistic Reservation in the Western Church*, 1965; C. E. Pocknee, *The Christian Altar*, 1963.

C. E. POCKNEE

Quadragesima *see* Lent

Quaker Worship

Ecumenical discussion recognizes the existence of three broad types of worship, often referred to as 'altar-centred', 'pulpit-centred' and 'waiting upon the Spirit'. Traditional Quaker worship, with its abandonment of prearranged form, ordained ministry, and sacraments, is then seen as the extreme example of this third type. Its true character is positively determined, however, by the full seriousness with which it witnesses to the reality behind the words 'Where two or three are gathered together in my name, there am I in the midst'. It is thus the central activity of a fellowship committed to the discerning and 'answering' of him who, as 'the light that enlightens every man, coming into the world', is hiddenly present in every situation and relationship. Such a group seeks to *offer*, in attentive and expectant waiting, its present experiences, needs, confessions, thanksgivings and intercessions. It *awaits* a word, expressed either 'inwardly' or in such spoken words as the Spirit may prompt in any person present. Such words may include prayer, exhortation, reflection upon experience, exposition of a biblical passage or theme. The keynote of Quaker worship is, therefore, not the quest for mystical absorption, nor preoccupation with individual meditation and private devotions. It is, rather, the profoundly simple intention, by a gathered group, of opening itself to the presence of Christ, to the implications of the discovery that Christ's presence in the Spirit requires no other mediation and is that by which isolation is overcome and communion is experienced.

Inseparable from this conception of worship is a no less profoundly simple conception of ministry. Worship is both nourished by ministry and issues in ministry. The form this ministry takes, whether in word or in action, will depend for each individual upon personal gifts, responsibilities and opportunities. But ministry is seen as a function, not a profession; for Quakers the difference between cleric and layman is irrelevant. All Christ's followers, men and women equally, are 'ordained' and, in the Spirit, have access to gifts and graces sufficient for their several needs.

This richly varied and fully shared ministry is directed towards the needs of the world, either indirectly, by the building up of the life of the worshipping community, or directly, through the rendering of service by the community corporately or by any member of it. As the members become sensitized in this corporate life, through worship and faithful caring for one another, they become painfully aware of areas of darkness and oppression, both in and among themselves and also in the world around them. These are seen as areas in which the strivings of the Spirit of God in human life are being ignored or withstood. In relation to them, individuals or groups may find themselves 'under concern' to bear witness and to accept obligations, so that liberation and true community may be more truly known and more widely shared.

The early Quaker attitude to the sacraments expressed the conviction that no external rite could effect spiritual change and that clerical celebration was a limitation upon the 'priesthood of all believers'. Quakers regarded 'water baptism' as merely diverting attention from the reality of 'baptism in the Spirit'. They understood themselves to be obeying Christ's command 'Do this in remembrance of me' whenever, in everyday life, they took food and drink. They supported their convictions regarding worship and sacraments biblically and theologically by reference (1) to the 'New Covenant' whereby, with the coming of Christ, all ceremonial and 'typical' forms of worship were abrogated, and (2) to the 'offices of Christ' as prophet, priest and king, exercised in the gathered, worshipping group in such wise that silent, attentive and expectant waiting was the sole appropriate response. Their eucharist was inward: 'Behold, I stand at the door and knock; if any man open the door, I will come in and sup with him.'

The mode of worship so far described has continued, from the seventeenth century, to be practised in Britain, in overseas areas where Quaker groups have close links with Britain (e.g. Australia and New Zealand), on the continent of Europe, in Canada and in parts of the USA. In other parts of the USA, and in areas of Asia, Africa and Latin America influenced by Quaker evangelical missionary activity, a form of worship is practised similar to that of most Protestant 'Free Churches', and pastoral leadership is generally accepted. Rather less than half the total membership of the Society of Friends now worships in the traditional manner described in this article. The four World Conferences of Friends held since 1920 have made possible a growth of understanding among Friends of the psychological, theological and historical grounds of their diversities, and have encouraged mutual openness and appreciation as well as a desire to rediscover, in appropriate contemporary forms, the experience which gave birth, in seventeenth-century England, to the mode of worship here delineated.

Both for the Society of Friends and for the Christian church as a whole, this mode of worship today raises far-reaching questions. If it is not, as early Friends claimed, the *only* form of worship appropriate to the new covenant dispensation, what is it? Is it simply a mode which appeals to certain temperaments? Or is it an emphasis – even an exaggeration – justified so long as it is balanced or off-set by other emphases? Or is it possible that it represents an essential ingredient or dimension of worship which, historically, found separate expression in conscious opposition to others? To express the matter otherwise, is it possible to think that, with other forms, it points beyond itself and them towards an understanding of the fullness of worship appropriate to today?

The Reports on Worship adopted by the World Faith and Order Conference (Montreal) 1963 and the British Faith and Order Conference (Nottingham) 1964, and the Fourth Assembly of the World Council of Churches (Uppsala) 1968, emphasized the need to go beyond all our inherited and traditional patterns of worship. They also recognized the obstacles posed for many of our contemporaries by the prescribed forms of ecclesiastical ritual, embodying traditional formulations of doctrine. They also deplored the gulf which appears to many to separate worship from responsible life in the world. Is it inconceivable that a mode of worship which minimizes ritual, requires no doctrinal affirmations but, instead, strongly requires the full and equal responsible participation of every worshipper, issuing directly in his service in and to the world, may have a contribution to make far greater than might be inferred from the fewness of those who, for more than three centuries, have practised it?

Robert Barclay, *An Apology for the True Christian Divinity* . . ., 1675, Propositions xi, xii, xiii; H. Brinton, *Creative Worship*, 1931; *Christian Faith and Practice in the Experience of the Society of Friends*, 1960, chs. 3, 4, 5, 7; George Fox, 'Concerning Silent Meetings', *Gospel Truth Demonstrated*, 1657, p. 103; T. F. Green, *Preparation for Worship*, 1952; T. Edmund Harvey, *Silence and Worship: A Study in Quaker Experience*, 1923; L. V. Hodgkin, *Silent Worship, the Way of Wonder*, 1919; George Keith, *The Benefit, Advantage and Glory of Silent Meetings*, 1670; James Nayler, 'Concerning Worship', *Collected Works*, 1656, pp. 272 ff.; Isaac Penington, 'Concerning the Worship of the Living God', *Works*, 1681, Part I, pp. 350 ff.; 'A Brief Account of the Ground of Our Worship', *Works*, Part II pp. 258 ff.; 'A Few Words concerning the Worship which our God Hath Taught Us', *Works*, Part II, pp. 374 ff.; 'A Brief Account concerning Silent Meetings, the Nature, Use, Intent and Benefit of them', *Works*, Part II, pp. 256 ff.; D. V. Steere, *Where Words Come from*, 1955; John Woolman, *Journal and Essays* (1772), ed. A. M. Gummere, 1922, pp. 508 ff.; John Woolman, 'On Silent Worship', *Works*, ²1775.

M. A. CREASEY

Quinquagesima

The name denotes the Sunday preceding Lent, being *fifty* days before Easter, but there is less obvious relevance in Sexagesima, 'sixtieth', and Septuagesima, 'seventieth', the terms applied to the two preceding Sundays. Lent (q.v.) was a preparation for the Pascha; to prepare for Quadragesima was a development which may be regarded as a tendency towards unnecessary elaboration.

Before the fourth century had ended there were places where the period before the Pascha was longer than six weeks. With the growth of monasticism the discipline of fasting rooted itself more and more firmly in the course of the century. The increasing emphasis on fasting would lead in time to a gratuitously meticulous calculation of the forty days. Sundays, and in some regions Saturdays also, would be excluded from the computation. Manifestly, there were factors which were liable to affect the integrity of the original six-week period. There is evidence of a seven-week Lent and an eight-week Lent at various centres in the eastern Mediterranean during the latter part of the fourth century. But it appears that in the East generally the period of preparation came to be seven weeks.

The situation was different in the West where Lent retained its character of six weeks. But between the middle of the fifth century and the end of the sixth Quinquagesima, Sexagesima and Septuagesima emerged to form a preparatory cycle. Western practice outside Rome during the period of the sixth to the eighth centuries varied between two Sundays and one Sunday before Lent, although two predominated. On the other hand, there were no preparatory Sundays in the lectionary of Luxeuil or the Bobbio Missal. Septuagesima, Sexagesima and Quinquagesima were established at Rome before the end of the sixth century, and the spread of the Roman rite ensured their eventual acceptance throughout the West.

A. A. MCARTHUR

Reader

Etymologically, reader is simply the English translation of 'lector' (q.v.), one of the minor orders of the ministry. In the Church of Scotland after the Reformation readers acted as assistants to parish ministers and in a number of cases were given full pastoral responsibility for a parish. They were authorized to *read* the prayers, the lessons from scripture and a homily and, after 1572, to perform baptisms and marriages. In the Church of Scotland at the present time readers are nominated by presbyteries and authorized to conduct services when there is no minister. In the Anglican Church, laymen (and, more recently, women) have been licensed as 'lay readers' since 1866. They may take services and preach (except at the eucharist) and may be authorized to administer the chalice.

P. HINCHLIFF

Reformed Worship

The origins of Reformed worship in the strictly Calvinistic sense are to be found in Strasbourg, where in St John's chapel below the high altar of the cathedral the first German mass, translated and modified by the ex-Dominican Diebold Schwarz, was celebrated in 1524. It was simply the Latin eucharist translated into plain homely German designed to express the new spirit, while retaining as far as possible the old familiar things. The ceremonial, e.g., was not appreciably altered – that is to say the action itself looked much the same as before. The words also were not much changed, except unobtrusively to remove from the canon (the consecration prayer) phrases which seemed to confirm the Roman doctrine of the sacrifice of the mass as a repetition of what took place on Calvary. The really far-reaching change, however, was to say the whole service in a clear audible voice and in the vernacular tongue. Low mass had been the popular form of service for a considerable period before the Reformation, and this meant that the old service had been said in Latin and also inaudibly. Now, for the first time, the people both heard the words and understood them, while at one stroke the old secret prayers disappeared and the central rite stood clear of its medieval accretions. It was in fact very similar to the new liturgical revolution which has taken place in the Roman Church during the last few years, even in some respects perhaps less radical.

During the next five years the reforms were carried farther (and independently) in Strasbourg. German metrical psalms and hymns were introduced to enable the people to take an active part in the worship, and more than one observer remarked that the church was full of the people's song. The Apostles' Creed, as simpler, is offered as an alternative to the Nicene; the lectionaries are abandoned, and the epistle and gospel read in course and at greater length; sermons are preached at every service; and the ceremonial is much reduced. The ancient basilican posture of the celebrant, when he stood behind the holy table facing the people, replaces the eastward position (q.v.), and the holy table itself, now no longer called the altar (q.v.) is moved forward in the sanctuary to be nearer to the people.

From 1530 onwards Bucer's influence became dominant and the reforms more radical. Choices were offered in the prayers, necessitating departure from the old text; each successive variant was more verbose and didactic. The responses long ago of course had disappeared from the people's usage, but now they were excised from the text. Sermons were very long, an hour or so in length, and the abandonment of the old lectionary which could have been profitably revised was a loss, as in fact reading the scriptures in course is unworkable for weekly worship. The eucharistic vestments (q.v.) now gave way to cassock and bands, black gown and scarf (or tippet), formerly the outdoor and preaching garments of the clergy. The *Orate fratres*, a bidding to prayer where no prayer then existed, was expanded into a long didactic exhortation and fencing of the table; and such exhortations became a feature – in truth, a somewhat tedious feature – of every subsequent Reformed liturgy. A central and important reform was the restoration of weekly communion, to replace the yearly communion of the medieval church. This became a primary principle of nearly all the Reformers (Zwingli, e.g., was an exception), though it was not always successfully given effect to. In Strasbourg there were weekly celebrations in the cathedral and monthly celebrations in the parish churches. When holy communion was not celebrated, all except that immediately pertaining to communion was retained, the eucharist thus remained the norm of worship, and in the *BCP* later issued it was described as antecommunion. Communion was received standing. It will be seen that to give effect to such reforms as we have mentioned, servicebooks became necessary for the people's use, and these were prepared and issued. Such books were unknown in the medieval church (there were rare exceptions); thus the people's prayer-books were an invention of the Reformers, and were in use thereafter in every Reformed church, though abandoned by some in the seventeenth century.

This was the situation when Calvin came to Strasbourg late in 1538, exiled from Geneva because of differences with the magistracy. Bucer and the other Reformers there welcomed him (after a while Bucer even found this somewhat reserved young man a charming wife) and gave him charge of the small congregation of French exiles in the city. The condition was that the same form of worship as used in the German churches be adopted and holy communion be celebrated once a month. This was very congenial to Calvin, and as he did not speak German he had prepared a Latin translation of the German service-book, then cast it into French. He made minor changes, such as substituting a metrical decalogue (divided into two tables by a collect) for the *Kyries* and the *Gloria in excelsis*.

Persuaded upon urgent invitation of the magistrates to return to Geneva in 1541 he took this book with him for use there. By this time it included an order for holy baptism, directions for the ordination of ministers, and other occasional offices, and metrical psalms were gradually added to it as they became available. Entitled *La Forme de Prières*, it became the standard of Reformed worship among Calvinists everywhere. During Mary's reign it was translated into English, slightly revised, and used in the Congregation of Marian exiles in Geneva, of which such men as John Knox and Whittinghouse were ministers. Thus after Mary's death it was taken back to Britain to be used in Scotland and among many Puritans in England. In 1560 it became the official service-book of the Church of Scotland, passing through over sixty editions between 1564 and 1638, variously known as the *Forme of Prayers*, the *Book of Common Order* and the *Psalm Book*, and later nicknamed Knox's Liturgy. In England it was generally known as the *Forme of Prayers*, 'the Waldgrave Liturgy', the 'Middleburg Liturgy', the 'Genevan Form', etc. The last editions known were printed in London in 1641, 1642 and 1644 for submission to Parliament and the Westminster Divines.

None, I think, would now hold the liturgical quality of this book or advocate it for present-day use. But it presented certain principles of enduring value, many of which have been forgotten by subsequent generations including our own. For example, it presupposed the Lord's Supper as the normative worship of the church, desired frequent communion, weekly to be preferred. Calvin declared infrequent communion to be 'an invention of the devil' and held that 'once a

week at the very least the Lord's Supper should be celebrated in the Christian Congregation'. This he made clear upon his first visit to Geneva, fought for it all his life, and declared that 'our practice is defection' because his purpose was not achieved, 'owing to ignorance' and other conservative opposition. The Sunday worship, even if there was no communion, was always based upon the eucharist.

One may summarize the Calvinistic rite as follows. It contained no order for daily prayer, though daily services took place, chiefly of a didactic nature with prayers added; and family prayers were also encouraged in the homes at a later period. The Sunday service consisted of (in this order): scripture sentence, Ps. 124.8; confession of sins, with scriptural words of pardon or absolution; the commandments sung in metre with Greek *Kyries* (q.v.) after each, the two tables divided by a collect for grace to keep God's law; a collect for illumination; scripture reading, and sermon; collection of alms; intercessions and Lord's Prayer (sometimes in a long paraphrase); Apostles' Creed in metre; metrical psalm; Aaronic blessing. In addition, as we learn from contemporary descriptions, one or two other metrical psalms were inserted at what were considered to be appropriate points. When holy communion was celebrated, the Lord's Prayer and blessing were omitted from the above and the prayer of consecration followed the creed and was completed by the Lord's Prayer. Then followed the words of institution, the fraction, the celebrant's communion, and the delivery to the people who came forward to the holy table standing to receive in both kinds during which a psalm was sung or the scriptures read. The service concluded with a brief post-communion thanksgiving, the *Nunc dimittis* in metre and the Aaronic blessing. Originally, Calvin's service was conducted from the communion table, with readings and sermon from the pulpit. Later, the whole service gravitated to the pulpit as any understanding of liturgical appropriateness disappeared, as it did also for a time in Anglican practice. The Christian year was followed widely in its main feasts, but not in detail. *See also* **Baptism** 15; **Books, Liturgical**, 15; **Liturgies** 15.

Strasbourg liturgies; F. Hubert, *Die Strassburger liturgischen Ordnungen im Zeitalter der Reformation*, 1920; for genealogy of *Form of Prayers* and text in use in Scotland, *see* W. D. Maxwell, *Genevan Service Book*, 1931, reprinted 1965, and for English translations of two Strasbourgian liturgies, *see* W. D. Maxwell, *An Outline of Christian Worship*, 1936 (both of these books contain extensive additional bibliography); Calvin's liturgy will be found in Calvin's *Opera*; William Cowan has given in the papers of the Edinburgh Bibliographical Society (vol. X, 1913) a *Bibliography of the Book of Common Order*, and a large number of Puritan liturgies of the period have been collected in Hall, *Reliquiae Liturgicae*, 1847, and *Fragmenta Liturgiae*, 1848. *See also* W. D. Maxwell, *The Book of Common Prayer and the Worship of the Non-Anglican Churches* (Dr Williams' Lecture, 1949).

WILLIAM D. MAXWELL

Reredos

In the English parish church of the later Middle Ages there was usually a large east window, or a series of lancet windows, the sill of which came down to within three or four feet of the altar-table. The intervening space on the wall between window and altar was filled in with a structure of wood or stone which extended the length of the altar, and this is the reredos. It was sometimes made of alabaster, but it was seldom, whether wood or stone, left without gilt and colour. In the middle was a crucifix and on either side there were carved or painted figures of the saints. The whole structure was encased in a frame. In some instances a fabric hanging of embroidery was preferred (*see* **Altar Hangings**).

In cathedrals and larger churches where there was a solid screen behind the high altar, e.g. Winchester Cathedral, England, the panel immediately above the altar was treated like the reredos in a parish church with more detailed and refined carving (*see* **Screen**).

In the Baroque era in France, Italy and Spain there was a great development of the reredos into a vast altar-piece with dramatic and theatrical details, e.g. in the Church of St Ignatius, Rome. But in England the altar-pieces designed by Wren and Hawksmoor seldom attained such proportions, although rising well behind the altar, since they usually had panels on which the Lord's Prayer and the ten commandments were inscribed.

J. W. Franklin, *The Cathedrals of Italy*, 1958; J. Harvey, *The Cathedrals of Spain*, 1957; C. E. Pocknee, *The Christian Altar*, 1963.

C. E. POCKNEE

Reservation

Reservation of the sacrament for the sick and dying has been customary in the church from the earliest times. Justin Martyr (*c.* 155) said that it was taken 'to those who were absent'. The faithful in the time of persecution were permitted to take the eucharist into their own homes, in order to give themselves holy communion. The clergy would keep the sacrament, for a sick call, in their houses, and after the Peace of the Church (313) often in the sacristy (q.v.). About the end of the ninth century, some churches issued regulations for reservation within the church itself, in close proximity to the altar.

The sacrament must have been reserved in both kinds, at least in some places, especially in northern countries, as it was often the custom to give the sick man the species of bread dipped in the chalice (intinction). By the twelfth century it became the normal practice to reserve the consecrated bread only.

The first official regulation for reservation in the Western Church comes from the Fourth Lateran Council of 1215, when it was already the custom to reserve the sacrament in cathedrals, parish churches and chapels of the religious orders on or, more usually, about the altar. The Council did no more than direct that the reserved sacrament should be kept with strict care under lock and key.

The mode of reservation in the Middle Ages differed in the various countries of Europe. A hanging pyx (q.v.) above the altar was usual in England and France (often in the form of a dove). Germany and the Low Countries developed the sacrament house, an elaborate structure, isolated from the altar. A niche in the wall of the sanctuary was customary in parts of Italy, Portugal, Sweden, Scotland and elsewhere. (*See* **Aumbry**.)

The Tridentine reform, which encouraged a more frequent reception of holy communion, prescribed, without formally forbidding other usages, a tabernacle (q.v.) fixed to the centre of the altar. In the brief reign of Queen Mary, when an effort was made to restore reservation, Cardinal Pole, archbishop of Canterbury, issued regulations for a tabernacle, but the bishop of London, Edmund Bonner, who was not so influenced by the Continent, envisaged a restoration of the hanging pyx. Since Trent, the tabernacle has become the usual mode of reservation in all Roman Catholic churches, although there are exceptions in Germany and Belgium, where the old sacrament houses are permitted to be used (*see* Plate 35).

Communion from the tabernacle is the norm on Sundays and feasts, as it is impossible to estimate the number of communicants. The liturgical commission, following up the findings of Vatican II, has again raised the question of the mode of reservation. The old altar against the east wall has been abandoned for a simple table in the middle of the sanctuary, with the celebrant facing the people. In such circumstances, a tabernacle is out of the question. If the old altar has been suffered to remain with its tabernacle, the celebrant can conveniently get the blessed sacrament to give communion to the people, but if, as in some places, the altar has been removed, an awkward pause would result while the celebrant went to a side chapel. The solution would seem to be an aumbry or sacrament house in close proximity to the present altar. This has been done in the cathedral churches of Cologne and Aachen. A hanging pyx would not solve the difficulty, as it would not hold sufficient hosts for communion.

In the latter part of the eleventh century, with the growth of a realization of the real presence of Christ in the eucharist, outward honour was paid to the reserved sacrament, which was increased over the years by theologians and councils. Prayers were offered to Christ present in the church under the species of bread. A feast was introduced for the express purpose of worshipping the sacrament: Corpus Christi, on the Thursday after Trinity Sunday. A form of devotion to the reserved sacrament is given in the 'Ancren Riwle', written for anchoresses in the thirteenth century. The Carmelite Sibert de Beka, who revised the ordinal of the order in the early years of the fourteenth century, added the words 'for the devotion of the choir' to 'for the use of the sick', as the purpose of reservation. Centuries later, St Alphonsus Liguori (d. 1787) encouraged the faithful to 'pay a visit' and pray before the tabernacle.

In the Middle Ages, the sacrament was reserved in what was known as the 'Easter

Plate 35 Sacrament house,
St Pierre, Louvain, Belgium

sepulchre' (q.v.) from Good Friday until the morning of Easter. There were elaborate ceremonies for the 'burial' (*depositio*), when the host was taken there and for the 'resurrection' (*elevatio*), when it was taken out and restored to the normal place of reservation. A watch was kept during the time that our Lord lay in the 'tomb', and there are contemporary accounts extant recording the number of pence given to the watchers for refreshments. The old ceremonies of the 'sepulchre' have been preserved in the rite of Braga, unless the recent liturgical changes have destroyed the distinctive Portuguese usages. The sacrament on Good Friday was taken in a bier to a side chapel, where it remained, without watchers, until the morning of Easter. Then, before the high mass, it was carried in a monstrance in a solemn procession to another chapel, where benediction was given.

Throughout Latin Christendom, the term 'sepulchre' has, since the Baroque period, been applied to the 'altar of repose', where the sacrament has been kept from Maundy Thursday until the Liturgy of Good Friday, surrounded by flowers and lights, with the faithful praying before the reserved sacrament. Since the recent Council, this has been simplified, with watchers only until midnight.

Extra-liturgical devotions to the sacrament belong exclusively to the Western or Latin Church and there is no trace of them in the Eastern Churches, except in those united to Rome.

Regulations for the renewal of the sacred species have varied over the years, but today the normal practice is once a week.

The custom of having a continual light burning before the reserved sacrament grew up in the Middle Ages.

The Eastern Churches, with the exception of Egypt and Ethiopia, reserve the sacrament, but without any exterior honour.

The Orthodox renew the consecrated bread annually on Maundy Thursday, when the bread is intincted from the chalice and dried by fire. It is moistened with a few drops of wine in giving communion to the sick.

The Copts equate the sacrament with the 'manna', which, they say, was supplied daily and not kept until the next day. A canon of the Ethiopian Church forbids the sacrament to be reserved.

In the Anglican Church, there were many instances of the sacrament being taken to the house of a sick person, but perpetual reserva-

tion began in a few churches in the nineteenth century. The bishops at first bitterly opposed the practice, especially in a tabernacle in the open church. The custom, however, continued, but more often in an aumbry, where there was less likelihood of extra-liturgical devotions. Parliament rejected the proposed prayer books of 1927 and 1928, largely because of the rubrics permitting reservation.

Reservation is now generally accepted and is found in several of the cathedral churches.

Official recognition of reservation exists in the rubrics of the Scottish prayer book of 1929 and in the South African rite of the same year.

A. A King and C. E. Pocknee, *Eucharistic Reservation in the Western Church*, 1965.

A. A. KING

Responsorial Psalmody and Responsories

These two terms signify two different modes of performance. In responsorial psalmody the chant was sung by a soloist in alternation with the congregation as opposed to the antiphonal psalmody (q.v.) of a later date, and was adopted from the Jewish liturgy. The congregation responded after each verse with a refrain such as 'Alleluia' or 'Amen'. A familiar example is Ps. 136 in which each verse ends with the refrain 'For his mercy endureth for ever'.

Responsories have a structure corresponding to rondo-form. The short ones come in prime (now discarded in the reformed office), the little hours of terce, sext and none, and at compline (*see* **Canonical Hours**). In the longer responsories, which come after each lesson in the nocturns of mattins, the procedure is more elaborate (*see* **Divine Office**).

ALEC ROBERTSON

Rite

A rite is a formal act constituting a religious observance; hence one refers to the sacrificial rites of the OT or to the eucharistic rite.

Rites are a universal phenomenon to be found in all the major religions. In origin they are based upon human actions, e.g. washing underlies baptism, and eating and drinking the Lord's Supper. Hence rites have a natural meaning which has been amplified and enriched by religious associations, without the new and additional meaning being forced arbitrarily upon the original. In other words, rites are not artificial constructions but rest in the natural order and in the sphere of human activities, and unless this connection is preserved they can easily degenerate into magic or intellectualism.

According to Cazeneuve, rites may belong to any one of three types: (1) Those whose object is to establish an intimate contact between man and the holy in order that man may control the divine power. These belong to the sphere of magic. (2) Those whose object is to isolate man from the holy which is regarded as dangerous. These are negative rites, relating to impurity, and are often connected with the idea of taboo. (3) Those whose object is to facilitate man's contact with the holy in such a way that man may be preserved and at the same time enter into a relationship with the source of his being.

The corollary of the last type, which is predominant within Christianity, is that rites are frequently regarded as being the work of the gods themselves, i.e. they are considered to have been instituted by the deity and their real agents are the god or gods working in and through them. So within Christianity, the eucharist is held to rest upon a command of Christ and he is the celebrant.

At the basis of religious rites are four further concepts: (1) That of *symbolism*. All have a symbolic character whereby the natural object or action symbolizes the divine, e.g. the bread of the eucharist symbolizes Christ who is the bread of life. (2) That of *consecration*. Their main function is to enable the human situation, in its entirety or in certain aspects, to share in a principle which goes beyond it and is its basis. (3) That of *repetition*. The divine power is thereby represented as being brought into the present. Rites are therefore representative actions, not in Schleiermacher's sense of the symbolic representation of the content of faith but in the sense of a representation of the original sacred action. So in the eucharist it is believed that the sacrifice of Christ on the cross is made present through its effects. (4) That of *remembrance*. They are the media for preserving and transmitting the founded tradition of the community and at the same time for sharing experience. This shared experience through the rites sustains the common faith and framework of understanding whereby the community is perpetuated and renewed.

L. Bouyer, *Rite and Man*, ET, 1963; J. Cazeneuve, *Les rites et la condition humaine*, 1958.

EDITOR

Ritual

Ritual refers to the prescribed form of words which constitute an act of worship. It is therefore not identical with ceremonial (q.v.) which relates to the actions. Nevertheless in common usage the two are treated as synonymous. Strictly speaking, however, ritual does not include such actions as processions nor the sign of the cross (qq.v.) and instead refers to the collect, the Lord's Prayer, the preface, etc.

EDITOR

Rogation Days

These days of intercession or prayer were much more frequent in earlier days, some occurring annually and others being arranged to suit local needs. But only four such days have been universally kept for many centuries – April 25 and the three days preceding Ascension Day.

April 25 was chosen to replace with a Christian procession the pagan Robigalia processions of that date. As this always occurred in the Easter season, it was not a fast day and the procession was festal, like the Easter week processions.

The other three days have their origin in France. In the fifth century, Mamertus introduced three days of fasting and prayer when disaster threatened Vienne and its neighbourhood. This practice spread to other places, but Rome did not adopt it for some while, since it thought fasting incompatible with Paschal joy. When it did adopt these rogation days, the fasting obligation was removed.

The feature of rogation days is the singing of the litanies (q.v.) of the saints in procession. April 25 is known as the greater litanies and the other three days as the lesser. Conflicting reasons have been given to explain 'greater' and 'lesser'. The litanies used are the same on all four days.

In the recent revision of the Roman liturgy, Ember and rogation days have been removed from the general calendar and their observance is now a matter of local arrangement.

The practice of processing round the parish

before Ascension Day is still retained in some Anglican churches.

J. CONNELLY

Roman Catholic Worship

In the Catholic tradition, both of the East and the West, worship from the earliest days was sacramental, communal and always associated with the proclamation of God's word. It was sacramental in the sense that it was held that the liturgy mediated to the worshipping community the saving power of Christ's redeeming work effected in his passion, death and resurrection. This view implied that the church was 'sacrament' manifesting and making Christ present in the here and now, and in the older Roman tradition (*Gelasian Sacramentary*, 432, ed. Mohlberg) the church is called the 'wonderful sacrament'. Worship was communal in the sense that its celebrants were the gathered people who, together with the clergy, celebrated the great events of salvation. The word was proclaimed by the reading of the scriptures, by preaching, but also by the very liturgical texts which unfolded the meaning of the sacramental celebration.

The liturgy, based on those foundations, remained in its main lines, even though from the fifth century onwards ceremonial became more elaborate. But as the sociological composition of the Christian people changed and with the entry of the northern races into the church, especially from the eighth century onwards, an increasing emphasis was laid on the sacramental *action*. Latin was not understood by the new races, and to compensate for the unintelligibility of the word, there was a further elaboration of ceremonial. At the same time, there is observable a tendency to the clericalization of the liturgy which became the preserve of a professional class. For reasons, it is true, of practical rather than theological significance, the cup was withdrawn from the laity (to avoid profanation) and the bread used became unleavened. The gap between the liturgy and the people was not closed by the proliferation of usages and observances of the later Middle Ages, though they did something to mitigate the rigours of a liturgy that had become remote. By the end of the Middle Ages liturgical 'pluralism' had become chaos and reform was necessary.

The reform initiated by the Council of Trent and carried out by the papacy aimed at uniformity, desired by many humanists and made possible by the printing press. The answer to the irreverence and chaos of the last phase of the Middle Ages was a corpus of rubrics that dictated every movement and word of the celebrant. Little enough attention was given to the people who were assumed to be devout onlookers and offerers in their secret hearts of the eucharistic sacrifice. Yet Catholic worship remained warm and devout, much assisted by the art and music of the Baroque era, and the murmured Latin mass with its periods of silence fitted the need of the devout whose spirituality had now become intensely individualistic. Moreover, what was lacking in liturgical worship was made up for by a great variety of popular devotions, expositions of the blessed sacrament, the rosary, processions, the stations of the cross (qq.v.) and others. By the end of the nineteenth century, when most of the laity attended only a low mass (q.v.), Catholic worship had become inward-looking, almost cosy, a devotional exercise.

The way of reform has been long, slow and painful. But with the coming of the Second Vatican Council (1962-65) a reform was initiated which, it is interesting to observe, takes sacramentality, communal celebration and the proclamation of God's word as the foundations of its theology of the liturgy as laid out principally in the *Constitution on the Liturgy* of 1963. Here we find that the liturgy 'is the action of Christ the priest and of his body, the church' which is made manifest in a worship made up of 'signs that are perceptible to the senses'. This sacramental liturgy mediates to the worshipping community, and beyond it to the world, the saving power of the mystery of Christ which consists of his passion, death, resurrection and ascension. Through the celebration of the liturgy the church looks on to the *eschaton* and up to heaven and sees the earthly liturgy as the counterpart of the heavenly. The whole Christian people, by virtue of their participation in Christ's priesthood, celebrate the liturgy, 'all liturgical services are celebrations of the church', both people and clergy, and from it they derive as from its source the true Christian spirit. For the liturgy is the summit of the church's activity and the source of all its power, and through its celebration the Christian people are able to make their own the saving mystery of Jesus Christ.

But Christ is known by the word and the liturgy itself, which must be within the people's grasp, must be self-explanatory. Hence liturgical reform must make it possible for the people to share fully in liturgical services; they must always hear God's word for which better provision must be made. If this was to be achieved, it was necessary that the language of the liturgy should be changed from Latin to modern vernaculars (q.v.).

These principles have been applied to the whole range of Catholic worship, including not only the eucharist but all the other sacraments, the divine office and the organization of the liturgical year. The reformed liturgy has also affected the style of celebration – the eucharist is normally celebrated facing the people – and necessitated the re-ordering of old churches and the designing of new ones. In particular, the emphasis on the importance of the word is striking, so much so that one can say 'No celebration without proclamation'.

In addition, new liturgical forms are emerging and the uniformity that was characteristic of post-Tridentine worship is no longer insisted on (*Constitution*, 39, 40). Adaptation is built into the new services.

Popular devotions continue alongside the official liturgy and it is recommended that they should do so but, as the *Constitution* observes (13), they are to be harmonized with the liturgy. Already new forms have emerged (*see* **Bible Services**) and if Catholic worship retains much of the warmth of the past, it has already become markedly biblical. It has been observed that the *Constitution on the Liturgy* does not emphasize mission very strongly, but it must be taken with the other documents of Vatican II, notably with the *Constitution on the Church in the Modern World*, which decisively turned Catholic Christians away from an exclusive concern with their own affairs to their mission in the world.

J. D. CRICHTON

Rosary

The rosary is a method of prayer. It combines repetition of familiar prayers with meditation on the mysteries of the faith. The prayers used are fifteen decades (i.e. groups of ten) of the 'Hail Mary', with each decade preceded by the 'Our Father' and followed by 'Glory be to the Father'. The mysteries are fifteen events in the life of Jesus or of his mother.

Normally, one third of the complete rosary is said at a time. It is divided into three groups of five: the joyful mysteries are the annuncia-

tion, visitation, nativity, presentation in the Temple and finding in the Temple; the sorrowful mysteries are the agony in the garden, scourging, crown of thorns, carrying of the cross, and crucifixion; the glorious mysteries are the resurrection, ascension, descent of the Holy Spirit, assumption of the Virgin and coronation of the Virgin. They are rightly termed 'mysteries', as they contain depths of spiritual meaning beyond anything the eye can see or the imagination describe. They have a relevance to daily Christian living and are not concerned only with a distant past or indefinite future. The introduction of these meditations, as the very essence of the rosary devotion, have been ascribed to a Carthusian two hundred years after the time of St Dominic.

The saying of repetitive prayers on a rosary is common to Buddhism and Islam, and a sculpture of ancient Nineveh depicts two females with rosaries in their hands.

Until the middle of the twelfth century, when the first part of the 'Hail Mary' came into Christian devotion, the 'rosary' consisted of the 'Our Father'. The lay brothers of Cluny in the tenth century counted them on knots made on a string. Such prayers became common in every part of Europe, aided by pebbles, berries or threaded discs of bone. They finally gave their name to beads (*see* **Bidding Prayer**). The devotion was called 'Pater Nosters' and in London the members of the craft who made these devices congregated in Paternoster Row.

Nowhere do we find the rosary associated with St Dominic (d. 1221) until the latter part of the fifteenth century, when a Dominican, Alan de Rupe (*c.* 1470-5) not only promulgated the devotion, which became very popular, but stated that the Saint had either instituted or revived it. Since that time, the rosary has been a universal devotion in Latin Christendom.

A. A. KING

Rostrum

Rostrum means literally the beak of a bird, and by transference it came to mean the beak-like prow of a ship. Then it was applied to the speaker's platform or tribune in the Roman forum because it was ornamented with the prows of ships taken from the people of Antium (the modern Anzio), in 338 BC. Hence the word has come to mean any platform from which public addresses or lectures are given.

C. E. POCKNEE

Rubrics

Rubrics are ceremonial (q.v) directions for the conduct of a service, and are so-called because in medieval books they were written in red (Lat. *ruber*) to distinguish them from the text of the services.

In the earliest liturgical books, few or no directions were given, simply the words to be used being provided. In time a special book, known as the *Ordinale*, was produced, being a directory for the arrangement of the altar service. Known also as the *Directorium* or *Pie*, this ·corresponded to the later rubrics which were included with the texts themselves.

Although at the present day rubrics are frequently not printed in red, the term is still used of the ceremonial directions.

On the so-called 'Black Rubric' *see* **Postures**, 2(*c*).

EDITOR

Sacred Heart

The devotion expresses our Saviour's love for us and our loving gratitude to him. It is based upon the symbolism of the heart as the emblem of love and self-sacrifice: 'The heart that has so loved men.' Devotion to the Sacred Heart is to the person of Jesus. The singling out of the heart as a symbol has grown out of private devotion, with a return of love and a desire to make reparation for the sins of men. Sinners are encouraged to find a sure refuge and a promise of pardon in the heart of Jesus. The devotion has sometimes been over-sentimentalized, but it has not ceased to be true and firmly rooted in Christian tradition. The development of the thought underlying the Easter-motif in the mystery of redemption led to a more subjective and psychological way of regarding the redeeming love of Christ, especially as revealed in the passion.

The first unmistakable devotion to the Sacred Heart developed in the German convent of Helfta, with St Mechtilde (d. 1298) and St Gertrude (d. 1304), as a private devotion of the mystical order. It became an objective devotion to the Five Wounds under the influence of the Franciscans, but it remained individual.

A church was dedicated to the Sacred Heart at Cuarapary in Brazil in 1585, but it was not until the seventeenth century that a public devotion was established. Its first expression, outside religious communities, was during the plague in Marseilles in 1720.

Several countries received permission to observe a feast of the Sacred Heart, and it was admitted into the Universal Calendar of the Roman rite in 1856, the second Friday after Corpus Christi.

A. A. KING

Sacristy

The room or repository in a church in which are kept the vestments, vessels, etc. Sacristies were introduced first in Syria, *c.* 400, as side chambers to the apse (q.v.). In the Middle Ages they were often placed on either side of, or behind, the high altar and were sometimes used for reservation (q.v.). In current usage, the term is virtually synonymous with vestry (q.v.).

EDITOR

Saints' Days

'By celebrating the passage of the saints from earth to heaven the Church proclaims the Paschal mystery achieved in those who have suffered and been glorified with Christ; she proposes them to the faithful as examples drawing all to the Father through Christ, and through their merits she pleads for God's favours' (*Liturgical Constitution of Vatican II*, para. 104). In this paragraph the Council sums up the church's reasons for honouring the saints.

The early Christians, like their pagan neighbours, kept the anniversaries of their dead, especially of the martyrs; for the martyrs had conquered in and for Christ and were now with Christ. At these anniversary services the eucharist was celebrated as the completion of the vigil service.

Lists of the earliest martyrs are practically non-existent, but later generations were exhorted to keep records of the date of the death of the martyrs, the *dies natalis*, and the place of their burial, *depositio*, for the anniversary celebrations depended on these facts. Such celebrations were naturally local at first, for they were held at the martyr's tomb, but some eventually became feast days for the whole church.

Some Christians acknowledged, *confessed*, Christ before men (*cf.* Matt. 10.32) not by death, but by imprisonment or exile. These were called confessors, *confessores* – a title which was eventually extended to men whose way of life was a confession of Christ and a proclamation of the Paschal mystery. The early confessors came to be honoured alongside the martyrs. Pope Sylvester, Anthony the Hermit and Martin of Tours seem to have been the first to be so honoured in the West.

Beside the feasts of martyrs and confessors, the Christian calendar contains feasts of those intimately connected with the work of salvation – John the Baptist, Mary, Joseph and the apostles.

J. CONNELLY

Saints' and Holy Days *see* All Saints, All Souls, Ember Days, Fast Days, Ferial, Rogation Days, Saints' Days

Salvation Army

In common with other churches the public worship of the Salvation Army always includes praise, prayer, a reading of scripture, together with an exposition of a selected Bible verse or portion. But, in addition, a recognized place is given to Christian testimony and, at the conclusion of a meeting, there is usually an invitation to Christian decision or dedication at what is known as the Mercy Seat or penitent-form.

Two further features should not be overlooked. One is that women take equal place with men in public worship, whether as leaders or as participants. The other is that the Salvation Army has no fixed liturgy, if by that is meant an order of service from which no deviation may be made. On the contrary, worship may commence with praise, or with prayer, or with a reading of scripture, nor is there any pre-determined place for the biblical exhortation. The leader of the meeting is at liberty to alter the order of that meeting in any way which may be for the greater spiritual good of the congregation.

This freedom, however, is not the fortuitous by-product of any casual approach to public worship, but the expression of a considered endeavour to act upon the principle that 'God is Spirit, and those who worship him must worship him in spirit and in truth' (John 4.24, NEB). The fact that there is no set liturgy upon which to lean requires everyone in the congregation to make a

personal effort to contribute to the worship of the whole. Yet this, far from giving rise to spiritual tenseness and overstrain, results in frequently that joy which is one of the first fruits of the Spirit and that liberty wherewith the children of God are set free.

Were this not made clear, it might be supposed that the absence of a set structure of worship might lead to a formless informality which, at its worst, could degenerate into a chaos which would defeat the very purpose of worship. But this is averted because, in the first place, Salvationists recognize – in the memorable phrase of van Unnik, quoted by C. F. D. Moule – that worship must always be 'within the magnetic field of the Holy Spirit'. As the Spirit's office is to glorify Christ, the worship which he guides will exalt that Christ as Saviour and Lord of men. Thus no contribution, whether of testimony or of prayer, becomes a private exercise in egoism, and the desire of the preacher is ever to speak 'in demonstration of the Spirit'.

In the second place, the congregation is not passive but active, and this seems to be in harmony with NT practice (I Cor. 14.26). In Salvationist parlance, one will have a prayer to offer, another a word of witness to give, another a 'Hallelujah' or an 'Amen' to utter – yet all will contribute to the edifying of the church. For the reality of Christian worship depends not on the use, or the refusal to use, a formal liturgy, but on the presence of the Holy Spirit.

Music and song play an integral part in the worship of the Salvationist. Here again his approach is truly catholic, for his song-book draws upon verses which have come down from the medieval church as well as the classic hymns of the Reformation, is undergirded by the two Wesleys, Watts and Doddridge, and does not pass by the Tractarians Faber and Newman. In addition, there is a substantial amount of original Salvationist material, some of which could well find a place in other hymn-books.

In like manner, the Salvation Army band can draw upon a Bach chorale, or a composition by one of the many gifted Salvationist musicians, to deepen the spirit of worship in a meeting. For such a contribution is not regarded as a programme item which might be applauded if decorum or convention allowed. But, as Walford Davies and Harvey Grace used to insist, there are moments when musical utterance becomes the highest expression of public worship.

Finally, it must be added that while worship, directed to the glory of God, is a worthy end in itself, that end is nullified if public worship does not strengthen the worshipper's public witness. Divine service does not end when the benediction is pronounced; it has only begun. The uniform worn by the Salvationist at his meetings – both in and out of doors – is his way of identifying himself as a soldier of Jesus Christ. He seeks the holy place on Sundays so that, by the renewal of grace, he may be a more effective Christian soldier on weekdays.

In the thought and practice of the Salvationist, worship and witness can never be divided – save to the impoverishment of both. As has been well said: 'What we become in the presence of God, that we can be all day long.'

The Handbook of Doctrine, 1969; *The Year Book of the Salvation Army*.

F. COUTTS

Sanctuary

In relation to religious architecture, the term sanctuary may be applied in three different ways: (1) Originally it designated that part of a church which was reserved for the clergy, which was often fenced off by chancels (q.v.) or balustrades. (2) It may also be used of the limited area immediately around an altar, often demarcated by an altar-rail (q.v.). These two different uses can lead to confusion, because while according to the first the term describes the whole of an area, according to the second it refers to a subdivision of the whole. (3) Occasionally it is employed of the church building as a whole.

EDITOR

Sanctus

An anthem which in most eucharistic liturgies forms part of the thanksgiving with which the eucharistic prayer or anaphora (q.v.) commences.

W. JARDINE GRISBROOKE

Screen

This article deals only with screens in Western Christendom. For the screen in the Eastern Orthodox Church, *see* **Iconostasis**.

1. There were screens in the Roman and other basilicas, which separated the altar from the nave (qq.v.). These screens were constructed of stone and had carved or decorated panels rising from the floor about four feet in height. Above this were columns of marble or porphyry which supported an architrave or beam from which votive lamps were sometimes suspended. Thus the altar was visible through the columns of the screen. On the nave-side immediately outside the screen were the singers or the *schola cantorum*. Many of these screens were pulled down in the baroque era.

2. The chancel screen in the English parish church developed in the Middle Ages from the narrow opening in the wall that separated the nave and the altar. By the fifteenth century, the English parish church had developed in style, and in the large parish churches there was frequently a wooden screen both carved and decorated with colour of great beauty. This screen extended not only across the main chancel but also across the aisles, thus forming chapels for lesser altars, e.g. the one in Southwold, Suffolk. Where this was the case there were lesser *Parclose* screens, separating the side chapels from the high altar as we can see at Southwold.

Above the chancel screen there was a loft with parapets and above this a beam, the rood beam, upon which were tenoned the crucifix with the figures of the Blessed Virgin Mary and St John. Hence the old term for this screen was rood screen. Unlike the Roman basilica, such churches usually accommodated the choir inside the screen in proximity to the altar.

3. In cathedral and the larger conventual churches there was a solid stone screen known as the *pulpitum* with an opening in the centre, which filled one bay of the arcade west of the choir. On the nave-side there were usually lesser altars on either side of the opening. The loft on the top of the pulpitum usually supported the pipe organ, as we can still see at the cathedral church at Norwich, while on occasions singers used the loft. Also on festivals the gospel was sung from this loft.

4. In the larger churches where there was the body of a notable saint, e.g. St Albans Cathedral, England, from the end of the fourteenth century, the increasing number of pilgrims coming to pray at the shrine of the saint necessitated separating the shrine by a solid screen from the high altar as we can still see at Westminster Abbey and Winchester Cathedral. On the west side the screen rose above the high altar and this side was usually decorated with tabernacle-work with the

statues of the saints. A canopy was projected out from the screen over the altar and a hanging pyx was suspended from this containing the reserved sacrament. *See also* **Reredos**.

F. E. Howard and F. H. Crossley, *English Church Woodwork*, ²1927; A. A. King and C. E. Pocknee, *Eucharistic Reservation in the Western Church*, 1965; C. E. Pocknee, *The Christian Altar*, 1963; A. Vallance, *English Church Screens*, 1936.

C. E. POCKNEE

Secret *see Super Oblata,* Silent Prayer

Secularization and Worship

Secularization is an imprecise term, since it can be used with a variety of meanings. It may refer, for example, to a process of social differentiation, involving the division of labour and the separation of home and work as well as a continuing specialization of social groups and institutions. Again, it can be applied to a shift of responsibility from ecclesiastical authority to worldly authority; so the secularization of the monasteries at the Reformation involved the transfer of property from church ownership to private tenure. For the purposes of this entry, however, the term is employed to refer to the process of change from a sacral to a secular universe.

A sacral universe is one in which the functioning of nature and society is explained in terms of the divine. In the sacral universe, man is at the mercy of nature; not only is he dependent upon it, but he finds himself largely unable to control it. Nature appears to be superior and sovereign, while man is weak and helpless. Nature is the central factor in his life, but in a pre-technical age, he is powerless to impose his will upon it. Unable to master nature, man then has to seek divine assistance, in order even to live. Nature appears to have almost divine features; it is an epiphany of God himself and the workings of nature are understood as the workings of God.

Within this sacral universe religion has a dual function. It acts as a preserver of society and it provides rituals to protect man against a world which he dominates neither intellectually nor materially. Worship is then a *cultus publicus*, securing the public

well-being and fulfilling the supreme end of the state. It safeguards man from the uncontrollable forces of nature and channels the divine assistance in his direction.

With secularization man enters a secular universe. This is one in which the functioning of nature and society is explained in terms of themselves. No longer is recourse had to the divine in order to understand either the material world or man. The natural sciences seek out the 'laws' of nature, their interrelationships and their workings; sociology analyses society, while man himself is investigated in terms of biology, psychology, etc. In the secular universe man is no longer at the mercy of nature, rather he is its master. Through the development of technology, man can control his environment; to a large extent he is therefore liberated from nature, in the sense that he has ceased to be dependent upon its changes and chances. This newly-won domination, precarious though it may be in the face of pollution and the need for conservation, results in a reversal of roles. Whereas previously man was in submission to natural forces, now he can bend them to his will. This change in the relationship of man and nature leads to a new concept of man in the universe. Man and his power become fundamental values which direct his efforts towards research into development and progress. So man fast becomes the lord of nature, dominating it by scientific and technological means. So far from being static and rigid, society now enters into a process of change – change that is constant and never ending. Society becomes also pluriform with different cultures and subcultures existing side by side. The mobility which technology brings breaks open the uniformity of society.

The result is that within the secular universe, religion loses the functions it exercised previously in the sacral universe. When change is the keynote, religion can no longer perform the role of preserver of society; if it tries to do so, it will be regarded as a bulwark against progress and a supporter of social stagnation. Moreover, when society is pluriform, there can be no *cultus publicus*. All religions tend to become *cultus privati*, with the abandonment of the public sector of life and with concentration upon forms of individual piety. When man dominates the universe, he no longer needs rituals to protect himself. If in former days it seemed reasonable to sprinkle water on an ox that was ill, today few would think of doing this to a tractor that has broken down.

Consequently the association of the words secularization and worship points, in the first instance, to a crisis of worship, because the passage from the sacral to the secular universe (secularization) renders those liturgical forms created within and for the sacral universe void of meaning and relevance within the new context of existence in the modern world. This crisis is intensified by another factor comprehended under secularization as social differentiation. Today, with the progress of urbanization, social life is very different from what it was in medieval Christendom. This latter was integrated with a civilization based largely upon agriculture and village units. The village was a social unity; it was a territorial area of restricted dimensions within which everyone knew everyone else. Its population found its residence, its work and its play all within its boundaries. There was an unavoidable interchange which promoted interest in other people, over and above any utilitarian project in which they may have been engaged. Worship, in this situation, was the occasion when those who knew one another gathered together and strengthened the ties that bound their already existing community, i.e. it was an assembly of a pre-existing community. The Sunday service was an important occasion for going out of the house and encountering one's fellow villagers; hence the importance, too, of conversation and inter-personal contacts, before, during and after the service. This pattern of life and worship favoured stability, respect for tradition and for nature and it allowed for the development of primary relations.

In the modern urban situation, however, specialization and diversification lead to the dispersal of man's social functions over a very wide area indeed. The husband goes to work in one quarter, the wife may shop in another, the children may go to school in a third, while the family as a whole will seek entertainment elsewhere. The consequence is that in a residential area personal relations may be non-existent and without this direct contact and sharing of interests, ideas and news, there exists no local community within which anyone can be integrated. The result of this transformation is that relations between fellow citizens become less and less primary, i.e. face-to-face, and more and more func-

tional. What is the effect of the demise of the village and the neighbourhood-based community upon worship? Clearly worship in this new context can no longer be understood in terms of the gathering of a pre-existing village type community. So worship loses its communal dimension and its necessary basis in inter-personal relations.

It now has to be affirmed that the association of the words secularization and worship points, in the second instance, to the need for a reformulation of the meaning and function of the latter in the light of the former. The inherited forms of worship are rooted in the view that it is an activity whereby we retire for a time from the secular world and, leaving all that is common behind, penetrate into another, sacred, world, where we enter the presence of the all-holy God and sing his praises in company with the heavenly choir of angels, archangels and saints. So worship is a special, religious activity, performed in special holy buildings; it may strengthen us to fulfil the divine purpose within our daily lives but it is, in itself, something separate from our daily lives in the world. In contrast to this, if worship today is to have any meaning in the face of secularization, it has to be redefined as an activity which springs out of life in the world; it is a celebration of that life. Instead of involving a divorce from the secular, it takes the secular or common as its basis, and so the cultic action is a means whereby we express the unity of the sacred and the secular. It does not need for its performance holy shrines, and while it is essentially a coming to awareness of and a response to God, this is achieved through that which is human and secular.

'Secular' worship, then, has a festive character in that it is a highlight in everyday existence and is based upon world involvement and not upon world rejection. It is an encounter with the divine and expresses and makes explicit the unity of the sacred and the secular by showing how the holy is a dimension of the whole of life. It is a sensitizing process, shaping our perception of the divine so as to open the secular to the holy and assist us to find the holy in everyday life. In a world in rapid change, it must also be a vehicle of social criticism and so a celebration of hope, bringing the hoped-for future into contact with the present and providing a stimulus for re-shaping the world. It points to the service of others; it expresses the love of neighbour and it comprises commitment and acceptance of responsibility for one another.

Since worship must have a communal basis, it has to be celebrated primarily in small groups, involving face-to-face encounters, social interaction, participation, mutuality, reciprocity and corporateness. It then fosters inter-personal relations and functions in terms of personalization and community identity. It is a shared activity, which is both intelligible to all and is related to past and future.

The norm of the worshipping community then becomes the primary group and the large liturgical assembly has to be redefined as a gathering of groups. The small group is a key factor in promoting participation in the large one; an occasional coming together allows for integration in the greater whole.

The meaning and function of worship as thus redefined in the light of secularization corresponds closely with that to be found in the N T, which, after all, belongs to the period before the emergence of Christendom. The disintegration of the latter, although producing a crisis, allows for a more radical interpretation of worship, in the sense that it compels theologians to reassess their roots. Clearly this understanding has to be embodied in new forms, but that is a subject to be considered elsewhere (*see* **Experimental Forms of Worship**).

J. G. Davies, *Every Day God*, 1973; W. Vos, ed., *Worship and Secularization* (Studia Liturgica 7, 2/3), 1970; J. F. White, *The Worldliness of Worship*, 1967; *Worship in the City of Man* (Liturgical Conference, Washington D.C.), 1966.

EDITOR

Sentences

Short passages of scripture read out during services. They have two separate purposes. First, they may serve as an introduction to or commentary upon the next stage in the act of worship. So the sentences in the 1552 *BCP* for use at the beginning of morning and evening prayer preface the confession and absolution with scriptural thoughts of penitence and of the assurance of forgiveness. Similarly the sentences used in association with the funeral procession declare the nature of death and the hope of resurrection. The sentences that accompany the offertory (q.v.) frequently stress the necessity of almsgiving.

The second purpose for which sentences may be used is to relate a particular act of worship with seasons, festivals, saints' days and other special occasions.

EDITOR

Septuagesima *see* Quinquagesima

Sepulchre *see* Easter Garden

Sequence
see Chants of the Proper of the Mass

Sermon

The preaching of a sermon in the liturgy is rooted in the synagogue practice (*cf.* Luke 4.16ff.; Acts 13.14ff.) of following the readings of scripture by exposition. Paul is related to have discoursed at Troas before breaking the bread (Acts 20.7ff.) and, although not specified, the prior reading of scripture is probably to be presumed. Preaching by prophets or by tongue-speakers was a feature of the assemblies at Corinth (I Cor. 14). The fourth gospel says that the Paraclete 'will take of mine and declare it to you' (John 16.14f.), suggesting that in the Christian assemblies the Jesus tradition, as well as the O T scriptures, became preaching material. The evident intention of Paul that his letters should be read in the assembly (I Cor. 16.22-24; *cf.* Col. 4.16) led to the reading and exposition of 'apostolic' writings also.

In the pre-Nicene church the bishop succeeded the prophet as the preacher of the sermon after the reading of the lections, as he also recited the great eucharist prayer (*cf. Mart. Pol.* 16 where the bishop is called a 'prophetic teacher'). (For a second-century bishop's understanding of his preaching *see* Irenaeus, *Adv. Haer.* I, x, 2.) An example of such liturgical preaching has survived in Melito of Sardis' homily *On the Passion*.

After Nicea the sermon continued to be a normal part of the liturgy. Thus, for Egypt, Serapion (*c.*340) instructs the bishop to pray for the Holy Spirit to assist him in proclaiming the message of the scriptures to the congregation.

During the dark ages a number of factors (mass conversions, the multiplication of presbyteral masses, the decay in educational standards, the Western development of low mass) contributed to the decay of preaching, so that the sermon ceased to be a normal part of the liturgy.

Medieval revivals of preaching (e.g., the friars) occurred largely outside the context of the liturgy, and it was devotional and moralistic rather than expository. The conservative Reformers sought to re-establish a liturgical sermon (*cf.* Luther's 'postils' and the rubric of the *BCP* requiring a sermon), but although there was much expository preaching in the Reformation churches, its integral relation to the liturgy was obscured in Protestant orthodoxy, pietism and rationalism. In reaction, the nineteenth-century liturgical revival in Anglicanism was often accompanied by a depreciation of preaching. Only with the twentieth-century Liturgical Movement (q.v.) has the sermon come to be understood once more as an integral part of the liturgy in which the word of God read in the lections is proclaimed for the present and becomes the material of the thanksgiving (*cf.* Vatican II, *Constitution on the Sacred Liturgy*, IV.35).

Y. Brilioth, *Landmarks in the History of Preaching*, 1950; G. Dix, *The Shape of the Liturgy*, [2]1945; B. S. Easton and H. C. Robbins, *The Eternal Word in the Modern World*, 1937; D. Ritschl, *A Theology of Proclamation*, 1960.

R. H. FULLER

Server

Though not ordained, the server performs many of the functions which originally belonged to the office of acolyte (q.v.). He prepares the altar and sanctuary before the eucharist, makes or leads the responses, brings the bread and wine to the celebrant at the offertory, etc. In the Roman Catholic Church only male persons are permitted to act as servers, and most Anglicans follow the same custom. In the Church of England the term is loosely used to describe any lay person who assists the officiant at any service and in practice the modern server has inherited many of the functions of the parish clerk.

P. HINCHLIFF

Seventh-day Adventist Worship

According to Seventh-day Adventist belief and practice, public worship is the corporate assembly of the community of faith for the adoration and praise of God, for thanksgiving, sacrifice and communion. 'The duty to worship God is based upon the fact that He is the Creator' (E. G. White, *The Great Controversy between Christ and Satan*, [1900], p. 436). Worship is the wholeheated response of the creature to his Creator and Redeemer, otherwise the coming together of worshippers is of no avail (*see* Matt. 15.8, 9). Worship involves an attitude of mind and heart which enables man to love God with all his being. Adventists recall that Christ said this was the fulfilment of the first great commandment. True worship is the fruit of the working of the Holy Spirit and is tied to conduct based on willing obedience to all God's requirements, for 'without obedience to his commandments, no worship can be pleasing to God' (White, *loc cit; see* Matt. 15.3-9; I John 5.3 and Prov. 28.9). The experience of worship must merge into a worshipping life.

In contrast to most other Christians, Seventh-day Adventists assemble for the weekly divine worship service on Sabbath, the seventh day of the week. They believe that the biblical Sabbath is a weekly memorial of God's creative act as recorded in the OT and of Christ's redemptive or re-creative act in the NT. The importance of the Sabbath as a day of rest and worship is that it keeps ever present the true reason why worship is due to God – because he is the Creator and Redeemer. The Sabbath, therefore, in Adventist theology, lies at the very foundation of Christian worship and continues to have heterocentric significance for modern man. The historical process which brought about a change in the *day* of worship also modified the *way* of worship (*see* N. F. Pease, *And Worship Him*, pp. 25-35). While Adventists have no quarrel with the dictum *lex adorandi est lex credendi*, they further believe that the worship of the church never rises higher than its theology, for worship is also a reflection of theology.

Because Adventist worship is 'free', charismatic, rather than liturgical, the emphasis is on extempore prayer, circumstantial, spontaneous inspiration, rather than on a formal liturgy and set prayers. However, the *Seventh-day Adventist Church Manual* does provide three suggested orders of worship and guidelines. On certain occasions, such as marriage, burial and ordination services and the Lord's Supper, the service is more formal.

Ceremonial is usually quite limited. Vestments are not used, except on occasion academic gowns and choir and baptismal robes. In some churches there is a choir procession. When the platform party (consisting customarily of the minister and one or more lay elders) steps up to the pulpit they kneel in silent prayer, while the congregation stands or remains seated (in some churches the congregation kneels). Adventists believe that usually the most appropriate and reverential attitude in prayer is shown in the bending of the knee. In public worship both ministers and congregation kneel for prayer facing the pulpit, whence go forth messages from God's holy word.

After an organ prelude, the service may begin with a scriptural or musical call to worship or a hymn. Invocation, hymns, one scripture lesson (either from the OT or the NT), pastoral prayer, offering, special music and sermon follow in one order or another. After the benediction is pronounced there may be an organ postlude. While the pastoral prayer represents perhaps the 'holiest exercise of the whole service' (*Seventh-day Adventist Church Manual*, p. 113), the reading and expounding of the scriptures constitute the central act of Adventist divine worship. For this reason the pulpit is normally in the centre of the rostrum, with the communion table in front.

The Seventh-day Adventist Church generally pays less attention than do more liturgical churches in worship services to the 'church year'. However, for over half a century it has had its own yearly calendar, with considerable emphasis on evangelistic outreach. Approximately forty special days, weeks and offerings are included.

The ethos of Seventh-day Adventist worship is best conveyed in the idea of a closely knit *koinonia of believers*, meeting for adoration, consecration and communion and desiring in unity to pattern their lives in closer harmony with the will of God and increase the church's evangelistic witness in preparation for the Second Advent of Christ. The intention of the service is to make the power of saving grace a joint reality in the life of the congregation.

W. R. Beach, *Dimensions in Salvation*, 1963, pp. 183-192; Harold B. Hannum, *Music and Worship*, 1969; 'Highways of Worship', *Sabbath School Lesson Quarterly*, Adult Division, No. 307, First quarter, 1972; *Manual for Ministers*, 1965; N. F. Pease, *And Worship Him*, 1967; *Seventh-day Adventist Church Manual*, 1967; E. G. White, *The Desire of Ages*, 1946, pp. 157-189; E. G. White, *Testimonies for the Church*, V, 1948, pp. 491-500.

B. B. BEACH

Sexagesima *see* Quinquagesima

Sext *see* Canonical Hours

Shinto Worship

Shinto, the traditional national religion of Japan, is of particular importance in the comparative study of worship in that of all the world's 'greater' religions it is the one nearest to a 'natural' religion; in the sense in which a Westerner understands the terms, it has no founder, no canonical scriptures, no creeds, and no developed dogmatic theology. The word *shinto* itself means 'the way of the gods', but the word *kami*, translated as 'god' or 'gods', has a much wider connotation than the translation normally bears in Western languages; in the words of a distinguished Shinto scholar, 'the term is an honorific for noble, sacred spirits which implies a sense of adoration for their virtues and authority. All beings have such spirits, so in a sense all beings can be called *kami*.' Shinto worship, then, is the worship of divinity perceived in and through the whole of creation; in Western terms it is both pantheistic and polytheistic. The whole of life, properly lived, is regarded as an act of worship; its worshipful character is ensured by specific ceremonial acts of worship at particular times and in particular places, notably by the daily devotions which a devout Shintoist performs before the domestic shrine (*kami-dana*, literally 'god-shelf') in his home, and his participation in the services celebrated on the many festivals in public temples or shrines, as well as by more informal devotional visits to the latter on other occasions.

There are about 100,000 Shinto shrines in Japan. While there is no linguistic ground for the common practice of translating *jinja* as 'shrine' rather than as 'temple', it does perhaps make clearer the essential nature of these sanctuaries, which are regarded primarily as divine dwelling-places, and only consequently as places of meeting for worship. The original shrines appear to have been 'natural' holy places – sacred mountains, sacred forests and so forth – without added buildings; the persistence of the *himorogi*, or small enclosure containing a sacred tree, appears to witness to the next stage in the development of the shrine. The great majority of shrines today, however, take the form of an enclosure containing a complex, simple or elaborate, of buildings; where possible, surroundings of natural beauty and impressiveness are chosen, and even in the great modern conurbations the attempt is made to provide a shrine with an attractive garden enclosure.

The centre of the shrine is the symbol of the *kami* to whom it is dedicated (which may take any of a number of forms, but is usually not a representative image), in which the spirit or power of the *kami* is believed to dwell in a particular manner for the benefit of the worshippers, and which is enshrined in the *honden* or sanctuary. The other principal buildings common to most shrines are the *heiden* or hall of offerings, and the *haiden* or hall of prayer. Other buildings of various kinds are also found in the enclosure; a structure which is universal is the *torii* or sacred gateway which marks each of the public entrances to the enclosure.

Shinto worship comprises a great and rich variety of observances, ranging from the extremely simple to the extremely elaborate. The regular forms of worship, however, whether simple or elaborate, always include four essential elements – purification, offering, prayer, and a sacred meal. They are seen at their simplest in the daily private devotions at home: the worshipper washes his hands and rinses his mouth, places a fresh food offering before the symbol of the *kami*, stands or sits before the shrine, and prays briefly as he will, bowing before and after; the food offering is removed and served at a later meal. When he wishes to pay his devotions at a shrine, the worshipper washes with particular care, puts on clean linen, on arrival at the shrine removes his outdoor clothes, and purifies his mouth and hands with holy water, proceeds to the hall of prayer, places an offering (today usually money) in the box provided, and prays, as at home, as he will; he may also request the celebration of a votive office by one of the priests, for which he makes a small offering. Offices of this kind are frequently requested, on all kinds of occasions, both by individuals and by groups. The regular shrine services, which commonly centre round morning and evening offerings of food, follow approximately the same pattern as the domestic devotions of the faithful, although each of their constituent parts is, of course, more formal and more elaborate. Most elaborate of all are the observances of festivals, of which there are a great number, and which, as many of them are of a local character, vary greatly from place to place in accordance with the traditions of different shrines. Those taking part, especially the officiating priests, prepare themselves by rituals of purification, and by a period of abstinence and recollection which can vary from half an hour to a week or more; the offerings of food are numerous and complicated, and presented with solemn ceremony accompanied by the playing of sacred music; and often sacred dances are performed. Processions, either within the shrine enclosure or through the streets, are a prominent feature of many festivals, as are also traditional entertainments of various kinds, which are regarded both as an offering to the *kami* and as a carnival for the worshippers.

Lack of space precludes even the mention of many important and interesting features of Shinto worship, but two basic characteristics of the whole of its rich variety of liturgical observance stand out. The first is the essential simplicity and 'naturalness' of Shinto rites, even of the most elaborate; the second is their high aesthetic quality – beauty, as both a manifestation of divinity and a tribute to it, is sought for, and commonly achieved, in order to express both the transcendence and immanence of the divine, and the power of the divine to transfigure the whole of life.

J. Herbert, *Shinto*, 1967.

W. JARDINE GRISBROOKE

Sick, Visitation of the

The Sarum 'order for visiting a sick man' begins with nine prayers for the sick man's recovery, for which scriptural precedents are freely invoked; it is nowhere suggested that his illness is due to sin. At first there is no hint that recovery is unlikely, but before long he is told that he is 'about to go the way of all flesh' (hence the name *viaticum*). So when he has professed his faith, he is exhorted to have hope and charity, and to make a full confession, since soon he will not be able to do so. No penance is given: instead, he is to give alms. Two absolutions and two more collects for renewal and restoration to the church end the service, which may be followed immediately by extreme unction (q.v.). After this, the priest administers communion; if the sick man is too ill to receive in a seemly way, the priest assures him, 'only believe, and you have eaten'.

Popular opinion in the Middle Ages regarded unction as a sign of terminal illness rather than as a means to health, and attached gross superstitions to it. But the service was certainly intended for chronic illness also, and one bishop suggested that weekly communion and yearly unction was sufficient.

As usual, Cranmer greatly abbreviated the medieval rite, keeping, for instance, only two of the nine collects. These are followed by an exhortation to acceptance of suffering, based on Heb. 12.6-10,. which is also the proper gospel. This introduces a new view of illness, that it is God's will for purposes of discipline. The sick man's faith is tested by putting the creed to him in interrogatory form, as in baptism; after which the minister is to exhort him to forgive others, make reparation, make his will, and discharge all his debts. All this is included in being 'in charity with all the world', but no mention of hope is kept. The sick man is then to 'make a special confession, if he feel his conscience troubled with any weighty matter': as in the communion service, it is not regarded as normal and mandatory. The absolution still speaks of Christ's 'authority committed to me'. Unction (of forehead or breast only) is accompanied by a collect assembled from four separate Sarum prayers, on the themes of recovery, forgiveness, and grace to withstand temptations.

Two methods are suggested for the communion of the sick: the priest should either reserve sufficient 'at the open communion', or say the whole service in the house in the short form appointed for weekdays. In the latter case there is a proper psalm, collect, epistle, and gospel. Rubrics lay down that there must always be 'some of his own house, or else of his neighbours' to communicate with the sick man. If he is unable to receive, he must be instructed that 'if he do truly repent . . . and stedfastly believe that Jesus Christ hath suffered . . . for him . . . he doth eat and drink spiritually . . .'.

Bucer regarded the service as 'agreeing sufficiently with holy scripture', and commended the practice of communicating the sick directly from the Lord's table, rather than from the reserved sacrament. Peter Martyr, on the other hand, would only approve the use of the complete service in the house. His view prevailed, and the first method is omitted in the 1552 BCP. Unction, being too closely bound up with superstitious ideas, also disappears completely. Curiously enough, the absolution remains untouched.

The service seems never to have become generally acceptable, and Canon 67 of 1604 says that the minister shall instruct and comfort the sick 'in their distress according to the Order of the Communion Book, if he be no preacher; or if he be a preacher, then as he shall think most needful and convenient'. Individual services have survived by Lancelot Andrewes, John Cosin, Jeremy Taylor, and Denis Granville, which shows that the liberty offered by the canon was readily accepted, and there is abundant evidence of confession in articulo mortis throughout the seventeenth century.

In 1662, in response to Puritan criticisms, the minister is directed to move the sick man to make his confession, and absolution is only to be given 'if he humbly and heartily desire it'. The second collect was enlarged to stress the need for faith and repentance, and the third to include prayer for the presence of the Spirit. Most important of all, four new prayers by Robert Sanderson were added. In these there is no suggestion that illness is God's will, and the titles imply that the service may be used in cases of chronic illness as well as terminal.

Even these changes proved insufficient, and demands for an improved office continued to be made. In recent times organizations such as the Guild of St Raphael have put out their own unofficial forms. In the 1928 BCP the service was printed in five sections, as suggested by W. H. Frere. The first exhortation is replaced by a list of subjects upon which the minister may make an exhortation of his own. New material includes a form of confession, a litany, two prayers from Sarum, and 'Go forth upon thy journey, Christian soul'. An appendix suggests twenty-five collects, sixteen psalms, and forty passages of scripture as especially useful. Provision was made for reservation (q.v.). In this form the service is enormously improved, and was adopted by other revisions; but, as has been pointed out, the result really belongs to a manual for parish priests rather than to a *BCP*. This may well be true of any attempt to provide for a private occasion of this character.

The Roman rite, now in process of revision, has a form for communion of the sick who are in danger of death, and another for extreme unction (q.v.). The service of visitation consists of Pss. 6, 16, 20, 86, 91, between which is read a healing miracle from each of the four gospels in turn, followed by a collect. The penitential psalms and the litany of the saints are also appointed for use in the sickroom.

F. E. Brightman, *The English Rite*, 1915, I, pp. cxxv, cxxvi, clxiv, ccxx, ccxxi; II, pp. 818-847; A. J. Collins, *Manuale Sarum,* 1960, pp. 97-114; William Maskell, *Monumenta Ritualia Ecclesiae Anglicanae*, 1846, I, pp. 66-95.

G. J. CUMING

Silent Prayer

Silent prayer within the liturgy falls into three categories: (1) periods of silent prayer which are integral to the structure of the service; (2) the silent, or nearly silent (technically 'secret'), recitation of certain prescribed prayers of private devotion by one or other of the ministers; (3) the similar recitation of prayers which should properly be recited aloud, or at least were originally so recited.

The second of these categories calls for little comment: such prayers are to be found in most of the historic liturgies, in which they were inserted in the Middle Ages. The most outstanding example of the third category is the eucharistic prayer itself, large parts of which are recited secretly in many of the historic liturgies.

This custom appears to have arisen from the desire to express and evoke an attitude towards the eucharistic mystery of awe and fear, the use of the secret voice being psychologically effective to this end. Such an attitude certainly existed to some extent from the very beginnings of Christian worship, as is clear from I Cor. 11.26-33, but it was in fourth- and fifth-century Syria that it came to dominate the approach to the eucharist, and it is in a Syrian document of the end of the fifth century, *The Liturgical Homilies of Narsai*, that we have the first definite evidence for the silent recitation of the anaphora

(q.v.). By the second half of the sixth century the practice had become widespread, although it was as yet by no means universal: in 565 the Emperor Justinian found it necessary to legislate against it. His legislation produced no lasting effect, and by the end of the eighth century the practice had become the established usage in the Byzantine rite. The first definite evidence of it in the West is found in the second Roman *Ordo* of almost exactly the same date. It became and remained the normal usage in the Roman rite until 1966, when the recitation of the canon aloud was again prescribed.

The silent recitation of the eucharistic prayer is undoubtedly a corrupt practice, but however undesirable it may be liturgically, the spread and persistence of the practice bear witness to an evident devotional need for silence and for its psychological fruits in worship. This need should, however, be provided for in other ways.

Among the possibilities are the provision of a space for silent prayer between any bidding to prayer and the formal prayer following it, of a space for silent meditation after readings from scriptures and after communion, and of a space for silent recollection between major sections of any service. Some of these provisions have been included in several recent liturgical reforms, and it is to be hoped that they will become more thorough and more widespread, for in an age of far too little silence they could be of great devotional and psychological value.

W. JARDINE GRISBROOKE

Sitting *see* Postures (2*d*)

South India Church
see Church of South India Worship

Spirituals

The spiritual was born in the American Negro Christian community. Opinions vary regarding its origin and function. It is considered as a misinterpreted hymn of the white Christians (G. P. Jackson), as a 'confession of faith' of the Negro church (S. Läuchli, T. Lehmann and many others), as the 'clearest exponent of the Negro's real self' (H. W. Odum), as a reminiscence of historical events in the history of the American Negro (M. M. Fisher), as a protest against social injustice (J. Lovell), as an adaptation of African songs (H. E. Krehbiel, W. E. Burghardt Du Bois), as originating in the camp meetings (q.v.) of the white revival movement (B. T. Washington), as the products of Negro bards like 'singing Johnson' and 'Ma White' (J. W. Johnson), and a blending of American and European melodies with African rhythm (E. M. v. Hornbostel, B. Nettl). Whatever the history of the spiritual, it is the origin of at least four musical trends today. (1) The different styles of jazz, including the blues. (2) It has been taken up, greatly changed and adapted to the white ear in the Pentecostal churches, particularly in USA, where Pentecostalism originated in a Negro church in Los Angeles and where some of the earliest Pentecostal hymn writers were Negroes. (3) It is further cultivated in a manner faithful to the original tradition in the American Negro Pentecostal churches and in some Negro Baptist churches. (4) Attempts have been made to adapt it to European and American traditional church music (example: Michael Tippett, *A Child of Our Time*, 1944). There is great controversy whether the Negro spiritual has a place in a non-Negro church service, a controversy which becomes even sharper if the spirituals are translated into French or German, or if they are sung in English in a non-English congregation.

Recently church musicians recognized that it was useless to introduce the songs of a contemporary, yet foreign sub-culture. Some of them therefore discovered a popular (not a pop-) musical language in the sub-culture of their own language groups and created new masses, ballads and community hymns (e.g. in Czechoslovakia, East and West Germany, Scandinavia). Some of these songs were created not by church musicians, but by folksingers and chansonniers who took up biblical topics in their chansons (Latin America, France).

T. Lehmann, *Negro Spirituals, Geschichte und Theologie*, 1965; J. Lowens, in *Musik in Geschichte und Gegenwart*, XII, 1965, pp. 1050-4; R. M. Stevenson, in *New Catholic Encyclopaedia*, XIII, 1966, pp. 609-10.

W. J. HOLLENWEGER

Stations of the Cross

Since the Peace of the Church under Constantine (313), many Christians have wished to walk where Christ walked in the week of his passion. Crowds of pilgrims have achieved

this over the centuries, but for the majority it was an unrealizable dream.

Some churches in the Middle Ages had chapels to commemorate an event in the passion of Jesus and, from these, the Franciscans, since the fifteenth century, have developed the devotion that has come to be called the Stations of the Cross. The word 'station' (*statio*) implies either 'standing still' or 'gathering at a place'.

It was not until the seventeenth century that stations came to be erected in churches, ranged at intervals around the walls. They took the form of wooden crosses, with a representation of an event in the passion underneath to fix the incident in mind. They are now almost universal in Roman Catholic churches of the Latin rite and also in many Anglican churches.

At first, the number of stations varied considerably, and at Birnau on Lake Constance there are eight superb examples of the rococo period (1724). In 1731, the number was finally fixed by Clement XII at fourteen: nine commemorating events related in the gospels and five from early tradition.

The devotion can be either public or private. Prayers are said at each station, with a short meditation on the scene from the passion. When it is public and taking the form of a church service, a verse from the hymn *Stabat Mater* is sung between each of the stations. An English version of this hymn, 'At the Cross her station keeping', can be found in *Hymns Ancient and Modern Revised* (1950), no. 118.

Every Friday in the year a Franciscan makes the stations along the authentic Way of the Cross in Jerusalem, although the ground has risen considerably since the time of our Lord. Since 1773, it is possible for invalids, prisoners and those at sea to make the devotion on a crucifix blessed for the purpose.

A. A. KING

Stole *see* Vestments (1*d*)

Stoup

A vessel for holding holy water placed near the entrance of churches, into which the faithful who enter dip the fingers of the right hand, blessing themselves with the sign of the cross. Holy water stoups (also called stocks) are probably derived from the fountains in the atrium of the older basilicas (e.g. old St

Peter's, Rome) in which those who were entering the church washed their hands and faces. They seem to have come into more general use from the ninth century, when the custom of sprinkling the people with holy water known as the *Asperges* (q.v.) before the Sunday mass became widespread. The blessing of the water into which salt was thrown crosswise with an invocation took place before this ceremony, and the stoups at the entrance to the church were replenished. The significance of the ceremony of holy water was to remind the worshipper of the promises made at his baptism and that the water had cleansed not only his body but also his soul for which Christ shed his blood.

In English medieval churches the stoup is usually found in a niche inside the porch in the form of a stone basin. But in France and Italy stoups are found inside the church itself, often standing on a stem or pillar. Holy-water stoups are in use in the Roman Catholic Church and in the churches of the Anglican Communion there has been a revival of their use.

F. Bond, *The Chancel of English Churches*, 1916.

C. E. POCKNEE

Subdeacon

The office seems to have originated in Western Christendom in the middle of the third century and its function seems to have been chiefly to provide assistance to the deacon. The principal liturgical duties of the subdeacon were to read the epistle and to prepare the elements and vessels for the offertory. The office was regarded as one of the minor orders in the West until the thirteenth century and still is so regarded in the East. In the Roman Catholic Church the subdiaconate is now the lowest of the major orders, and those admitted to it are normally bound to celibacy. It is usually no more than a stage through which candidates for the priesthood pass, and the vestigial ceremonial duties of the subdeacon at a high mass are performed by a priest, a deacon or even a layman. The office has recently been revived in some parts of the Anglican Communion where it is the equivalent of that of a lay reader (q.v.) with additional authority to administer the chalice, a curious device, since the administration of the elements does not seem to have been a traditional part of

the subdeacon's duties.

P. HINCHLIFF

Suffrages

Suffrages (Lat. *suffragia*, prayers seeking favour or support) are found in the divine office in the historic Western rites, and in some rites derived from them, e.g. in morning and evening prayer in the *BCP*. They are always petitionary, sometimes intercessory; they are usually couched in general, but sometimes in particular terms; they are normally in the form of versicles and responses, commonly include the Lord's Prayer, and usually conclude with a collect or collects.

Suffrages were no part of the original Roman offices; they were added to them when the latter were adopted in the Frankish lands, where they were probably part of the Gallican offices, and were then accepted at Rome. Their use has been all but completely suppressed in the latest reform of the Roman breviary.

The suffrages in the morning and evening offices of the *BCP*, comprising the material from the creed to the third collect, are typical; they are largely derived from those found in the Sarum books.

W. JARDINE GRISBROOKE

Sunday

The Lord's Day is the foundation of the entire structure of the Christian year. In the Jewish system, the days of the week were known simply as the first day, the second day, and so on. The last day of the week had a title, the Sabbath, and, dependent on this, Friday was called the preparation. The Sabbath set the pattern of a weekly day of worship, but in Christianity it was 'the first day of the week' (Acts 20.7) which took this position. By the end of the first century that designation had given place to one which more adequately conveyed the day's significance – the Lord's Day. The use of the name Sunday dates from about the middle of the second century. In 321 the official recognition by the Roman state of Sunday as the day of Christian worship and as a day of public rest meant that the Sabbath had now been incorporated into and transformed by the Christian tradition.

As the Sabbath provided the model of a weekly day of worship, so its general influence is demonstrated by the fact that for a considerable period the Christian Sunday began about 6 p.m. on the Saturday evening, the hour at which the Sabbath began on the Friday evening. Centuries passed before the old Semitic reckoning from sunset yielded completely to the Roman conception of the day as beginning at midnight. About the middle of the fourth century the *Testament of our Lord* refers to the evening as the beginning of the day. The 'eves' of the great festivals represent the survival of the beginning of the Semitic day, the 'eve' being part of the festival itself. It was natural enough that when this reckoning had disappeared from common use, it should remain in connection with the outstanding days of the Christian year.

The relationship between the Lord's Day and the Sabbath of the old covenant serves as the context within which to emphasize the immense difference between these liturgical days. The gospel narrative of the resurrection furnishes the true normative use of the designation 'the first day of the week' as a proper name for the Christian day of worship. When we remember that primitive worship took place at an early hour of the morning, the binding link between Sunday and the resurrection becomes more obvious. Late in the fourth century at Jerusalem the central service of Christendom, consisting of the reading and preaching of the word and the celebration of the sacrament, was held at daybreak. Thus the true note of the Lord's Day must always be joy, thanksgiving, victory. It is surely from the lordship of Jesus Christ, made manifest in the resurrection on 'the first day of the week' (Mark 16.2), that the title 'the Lord's Day' is ultimately derived. The early church never lost this conception of Sunday as the sign of the inbreaking of the eternal order of God, and it remained a day of praise and triumph. Fasting and the penitential observance of kneeling in prayer were strictly forbidden.

The profound revolution which substituted the Christian Sunday for the Jewish Sabbath took place within the first generation of the church's life. Certainly by the middle of the sixth decade when Paul, writing to Corinth, refers to 'the first day of every week' (I Cor. 16.2), the Lord's Day must long have been supreme. In the second century there was a group of Jewish Christians who celebrated the Sabbath as well as Sunday. But the church in general would tolerate no compromise and delivered itself from the impoverishment of Judaizing Christianity. Early in the third century there is the hint of a tendency to make the Sabbath a liturgical day, but it is in the fourth century that the whole question moves into the foreground. The liturgical commemoration of the Sabbath brought with it the holy communion on that day. It can scarcely be doubted that, although the celebrations on the station days (*see* **Good Friday**) have a longer history, those on Saturdays and other days are the result of developments in the fourth century. It is when we appreciate the eucharistic unity of the passion and victory of Christ Jesus that we understand the uniqueness of Sunday. To set weekdays as such beside Sunday as days for celebrating the holy communion served to obscure the uniqueness of Sunday and may have affected the understanding of the sacrament, for it weakened the connection between the resurrection, the Lord's Day and the eucharist.

A. A. McArthur, *The Evolution of the Christian Year*, 1953; H. B. Porter, *The Day of Light. The Biblical and Liturgical Meaning of Sunday*, 1960; W. Rordorf, *Sunday*, 1968.

A. A. MCARTHUR

Super Oblata

Since the mid-fifth century, the offertory ceremony in the Roman rite has been concluded with a prayer called originally, and again since 1969, the *oratio super oblata* ('prayer over the offerings'), but for many centuries called the *secreta* ('secret'). As the latter name first appears in France and Germany, where the custom of saying the prayer in a low voice (*secreto*) originated, it probably refers to this custom, although other meanings are possible. At Rome it was anciently sung, and the singing or saying aloud of it has been restored in the new *Ordo Missae* of 1969.

The prayer, which varies according to the day, is in form a variant of the collect type; its basic content is always a prayer for the divine acceptance of the gifts just placed on the altar within the context of the eucharistic mystery about to be accomplished. A prayer parallel to the *oratio super oblata* in function and content is found in a corresponding place in most of the historic liturgies.

J. A. Jungmann, *The Mass of the Roman Rite*,

II, 1955, pp. 90-97.
W. JARDINE GRISBROOKE

Superintendent

The Greek term *episcopos*, from which 'bishop' is derived, means 'overseer'. In the Reformation period, when a term was wanted which would express the element of oversight while avoiding the hierarchical and prelatical overtones of 'bishop' (q.v.), the title 'superintendent' seemed an obvious choice. Many of the churches of the Reformation used the term. In German Lutheranism there were superintendents until the 1920s, when the title of bishop was revived. In the Church of Scotland, five superintendents were appointed in 1561 and they, with three bishops who threw in their lot with the Reformation, exercised oversight over other clergy. The superintendent was required to minister in a congregation of his own besides overseeing the work of other men. The office was subsequently discontinued, and there has been a good deal of controversy about whether it was intended as a reformed and permanent, if limited, episcopate or whether it was a temporary expedient made necessary as ministers could not be found for every parish. In the Methodist Church the superintendent minister is the minister in charge of a circuit.

P. HINCHLIFF

Surplice *see* Vestments (2c)

Synaxis

The name *synaxis* (Greek 'meeting' or 'assembly'), anciently used in the Christian church of any meeting for public worship, is today normally used only of that service which is the most ancient and archetypal of them all, the office of readings and prayers which precedes the celebration of the eucharist, and which has indeed, from a very early date, come to be reckoned as a part of the eucharistic liturgy.

The close relationship of *synaxis* to *synagogue* (Greek 'gathering' and hence 'gathering place'), although it is intrinsically no more than a grammatical one, serves to underline the essential character of the first part of the eucharistic liturgy, as an inheritance from, and development of, the worship of the synagogue. The earliest Christians, as we learn from the Acts of the Apostles, continued to worship in the synagogue, while celebrating the eucharist in their own houses; when they were expelled from the synagogue they prefixed the essential elements of the synagogue service to the eucharist, and made one service of the two (except on certain occasions when the eucharist was preceded by some other function, e.g. the baptismal vigil at Easter).

The synagogue service was composed basically of three elements – reading from the scriptures, psalmody, and prayer, and these three are from the beginning the constant basic elements of the Christian synaxis, which is characterized by Jungmann as essentially a biblical instruction. It appears originally to have opened abruptly with the readings, preceded by no more than the exchange of a mutual greeting between the president (bishop or presbyter) and the assembly. Neither the number nor the order of the readings can be definitely gathered from the earliest evidence, but it seems likely, from a comparison with the synagogue, and from the evidently archaic arrangements of the synaxis which survive in some of the Eastern rites, as well as on certain days in the Roman and Byzantine rites, that there were originally at least four readings in a normal synaxis – from the law, the prophets, the epistles, and the gospels. From earliest times the readings appear to have been followed by a sermon expounding them. From the fourth century onwards there was a universal and rapid tendency towards disuse of the readings from the OT, and nearly everywhere in Christendom the ordinary synaxis came to include only two readings, the epistle and the gospel. During the Middle Ages the sermon also came to be a less frequent feature of the synaxis than in earlier times.

The earliest form of psalmody at the synaxis of which we have any evidence is the singing of selected psalms in a responsorial manner (i.e. the psalm sung by a soloist, and an unvarying refrain sung after each verse by the congregation) between the readings. This survives in all the historic rites, although commonly in a very reduced form (e.g. the gradual – since 1969 replaced by a return to a more extended responsorial psalm – and alleluia of the Roman rite, and the prokeimenon and alleluia of the Byzantine rite) (*see* **Liturgies** 2).

The element of prayer in the early synaxis took the form of more or less extended intercessions which followed the readings and sermon. The oldest formal arrangement of these is probably that still found in the Roman rite on Good Friday – a series of biddings by the deacon, each followed by a period of silent prayer by the congregation and a collect by the president or a concelebrant presbyter; a parallel form still exists in the Alexandrine rite. From the late fourth century onwards a litany (q.v.) became a more common form in most parts of the Christian world; in the Roman rite the older form was replaced by a litany (elsewhere in the service) late in the fifth century, and by the seventh century this also had fallen out of use, with the result that with the spread of the Roman rite in the former Gallican lands the common prayers of the synaxis disappeared for many centuries over the greater part of Western Christendom.

While between the fourth and eighth centuries there was an almost universal tendency to reduce the quantity of readings and psalmody, there was a simultaneous universal tendency to add secondary matter to the synaxis: notably, parallel introductory rites developed everywhere during this period. The order and contents of these vary considerably, but there are constant features, such as the introit or entrance psalm, an introductory hymn of prayer and praise – e.g. the *Gloria in excelsis* or great doxology (q.v.) in the Roman rite and the *Trisagion* (q.v.) in the Byzantine rite – and an introductory prayer by the president – e.g. the collect of the day in all the Western rites and the prayer which accompanies the *Trisagion* in the Byzantine rite. During the Middle Ages a further parallel development led to the widespread prefixing of preparatory rites of various kinds to the introductory rite itself – e.g. the enarxis (q.v.) of the Byzantine rite, and the preparatory prayers and confession of the Roman rite.

Modern revisions of the synaxis, whether in the great historic rites themselves or in the post-Reformation liturgies (in most of which the principal features of the synaxis, so far as they had been preserved during the Middle Ages, survived in a recognizable form), tend to concentrate on the restoration of the integrity of its primary elements – readings, psalmody and common prayers – and the rationalization (and in part elimination) of the secondary and tertiary growths of introductory and preparatory matter. In particular there is an all but universal move towards the recovery of the OT material – reading and psalmody – which had come over the centuries to be greatly abbreviated or even, in some post-Reformation liturgies, completely eliminated.

The original relationship between the synaxis and the divine office is an obscure and complex problem, but there seems little doubt that the morning and evening services of the early centuries (corresponding to the mattins and lauds and the vespers of the later office) bore considerably more resemblance to their common synagogal origins with the synaxis than do their later forms: a brief consideration of this question will be found under the heading **Cathedral Office**.

Further information on the synaxis and its component parts will be found in most books dealing with Christian worship in general, and especially in those dealing with the eucharistic liturgies of the several rites.

W. JARDINE GRISBROOKE

Tabernacle

This term has been employed to describe a number of disparate objects.

1. It has been used to describe the silk 'tent' or canopy which covered the pyx (q.v.) suspended over the altar in medieval England and France.

2. The term is applied to niches with a carved canopy which housed the statue of a saint.

3. The term was also used in the Middle Ages for a type of altar-piece with carved niches and having hinged wings.

4. Its more usual application now is to the safe or cupboard which stands in a central position at the back of the altar or immediately over it for the reservation (q.v.) of the blessed sacrament. This is the normal method of reservation in the Roman Catholic Church today; the tabernacle has to be circular in design, so that the whole structure of metal is completely enveloped by a silk or fabric veil of white or the appropriate liturgical colour. The term 'tabernacle' to denote this kind of receptacle fixed to the altar for the reserved sacrament was introduced by the reforming bishop of Verona, Matthew Giberti, about 1525; his ideas were later endorsed by the Council of Trent.

A. A. King and C. E. Pocknee, *Eucharistic Reservation in the Western Church*, 1965.

C. E. POCKNEE

Table Prayers
see Ante-Communion

Tenebrae

A quasi-popular term, found in the Roman books not before the twelfth century, for mattins and lauds of the last three days of Holy Week (q.v.). The reason was that to allow the easier participation of the people, these offices were anticipated to the evening before the day to which they referred (thus *tenebrae* of Maundy Thursday was sung on the evening of Wednesday). The term came into use most probably because the lights (candles) were gradually extinguished in the course of the office and all departed in darkness (*tenebrae*) and silence.

Mattins and lauds of these days were originally simply the ordinary offices sung by monastic or quasi-monastic communities serving the Roman basilicas and other collegiate churches throughout Europe (*see* **Canonical Hours**). In their form they reveal certain primitive features of the Roman (cathedral) office. Thus, there were no hymns, no invitatory, no introductory versicles and responses and the *Gloria Patri* at the end of each psalm was suppressed. Mattins consist of nine psalms and nine readings (Lamentations, patristic readings and NT), the old Roman pattern. The Lamentations were sung to a chant of peculiar poignancy and all the readings were divided by responsories of great musical beauty. They almost certainly derive from the Roman *schola cantorum* of the seventh, eighth and ninth centuries.

These offices are a prolonged meditation on the events of salvation running from the Last Supper to the entombment. The note of betrayal is sounded in Thursday *tenebrae*, the judgment, crucifixion and death of Christ on Friday and his burial and the expectation of his resurrection on Saturday.

A unique feature of the offices of these days was the triangular candlestick which stood in the choir and on which fifteen candles of natural, dark-coloured wax were placed. They were extinguished one by one after each psalm (nine for mattins and five for lauds) until one only remained. During the *Benedictus* this was hidden either behind the altar or elsewhere in the church and when the signal for departure (*strepitus*) was given it was replaced on the top of the candlestick. This has been understood as an anticipated sign of the resurrection, but probably was no more than a way of providing light for the congregation to depart.

The eventual appearance of the part of the breviary giving the Holy Week offices may modify this inevitably provisional statement.

J. D. CRICHTON

Terce *see* Canonical Hours

Thanksgiving *see* Prayer (5)

Three-hours Service

In fourth-century Jerusalem the custom originated by which the events of redemption were celebrated each year on what were believed to be their original sites, and in their original chronological sequence. Accordingly the three hours of Jesus' passion were observed by a service from the sixth to the ninth hour on the day now called Good Friday (q.v.). The bishop presided and the service included readings from all passages of scripture which relate to the passion interspersed with prayers and ending with the passion story from St John's gospel. Although many features of the Jerusalem observances, e.g. Palm Sunday, were adopted throughout Christendom, this particular observance was not, probably because it intruded on the liturgical activities which had already developed in the West, notably the preparation of catechumens (q.v.) for baptism. The three-hours service as it is known today originated in Peru as an extra-liturgical devotion as recently as the late seventeenth century and has since been adopted in many Roman Catholic and Anglican churches. In Peru it consisted in essence of addresses on the seven words from the cross, and this remains the common basis of the service today. But it interferes with the proper observance of the traditional liturgy, and in the Church of England the attempt is sometimes made to observe the three hours with a complete use of the official liturgy, mattins, litany, and ante-communion, and to end with evensong (qq.v.). Changing social patterns, however, make it very uncertain whether it is any longer desirable to adhere to the hours in question, which are commonly understood to be twelve noon to three o'clock, as a means of presenting the Lord's passion either to the church or to the world.

J. G. Davies, *Holy Week*, 1963; J. W. Tyrer, *Historical Survey of Holy Week*, 1932.

E. C. WHITAKER

Thurible

More commonly termed in English *censer*. A metal pan designed to hold heated charcoal upon which powdered or granulated perfumed gums, the most common being *olibanum*, are sprinkled. The most usual form of the censer is now a pan having a cover which is pierced with a number of apertures so that the fumes of the incense may be exuded as the censer is swung to and fro on the chains to which it is attached. The use of incense (q.v.) in pagan religions as well as in OT rites and also its association with the deification of the Roman emperors probably accounts for its rejection by Christians in the first three centuries. It is unlikely, therefore, that the reference to a censer in Rev. 8.5 reflects the custom of Christian worship at the end of the apostolic era. About AD 200, Tertullian in North Africa rejects the use of incense because of its association with emperor worship (*Apol.* 30).

The first definite evidence for the use of incense in Christian worship is at the end of the fourth century in *The Pilgrimage of Etheria*, describing the services in Holy Week and Easter at the Church of the Holy Sepulchre, Jerusalem. Also the Pseudo-Dionysius refers to the act of censing about AD 500. The earliest use of the censer was in processions when it was carried before the bishop at the entrance of the ministers, and also in the procession which preceded the reading of the gospel at the mass. In both these instances its use was probably honorific. This custom may have been derived from imperial usage, since it was customary for torches and incense to be carried before the emperor, and when the bishop acquired a status as a court dignitary in the fourth century this custom may have applied to him. As time went on, the use of the censer was elaborated to include the censing of the ministers and congregation as well as the elements of bread and wine as they were carried in and offered at the altar. After the thirteenth century, with the introduction of the new ceremony of the elevation of the host, the consecrated element was censed as it was lifted up by the celebrant. The censer was also used at the offices of lauds and vespers on festivals.

The use of censers did not entirely cease after the Reformation in England, as the records from the reign of Elizabeth I clearly show, and the use of a censer was maintained at Ely cathedral until 1752. Also a pan with a handle for the use of incense was part of the ceremonies in the coronation processions of all the Stuart kings including James II.

In the Eastern Orthodox Church the censer is used with considerable elaboration not only in the celebration of the eucharistic liturgy, but also in the rites associated with baptisms, marriages and funerals.

Another form of the censer is to be seen in the cathedral at Lyons, France, where at the pontifical high mass a large urn is in use on either side of the altar and these are replenished with incense at certain stages of the progress of the liturgy. The grains of incense are usually kept in a metal container known as a 'boat' on account of its shape.

M. Andrieu, *Les Ordines Romani du haut moyen age*, 5 vols., 1931-61; E. G. C. Atchley, *History of the Use of Incense*, 1909; J. Wickham Legg, *Church Ornaments and their Civil Antecedents*, 1917.

C. E. POCKNEE

Thurifer

The person who, in processions or on liturgical occasions, carries the thurible (q.v.) or censer (a metal brazier hanging from chains and fitted with a lid) in which incense (q.v.) is burnt.

P. HINCHLIFF

Tower

The most familiar use of this term is a stone, brick or wooden structure attached to a church building often containing one or more bells. The term has also been applied to a tower-like vessel used at the eucharist in the Gallican rites. There is some difference of opinion among ecclesiologists as to whether this tower housed the reserved sacrament or whether the bread it contained was for consecration at the eucharist. In our opinion the poem written by Venantius Fortunatus (*Carm.* XX) indicates that the tower given by Felix, Bishop of Bourges, *c.*573, was for the purpose of reservation (q.v.).

C. E. POCKNEE

Tract

The name given to the psalm sung after the
epistle and gradual instead of the alleluia
during Lent and other penitential seasons and
at masses for the dead in the Roman church.
English versions are printed in the *English
Hymnal* under 'Introits and Other Anthems'.

EDITOR

Transept

The transept is the transverse part of a
church at right angles to the nave and usually
inserted between it and the chancel (q.v.).

Transepts originally filled two functions
and can therefore be classified as (1) a
transept-martyrium, which provided a large
space around the tomb of a saint; (2) a
transept-prothesis, which provided an area
for the tables on which the congregation
placed the gifts at the offertory (q.v.).

A second classification, by form instead
of function, allows transepts to be divided
into six groups (*see* Figs. 19-23): (1) *Continuous transept*. The transverse space is
undivided, the colonnades being cut short
to leave an open rectangle, e.g. St Peter's,
Rome. (2) *Cross transept*. The colonnades

Fig. 21   Basilica A, Philippi, Macedonia

Fig. 22   Church of the Nativity,
Bethlehem, Israel

Fig. 23   Hermopolis (Ashmunein), Egypt

Fig. 19   St Peter's, Rome, Italy

Fig. 20   St Menas, Abu Mina, Egypt

are turned at right angles into the wings and
then envelop them on three sides, e.g. St
Menas, Abu Mina. In a reduced cross transept, the colonnades are bent at right angles
and then turn through another to join the
east wall, e.g. Basilica A, Philippi. (3) *Trefoil
transept*. The two extremities of the transept
are provided with apses, and these, with the
sanctuary, produce an integrated design with
three semi-circles, e.g. the Church of the

Nativity, Bethlehem. (4) *Triconch transept.*
This is similar to the former, but nothing
intervenes between the sanctuary and the
transept apses, so that the plan is like that
of a three-leaved clover, e.g. the cathedral
of Hermopolis (Ashmunein). (5) *Dwarf transept.* This form is not discernible from the
plan, since it relates to the elevation and
designates a transverse space whose wings
are lower in height than the nave. (6) *Tripartite transept.* This, too, refers to the
elevation, when the wings are shut off by
arcades from the central area.

EDITOR

Transfiguration

This commemoration on 6 August, deriving
from the Eastern Church, became general in
the west in the fifteenth century. It is not
related to the structure of the liturgical year
formed by the festivals of Christmas, Epiphany, Good Friday, Easter, Ascension and
Pentecost (qq.v.).

A. A. MCARTHUR

Trinity Sunday

This festival is different in character from
those which commemorate the historical
events of salvation. It is also remote in time,
originating in the West in the tenth century.
Late in the following century Pope Alexander
II was not persuaded that the festival was a
valid development, but Rome adopted it in
the fourteenth century.

A. A. MCARTHUR

Trisagion

The name (Greek, lit. 'the thrice-holy') of a
hymn in the Byzantine rite which is sung
after the little entrance (q.v.) at the pre-
eucharistic synaxis (q.v.), its place and purpose corresponding to the *Gloria in excelsis*
(*see* **Doxology**) in the Roman rite. Also used
at many other points in the services of the
Byzantine rite, it consists of the invocation
'Holy God, Holy and Mighty, Holy and
Immortal, have mercy upon us' three times,
followed by the lesser doxology (q.v.) and
in some contexts a final repetition of the
invocation.

The Byzantine form of the *Trisagion* is
occasionally met with in the historic Western
rites also, notably in the Roman rite on Good
Friday at the veneration of the cross. Another form of the *Trisagion*, of a more festal
character, appears to have been in use in the

ancient Hispano-Gallican liturgy, as an acclamation before the singing of the gospel.

The *Trisagion* should *not* be confused with
the *Sanctus* (q.v.); the use of the Latin name
of the *Trisagion* – *Tersanctus* – as a title for
the latter by some writers is a misleading
error.

H. Holloway, *A Study of the Byzantine
Liturgy*, 1933, pp. 59-62.

W. JARDINE GRISBROOKE

Tunicle *see* Vestments (1*g*)

Unction

The anointing of persons and things is
ancient and widely used in a great many
religions, not merely in those of the Mediterranean basin. Various substances (oil, fat,
blood, water, saliva) were used at different
times and in different places with various
significance. Of these, consecration or the
making of a person or thing sacred seems to
have been the dominant one.

This was so in OT. Things, Jacob's stone
(Gen. 28.18), the ark and tabernacle furniture
were consecrated with oil (Ex. 310.25ff.).
Kings were the special object of unction (I
Sam. 10.1ff.; 16.13; etc.) as also were priests
(Lev. 8.12, high priest; Lev. 8.30, other
priests). There is a possible reference to the
anointing of prophets (Ps. 105.15), though
the injunction to anoint Elisha (I Kings
19.16) seems never to have been carried out.
None the less, the consecration with oil with
which 'priests, kings and prophets' were
anointed by God was destined to have a long
history in the Christian liturgy.

In the NT there is a reference to the
apostles' healing with oil (Mark 6.13) and
what in the Catholic tradition is regarded as
a ritual use of oil for healing in James 5.14-15.
However, the key-factor in the use of unction
in the liturgy seems to have been the figure
of Jesus, the Messiah ('Anointed', *Christos*),
who was 'anointed' at his incarnation (Heb.
1.9), for his messianic ministry at baptism
(Mark 1.9-11 and par.), and who was
conscious of the presence of the Spirit with
him in his saving work (Luke 4.16-22). After
his death and resurrection he becomes the
source of the Spirit (Acts 2.33) whom he
sends upon his church. This coming of the

Spirit to the individual Christian is symbolized in the liturgy both by the laying-on of hands and in a great variety of ways by unction. The precise purpose (whether gift, grace or ministry) intended by unction has to be discerned both from the circumstances in which it is given and the words that accompany it. However, the overriding significance of anointing is that it conveys the Spirit of Christ who is at once the source of the Spirit and the exemplar of the life of the Christian.

The relationship between the anointing and the Spirit-filled Christ can be seen in a very striking manner in the post-baptismal unction, usually called chrismation. Apart from the Syrian Church which most probably has never had it (E. C. Whitaker, *Documents of the Baptismal Liturgy*, [2]1970, Introduction), all liturgies with remarkable unanimity have had this rite. The oil used is *chrisma* (from the same verb *chrio* as *Christos*) and it signifies the positive side of baptism, the conformation of the Christian to Christ, his participation in the priestly, royal and prophetic quality of Christ and the giving of the Spirit (*cf.* the prayer of consecration, Roman pontifical, liturgy of the chrism mass). But as in OT unction signified richness and abundance of life, the chrism acquired a very rich symbolism. This is particularly noteworthy in the Eastern Church where from the fourth century onwards chrism was called *myron* (Cyril of Jerusalem, *Cat. Myst.*, III, 2, 3, 7) on account of the many aromatic ingredients that went to its composition. It was accordingly interpreted as 'the good odour of Christ' (*cf.* II Cor. 2.15) which should perfume the life of the Christian who has died and risen with Christ and who henceforth should live with him (*Apostolic Constitutions*, VII, 44). To this the Council of Laodicea adds that it makes the candidate a sharer in the kingdom of God (can. 48). To this the anointing with chrism in confirmation, when it came to be combined with the imposition of hands, adds the significance of completion and the giving of the fullness of the Spirit (*Ap. Trad.*, 22. 1, 2).

The pre-baptismal anointing is more closely related to the culture of the Greco-Roman world where the anointing of athletes before the *agon* was well known. This rite, which is found in every baptismal liturgy until the sixteenth century, signifies the strengthening of the candidate for the struggle with the powers of darkness he will meet in the waters into which he will be plunged. Originally, he was anointed all over as were the ancient wrestlers so that the opponent could not get a firm grip on him – a symbolism that was known to St Gregory the Great. This anointing was really an exorcism and this fact gave its name to the oil which in more recent centuries has been called the 'oil of catechumens'.

In spite of James 5.14-15, the use of unction for the healing of the sick is not attested until the first decades of the third century (*Ap. Trad.* V). The oil is blessed after the eucharistic prayer and is very clearly intended for healing. The prayer envisages the sick persons as not only being anointed with it but also as drinking it. This is found also in the *Sacramentary* of Serapion (*c.* 350, ed. Funk, 17[1905], pp. 178-181) where the terms are strongly medical (the oil is a healing *medicine*) but there is also an element of exorcism in the prayer. This is not surprising since both in OT and in the Graeco-Roman world physical illness was connected with sin and evil. The emphasis on healing in the liturgical tradition is marked, and the main elements of the prayer of the Apostolic Tradition have remained in the Roman Pontifical to this day. The modern version of the prayer has omitted the mention of people touching and drinking the oil but this was a very common practice. They used to bring their phials of oil to church (not only on Maundy Thursday) and when ill anoint themselves or get others to do so for them. Several ecclesiastical writers recommend them to do so, no doubt to eliminate superstitious practices.

At first there was no particular order of anointings and some texts suggest that the oil should be applied where the pain was greatest. It was only when the anointing of the sick became entangled with current penitential practice in the tenth century that the anointing of the separate senses to remove sin committed through them became customary.

In the Roman Catholic church sick persons in danger of death are still anointed, usually in conjunction with confession, absolution and communion where these are possible (Last Rites).

The use of unction in the ordination (q.v.) of bishops and priests undoubtedly came in under the influence of the Carolingian practice of anointing kings. Behind this is the influence of OT, which was dominant in all the liturgy of that time. It was easy to make the transference from the anointing of kings in OT (and one or two texts in the consecration of the oils suggested it) to the anointing of Gallic monarchs. Once this transference was made, it was felt that bishops and priests, too, must be anointed. The rites are first found in the Romano-German pontifical of the end of the tenth century. The bishop was anointed on the head but the text suggests that his whole body was regarded as being anointed. He became a sacred, even a sacrosanct, person. The hands of the priest were anointed and made sacred for the celebration of the eucharist and the handling of the sacred elements.

Unction was and is used in rites that are not strictly sacramental, in consecrating chalices and bells and above all in the dedication of a church (q.v.). This ritual, very elaborate until recently and still undergoing revision, saw the physical church as a symbol of the Christian people and the anointings with chrism were parallel to the initiation rites of baptism and confirmation. But all these later anointings had for their over-riding purpose the consecration of persons and things, setting them apart from the 'profane' world so that they might accomplish their ministry or the purpose for which they were made.

L'Eglise en Prière, ed. A. G. Martimort, 1961, Part 3 on the sacraments, where the meaning of unction in connection with various sacraments is given; cf. pp. 169-183 for dedications of church, etc.; Bruno Kleinheyer, Die Priesterweihe im Römischen Ritus, 1961 (for priesthood only); L. L. Mitchell, Baptismal Anointing, 1966; Mario Righetti, Storia Liturgica, ²1959, IV (on the sacraments, dedication of churches, etc.); Dictionnaire d'Archéologie Chrétienne et de Liturgie VI, cc. 2777-2791 (Cabrol) s.v. 'Huiles'; ibid. XII, cc. 2116-2130 (Leclercq) s.v. 'Onction'; ibid. XII, cc. 2130-2147 (Leclercq) s.v. 'Onction dans l'Ordination'.

J. D. CRICHTON

Unitarian Worship

Manchester College, Oxford, which is affiliated to the General Assembly of Unitarian and Free Christian Churches, is dedicated to Truth, to Liberty and to Religion. This is a principle dear to Unitarians the world over. Guided by reason and conscience, but not unmindful of continuing revelation and tradition, the Unitarians seek to serve the Lord in sincerity and truth.

Unitarianism, at its worthiest, is a rational mysticism, and tolerance a genuine article of faith. This goes far to explain variations of church government and modes of worship. Unitarians see no inconsistency in having a General Assembly in Britain and a succession of bishops in Transylvania in continuous line from the Reformation. A revised BCP is still found in use at King's Chapel, Boston, Massachusetts, where English governors once worshipped. But at Dr Preston Bradley's famous 'People's Church' in Chicago emphasis is laid on the sermon. Not infrequently in America the sermon is followed by discussion.

The 'free services' of Nonconformity and a vigorous liturgical tradition have coexisted in England for two centuries. Traces of Calvinist worship, notably the Great Prayer, long survived among the 'English Presbyterians' from whom the Unitarians are in the main derived. But in the eighteenth century these 'Rational Dissenters' began to bring forth prayer books of their own. Even Joseph Priestley produced Forms of Prayer for the use of Unitarian Societies (1783). Nor did theological change stem the flow. From 1741 to our own day over a hundred liturgies have been forthcoming. For the purpose of this article it is the liturgies that are examined. They illustrate the development of doctrine common to all congregations, the majority always preferring conceived prayer. The Rational Dissenters were profoundly influenced by Locke's common-sense psychology and Newton's mathematical cosmology. Their service-books were scriptural in language, and often incorporated many responses for minister and people. They were dignified and devout and, what appealed to the spirit of the Age, entirely devoid of 'enthusiasm'.

Anglican worship entered these churches with the advent of Theophilus Lindsey who much admired the great Semi-Arian Samuel Clarke. Lindsey resigned his living to establish a Reformed Church of England with a revised BCP. In fact he established the first avowedly Unitarian church in the country in 1774. At Essex Street, London, he used The Book of Common Prayer reformed *according to the Plan of the Late Dr Samuel Clarke*. This soon attained an enormous popularity among the English Presbyterians now venturing into Biblical Unitarianism. The services amended were usually mattins and evensong. Lindsey followed Clarke in addressing all prayers to the Father. The virgin birth was rejected as unhistorical. Satan was expelled from the litany!

In 1862 Sadler and Martineau published *Common Prayer for Christian Worship*; it is the finest of the Unitarian liturgies. The last two services by Martineau are historic. For the first time Nonconformity had produced a liturgical editor of rare genius. The haunting beauty of the prayers, the timely responses, and the scripturally inspired canticles attain poetic felicity and prophetic piety.

But Martineau was troubled in conscience. He sang the song of the Lamb, but like Lindsey before him he objected to the perpetual termination of every prayer *'per Jesu Christum, Dominum nostrum'*. He did not rest until these words were deleted. *Ten Services of Public Prayer*, a revised edition published in 1879, repudiates the redemptive and intercessory functions of Christ.

No noteworthy change is to be found in *Orders of Worship* published in 1932. Nor is there any approach to a eucharistic norm. But the many fine prayers have been adopted by non-liturgical congregations to their spiritual enrichment.

Infant baptism is common among Unitarians although they reject the doctrine of original sin. The triune formula is to be found in many of the older liturgies. But *A Book of Occasional Services* (1932) and *In Life and Death* (1968) suggest 'I baptize thee in the name of God our Father, and in the spirit of his Son, Jesus Christ'. Holy communion is for Unitarians memorialism. The rite often varies as there is no rigidly prescribed form, still less a eucharistic doctrine. But the ancient Christian piety makes this service sacred and sanctifying. There is always a celebration at the General Assembly in Great Britain.

Dr Rowe's *Book of Occasional Services* and a similar compilation by the Rev. Kenneth Twinn, *In Life and Death*, are useful aids to ministers. Both, rather surprisingly, include 'Thanksgiving after Childbirth'. Mr Twinn's book contains a remarkable number of very appropriate extra-biblical readings.

Especially is this true of his funeral service.

Unitarians seem always to have encouraged the people of God to take an active part in worship. Litanies and responses are part of their heritage. An admirable modern example is the American *Hymns for the Celebration of Life* (1964). This book includes litanies and responses derived from many sources. The themes are most comprehensive and include science, the countryside, and the democratic way of life.

A quest for more meaningful worship among the younger English Unitarians has given rise to some experimentation. The impulse undoubtedly comes from contact with some of the Unitarian-Universalists in America. The Americans are making greater use of music and of periods of silence. In America and England alike there is a tendency in some quarters to depart from the preacher-hearer tradition and to develop a dialectic. But it is dangerous to generalize about Unitarians anywhere!

Unitarians have been accused of being 'cold' in their worship. This has never been true but the older piety was perhaps too unobtrusive and almost shy. The secret of their piety is disclosed in their own fine hymns. Such names as Sarah F. Adams and Oliver Wendell Holmes come to mind.

Unitarian sermons tend to be thoughtful meditations; for the English have remained Rational Dissenters, and the Americans have not forgotten their roots in Boston and Harvard. Alike they remember an abiding aspiration for the Beauty of Holiness.

A. E. PEASTON

Utensils *see* Aumbry, Alms-dish, Bells, Candles, Chalice and Paten, Chrismatory, Ciborium, Cruet, Fan, Monstrance, Paschal Candle, Pyx, Stoup, Tabernacle, Thurible, Tower

Veil

1. A veil or curtain was drawn before the altar at certain points in the liturgy from the fourth century onwards; and some of the Greek fathers liken this veil to that which hung before the holy of holies in the temple at Jerusalem. This custom has continued until today in the lesser Eastern churches such as the Armenian and the Coptic. But the need

Plate 36
Lenten array and
veiling, Southwark
cathedral, London

for this veil has been obviated in the Eastern Orthodox rite with the development of the solid iconostasis (q.v.).

2. In the West this veiling has not developed to the same extent as in the East. But during the season of Lent in the Middle Ages in England and elsewhere, the altar was shrouded from the congregation by the Lenten veil drawn across the sanctuary, which was only drawn aside at the reading of the gospel at the parish mass on Sundays. This veil is not to be confused with another veil which hung before the crucifix on the rood beam during Lent. Both these veils were made of unbleached linen or holland; they formed part of the general shrouding with this material which took place in all churches at the beginning of Lent and continued until the eve of Easter Day. This shrouding is known as the *Lenten Array* (*see* Plate 36). It covered every crucifix, statue, and reredos (q.v.), including the three figures on the rood beam. The veils often had emblems of red, black or blue stencilled on them; and the emblem frequently gave a hint of the object that it veiled. The Lenten Array has been revived in a number of the cathedrals and parish churches in Britain.

In the modern Roman rite it is customary to veil all crucifixes, statues and pictures with purple-toned veiling from the eve of the fifth Sunday in Lent, commonly called Passion Sunday, until the eve of Easter Day.

A. A. King, *The Rites of Eastern Christendom*, 2 vols., 1947; C. E. Pocknee, *The Christian Altar*, 1963; C. E. Pocknee, *Cross and Crucifix*, 1962; H. B. Walters, *London Churches at the Reformation*, 1939.

C. E. POCKNEE

Veneration of the Cross

The Veneration of the Cross, which forms a part of the liturgy for Good Friday, originated in Jerusalem after the finding of the cross by St Helena (325). At the end of the fourth century, a relic of the cross was venerated in silence, as witnessed by the bishop, Cyril, and the pilgrim Etheria. Relics were sent to other churches; to Rome in the seventh century, probably from Greece. Here, at first, the same austere ceremony took place as in Jerusalem, but at the end of the eighth century a service-book records the singing of 'Behold the wood of the cross' and Ps. 118. Churches in the West, which were without a relic, substituted a plain wooden cross, which later was changed for a crucifix.

The ceremony was more dramatized in the churches of Spain and Gaul, and all the elements of the present rite are found in the Roman-German pontifical of Mainz about the year 950.

By the eleventh century, the Roman liturgy had introduced this more solemn form of the Veneration of the Cross. It included the showing and kissing of the cross, a dialogued chant of the 'reproaches' ('My people, what have I done to you?'), the Byzantine *Trisagion* ('Holy God, Holy and strong'), an antiphon ('Lord, we worship thy cross') and the hymn, 'Sing, my tongue, the glorious battle' (*Hymns Ancient and Modern*

Revised, 1950, 97). The chants are mainly Eastern in origin, and are sung as the ministers and people come up and kiss the cross.

In the Middle Ages, the ceremony was called 'Creeping to the Cross'. In 1955, the 'Restored Order of Holy Week' added to the solemnity of the rite, which in future is to take place in the afternoon and not in the morning, as has been the case for many centuries.

The veiled crucifix, taken from the sacristy (q.v.) to the altar between two taper bearers, is unveiled in three stages, at each of which 'Behold the wood of the cross' is sung, with the response 'Come, let us worship'. The crucifix is held upright, flanked by two candles, and the feet of the Crucified are kissed first by the ministers and then by the people, while the chants and hymn are sung.

The veneration and kissing of the cross on Good Friday are an act of worship to Christ the Redeemer of the world, and a wooden cross is merely an aid to this devotion.

A. A. KING

Vernacular

Liturgy is of its nature social worship, and therefore must involve the use of audible communication between members of the worshipping community. *A priori* one would expect that the speech used would be in a language intelligible to all present, i.e. a vernacular. This is the natural, sensible and practical means of intercommunication.

History shows that all liturgies did, in fact, come into being in vernacular forms. No religious body using a liturgy has ever deliberately chosen to start with a liturgy in an unintelligible language. (Glossolaly constitutes no exception since it never hardened into liturgical forms.) Yet history shows also another fact which seems surprising: nearly all religions have come to, or passed through, a stage where they employed, either wholly or in part, a liturgy which worshippers understood with difficulty or not at all. The language was antiquated, dead or even foreign. There has been a contradiction between what would seem the natural thing and what actually happened.

No single cause suffices to explain this phenomenon; but some of the factors which produced it are these: (1) Mankind is innately conservative in matters of religion. For religious things are holy things; they are thought to partake in some way of the unchangeableness of the divinity in whose honour they are said or done; it is felt to be improper to change them. Once a liturgy has settled down into a definite form, this form tends to persist from generation to generation as a precious heritage. Yet it is an inescapable fact that living languages change. Therefore if the language of a liturgy remains unchanged it becomes archaic; in time it becomes a dead language. (2) An antiquated or dead language, precisely because it is not a vernacular, comes to be considered as a sacred language. Its exclusive use in liturgy is rationalized in terms of the reverence due to the divinity who, it is felt, ought not to be addressed in the language used for fellow men (equals) but only in a very special and sacred style or language. Any attempt to change this sacral language is denounced as impious desecration. (3) A dead language is totally unintelligible. Its use in liturgy produces in the popular mind a mystification which, when allied to its 'sacredness', results in a 'sense of mystery' (more correctly described as a 'sense of the numinous'). As this is a very important element in any religion the fact that an unknown tongue fosters it militates against change. (4) It has often happened that some nation has been evangelized by foreign missionaries who already possess a traditional liturgy; this they have imposed, without any change in language, upon their converts. Thus, even if the language is living or merely archaic for the missionaries, it starts off among the converts as something unintelligible and foreign.

For these and other reasons there exists in all liturgies a tension between the need for intelligibility and the tendency to become stabilized, sacralized and mysterious. It is only when this tendency has become excessive that a reaction may set in and cause a demand for the use of the vernacular.

The Christian religion was faced with a choice at its very beginning, for it originated among the Jews. But they, in their temple liturgy and in their scriptures, employed the Hebrew language, a tongue that was archaic and hardly understood except by the learned. But in their synagogues Jewish worship, though partly in Hebrew, was largely in Aramaic, the then vernacular which was closely allied to Hebrew. Throughout the diaspora the Aramaic was replaced by Greek, then the common language outside Palestine. Faced with a choice of a dead or a living language, the Christian church unhesitatingly chose the latter. In Palestine the early Christian liturgy took shape in Aramaic; outside Palestine in Greek. But, though Greek was widely spoken in urban areas, it had never completely driven out native languages which were the vernaculars of country people. So when the Gentiles began to be converted they worshipped in their own tongues – Syriac, Armenian, Coptic and many others.

The early church had no inhibitions whatever about changing its liturgical language or translating scriptures into vernaculars. The classic instance of this flexibility is Rome itself where the liturgy started in Greek. This was because the first converts were the poor and humble, almost all from the Greek-speaking slave class. By the third century, however, many Christians were speaking Latin; during the next hundred years Greek died out in Rome. So the Greek liturgy was gradually replaced by Latin until Latin was the sole language for worship. However, in the seventh century many Greek merchants and craftsmen immigrated into Rome and formed quite a large colony there. This resulted in a partial return to Greek in public worship; the scriptures at mass and at vigils were read in Greek as well as in Latin; baptism and other sacraments were administered in either language. This practice continued as long as there was any need for both vernaculars. When Greek died out again only Latin (the remaining vernacular) sufficed. The original policy of the church was undoubtedly to use vernacular languages in worship, and this policy has remained unchanged in the East.

But in the West conditions were different, and a different policy ultimately prevailed. The East was fairly well civilized and its languages were developed; even though Greek became spoken almost everywhere, the other languages survived. But when the Romans conquered the West, its peoples were still uncivilized, and there were no developed languages. By the time Christianity began to spread into the West nearly all the inhabitants of the Roman empire spoke Latin, even if only vulgar Latin. For Latin had now become the vernacular; it had driven out all the undeveloped native languages which hardly survived anywhere.

Different liturgical rites, such as the Roman, the Gallican, the Celtic did indeed arise, but they were all in Latin from their very beginning. No other possibility existed.

This complete hegemony of Latin explains why the West has differed from the East in its policy about liturgical language. Latin was kept even when it ceased in later centuries to be the vernacular. As living languages always do, it gradually changed in different parts of the empire; there arose dialects which, after centuries of development, have ended up as Italian, French, Spanish and Portuguese. But Latin was retained as the language of the liturgy because it, too, had matured and given rise to Christian literature. All educated persons in the West remained able to speak and write Latin fluently until at least the fifteenth century. It was the language of culture, of government, of theology and even of commerce. But it was not the language of the common people who now could not understand the liturgy.

From time to time the need for the people to understand their worship was perceived and voiced, but the demands for a vernacular liturgy were usually small, localized and without result. A notable exception, however, was the missionary activity of St Cyril and St Methodius who, in the ninth century, evangelized the Slavonic peoples of Moravia. The whole story is immensely complicated, involving political intrigues, the Photian schism, forged documents and contradictory rulings by successive popes; but it all ended up with the establishment of a vernacular liturgy in the Slavonic tongue. In time permission was granted for the use of Dalmatian, Croatian, Slovenian and Czech (all of them Slavic languages). These are genuine vernaculars even today, though the tongue used by Cyril and Methodius, called Staro-Slav, is now archaic and thus but partially intelligible.

In the fourteenth century the Dominicans who had a house in Constantinople were allowed to celebrate their own (Latin) rite in the local Greek; others, working among the Armenians in Cilicia, translated the Dominican liturgy into Armenian. Missionaries in Georgia were likewise permitted to translate their Latin rite into the local vernacular.

In the sixteenth century came the great upheaval of the Reformation. Almost all Protestant Reformers demanded the use of the vernacular in the liturgy, but their reasons for this always involved dogmatic contentions judged by the Council of Trent to be heretical. The question was very thoroughly discussed at the Council; many of the bishops saw clearly that the replacement of Latin by vernacular languages (at least in parts of the liturgy) was in itself desirable. That is why the Council was careful not to condemn the vernacular as such; it decreed that its introduction was not at that time expedient. Because the language question was, in those days, so inextricably bound up with dogmatic positions, the Council could hardly have decided otherwise. Hence, for the next four centuries, Latin continued to be the official liturgical language of the western patriarchate of the Roman Catholic Church.

The Protestants, of course, took to the vernacular very quickly for some (usually for all) of their worship. Some of the churches dating from that era have vernacular liturgies of which the prayer-texts are 400 years old. As a result these texts have reached the stage of being archaic, and many voices are being raised in favour of modernization. There are new versions of prayers, new translations of holy scripture being used in public worship with or without authorization; there is a process of liturgical reform going on in nearly all the churches, and this usually entails a reform of rites and of texts now expressed in twentieth-century language, that is, in the current vernacular. These churches are acting before the original languages of their liturgies have become dead languages.

In the Roman Catholic Church the liturgical language had certainly reached the stage of being a dead language; its liturgical movement, which began with an aesthetic and archaeological phase about a century ago, became pastoral early in the present century. By the time of Pius XII it had become a reforming movement and its leaders were urging (against much powerful opposition) that the Latin liturgy should not only be reformed but also put, wholly or in part, into the vernacular. Partial concessions were granted to several countries and missionary dioceses; the movement grew in intensity and influence till the whole question was examined at the Second Vatican Council convened by Pope John XXIII. The upshot has been a radical reform which has included an almost complete adoption of the vernacular wherever this is feasible.

CLIFFORD HOWELL, SJ

Vespers *see* Canonical Hours

Vestments

There are four basic types of ecclesiastical vesture. First, the garments which are worn for the cultus, i.e. at the eucharist and at other sacramental ceremonies – these are vestments in a strict sense. Secondly, there is vesture which may be worn on other liturgical occasions. Thirdly, there are various items of clothing which indicate rank or specific role – including those of religious orders. Fourthly, there are garments which are, or have been, customary clerical dress on non-liturgical occasions – the civilian dress of the clergy.

A cross-division of these types also has to be made between the vesture of different sectors of the whole church – Eastern Orthodox Churches, Roman Catholic Church and various Reformed Western Churches. Further, it is necessary to consider in outline the historical succession of comparable garments and to trace derivation and development when this has occurred.

In addition to a purely descriptive account of vestments, it is also desirable to consider their significance as a means of communication – both liturgical and theological, and even political and personal.

The organization of such a mass of material creates many problems in the matter of presentation, and some framework of reference is necessary. At the risk of over-simplification, it is possible to state that ecclesiastical vesture can be studied from the proposition that there are two main garments and many accessories. The basic garments are: 1. an *indoor tunic*; 2. an *outdoor cloak*. The classical Christian form of the tunic is the white *alb*, while the cloak exists as both the *chasuble* and the *cope*. Derivatives and variations of the tunic include the following garments: tunicle, dalmatic, rochet, surplice and cotta. Obviously, in clement weather, indoor clothing may also be worn outside without an overgarment, just as, conversely, for ceremonial reasons, outdoor robes may be worn indoors. It should also be remembered that, though worn under a chasuble or cope, the tunic is an outer-garment rather than an under-garment.

The ecclesiastical accessories correspond generally to the accessories of convenience which are normally found in association with civilian dress at any period (e.g. handkerchief and napkin), and also with the rank insignia of the ceremonial dress of the officers of any institution or society. Ecclesiastical accessories, like the garments themselves, are conveniently considered under the following headings:

1. Liturgical (*a*) eucharistic or generally sacramental; (*b*) 'choir' or generally for other services of worship.

2. Non-liturgical (*a*) ceremonial; (*b*) civilian.

Since any classification is being imposed upon a range of costume which has developed 'organically' under a variety of influences, there are likely to be some items of dress which are difficult to classify or include in any general scheme. This qualification applies to those which are characteristic of a particular locality or period, and which belong mainly to the non-liturgical dress of dignitaries (e.g. Anglican apron and gaiters): for this reason, apart from pontificalia, they need not be discussed in this context. Several further considerations may be noted before a systematic description and discussion of the liturgical garments. First, the Christian vestments are derived primarily from the civilian dress of the late Roman empire and owe nothing directly to the vesture of the Jewish priesthood: the original differentiation and development from lay attire took place from the fourth to the ninth centuries. Secondly, they have undergone some changes corresponding to differences in the actual mode of conducting the rites and to the addition or omission of particular ceremonies. Thirdly, they have been subject to fashion, and to the availability of various types of material used for their manufacture and embellishment. In this connection the influence of the commercial church furnishers and haberdashers is not without significance. Fourthly, the changes in style reflect to some extent various ecclesiological and sacramental doctrines concerning the status and role of the ministers of the church and the nature of worship in general. Fifthly, like most ceremonial garments, some of their features have lost their original usefulness and survive as vestigial appendages which are no more than visual reminders of the continuity of Christian worship and

which, ultimately, may be abandoned (e.g. the maniple). Sixthly, vestments (in common with other 'church furnishings') have undergone periods of rejection and revival in the Western church and, at times, have become objects of controversy and symbols of party: their use may also be subject to law – both internal ecclesiastical regulations and external national enactments.

Each item of vesture will now be considered within the following scheme:

1. *Vestments of the Cultus*: alb, amice, girdle, stole, maniple, chasuble, dalmatic and tunicle.

2. *Other Liturgical and Clerical Garments*: cope, cassock, surplice, tippet and hood, almuce, mozetta, pallium, chimere, rochet and mitre.

3. *Eastern Orthodox Vesture.*

1. *Vestments of the Cultus*

(*a*) *Alb.* The ecclesiastical alb is directly derived from the *tunica alba* of classical times. It is now usually a long white tunic reaching to the feet, made of linen, and belted with a girdle or cincture at the waist: it has close-fitting sleeves and is collarless.

In antiquity such a garment existed in two forms – short and long. The knee-length Greek *chiton* was more like a modern shirt and was sometimes sleeveless. The long type, *chiton poderes* or *tunica talaris*, has either narrow sleeves (corresponding to the alb) or wide sleeves (corresponding to both the dalmatic and the surplice). If made of linen, the garment might be called *tunica linea*. On occasion two tunics might be worn – one as an undergarment and the other as an outer garment.

In the NT the word *chiton* is used in the saying: 'If a man wants to sue you for your shirt (*chiton*), let him have your coat (*himation*) as well' (Matt. 5.40). It is also used of the seamless tunic worn by Jesus (John 19.23) in contrast to his other garments (*himatia*) which were shared by the soldiers, and *chiton* is also implied in the description of the visionary personage of Revelation as being 'robed to his feet' (*chiton poderes*) (1.13).

The long white tunic was sometimes decorated with *clavi*, i.e. full length thin strips of purple or russet material – either a single stripe down the middle (front and back) *latus clavus*, or one such stripe over each shoulder. This elementary decoration probably served to cover and strengthen joins in the material, and was discontinued if the alb was to be worn under a dalmatic. Tunics so embellished were generally worn without a girdle and thus their character of verticality was emphasized. In addition, some early tunics carry similar decoration around the hem near the ground and thus suggest a basis for the medieval application of apparels.

The long white tunic which was worn generally by professional people did not really begin to become a specifically Christian vestment until the beginning of the fifth century. For example, in a transitional stage, Jerome (341-420) distinguishes between everyday clothing and a special 'suit of clean clothes' for wear in church. The mosaics at Ravenna show that by the sixth century it had become customary for bishops to wear not only the *paenula* (or chasuble) but also a wide-sleeved tunica (or dalmatic) over a narrow-sleeved alb (*see* Fig. 24). In S. Vitale, this is quite clear in the case of Archbishop Maximianus – the narrow sleeve of the under-tunic shows at his wrist; moreover, the edges of the wide surplice-like sleeves of his 'dalmatic' (like those of his two clerical attendants) are embellished with double

Fig. 24   Sixth-century vestments, Ravenna

purple stripes which correspond with the two full-length clavi. (It is not clear whether or not the assistants are wearing albs under their dalmatics.) Similarly, in S. Apollinare in Classe the narrow sleeves of the bishop's alb are plainly seen to emerge from the broader sleeves of his dalmatic.

Incidentally, the sleeves of the alb (or, more correctly in the East, the *sticherion*) are also decorated with double bands of what appears to be golden embroidery, corresponding to the later Eastern *epimanika* (detachable cuffs) and, more remotely, to wrist apparels of the alb in the West. This vestment, which is common to all the clergy in the Ravenna mosaics, is remarkably like the long medieval surplice in shape, but because of its context and its decoration is best understood as the forerunner of the later tunicle and dalmatic.

All ranks of the clergy wore the plain alb until the eleventh century, but at about this period two changes occurred in the West. First, a wide-sleeved and somewhat shorter version of the alb, namely the *surplice*, began to replace it as the clerical vestment for non-eucharistic worship, and also for wear by clergy and monks in choir. Secondly, there grew up a custom of applying apparels (*paramenta*), i.e. oblong pieces of richer material or embroidery attached to the cuffs, and also front and back in the middle near the ground: these *alba parata* were, perhaps, being forbidden by implication in the *First English Prayer Book* which orders 'a white Albe plain' to be worn by the priest.

The alb, plain or with apparels, and with only minor changes in fashion (e.g. amplitude of cut, use of lace or other decoration), has continued to be worn until the present day and, in a sense, is to be thought of as the archetypal 'white robe' of Christianity.

(*b*) *Amice*. The amice is a rectangular piece of linen which originated as a neckerchief used to protect other vestments from sweat. The Latin name *amictus* is derived from *amicio* which means 'to wrap around'. The Ravenna and other mosaics show that such a neck-cloth was not worn before the sixth century, and in the Eastern Orthodox churches it has never become an official vestment.

In the West, the amice slowly became adopted as an essential mass vestment from the eighth century onwards. The *Ordo Romanus Primus* refers to the amice (*ana-*

golagium) as being part of the pope's vesture, but *Ordo IV* (*c.*800) indicates that sub-deacons wore amices only when the pontiff was vested in a dalmatic. Other names used of the amice are *humerale* (shawl), *super-humerale* and *anaboladium*.

Originally, as was natural, the amice was not assumed until the alb had been put on. This earlier mode survives in the liturgies of Lyons and Milan, but generally the amice is now the first vestment to be donned. The latter custom derives from the tenth century when a longer hair style was fashionable and, in order to protect the other garments during vesting, the amice was first put on like a helmet and kept there until all the other vestments were in place. Thus the amice is provided with long tapes which are tied around the waist in order to keep it over the hair until vesting is complete. This procedure is further facilitated if a long narrow apparel is attached to the front of the amice so that when the 'helmet' is pushed back from the head the apparel forms a kind of collar. Medieval apparels accorded in colour with the stole and maniple and contrasted with that of the chasuble or dalmatic.

In spite of the medieval development of the amice into a hood, its origin as a pro-tective neckerchief is attested by the admoni-tion at the ordination of a sub-deacon that he receives the amice as the *castigatio vocis*.

(c) *Girdle*. It was normal to wear a girdle of some sort with the classical *tunica* simply for the sake of convenience in moving about. Thus, when the long *tunica alba* emerged as a Christian vestment it was accompanied by the customary *cingulum* and was recognized as such in the eighth century. Worn with a very full alb, the girdle is not visible and may be referred to as the *subcingulum* – especially in connection with the attachment to it of a deacon's napkin. In the Eastern Orthodox churches the deacon wears an ungirdled *sticharion*, and the corresponding belt, *zone*, is worn only by priests and bishops.

In the past, the girdle has taken the form of a broad belt or cincture of white or coloured material. Today it is usually a long white rope with tasselled ends. It is put on immediately after the alb and the ends of the stole are customarily tucked under or through it.

(d) *Stole*. The stole is a strip of material about four inches (ten centimetres) wide and up to twenty-six feet (eight metres) long. It may be made of white or coloured textiles and may be plain or embroidered. It is worn over one or both shoulders in distinctive ways by bishops, priests and deacons. It is normally worn immediately over the alb and under any other outer vestment, though there are some exceptions.

The remote origin of the stole is obscure: it may have been some sort of napkin or kerchief or, alternatively, it is more likely to have been a ceremonial garland worn in honour at a festival. However, there can be no doubt that its Christian use derives directly from a scarf worn by Roman officials as an ensign of rank, and there is much to be said for the view that the stole and the *pallium* (*see below*) have a common origin as a status symbol.

Under the civil law in the Theodosian Codex (AD 395) senators and consuls were ordered to wear a coloured scarf or pall over alb and paenula as a badge of office (cf. a mayor's chain). There seems little doubt that by this time the dignitaries of the church had adopted a similar ensign: bishops wore a *pallium* (*see* Plate 37) (equivalent to the Eastern *omophorion*) over the chasuble, while priests and deacons wore a corresponding scarf known as the *orarium*. This *orarium* was forbidden to sub-deacons by the Council of Laodicea (*c.*372), and is certainly the same vesture which, in the ninth century, is referred to as the *stola* received by deacons at ordi-nation.

In the East the corresponding vestment of the deacon is still called the *orarion* and is a long narrow strip hanging down, back and front, from the left shoulder, while that of the priest is joined together in front and slipped over the neck – hence the name *epitrachelion*.

Much confusion has been caused by the fact that in the classical period, the Latin *stola* was the name of a long outer garment and, further, that this name corresponds to the NT use of *stole* for a similar flowing or festal raiment (e.g. Mark 16.5; Luke 15.22; Rev. 6.11). In a very remote way it is possible that the Roman scarf (or pallium) itself is derived from an earlier toga-like garment (also called pallium) which came to be closely folded length-wise and worn as a sign of rank, but even this possible derivation in no way connects the ecclesiastical stole with the classical *stola* or biblical *stole*. It is not known why the name was changed from the tra-

Plate 37 Pallium worn by Bishop Apollinare. The originally mid-sixth century apse mosaic in Ravenna, S. Apollinare in Classe, depicts the founder bishop vested in two albs – a tight-sleeved under-tunic decorated on the forearms with coloured bands and over this a wide-sleeved alb with vertical *clavi*. Over these he wears a chasuble, or phelonion, surmounted by the episcopal pallium. The saintly bishop stands in the *orans* posture of prayer with arms outstretched and hands upraised.

ditional *orarium* to *stola* from the ninth century onwards and, regrettable though it may be, there is now no alternative but to continue to use the word which was universally accepted by the thirteenth century.

Historically there have been many different ways of wearing the stole, but today the general Western practice is as follows: a deacon wears a stole as a sash over the left shoulder, fastening or looping it below the right arm; a priest wears the stole round the back of his neck and, when worn over an alb, crosses it on the breast, while, over a surplice, the ends are allowed to hang down vertically; a bishop always wears a stole in the latter manner.

The current Western custom that the bishop should wear a stole hanging straight down from both shoulders is not supported by the Byzantine mosaics at Ravenna where, with one exception, the bishops there depicted all wear a pallium over a chasuble instead of a stole beneath it: the exception is Archbishop Ecclesius (in the apse of S.

Vitale) who appears to be wearing both (The validity of this evidence has been doubted, and it has been suggested that the mosaic in question was inaccurately re-made in the twelfth century.)

Apart from being worn at the eucharist, the stole is commonly worn in the Roman Catholic Church when administering the other sacraments, when preaching, and when hearing confessions.

In the course of time its form has been modified and its decoration varied. It remained long and narrow until the late Middle Ages, when it was shortened and the ends were made wider to accommodate more extensive decoration. From about the tenth century it became customary to embellish stoles with embroidery – usually with simple geometric patterns: sometimes fringes were attached to the ends. In the baroque period stoles became very short indeed and very heavily decorated. Stoles also came to be made of coloured material – originally, like orphreys and apparels, in contrast to the colour of the chasuble or other vestment, but in the post-Reformation period when the sequence of liturgical colours (q.v.) was stabilized, stoles were worn in the same colour as the chasuble or dalmatic.

During the Gothic revival stoles were again lengthened and commonly decorated with three crosses – one in the middle and one at each end. In the Evangelical sector of the Anglican Church, the stole is the only item of the early suit of liturgical vestments which is generally found acceptable.

(e) *Maniple*. The maniple of today is a strip of material some two to four inches wide (6-10 cms.), varying in length up to three feet (1 metre) or thereabouts: it is looped over the left wrist with some sort of fastening beneath. The maniple normally matches the stole both in material and decoration; its use is now discouraged in the Roman Catholic Church and it is not even mentioned in the new missal.

There is no doubt that this vestment derives directly from the rank ornament of a consul, the *mappa*, which he held in his right hand and waved as a signal for the games to begin: correspondingly, in the seventh century, the maniple of the pope was used as a signal for the beginning of a stational mass.

The *mappa* itself originated as a folded handkerchief or napkin which, since pockets were not a feature of classical clothing, was normally carried in the hand. Thus, a purely practical rectangle of linen developed into an ensign of rank and authority in the empire and in the church, and in the course of this development was known variously as *manipulus, mappula, sudarium, mantile, fano, manuale* and *sestace*.

For a long time the maniple continued to be carried in the hand (e.g. Archbishop Stigand in the Bayeux Tapestry) and, so far as deacons and sub-deacons were concerned, may well have served practical purposes well into the medieval period. However, it eventually became solely an ornament worn on the wrist, and other cloths were used to wipe the sacramental vessels and the hands and faces of the ministers.

Further, in the Middle Ages the maniple was commonly worn by all clerics, but it was subsequently restricted to those of at least the rank of sub-deacon.

(f) *Chasuble*. Chasuble and cope (*see below*) alike are derived from an outer cloak, *byrrhus, paenula*, or *lacerna*, generally worn in the Graeco-Roman world by all classes and both sexes. Made from a semi-circle (or more usually two quadrants) of about twelve feet (four metres) in diameter of woollen material, the two edges could be either sewn together to form a conical or tent-shaped cloak (a hole being left for the head), or joined together by a clasp to form an enveloping cape – in either case the garment would fall to cover the hands. The former type became known as a *casula*, or 'little house', from which the name chasuble is derived, while the latter type is the forerunner of the cope, or *cappa*, signifying 'topmost' garment. The 'overcoat' left by Paul at Troas is called *phelones* (II Tim. 4.13), and related words are used in the Eastern Orthodox churches for the vestment which corresponds to the chasuble – *phelonicon, felon, phenolion*, and *phainoles* – various equivalents of the Latin *paenula*.

The *paenula*-type chasuble has undergone many changes in the course of its ecclesiastical history (*see* Fig. 25) – mainly by way of reduction in size and increase in decoration, but also through being (so to speak) turned through a right-angle. The two quadrants of material which comprised the original chasuble were joined by two seams which appeared vertically in the middle of the front and back of the garment when worn: these seams were strengthened and hidden by narrow strips of braid which, since they often were woven with gold thread, came to be known as *orphreys* (*auriphrygia* or *Phrygian* gold). Subsequently the conical chasuble was cut away at the sides to give greater freedom to the arms, and eventually it was found to be more convenient to make this reduced chasuble by joining two shield-shaped pieces of material in such a way that the seams came along the shoulders and down the sides. The seams of such chasubles are not usually decorated, but non-functional vertical orphreys are often applied and provided with 'arms' to form a kind of cross – back and front.

Starting from a semi-circular design, it is obvious that this shape is easily modified, e.g. by increasing or reducing the extent of the notional circle by making the semicircle a semi-oval, or by making the front smaller than the back.

Illustrations of various kinds from the sixth century onwards (by which time the chasuble had become a specifically ecclesi-

Plate 38   Full Gothic chasuble,
fourteenth-century Germany.

astical vestment) show that such modifications were made, but that, in general, the full
conical chasuble with its characteristic cres-
cent-shaped folds persisted until the thirteenth century. One variation was that there
was at times a tendency to make the bottom
of the front more pointed (e.g. the *phelonion*
of S. Apollinare in the apse mosaic at
Classis), and in the eleventh century there
appears to have been a temporary fashion
for cutting away a considerable part of the
front – not unlike the subsequent development of the *phelonion* in the Eastern Orthodox
churches.

From the tenth and eleventh centuries in
the West chasubles began to be made of much
richer materials, when the church became
wealthier and as silks became less expensive.
Until this time they had been made principally of fine wool and had been worn
generally by the clergy. The eighth-century
Ordo Romanus Primus documents the gradual

emergence of the chasuble as the distinctive
outer garment of the presiding celebrant
at the eucharist: at the stational mass only
the pontiff retained his *paenula* for the whole
of the mass. And in the ninth century
Amalarius of Metz reports that at the mass in
Rome the deacon removed his *paenula* before
the gospel and thenceforth rolled it in such a
way that he could wear it with his stole over
the left shoulder and under his right arm –
the so-called 'broad stole'.

By the thirteenth century, then, the
chasuble was established a rich 'high-priestly'
ornament (*see* Plate 38), but one which had
not lost the essential character of the original
garment. At this time, however, the ceremonial of the elevation of the host (q.v.) was
introduced into the eucharist. This meant
that the president had to raise his hands high
above his head in order that the congregation
might see the eucharistic bread since, by this
time, he no longer faced the worshippers but

Fig. 25 HISTORY OF THE CHASUBLE

Penula

VI.–X. Ravenna
Mosaic VI

VI.–X. Ravenna
Mosaic VI

VII.–IX. Roma
S.Agnes Mosaic VII

VIII.-IX. Frankfort
Ivory IX

X. Havre
msx

X. Paris
Nat. Libr. msx

XI. Roma
Minerva, Pontificale

XI. Roma
S. Clement

XI. Bayeux
Tapestry

XI. Mayence
Ch. S. Willigise

XI. Metz
Ch. S. Stephen

XI. Bayeux
Ch. S. Regnobert

XII. Florence
Ch. B. Bernardo

XI. Hildesheim
Ch. S. Godehard

XII. Brauweiler
Ch. S. Bernard

XII. Tournay
Ch. S. Thomas

XII. Sens
Ch. S. Thomas

XIII. Louannec

XIII. Provins
Ch. S. Edme

XIII. Angers
V. Montfaucon

XIII. Angers
V. Montfaucon

XIII. Maubeuge

XIII. Brienon
Ch. S. Loup

BY THE MONUMENTS

XIII. Reims | XIII. Reims Ch. for Deacon | XIII. Brunswick mus. | XIII. Dreux v. Montfaucon | XIII. Brussels v. Bollandists

XIV. Aix la Chapelle | XIV. Roma S. M. Transtav. tomb | XIV. Brussels v. Bollandists | XIV. Cologn Dominican Church | XIV. Vatican Pontifical | XV. Roma S. Peter a Vinc. tomb

XV. V. Baluze | XV. Coire | XV Dantzig N. Dame | XV. Binche Ch. S. Ursmer | XVI. Bern Museum | XVI. Roma Pict. Titian

XVI. Roma Pict. Tintoretto | XVI. Florence Cathedral | XVI. Brussels Museum | XVI. Brussels Museum | XVII. Roma Pict Sacchi | XVII. Roma Pantheon | XVII. Brussels Museum | XVIII. Brussels Museum

XVIII. Rheims Cathedral | . Roman Shape | Roman Shape Cross at the back | French | Belgian

Austrian | Spanish | Brazilian | Polish | Austrian | Gothic | Large Gothic

Plate 39 Elevation in the eastward position at a medieval mass. Priest vested in a very full alb (girdle covered) with apparels on skirt and cuffs and on amice; stole not visible but maniple worn on left wrist. Chasuble thrown back for the elevation. Characteristic medieval altar with front and reredos. (*The Mass of St Giles*. Flemish diptych *c.* 1495. National Gallery, London.)

Plate 40 The Clare chasuble. Originally a full Gothic chasuble made and embroidered at the end of the thirteenth century – a splendid example of the *Opus Anglicanum*. Cut down to a baroque shape in the seventeenth or eighteenth century. (Victoria and Albert Museum, London.)

had his back to them. Therefore, either the front of the chasuble had to be thrown back over the shoulders, or the vestment had to be re-designed with cut-away sides giving greater freedom to the arms (*see* Plate 39). The latter practice prevailed and was carried a stage further still in the baroque style of the Counter-Reformation (*see* Plate 40).

From the late medieval period, the embellishment of the vestment with embroidery was vastly extended and this, together with an increased regard for liturgical colours (q.v.), endangered the very character of the vesture. The front of the chasuble was cut away even more and the way was prepared for the baroque 'ornament' which, by the seventeenth century, had really ceased to be a garment and had become merely a vehicle for the display of the highly developed art of embroidery with rich silks, velvets, metallic threads, pearls and jewels.

Such vestments continue in use, but the nineteenth-century Romantic Movement includes much ecclesiastical harking back to the fashions of the medieval period – real or supposed. This neo-medievalism of the Cambridge Ecclesiologists and of the Ritualists led to the advocacy of the so-called Gothic chasuble together with matching stole and maniple, and their mass-production by commercial interests in a period of rapidly expanding population and religious revival. These 'reproduction antiques' have been accepted as the only alternative to the baroque style up to the middle of the twentieth century, but recently further research and new designs have begun to replace them.

(*g*) *Dalmatic and Tunicle.* The dalmatic, like the tunicle, is essentially a variant form of the *tunica alba* or alb: the name *tunica dalmatica* would seem to indicate an origin

Vestments

in the region of Dalmatia. As a wide-sleeved over-tunic it was a popular garment in second century Rome and, in a somewhat shortened version, appears to be the garment worn by some praying figures in catacomb frescoes.

By the fourth century the dalmatic was commonly worn over an alb as part of the distinctive 'uniform' of both bishops and deacons, as may be clearly seen in the mosaic of Maximianus and his attendants in S. Vitale. The dalmatic did not, however, become a vestment until the ninth century or thereabouts. At this time it was formally accepted in the West that over the alb at the eucharist the priest wore a chasuble, the deacon a dalmatic, and the subdeacon a tunicle. In the Latin rite the dalmatic is bestowed upon the deacon at his ordination and, correspondingly, a simpler version of it, the tunicle, belongs to the subdeacon. The bishop continued to wear the dalmatic under the chasuble and, in the ninth century, some bishops adopted the practice of wearing a tunicle under the dalmatic on solemn occasions.

Originally, the dalmatic was made of white linen or wool, and, like the alb (see above), was decorated with two coloured strips, clavi, running from front to back over the shoulders: the original tunicle lacked such clavi. Later, the dalmatic was shortened to knee-length, the sleeves were cut broader still and slits were introduced at the sides. From the tenth century onwards the dalmatic, and to a somewhat lesser extent the tunicle, came to be made of richer materials and to be more elaborately decorated with apparels, orphreys, fringes and tassels. Thus, like the chasuble, dalmatic and tunicle tended to become ornaments rather than garments. They have, indeed, been regarded as festal vestments not to be worn in penitential seasons.

In Eastern Orthodox churches, a dalmatic-like vestment, the sakkos (see below), is worn only by bishops and, since the sixteenth century, has replaced the chasuble (phelonion) as the liturgical outer garment of Greek metropolitans and all Russian bishops.

(It may also be noted that during the coronation ceremony, the English sovereign is vested in a dalmatic.)

2. Other Liturgical Garments

(a) Cope. The cope, like the chasuble (see above), is a ceremonial version of an outdoor cloak commonly worn in the Roman empire. Basically it is a semi-circular piece of cloth worn around the shoulders and held together at the front by a clasp (morse). Apart from a curious deviation in the Church of England (see below), the cope is worn at non-eucharistic ceremonies (e.g. baptism, marriage, procession) in place of the chasuble: it may also replace the dalmatic or tunicle since its use is not restricted to bishops and priests.

The forerunner of the ecclesiastical cope was known by the name cappa (signifying 'topmost' garment) by the end of the sixth century, and other names by which it was known include pluviale (rain-coat'), planeta (possibly from the Greek word meaning 'to wander' or travel around) and amphibalus (a Gallican term).

The original paenula or cappa was often fitted with a hood, and as a functional garment made of thick black material (cappa nigra) continued to be worn in choir as a protection against cold throughout the Middle Ages. As increasingly the cappa became a ceremonial garment (probably from the sixth century onwards), so the hood ceased to be functional and eventually was reduced to a triangular or shield-shaped decoration on the back.

The employment of silks and other expensive materials, together with the use of embroidery and other means of embellishment of the cope, has run parallel to that of the chasuble. A certain variation in style has occurred, but apart from the reduction of the hood to a vestigial flap, there has been no substantial change in its form. In the West the cope is a general ecclesiastical robe of splendour and has never been a distinctive clerical vestment. There is no liturgical equivalent to the cope in the Eastern Orthodox churches, though cope-like mantles are worn on occasion by some bishops.

At the time of the Reformation in England, the BCP of 1549 ordered the parish priest at the eucharist to wear 'a vestment (i.e. chasuble, stole and maniple) or cope': this rubric was withdrawn in 1552, but in Canon XXIV (1604) it was ruled that the principal minister at the communion in cathedrals and collegiate churches should wear a coloured cope over a plain alb. This custom is still observed in some cathedrals and ex-collegiate churches in spite of the fact that a cope is an extremely inconvenient garment in which to perform the eucharistic actions and gestures.

Oddly enough, in the S. Vitale mosaic of Melchizedek offering bread, the priest-king appears to be attired in a 'cut-away' cope: this is probably an imagined Jewish vestment, though it may reflect some aspects of sixth-century Christian ceremonial clothing.

Also in S. Vitale the emperor Justinian is shown wearing a hoodless ceremonial *paenula* fastened with a clasp on his right shoulder, thus leaving his right arm free. Some modern copes may be worn in this way as well as in the more customary manner.

(*b*) *Cassock.* The cassock is now an ankle-length tunic with long narrow sleeves; it is usually girt at the waist with a belt or cincture, but may be buttoned from neck to foot; it may be of any colour (*see* **Colours, Liturgical**). Its form and use demonstrate the difficulty of classifying the garments worn by the clergy: thus, it is universally worn under the eucharistic vestments and all other liturgical garments, but it is not itself a vestment. Again, although it is an under-garment, as the Latin name *subtanea* (soutaine) indicates, it is also worn as an over-garment for wear indoors and outdoors. Further, the cassock is not an exclusively clerical garment and may be worn by servers, choristers, vergers and other ecclesiastical persons.

The word in English is derived from Italian *cassaca*, or French *casaque*, possibly themselves derived from the name of a barbarian tunic known in the second century as *caracalla*. A long tunic, *vestis talaris*, was part of normal civilian dress in the late Roman empire, but when under barbarian influence (*c.* sixth century) lay fashions became shorter and more military, the clergy retained the ankle-length coat. Its use was ordered by the Council of Braga (572) and, in one form or another, it has subsequently been an important element in the distinctive attire of the clergy. Thus, the Anglican Canon LXXIV (1604) forbade beneficed clergy to go out in public 'in their doublet and hose without coats or cassocks' and, together with gown, hood, scarf and square cap, this comprised the outdoor dress of the clergy until the beginning of the nineteenth century. (Correspondingly, Roman Catholic clergy were forbidden by law to wear cassocks in public in England.) Cassocks have from time to time been fitted with hoods or capes and, unless worn with an academic hood, are often still so designed. In the medieval period in cold regions cassocks were lined with fur or

sheepskin (*pellicia*), hence the wide-sleeved full alb worn over the bulky lined cassock acquired the name 'surplice'. Very full cassocks with a train were fashionable for prelates in the fifteenth and sixteenth centuries but are no longer favoured. In contrast, in the eighteenth century the cassock was shortened to form an 'apron' for horse-riding bishops, deans and archdeacons and, together with corresponding gaiters, forms an outfit still affected by some dignitaries. The ministers of the Reformed churches (apart from some Methodists) do not normally cover their civilian clothes with a cassock, but prefer simply to wear a version of the medieval gown (known as 'Geneva' gown) with or without an academic hood, for liturgical or other ceremonial occasions. Gowns and hoods are not, of course, exclusively items of ministerial attire and are worn as ceremonial dress not only by churchmen but by academics and lawyers: it is often the case that two linen strips called 'bands' are worn in place of a tie or stock when a cassock or gown is worn. The decline in the practice of wearing a cassock as distinctive outdoor dress by clergy of the Church of England coincided with the separation of the neckerchief into collar and tie shortly before the middle of the nineteenth century. At about this time the back-fastening so-called Roman collar was devised to be worn with a black stock and without a tie. Until recently it was universally worn as a 'label' by ministers of virtually all denominations, sects and faiths, and the cut of the neck of cassocks was adjusted to accommodate it. Since about 1965 increasing numbers of clergy have abandoned the clerical collar and in their outdoor everyday attire are as indistinguishable from their fellows as were their predecessors in the first five centuries or so in the life of the church.

(*c*) *Surplice.* The surplice is a wide-sleeved ample version of the linen alb which was adopted in northern countries in the twelfth century for wear over fur-lined cassocks, hence the name: *superpelliceum* = over a fur garment. The actual shape of the surplice (as distinct from the name) is much earlier, as may be seen in the sixth-century mosaics of the bishops in S. Apollinare in Classe; apart from the decorative *clavi*, their albs are identical in form with the medieval surplice.

From the twelfth century onwards the surplice became the distinctive dress of the lower clergy and was worn by priests outside the mass: today it is commonly worn over the cassock by both clerics and laymen in choir or otherwise assisting in the conduct of worship.

Originally ankle-length, the surplice was progressively shortened and by the eighteenth century on the Continent barely reached the waist and had short sleeves: in this form it is known as the *cotta*. In the Roman Catholic Church it has also been trimmed with lace from the sixteenth century onwards. The surplice now exists in many different styles and, from time to time, attempts are made to restore its original simplicity and amplitude.

In the Church of England it has been a prescribed eucharistic vestment since Elizabethan times (*see below*).

(*d*) *Tippet and hood*. The long black scarf worn by Anglican clergy over the surplice. The exact origin of this ecclesiastical accessory is as obscure as its Latin name *liripipium* (liripipe or typet), though it is probable that it derives from an appendage of the medieval hood – either the 'poke' which hung down at the back or extensions of the cape which hung down at the front. In either case, hood and scarf would appear to be separated parts of the same garment – just as collar and tie are derived from the single neckerchief. In the fifteenth century the hood was commonly worn over the surplice and then, having been adopted by the universities as a token of graduation and given distinctive colours and linings, was further accepted in its academic form in the emergent Anglican Church as part of the choir habit of the clergy. The 1549 *BCP* recommends the hood as 'seemly' for preachers and the 1604 Canons (XXV and LVIII) order it for all graduate ministers. Correspondingly, non-graduates are ordered to wear a tippet instead of a hood in church. For outdoor wear Canon LXXIV orders all clergy to wear the tippet over a gown (*see below*).

(*e*) *Almuce*. This garment originated as a protection for the head and shoulders against the winter cold of medieval churches and, in the course of time, became a mark of rank or distinction. Originally either a lined hood or a fur scarf worn over the surplice, it emerged as a fur-lined hood with two ends hanging down in front and was regarded as part of the choir habit. The colour and the type of fur of the almuce came to have hierarchical significance – grey squirrel being the highest ranking and reserved for bishops and cathedral canons. Its used was discontinued in the Established

Church under Elizabeth I when it became customary to wear a black tippet or scarf.

A transitional stage may be noted at St Paul's Cathedral when in 1549 it is recorded that minor canons wore 'tippets like other priests' instead of their almuces.

The name almuce (Latin *almutia*) sometimes appears as 'amess' or even 'amice', and confusion with the eucharistic amice must be avoided.

(*f*) *Mozetta*. A short hooded cape of coloured silk or fur worn over a cope by pope, cardinals, abbots, bishops and other dignitaries of the Roman Catholic Church. Probably derived from the almuce (*see above*) which it has largely replaced.

(*g*) *Pallium*. A narrow band of white woollen material, marked with six dark crosses, and worn in one way or another around the neck and over the shoulders by patriarchs, archbishops and some other bishops. In the Roman Catholic Church it is now usually in the form of a circular band with two hanging strips back and front, but in the Ravenna mosaics the bishops all wear a straight band looped over the shoulders with the ends hanging down back and front from the left shoulder: it is still so worn in the Eastern Orthodox Churches and is called the *omophorion*.

In the Codex of Theodosius (395), a scarf or pall of several colours is ordered to be worn over the *paenula* by senators as an ensign of their rank; shortly afterwards this civil ornament became a distinctive badge of episcopal status. In the West the custom grew of reserving the pallium to archbishops who received it directly from the pope as a sign of their jurisdiction: the pope also acquired discretion to confer it on other bishops.

(It is a matter of dispute whether or not the 'scarf-pallium' is derived from the classical 'wrap-round' toga-like *pallium*: some writers believe that the latter was folded to form a narrow bundle and then reduced to the size of an ornament.)

(*h*) *Chimere*. A silk or satin sleeveless gown, black or scarlet, now worn by Anglican bishops and doctors of divinity. The name may be derived from the Spanish *zamarra*, and by the twelfth century the chimere was a short cloak worn by bishops when riding horseback. In a longer version it soon became part of the customary attire of bishops on both liturgical and civil occasions.

(*i*) *Rochet*. A variant form of the alb with

narrow sleeves, or without sleeves, which was in general use by clerics, sacristans, servers, etc., up to the thirteenth century. Later it became the prerogative of bishops, cardinals and canons regular.

Contrary to its origin as a convenient sleeveless 'dust-coat', the rochet of Anglican bishops (as worn under the chimere) acquired full lawn sleeves gathered at the wrist: in the eighteenth century the sleeves became so voluminous that they were commonly sewn to the chimere.

(*j*) *Mitre.* The origin of the mitre is obscure, but by the eleventh century it has emerged as the distinctive liturgical hat of bishops. Its shape has undergone many changes, starting from a simple conical cap of white linen with two lappets (or fanons) hanging down at the back. Subsequently, in the twelfth century, there was a front-to-back dent in this cap, but a century later the dented cap was being worn the other way round and the present form of a tall divided hat began to develop. In the thirteenth century three types of mitre are recognized in Roman ceremonial corresponding with different degrees of ceremony – *mitra pretiosa* (jewelled), *mitra aurifrigiata* (decorated without jewels) and *mitra simplex.*

The wearing of a mitre is not entirely restricted to bishops in the West, and some abbots and cardinals have been granted the privilege.

The Eastern Orthodox form of the mitre (*mitra*) resembles the Byzantine imperial crown and is sometimes worn by archpriests.

3. *Eastern Orthodox Vesture.* Deriving from the same source, the vestments and ornaments of the Eastern Orthodox churches are basically similar to those of the West. The differences arise either from the 'fixing' of a particular form or style in the East in contrast to Gothic and subsequent developments in the West, or to minor additions or variations following the Great Schism which have no parallel in the West. Broadly speaking, the vestments in use in the Eastern Orthodox churches are all 'eucharistic', and with only minor modifications are worn at all services; i.e., such garments as cope, surplice, tippet, hood, etc., have never come into existence.

Most of the corresponding Eastern vestments have been mentioned in the above account and the same order will be followed in this summary:

(*a*) *Corresponding vestments*

Sticharion or Stikir. The liturgical tunic, equivalent to the alb, but usually of coloured material.

Zone. Equivalent of the girdle but usually fitted with a clasp.

Epitrachelion. Corresponding to the stole, but a broad band with the ends joined together from the chest downwards to leave an opening for the head. Usually made of silk or brocade and ornamented with metal and jewels. Worn by bishops and priests.

Orarion. A narrow band of silk, also corresponding to the stole, but worn by deacons over the left shoulder with ends either hanging straight down back and front or arranged otherwise.

Phelonion. Equivalent to the Western chasuble and worn by all bishops and priests. From the eleventh century the white phelonion of a patriarch began to be embroidered all over with crosses (*polystaurion*), and from the fourteenth century this decoration was used for the vestments of all bishops. In the Russian church the phelonion (or *felon*) is cut away at the front from the breast downwards while at the back it falls to the feet and covers the arms at the sides. Since the fall of Constantinople in 1453 the phelonion has been replaced by. the *sakkos* (*see below*) in the Byzantine rite by all bishops.

(*b*) *Western vesture without equivalent, in Eastern Orthodox churches*

Amice.

Maniple (but see *Epimanikia*).

Cope (a modern form of phelonion in the Armenian and Syrian churches is open at the front like a cope).

Dalmatic (but see *Sakkos*).

(*c*) *Eastern vesture without equivalent in the West*

Epimanikia. Cuffs of embroidered silk worn over the sleeves of the sticharion of bishops and priests and known from the eleventh century. They take the place of the Western maniple but are not really its equivalent.

Epigonation. A lozenge-shaped ornament suspended from the *zone* on the right side in the Greek and Armenian churches (*see* Fig. 26) (*cf.* the decoration worn by Emperor Justinian and his courtiers in the mosaic in Ravenna, S. Vitale). It probably originated as a functional handkerchief and, in this . sense, would correspond to the Western maniple.

Fig.26 Epigonation

Fig. 27 Sakkos

Sakkos. An ample tunic with short wide sleeves and slit at the sides (*see* Fig. 27). Such a garment was one of the ceremonial vestments of the Byzantine emperors and it may well have a common origin with the Western dalmatic. As a liturgical vestment it appears at first to have been a mark of imperial favour for selected patriarchs, but by the thirteenth century it was worn by all patriarchs and metropolitans at Christmas, Easter and Whitsun. After the fall of Constantinople it gradually came to be worn generally by all bishops.

The outdoor dress of Eastern Orthodox clerics is basically cassock, gown and hat: priest-monks and bishops wear a veil on the hat. There is considerable variety from one country to another in the type of hat. Black is most usual colour, but some patriarchs wear white and other hierarchs wear Roman purple belts.

4. *The Role of Vestments.* Liturgical vestments comprise a special case of ceremonial clothing and are, therefore, part of a complex pattern of communication. They serve both to express the nature of the occasion when they are worn and to distinguish the respective role and rank of each participant. Until the church began to be 'imperialized' under Constantine, the ministers (bishops, presbyters and deacons) wore their everyday civilian clothing in the acts of worship of the community: at the Reformation, and again recently, attempts have been made to revert to the principle that contemporary lay clothes should be worn by all at the eucharist and other services. Thus, characteristically clothing becomes an item in a movement of protest – in these cases against alleged distortions of both sacramental doctrine and hierarchial authoritarianism. And in this way, vestments (themselves derived from ordinary clothing) become badges of party in ecclesiastical conflicts.

This 'political' significance of vestments is, of course, in addition to the allegorical meanings which have been attributed to them and to their more profoundly religious significance associated with concepts of transcendence, incarnation, majesty, priesthood, mystery, revelation, sacrifice and communion. However, on all sides, it is recognized that whatever particular meanings vestments may have acquired, there must, from time to time, be an appraisal of the symbolism of vesture and its relevance and effectiveness in the total communication pattern of worship. Psychologically, it seems that people who engage in the corporate performance of ritual desire that some, if not all, of the participants should wear special clothing. The question then tends to resolve itself into: What type of special clothing? In the church the emphasis has tended to be upon the expression of historical continuity and, hence, each succeeding style has been a modification or a revival of a previous one. Thus, any sector of the church is faced with the further question: To what point in the historical development of vesture shall we seek to return? Roman Catholics, some Anglicans and some Lutherans favour modern versions of Gothic, Gothic-revival and even Baroque styles, while Protestants generally are content with the everyday gown as worn by Renaissance Puritans.

There are, then, three basic choices: first, to dispense with ceremonial clothing; secondly to modernize or modify a particular historic style; thirdly, to attempt to design vestments which express a renewed understanding of Christian liturgical celebrations (*see* Plate 41).

Plate 41 Roman Catholic priest in lay dress for liturgy. At this experimental mass in a Jesuit high school chapel in Amsterdam the priest wore lay clothes for the synaxis but put on a grey gown for the eucharist itself.

The first choice perhaps needs to be made from time to time in order to highlight the underlying problems, but only a minority of worshippers is ever likely to accept the absence of all special clothing as a permanent solution.

The second choice finds clear expression in the most recent Roman Catholic regulations:

the *Ordo Missae* (1969) states unequivocally that 'the vestment common to all ministers is the alb' and that, if necessary, it should be tied at the waist with a cincture. Also optional is the amice, and the maniple is not mentioned at all. A surplice may replace the alb: a stole may be worn with it, but not a chasuble, dalmatic or tunicle. A cope may be worn in processions and some other services. Vestments may be made of either traditional materials or natural regional fabrics; artificial fabrics may be used for vestments provided they are 'in keeping with the dignity of the sacred action and the person wearing them'. The 'instruction' assumes that the traditional vestments (except the maniple) will be worn for the celebration of the mass and that they will constitute an external demonstration of the diversity of function of members of the body of Christ in worship: the possibility that the ministers should wear ordinary lay clothes is not considered.

This attitude, welcome though it is, does not really go far enough at a time when there is a confluence of the Liturgical Movement (q.v.) and the Ecumenical Movement, creating a situation in which all 'sides' may be willing to accept similar well-designed simple robes. Increasingly, Roman Catholics realize that most of their customary vestments now have little meaning, while some Protestants recognize the fact that quasi-academic gowns are not entirely appropriate for the *celebration* of sacraments. The restoration of greater lay participation in the ceremonies provides an opportunity for a fresh appraisal of the *functional* character of vestments in a purely practical sense of convenience for movement, posture and gesture as well as in the symbolic senses of cultic hierarchy and historical continuity.

Outstanding in the field of re-designed vestments is the work of Sr Flüeler (*see* Plate 42): she has designed and made a new form of wide-sleeved *tunika* which may be worn directly over the civilian clothing of the minister. In a single off-white garment – at once dignified and practical – the functions of both alb and cassock are combined: as a free-falling tunic it is essentially an outer garment and, therefore, does not require a chasuble to be worn over it because it already has the 'enshrouding' quality of sacred vesture, though, obviously, either a chasuble or a cope may be worn over it, if desired (*see* Plate 43). A long stole has been designed to

Plate 42   Basilican mass in modern vestments. The vestment worn by all the sacred ministers is the wide-sleeved *tunika* designed by Sr Flüeler at Stans, Switzerland. The celebration is in the modern college chapel at Sarnen.

Plate 43   Modern alb, stole and chasuble. The wide-sleeved alb functions as both cassock and alb and may be worn directly over everyday clothes: the *tunika* is made from commercially produced material but the stole is hand-woven. The chasuble is optional and the vestments appear 'complete' without it; alternatively, a cope may be worn with the fastening either at the centre or on the right shoulder. Vestments designed by Sr Flüeler at Stans.

wear with the *tunika* in such a way that a pleasing draped effect can be obtained and, further, a number of variations of the basic garment have been designed to make possible a distinction between the various ranks of ministers. It is easy to imagine that such new garments would be perfectly acceptable to most Protestants and, thus, it would be possible to use a vestment as an aid to Christian unity and not as a badge of division. This is already happening in an Anglican-Methodist shared church in Birmingham where the vesture of the ministers is identical, namely, an inexpensive version of the off-white combined cassock-alb now commercially available in England.

Archbishop's Commission, *The Canon Law of the Church of England*, 1947; G. R. Balleine, *A History of the Evangelical Party*, 1908/51; J. Braun, *Die Liturgische Gewandung im Occident und Orient nach Ursprung und Entwicklung, Verwandung und Symbolik*, 1907; O. Chadwick, *The Victorian Church*, 1966; H. J. Clayton, *The Ornaments of the Ministers as shown on Monumental Brasses*, 1919; H. J. Clayton, *Cassock and Gown*, 1929; Convocation of Canterbury, *The Ornaments of the Church and its Ministers: Upper House Report 416*, 1908; P. Dearmer, *The Ornaments of the Ministers*, 1908/20; P. Dearmer, *The Linen Ornaments of the Church*, 1929; A. Flüeler, *Das Sakrale Gewand*, 1964; A. K. Fortescue, *The Vestments of the Roman Rite*, 1912; A. K. Fortescue and J. B. O'Connell, *The Ceremonies of the Roman Rite*, 1917; H. Gee, *The Elizabethan Prayer Book and Ornaments*, 1902; J. A. Jungmann, *The Mass of the Roman Rite*, rev. ed., 1959; J. W. Legg, *Church Ornaments and their Civil Antecedents*, 1917; J. T. Micklethwaite, *The Ornaments of the Rubric*, 1897; H. Norris, *Church Vestments*, 1949; *Ordo Missae* 1969; C. E. Pocknee, *Liturgical Vesture*, 1960; C. E. Pocknee, *The Christian Altar*, 1963; F. Procter and W. H. Frere, *The Book of Common Prayer*, new rev. ed. 1961.

GILBERT COPE

Vestry

A side room in a church where the clergy and/or choir may vest or dress. The term is virtually synonymous with sacristy (q.v.).

EDITOR

Visitation *see* Mariological Feasts

Watch-Night

Watch-night is the British Methodist form of vigil-service, now generally confined to the New Year's Eve.

The watch-night began in spontaneous meetings held by enthusiastic Methodists in Kingswood (a mining area near Bristol), who often spent 'the greater part of the night in prayer, and praise, and thanksgiving'. Discovering these unofficial gatherings, probably in the early spring of 1742, John Wesley adopted and regularized the idea (*see* **Covenant Services**).

Within a few months the watch-night had become a regular event at the main Methodist centres (Bristol, London, Newcastle), held from about 8.30 p.m. to about 12.30 a.m. on the Friday nearest the full moon, so that members walked safely home through moonlit streets. It was also held on public and Methodist fast-days, and especially on New Year's Eve. (This may have been suggested by folk-customs of 'seeing in' the New Year; where such folk-customs are still lively, the watch-night remains popular.) Through the nineteenth century, the watch-night came to be restricted to the New Year, possibly because such a service, to be psychologically effective, needs some defined moment to aim at (namely, the 'seeing in' of the year). In some areas, Anglican and Free Churches adopted this New Year watch-night. At present, services of a 'vigil'-type for great festivals (Christmas midnight communion) and nights of intercession for world need appear to be winning favour in Methodism, while the New Year's Eve service is losing it.

The first watch-nights were preaching-services designed to deepen the spiritual life. Later themes are light and darkness, newness of Christian life, shortness of human life and imminence of judgment, or 'solemn praise to God for continuing his great work in our land' (John Wesley, *Journal*, 31 December 1777).

L. F. Church, *More about the Early Methodist People*, 1949; Charles Wesley, *Hymns for the Watch-Night*, 1744; Charles Wesley, *Hymns for New Year's Day*, 1750, 1766; John Wesley, *Journal*, ed, N. Curnock, 8 vols., 1909-16; John Wesley, *Plain Account of the People called Methodists*, 1749.

DAVID TRIPP

West Syrian Worship

1. *Introduction.* The West Syrian Church, known to many as 'Jacobite' (after Jacob Baradeus, the sixth-century reorganizer of the West Syrian Church) and as Monophysite (after the erroneous idea prevailing in Byzantium and the Latin West that the West Syrians believed only in the divine nature of Christ), historically inherited the Semitic, Palestinian tradition of Christianity, though not uninfluenced by the Hellenistic milieu in which they lived.

The Syrian tradition broke up soon into four families – the East Syrian (Edessa), the West Syrian (Antioch), the Melchite (Greek), and the Maronite (Lebanon).

2. *Liturgical rites.* The West Syrian Church has probably the richest and most diverse heritage in respect of eucharistic anaphorae and canonical offices (qq.v.). In addition to these there are the rites of baptism and chrismation of which three different forms are known. Ordination rites also vary substantially; the whole liturgical corpus also includes rites of matrimony (separate rites for first and second marriages), burial (different for clergy, laymen, women and children), anointing of the sick (not extreme unction – again different for clergy and laity), profession of monks, consecration of churches and altars, translation of relics, etc.

3. *The eucharistic liturgy.* The liturgy is nowadays celebrated mostly in the vernacular – Arabic in the Middle East, English in America, Malayalam in India and so on – though certain portions may still be said by the priest in Syriac. The officiating priest and the people alternate in practically all the prayers, and the deacon plays an important part, admonishing and directing the people to stand with fear, pray and understand the nature of the event that is going on in the liturgy. Choirs have not been allowed to usurp the place of the congregation as in certain other Eastern liturgies.

Some scholars have spoken of a hundred different West Syrian anaphorae, though only about seventy can be traced by the present writer. Some of these, especially the principal Anaphora of St James, go back in their basic structure to the Jerusalem church of apostolic times. Other anaphorae come from the second (Ignatius of Antioch) to the fourteenth centuries, if we take the names of the anaphorae at face value. New liturgies continued to be created in every century up to the fourteenth, though production was most prolific from the fourth to the seventh. The twelfth century produced at least six new anaphorae and about the same number was produced in the thirteenth. With the thirteenth century the development reached its peak in Gregory Bar-Hebreus and has remained more or less static ever since.

Two peculiarities of the West Syrian rite are (1) the liturgy of incense between the liturgy of the word and the liturgy of the eucharist proper; (2) the prayer of adieu to the altar at the end of the liturgy. The liturgy of incense, which recalls the offering of incense in the Temple (Ex. 30.1-10), seems to have replaced the dismissal of the catechumens, and comprises a general absolution of the priest and people before the offering of the eucharistic sacrifice. It also represents a sort of offertory; incense (q.v.) symbolizes the good works and prayers which are well-pleasing to God. It symbolizes also the prayers of the departed saints which mix with those of the congregation, as a true spiritual offering of praise and adoration.

The epiclesis occurs in all the seventy known liturgies, though the form of the epiclesis varies verbally from anaphora to anaphora, as also does the verbal content of the 'words of institution'.

Not all the seventy anaphorae are in common use. The ones most commonly used in India are St James (on all principal feasts, for the first eucharist offered by a priest, or offered at a new altar), Dionysius Bar Salibhi, St John Chrysostom and St John the Evangelist.

The canonical offices for ordinary days are called the *Shimo,* and have recently been translated into English by the Benedictine Fr Griffiths. The more elaborate office, the *Fenqith,* has not yet been translated into English or Malayalam and is rarely used even in the Syriac. The Syriac text of the Fenqith is available in an Indian edition as well as in a Mosul edition (1886-1896).

One major feature of the eucharistic liturgy and the daily offices is the *Sedro,* a long meditative-homiletical prayer, preceded by a proemion which seems to be an elaborated form of the *Gloria.* These prayers are rich in theological content, and play a considerable role in the religious education of the faithful, especially in the absence of biblical preaching.

An introduction and critical text of the Syriac anaphorae with Latin translation have been published by the Pontifical Oriental Institute in Rome (*Anaphorae Syriacae*, 1953). The ninth-century commentary of Moses Bar Kepha on the Syrian liturgies was published with an English translation by R. H. Connolly and H. W. Codrington (*Two Commentaries on the Jacobite Liturgy*.).

The people communicate rather rarely, the legal minimum of once per year being observed by most, usually on Holy Thursday. Communion is in both kinds, usually by intinction for the laity. The priest usually administers, though the deacon is allowed to serve communion to the laity.

Reservation of the sacrament for adoration is forbidden; it may be reserved in case of need for the sick, and for those who fast till the evening.

Confession before communion is often demanded, though this is not necessary for those who communicate frequently. Fasting from the previous midnight is required.

The lections during the liturgy of the word are three, one from the Acts or catholic epistles (representing the twelve), then from the Pauline epistles, and then finally the gospel, which is read with great ceremony by the officiating priest. Sermons had gone out of use, but are coming back more recently as priests become better trained.

The creed recited is the Niceno-Constantinopolitan, introduced into the liturgy by Peter the Fuller in the fifth century as an anti-Chalcedonian measure.

Two of the West Syrian anaphorae, those of Matthew the Shepherd and Sixtus of Rome, lack the actual words of institution. The latter says: 'He, when he was prepared for his saving passion, by the bread which by him was blessed, broken and divided among his holy Apostles, gave us his propitiatory body for life eternal; in a like manner, also by the cup . . .'.

The canon of the mass, with words of institution, anamnesis and epiclesis (qq.v.) is said aloud by the priest, with responses from the people.

A. Fortescue, *The Lesser Eastern Churches*, 1913; W. de Vries, *Sakramententheologie bei den Syrischen Monophysiten*, 1940; I. Ziade, 'Syrienne' (église), *DTC*, XIV, cols. 3017-88.
PAUL VERGHESE

Westward Position
see Postures (1*c*)

Whitsunday
The English title for Pentecost (q.v.), so-called from its association with the white robes of baptism.

Words of Administration
The words of administration are those that accompany the giving of the sacramental bread and wine to the communicants at the eucharist. The earliest recorded formula is that preserved by Hippolytus (*Ap.Trad.* 23.5) concerning the bread: 'The bread of heaven in Christ Jesus', to which the recipient responds with 'Amen'. The same answer is made to the words of the priest in the Ambrosian rite – 'The Body of Christ' – and in the *Apostolic Constitutions*, where the formulae are: 'The Body of Christ . . . The Blood of Christ, the Cup of Life.' In the Byzantine liturgy the formula reads: 'The servant of God N. partakes of the precious and holy Body and Blood of our Lord and Saviour Jesus Christ for forgiveness of his sins and life eternal.' The form in the Roman mass is that of a blessing, adopted in the eighth century: 'The Body of our Lord Jesus Christ preserve thy soul unto everlasting life.' Indeed, the words in all orders are variations and expansions of those current in the patristic period; so, for example, those in the rite of the Church of South India are: 'The Body of our Lord Jesus Christ, the Bread of Life . . . the Blood of our Lord Jesus Christ, the True Vine.' Within the Church of England, there was a fusion in 1559 of the 1549 words, which were close to the old formulae, and those of 1552, which were substituted in accordance with the views of the European Reformers and avoided calling the elements the body and the blood of Christ.

EDITOR